Werner Nicolaas Nel

Grievous religious persecution: A conceptualisation of crimes against humanity of religious persecution

The cover art depicts the image of *Iustitia* (Lady Justice), the goddess of Justice within Roman mythology. Her allegorical personification and metaphoric symbols represent the moral virtues of justice, truth and fairness. It is indicative of the philosophical attitude that embodies justice, in Celsus' words "*ius est ars boni et aequi*" – the law is the art of the good and the fair. This reminds us that the conscience of humankind cannot remain silent about gross human rights violations and mass atrocity crimes. It is a call to change, it is the hope and belief that there can be justice for those who suffer for their faith. Ultimately, it relentlessly insists that the gloating triumph of persecutors over their victims be not the last word in history.

Religious Freedom Series (IIRF)

Volume 5

Vol. 1: Charles L. Tieszen. Re-Examining Religious Persecution: Constructing a Thelogical Framework for Understanding Persecution.

Vol. 2: Christof Sauer, Richard Howell (Hg.). Suffering, Persecution and Martyrdom: Theological Reflections.

Vol. 3: Heiner Bielefeldt. Freedom of Religion Belief: Thematic Reports of the UN Special Rapporteur 2010 – 2016.

Vol. 4: Christine Schirrmacher. „Let there be no Compulsion in Religion" (Sura 2:256): Apostasy from Islam as judged by contemporary Islamic Theologians – Discourses on Apostasy

Vol. 5: Werner Nicolaas Nel. Grievous religious persecution: A conceptualisation of crimes against humanity of religious persecution

Werner Nicolaas Nel

**Grievous religious persecution:
A conceptualisation of crimes against
humanity of religious persecution**

WIPF & STOCK · Eugene, Oregon

Wipf and Stock Publishers
199 W 8th Ave, Suite 3
Eugene, OR 97401

Grievous Religious Persecution
A Conceptualisation of Crimes Against Humanity of Religious Persecution
By Nel, Werner Nicolas and Bielefeldt, Heiner
Copyright © 2020 Verlag für Kultur und Wissenschaft Culture and Science Publ.
All rights reserved.
Softcover ISBN-13: 978-1-7252-9514-8
Hardcover ISBN-13: 978-1-7252-9515-5
Publication date 12/7/2020
Previously published by Verlag für Kultur und Wissenschaft Culture and Science Publ., 2020

This edition is a scanned facsimile of the original edition published in 2020.

Contents – Overview

Foreword 13

Acknowledgements 15

Summary 17

Keywords 18

1 Chapter One: Introduction 19

2 Chapter two: The Contextual Spectrums of the Notion of Persecution 27

3 Chapter Three: The Crime of Persecution in International Criminal Law 49

4 Chapter Four: The Role of Religious Identity in Determining the Grounds of Persecution 107

5 Chapter Five: 'Motive' and its Effect on the Classification of Religious Persecution 153

6 Chapter Six: A Taxanomy of Crimes Against Humanity of Religious Persecution 179

7 Chapter Seven: Counteractive Responses to Religious Persecution ..199

8 Chapter Eight: Conclusions 233

Appendix A: Overview of the Basic Principles of International Criminal Law 255

Appendix B: Freedom of Religion or Belief in the Context of Religious Persecution 315

Appendix C: Assessing 'Grievous Religious Persecution' in the Context of the Atrocities Committed by *Da'esh* 393

Biliography 467

Contents – in Detail

Foreword 13

Acknowledgements 15

Summary 17

Keywords 18

1 **Chapter One: Introduction** 19
   1.1 Introductory remarks 19
   1.2 Chapter synopsis 21
   1.3 Final introductory remarks 25

2 **Chapter two: The Contextual Spectrums of the Notion of Persecution** 27
   2.1 Introduction 27
   2.2 A Colloquial Conception of Persecution 29
   2.3 A Sociological Perspective on Persecution 30
   2.4 Suffering and Persecution in the Context of Religious Epistemology 35
      2.4.1 Varying theological ideologies of suffering and persecution 36
      2.4.2 Suffering persecution and it's relation to commitment 37
   2.5 Persecution in the Sphere of Asylum and Refugee Protection 41
   2.6 Conclusion 47

3 **Chapter Three: The Crime of Persecution in International Criminal Law** 49
   3.1 Introduction 49
   3.2 The Origins and Evolution of the Crime of Persecution in International Criminal Law 50
      3.2.1 The origins of the crime of persecution 50
      3.2.2 Persecution in terms of the Rome Statute 53
   3.3 The Definitional Elements of the Crime of Persecution 54
      3.3.1 The *actus reus* of 'grievous persecution' 56
      3.3.2 The *mens rea* of 'grievous persecution' 71
      3.3.3 The threshold of severity 85

Contents

- 3.4 'Grievous Persecution' in the Context of International Human Rights Law 92
  - 3.4.1 International human rights law 92
  - 3.4.2 The relationship between international human rights law and international criminal law 96
  - 3.4.3 Persecution as a deprivation of fundamental human rights 99
- 3.5 The Relationship Between Persecution and Other International Crimes 101
  - 3.5.1 Persecution and war crimes 101
  - 3.5.2 Persecution and ethnic cleansing 101
  - 3.5.3 Persecution and genocide 103
- 3.6 Conclusion 105

4 Chapter Four: The Role of Religious Identity in Determining the Grounds of Persecution 107
- 4.1 Introduction 107
- 4.2 Religion and Persecution 110
  - 4.2.1 A doctrine of 'religion' 110
  - 4.2.2 A preliminary characterisation of religious persecution 115
- 4.3 The Notion of Identity and the Role of Religion or Belief in Forming Personal Identity 118
  - 4.3.1 Personal identity 119
  - 4.3.2 The role of religion in forming an identity 121
- 4.4 Collective Religious Identity 126
  - 4.4.1 Group identity and persecution 127
  - 4.4.2 The nature of a collective religious identity 127
  - 4.4.3 Religious persecution and a collective religious identity 129
- 4.5 Identity and the Protected Grounds of Persecution 130
  - 4.5.1 Distinguishing the grounds of persecution with the use of the identity element 131
  - 4.5.2 The multiplicity and complexity of identity 132
  - 4.5.3 Intersectionality of grounds of persecution with religion 133
- 4.6 The Primacy of 'Religious Identity' as the Basis of Discrimination in the Context of Religious Persecution 145
  - 4.6.1 'Religious identity' as the basis of discrimination in the context of religious persecution 145
  - 4.6.2 The primacy of a religious identity 148
- 4.7 Conclusion 150

5 Chapter Five: 'Motive' and its Effect on the Classification of
   Religious Persecution 153
   5.1 Introduction 153
   5.2 Distinguishing Religiously Motivated Persecution from
        Religious Persecution in International Criminal Law 154
        5.2.1 Religious discriminatory intent and persecution
               (persecution 'by reason of' religious identity) 155
        5.2.2 Religiously motivated persecution (persecution in the
               name of religion) 156
        5.2.3 Instances of entanglement and disentanglement 157
   5.3 Motivational Triggers of Religious Persecution 161
        5.3.1 Religious antagonist impulse 163
        5.3.2 Exclusivist impulse 166
        5.3.3 Secularist impulse 171
        5.3.4 Exploitative impulse 174
   5.4 Conclusion 177

6 Chapter Six: A Taxonomy of Crimes Against Humanity of
   Religious Persecution 179
   6.1 Introduction 179
   6.2 Proposed Taxonomy of Crimes Against Humanity of
        Religious Persecution ('Grievous Religious Persecution') 180
        6.2.1 Substantive elements of 'grievous religious persecution' 180
        6.2.2 Religious persecution taxonomy checklist 194
        6.2.3 Defining crimes against humanity of religious
               persecution 196
   6.3 Conclusion 197

7 Chapter Seven: Counteractive Responses to Religious Persecution .. 199
   7.1 Introduction 199
   7.2 The Notion of Responses to Religious Persecution 200
   7.3 Response from the Perspective of the Religious Community 202
        7.3.1 Internal response to persecution in the name of
               religion 202
        7.3.2 External response to persecution from the religious
               victim groups perspective 204
   7.4 Governmental Responses in Line with Human Rights
        Obligations 207
   7.5 International Humanitarian Respsones 210
        7.5.1 Religious freedom advocacy 211
        7.5.2 Human rights mechanisms 213

7.6 International Criminal Prosecutions as a Response to
'Grievous Religious Persecution' 214
   7.6.1 The suitability of international criminal prosecutions 214
   7.6.2 The principle of legality and a charge of persecution 217
   7.6.3 Legal liability for religious persecution 222
7.7 Conclusion 230

8 Chapter Eight: Conclusions 233
8.1 Introduction 233
8.2 The Persecution Phenomenon in International Criminal Law .. 233
8.3 Establishing the Role of 'Religion' in Religion-Based
Persecution 237
   8.3.1 'Religious identity' 239
   8.3.2 The role of religious identity in determining the 'mode
   of persecution' as a crime against humanity 243
8.4 Proposing and Endorsing the Conceptualisation 245
   8.4.1 The taxonomy of 'grievous religious persecution' as a
   crime against humanity 245
   8.4.2 Testing the taxonomy in a case study 246
   8.4.3 Anticipated outcomes of the conceptualisation 249
8.5 Limitations and Future Research 250
   8.5.1 Limitations of the proposed conceptualisation 250
   8.5.2 Potential for future studies 251
8.6 Final Remarks 253

Appendix A: Overview of the Basic Principles of International
Criminal Law 255
1 Introduction 255
2 The basic characteristics of international criminal law 256
   2.1 An introduction to international criminal law 256
   2.2 Role and characteristics of the International Criminal
   Court 262
   2.3. International crimes 264
   2.4 Jurisdiction 274
3. The contextual framework of crimes against humanity in
terms of the Rome Statute 279
   3.1 The notion of crimes against humanity 283
   3.2. Conditions of applicability of crimes against humanity 284
4 Individual criminal responsibility 296
   4.1 The principle of *ne bis in idem* 298
   4.2 Forms of individual criminal responsibility 299

5   Grounds for contesting criminal responsibility 305
     5.1.   Immunity in international criminal proceedings 305
     5.2.   Defences for excluding criminal responsibility 308
6.   Principles of Criminal procedure before the ICC 310
7.   Conclusion 312

Appendix B: Freedom of Religion or Belief in the Context of Religious Persecution 315

1   Introduction 315
2   Applicable international human rights standards of religious freedom 316
3   The normative core values of the right to freedom of religion or belief 321
     3.1   Freedom to choose a religion or belief 323
     3.2.   Right to manifest one's belief, either publicly or in private, through teaching, practice, worship, and observance 325
     3.3.   Freedom from coercion 328
     3.4.   Right to conversion – the right to adopt, change or renounce one's religion 330
     3.5.   Freedom from discrimination and the right to equality 338
     3.6.   Principle of non-derogability and religious freedom 354
     3.7.   Freedom from impermissible restrictions or limitations on the right to freedom of religion or belief 356
4   'Recognition' of a religion and a religious group 361
     4.1.   'Recognition' of the individual's status as a bearer of human rights 361
     4.2.   'Recognition' of religious options 361
     4.3.   Registration procedures for the recognition of legal personality 365
5   Intersection of freedom of religion or belief with other human rights 367
     5.1.   Freedom of religion or belief and due process 369
     5.2.   Freedom of religion or belief and freedom of expression 370
     5.3.   Freedom of religion or belief and privacy 373
     5.4.   Freedom of religion or belief and gender issues 374
     5.5.   Freedom of religion or belief and the freedom of collective participation 375
6   Patterns of deprivations of religious freedom 377
     6.1.   Governmental restrictions and violations by State actors 377

    6.2.   Social or societal hostility and religious persecution 384
7   Varying intensities of deprivations of religious freedom........... 386
8   Conclusion 388

Appendix C: Assessing 'Grievous Religious Persecution' in the Context of the Atrocities Committed by *Da'esh* 393

1.   Introduction 393
2.   The Global Trend of Fear Relating to Religious Extremism........ 394
    2.1. The nature of religious extremism.. 395
    2.2.   Religious motivation and extremism 396
    2.3.   The adverse effect of religious extremism on associated religious communities 397
    2.4.   The rising trend of fear relating to Islamic extremism 399
3.   The Evolution of *Da'esh* 402
    3.1.   The emergence of *Da'esh*.. 403
    3.2.   Military and leadership structures 406
    3.3.   Resources and funding.. 407
    3.4.   *Da'esh* propaganda 408
    3.5.   Arms and ammunition.. 409
    3.6.   In pursuit of justice for *Da'esh* offences 409
4.   *Da'esh* Ideology 410
    4.1.   Inter-denominational hostility between Sunnis and Shias 411
    4.2.   Interpreting and justifying *jihad* 413
    4.3.   *Da'esh*'s interpretation of '*jihad*' 415
5.   The Pattern of Abuses, Atrocities and Crimes Committed by *Da'esh* 418
    5.1.   Acts of terror and terrorism 420
    5.2.   War crimes committed in Iraq and Syria 424
    5.3.   Possible genocide against the Yazidi community............. 427
    5.4.   Ethnic cleansing on a historic scale 436
    5.5.   Several inhumane acts of crimes against humanity.......... 439
6.   Charging *Da'esh* with 'Grievous Religious Persecution'............. 440
    6.1.   Applying the taxonomy checklist 441
    6.2.   Multiplicity of the grounds of persecution....................... 457
7.   Conclusion 460

Biliography 467

Foreword

Violations of freedom of religion or belief take place in virtually all parts of the globe, they occur under various political or ideological auspices, and they reach quite different degrees of intensity. Sometimes they even assume the character of crimes against humanity. This term suggests that atrocities can reach such a dimension as to affect humanity as a whole. The 1948 Universal Declaration of Human Rights, the "mother document" of international human rights protection, reflects the same idea when pointing in its preamble to "barbarous acts which have outraged the conscience of mankind". The two notions – "crimes against humanity" and "conscience of mankind" – obviously resemble each other. Crimes against humanity do not only concern specialized lawyers; they demand a worldwide moral outcry, which itself can only be credible in connection with the willingness to adopt practical measures. The idea of a "conscience of mankind" can only make sense when driving the international community to take action.

While the media provides us with daily information about mass-scale violations of people's human rights and freedom of religion or belief, we may often feel that the conscience of humankind remains deafeningly silent. This is a disturbing experience. What are the reasons? The accelerating crisis of multilateralism has seriously weakened the global infrastructure of human rights protection. Once promising projects, like the international political commitment to the "responsibility to protect" appear to belong to a bygone era. In the eyes of critics, the International Criminal Code, established less than a generation ago with the purpose of putting an end to the culture of impunity, has meanwhile become the symbol of lost aspirations. There is an increasing danger that political resignation, when remaining unchecked, breeds collective cynicism.

Werner Nicolaas Nel's dissertation does not fit into the current political climate of resignation. This accounts for the significance of his work, which is a very timely contribution in times of growing political fatalism. Nel forcefully sticks to the idea that international criminal law has an important task to fulfil by relentlessly insisting that the gloating triumph of perpetrators over their victims be not the last word in history. When tackling crimes against humanity, international criminal law may proceed in representation of the conscience of humankind, which might regain strength – or so we may hope.

In his dissertation, Nel focuses on grievous religious persecution as one manifestation of crimes against humanity. In spite of shocking reports in recent years about mass-scale atrocities committed against Yezidis in Iraq, Christian minorities in the Middle East, Muslim Rohingyas in Myanmar, Buddhists, Christians and Muslims in China and elsewhere, the issue of religious persecution so far has received comparatively limited attention in academic literature. By meticulously putting together the various elements that jointly define religious persecution, Nel's dissertation fills a frequently felt gap.

Within the broader human rights framework, freedom of religion or belief plays a crucial role. Indeed, it has an indispensable significance by pointing to a dimension of human life that the human rights approach cannot ignore. We humans are complicated beings, driven by our never-ending search for an ultimate meaning in life. We can adopt and develop profound convictions and try to live our lives – closely together with others – in conformity with our existential beliefs. Violations of freedom of religion or belief may therefore affect people in the innermost nucleus of their personal or communitarian identity. To use an old metaphor once coined by Roger Williams, abuses in this area can amount to forms of "soul rape". Werner Nicolaas Nel offers us profound insights into what is at stake when religious minorities experience systematic persecution. Moreover, he reminds us that humanity cannot remain silent about manifestations of grievous religious persecution, which after all are crimes against humanity as a whole.

Heiner Bielefeldt
Professor of Human Rights and Human Rights Policy at the University of Erlangen-Nürnberg, Germany
Former United Nations Special Rapporteur on freedom of religion or belief (2010–2016)

Acknowledgements

The noble aspirations of those determined to change what is unjust, are often considered to be impractical pursuits of idealistic goals. While some may consider this work such an idealistic goal, I wish to thank those individuals whose gracious support and belief invigorated my aspiration to make a difference with this work.

In particular, I wish to express my most sincere gratitude to Christo Botha and Christof Sauer for providing their invaluable guidance, comments and encouragement throughout the course of this study. Professor Sauer, thank you for your dedication to my cause, the inspirational example you are as a human being and a Christian, and your enthusiasm in fostering young scholars and researchers. Thank you to Thomas Schirrmacher for his persistent desire to see the work published, as well as the generous assistance of Titus Vogt in editing the book. I also wish to express my thanks to Heiner Bielefeldt for writing the foreword, your dedication to, and impact on, furthering religious freedom and pluralism worldwide is truly an inspiration.

A final thanks is due to my family, without whom none of this would have been possible. To my wife, Inge, I love you for this journey together, the trust, and the absolute confidence that you have in me. Thanks you for sticking with me and for the sacrifices that you had to make in order to help me bring this work to fruition. I also wish to express my most sincere gratitude to my parents, Anton and Baretta. Words fail to explain how much your love, support, and encouragement has meant to me. Finally to my children, Mieke (6) and Ethan (2), thank you for the countless hours playing, so often it was the distraction I needed to renew my determination and restore my morale.

All praise be to God, my heavenly Father. Through Him all things are possible. In rememberance of the suffering of Jesus Christ and dedicated to those persecuted for His name's sake.

Werner Nicolaas Nel
Johannesburg, December 2020

Summary

International criminal law functions as a legal mechanism that contributes to the protection of human rights by, suppressing and punishing individuals responsible for, *inter alia*, the commission of mass discriminatory crimes constituting severe human rights deprivations. In relation hereto, particular incidences of religious persecution are, because of their scale, severity, and discriminatory motivation, so heinous that they may be justifiably categorised as crimes of serious concern to the international community, constituting one of the enumerated inhumane acts of crimes against humanity. Despite its proscription under international criminal law, religious discrimination and religion-based persecution remain a major human rights issue. In response, international prosecution systems are to be resorted to in pursuit of criminal accountability. However, the incessant impunity for persecution is not due to the lack of proscription in international law, but stems rather from definitional instability and legal vagueness. Consequently, such opacity may be responsible, at least in part, for the international criminal justice systems' perceived reluctance to enforce prosecution measures based on religious persecution.

The primary aim of this study is to unveil the legal opacity surrounding crimes against humanity of religious persecution (coined 'grievous religious persecution') by proposing a justifiable, comprehensively formulated and pragmatically verified conceptualisation. In this regard, a relevant taxonomy is proposed which differentiates between various forms of persecutory conduct, discusses the *mens rea* requirement, establishes the intensity threshold, recommends an effective definition, and is finally applied to a relevant case study in order to analyse its practical efficiency.

In furtherance thereof, the writer takes a multidisciplinary approach, briefly examining the exact denotation and connotation of religion and religious identity, its role in characterising a situation as *religious* persecution, and the influence of the right to freedom of religion or belief on such an assessment. By proposing a detailed conceptualisation from the perspective of religious identity and religious freedom, the legal semantics and discourse regarding 'grievous religious persecution' is developed, which may positively influence its substantive understanding and may potentially lessen the political and judicial unease regarding its perceived scope and application. It is argued that such a conceptualisation may have various implications, including to strengthen the efforts of human rights defenders *in re* religious freedom, and advance criminal accountability and counteract impunity for 'grievous religious persecution'.

Keywords:

International Criminal Court, international criminal law; international human rights law, right to freedom of religion or belief, crimes against humanity, religious identity, religious discrimination, counteracting impunity, human rights deprivations, 'grievous religious persecution'.

This research monograph is based on the core thesis of Werner Nel's doctoral dissertation, entitled: International criminal accountability for religious persecution in terms of the Rome Statute: A taxonomy of crimes against humanity of religious persecution. The LLD – Doctor Legum (Doctor of Laws) in International Criminal- and Human Rights-Law, was conferred upon him by the Department of Public Law, Faculty of Law, University of Pretoria in September 2019. He was supervised by Prof Christo Botha, University of Pretoria, and Prof Dr Christof Sauer, Freie Theologische Hochschule Gießen, and Evangelische Theologische Faculteit, Leuven. The dissertation was a multidisciplinary study with the main dissertation focus being religious persecution and religious freedom in the context of International Criminal Law and Human Rights. The dissertation is available at: https://repository.up.ac.za/handle/2263/72657.

Chapter One: Introduction

1.1 Introductory remarks

The noble aspirations of those determined to change what is unjust, are often considered to be impractical pursuits of idealistic goals. While some may consider the thesis of this book to be such an idealistic goal, it is beneficial to be reminded of the outrageous adventures of the beloved character of Don Quixote and the disenchanting central ethic of the story, which is that individuals can be right while society is quite wrong.

A founding work of modern literature and one of the earliest canonical novels, *The Ingenious Nobleman Mister Quixote of La Mancha* follows the adventures of Don Quixote, a delusional hidalgo. Quixote, beseeched by grand notions of romance and antiquated knighthood, embarks on a quest to revive chivalry, undo wrongs, and bring justice to the world. This self-proclaimed knight-errant dons an old suit of armour, saddle's his exhausted horse 'Rocinante' and recruits a faithful squire, in order to prove his chivalric virtues. Don Quixote's humourist attempts at grandeur repeatedly end in utter failure, yet the inadequacies of his 'heroic' attempts are not due to his lack of commitment to a valiant cause or his meagre abilities, but rather because of the privation of rational clarity. In the same way, the existing impunity for severe religious persecution[1] is not due to the lack of conviction or proscription in international law, but predominantly stems from "definitional instability and judicial unease, notable due to the fact that the crime itself falls short of a definitive and comprehensive definition".[2] Thus, despite its extensive acceptance as an enumerated inhumane act of crimes against humanity under customary international law,[3] the complexity and inconsistency of a substantive understanding of persecution may well be its prime debilitating factor. As a result, the crime of persecution has been void of jurisprudential clarity and prosecutorial

---

[1] The phrases 'persecution on the basis of religion', 'religious-orientated persecution', 'religious persecution', or otherwise, are used as contextually similar expressions.

[2] Fournet, C & Pégorier, C. *'Only One Step Away From Genocide': The Crime of Persecution in International Criminal Law.* International Criminal Law Review, Vol. 10, Issue 5, pages 713 – 738. Marthinus Nijhoff Publishers. (2010), pg 713.

[3] *Summary of Appeal Judgement (KAING Guek Eav)*, Case File 001/18-07-2007/ECCC/SC, Extraordinary Chambers in the Courts of Cambodia, 3 February 2012, par 225.

conviction, depriving it of constant and uniform State practice and subsequently failing to instil a sense of legal obligation (*opinio juris*) amongst States. Consequently, the crime of religious persecution, has remained a controversial and relatively underdeveloped international crime. Therefore, as with Don Quixote's noble aspirations, any course of action by those engaged in advocating on behalf of the religiously persecuted,[4] may amount to 'tilting at windmills' if the substantive complexity of, and ambiguity in, persecution is not addressed. Thus, in a chivalrous attempt to address the perpetuation of impunity, the primary aim of this paper is to unveil the legal opacity surrounding crimes against humanity of religious persecution, simply coined 'grievous religious persecution'.[5]

In this endeavour to definitively conceptualise 'grievous religious persecution', the strategy is to recommend a legally justifiable conceptualisation or taxonomy. In terms of this conceptualisation, different forms of persecutory conduct will be identified, the *mens rea* requirement will be discussed, the intensity threshold will be established, and a comprehensive definition will be proposed. Thus, it will function as a substantive synopsis of the legal preconditions for establishing the International Criminal Court's (ICC) subject-matter jurisdiction over conduct constituting 'grievous religious persecution'.[6] In addition, such a conceptualisation may affect the interpretation of persecution in the context of the International Law Commission's (ILC) proposal for a *Convention on the Prevention and Punishment of Crimes against Humanity*.[7]

At the core of such proscriptions is the fundamental proposition that religious discrimination and persecution remain "a major human rights issue of national and international concern, [accordingly] international prosecution systems, as provided by the International Criminal Court

---

[4] Throughout this book, the term 'religiously' is used in the sense of religiosity, i.e. 'pertaining to a religion' or 'related to religion', and is used so as not to disturb the syntax in certain instances. 'Religiously' is not used in relation to its secondary meaning, signifying a 'devotion' to a cause, acting 'meticulously' or 'regularly'.

[5] 'Grievous religious persecution' is a term coined by the writer in order to distinguish situations which satisfy the intensity threshold for crimes against humanity of religious persecution, from other 'subsidiary' forms of persecution.

[6] *Rome Statute of the International Criminal Court*, Doc. A/CONF.183/9 of 17 July 1998 in force 1 July 2002. Art 7(2)(g) read together with Art 7(1)(h) (*Rome Statute*).

[7] UN General Assembly, *Report of the International Law Commission*, 69th session (1 May-2 June and 3 July-4 August 2017), 2017, A/72/10, pg 10. See also UN General Assembly, *Report of the International Law Commission*, 66th session (5 May-6 June and 7 July-8 August 2014), 2014, Supplement No. 10, A/69/10.

1. Introduction

(ICC), are to be resorted to in pursuit of criminal accountability".[8] In other words, the criminalisation of 'grievous religious persecution' is aimed at protecting individuals and groups against severe deprivations of their religious freedom,[9] *inter alia*, and other atrocities on the basis of their religious identity, or lack thereof.[10] As a result, 'grievous religious persecution' finds itself naturally placed between the legal recognition, enforcement and protection of fundamental human rights in terms of international human rights law, and the suppression and punishment of individuals responsible for, *inter alia*, the commission of mass discriminatory crimes that result in severe deprivations of such fundamental values, in terms of international criminal law. Thus, in relation to occurrences of 'grievous religious persecution', international criminal prosecution mechanisms constitute a justifiable and appropriate response to address severe and discriminatory deprivations of fundamental human rights. Unfortunately, as mentioned, the ultimate failure of the current system is that the crime of persecution is plagued by definitional instability and legal vagueness, blunting the enforceability of international criminal prosecutions as a robust sanction-based mechanism, and resulting in a lack of resolve in addressing emerging patterns of human rights atrocities.

With this legal obstacle in mind, it is argued that the envisioned conceptualisation may provide greater legal certainty regarding the definitional elements of 'grievous religious persecution', which would strengthen the enforceability of, and resolve to pursue, international criminal prosecutions. In addition, it provides a legal framework that promises greater credibility, objectivity and legal accuracy to the efforts of those advocating for the religiously persecuted.

1.2   Chapter synopsis

The notion of persecution does not only have legal significance for the purposes of human rights law and criminal justice. It encapsulates a certain universal perception based on its historic roots, yet its exact meaning is complicated by multiple spectrums. Despite a common familiarity with the

---

[8]   Van Boven, T. *Racial and Religious Discrimination. Max Planck Encyclopedia on Public International law*, Wolfrum, R. (ed.), Heidelberg. Oxford University Press. (2009), par 22.

[9]   The phrase 'religious freedom', as interpreted in terms of international human rights law, must be understood in its broadest sense to include all aspects and dimensions of the right to freedom of thought, conscience, and religion or belief.

[10] Thames, H. *et al. International Religious Freedom Advocacy: A guide to Organizations, Law and NGO's*. Baylor University Press. (2009), pg 10–11.

term 'persecution', its exact conceptualisation, its various contextual forms, gradations and manifestations, and its definition have remained perplexingly enigmatic. Chapter Two discusses the differing contextual understandings of persecution and its effect on the assessment of the notion of *religious* persecution. Persecution has significant importance from the perspective of religious studies and missiology, as well as aspects of psychology, anthropology and sociology. These perspectives highlight the 'existential dimensions' of persecution, which is subsequently distinguished from the 'legal dimensions'. In the latter context, 'persecution' is first considered as a core concept of asylum and refugee protection, which functions primarily to protect individuals and groups from human rights violations. Furthermore, international criminal law in conjunction with human rights law, primarily seek to protect the religious identity of an adherent or religious group in relation to the right to freedom of religion or belief.

In other words, the notion of persecution includes various obvious 'subsidiary' forms of persecution.[11] However, the focus of this book will eventually be limited to the most extreme instances of religious persecution in the context of international criminal law. In order to distinguish extreme forms of persecution from other subsidiary forms, the preferred prefix will be 'grievous'. Considering the multidisciplinary audience of this book, Appendix A provides a brief overview of international criminal law and it's relation to international human rights.

Subsequent to a broad understanding of the notion of persecution, Chapter Three shifts the focus to a discussion of crimes against humanity of persecution in its 'generic' sense, or 'grievous persecution'. In terms of this broad generic understanding of persecution, the *Rome Statute* provides an expansive list of prohibited grounds of persecution.[12] The persecutor's intention to discriminate (categorise, differentiate and target) 'by reason of' an identifiable aspect of the victim's identity (identifying element), is

---

[11] It should be made clear that using the phrase 'subsidiary' forms of persecution should in no way be construed as to diminish the damaging physical and psychological harm to individuals or communities, associated with such forms of persecution that may not satisfy the intensity threshold for 'grievous persecution'. This distinction is therefore purely made for the purpose of differentiating the various spectrums of persecution.

[12] The following grounds of persecution are considered to be identifiable protected grounds in terms of the *Rome Statute*: political, racial, national, ethnic, cultural, religious, gender, or other grounds that are universally recognised as impermissible under international law.

I. Introduction

instrumental in classifying the ground of persecution (for example, political persecution or persecution based on ethnicity).[13]

While a generic understanding of persecution may provide the foundation for understanding the crime of persecution, the focus of this book necessitates the separation of 'religion' from the other grounds of persecution. Although a 'religious identity' is an important aspect of personal and communal conceptions of identity, it also serves as the elementary *nexus* that determines the mode of persecution as religiously orientated. The notion of 'religious identity' is completely dependent on the recognition and protection of the right to freedom of thought, conscience, religion or belief, in the context of international human rights law. Bearing in mind the multidisciplinary audience, Appendix B provides an overview of the principles of the right to freedom of religion or belief in the context of international human rights law. These international legal standards applicable to religious freedom play a pivotal interpretive role in the context of religious persecution, including: (1) defining the parameters of protection of religious freedom in order to gauge potential infringements, such as religious persecution; (2) recognising and contextualising equality on the basis of religion and the protection against religious discrimination as the core element of the notion of 'religious persecution'; and (3) formulating what constitutes a 'religious identity' as a deep existential view, as an identifying element, and as a way of life. Therefore, Chapter Four will consider the notion of 'religion' in the context of religious freedom, before examining the role of religious identity in determining the ground of persecution. Importantly, religion and religious identity are aspects of the "inner existential dimension of a person's conscience".[14] Consequently, it is impossible to deliberate such topics holistically without due consideration of certain sociological, theological and anthropological aspects,[15] to the extent that they are relevant to the aim of the conceptualisation.

---

[13] Please note that the terms 'intent' and 'intention', as used throughout this paper, are concomitantly similar expressions which refer to a form of culpability or fault which may be defined as 'the blameworthy state of mind' of a criminally responsible person who performs an unlawful act with the will to perform such act or cause such consequence while knowing that this conduct is unlawful.

[14] Bielefeldt, H. *Misperceptions of Freedom of Religion or Belief*. Human Rights Quarterly, Volume 35, Number 1, pp. 33–68 (Article). Published by The Johns Hopkins University Press (2013), pg 46–47.

[15] It should be noted that the discussions regarding these 'religious' aspects should in no way be construed as a claim to scholarly expertise in this field. This discus-

Chapter Five considers the manifold root causes and motivations of religious discrimination and persecution. In this regard, a clear distinction is made between religious persecution and religiously motivated persecution (persecution in the name of religion).

The integration of the preceding framework allows for a holistic and definitive conceptualisation of 'grievous religious persecution'. Thus, Chapter Six addresses the primary aim of the book, *viz.* to lift the veil on the obscure notion of religious persecution by proposing a justifiable and comprehensively formulated conceptualisation in the context of international criminal law. This conceptualisation or taxonomy will comprise a focussed discussion of the definitional elements of 'grievous religious persecution', including the different forms of persecutory conduct, the *mens rea* requirement, the intensity threshold, and the conditions of applicability for crimes against humanity. A comprehensive definition in the context of the *Rome Statute* will also be proposed. Optimistically, this conceptualisation will improve advocacy efforts for a more effective utilisation of international prosecution mechanisms in relation to ocurrences of 'grievous religious persecution'. It could be argued that this conceptualisation will be more persuasive if it is tested with the use of a suitable contemporary case study. Therefore, Appendix C will consider the pattern of offences and human rights atrocities committed by *Da'esh* in northern Iraq and Syria. For the purposes of the book, the outcome of the case study is less important than the pragmatic efficacy of the conceptualisation itself.

The scattered spectrum of concurrent persecution phenomena may result in a variety of responses to persecution. Chapter Seven provides a non-exhaustive overview of some of the most adequate and appropriate responses to manifestations of religious persecution. As an alternative to the use of international prosecution mechanisms, aspects such as religious advocacy efforts, interventions by States and NGO's, and the response from associated and persecuted religious communities will be considered. The suitability of international criminal prosecutions as a response to religious persecution, is discussed, including concerns regarding a charge of persecution in the light of the legality principle. In addition to individual criminal responsibility, the international responsibility of a State for the commission of 'grievous religious persecution' is also discussed.

---

sion is merely an attempt of using some secondary literature for sketching a rudimentary picture and extracting information relevant for conceptualising 'grievous religious persecution'.

1. Introduction

In conjunction with providing some final inferences, Chapter Eight will also consider certain inherent restrictions on the application of the conceptualisation. Importantly, the contribution and practical applications of this study will be supplemented by referencing various possible research contributions that may have the potential to further develop the topic at hand.

1.3 Final introductory remarks

Lifting the veil on the obscure notion of religious persecution may serve the purpose of conserving fundamental human rights and speak to the necessity to end impunity for severe acts of religious persecution through international criminal prosecution mechanisms. In so doing, the aim is to advocate for greater recognition of the occurrence of religious persecution globally, and pursue justice for those who have been, or are continually being, persecuted because of their religious identity.

In serving this purpose, the unique multidisciplinary approach of this book provides for a deeper, more comprehensive understanding of the notion of religious persecution and the *materiae* of the crime of persecution. This multidisciplinary approach results in an intersection of various related disciplines, including law, religion, human rights, politics and international relations. Though each discipline would bring a different perspective and focus on the topic, it is argued that the conceptualisation of persecution in this book may be beneficial to both academics and practitioners in these fields, especially those engaged with criminal justice issues and human rights advocacy.

As a result, the study is conducted as an impartial legal analysis of religious persecution, regardless of the writer's personal religious identity. As such, this study is not intended to either implicate, disrespect or attack, nor act in defence of, any particular religious group or religion. Any reference, case study, or example implicating a religion, a religious group or a *de facto* authority, was selected on the basis of their practical and substantive relevance.

Chapter Two: The Contextual Spectrums of the Notion of Persecution

2.1   Introduction

The term 'persecution' is derived from the Latin *persequor*, which can be translated to mean "to follow with hostile intent".[1] Bassiouni points out that:

> Throughout history... the terms 'persecute' and 'persecution' have come to be understood to refer to discriminatory practice resulting in physical or mental harm, economic harm, or all of the above... The words 'persecute' and the act of 'persecution' have come to acquire a universally accepted meaning... [including] the infliction upon an individual of harassment, torment, oppression, or discriminatory measures... because of the victim's beliefs, views, or membership in a given identifiable group (religious, social, ethnic, linguistic etc.), or simply because the perpetrator sought to single out a given category of victims for reasons peculiar to the perpetrator.[2]

At first glance 'persecution' seems to encapsulate a seemingly undisputed common understanding. However, its exact meaning is complicated by a diversity of concurrent contextual understandings, perceptions and utilisations. Accordingly, a recurrent obstacle in conceptualising religious persecution is a lack of clarity regarding the different spectrums of the persecution phenomena. This may be understandable, "given the endless variety of situations the term might cover",[3] and considering that "the nature of persecution and our understanding of it keep changing".[4] In line with this multidimensional understanding of 'persecution', a universal conceptualisation remains problematic. Whilst there are certain definitional elements common in all the contextual understandings of religious

---

[1]   Tieszen, C.L. *Re-Examining Religious Persecution: Constructing a Theological Framework for Understanding Persecution.* Religious Freedom Series. Vol 1 (2008), pg 38.
[2]   *Prosecutor v Duško Tadić (Trial Judgement)*, Case No. IT-94-1-T, ICTY, 7 May 1997, par 695, quoting Bassiouni, M. C. *Crimes Against Humanity in International Criminal Law.* Martinus Nijhoff: Dordrecht (1992).
[3]   Vaughns, K.L. *Taming the Asylum Adjudication Process: An Agenda for the Twenty-First Century*, 30 San Diego L. REV. 1, (1993), pg 63.
[4]   Ramji-Nogales, J. et al. *Refugee Roulette: Disparities in Asylum Adjudication*, 60 STAN. L. REV. 295, (2007), pg 379.

persecution, there are often conflicting language used in describing such. In addition to the conflicting use of terminology, a lack of appreciation of the diversity of concurrent contextual understandings of religious persecution has resulted in the careless overuse of the term 'persecution'. This has reduced the impact when describing an actual situation of religious persecution,[5] making it much more difficult to advocate on behalf of the persecuted, and to encourage an appropriate response.[6] As a result, 'persecution' has become a neatly packaged 'catch-phrase', often used by media outlets to sensationalise reports and generate revenue. Similarly, some of those concerned with religious persecution, including non-governmental organisations and humanitarian aid groups promoting the interests of certain religious groups, are occasionally inclined to deliberately misuse language in order to attract widespread response, support and even financial contributions. In other circumstances, the use of persecution terminology has been trivialised. These, and other, misperceptions regarding religion and 'religious persecution' trigger misnomers that undermine the fundamental status of religious freedom and underrates the necessity for enforcing prosecution mechanisms to end impunity.

Therefore, Chapter Two will distinguish between the varying contextual uses of the term persecution, which is essential in understanding and conceptualising the persecution phenomenon holistically, and also in limiting the scope of this book. This will require a multidisciplinary understanding of the persecution.

In terms of the 'legal dimension', the concept of persecution is prominent in three different legal contexts, refugee law, international criminal law and international human rights law. Each of the legal uses of the term 'persecution' have specific contextual interpretations and purposes, and generally entail a high threshold of severity of harm. However, as Bielefeldt points out, "the language of law is not an existential language",[7] and therefore, cannot exhaustively cover all existential experiences of religious persecution. Consequently, the 'existential dimension' considers the experience and surrounding ideology from the viewpoint of those persecuted, and from the viewpoint of the persecutor (whether committed in the name of religion or some other root cause). Accordingly, the phenom-

---

[5] Thames, K. H. et al, *International Religious Freedom Advocacy: A guide to Organizations, Law and NGO's*. Baylor University Press (2009), pg 6.
[6] Thames et al. *International Religious Freedom Advocacy* (2009) 6.
[7] Bielefeldt, H. *Misperceptions of Freedom of Religion or Belief*. Human Rights Quarterly, Volume 35, Number 1. The Johns Hopkins University Press (2013), pg 46.

enon of persecution is considered from sociological, philosophical, psychological and theological perspectives. Although each of these contextual uses of 'persecution' differ, in some or other way, each of these perceptions contribute to the overall conception of the persecution phenomenon. Below, this scattered spectrum of concurrent interpretations of persecution will be briefly discussed, contextualised and distinguished.

2.2 A Colloquial Conception of Persecution

'Persecution' is a well-known term in everyday language.[8] The lexical entry of 'persecution' as a noun, includes the act of *persecuting*, the state of being *persecuted*, and a program or campaign to exterminate, drive away, or subjugate people based on their membership in a religious group, *inter alia*.[9] In its verb form, 'persecuted' and 'persecuting', means to pursue with harassing or oppressive treatment, especially because of religious or political beliefs, ethnic or racial origin, gender identity, or sexual orientation; or to annoy or trouble persistently.

Historically, persecution explicitly referred to the violent oppression of a given category of victims because of their religious practices and beliefs. Thus, 'persecution' constituted a hostile reaction against the perceived threat that a particular religious view posed to the mainstream society, the autonomy of other religions, or political power. A twenty-first century understanding of persecution reflects a wider scope of protection. Contemporarily, persecution refers to unfair or abusive treatment toward a person or group of people because of race, religion, ethnicity, sexual orientation, gender, or social status.[10] Tieszen defines 'persecution' in its most general and basic form as:

> An unjust action of varying levels of hostility with one or more motivations directed at a specific individual or a specific group of individuals resulting in varying levels of harm as it is considered from the victim's perspective.[11]

Therefore, persecution is commonly understood as a spectrum of hostility towards an individual or group by another individual or group, based on

---

[8] Fournet, C. & Pigorier, C. *'Only One Step Away From Genocide': The Crime of Persecution in International Criminal Law.* International Criminal Law Review 10 (2010), pg 713.

[9] Dictionary.com: https://www.dictionary.com/browse/persecution?s=t. Accessed 25/07/2019.

[10] Vocabulary.com Dictionary. https://www.vocabulary.com/dictionary/persecution. Accessed 17/10/2017.

[11] Tieszen *Re-Examining Religious Persecution* (2008) 41.

the identity of the victim, such as the victim's religious identity or political allegiances. Consequently, it is common to encounter persecution in the context of, and within the understanding of, discrimination.[12] However, persecution may be distinguished from discrimination because the former requires not only a form of intolerance, but also consequential harm.[13] The infliction of suffering, harassment, imprisonment, internment, fear, or pain are all factors that may embody harm within a colloquial perspective of persecution. Accordingly, the core elements of persecution relate to deliberate hostility directed arbitrarily at a specific person or group because of a certain identity element they posses, resulting in a variety of harmful consequences.[14]

2.3 A Sociological Perspective on Persecution

The social and anthropological sciences are concerned with social conditions and behaviour within human society. An observation of the social matter in society includes aspects of the self as an autonomous and sociably connected being.[15] In each person, this connection between individuality and solidarity may take on different levels of consciousness regarding societal ideas, feelings, rules, and habits. A complex interplay exists between individuality and solidarity or connections, which make up part of the irreducible social datum. At a minimum, it can be said that each person's connection to society results in at least a "vague sentiment of overall solidarity".[16] Consequently, there is at least a tacit acceptance of societal rules, whether consciously or unconsciously. However, this solidarity does not imply that all members of the group must know about or will endeavour to comply with the social constructs of the group. Within the context of criminal law, this indicates that:

> If society has the right to punish, it is not because wrongdoers have formally agreed to the penal laws, but because they have accepted in a general manner the solidarity of the social group, of which penal laws make up one part.[17]

---

[12] UN General Assembly, Resolution 103(I) Persecution and Discrimination, 19 November 1946.
[13] Tieszen *Re-Examining Religious Persecution* (2008) 38.
[14] Tieszen *Re-Examining Religious Persecution* (2008) 41.
[15] Hauriou, M. and Gray, C. *Tradition in Social Science*. Amsterdam: Brill Academic Publishers. (2011), pg 7.
[16] Hauriou & Gray *Tradition in Social Science* (2011) 4.
[17] Hauriou & Gray *Tradition in Social Science* (2011) 4.

2. The Contextual Spectrums of the Notion of Persecution

Therefore, rules of conduct, especially legal rules, have a significant function in society and in the social sciences, which is to govern how people should act and interact in society, in an attempt to deter what is generally considered antisocial behaviour.[18] This results in a variety of perspectives on persecution, depending on which side a person's solidarity with a social group lies. Thus, the perception of persecution may vary from a social phenomenon, to a social defect, or even acceptable social behaviour. Most importantly, 'persecution' must be considered as a form of social behaviour from the perspectives of those involved or affected. Consequently, a sociological perspective on persecution considers acts of religious hostility by private individuals, organisations or groups in society, i. e. persecution in the form of social hostility.[19] The most significant forms of social hostility towards religion or religious groups includes "social groups harassing members of a certain religion, as well as organised groups attempting to dominate public life with their perspective on religion".[20] Within a hostile social environment, those involved or affected often have diverging views on the nature and legitimacy of their persecutory experience or conduct. Therefore, a sociological perspective considers two main perceptions: persecution experienced from the viewpoint of those persecuted, versus the perception of those who attempt to justify their persecutory conduct, i. e. the persecutor or antagonist's viewpoint.

Tieszen contends that from a sociological perspective, the victim's perspective is the most important.[21] The persecuted victim generally experiences varying degrees of animosity, resulting in different levels of suffering or harm, which stem from multiple motivations.[22] Therefore, the

---

[18] Lempert, R. & Sanders, J. *An Invitation to Law and Social Science: Law in Social Context Series*. University of Pennsylvania Press. (1989).
[19] Pew Research Center, Washington, D.C. *Global Uptick in Government Restrictions*. June 21, 2018, pg 4. http://www.pewforum.org/2018/06/21/global-uptick-in-government-restrictions-on-religion-in-2016/. Accessed 22/11/2018.
[20] Pew Research Center *Global Uptick in Government Restrictions* (2018) 19.
[21] From this sociological perspective, Tieszen defines religious persecution as: "an unjust action of varying levels of hostility directed at a believer or believers of a particular religion or belief system through systematic oppression or genocide, or through harassment or discrimination which may not necessarily limit these believers' ability to practise their faith, resulting in varying levels of harm as it is considered from the victim's perspective, each action having religion as its primary motivator." – Tieszen *Re-Examining Religious Persecution* (2008) 41.
[22] The *Bad Urach Statement* published as part of the compendium on the *Bad Urach Consultation: Suffering, persecution and martyrdom – Theological reflections*. Edited by

victim group is identified and distinguished from others for the sake of a cause, or based on a belief or an aspect of their identity. The basis or reason for this discrimination is usually assessed from the victim's perspective. In other words, a victim may often 'feel' or believe that he/she is being persecuted, and may well form a subjective conclusion as to the reason or basis for such persecution.[23]

Sometimes this belief of persecution may create various difficulties, in that the individual may subjectify his/her experience, and associate their suffering with a perceived cause, belief or aspect of personal identity. 'Scotomisation', or the confirmation bias, refers to the psychological tendency in people to perceive a situation or information in a way that confirms one's pre-existing beliefs or hypotheses, rather than an interpretation based on an objective analysis.[24] In Don Miguel Ruiz's words:

> We only see what we want to see; we only hear what we want to hear. Our belief system is just like a mirror that only shows us what we believe.[25]

In psychology, individuals who experience an upsurge of suspicious feelings and thoughts with high levels of threat may be considered to suffer from "persecutory delusion".[26] This intensified perception of persecution not only manifests in the mind of individual victims, but may also occur within a larger group or community dynamic. A compulsive and subjective fixation on persecution by those concerned with persecution or engaged with promoting the interests of certain persecuted groups, such as non-governmental organisations and humanitarian aid groups, may also result in 'persecutory scotomisation' or even 'persecutory delusion'. Nonetheless, the experience of persecution from a victim's or targeted group's perspective may be vital in understanding the proper context of persecution.

Conversely, persecution from the persecutor's perspective provides similar concerns regarding the subjective perception and justification of persecutory conduct from the *boni mores* viewpoint. For example, Turkish

---

Sauer, C. & Howell, R. Religious Freedom Series: Suffering, Persecution and Martyrdom. Vol 2. (2010), Kempton Park: AcadSA Publishing / Bonn: VKW (2010), pg 40.

[23] *Bad Urach Statement* (2010) 40.
[24] Plous, S. *The Psychology of Judgment and Decision Making*. Published by McGraw-Hill Education (1993), pg 233.
[25] BrainyQuote website/Don Miguel Ruiz. https://www.brainyquote.com/authors/don_miguel_ruiz. Accessed 17/10/2017.
[26] Preti, A. & Cella, M. *Paranoia in the 'normal' Population*. Nova Science Publishers, Inc, New York (2010), pg 21.

2. The Contextual Spectrums of the Notion of Persecution

nationalism provided the justification for the Armenian Genocide carried out during and after World War I. In this context, the *boni mores* of the Ottoman society contained a false perception about ridding their country of what, to them, were foreign and evil influences.[27] Therefore, manifestations of collective hatred towards certain identifiable groups or identities often legitimize persecutory conduct. In such instances the persecutors may perceive themselves, and those likeminded, as the protagonists or protectors of a certain cause, belief or identity.

The justification for vilifying and persecuting certain groups is often based on perceived objects of fear. This may happens when complex societal problems are simplified by social or institutional narrow-mindedness, gradually cultivating feelings of vulnerability, mistrust and fear. Such instances of fear, whether actual or perceived, generally result in a fight or flight response, harbouring serious risks of an over-emotional and hostile reaction. In the context of concomitant fear, members' sense of responsibility for those with whom they share a commonality or solidarity, may further exaggerate such reactions. Consequently, fears often result in violent action or may create a demand for a scapegoat on whom to project such fears. These perceived objects of fear may become powerful tools that could fuel propaganda, collective paranoia and public dehumanisation. By addressing the object of concern (i. e. vilified group) with discrimination and persecution, the persecutor (or perceived protector) believes his/her actions promote the interests of the common good. For example, the anti-Semitic policy that led to the Jewish Holocaust, was largely based on Nazis propaganda that blamed the German-Jews for the troubles with which the nation was afflicted following World War I.[28] Subsequently, the systematic extermination of the Jews became a simplified and final solution to a complex societal fear indoctrinated into the psyche of populations in parts of Europe.

Given the complexity of human nature and collective solidarity, feelings of vulnerability and fear can be connected to many different interests.[29] Within a group dynamic, associated communities may fear for their social or economic status, ideals or morals, or even the demise of their collective identity, based on aspects such as language, culture or religion. Bielefeldt notes that in the constructs of religious communities, "rapid

---

[27] Tieszen *Re-Examining Religious Persecution* (2008) 40.
[28] *The Trial of German Major War Criminals, Proceedings of the International Military Tribunal Sitting at Nuremberg, Germany.* International Military Tribunal, Judgment of 1 October 1946, pg 20.
[29] Bielefeldt, H. *Freedom of Religion or Belief: Thematic Reports of the UN Special Rapporteur 2010 - 2016.* Religious Freedom Series of the International Institute for Religious Freedom, Vol 3, 2nd and extended edition, Bonn (2017), pg 195.

changes in societies may cause feelings of gradual dissolution of one's familiar religious lifeworld and concomitant fears of a decline in religious values".[30] Such societal changes may include notions of doctrinal secularism, humanism, and even pop-culture.

In view of such imagined threats as the pretence to the persecutor's moral superiority, identifying the true antagonist may often depend on the perspective of the relevant subject. Whereas those against whom social hostilities are directed will rightly consider themselves as the persecuted, those responsible for such hostilities may feel vindicated as 'protectors' of the collective values, cause, belief or identity. Therefore, it is imperative to corroborate any subjective perceptions of persecution with external factors or evidence. Without an objective standard-setting framework, the analysis of persecution by those affected, those responsible, or even other interested parties, may harbour serious risks of persecutory delusions and bias.

First-hand contextual knowledge of those persecuted allows for critical judgements regarding the nature or mode of persecution. By contrast, incidental knowledge may be subjective and lack the contextual knowledge necessary for critical thinking.[31] In the absence of contextual knowledge or first-hand experience, the "source of information on such events, which will almost always be stylised to conform with the popular culture, is a closed one and often limited to certain official government or establishment sources".[32] Sources that lack contextual objectivity may inevitably filter through rumours built on hearsay or by community authorities, whether leaders or politicians, writers or journalists, or other 'official' sources. This is because our perception of reality and facts regarding distant events is based on the objective accuracy of the source, which, in turn, influences our conclusions and motivates our actions.[33] An impartial information environment is thus crucial to assess the occurrence and nature of persecution from an objective point of view. However, an overemphasis on the victim's perception about persecution may result in a subjective interpretation regarding the motive and discriminatory mindset of the perceived persecutory antagonists in the situation.[34]

---

[30] Bielefeldt *FORB: Thematic Reports* (2017) 195.
[31] Davidson, L. *Cultural Genocide*. Rutgers University Press, New Brunswick, N.J. (2012), pg 118–119.
[32] Davidson *Cultural Genocide* (2012) 119.
[33] Davidson *Cultural Genocide* (2012) 120.
[34] It will be discussed later that in the context of 'grievous persecution', the motive for the persecutory acts are irrelevant to the determination of the ground of persecution.

2.4 Suffering and Persecution in the Context of Religious Epistemology

In general, 'suffering' is "a human experience which a person undergoes against his or her wish".[35] Human suffering may result from natural causes, such as illness, injury or grief, but it may also result from external factors, such as anxiety because of financial problems or work-related stress.

From a theological perspective, the commitment to a religious identity implies that adherents must often abstain from certain conduct or endure certain hardships in conformity with their belief-convictions. Such a phenomenon may be understood as the suffering of adherents for the sake of their religious identity, and has nothing to do with persecutory suffering.[36] However, adherents may also endure suffering because of their chosen commitment to a religious or belief-identity in the form of persecution. Importantly, the suffering and persecution endured by a religious person or group does not automatically constitute religious persecution,[37] unless the persecutor deliberately targeted the victim group because of their chosen commitment to a religion or belief.[38] In other words, in the context of suffering as a result of a religious conviction, 'choice' is the difference between enduring 'suffering' for the sake of one's faith, versus being forced to suffer religious persecution 'by reason of' one's faith.

Suffering in the form of religious persecution is an aggravated form of human suffering because the persecutor consciously and deliberately inflicted such harm on the basis of religious discrimination. Generally, the persecuted victim not only experiences the effects of a form of harmful conduct, but also the discriminatory deprivation of his or her fundamental rights. Consider the following example: the universally accepted crime of rape will inevitably result in physical and psychological suffering for the victim. In other words, the criminal conduct has brought about a form of human suffering. However, if acts of rape are consciously and discriminately directed at a victim based on a protected ground, such as the victim's gender or ethnic identity, such conduct constitutes an aggravated form of rape, viz. persecution. In such instances, the additional discriminatory intent to target a victim based on their identity, elevates the extent of suffering for the victim. It is unfortunate to note the universality of rape

---

[35] The *Bad Urach Statement* (2010) 34.
[36] The *Bad Urach Statement* (2010) 22.
[37] Tieszen *Re-Examining Religious Persecution* (2008) 42.
[38] This will be discussed in Chapter Four.

and intimate violence against women in conflict, arguably becoming a necessary concomitant of male aggression during war.[39] Dishearteningly, gender-based violence and persecution is not limited to war zones, but are a common occurrence in many domestic households.

Clearly, religious persecution implies a particular discriminatory form of human suffering. Two interesting aspects should be noted here.

2.4.1 Varying theological ideologies of suffering and persecution

Religions or beliefs are likely to differ in terms of their religious epitimological or theological interpretation and perspective of religious persecution. For example, the Christian faith, unlike others, was – and is – built on the "strength in weakness" and "wisdom in foolishness".[40] An orthodox interpretation of Christianity may consider 'persecution' a privilege which accentuates the Christian virtues of dependency on, and vulnerability in, Christ. In other words, "suffering for the sake of Christ" remains a cornerstone of the Christian faith, and whilst violent persecution is not sough out or encouraged, it is to be expected and endured as part of taking up one's daily cross for the sake of following Christ. In a certain interpretational context, Islamic theology provides for a similar expectance and forbearance of suffering associated with 'struggling' or 'striving' in the way of Allah.[41] In this context, *jihad* (*jihād al-nafs*) is an eternal directive of the *Shari'ah* and implies an internal, spiritual struggle, which require "the practice of 'patient forbearance' by Muslims in the face of life's vicissitudes and toward those who wish them harm".[42] Thus, in the religious and ethical realm, *jihad* implies the human struggle and suffering associated with promoting what is right and preventing what is wrong in the eyes of Islam. However, this is as far as the similarities go in this regard. The *Qur'an* (Koran) states that:

---

[39] Chertoff, E. *Prosecuting Gender-Based Persecution: The Islamic State at the ICC*. The Yale Law Journal (2017), pg 1077, fn 112.

[40] Burnard, M. *Understanding Persecution: Recalibrating a theology of suffering with the reality of Easter*. INcontext international. (2019). Available at: https://www.incontextinternational.org/wp-content/uploads/2016/09/1904-EasterPersecution.pdf. Accessed 26/07/2019.

[41] Mahmoudi, S. *Islamic approach to international law*. Max Planck Encyclopedia on Public International law, Wolfrum, R. (ed). Heidelberg. Published by Oxford University Press (2011), pg 391.

[42] Afsaruddin, A. *Jihad – Islam*. Encycloaedia Britannica, last updated on 15 January 2019. https://www.britannica.com/topic/jihad. Accessed 01/02/2019.

2. The Contextual Spectrums of the Notion of Persecution

Permission to take up arms is hereby given to those who are attacked because they have been oppressed [persecuted] – Allah indeed has power to grant them victory – those who have been unjustly driven from their homes, only because they said: 'Our Lord is Allah'. (22:39–40)

In more specific terms, literal interpretations of further verses (4:75–6) direct Muslims to take up arms against people who are responsible for *fitnah* ('persecution'), meaning those who force Muslims to give up their religion, and to continue this aggression until the persecution is uprooted from Arabia.[43] In other words, in certain Islamic traditions, oppression or persecution is something that should be resisted, through violence if required.[44]

2.4.2 Suffering persecution and it's relation to commitment

The extent or parameters of suffering persecution may often depend on the level of commitment of the individual believer. Generally, the more committed an adherent is to a belief, the higher the intensity of religious self-identification and faithfulness to such a belief. Consequently, such a devoted believer is more likely to encounter and possibly suffer harsher religious persecution. In short, the more dedicated to the cause, the greater the level of threat such beliefs might pose to the perpetrator.[45] This cuts both ways, in the sense that a commitment to a belief may escalate into, or justify, religious fundamentalism and extremism. In another sense, it could be argued that those who stand resolute in their belief may suffer more severe persecution than others.

In the latter sense and for the purposes of this study, one may distinguish between 'census believers', 'parishioners', 'habitual believers' and 'faithful followers'.[46] Within certain settings, each of these groups will experience suffering for their belief and possibly persecution to a different

---

[43] Ghamidi, J. A. *The Islamic Law of Jihad*. Studying Islam website: http://www.studying-islam.org/articletext.aspx?id=771. Accessed 20/08/2014.
[44] It should be noted that the discussion regarding Islamic law and tradition should in no way be construed as a claim to scholarly expertise in this field. This discussion was merely an attempt at using some secondary literature for sketching a rudimentary picture of Islamic theology on persecution.
[45] Tieszen *Re-Examining Religious Persecution* (2008) 45–46.
[46] Adapted from Marshall, P. *Persecution of Christians in the Contemporary World*. International Bulletin of Missionary Research, Vol. 22 issue 1 (1998), pg 4, and from Barrett, D, B. *et al. World Christian Encyclopaedia*. New York: Oxford University Press, 2nd edition, Vol 2. (2001), pg 651–662.

extent based on the varying levels of commitment.[47] As such, 'census believers' are connected to a specific belief merely by other factors, such as ancestry, ethnicity, and nationality or otherwise. Their lack of dedication and sacrifice to an associated belief unburdens them from any suffering associated with such a commitment. 'Parishioners', those who merely associate with a belief without any level of involvement or attendance, and 'habitual believers', those who are involved in the manifestations of beliefs out of habit or tradition, lack true conviction and commitment to a belief. As a result, these 'detached believers' will arguably only suffer persecution under very specific circumstances, because their conviction will likely not endure in situations where persons are persecuted for a failure to denounce their beliefs. Those who are truly committed to their conviction, the 'faithful followers', will encounter religious persecution on every level of intensity and harm, and will undergo more systematic suffering based on their religious identity than the preceding groups.

It should also be mentioned that in the context of intra-religious persecution,[48] a lack of commitment may have an opposite effect than outlined previously. In certain religious groups, an adherent's lack of commitment may consequently designate such a lackadaisical believer as the object of ridicule and persecution. Religious extremism and related terrorism illustrate this tendency of intra-religious persecution towards ideologies that do not purport the same level of fundamentalism or perceived commitment. For example, a report on terrorist incidents by the *American National Counter-terrorism Center* concluded that Sunni terrorist groups, more than any other subnational group, conducted the largest number of hostile incidents with the highest casualty totals in various countries.[49] Significantly, the report found that Muslims from other denominations constituted the most substantial share of the victims of these terrorist attacks.[50] Celso's observations echo these findings:

---

[47] This perspective was taken from a theological study on the persecution of Christians specifically and may not be inherently similar to all religious groups and their persecution.

[48] Intra-religious persecution or intra-denominational religious persecution refers to persecution within the same religion, or between different sects, or amongst members of the same sect, or a combination of both.

[49] American National Counterterrorism Center – *Report on Terrorist Incidents* 30 April 2006 – https://web.archive.org/web/20090326171214/http://wits.nctc.gov/reports/crot2006nctcannexfinal.pdf. Accessed 16/07/2017.

[50] *Report on Terrorist Incidents* (2006) 11.

2. The Contextual Spectrums of the Notion of Persecution

Jihadism's propensity for violence knows no bounds and seeks to eviscerate that which lies in its immediate path. A fact underscored by the bloody history of Jihadism waged primarily against [other] Muslims.[51]

In instances where a person's belief status is assigned through religious registration, the level of commitment to such a religious identity may have less of an impact on the extent of religious persecution. Religious registration refers to situations where all persons must choose, or are assigned, a certain belief status.

> Religious registration identifies every person with a particular faith, making them part of a religiously defined community. This identification is maintained irrespective of the individual's religious belief or practice, which prompts profound questions as to what it means to be a Muslim, Christian, and so on.[52]

Religious registration allows domestic courts or tribunals to handle private law matters, such as inheritance and divorce, according to the traditions and beliefs of the persons involved.[53] Usually, adherents registered to the mainstream religious identity will escape persecution. In such cases, religious persecution is most often directed against a minority religion. Therefore, the experience of persecution of those assigned with such a religious identity will not necessarily be proportional to their level of commitment. The rationale is that they are persecuted based on their assigned religious identity, which they cannot easily escape. Their experience will only cease if they formally convert or abandon their assigned religious identity in favour of the mainstream religious identity. In most situations, the reality of conceding to forced conversion or coercion in order to escape religious persecution is probably true for all adherents, regardless of their level of commitment.

The intensity of religious faithfulness or commitment to a religious identity is often proportional to the degree of an adherent's suffering, persecution, or the likelihood to suffer martyrdom.[54] The term 'martyr' and 'martyrdom' is derived from Greek, meaning 'bearing witness even unto

---

[51] Celso, A. *Jihadist Organizational Failure and Regeneration: The Transcendent Role of Takfiri Violence*. Political Studies Association Meeting. Manchester, England. 14 – 16 April 2014, pg 5. https://www.psa.ac.uk/sites/default/files/conference/papers/2014/PSU%20presentation.pdf. Accessed 14/02/2016.
[52] Andrews, J. *Identity Crisis: Religious Registration in the Middle* 24.
[53] Andrews *Identity Crisis* (2016) 24.
[54] Tieszen *Re-Examining Religious Persecution* (2008) 45-46.

death'.[55] The term has varying theological interpretations throughout different religious beliefs, therefore the following secular understanding of martyrdom may be proposed for the purposes of this discussion:

> A martyr must be regarded as the victim of religious persecution by a perpetrator hostile to the individual's religious identity, ultimately resulting in the death of the individual as the penalty for observing or defending his belief, or refusing to renounce such a belief, principle or manifestation associated thereto.[56]

Suffering persecution in the context of a commitment to one's belief is distinctly obvious in the context of martyrdom as one cannot experience martyrdom apart from experiencing persecution.[57] However, the opposite is not necessarily true. A believer may well experience religious persecution, without being martyred to death for practising or holding a certain religious identity. The actual death of an individual qualifies him or her as a martyr if such a death is suffered in relation to, or on the grounds of, his or her religious identity. It could be argued that this phenomenon should be distinguished from instances where religious extremists (terrorists) enact suicide bombings against civilian targets in order to obtain a 'divine' status as 'martyr' in the name of their religion. Martyrdom is a specific manifestation of persecution, but does not constitute its only effect, nor is it indicative of the level of severity required of persecution under international criminal law. Therefore, martyrdom constitutes an extreme and severe form of religious persecution, which may be indicative of 'grievous religious persecution'. Furthermore, instances of religious martyrdom often afford the most unambiguous examples of religious persecution in contemporary society and seemingly provide "the simplest way in which to quantify not only martyrs, but the presence of persecution as well".[58] However, the relation of martyrdom to persecution should not be overestimated, because although martyrdom may constitute a manifestation of persecution, an overemphasis on religion-related executions as persecution may ultimately belittle other 'subsidiary' forms of religious persecution.[59]

---

[55] The *Bad Urach Statement* (2010) 41.
[56] Based on the definition of a martyr and martyrdom in terms of the *Bad Urach Statement* (2010) 42.
[57] Tieszen *Re-Examining Religious Persecution* (2008) 33.
[58] Tieszen *Re-Examining Religious Persecution* (2008) 33.
[59] Tieszen *Re-Examining Religious Persecution* (2008) 33.

It is important to realise that each situation, and each religion, is different. Therefore, this proportionality between commitment and the extent of persecution is only applicable in some instances. In other instances, a person may experience religious persecution because they lack a specific religious identity or their perceived level of commitment to a religious identity is not considered adequate. The context and motive for religious persecution are unique in each setting and must be considered on a case-by-case basis. Unfortunately, in many instances the only way to escape religious persecution is to forsake such a cause, convert or flee.

2.5 Persecution in the Sphere of Asylum and Refugee Protection

Within the broader field of human rights law, refugee law functions primarily to protect individuals and groups of individuals from human rights infringements suffered within their country.[60] The interest here focusses on the question under which conditions a foreign State is obliged to grant asylum to a person who claims persecution. The extensive nature of persecution is thus an integral concept in the administrative process for asylum seekers and the protection of refugees.[61]

> Throughout history, people have fled their homes to escape persecution... the international community included the right to seek and enjoy asylum in [order] to protect and assist refugees...[62]

'Persecution' and the consequent principle of *non-refoulment*,[63] is framed with the victim in mind in an attempt to prevent or protect against human rights infringements. Accordingly, the *Refugee Convention* states that the term 'refugee' shall apply to any person who:

---

[60] Rempell, S. *Defining Persecution*. Utah Law Review, Vol. 2013, No. 1 (2013), pg 22.
[61] Rempell *Defining Persecution* (2013) 1.
[62] UN High Commissioner for Refugees (UNHCR), *Handbook and Guidelines on Procedures and Criteria for Determining Refugee Status under the 1951 Convention and the 1967 Protocol Relating to the Status of Refugees*, December 2011, HCR/1P/4/ENG/REV. 3, pg 345.
[63] As contemplated in Art 3 of the UN General Assembly, *Declaration on Territorial Asylum*, A/RES/2312(XXII), 14 December 1967. For a detailed discussion on the non-refoulement, see Lauterpacht, E. and Bethlehem, D. *The Scope and Content of the Principle of Non-Refoulement (Opinion)*, 20 June 2001, pg 87–162 published in the Office of the United Nations High Commissioner for Refugees, *Refugee Protection in International Law: UNHCR's Global Consultations on International Protection*. Feller, E. et al. (eds.) Cambridge University Press (2003).

> ...[O]wing to well founded fear of being persecuted for reasons of race, religion, nationality, membership of a particular social group or political opinion, is outside the country of his nationality and is unable or, owing to such fear, is unwilling to avail himself of the protection of that country; or who, not having a nationality and being outside the country of his former habitual residence as a result of such events, is unable or, owing to such fear, is unwilling to return to it.[64]

A determination of refugee status will primarily require an evaluation of the applicant's subjective fear of persecution, including membership of a targeted group. Such a fear of persecution must be accompanied by an external determination of whether, to a reasonable degree, the applicant's continued presence in, or return to, such a country may be intolerable to the applicant.[65]

> ...[I]t is not only the frame of mind of the person concerned that determines his refugee status, but that this frame of mind must be supported by an objective situation.[66]

The drafters of the Refugee Convention deliberately omitted a definition of the term for fear of being too restrictive.[67] In the oft quoted words of Grahl-Madsen, "...[the drafters] capitulated before the inventiveness of humanity to think up new ways of persecuting fellow men."[68] We also do not find a definition universally agreed by legal experts. It is clear that

---

[64] Art 1 A(2) of the United Nations General Assembly Resolution 429(V) of 14 December 1950, UN High Commissioner for Refugees (UNHCR), *Convention and Protocol Relating to the Status of Refugees*. https://www.unhcr.org/3b66c2aa10. Accessed 13/02/2019. (Hereinafter referred to as the *Refugee Convention of 1951*).

[65] UNHCR *Procedures and Criteria for Determining Refugee Status* (2011) par 39–41. See also the United States of America: *Immigration and Nationality Act* (last amended March 2004), 27 June 1952 (INA), 8 U.S.C. § 1101(a)(42)(A). Available at https://www.law.cornell.edu/uscode/text/8/1101. Site accessed 19/10/2016.

[66] UNHCR *Procedures and Criteria for Determining Refugee Status* (2011) par 38.

[67] Storey, H. *What constitutes persecution: Towards a working definition of persecution.* (2014), pg 1. Paper for European Chapter Conference, Goteborg, Sweden, 21–22 November on Recent Developments in European Asylum Law Conference, in co-operation between the Migration Courts in Sweden and the IARLJ. This paper is based on the article by Storey, H. *Persecution: Towards a Working Definition*, in V. Chetail & C. Bauloz (eds.), Research Handbook on Migration and International Law, Cheltenham: Edward Elgar Publishing (2013).

[68] Grahl-Madsen, A. *The Status of Refugees in International Law, Volume I - Refugee Character.* Leiden: Sitjthoff (1966).

2. The Contextual Spectrums of the Notion of Persecution

most writers concur that historically speaking, the persecution phenomenon has been a continuously adaptable manifestation of the wicked ingenuity of humankind and therefore the nature of persecution is self-identifying.[69] However, Storey argues that:

> to say that persecution is too protean to try and 'freeze- frame' into a definition is an objection only to an approach which seeks to define persecution exhaustively or in absolutist terms. It is not an argument against a non exhaustive approach or an approach that seeks to define its material scope defeasibly.

The English Court of Appeal in *Sandralingham Ravichandran*, stated that "persecution is most appropriately defined as the sustained or systemic failure of state protection in relation to one of the core entitlements which has been recognised by the international community."[70] Storey contends that in order to theorise a definition of persecution, one needs to "conceptualise what its underlying criteria should be or should look like".[71]

Rempell's definition focusses on the elements of persecution, which for purposes of asylum protection, should be defined as "the illegitimate infliction of sufficiently severe harm".[72] In this context, the core elements of persecution are manifestations of harm or harmful conduct, severity, and an assessment regarding the legitimacy or permissibility of such harm.[73] Within this context, harm relates to conduct that is intentionally committed by a perpetrator with a discriminatory mind-set against, or in relation to, a specific individual or group, based on their identity, and has a severely harmful effect. Therefore, it is the discriminatory intention with which harmful acts are perpetrated that distinguishes persecution from otherwise harmful conduct.

The manifestation of harm must be sufficiently tethered to an identifiable group or collectivity on one or more of the five protected grounds, including membership in a particular religious community.[74] A successful claim for asylum presupposes that "the State perpetuates the harm or abdicates in its responsibility to control the actions of private actors".[75]

---

[69] Storey *What constitutes persecution* (2014) 2-3.
[70] *Senathirajah Ravichandran v. Secretary of State for the Home Department*, United Kingdom: Court of Appeal (England and Wales), 11 October 1995, pg 107.
[71] Storey *What constitutes persecution* (2014) 6.
[72] Rempell *Defining Persecution* (2013) 52.
[73] Rempell *Defining Persecution* (2013) 52.
[74] Rempell *Defining Persecution* (2013) 52.
[75] Rempell *Defining Persecution* (2013) fn 47, pg 9.

Harmful conduct, or the cumulative effect of harm, may constitute *prima facie* evidence of persecution, provided such harm was deliberately imposed.[76] In terms of refugee law, the hesitation to define persecution is once again attributable to vagueness, especially given the large "variety of inflicted harms that may fall under the persecution rubric".[77] In the context of refugee law, 'harm' may include physical harms,[78] restraints and deprivations of privacy,[79] resource and opportunity limitation,[80] psychological harms,[81] and infringements on human rights.[82] It may be inferred from Article 33 of the Refugee Convention that:

> [A] threat to life or freedom on account of race, religion, nationality, political opinion or membership of a particular social group is always persecution. Other serious violations of human rights – for the same reasons – would also constitute persecution.... Whether other prejudicial actions or threats would amount to persecution will depend on the circumstances of each case...[83]

Severity of harm implies that the harm caused will only amount to persecution when a certain degree or threshold of severity has been reached. However, the threshold of the severity of harm is a contentious issue.[84] Rempell suggests a continuous suffering model, whereby harm is not only

---

[76] Rempell *Defining Persecution* (2013) 52.
[77] Rempell *Defining Persecution* (2013) 4.
[78] The different types of physical harm constituting persecution may well be too numerous to provide an exhaustive list, but may include *inter alia*: torture or other cruel and inhumane treatment or punishment, rape, murder and mutilation – Rempell *Defining Persecution* (2013) 10.
[79] Restraints and deprivations of privacy in this sense refers to personal liberty and freedom of movement, and may include *inter alia*: arbitrary confinement; extrajudicial surveillance, searches and seizures; and any form of slavery or forced labour – Rempell *Defining Persecution* (2013) 11.
[80] Civic or economic disadvantages or resource and opportunity limitation include various actions that generally relate to or have a direct influence on a person's patrimony or monetary means – Rempell *Defining Persecution* (2013) 12-13.
[81] Psychological harms refers to the derivative effect that other forms of persecution may have on the internal mental and emotional suffering of a person. – Rempell *Defining Persecution* (2013) 52.
[82] Virtually all forms of persecutory conduct may, directly or indirectly, result in the infringement or violation of one or more human rights and it may therefore prove redundant to expressly discuss the human rights grounding of each harm relevant to a particular case – Rempell *Defining Persecution* (2013), 24.
[83] UNHCR *Procedures and Criteria for Determining Refugee Status* (2011) par 51-52.
[84] Rempell *Defining Persecution* (2013) 25.

assessed as a sufficiently harmful isolated incident, but also based on the cumulative harmful effect that a range of actions may have on the individual's continuous experience.[85] Therefore, a person may have been subjected to various manifestations of discriminatory measures that do not independently constitute persecution. However, if the discriminatory measures are combined with other adverse factors, such as a general atmosphere of insecurity in the country of origin, its cumulative harmful effect may "produce an effect on the mind of the applicant that can reasonably justify a claim to well-founded fear of persecution on 'cumulative grounds'".[86] Furthermore, even in situations where the conduct satisfies the threshold of severity, such harm will not amount to persecution if "the inflicted harm is normatively justified or otherwise permissible".[87]

Most importantly for this study, refugee law includes protection against persecution on the grounds of religious orientation or identity. According to the former UN Special Rapporteur on Freedom of Religion or Belief, Heiner Bielefeldt, the experiences of asylum seekers persecuted for their religion or belief fails to receive appropriate attention and recognition.[88]

> [W]hen applying for asylum because of violations of their freedom of religion or belief, refugees have sometimes experienced that their claims are not taken seriously. Some of them have been given bizarre recommendations, such as to avoid public exposure and to keep their faith to themselves.[89]

The Rapporteur noted diverging views and implementations of States and governments in honouring their responsibility to accommodate refugees, including those who are fleeing serious deprivations of their freedom of religion or belief.[90] While some governments have demonstrated solidarity and provided refugee protection, other governments have been reluctant to assist refugees.[91]

> Yet other Governments have indicated that they would be merely willing to accommodate refugees from religious backgrounds close to their own pre-

---

[85] Rempell *Defining Persecution* (2013) 52.
[86] UNHCR *Procedures and Criteria for Determining Refugee Status* (2011) par 53.
[87] Rempell *Defining Persecution* (2013) 39.
[88] Bielefeldt *FORB: Thematic Reports* (2017) 360–361.
[89] Bielefeldt *FORB: Thematic Reports* (2017) 360.
[90] Bielefeldt *FORB: Thematic Reports* (2017) 361.
[91] Bielefeldt *FORB: Thematic Reports* (2017) 361.

dominant religious traditions. However, this would amount to a (re)territorialization of religion and thus would clearly be at variance with the freedom of religion or belief, which protects human beings in their diverse convictions and practices instead of fostering religiously homogeneous territories.[92]

Although it is conceivable that the same conduct may give rise to both a legitimate claim for refugee status as well as constituting an international crime, the differing contexts of 'persecution' contain fundamental disparities. The norms of recognising persecution in the context of asylum and refugee law are distinct, and "cannot readily be applied to customary international criminal law entailing individual criminal responsibility".[93] There are a number of important reasons for this.

Firstly, the gravity threshold under international criminal law is much higher. In refugee law, a harm taxonomy includes, but is not limited to, human rights infringements. Conversely, the proscription of 'grievous persecution' is specifically based on persecutory conduct that results in a severe deprivation of fundamental rights.[94]

Secondly, the determination of refugee status is premised on a subjective fear, supplemented with external corroboration of such a fear.[95] Therefore, the applicability of 'persecution' is considered either retrospectively or hypothetically, rather than an objective consideration of the situation prevailing in the applicant's country of origin.[96] Whilst such a determination of persecution is understandable and necessary in the context of refugee law, an assessment of 'grievous persecution' requires an objective analysis of evidence by a court of law.

Thirdly, in accepting persecution as a 'well-founded fear', refugee law essentially seeks to prevent persecution and human rights infringements. International criminal law, on the other hand, is applied *ex post facto* with

---

[92] Bielefeldt *FORB: Thematic Reports* (2017) 361.
[93] *Tadić (Trial Judgement)* par 694.
[94] Art 7(1)(h) read with art 7(2)(g) of the *Rome Statute of the International Criminal Court*, Doc. A/CONF.183/9 of 17 July 1998 in force 1 July 2002.
[95] Art 1 A(2) of the *Refugee Convention of 1951* provides that the term 'refugee' shall apply to any person who subjectively establishes a well-founded fear of being persecuted. Asylum seekers must show a well-founded fear of persecution which can either be assessed *ex post facto* or based on a reasonable fear of persecution in the future. Although a well-founded fear must be objectively considered to be reasonable, the prevailing factor of refugee status must normally be determined on an individual basis. This fear must be assessed by a competent administrative authority.
[96] UNHCR *Procedures and Criteria for Determining Refugee Status* (2011) par 37.

2. The Contextual Spectrums of the Notion of Persecution

the aim of retribution for, and to a lesser extent deterrence of, existing or continuing human rights deprivations.

Finally, refugee law is concerned with the protection of persons against human rights violations perpetrated by their own government.[97] Conversely, the criminalisation of persecution is directed at the responsible individual, regardless of whether State or non-State actors inflicted the human rights infringements.[98]

2.6 Conclusion

Although the words 'persecute' and the act of 'persecution' have come to acquire a universally accepted meaning, an exact definition thereof has remained somewhat of an enigma. An understanding of persecution may range between contextual understandings, which exacerbates its opacity. It thus seems imperative that those engaged in advocating on behalf of the persecuted should possess a working knowledge of the various contextual spectrums, conceptualisations and applications of 'persecution', and its related terminology. As a starting point, it is advisable to clearly indicate the contextual framework within which one intends to use the terms 'persecution' and 'religion'. Although a contextual and existential awareness may assist in limiting contradictions and overuse, the notion of persecution remains prone to ambiguity and exploitation. Therefore, conceptualising the notion of 'persecution' is not a foregone conclusion, considering that the lack of a coherent, succinct definition is partly the result of:

---

[97] Human rights violations include government transgressions of the rights guaranteed by national, regional, and international human rights laws and acts and omissions directly attributable to the State involving failure to implement legal obligations derived from human rights standards. Any discrimination on grounds of race, colour, sex, language, religion, political or national or social origin, property, birth or other status with the purpose or effect of nullifying or impairing the equal enjoyment or exercise of any human rights constitutes a violation of human rights – Office of the United Nations High Commissioner for Human Rights. *Professional Training Series No. 7, Training Manual on Human Rights Monitoring*. United Nations Publication. (2001), pg 10 https://www.ohchr.org/Documents/Publications/training7Introen.pdf. Accessed 16/01/2019. As discussed in Horton, G. *Dying Alive - A Legal Assessment of Human Rights Violations in Burma*, a report co-funded by the Netherlands Ministry for Development Co-operation. Images Asia (2005), par 5.18.

[98] Human rights abuses on the other hand, "describes conduct inflicted by non-State actors" – OHCHR *Training Manual on Human Rights Monitoring* (2001) 10, and discussed in Horton *Dying Alive* (2005) par 5.17.

- the variety of situations and contextual understandings the term might cover;
- the various possible manifestations of hostility and conduct;
- the varying roles and emphasis of the perception of those involved; and
- the varying levels of severity of harm that results from such persecution.

Arguably, some of these identified obstacles may be overcome by addressing the opacity relating to religious persecution. Thus, the spectrum of contextual understandings of persecution was clearly demarcated and distinguished in this chapter.

Despite the fact that all of these contextual perspectives are in agreement that discrimination is at the core of understanding persecution, such discrimination will only amount to persecution if there is some form of consequential harm.[99] Essentially, the severity of this 'harm' is one of the key aspects that differentiate between the contextual uses of the term 'persecution'. In other words, while 'persecution' has a universal understanding, it is only when certain gravity thresholds are satisfied that persecution is considered from a 'legal dimension'. While having the benefit of being based on international norms, none of the legal uses of the term 'persecution' are meant to exhaustively cover all existential experiences of persecution. However, though a holistical understanding of religious persecution must always reflect an 'existential' understanding, referring to a broad colloquial, religious epistemological, sociological and psychological context, the 'legal dimension' is generally limited to relatively severe instances of religious persecution.

In refugee law, 'persecution' is used as an assessment criterion in order to determine the eligibility for asylum and refugee protection. This assessment, however, does not conform to the legal qualifications of international criminal law. Therefore, even within the 'legal dimensions', the contextual use of persecution contains fundamental disparities and should be distinguished. It is mainly for this reason that the writer prefers to use the prefix 'grievous' when referring to persecutory conduct that satisfies the severity threshold for crimes against humanity under international criminal law.[100] In Chapter Three this latter context will be discussed in more detail. At this point, it is advisable to readers unacauinted with international criminal law, to first read Appendix A for an overview of the topic.

---

[99] Tieszen *Re-Examining Religious Persecution* (2008) 38.
[100] *Tadić (Trial Judgement)* par 694.

Chapter Three: The Crime of Persecution in International Criminal Law

3.1 Introduction

Within the broader scattered spectrum of concurrent contextual notions of persecution, particular incidences of religious persecution are, because of their scale, severity, and discriminatory motivation, so heinous that they may be justifiably categorised as human rights atrocities of serious concern to the international community. Consequently, persecution in its most grievous form constitute one of the enumerated inhumane acts of crimes against humanity. In this context, persecution has been repeatedly and indisputably recognised since its inception into contemporary international criminal law.[1] The most notable reason for that is the acceptance that widespread or systematic discrimination should be the concern of the international community. As a result, grievous persecutory conduct necessitates individual criminal responsibility, provided the relevant prerequisites are satisfied.

The foremost purpose of this chapter is to analyse the current legal understanding of crimes against humanity of persecution in its non-specific or generic sense. First, the history and evolution of the crime of persecution in international law is briefly examined. Second, 'grievous persecution' will be contextualised as an underlying inhumane act of crimes against humanity in terms of the *Rome Statute*.[2] In order to address the substantive ambiguities of persecution, a clarification of the *actus reus*, *mens rea*, and legal threshold of severity will be crucial. It should be noted that the conditions of applicability for crimes against humanity is discussed in Appendix A. Third, 'grievous' persecution is confirmed as a crime of international concern based on its related deprivation of fundamental human rights. Last, the lack of precision regarding persecution means that its characterisation has, at times, been intertwined with other international crimes, especially genocide. The section concludes by clearly distinguishing 'grievous' persecution from other international acts and crimes.

---

[1] The crime of persecution has been included in all the statutes of the major international criminal tribunals.
[2] *Rome Statute of the International Criminal Court*, Doc. A/CONF.183/9 of 17 July 1998 *in force* 1 July 2002.

3.2 The Origins and Evolution of the Crime of Persecution in International Criminal Law

This section briefly examines the history of persecution as a crime against humanity. In doing so, it will become clear that the emblematic nature of persecution served a functional role in defining the parameters and normative insights of international criminal law, especially in terms of its relation to the protection of fundamental human rights.[3]

3.2.1 The origins of the crime of persecution

> The story behind the recognition of persecution as a crime of international concern is a key chapter in the development of international criminal law. In short, acceptance ... that widespread or systematic discrimination should be the concern of the international community – not simply the territorial state – was instrumental in defining the parameters of the contemporary international criminal law framework. Ongoing international efforts ... to repress persecutory conduct were a primary impetus – if not the primary impetus – behind the delineation of the category of crimes against humanity, of which the crime of persecution is a part.[4]

Historically, persecution had been situated on the cusp between discriminatory conduct constituting the exclusive concern at the domestic level, and mass discrimination rising to the level of international concern.[5] The origin of international concern with persecution is evident in the first multilateral efforts to respond to such conduct in the wake of the First World War.[6] Unfortunately, the failure in attempts by the League of Nations to criminalise such conduct, was ultimately "evidenced in the rise of the mass persecution of groups on, *inter alia*, racial, religious and political grounds in the lead-up to and throughout the Second World War".[7]

---

[3] Brady, H. and Liss, R. *The Evolution of Persecution as a Crime Against Humanity*, in *Historical Origins of International Criminal Law: Volume 3*, Bergsmo, M. et al. (eds). Torkel Opsahl Academic EPublisher, Brussels (2014), pg 430.
[4] Brady, H. & Liss, R. The Evolution of Persecution as a Crime Against Humanity, in Historical Origins of International Criminal Law: Volume 3, Bergsmo, M. et al. (eds). Torkel Opsahl Academic EPublisher, Brussels (2014), pg 429
[5] Brady & Liss *Evolution of Persecution* (2014) 430–431.
[6] Brady & Liss *Evolution of Persecution* (2014) 433.
[7] Brady & Liss *Evolution of Persecution* (2014) 433.

Consequently, persecution as a crime under international law emerged in the aftermath of the atrocities and human rights infringements committed by the Nazi regime.[8] The Nuremberg Charter included persecutions on political, racial or religious grounds amongst the crimes against humanity over which the Nuremberg Tribunal had jurisdiction.[9] The Tribunal described the Nazi persecutions as "a record of consistent and systematic inhumanity on the greatest scale".[10] After the Nuremberg Trials, international policymakers and lawyers recognised

> that certain acts – because of their scale, their severity, and, in some cases, their motivation – were so heinous that they aptly could be called crimes against the whole of mankind and the international order.[11]

As a result, persecution as a crime against humanity was recognised in a number of other post-war legal instruments, including the *Tokyo Charter*,[12] *Control Council Law No. 10*,[13] and the *Nuremberg Principles*.[14]

The crime of persecution experienced a 'kind of renaissance' in the 1990s. On the one hand, the progression of persecution was promoted by the International Law Commission (ILC). In the commentary to Article 21 of the 1991 *Draft Code of Crimes against the Peace and the Security of Mankind*, the ILC stated that persecution relates to human rights deprivations, which "seek to subject individuals or groups of individuals to a kind of life

---

[8] Brady & Liss *Evolution of Persecution* (2014) 434.
[9] Art 6(c) of the United Nations, *Charter of the International Military Tribunal – Annex to the Agreement for the prosecution and punishment of the major war criminals of the European Axis ("London Agreement")*, 8 August 1945.
[10] *The Trial of German Major War Criminals, Proceedings of the International Military Tribunal Sitting at Nuremberg, Germany*. International Military Tribunal, Judgment of 1 October 1946, pg 247. The Tribunal devoted a section of its judgement on outlining the persecutory acts that were perpetrated as part of the Nazis' systematic persecution of the Jews – *IMT Judgment* (1946) 463.
[11] Chertoff, E. *Prosecuting Gender-Based Persecution: The Islamic State at the ICC*. The Yale Law Journal (2017), pg 1065–1066.
[12] Art 5(c) of the *Charter of the IMT for the trial of the major war criminals in the Far East*, proclaimed at Tokyo on 19 January 1946.
[13] Art II(c) of the *Control Council Law No. 10, Punishment of Persons Guilty of War Crimes, Crimes Against Peace and Against Humanity*, 20 December 1945, Official Gazette of the Control Council for Germany, No. 3, 31 January 1946, available at http://avalon.law.yale.edu/imt/imt10.asp. Accessed 20/06/2016. Several of the US Military Tribunals sitting in Nuremberg, operating under the auspices of *Control Council Law No. 10*, explored the ambit of the crime of persecution – Byron, C. *War Crimes and Crimes Against Humanity* (2009), pg 225–226.
[14] UNGA *Resolution 95(1) on the Affirmation of the Principles of International Law* 1946.

in which enjoyment of some of their basic rights is repeatedly or constantly denied".[15] The 1996 *ILC Draft Code* provided for the crime of persecution "on political, racial, religious or ethnic grounds".[16] In the commentary to Article 18, the ILC stated that the "inhuman act of persecution may take many forms with its common characteristic being the denial of the human rights and fundamental freedoms to which every individual is entitled without distinction".[17] On the other hand was the criminalisation and prosecutions before the two UN International Criminal Tribunals for Rwanda and the former Yugoslavia respectively.[18] The jurisprudence of the ICTY[19] provides the most thorough analysis of the crime of persecution to date.[20] The ICTY jurisprudence makes it clear that at the core of the articulation of persecution is "some form of discrimination that is intended to be and results in an infringement of an individual's fundamental rights".[21] There are fewer judgements on persecution by the ICTR,[22] which tend to follow the ICTY jurisprudence. Both Tribunals have consistently defined

---

[15] International Law Commission, 1991 *Draft Code of Crimes against the Peace and the Security of Mankind,* Yearbook of the International Law Commission, 1991, Vol II Part One, document A/CN.4/435 and Add.1. (Hereinafter referred to as the *1991 ILC Draft Code*).

[16] Art 18(e) of the International Law Commission, *Draft Code of Offences against the Peace and Security of Mankind with commentaries 1996,* Yearbook of the International Law Commission, 1996, Vol. II, Part Two, par 50. http://www.legal-tools.org/doc/5e4532/. Accessed 13/02/2019. (Hereinafter referred to as the *1996 ILC Draft Code, with commentary*).

[17] Par 11 commenting on Art 18 – *1996 ILC Draft Code, with commentary* (1996) 46–48.

[18] Brady & Liss *Evolution of Persecution* (2014) 500.

[19] UN Security Council, *Statute of the International Criminal Tribunal for the Former Yugoslavia (as amended on 17 May 2002),* 25 May 1993. (*Statute of the ICTY*). Persecution on political, racial or religious grounds are provided for in terms of art 5(h) of the *Statute of the ICTY*.

[20] Byron, C. *War Crimes and Crimes Against Humanity in the Rome Statute of the International Criminal Court.* Manchester University Press (2009), pg 226.

[21] *Prosecutor v Duško Tadić (Trial Judgement),* Case No. IT-94-1-T, ICTY, 7 May 1997, par 696.

[22] UN Security Council, *Statute of the International Criminal Tribunal for Rwanda (as last amended on 13 October 2006),* 8 November 1994. (*Statute of the ICTR*). In the hallmark case of *Riggiu,* a civilian journalist and broadcaster was charged and convicted by the ICTR Trial Chamber for persecution based on his actions which resulted in propagating the Hutu extremist ideology, by systematically inciting ethnic hatred, persecution and violence against the entire Tutsi minority – *Prosecutor v Georges Ruggiu (Trial Judgment),* Case No. ICTR 97-32-I, 1 June 2000, par 19.

3. The Crime of Persecution in International Criminal Law 53

'persecution' in parallel,[23] from which the following skeletal framework was formed:

> The *actus reus* required an act or omission that (1) discriminated in fact; (2) denied or infringed upon a fundamental right laid down in customary international law or treaty law; and (3) where not specified as a crime under the relevant provision on crimes against humanity, the cumulative effect of the underlying acts of persecution reached a level of gravity equivalent to that for other crimes against humanity. The mens rea required that the underlying act or omission was (1) carried out deliberately/intentionally and (2) with the intention to discriminate on political, racial, or religious grounds.[24]

These developments ultimately fuelled the adoption of the *Rome Statute* of the ICC, constituting the most advanced and acceptable codification of persecution yet.

3.2.2 Persecution in terms of the Rome Statute

'Grievous persecution' constitutes an enumerated inhumane act of crimes against humanity in terms of the *Rome Statute*. Article 7(2)(g), read together with Article 7(1)(h), defines persecution in the context of crimes against humanity, as:

> ... the intentional and severe deprivation of fundamental rights contrary to international law by reason of the identity of the group or collectively... against any identifiable group or collectivity on political, racial, national, ethnic, cultural, religious, gender, or other grounds that are universally recognized as impermissible under international law, in connection with any act referred to in this paragraph or any crime within the jurisdiction of the Court.[25]

---

[23] *Prosecutor v Milorad Krnojelac (Appeal Judgement)*, Case No. ICTY-97-25-A, ICTY, 17 September 2003, par 185, followed by *Prosecutor v Mitar Vasiljević (Appeal Judgement)*, IT-98-32-A, ICTY, 25 February 2004, par 113; *Prosecutor v Tihomir Blaškić (Appeal Judgement)*, Case No. IT-95-14-A, ICTY, 29 July 2004, par 131; *Prosecutor v Dario Kordić, Mario Cerkez (Appeal Judgement)*, Case No. IT-95-14/2-A, ICTY, 17 December 2004, par 101; *Prosecutor v Miroslav Kvočka et al. (Appeal Judgement)*, IT-98-30/1-A, ICTY, 28 February 2005, par 320; *Prosecutor v Miroslav Deronjić (Judgement on Sentencing Appeal)*, IT-02-61-A, ICTY, 20 July 2005, par 109; *Prosecutor v Milomir Stakić (Appeal Judgement)*, IT-97-24-A, ICTY, 22 March 2006, par 327.

[24] Brady & Liss *Evolution of Persecution* (2014) 504.

[25] Fournet, C., & Pégorier. *'Only One Step Away From Genocide': The Crime of Persecution in International Criminal Law*. International Criminal Law Review, Vol. 10, Issue 5, pages 713 - 738. Marthinus Nijhoff Publishers (2010), pg 713.

Unfortunately, this definition is still hindered by a lack of substantive and practical clarity, definitional precision and a distinct characterisation. Nevertheless, it does provide a contemporary understanding of persecution as a crime against humanity for the purposes of individual criminal responsibility. The *Rome Statute* does provide more clarity in regards to what constitutes an underlying offence by specifying that the conduct must have been committed in connection with any act that may constitute crimes against humanity or any other crime within the jurisdiction of the Court. Furthermore, the *Rome Statute* has broadened the list of discriminatory purposes or grounds to also include national, ethnic, cultural, gender, or 'other grounds that are universally recognised as impermissible under international law'.

In *Duch*, the Supreme Court Chamber of Cambodia Tribunal, concluded that persecution has been a crime against humanity under customary international law since 1975.[26] Therefore, it is clear that persecution is conferred a position of great prominence.[27]

3.3 The Definitional Elements of the Crime of Persecution

'Grievous persecution' constitutes an enumerated inhumane act of crimes against humanity in terms of the *Rome Statute*. According to the conditions of applicability, persecution may amount to crimes against humanity if: (1) the *chapeau* elements are satisfied, and (2) certain *sui generis* definitional requirements or elements of persecution are also satisfied. These definitional elements will form the crux of the discussion that follows.

The ICTY jurisprudence makes it clear that at the core of the articulation of the *actus reus* and *mens rea* of persecution is "some form of discrimination that is intended to be and results in an infringement of an individual's fundamental rights".[28] Although the crime of persecution has been extensively analysed in the jurisprudence of the *ad hoc* tribunals, "[n]one of the judgments before the ICC have addressed the elements of this crime".[29] The *ICC Elements of Crimes* lists the following elements for 'grievous persecution':

---

[26] *Appeal Judgement (Kaing Guek Eav alias Duch)*, Case File 001/18-07-2007/ECCC/SC, Extraordinary Chambers in the Courts of Cambodia, 3 February 2012, par 225. (Hereinafter referred to as *Duch Appeal Judgement*)
[27] *Prosecutor v Kupreškić et al. (Trial Judgement)* 597.
[28] *Tadić (Trial Judgement)* par 696.
[29] Klamberg, M. (ed.). *Commentary on the Law of the International Criminal Court*, TOAEP, Brussels (2017), pg 55–56.

1. The perpetrator severely deprived, contrary to international law, one or more persons of fundamental rights.
2. The perpetrator targeted such person or persons by reason of the identity of a group or collectivity or targeted the group or collectivity as such.
3. Such targeting was based on political, racial, national, ethnic, cultural, religious, gender, or other grounds that are universally recognised as impermissible under international law.
4. The conduct was committed in connection with any act referred to in Article 7, paragraph 1, of the Statute or any crime within the jurisdiction of the Court.
5. The conduct was committed as part of a widespread or systematic attack directed against a civilian population.
6. The perpetrator knew that the conduct was part of, or intended the conduct to be part of, a widespread or systematic attack directed against a civilian population.

The phrase 'contrary to international law' refers, in general, to the unlawfulness or unjustifiability of the conduct, which may be inferred from general principles of criminal law.[30] It was also mentioned that 'knowledge' is considered inclusive of the cognitive appreciation of the unlawfulness of the prohibited act or result. In the context of 'grievous persecution', consequential severe deprivation of fundamental human rights, is a *prima facie* indicator of unlawfulness.

The following assessment of the definitional elements of 'grievous persecution' is offered in the context of the *Rome Statute*. The elements of persecution may be divided into three main categories: the *actus reus* of persecution, i. e. the required material elements or criminally liable conduct; the *mens rea* of persecution, i. e. the required mental elements or subjective mindset of the perpetrator; and the required threshold of severity. The contextual elements specific to crimes against humanity of persecution will be integrated amongst these categories.

---

[30] International Criminal Court (ICC), *Elements of Crimes*, 2011, Official Records of the Review Conference of the Rome Statute of the International Criminal Court, Kampala, 31 May–11 June 2010 (International Criminal Court publication, RC/11), General Introduction, par 6.

3.3.1 The *actus reus* of 'grievous persecution'

The *actus reus* (material element) focusses on the act or omission (conduct), consequences and circumstances associated with each crime. The crime of persecution essentially pertains to discriminatory conduct (a voluntary act or omission), which need not be criminal in nature or elicit a criminal effect, and which results, separately or cumulatively, in the severe deprivation of fundamental rights contrary to international law.[31] In defining the objective element (*actus reus*) of persecution in terms of the *Rome Statute*, the following elements may be identified:

- an underlying discriminatory act or omission (persecutory conduct);
- committed in connection with any acts of an inhumane nature or any other jurisdictionally relevant international crime (connection requirement);
- resulting in the deprivation of a fundamental right (the causation requirement).

3.3.1.1 An underlying discriminatory act or omission (persecutory conduct)

Persecutory conduct must be understood as a voluntary (will-controlled) and discriminatory human conduct, which may be either a 'positive act' or a 'failure to act' (omission) under circumstances where there is a legal duty upon somebody to perform a certain type of positive act.[32]

In terms of a persecutory omission, such conduct may be based on an organisational policy that exhibits a deliberate failure to take action. For example, if the State perpetuates the harm or abdicates in its responsibility to control social hostility discriminately directed at a certain protected group, through the deliberate inaction of responsible office bearers.

Regarding positive persecutory conduct (discriminatory practices and acts), such underlying acts of persecution have remained an aspect of definitional concern. In *Kordić*, the ICTY noted that "neither international treaty law nor case law provides a comprehensive list of illegal acts encompassed by the charge of persecution".[33] Therefore, persecutory

---

[31] *Prosecutor v Miroslav Kvočka et al. (Trial Judgement)*, Case No. IT-98-30/1-T, 2 November 2001, par 186. See also *Duch (Appeal Judgement)* paras 226, 240, 267 and 278.
[32] Snyman, C.R. *Criminal law*. LexisNexis, 6th edition (2014), pg 51–54.
[33] *Prosecutor v Dario Kordić, Mario Cerkez (Trial Judgement)*, Case No. IT-95-14/2-T, 26 February 2001, par 694.

3. The Crime of Persecution in International Criminal Law

conduct is not based on a specific list of prohibited actions. In *Tadić*, the tribunal concluded that:

> the crime of persecution encompasses a variety of acts, including, *inter alia*, those of a physical, economic or judicial nature, that violate an individual's right to the equal enjoyment of his basic rights.[34]

Based on the jurisprudence of the *ad hoc* tribunals, three broad classes of acts that may amount to persecution can be identified, provided they contribute significantly to the overall cumulative effect of persecutory conduct: "[s]erious bodily and mental harm; infringements upon freedom; and attacks against property".[35] Thus, it is clear that the crime of persecution encompasses numerous acts of varying severity, yet this list is non-exhaustive.[36] Nonetheless, there is "a limit to the acts which can constitute persecution".[37] Persecutory conduct must be directed discriminately and must result, alone or cumulatively, in a severe deprivation of fundamental rights.[38] In other words, persecutory conduct must involve the deprivation of a fundamental right, the consequential effect of which must be of sufficient gravity, whether considered separately or cumulatively.[39]

In *Tadić*, the prosecution asserted that "the crime of persecution encompasses any acts of an inhumane nature directed against a civilian population when committed with discriminatory intent on the specified grounds".[40] Consequently, it is not necessary to have a separate act of an inhumane nature to constitute persecution, provided the common ele-

---

[34] *Tadić (Trial Judgement)* par 710.
[35] *Prosecutor v Tihomir Blaškić (Trial Judgement)*, Case No. IT-95-14-T, 3 March 2000, par 556.
[36] In terms *Kordić*, the Tribunal summarised some of the acknowledged forms of persecutory acts. They include: the seizure, collection, segregation, deportation and forced transfer of civilians to camps; beatings and killings; murder, imprisonment, and deportation, and such attacks on property as would constitute a destruction of the livelihood of a certain population; the destruction and plunder of property, unlawful detention of civilians; physical and mental injury; and infringements upon individual freedom – *Kordić (Trial Judgement)* par 198. In addition, *Kovack* added psychological harm, humiliation, and harassment as possible forms of persecution, provided of course it contributes significantly to the overall cumulative effect of persecutory conduct – *Kvočka (Trial Judgement)* par 190.
[37] *Tadić (Trial Judgement)* par 707.
[38] Ambos, K. & Wirth, S. *The Current Law of Crimes Against Humanity: An Analysis of UNTAET Regulation 15/2000.* Crim LF, 13 (2002), pg 79.
[39] Ambos & Wirth *The Current Law of Crimes Against Humanity* (2002) 79.
[40] *Tadić (Trial Judgement)* par 699.

ment of discrimination in regard to the enjoyment of a basic or fundamental right is present.[41] Therefore, depending on the circumstances, "the discrimination itself makes the act inhumane".[42] Accordingly, persecutory conduct may entail a serious form of discrimination, to the extent that it may be termed inhumane or offensive to humanity.

Implicit in the use of the phrase 'inhumane act' or 'conduct of an inhumane nature', is the severe infringement of a fundamental right for a discriminatory purpose. As a result, conduct of an inhumane nature, whether considered separately or cumulatively, inherently entails a severe human rights deprivation. In other words, the nature and gravity of the discriminatory act itself, or the cumulative effect of a course of discriminatory conduct, must be severe enough to be termed inhumane or offensive to humanity. Thus, 'persecutory conduct' is not, in itself, premised on the commission of a distinct underlying inhumane act, because the discrimination itself or the effect thereof may constitute conduct of an inhumane nature, i.e. a severe deprivation of a fundamental right. Therefore, whether "[s]eparately or combined, the acts must amount to persecution, though it is not required that each alleged underlying act be regarded as a violation of international law".[43]

Consequently, Ambos distinguishes between two types of discriminatory conduct which may constitute persecutory conduct:

> acts which are sufficiently serious to constitute persecution on their own even if only one act is committed; [and] acts which are less serious but which, together with other acts, through their cumulative effect reach the necessary level of gravity.[44]

We can, therefore, distinguish between 'Inhumane-type' conduct, which is based on an act or acts that are sufficiently serious to constitute persecution (inherently inhumane acts or crimes), and 'Other-type' conduct, which refer to less serious (including non-felonious) acts that, together with other acts, through their cumulative effect, satisfy the necessary severity threshold.

---

[41] *Tadić (Trial Judgement)* par 697.
[42] *Tadić (Trial Judgement)* par 697. See also *Fédération Nationale des Déportés et Internés Résistants et Patriotes and Others v. Barbie*, Court of Cassation (Criminal Chamber), 20 December 1985, 78 I.L.R. 125, pg 143.
[43] Zgonec-Rožej, M. (Principal author). *International Criminal Law Manual*. International Bar Association (IBA) (2013), pg 158.
[44] Ambos & Wirth *The Current Law of Crimes Against Humanity* (2002) 76.

a) Inhumane-type conduct

Inhumane acts or conduct of an inhumane nature refers primarily to the inherent cruelty of the conduct or the brutality of its consequences. In this regard, the discriminatory act or acts themselves are severe enough to be considered as inhumane. An act of an inhumane nature is the general characteristic of all the underlying acts constituting crimes against humanity, such as murder, rape or torture. In *Tadić*, the ICTY concluded that

> [g]iven the fact... [that] only the persecution type requires discriminatory intent, there would seem to be no difficulty in attaching additional culpability to acts which fall within the 'inhumane act' category of crimes against humanity if motivated by discrimination.[45]

Therefore, the commission of any of the underlying acts constituting crimes against humanity may be considered as 'inhumane acts' for the purposes of the *actus reus* of persecution. Cassese justly concludes that:

> All of these crimes [enumerated inhumane acts], if found to be pursued with a specific discriminatory purpose, can fall under a persecutions charge.[46]

It is obvious that "all of the inhumane acts enumerated in Article 7(1) of the *Rome Statute* amount to severe deprivation[s] of fundamental rights and can constitute persecution",[47] provided the persecutory acts were committed with the required discriminatory intent.[48] Thus far at the ICC,

---

[45] *Tadić (Trial Judgement)* par 702.
[46] Cassese, A. et al. *International Criminal Law: Cases and Commentary*. Oxford University Press (2011), pg 184.
[47] Ambos & Wirth *The Current Law of Crimes Against Humanity* (2002) 74. The underlying acts of crimes against humanity in terms of the *Rome Statute*, include: (a) Murder; (b) Extermination; (c) Enslavement; (d) Deportation or forcible transfer of population; (e) Imprisonment or other severe deprivation of physical liberty in violation of fundamental rules of international law; (f) Torture; (g) Rape, sexual slavery, enforced prostitution, forced pregnancy, enforced sterilization, or any other form of sexual violence of comparable gravity; (h) Persecution against any identifiable group or collectivity on political, racial, national, ethnic, cultural, religious, gender as defined in paragraph 3, or other grounds that are universally recognised as impermissible under international law, in connection with any act referred to in this paragraph or any crime within the jurisdiction of the Court; (i) Enforced disappearance of persons; (j) The crime of apartheid; (k) Other inhumane acts of a similar character intentionally causing great suffering, or serious injury to body or to mental or physical health.
[48] *Tadić (Trial Judgement)* par 700.

persecutory conduct has been incidental to charges for acknowledged inhumane-type acts, which are part of the enumerated inhumane acts under the *Rome Statute*, and were committed with the additional discriminatory intent.[49] For example, the application for an arrest warrant against Laurent Koudou Gbagbo, relied on separate charges of murder and rape as the underlying acts of persecution.[50]

The enumerated inhumane acts in terms of the *Rome Statute* also include a category referred to as 'other inhumane acts'.[51] This category of inhumane acts includes "conduct not specified by the other specific crimes contained within crimes against humanity".[52] As a minimum, an 'inhumane act' must cause great suffering, or serious injury to body or to mental or physical health, which must be equal in gravity, and similar in nature to other underlying crimes against humanity.[53] An 'inhumane act' or an act of an inhumane nature thus includes any conduct of which its nature and gravity are similar to any of the underlying acts constituting crimes against humanity.[54]

---

[49] *Prosecutor v. Gbagbo*, ICC PT. Ch. I, Decision on the Confirmation of Charges against Laurent Gbagbo, ICC-02/11-01/11-656-Red, 12 June 2014, par 204, compared with paras 193–199; *Prosecutor v. Muthaura et al.* ICC PT. Ch. II, ICC-01/09-02/11-382-Red, Decision on the Confirmation of Charges Pursuant to Article 61(7)(a) and (b) of the *Rome Statute*, 23 January 2012, par 283, compared with paras 233, 243, 257, 270–271, 275–277; *Prosecutor v. Ruto et al.* ICC PT. Ch. II, ICC-01/09-01/11-373, Decision on the Confirmation of Charges Pursuant to Article 61(7)(a) and (b) of the *Rome Statute*, 23 January 2012, paras 271–272, compared with paras 225–226, 228–239, 241–242, 248–251, 253–266, in Klamberg *Commentary on the Law* (2017) 56.

[50] *Prosecutor v Laurent Koudou Gbagbo* (ICC) Case No ICC-02/11-01/11, Public redacted version of 'Decision on the Prosecutor's Application Pursuant to Article 58 for a warrant of arrest against Laurent Koudou Gbagbo' (30 November 2011) ('*Gbagbo Arrest Warrant*'), as discussed in Zgonec-Rožej *International Criminal Law Manual* (2013) updated version at 16.

[51] Art 7(1)(k) of the *Rome Statute*.

[52] Cassese *et al. ICL: Cases and Commentary* (2011) 185.

[53] Art 7(1)(k) of the *Rome Statute*.

[54] Inhumane persecutory conduct may include the following acts: murder; extermination; enslavement; deportation; torture; rape; physical violence not constituting torture; and cruel and inhumane treatment amongst others. For an exhaustive list see Triffterer, O. & Ambos, K. *Commentary on the Rome Statute of the International Criminal Court: Observers' Notes, Article by Article*. Beck Publishers, second edition (2008), pg 258–260.

3. The Crime of Persecution in International Criminal Law

The underlying inhumane acts of crimes against humanity generally entail a physical element, a violent "smash",[55] which may be referred to as 'persecution atrocities'. However, persecution does not require physical harm because the "disadvantage to an identifiable group or collectivity or their individual members is an obvious consequence of a severe form of discrimination".[56] Therefore, sufficiently severe forms of discrimination that satisfy the 'inhumane' threshold may constitute the *actus reus* of persecution.[57] A discriminatory policy, such as apartheid or institutionalised discrimination, may be said to be inherently inhumane in nature. Thus, the nature of the discrimination itself makes the ideology inhumane, provided the ideology does 'discriminate in fact' and results in the severe deprivation of fundamental rights.

The connection of persecutory conduct to other underlying inhumane acts of crimes against humanity will form the category of persecutory conduct that most clearly satisfies the principle of legality. The reason for this is because it is more difficult to determine and legally justify the 'other-type' conduct, not inherently of an inhumane nature, as persecutory conduct.

b) 'Other-type' conduct

'Other-type' conduct refers to discriminatory non-enumerated conduct, not inherently of an inhumane nature, provided their cumulative effect offends humanity. It was confirmed in *Tadić*, that conduct other than the enumerated inhumane acts of crimes against humanity ('other-type' conduct), could be considered persecutory, provided the common element of discrimination in regards to the enjoyment of a basic of fundamental rights is present.[58] This means that "acts that are not inherently criminal may become criminal and persecutorial if committed with discriminatory intent".[59]

The underlying discriminatory conduct constituting persecution must be evaluated not in isolation, but in context, considering its cumulative

---

[55] Open Doors Analytical. *World Watch List Methodology*. November 2017, pg 17–18. Available at: http://opendoorsanalytical.org/world-watch-list-methodology-latest-edition-november-2017/. Accessed 09/01/2019.
[56] Triffterer & Ambos *Commentary on the Rome Statute* (2008) 257–258.
[57] *Prosecutor v Blagoje Simić et al.* (Trial Judgement), IT-95-9-T, ICTY, 17 October 2003, par 58.
[58] *Tadić* (Trial Judgement) par 703–710.
[59] *Kvočka* (Trial Judgement) par 186.

effect.[60] This is important for a number of reasons. Firstly, it means that each underlying act need not constitute a crime under international or national law, provided the cumulative effect thereof results in the severe deprivation of fundamental rights. Secondly, the persecutory conduct itself need not be inhumane in nature, but the cumulative effect of 'other-type' conduct must satisfy the 'inhumanity threshold'. Finally, this seems to imply that persecutory conduct should not be considered as individual underlying discriminatory acts, but rather as the accumulation of harm, consequential to a discriminatory policy. This is further evident in the necessity that the conduct must discriminate in fact, which means that the acts are only persecutory in nature if they had an actual discriminatory effect. Acquaviva clarifies this as follows:

> The question of whether a given act, such as harassment or humiliation, amounts to persecution is answered not with reference to its apparent cruelty but with reference to the discrimination the act seeks to inspire.[61]

In other words, persecutory acts may include known felonious conduct,[62] but may also include non-felonious conduct such as a discriminatory ideology, which precipitates an actual result or an overall consequence offensive to humanity. Regardless of the nature of the conduct, the overall consequence must be of an inhumane nature. In *Duch*, it was held that the cumulative approach to the gravity assessment is satisfied if the 'other-type' acts or omissions, when considered cumulatively and in context, result in a severe and intentional breach of fundamental rights to the extent that it is equal in gravity to the enumerated 'inhumane-type' conduct of crimes against humanity.[63] The threshold of 'inhumanity' is therefore at the crux of assessing whether 'other-type' persecutory conduct has satisfied the required level of gravity. What exactly constitutes 'inhumane' or 'offensive to humanity' depends on the circumstances of each case.

Discriminatory conduct, not inherently of an inhumane nature, may therefore include, *inter alia*, unlawful arrests, detentions, imprisonment or confinement of civilians, restrictions on movement to certain places and

---

[60] Cassese *et al. ICL: Cases and Commentary* (2011) par 622.
[61] Acquaviva, G. & Pocar, F. *Crimes Against Humanity. Max Planck Encyclopedia on Public International law*, Wolfrum, R. (ed). Heidelberg: Oxford University Press (2011), pg 4.
[62] *Kvočka (Trial Judgement)* par 186.
[63] *Duch (Appeal judgement)* par 257.

3. The Crime of Persecution in International Criminal Law

times, and registration of members of a group.[64] However, a comprehensive list of persecutory conduct is unattainable in the same way that it may prove impossible to provide a list of actions that may be used to kill a person for the purposes of defining such actions as murder. From a substantive point of view, the crime of persecution is a 'contextual crime' in the sense that it does not pertain to conduct or consequences unique unto itself, but exists as a crime incidental to other acts.

In summary, it has been established that persecutory conduct may consist of 'inhumane-type' or 'other-type' conduct. However, neither of these categories need to consist of physical acts, provided the common element of discrimination is present. Consequently, it is argued that the two acknowledged categories of persecutory conduct, may be further subdivided into two additional categories:

1. Physical 'persecution atrocities', which may be subdivided into:
   a) the commission of one or more of the enumerated inhumane acts of crimes against humanity on a discriminatory basis; or
   b) the commission of physical 'other-type' acts (that are not inherently inhumane in nature), provided their cumulative effect satisfies the severity threshold.

2. 'Iniquitous' persecutory conduct, which may be subdivided into:
   a) the enforcement of discriminatory ideology or policy that is either inherently inhumane in nature, or may be considered to offend humanity based on its cumulative effect; or
   b) persecutory omissions, based on an organisational policy that exhibits a deliberate failure to take action under circumstances where there is a legal duty upon the de facto authority to perform a certain type of positive act, provided their cumulative effect satisfies the severity threshold.

Therefore, persecutory conduct may be summarised as discriminatory acts, policies, practices, or omissions, which are offensive to humanity, whether based on their inherent nature or their cumulative effect.

---

[64] For a non-exhaustive list see Triffterer & Ambos *Commentary on the Rome Statute* (2008) 260–261.

3.3.1.2 Connection requirement (jurisdictional element)

As outlined, the particular acts that may constitute persecution remain essentially undeveloped.[65] However the connection requirement effectively includes the prohibited acts and crimes within the jurisdiction of the Court as underlying acts of persecution, if committed with discriminatory intent.[66] Although persecution must be part of a widespread or systematic attack, the *Rome Statute* requires that it must be linked to at least one other act or crime within the Court's jurisdiction in order to constitute persecution under Article 7.[67] Consequently, persecution must link to another enumerated inhumane act of crimes against humanity, or any other crime within the jurisdiction of the Court.[68] Ambos explains that the connection requirement of the *Rome Statute* results in a twofold application:[69]

1. If the persecutory conduct is linked to war crimes or genocide, the connection requires a link to a complete crime ("connection with ...] any crime within the jurisdiction of the Court").
2. If the persecutory conduct is linked to the individual criminal acts (not a multiplicity of acts) enumerated in Article 7(1) of the *Rome Statute*, the connection required need not relate to another crime against humanity but only to "any act" referred to in Article 7(1) of the *Rome Statute*. This implies that the persecutory conduct must only be connected to a (single) inhumane act, and not to an inhumane act that is part of a widespread or systematic attack consisting of other enumerated inhumane acts.

In other words, a multiplicity of grave human rights violations (which are not, as such, enumerated among the inhumane acts), e. g., severe attacks on personal property, can be transformed into the crime of persecution by a single connected murder.[70]

Subsequently, in terms of the latter application, the connection requirement establishes two types of persecution in the sphere of crimes against humanity:

---

[65] Cryer, R. et al. *An Introduction to International Criminal Law and Procedure*. Cambridge University Press (2007), pg 213.
[66] Cryer et al. *International Criminal Law and Procedure* (2007) 216.
[67] Triffterer & Ambos *Commentary on the Rome Statute* (2008) 221.
[68] Brady & Liss *Evolution of Persecution* (2014) 543.
[69] Ambos & Wirth *The Current Law of Crimes Against Humanity* (2002) 71–72.
[70] Ambos & Wirth *The Current Law of Crimes Against Humanity* (2002) 72

1. Persecution may be an autonomous crime if the persecutory conduct is committed through 'other-type' conduct, i. e. conduct not enumerated as inhumane acts under Article 7(1), but connected with an enumerated inhumane act.[71] In such instances, the connection requirement must be satisfied.

As the perpetrator can understand the gravity of such acts only if he or she knows about the other acts, the knowledge of these other acts is necessary for them to be culpable for a crime against humanity.[72]

2. Persecution may be an incidental crime if the persecutory conduct is based on 'inhumane-type' conduct, i. e. committed through an enumerated inhumane act with discriminatory intent. In such instances, persecution does not pertain to conduct unique unto itself, but constitutes an aggravated form of an enumerated inhumane act. The use of the phrase "any act" suggests to also include any other acts of persecution.[73] If the persecutory conduct (itself) is sufficiently widespread or systematic, the persecutory acts themselves can constitute the inhumane act. In instances where an enumerated inhumane act (including other acts of persecution) forms the underlying act of persecution, a further connection to yet another inhumane act is not required.[74] Therefore, the connection requirement is always fulfilled if persecutory conduct is based on an enumerated inhumane act in Article 7(1).

However, the connection requirement should not be construed to render persecution dependent upon the commission of other listed inhumane acts or crimes. In other words, the connection requirement should be distinguished from the issue whether conduct can amount to persecution.[75] The connection requirement merely entails an objective contextual link between the persecutory conduct and at least one underlying act or crime within the jurisdiction of the ICC.[76] Ambos provides some clarity as to when this connection requirement is established:

---

[71] Ambos & Wirth *The Current Law of Crimes Against Humanity* (2002) 72.
[72] Ambos & Wirth *The Current Law of Crimes Against Humanity* (2002) 82.
[73] Triffterer & Ambos *Commentary on the Rome Statute* (2008) 221.
[74] Ambos & Wirth *The Current Law of Crimes Against Humanity* (2002) 72.
[75] Ambos & Wirth *The Current Law of Crimes Against Humanity* (2002) 70.
[76] Byron *War Crimes and Crimes Against Humanity* (2009) 234.

The connection between the act or crime and the persecutory conduct exists if the goal of the persecution is supported by the act or crime or if the persecution supports the commission of the act or crime. A causal link is not required.[77]

An objective contextual link entails a clear and obvious connection if:

- The purpose or aim of the persecution is attained through the commission of the linked act. In other words, if the other inhumane act or crime was committed in order to satisfy the perpetrator's discriminatory intent.
- The purpose or aim of the inhumane act or crime can only be attained if the conduct is committed on a discriminatory basis.
- Multiple acts of persecution are committed by various perpetrators, but may be connected by a collective discriminatory intent underlying such acts.

Importantly, the connection requirement is not intended as a limitation or restriction for "legitimate prosecutions of persecutions, since it is satisfied by a linkage to even one other recognized crime (a killing or other inhumane act), which one would expect to find in a situation warranting international prosecution".[78] The requirement that persecution must occur in connection with at least one of the acts or crimes criminalised elsewhere in the *Rome Statute*, is aimed at ensuring that "relatively trivial acts of discrimination... do not form the basis for international criminal liability".[79] Consequently, the connection requirement must be interpreted to merely enforce the jurisdictional or contextual threshold for crimes against humanity.[80] It should, however, be mentioned that such a connection between a persecutory act and another crime or act is "not consonant with customary international law".[81]

As such, the connection requirement seems to reinforce the gravity or severity threshold for classifying persecutory acts in the context of crimes against humanity.[82] Effectively, the inclusion of the connection requirement "render unnecessary any requirement for 'equal gravity'

---

[77] Ambos & Wirth *The Current Law of Crimes Against Humanity* (2002) 87.
[78] Cryer et al. *International Criminal Law and Procedure* (2007) 214.
[79] Chertoff *Prosecuting Gender-Based Persecution* (2017) 1109.
[80] Ambos & Wirth *The Current Law of Crimes Against Humanity* (2002) 74.
[81] *Kupreškić et al. (Trial Judgement)* 580.
[82] Ambos & Wirth *The Current Law of Crimes Against Humanity* (2002) 73.

3. The Crime of Persecution in International Criminal Law

with other acts amounting to crimes against humanity or other crimes within the ICC Statute".[83]

The connection requirement should not be confused with the contextual knowledge required for all crimes against humanity. The connection requirement entails an objective link to another inhumane act or crime within the jurisdiction of the ICC. In terms of the *ICC Elements of Crimes*, the connection requirement is purely objective and no additional mental element (*mens rea*) is necessary other than that inherent in the conditions of applicability for crimes against humanity.[84] Therefore, the perpetrator does not have to be aware that the connection exists,[85] but must be aware of the risk that an 'attack' exists and that his conduct objectively forms part of it.[86]

In summary, persecutory conduct must be objectively linked (not causatively linked) to a single inhumane act (which need not be widespread or systematic), or any completed crime within the jurisdiction of the Court. The connection requirement confirms that persecution can be based on 'inhumane-type' or 'other-type' conduct and must thus be interpreted to be a merely jurisdictional requirement (objective conditions of punishability).[87] The connection requirement is satisfied if the act or crime supports the purpose of the persecution or *vice versa*. The connection requirement is satisfied if:

- Multiple acts of persecution may be linked to form the basis of the inhumane conduct, committed with the same discriminatory intent;
- the persecutory conduct can be linked with the commission of any other enumerated inhumane act (no additional discriminatory intent is required for such acts); or
- the persecutory conduct constitutes an aggravated form of an enumerated inhumane act committed with discriminatory intent.

---

[83] Brady & Liss *Evolution of Persecution* (2014) 543.
[84] *ICC Elements of Crimes* fn 22. See Cryer *et al*. *International Criminal Law and Procedure* (2007) 215.
[85] Byron *War Crimes and Crimes Against Humanity* (2009) 233.
[86] Ambos & Wirth *The Current Law of Crimes Against Humanity* (2002) 86.
[87] Ambos & Wirth *The Current Law of Crimes Against Humanity* (2002) 74.

3.3.1.3 Resulting in the severe deprivation of a fundamental human right (the causation requirement)

'Grievous persecution' requires an 'intentional and severe deprivation of fundamental rights', which is similar to the 'gross and blatant denial of fundamental rights' standard required by the ICTY and ICTR.[88] The phrase 'severe deprivation of fundamental human rights' has three important functions:

1. it is a *prima facie* indication of the unlawfulness or unjustifiability of the persecutory conduct;
2. it establishes the legal threshold of severity or gravity (which will be discussed separately below); and
3. it clarifies the causal link between the persecutory conduct and the deprivation of fundamental human rights, which is considered an obvious consequence of inhumane discriminatory conduct.

Effectively, all core crimes or inhumane acts of crimes against humanity constitute an infringement of human dignity and freedom, directly or indirectly. In other words, an infringement of human rights is not a *sui generis* result of persecution or any other inhumane act for that matter. In the case of persecution, the *Rome Statute* requires a *nexus* between the persecutory conduct and the severe deprivation of a fundamental human right. Therefore, while crimes against humanity are generally "intended to safeguard basic human values by banning atrocities directed against human dignity",[89] 'grievous persecution' "attacks these core aspects of 'humanness' more directly than any other crime against humanity".[90] Consequently, the 'severe deprivation of fundamental rights' should be a clear and obvious consequence of the persecutory conduct.

It should also be reiterated that the quintessential effect of the discriminatory intent inherent to persecution, determines that a severe form of discrimination will have an obvious consequence or disadvantage on a targeted identifiable group or its individual members.[91] This implies that either the nature and gravity of the discrimination itself, or the consequence of the discriminatory act/s or omission, may provide the causal link to the severe deprivation of fundamental rights.

---

[88] Brady & Liss *Evolution of Persecution* (2014) 545.
[89] *Prosecutor v Kupreškić et al.* (Trial Judgement) 547.
[90] Brady & Liss *Evolution of Persecution* (2014) 430.
[91] Triffterer & Ambos *Commentary on the Rome Statute* (2008) 257–258.

The word 'intentional' requires that the act of deprivation must have been committed intentionally, but should not be construed as to require that the perpetrator intended to deprive human rights specifically. It is not required that the perpetrator intended to deprive the targeted group of their fundamental human rights, because the deprivation of fundamental rights is an obvious consequence of the type of acts relevant to crimes against humanity. In other words, the act of deprivation on a discriminatory basis constitutes the prohibited condition or consequence of persecution (the material element), and must therefore be committed with the necessary *mens rea*. On the other hand, the severe deprivation of human rights is merely an inherent and inevitable consequence of conduct that satisfied the 'inhumane threshold'. Therefore, the deprivation of fundamental rights need not constitute the purpose or aim of the conduct (material element), and consequently, such a result need not have been committed with any form of criminal culpability. It is also not necessary that the perpetrator personally completed a particular value judgement pertaining to the mental elements of "inhumane" or "severe".[92]

Accordingly, some writers prefer to understand persecutory conduct as an act of deprivation of human rights because of the close proximity of the act and the consequential human rights infringement.[93] Although this interpretation is not mistaken, it is important to some extent to differentiate the act of deprivation from the human rights infringement. The persecutory conduct or act of deprivation is a material element of persecution, and must be done knowingly and intentionally (persecutive intent), while the human rights deprivation is considered an obvious consequence of the nature of the persecutory conduct, whether based on the nature and gravity of the act itself or its cumulative discriminatory effect. Consequently, while the causation requirement necessitates a causal link between the persecutory conduct and the severe deprivation of human rights, this *nexus* is only relevant in order to establish the intensity threshold for persecution as an inhumane act of crimes against humanity. In other words, while all forms of persecution will have a discriminatory effect on the enjoyment of human rights and freedoms 'grievous persecutory' conduct, whether considered individually or cumulatively, must result in a *severe* deprivation of *fundamental* rights.

---

[92] *ICC Elements of Crimes*, General Introduction, par 4.
[93] Cassese, A. (ed), *The Oxford Companion to International Criminal Justice*. Oxford University Press (2009), pg 454.

3.3.1.4 Participation context

In terms of the *chapeau* elements, the 'participation context' clarifies the accused's requisite involvement in the 'broader attack'. The accused's criminal responsibility for 'crimes against humanity' will depend on his participation in, or commission of, persecutory conduct, which must be sufficiently linked to the 'broader attack'.[94]

The course of conduct must be widespread and systematic, not the individual persecutory acts of the accused, provided his actions form part of the broader attack.[95] Thus, the accused's criminal responsibility may be based on a single specific persecutory act, provided such an act satisfies the other conditions of applicability. If, however, a course of persecutory acts exists (i.e. a course of discriminate practices), the acts could constitute the attack itself, provided their cumulative effect satisfies the contextual threshold of severity.[96]

The *ICC Elements of Crimes* confirms the listed grounds of discrimination designated by the *Rome Statute* but nevertheless requires that the persecutory conduct was committed as part of a widespread or systematic attack 'directed against a civilian population'. By extension to the listed grounds of discrimination, the use of the phrase 'directed against a civilian population' indicates that persecution, in the ambit of crimes against humanity, is not relevant in circumstances where a combatant group is targeted based on a specific aspect of their identity, for example, a militant religious extremist group. However, in such circumstances, the commission of war crimes may be satisfied.

Although the participation context relates specifically to participation in conduct which is related to a 'broader attack', 'participation' is also generally indicative of the modes of criminal responsibility or forms of participation set out in Article 25 of the *Rome Statute*, which is discussed in Appendix A.

Summary of *actus reus*. The severe deprivation of fundamental rights may be effected either through the cumulative effect of a series of 'other-type' acts or through the singular effect of an 'inhumane-type' act of extraordinary magnitude.[97] The 'connection requirement' is automatically satisfied if persecutory conduct is based on an enumerated inhumane act. However,

---

[94] Triffterer & Ambos *Commentary on the Rome Statute* (2008) 176.
[95] Triffterer & Ambos *Commentary on the Rome Statute* (2008) 176.
[96] Triffterer & Ambos *Commentary on the Rome Statute* (2008) 174.
[97] Art 18 (4) of the *1996 ILC Draft Code, with commentary* (1996).

if persecutory conduct is based on 'other-type' conduct, it must be objectively linked to a inhumane act or jurisdictionally relevant crime. It is not necessary to prove "that the perpetrator knew that his actions were inhumane, or rose to the level of crimes against humanity".[98] The *Rome Statute* does not specify the exact threshold of a 'severe' deprivation or the nature of 'fundamental rights', only that it must be committed by reason of the identity of the group or collectivity.[99] These aspects will be considered under the threshold of severity.

3.3.2 The *mens rea* of 'grievous persecution'

The mental element is what is unique about 'grievous persecution', which relates to the deliberate perpetration of an act or omission with the intent to discriminate on certain prohibited grounds.[100] According to the judgement in the *Tadić* case, intentional deprivation is "some form of discrimination that is intended to be and results in an infringement of an individual's fundamental rights".[101] In the *Stakić* case, the ICTY concluded that "the *mens rea* of the crime of persecutions, apart from the knowledge required for all crimes against humanity..., consists of (1) the intent to commit the underlying act, and (2) the intent to discriminate".[102] Byron summarises the mental element as follows:

> The mens rea requires the act to be carried out intentionally, against the person because of their connection with or identity as part of a group, or against a group as such, which was targeted on one of the listed grounds.[103]

Read with the *chapeau* elements, the *mens rea* of 'grievous persecution' contain the following mental elements:[104]

- Persecutive intent – The perpetrator intended to commit an underlying persecutory act or omission, or deliberately enforced a discriminatory policy, while reconciled to the knowledge of the substantial likelihood that such conduct is unjustifiable.

---

[98] Triffterer & Ambos *Commentary on the Rome Statute* (2008) 182.
[99] Ambos & Wirth *The Current Law of Crimes Against Humanity* (2002) 74.
[100] *Duch (Appeal judgement)* paras 226, 240, 267 and 278.
[101] *Prosecutor v Duško Tadić aka "Dule" (Sentencing Judgement)*, Case No. IT-94-1-T, 14 July 1997, par 697.
[102] *Prosecutor v Milomir Stakić (Trial Judgement)*, Case No. IT-97-24-T, 31 July 2003, par 738.
[103] Byron *War Crimes and Crimes Against Humanity* (2009) 234.
[104] Cassese *et al. ICL: Cases and Commentary* (2011) 184–188.

- Discriminatory intent – The perpetrator deliberately discriminated and targeted the victim or victims based on either an objective or subjective perception of their affiliation or membership to a civilian group with a protected identity.
- Contextual knowledge – The perpetrator knew that the conduct was part of, or intended the conduct to be part of, a widespread or systematic attack.

Therefore, as far as intention in the form of *mens rea* is concerned, it is submitted that these three categories of intent must be proven to qualify acts of persecution as crimes against humanity. Consequently, persecution may be considered as a multi-layered or heightened crime against humanity, requiring a specific *mens rea* in addition to the contextual intent required of all underlying crimes.[105]

3.3.2.1 Contextual knowledge

The contextual mental elements required for classifying persecution as a crime against humanity requires that:[106]

- the persecutor was aware of the widespread or systematic attack;
- was aware that it was directed against a civilian population based on certain discriminatory grounds; and
- knew or intended that his acts formed part of that attack or pattern of persecution.

Knowledge of the broader attack within which persecutory acts were committed[107] requires an awareness of the risk that the conduct can be objectively considered to form part of a broader attack, therefore a *dolus eventualis* standard is sufficient with regard to the contextual element.[108] The knowledge can be actual or inferred from the circumstances.[109]

---

[105] Fournet & Pigorier *Only One Step Away From Genocide* (2010) 716.
[106] ICC Elements of Crimes, art 7(1)(h) par 6.
[107] Blaškić *(Trial Judgement)* par 220.
[108] Ambos & Wirth *The Current Law of Crimes Against Humanity* (2002) 40. *Dolus eventualis*, which is "the minimum level of intention required to prove a *Crime against Humanity*, if the additional other criteria of *widespread or systematic* are met" – Horton, G. *Dying Alive – A Legal Assessment of Human Rights Violations in Burma*, a report co-funded by the Netherlands Ministry for Development Co-operation. Images Asia (2005), par 5.21. The ICC Pre-Trial Chamber in the case of *Thomas Lubanga Dyilo* had "no difficulty in reading the concept of *dolus eventualis* into Article 30 of the

3. The Crime of Persecution in International Criminal Law

3.3.2.2 Persecutive intent[110]

In terms of the *Rome Statute*, persecutive intent relates to the deliberate perpetration of persecutory acts or omissions.[111] As mentioned, the perpetrator need not have intended to severely deprive the victims of their fundamental rights, only that he deliberately committed the persecutory conduct, which had that effect. However, persecutive intent is not specifically required under all circumstances, especially considering that the specific discriminatory intent encapsulated by persecution activates the 'unless otherwise provided' proviso in Article 30 of the Statute.[112] Consequently, the application of the persecutive intent requirement will depend on the nature of the underlying persecutory conduct:

1. If the underlying persecutory conduct is based on physical acts, constituting 'persecution atrocities', these underlying acts, whether felonious or non-felonious, must be deliberately perpetrated. Additionally, if the underlying act of persecution is based on the commission of an enumerated 'inhumane-type' act, the mental element required for the other act must also be proven. For exam-

---

ICC Statute". - *Situation in the Democratic Republic of the Congo, in the case of the Prosecutor v Thomas Lubanga Dyilo*, Case No ICC-01/04-01/06, Decision on the Confirmation of Charges, ICC, 14 March 2012, paras 351–355.

[109] Triffterer & Ambos *Commentary on the Rome Statute* (2008) 182.
[110] Distinguish the term 'persecutive intent' from persecutory intent as used by the court in *Prosecutor v Tihomir Blaškić (Appeal Judgement)*, Case No. IT-95-14-A, 29 July 2004, par 165. In *Blaškić*, the Appeals Chamber clarified that the *mens rea* of persecution is dependent on a discriminatory intent, and it is therefore not necessary to establish that the perpetrator possessed a specific 'persecutory intent' behind an alleged persecutory plan or policy, i. e. removal of targeted persons from society or humanity. Persecutory intent, as it was interpreted by the court, referred to a specific intent with the discriminatory conduct. Such a specific intent is indicative of genocide, which consists of the special intent (*dolus specialis* or aggravated criminal intention) to destroy, in whole or in part, a protected group. The term 'persecutory intent', as a particular *dolus specialis*, should therefore be distinguished from the notion of 'persecutive intent' as a contextual form of *dolus*.
[111] Art 7(1) of the *Rome Statute*, read with the *ICC Elements of Crimes*.
[112] "As an additional mental element is, by definition, a mental element that has no corresponding material element, it would appear that Art 30 does not apply, as Art 30's definitions of 'intent' and 'knowledge' are required only with respect to the material elements of a crime". - Finnin, S. *Mental elements under Art 30 of the Rome Statute of the International Criminal Court: a comparative analysis.* ICLQ, Vol. 61, No. 2 (2012), pg 357.

ple, if the victim was singled out and murdered based on his political affiliations, the perpetrator must have intended to cause the death of the victim.
2. If the underlying persecutory conduct is based on non-physical discriminatory policies or omissions ('iniquitous persecution'), the conscious discriminatory policy is satisfactory in terms of the 'unless otherwise provided for' proviso in Article 30.

The perpetrator will be held criminally liable for at least his share of the persecutory conduct, provided the other elements are also satisfied.

3.3.2.3 Discriminatory intent

In addition to the persecutive intent, 'grievous persecution' requires an additional element of culpability. This additional mental element constitutes a higher standard of criminal intent, similar to *dolus specialis* or intent in the narrow sense of 'purpose' or 'aim'.[113] This additional mental element may be referred to as a conscious and deliberate discriminatory mindset.[114] The persecutor acts with discriminatory intent if he targets his victims on the basis of their membership (or perceived membership) in a specific protected group.[115] Discriminatory intent is an expressly required form of intent, which is an indispensable ingredient of the offence of persecution.[116] The Trial Chamber in *Blaškić* stated that:

> [P]ersecution may take many forms other than injury to the human person, in particular those acts rendered serious not by their apparent cruelty but by the discrimination they seek to instil within humankind.[117]

The origins, forms and contemporary manifestations of racism, xenophobia, discrimination and related intolerance are complex and multifaceted. This victimisation can take various forms, ranging in severity, including distinction, exclusion, restriction, hostility or differential treatment based on identity.[118] If left unchecked, such an intolerant attitude may ultimately

---

[113] Brady & Liss *Evolution of Persecution* (2014) 553.
[114] Cassese *Companion to International Criminal Justice* (2009) 453.
[115] Brady & Liss *Evolution of Persecution* (2014) 533.
[116] Triffterer & Ambos *Commentary on the Rome Statute* (2008) 182 at fn 103.
[117] *Blaškić (Trial Judgement)* par 227.
[118] Art 2(2) of the UN General Assembly, *Declaration on the Elimination of All Forms of Intolerance and of Discrimination Based on Religion or Belief*, UNGA Res 36/55, 73rd plenary meeting, 25 November 1981 (*Religious Discrimination Declaration*).

3. The Crime of Persecution in International Criminal Law

escalate into the denigration and dehumanisation of the targeted group, resulting in the negation of the essence of the victims or the group. As a result of this dehumanisation, the perpetrator views the 'others' as 'lesser' and unworthy of human dignity and respect, which overcomes the normal human revulsion against discrimination, persecution, violence and other human rights atrocities. Eventually, whether as its purpose or as its effect, a conscious discriminatory mindset will result in the nullification or impairment of the recognition, enjoyment or exercise of human rights and fundamental freedoms on an equal basis.

Importantly, in assessing the perpetrator's discriminatory intent, the root causes or motivations of such a discriminatory mindset is irrelevant. It is not even necessary that the perpetrator knows or fully understands the root causes or motivations of the broader discriminatory policy. What is important is that before a perpetrator can act with discriminatory intent, he must be aware of this discriminatory differentiation and based on this classification, identifies and targets his victims.

As a result of the necessity to show intentional discrimination on the listed grounds, 'grievous persecution' under the *Rome Statute* has a higher mental element than other inhumane acts.[119] According to a series of judicial decisions, the crime of persecution is to be considered an aggravated or heightened form of crimes against humanity, requiring additional elements for its qualification.[120] In *Kupreškić*, the Trial Chamber stated that "the *mens rea* requirement for persecution is higher than for ordinary crimes against humanity, although lower than for genocide".[121] Consider also that persecution and genocide share the underlying *mens rea* to discriminately target an identifiable group. Consequently, it is possible for inhumane acts inherently constituting persecution to escalate into genocidal acts, if they were committed with the additional genocidal intent to destroy, in whole or in part, such a protected group. *Vice versa*, persecution may constitute a type of 'competent verdict'[122] for situations which lacked the specific intent required for the crime of genocide.[123] Mettraux thus concludes that:

---

[119] Byron *War Crimes and Crimes Against Humanity* (2009) 234.
[120] Fournet & Pigorier *Only One Step Away From Genocide* (2010) 716.
[121] *Kupreškić et al. (Trial Judgement)* 636.
[122] In terms of South African criminal law, competent verdicts are regulated under the Criminal Procedure Act 51 of 1977 and refer to the situation where in a court of law the accused is charged with a certain crime but during the trial it appears that the accused in actual fact did not commit the crime he has been charged with but has committed a crime which has elements of a different crime.
[123] Par 11 of the commentary on art 18 – *1996 ILC Draft Code, with commentary* (1996).

Persecution may ... be a first step in a genocidal enterprise and it may serve from a prosecutorial point of view as a gap-filling criminal prohibition between other crimes against humanity which are not otherwise motivated by the persecutory agenda, and genocide.[124]

The *ICC Elements of Crimes* requires that the perpetrator targeted certain persons or groups by reason of the identity of a group or collectivity, and such targeting was based on political, racial, national, ethnic, cultural, religious, gender, or other grounds that are universally recognised as impermissible under international law. Discriminatory intent therefore requires that the perpetrator must consciously intend to discriminate based on the listed grounds, and target his victims accordingly.[125] Therefore, discriminatory intent encapsulates the following aspects:

- a preconceived classification between what is perceived as an acceptable identity and those who differ from or lack such an identity, affiliation or membership;
- a conscious mindset to differentiate and categorise those persons or groups with a conflicting or diverging identity;
- such a diverging identity is clearly identifiable based on the listed protected grounds; and
- the deliberate victimisation of the targeted group or identity.

In the sub-headings that follow, these aspects will be examined in more detail.

a) Conscious and deliberate discriminatory mindset

The jurisprudence of the ICTY found that persecution requires the presence of a particular intent to discriminate and not merely knowledge on the side of the perpetrator that his or her actions may result in unfair discrimination.[126] A conscious discriminatory mindset entails premeditation regarding the victim to be persecuted, wherefore the crime does not seem to cover conduct that had an unintended discriminatory effect. Thus, it is not "enough to show that the accused was merely aware that he was acting

---

[124] Mettraux, G. *International Crimes and the Ad Hoc Tribunals*. Oxford University Press (2006), pg 336.
[125] *Krnojelac (Trial Judgement)* par 435.
[126] *Kordić (Trial Judgement)* par 212; *Krnojelac (Trial Judgement)* par 435.

3. The Crime of Persecution in International Criminal Law

in a discriminatory manner, 'he must consciously intend to discriminate'".[127] Furthermore, in *Krnojelac*, the Trial Chamber held that the discriminatory intent need not constitute the primary intent with respect to the act, provided that the discriminatory intent was significant.[128]

By implication, this means that persecution consists of 'sufficiently serious discrimination' to the extent that it results in seriously disadvantaging a part of the population.[129] Although a discriminatory mindset often occurs at a societal or communitarian level, a persecutor may form his or her own personal discriminatory intent.

b) Against a group or collectivity

The discriminatory nature is directed towards a specific group, but the persecutory acts are nevertheless committed against individual members based on their affiliation to that group.[130] Therefore persecutory conduct may target either individual members of a group or the group itself, provided they were targeted by reason of the identity of the group or the individual's actual or perceived affiliation to the identity, which must be based on one of the protected grounds. Persecution against any identifiable 'group' or 'collectivity' appear interchangeably; however, in the situation when a number of groups are attacked, the sum of these groups could appropriately be referred to as a 'collectivity'.[131]

c) Discrimination must be on one of the listed grounds

The discrimination must have taken place on one of the listed grounds, and the perpetrator targeted certain victims based on such discriminatory grounds.[132] In terms of the *Rome Statute*, the listed prohibited grounds are political, racial, national, ethnic, cultural, religious, and gender.[133] Furthermore, the Statute also includes an open-ended category of 'other grounds that are universally recognised as impermissible under international law'.

---

[127] *Prosecutor v. Radoslav Brdjanin (Appeal Judgement)* par 996, in Byron *War Crimes and Crimes Against Humanity* (2009) 229.
[128] *Krnojelac (Trial Judgement)* par 435.
[129] Triffterer & Ambos *Commentary on the Rome Statute* (2008) 257-258, footnote 505.
[130] "...the persecutory act must be intended to cause, and result in, an infringement on an individual's enjoyment of a basic or fundamental right" – *Tadić (Sentencing Judgement)* par 715.
[131] Brady & Liss *Evolution of Persecution* (2014) 550.
[132] Cassese *et al. ICL: Cases and Commentary* (2011) 186.
[133] Under art 5(h) of the ICTY Statute and art 3(h) of the ICTR Statute, the prohibited grounds were limited to persecution on political, racial or religious grounds.

Such a category seems to be indicative of principles of customary international criminal and human rights law, including *jus cogens* or peremptory norms,[134] and obligations *erga omnes*.[135] These individual grounds of persecution and how they intersect with religion, will be discussed in Chapter Four.

d) An identifiable group

An 'identifiable group or collectivity' implies that its individual members are bound together by a collective identity, which suggests possible membership, affiliation, support or identification with the group.[136] The targeted group or collectivity and their individual members must be 'identifiable' based on one or more of the listed identity elements. 'Identifiability' is thus closely related to the question of the victim's identity, and whether an aspect of his or her identity made him or her the identifiable target of the persecutor's discriminatory persecutory conduct.

Once it is established that the group was identifiable, whether objectively or in the mind of the accused, on one of the listed grounds, it must be established that the listed ground constitutes the discriminatory basis upon which the persecutor chose his victim's. In other words, establishing that the victims may be identified as being part of the identifiable group is only the first step in identifying the ground of persecution. The second step is to establish whether the group's identity constituted the primary reason for their persecution, based on the persecutor's discriminatory mindset (identity element).

e) The identity of the group or collectivity (the identity element)

The reason why a person, group, or collectivity was targeted must be based on the identity of the group or collectivity as such, which must be identifiable on one of the listed grounds.[137] In other words, a victim or victim

---

[134] UN, *Vienna Convention on the Law of Treaties*, 23 May 1969, United Nations, Treaty Series, vol. 1155, p. 331. Art 53 states that "...a peremptory norm of general international law is a norm accepted and recognised by the international community of States as a whole as a norm from which no derogation is permitted and which can be modified only by a subsequent norm of general international law having the same character".

[135] Obligations *erga omnes* refer to obligations owed by all States towards the international community and in the enforcement of which all States have an interest.

[136] Brady & Liss *Evolution of Persecution* (2014) 430.

[137] Brady & Liss *Evolution of Persecution* (2014) 550.

3. The Crime of Persecution in International Criminal Law

group must have been targeted and persecuted "by reason of the identity of the group or collectivity".[138] The nature of persecution and the inherent discrimination it entails

> not only inflict wounds or death, but are aggravated by the voluntary, deliberate and gratuitous deprivation of the dignity of all men and women: these are victimised only because they belong to a group other than that of their persecutors, or do not accept their dominion.[139]

It is argued that although the perpetrator's guilty mind is essential in determining whether the act did discriminate in fact,[140] it is also crucial in establishing the ground or grounds of persecution.[141] The identifiable ground upon which the perpetrator's discriminatory intent is based becomes the identifying factor used to target the victims. Thus, the grounds of persecution are based on the identifying factor (listed ground) of the targeted person or group, rather than the nature of the rights which are infringed upon.[142] To put it differently, it is the nature of the denial of the right to equality, which contextualises the grounds of persecution. For example, political persecution is not premised on the infringement or denial of a citizen's ability to participate in the civil and political life of the State, but rather based on the victim's 'political identity', i. e. political membership or lack thereof.

The identity element entails a clear link between the persecutory conduct and the discriminatory intent to target a victim based on his or her identity. Therefore, this 'identity element' must be "interpreted in a broad sense referring to the common feature according to which the victims were singled out by the perpetrators".[143] The identity of, or affiliation to, a certain protected aspect of identity becomes the basis of the perpetrator's discrimination and persecution.

---

[138] Art 7(1)(h) read with art 7(2)(g) of the *Rome Statute*.
[139] Cassese, A. *Violence and Law in the Modern Age*. Princeton University Press. (1988) pg 112.
[140] *Krnojelac (Appeal Judgement)* paras 184–185.
[141] Acquaviva & Pocar *Crimes Against Humanity*. (2011) par 16.
[142] *Blaškić (Trial Judgement)* par 235.
[143] Ambos & Wirth *The Current Law of Crimes Against Humanity* (2002) 76.

f) 'By reason of' the identity of the group or collectivity

An important consideration is whether a discriminatory intent is satisfied even if the victim did not actually belong to the targeted group or collectivity. In *Duch*, the Supreme Court Chamber (SCC) of the Cambodia Tribunal had to decide whether there can be actual discrimination if the perpetrator is objectively mistaken as to the victim's membership in the targeted group.[144] While accepting that an act or omission is discriminatory in fact, where "a victim is targeted because of the victim's membership in a group defined by the perpetrator on specific grounds",[145] the SCC found that actual discrimination must be "connected to the requirement that the victim actually belong to a sufficiently discernible political, racial or religious group".[146] Therefore, the SCC found that the required discriminatory intent will be lacking when the perpetrator subjectively erred as to the victim's membership of the targeted group. Consequently, in the interpretation of the Cambodia Tribunal, the targeting would be indiscriminate in the absence of proof that the victim is a member of a 'discernible targeted group'.[147]

In the context of the *Rome Statute*, such an interpretation does not seem appropriate. Article 32 states that a mistake of fact shall be a ground for excluding criminal responsibility only if it negates the mental element required by the crime. In the context of persecution, the discriminatory intent cannot be excluded by *error personae*, because a mistake regarding the victim's identity does not exclude the persecutor's primary intention or the discriminatory effect on the fundamental rights of the victim. Where "the perception of the perpetrator provides the basis of the discrimination in question, the [discriminatory] consequences are real for the victim even if the perpetrator's classification may be incorrect under objective criteria".[148] Therefore, a mistake by the perpetrator regarding the true identity of the victim will not suffice to exclude the discriminatory intent itself.

Furthermore, if a persecutor commits a persecutory act against a person who is not in fact a member, supporter or otherwise identified in connection with a targeted group, such a mistaken belief by the perpetrator will not exclude his responsibility before the Court. The *Rome Statute* allows

---

[144] *Duch (Appeal judgement)* par 269.
[145] *Duch (Appeal judgement)* par 272.
[146] *Duch (Appeal judgement)* par 274.
[147] Zgonec-Rožej *International Criminal Law Manual* (2013) updated version at 17.
[148] Judgment (Kaing Guek Eav alias Duch), Case File/Dossier No. 001/18-07-2007/ECCC/TC, Extraordinary Chambers in the Courts of Cambodia, 26 July 2010, par 317.

3. The Crime of Persecution in International Criminal Law 81

for the possibility of attempted crimes (unlike the *ad hoc* tribunals), wherefore such a persecuted person could, in any event, be considered the victim of attempted persecution.[149]

The *Rome Statute* requires only that the individuals must be targeted 'by reason of' the identity of the group or collectivity. It has been noted that this element was included to "ensure that those persons who were not part of the group, and yet were targeted because of their association with or support of the group, would also be protected".[150] In other words, persons who are, for example, "targeted because of their former membership in a targeted political party, or because they are married to persons belonging to the targeted ethnicity may, depending on the circumstances, be considered victims of persecution".[151]

The use of the term 'identifiable' as in Article 7(1)(h), implies a subjective notion in terms of the identifiability of the group or collectivity.[152] Whether a victim was targeted 'by reason of' an aspect of his or her identity may be determined "based on objective criteria or in the mind of the accused".[153]

Therefore, the targeted group must be interpreted broadly to include not only actual membership but other persons who are perceived by the perpetrator as belonging to the victim group due to their close affiliations, support or sympathies for the victim group.[154] Thus, it is "the perpetrator who defines the victim group while the targeted victims have no influence on the definition of their status".[155] Consequently, discriminatory intent is satisfied even if the victim did not actually belong to the targeted group or collectivity, yet was targeted by reason of such a perceived identity in the mind of the persecutor.

g) Proving discriminatory intent

In terms of the *Rome Statute*, the ICC has suggested that two types of evidence may prove the identity element in persecution cases.[156]

---

[149] Brady & Liss *Evolution of Persecution* (2014) 551.
[150] Byron *War Crimes and Crimes Against Humanity* (2009) 230.
[151] Acquaviva & Pocar *Crimes Against Humanity* (2011) par 17.
[152] Triffterer & Ambos *Commentary on the Rome Statute* (2008) par 60.
[153] Triffterer & Ambos *Commentary on the Rome Statute* (2008) 217.
[154] *Prosecutor v. Mladen Naletilic aka "Tuta", Vinko Martinovic aka "Stela" (Trial Judgement)*, IT-98-34 T, International Criminal Tribunal for the former Yugoslavia (ICTY), 31 March 2003, par 636.
[155] *Naletilic and Martinovic (Trial Judgement)* par 636.
[156] Chertoff *Prosecuting Gender-Based Persecution* (2017) 1107.

First, a discriminatory intention may be proven by way of direct evidence (direct discriminatory intent) regarding an explicit, official organisational policy to target a covered identifiable group. For example, where an explicit or systemised policy of conscious and intentional discrimination existed within a structured group, or in instances where a *de facto* authority subscribes to a deliberate policy of passive toleration which is consciously aimed at encouraging such discrimination and persecution. However, the existence of such a policy cannot be inferred solely from the absence of governmental or organisational action.[157]

Second, discriminatory intent may be inferred from the surrounding circumstances (inferred discriminatory intent).[158] This does not mean that a discriminatory intent may be automatically inferred directly from the general discriminatory nature of the persecutory conduct.[159] It has been noted that "evidence of an overt policy to persecute a particular group because of bias can be difficult to obtain".[160]

According to the jurisprudence of the ICTY, a discriminatory intent "may be inferred from such a context as long as, in view of the facts of the case, circumstances surrounding the commission of the alleged acts substantiate the existence of such intent".[161] However, the general discriminatory nature in a given context may provide evidence of the discriminatory intent of the accused.[162]

The jurisprudence of the ICC may also provide some guidance. In *Harun*, the Pre-trial Chamber found 'reasonable grounds to believe' that the Sudanese government had persecuted the ethnic *Fur* people of Darfur based on evidence that inferred an overt policy.[163] Similarly, in *Gbagbo* the Pre-trial Chamber found 'substantial grounds' to infer an overt policy to persecute a particular group.[164] In other words, a link may be inferred from circumstantial evidence that shows at least 'reasonable proof' of an apparent pattern of discrimination against a particular identifiable group.

Consequently, the requisite discriminatory intent may be inferred from the surrounding circumstances of the case, provided such inference is the only reasonable conclusion to be drawn, in the opinion of the

---

[157] ICC *Elements of Crimes*, art 7, Introduction, footnote 6.
[158] Brady & Liss *Evolution of Persecution* (2014) 536.
[159] *Krnojelac* (Appeal Judgement) par 184. Confirmed in *Blaškić* (Appeal Judgement) par 164, and *Kordić* (Appeal Judgement) par 110.
[160] Chertoff *Prosecuting Gender-Based Persecution* (2017) 1107.
[161] *Krnojelac* (Appeal Judgement) par 184.
[162] *Krnojelac* (Appeal Judgement) par 184.
[163] *Harun* (Decision on the Prosecution Application under Article 58(7) of the Statute), 74-75.
[164] *Gbagbo Arrest Warrant*, par 204.

Court.¹⁶⁵ The context may include the systematic nature of the crimes committed against a specific identity and the general discriminatory attitude of the perpetrator as seen through his behaviour.¹⁶⁶

h) Negative discriminatory intention (*dolus indeterminatus*)

The notion of a 'negative discriminatory intention' refers to the deliberate victimisation or targeting of individuals or groups not belonging to a particular persuasion or identity.¹⁶⁷ In this sense, 'by reason of' the identity of a group or collectivity is interpreted to indicate the lack of a certain identity. Triffterer and Ambos surmise that:

> The group or collectivity might therefore also be identifiable by the accused, both as a group or collectivity by virtue of objective criteria, and as a group or collectivity not being the same as the group or collectivity the accused belongs to him or herself.¹⁶⁸

In other words, if a person or group is specifically targeted by reason of their membership or affiliation to a protected identity, such discrimination is narrowly applied and may be referred to as a 'specific discriminatory intention'. However, a discriminatory mindset may also consist of a non-specific or negative discriminatory intent.¹⁶⁹ Thus, a perpetrator may also act with discriminatory intent in the form of *dolus indeterminatus*, i. e. the perpetrator intentionally directed his persecutory conduct at any indiscriminate victim simply because he or she had a diverging identity to that of the persecutor.¹⁷⁰ A 'negative discriminatory intention' relates to a situation where victims are targeted because they either lacked a certain identity, did not conform to a particular identity, or opposed a certain identity. Simply put, the perpetrator's discriminatory intention is broadly applied. For example, a persecutor will act with a 'negative religious dis-

---

[165] *Krnojelac (Appeal Judgement)* par 186 and 202.
[166] *Kvocka et al. (Appeal Judgement)* par 460.
[167] Byron *War Crimes and Crimes Against Humanity* (2009) 229–230.
[168] Triffterer & Ambos *Commentary on the Rome Statute* (2008) 217.
[169] *Tadić (Trial Judgement)* par 714; *Blaškić (Trial Judgement)* par 236; *Kvočka (Trial Judgement)* par 195.
[170] Snyman (2014) 196–197.

criminatory intention' if he deliberately targets all those adherents not belonging to his particular political persuasion.[171] According to the jurisprudence of the ICTY, such a negative discriminatory intent would be a sufficient *mens rea* for the offence of persecution.[172]

In summary of *mens rea*, the discriminatory purpose of persecution entails a conscious intent in terms of which the perpetrator must "commit the underlying crime or act on a discriminatory basis".[173] In this regard, the perpetrator's conduct forms part of a widespread or systematic attack, discriminately intended and resulting in the deprivation of a person of any of his fundamental rights because that person belongs to, or is a member of, an identifiable group. A person may be considered to be the victim of persecution where that person was affiliated with a certain identity based on:[174]

- his/her voluntary identification with, or sense of belonging to, association with, or support of the targeted group;
- the acceptance of the person into the group by other members of the group;
- the designation of a perceived identity of the victim, whether in the mind of the perpetrator or others; or
- based on objective criteria, and circumstantial evidence.

It is essential to determine or prove that the persecutor acted with a discriminatory intent; whether a specific or negative intent. Proof that the perpetrator targeted his victims based on their collective affiliation or lack thereof, may be established through an explicit policy or ideology to target an identifiable group, or through an objective deduction of an overt policy inferred from circumstantial evidence, such as the collective identity of the 'other' victims. Ultimately, discriminatory intent implies that specific victims were targeted, either because they have, or because they lack, a certain identity. The perpetrator's motive for his discriminatory conduct is irrelevant.

---

[171] Byron *War Crimes and Crimes Against Humanity* (2009) 229–230.
[172] Tadić *(Trial Judgement)* par 714; Blaškić *(Trial Judgement)* par 236; Kvočka *(Trial Judgement)* par 195.
[173] Cassese *Companion to International Criminal Justice* (2009) 453.
[174] Prosecutor v Bagosora, Case No. ICTR-98-41-T, 18 December 2008. par 2208.

3.3.3 The threshold of severity

Although persecution may be perpetrated by a variety of regimes and actors, and manifest in varying degrees of severity,[175] the persecutory conduct and the context within which it occurred, must reach a certain level or grade of severity before such an act will constitute criminal persecution. In this regard, the Court's jurisdiction is limited to "unimaginable atrocities that deeply shock the conscience of humanity".[176] Consequently, it is the function of the threshold of severity to limit the scope of application of 'grievous persecution' to mass atrocity crimes against the whole of mankind and against international norms.[177]

Considering that persecution constitutes one of the enumerated inhumane acts of crimes against humanity, the threshold of severity sets two distinct requirements: (1) the *chapeau* elements provides for the contextual threshold of the attack or pattern of persecution (internationalising factor); and (2) the nature and gravity of the persecutory conduct, or its cumulative effect, must satisfy a certain intensity threshold.

3.3.3.1 Contextual threshold of severity

'Grievous persecution' is almost always part of a widespread or systematic campaign of persecution or other listed acts of crimes against humanity. The contextual threshold of severity serves to distinguish isolated or sporadic discrimination and related acts, from a discriminatory policy or a consistent pattern of persecution, which constitutes 'grievous persecution'.[178] Consequently, the contextual threshold or international element is an intensity criterion regarding the severity or intensity of the *attack*. In terms of the *chapeau* elements, the persecutory conduct must have been committed as part of a widespread or systematic course of conduct involving the multiple commissions of inhumane acts, actively promoted, encouraged, or tolerated (through deliberate inaction), by way of an asserted policy, plan or ideology by a *de facto* authority

---

[175] University of Notre Dame – Under Caesar's Sword: Christian Response to Persecution. *In Response to Persecution: Findings of the Under Caesar's Sword Project on Global Christian Communities*. Report released on April 20, 2017 in Washington D.C. http://ucs.nd.edu/report/. Accessed 19/02/2018, pg 10.
[176] Preamble of the *Rome Statute*.
[177] Chertoff *Prosecuting Gender-Based Persecution* (2017) 1065–1066.
[178] Triffterer & Ambos *Commentary on the Rome Statute* (2008) 176.

(which need not be publicised),[179] and directed against a civilian population targeted by reason of their identity.

3.3.3.2 Intensity threshold of persecution

In the context of the *ad hoc* tribunals, the threshold of severity is satisfied if the persecutory conduct or the cumulative effect thereof constitutes a gross or blatant denial, on discriminatory grounds, of a fundamental right, laid down in international customary or treaty law, reaching the same level of gravity as the other crimes against humanity.[180]

In terms of the *Rome Statute*, 'reaching the same level of gravity' criteria has been replaced by the intensity threshold of severe deprivations of fundamental rights. Therefore, a mere discriminatory intent is not sufficient; the persecutory act or omission must also have discriminatory consequences, *viz.* a 'severe deprivation of fundamental rights'. Thus, not every denial or infringement of a human right is sufficient to qualify persecution as a crime against humanity.

The deprivation of fundamental rights refers to the material effect of persecutory conduct. Thus, when considering 'grievous persecution' in the context of the *Rome Statute*, the effect of the persecutory conduct whether considered individually or cumulatively, must result in a 'severe deprivation of fundamental rights'.[181] Therefore, the intensity requirement "does not refer to the character of the act of persecution as such... [i]t refers to the character of the deprivation of fundamental rights".[182] Consequently, the persecutory conduct or its consequential effect, whether considered separately or cumulatively, must result in (causation requirement) a deprivation of a fundamental right in terms of international law and, simultaneously, be severe.[183]

However, evaluating this severity threshold remains somewhat problematic. Two important aspects must be considered: (1) which human rights or freedoms are *fundamental* in nature? (2) what will constitute as a *severe* deprivation of such rights?

---

[179] Ambos & Wirth *The Current Law of Crimes Against Humanity* (2002) 26-27.
[180] Kupreškić *(Trial Judgement)* from Cassese et al. *ICL: Cases and Commentary* (2011) 187.
[181] See Art 7(2)(g) of the *Rome Statute*.
[182] Triffterer & Ambos *Commentary on the Rome Statute* (2008) 257.
[183] Ambos & Wirth *The Current Law of Crimes Against Humanity* (2002) 74.

a) The 'fundamental' nature of human rights deprivations

It has been commented that the "inhumane act of persecution may take many forms with its common characteristic being the denial of the human rights and fundamental freedoms to which every individual is entitled without distinction".[184] Thus, the human rights which are deprived must be of a fundamental nature, i. e. elementary and inalienable rights.[185] 'Fundamental human rights' may be understood as "the rights which concern people's primary material and non-material needs [and if] these are not provided, no human being can lead a dignified existence".[186] In other words, it includes those rights and freedoms that are an essential necessity for an existence worthy of human dignity. However, the realm of human dignity in terms of human rights and freedoms is a dynamic and expansive notion, complicating an assessment of which rights constitute a fundamental right.[187]

In essence, *fundamental* rights encapsulates certain higher norms of international law and have the character of *jus cogens*, and are thus non-derogable rights.[188] Effectively, fundamental rights refer to values or norms which are "recognised and accepted on a universal level, that is to say, those rules applicable *vis-à-vis* the State, either because they constitute international custom as a source of international law or because the State has accepted them through its conventional obligations".[189] Fundamental human rights will include,[190] *inter alia*: the right to life; discrimination and other acts which impinge on human dignity; and freedom of thought, conscience and religion.[191]

---

[184] *Commentary on the 1996 ILC Draft Code*, par 11.
[185] *Blaškić (Trial Judgement)* par 220.
[186] Sepúlveda, M. et al. *Human Rights Reference book*. University for Peace Publisher (2004), pg 11.
[187] Cassese *ICL: Cases and Commentary* (2011) 187.
[188] For a list of non-derogable rights, see par 8 of UNHRC, *General Comment No. 24: Issues relating to reservations made upon ratification or accession to the Covenant or the Optional Protocols thereto, or in relation to declarations under article 41 of the Covenant*, par 10. From the UN International Human Rights Instruments, Compilation of General Comments and General Recommendations Adopted by Human Rights Treaty Bodies, 12 May 2004, HRI/GEN/1/Rev.7.
[189] *Summary of Statements made in Plenary in Connection with the Adoption of the Report of the Working Group on the Rules of Procedure and Evidence and the Report of the Working Group on Elements of Crime*, Preparatory Commission document PCNICC/2000/INF/4, 13 July 2000, p 3.

Although the *ad hoc* tribunals have deviated from a strict interpretation of 'fundamental rights', it has been found that persecution requires a 'gross or blatant denial' of a fundamental right,[192] which reaches the same level of gravity as other acts prohibited as crimes against humanity.[193] Accordingly, in the following sections the possibility of two likely criteria to establish which rights could be considered as 'fundamental' will be discussed.

a.i) Identifying the 'fundamental' nature of human dignity

The first criteria to establish 'fundamental human rights' relates to the standard of human dignity as found in the principles of international human rights. The defined parameters for the definition of human dignity can be construed from the international standards on human rights, such as those laid down in the *'International Bill of Rights'*.[194] It may, therefore, be "possible to identify a set of fundamental rights appertaining to any human being, the gross infringement of which may amount, depending on the surrounding circumstances, to a crime against humanity".[195] The deprivation of fundamental rights would thus consist of a brutal attack on those rights identified in drawing upon the various provisions of international human rights.[196] This interpretation is in "full accordance with the purpose of crimes against humanity, the protection of human rights, and also with article 7(1)(g) of the *Rome Statute*".[197]

However, considering the deliberately flexible nature of the crime of persecution and the complexity of the notion of human dignity, it would not be in the interests of justice to provide a list of rights which constitute fundamental rights for the purpose of persecution.[198]

---

[190] Sepúlveda *Human Rights Reference book* (2004) 11.
[191] Brady & Liss *Evolution of Persecution* (2014) 547. A detailed discussion of the fundamental nature of the right to freedom of religion or belief is provided in Appendix B.
[192] *Kupreškić et al. (Trial Judgement)* par 618–621.
[193] *Blaškić (Appeal Judgement)* par 135.
[194] Includes the UN General Assembly, *Universal Declaration of Human Rights*, 10 December 1948, Resolution 217 A (III) (hereinafter referred to as *UDHR*), the UN General Assembly, *International Covenant on Civil and Political Rights*, 16 December 1966 (ICCPR) with its two Optional Protocols and the UN General Assembly, *International Covenant on Economic, Social and Cultural Rights*, 16 December 1966 (ICESCR).
[195] *Kupreškić et al. (Trial Judgement)* par 621.
[196] Cassese et al. *ICL: Cases and Commentary* (2011) 187.
[197] *Kupreškić et al. (Trial Judgement)* par 617.
[198] Cassese et al. *ICL: Cases and Commentary* (2011) 187.

> [T]he explicit inclusion of particular fundamental rights could be interpreted as the implicit exclusion of other rights (*expressio unius est exclusio alterius*).[199]

It is, therefore, "immaterial to identify which rights may amount to fundamental rights for the purpose of persecution [because persecution] … can consist of the deprivation of a wide variety of rights, whether fundamental or not, derogable or not".[200] Nonetheless, it may be concluded with relative certainty that those human rights principles, which have become part of customary international law, and *a fortiori* have the character of peremptory norms, constitute 'fundamental rights'.[201] However, it should not be overlooked that severe deprivations of fundamental rights may "also include the denial of other fundamental human rights, provided they are of equal gravity or severity".[202] It is feasible that:

> [T]he open-ended definition of the actus reus of persecution would seem to facilitate the incorporation of a growing range of fundamental human rights violations into the class of crimes against humanity.[203]

It should be recalled that the nature of the fundamental human rights that are deprived for the purposes of persecution is inconsequential for purposes of identifying the relevant ground/s of persecution.

a.ii) Severe deprivations of fundamental rights ejusdem generis (of the same kind)

The criteria of severe deprivations of fundamental rights *ejusdem generis* (of the same kind) may be used to determine the parameters of fundamental human rights in the context of the ICC. Based on the 'connection requirement', the objective link between the persecutory conduct and a separate inhumane act or jurisdictionally relevant crime provides a framework of inhumane-type acts or crimes. As mentioned, all such inhumane acts or crimes amount to severe deprivations of fundamental rights.[204] Consequently, inhumane acts or other jurisdictionally relevant crimes may be considered *ejusdem generis* for the purposes of an assessment of

---

[199] Cassese *et al. ICL: Cases and Commentary* (2011) 187.
[200] *Stakić (Trial Judgement)* par 773.
[201] Sepúlveda *et al. Human Rights Reference book* (2004) 23.
[202] *Prosecutor v Radislav Krstic (Trial Judgement)*, Case No. IT-98-33-T, ICTY, 2 August 2001, pg 187.
[203] Acquaviva & Pocar *Crimes Against Humanity* (2011) par 24.
[204] Ambos & Wirth *The Current Law of Crimes Against Humanity* (2002) 74.

'fundamental rights'.[205] The ICTY concluded that in "applying the maxim *ejusdem generis*, it holds that a human rights violation must be at least as grave as one of the other, more concrete enumerated inhumane acts".[206]

Thus, the connection requirement makes it possible to infer which rights may be considered 'fundamental', based on the nature and gravity of the deprivation incidental to the commission of the enumerated inhumane acts or other jurisdictionally relevant core crimes.[207]

Although certain human rights clearly constitute 'fundamental rights', the nature of human dignity and the evolving inhumanity of acts and offences makes a precise list of 'fundamental rights' very difficult to attain, but also redundant based on the interests of justice. Ultimately, it will be for the Court to decide on a case-by-case basis, whether a certain right, considered in context, may be considered a 'fundamental right'.

b) The severity of the nature and gravity of the deprivation

The deliberate flexible nature of the crime of persecution is not intended "to define a core assortment of acts and to leave peripheral acts in a state of uncertainty ... [however] there must be clearly defined limits on the types of acts which qualify as persecution".[208]

In the context of the ICC, the deprivation of fundamental rights must be 'severe'. 'Severe'[209] establishes the level or threshold of severity. Severity refers to the nature and gravity of the infringement of fundamental rights and therefore does *not* refer to the character of the persecutory conduct.[210] The level of gravity required to classify acts of persecution as crimes against humanity is established when "the overall consequence ... offend humanity in such a way that they may be termed inhumane".[211]

---

[205] Although the *Rome Statute* does not require that the persecutory conduct must reach 'the same level of gravity as the other crimes against humanity' as found in the ICTY Statute, the connection requirement may arguably serve the same purposes; at least in situations where the underlying persecutory conduct is based on a inhumane act.

[206] *Prosecutor v Kupreškić et al. (Trial Judgement)* par 620.

[207] For example, a denial of the right to life associated with murder, the infringement of the right to bodily integrity associated with rape, or the unjustifiable restriction on the freedom of movement associated with forced displacement.

[208] Cassese et al. *ICL: Cases and Commentary* (2011) 186.

[209] In terms of the *ICC Elements of Crimes* (2011), General Introduction, par 4, it is unnecessary that the perpetrator personally completed a particular value judgement pertaining to the mental elements of "inhumane" or "severe".

[210] Byron *War Crimes and Crimes Against Humanity* (2009) 230.

[211] Cassese et al. *ICL: Cases and Commentary* (2011) par 622.

3. The Crime of Persecution in International Criminal Law

Cassese finds that "the only conclusion to be drawn from its application is that only [severe] gross or blatant denials of fundamental human rights can constitute crimes against humanity".[212] It may be argued that a similar approach is plausible in interpreting persecutory conduct in the context of the *Rome Statute*, especially considering that 'inhumane-type' conduct may constitute an aggravated form of 'grievous persecution'.

The inferred *ejusdem generis* of inhumane acts or other jurisdictionally relevant crimes discussed earlier may also assist in assessing what will constitute as a 'severe deprivation'. Consequently, it may be inferred that the deprivation of fundamental rights must be so severe (gross or blatant) as to be considered similar in nature to other acts of an inhumane nature. It should not be overlooked that persecutory conduct may also consist of 'other-type acts' that are not inherently inhumane, provided their overall effect offends humanity.[213] Essentially, this implies that the intensity threshold of 'severe' deprivations is likely to be deprivations that are of equal gravity or severity to the deprivations associated with the other inhumane acts of crimes against humanity, or comprise of conduct of a similar nature. While not every denial of a right will be serious enough to constitute persecution, it is clear that the 'underlying act' itself need not constitute a crime in international law. Consequently, the cumulative effect of several connected acts could satisfy the severity threshold of human rights deprivation.[214]

> [T]he crimes must be examined in terms of their cumulative effect, and thus, although individual acts may not be inhumane, if their overall consequences offend humanity they could amount to the actus reus of persecution.[215]

The nature and gravity of persecutory conduct are therefore based on the contextual result or effect of the conduct, rather than the severity or character of the persecutory act itself. Although the intensity threshold for persecution may be more readily assessed by the commission of a particular inhumane act, the aggregate intensity of various persecutory acts or the effect of a discriminatory ideology may also satisfy this threshold. Nevertheless, the ICC will have to assess whether the deprivation of a certain fundamental right, considered in context, may be considered as sufficiently 'severe' on a case-by-case basis.

---

[212] Cassese *et al. ICL: Cases and Commentary* (2011) 187.
[213] *Tadić (Trial Judgement)* par 715.
[214] Byron *War Crimes and Crimes Against Humanity* (2009) 230.
[215] *Tadić (Trial Judgement)* par 715.

3.4 'Grievous Persecution' in the Context of International Human Rights Law

The nature of persecution as a crime against humanity, finds itself naturally placed between international criminal law (considering that persecution is an underlying inhumane act of crimes against humanity), and fundamental human rights (considering that persecution involves the discriminatory deprivation of international human rights). Consequently, unveiling the legal opacity of 'grievous persecution' will help preserve international human rights norms and validate the enforcement of prosecution mechanisms. Protecting human rights through criminal proceedings is aimed at ending impunity for deprivations of fundamental rights, thus justifying an exploratory discussion regarding the nature of international human rights and its connection with international criminal law.

3.4.1 International human rights law

Human rights are generally considered "to be universal in the sense that most societies and cultures have practised them throughout most of their history".[216] Therefore, the origins of human rights cannot be accurately derived from a singular source, as the common values inherent to human dignity, freedom and equality are underlying principles in many world religions and cultures.[217] In this regard, Bielefeldt stresses the role of human dignity:

> [T]he concept of human dignity has a long history and it strongly resonates within most religious, philosophical and cultural traditions, including the Bible, the Qur'an, the work of Confucius, or Stoic philosophy, to mention a few examples. This denotes the possibility that human dignity could become the center of an overlapping normative consensus shared by people from different religious or non-religious backgrounds, who otherwise may continue respectfully to disagree on many questions of ultimate concern.[218]

A detailed analysis of the historical background and development of international human rights is beyond the scope of this book and it will thus

---

[216] Bhuiyan, J. H. & Chowdhury, A. R. *An Introduction to International Human Rights Law*. Leiden: Brill / Nijhoff. (2010), pg 6.
[217] Sepúlveda, M. et al. *Human Rights Reference book*. University for Peace Publisher (2004), pg 3.
[218] Bielefeldt, H. *Misperceptions of Freedom of Religion or Belief*. Human Rights Quarterly (2013), pg 68.

3. The Crime of Persecution in International Criminal Law 93

suffice to highlight some essential developments in the field of international human rights.

It was during the Age of Enlightenment (18th century) in Europe that the explicit conception of human rights emerged in terms of which the individual, endowed by nature, was the beneficiary of certain inalienable fundamental rights which was henceforth regarded as a necessity for an existence worthy of human dignity.[219] The internationalisation of human rights occurred in the aftermath of the widespread atrocities perpetrated during World War II. The international community unified in their endeavour to prevent the recurrence of such despicable events, and subsequently formalised their resolve by signing the UN Charter on 26 June 1945.[220] This consensual appreciation of the necessity of human rights protection established itself within the sphere of international law and regarded *de facto* authorities as the primary addressees responsible for its implementation.[221] The UN Charter acknowledges that "promoting and encouraging respect for human rights and for fundamental freedoms for all without distinction as to race, sex, language or religion"[222] is a primary objective.

The subsequent UN activities on human rights included the establishment of the *UN Commission on Human Rights* (UNCHR) in 1946. Furthermore, the *UN General Assembly* (UNGA) unanimously accepted a draft *Universal Declaration of Human Rights* (UDHR) by the UNCHR, which was adopted in Paris on 10 December 1948.[223] However, the "ideological differences between East and West made it impossible to produce a single multilateral treaty giving legal effect to the Universal Declaration" which resulted in the adoption of the two significant covenants to back up the UDHR, namely: *International Covenant on Civil and Political Rights* (ICCPR) and the *International Covenant on Economic, Social and Cultural Rights* (ICESCR). Collectively known as the *International Bill of Human Rights*, it symbolizes the core principles of international human rights upon which numerous subsequent international documents and national constitutions are based.[224] When one considers State practice in this regard, it is possibly

---

[219] Sepúlveda *et al. Human Rights Reference book* (2004) 3.
[220] United Nations, *Charter of the UN*, 24 October 1945, 1 UNTS XVI (hereinafter referred to as UN Charter).
[221] Sepúlveda *et al. Human Rights Reference book* (2004) 5.
[222] Art 1(3) of the UN Charter. The *UN Charter* refers to human rights in the Preamble and Arts 1, 8, 13, 55, 56, 62, 68 and 76.
[223] UN General Assembly, *Universal Declaration of Human Rights*, 10 December 1948, Resolution 217 A (III) (hereinafter referred to as UDHR).
[224] Sepúlveda *et al. Human Rights Reference book* (2004) 21.

beyond contestation to assert that contemporary international law recognises the principles laid down in the *International Bill of Rights* as part of customary international law (and *a fortiori* they have the character of peremptory norms). Such principles and values are binding upon all States regardless of formal recognition, and in terms of which no reservations are allowed.[225]

In the context of international law, human rights are generally understood as "inalienable fundamental rights to which a person is inherently entitled simply because she or he is a human being".[226] Consequently, the protection of human rights has become a core aim of international law.[227] As Bielefeldt explains:

> ... human rights represent the aspiration to empower human beings – on the basis of equal respect and equal concern for everyone's freedom – to develop and pursue their own specific life plans, to freely express their most diverse opinions and convictions, and to generally enjoy respect for their irreplaceable personal biographies, alone and in community with others.[228]

The international standards in the field of human rights have clarified certain guidelines in terms of defining or understanding human rights.[229] Yet, international human rights comprise certain characteristics that often distinguish them from other rights.[230] These basic characteristics of human rights include:

- normative universalism of human rights (i. e. all human beings are inherently entitled to human rights by virtue of their humanity alone);
- the inalienability of human rights within qualified legal margins;

---

[225] Sepúlveda *et al. Human Rights Reference book* (2004) 23.
[226] Sepúlveda *et al. Human Rights Reference book* (2004) 3.
[227] Dugard J. *et al. International Law: A South African Perspective.* Juta, 4th edition (2005), pg 308.
[228] Bielefeldt *Misperceptions of Freedom of Religion or Belief* (2013) 51.
[229] UN General Assembly, *Setting international standards in the field of human rights*, Resolution 41/120 of 4 December 1986, 97th plenary meeting, A/RES/41/120. A human right must essentially: (1) be consistent with the existing body of international human rights law; (2) be of fundamental character and derive from the inherent dignity and worth of the human person; (3) be sufficiently precise to give rise to identifiable and practicable rights and obligations; (4) provide, where appropriate, realistic and effective implementation machinery, including reporting systems; and (5) attract broad international support.
[230] Sepúlveda *et al. Human Rights Reference book* (2004) 4.

- equality and freedom in the application and protection of human rights (i. e. all persons are entitled to fundamental human rights and may exercise such rights free from discrimination);
- the indivisibility of human rights (i. e. human rights are inextricably connected or related); and
- the identification of the State as the primary addressee of legal duties *in re* human rights (although human rights law also requires vertical adherence).[231]

The foremost consideration of human rights law is centred around safeguarding the individual against breaches of fundamental principles of humanity, including the uncontrolled and arbitrary exercise of discretion or misuse of power, usually by a person's own State or government.[232]

The enforcement of human rights occur in an interrelated manner on the domestic, regional or international levels. States that ratify human rights treaties commit themselves to respect those rights and ensuring that their domestic law is compatible with international standards. When domestic law fails to provide effective protection or an unprejudiced remedy for human rights infringements, parties may be able to resort to regional or international mechanisms. Werle and Jessberger explain that:

> Victims often remain unprotected, especially from the worst human rights violations. In such cases, protection at the national level fails. The internationalization of human rights protection is a step towards ending this unfortunate state of affairs.[233]

Therefore, a very important implication of the nature and characteristics of human rights in general, is that the protection, enforcement and implementation of such rights are dependent upon the effective and unbiased rule of law.[234]

---

[231] Sepúlveda *et al. Human Rights Reference book* (2004) 4.
[232] Triffterer & Ambos *Commentary on the Rome Statute* (2008) 24.
[233] Werle, G. & Jessberger, F. *Principles of International Criminal Law.* Oxford University Press (2014), par 140.
[234] Sepúlveda *et al. Human Rights Reference book* (2004) 6. "The rule of law implies that rights must be protected by law, independently of the will of the ruler. Individual rights and freedoms are to be protected against any manifestation of arbitrary power by public authorities". – Sepúlveda *et al. Human Rights Reference book* (2004) 30.

The protection and enforcement of human rights under international law is therefore based on a wide range of mechanisms for monitoring compliance with, and the protection of, human rights at an international level.[235]

3.4.2 The relationship between international human rights law and international criminal law

The two legal fields of international human rights and international criminal law act as auxiliary components of each other. International criminal law "contributes significantly to strengthening and further developing the protection of human rights".[236] On the other hand, human rights law has been instrumental in the development of international criminal law. International human rights law "has expanded or strengthened, or created greater sensitivity to, the values to be protected through the prohibition of attacks on such values".[237] The serious human rights atrocities and mass crimes committed during the twentieth century paved the way for the direct criminalisation of gross and systematic human rights deprivations. Subsequently, States have viewed the maltreatment of human dignity, freedom, and equality, as a global concern justifying humanitarian intervention in some instances.[238]

Although the *Rome Statute* does not explicitly refer to the applicability of international human rights law, such legal provisions are codified in widely ratified treaties that are viewed as evidence of 'rules and principles of international law'[239] which constitute an important source of law under the Statute.[240] At the same time, human rights principles provide the basis for ensuring procedural fairness and the rights of the accused in judicial proceedings before the Court.[241] Furthermore, the application

---

[235] Such as the *United Nations Human Rights Committee* and the *Committee on the Rights of the Child*, and regional systems, such as the *African Commission on Human and Peoples' Rights*, the *European Court of Human Rights* and the *Inter-American Court and Commission of Human Rights*.
[236] Werle & Jessberger *Principles of International Criminal Law* (2014) 53.
[237] Cassese *International Criminal Law* (2003) 18.
[238] Barrie, G.N. *Humanitarian Intervention in the Post-Cold War Era.* South African Law Journal (2001), pg 155.
[239] Pellet, A. *Applicable Law,* in Cassese, A. et al. (eds), I, *The Rome Statute of the International Criminal Court: A Commentary* (OUP, Oxford 2002) 1051, 1067–1072, 1077–1082, in Zgonec-Rožej *International Criminal Law Manual* (2013) 39.
[240] Art 21(1)(b) of the *Rome Statute*.
[241] In this regard, see Appendix A for more detail.

3. The Crime of Persecution in International Criminal Law 97

and interpretation of law pursuant to the *Rome Statute* must be consistent with internationally recognised human rights.[242]

The law of human rights comprises legal duties upon States, as the primary addressees, to implement the prohibitions contained in human rights law; whereas international criminal law serves to criminalise and punish the breach of such prohibitions by holding individuals criminally responsible. International human rights legitimise individual criminal responsibility, but serve as an important aspect in limiting the application thereof, mainly regarding the principle of legality, the principle of personal culpability, and due process. International human rights law is also pivotal in understanding the obligations of States in connection with international crimes, including, *inter alia*: the exercise of universal jurisdiction and the principle *aut dedere aut judicare*. The primary international duty of all States is to protect every person on its territory from human rights infringements or denials. In support, the international community is responsible for supporting individual States in their duty of protection. Should these protection mechanisms fail, a subsidiary legal duty arises on the part of the international community, which requires the suppression of human rights atrocities and core crimes.[243]

In this regard, there are a number of universal human rights conventions explicitly requiring criminal prosecution, including, *inter alia*: the *Genocide Convention*; the *Convention against Torture*;[244] the *Convention on the Non-Applicability of Statutory Limitations to War Crimes and Crimes Against Humanity*;[245] the *Apartheid Convention*;[246] and the *International Convention on the Elimination of All Forms of Racial Discrimination*.[247] However, individual criminal responsibility for international crimes remains a mechanism of last resort in the context of human rights protection. In this regard, it should be explicitly mentioned that during the course of this book, and unless otherwise indicated, human rights *abuses* will refer to the conduct inflicted

---

[242] Art 21(3) of the *Rome Statute*.
[243] Werle & Jessberger *Principles of International Criminal Law* (2014) par 141.
[244] UN General Assembly, *Convention against Torture and Other Cruel, Inhuman or Degrading Treatment or Punishment: resolution / adopted by the General Assembly.*, 10 December 1984, A/RES/39/46.
[245] UN General Assembly, *Convention on the Non-Applicability of Statutory Limitations to War Crimes and Crimes Against Humanity*, 26 November 1968, A/RES/2391(XXIII).
[246] UN General Assembly, *International Convention on the Suppression and Punishment of the Crime of Apartheid*, U.N Doc. A/Res/3068 (XXVIII), 30 November 1973 entered into force on 18 July 1976 (*Apartheid Convention 1973*).
[247] UN General Assembly, *International Convention on the Elimination of All Forms of Racial Discrimination*, 21 December 1965, United Nations, Treaty Series, vol. 660.

by non-State actors, whereas human rights *violations* describe transgressions by a government or *de facto* authority. References to human right denials, infringements or deprivations (as used in the *Rome Statute*) are thus considered neutral in this regard.

It is conceivable that most international crimes have a consequential harmful effect on human rights, however, not every abuse or serious violation of a human right will be directly punishable under international criminal law.[248] Direct criminalisation and subsequent individual criminal responsibility for serious deprivations of fundamental human rights is the highest level of protection that specific human rights can achieve under international law.[249] Although the exact scope of human rights that will satisfy this threshold remains elusive, Werle and Jessberger contend that

> The human rights-protecting function of international criminal law is especially clear for crimes against humanity and criminalizes systematic attacks on fundamental human rights, ... [thus] [t]he idea of humanity as the foundation for human rights protection and of international criminal law is visible here.[250]

Triffterer and Ambos conclude that international criminal law functions, namely

> to protect in a subsidiary way legal values which primarily and originally belong to the national legal order in situations in which State organs or Government officials commit or participate at least tacitly in the commission of the crime and the relevant national jurisdictional systems, therefore, may not be willing or in the position to properly prosecute such behaviour.[251]

Prosecuting and punishing persons responsible for such criminal conduct may therefore use international criminal law as a procedural instrument to counteract serious infringements of human rights. Prosecution mechanisms afford an effective remedy[252] that may function to prevent further deprivations and provide redress in the attainment of justice.[253] Criminal prosecution may also serve as a deterring factor on

---

[248] Werle & Jessberger *Principles of International Criminal Law* (2014) 53. See also Cryer et al. *International Criminal Law and Procedure* (2007) 10.
[249] Werle & Jessberger *Principles of International Criminal Law* (2014) 53.
[250] Werle & Jessberger *Principles of International Criminal Law* (2014) 53.
[251] Triffterer & Ambos *Commentary on the Rome Statute* (2008) 24.
[252] Art 8 of the *UDHR*; arts 2(3), 9(5) & 14(6) of the *ICCPR*; and art 2(1) if the *ICESCR*.
[253] Shelton, D. *Human Rights, Remedies. Max Planck Encyclopedia on Public International law*, Wolfrum, R. (ed). Heidelberg: Oxford University Press (2011), pg 1097.

both States and individuals as potential perpetrators, thereby compelling them to respect such fundamental human rights and refrain from acts constituting such serious crimes.[254]

3.4.3 Persecution as a deprivation of fundamental human rights

While the efforts to establish a robust international criminal law proscription of persecution were stalled during the Cold War period, "interest shifted to the protection of the individual through internationally guaranteed human rights".[255] The consequent growth of human rights standards was specifically influential on persecution, and developed "the notion that the crime of persecution may be used as a means to protect fundamental human rights".[256] Persecution has therefore crystallised as a form of discrimination that is intended to be, and which results in, the infringement or denial of an individual or group's fundamental human rights.[257] Brady and Liss points out that:

> In the common form of the offence, a perpetrator harms or encroaches upon the fundamental human rights of a person because of that person's membership, affiliation or identification with a group.[258]

International concern and criminalisation of 'grievous persecution' are therefore justified by the notion that severe persecutory conduct attacks, more directly than any other crime against humanity, the core aspects of humanity, constituting a global human rights concern.[259]

Thus, persecution attacks the two fundamental aspects of being human, namely:

1. the persecuted victim's individuality, given that persecution reduces a victim to a specific identity based on his or her membership in a group; and
2. the victim's ability to freely choose an identity and in terms thereof associate with others.[260]

---

[254] Triffterer & Ambos *Commentary on the Rome Statute* (2008) 24.
[255] Brady & Liss *Evolution of Persecution* (2014) 498.
[256] Brady & Liss *Evolution of Persecution* (2014) 499.
[257] Cassese et al. *ICL: Cases and Commentary* (2011) 186.
[258] Brady & Liss *Evolution of Persecution* (2014) 430.
[259] Brady & Liss *Evolution of Persecution* (2014) 430.
[260] Luban, D. *A Theory of Crimes Against Humanity.* YJIL, Vol. 29 (2004), pg 116–117.

Persecution constitutes, first and foremost, "the violation of the right to equality in some serious fashion".[261] In the case of persecution, the required discriminatory intent invariably constitutes a serious infringement of the fundamental right to equality and non-discrimination based on one or more of the listed grounds of identity, and the subsequent conduct (or its effect) ordinarily deprives those persecuted of other interrelated rights and/or freedoms. While the nature of the fundamental rights infringed is relatively unimportant for purposes of the establishing the ground or mode of persecution, the nature of the denial of the right to equality or the basis upon which discrimination occurred, contextualises the ground or mode of persecution. In other words, the nature of discrimination, which must be on one of the listed grounds, may signify the mode of persecution, whether political, ethnic, religious, or otherwise.

Whereas the nature of the discrimination provides context to the ground of persecution, the severe infringement of fundamental rights constitutes the legal threshold for 'grievous persecution'. Cassese justly states that:

> Although the realm of human rights is dynamic and expansive, not every denial of a human right may constitute a crime against humanity.[262]

So far, prosecution for acts of persecution at the ICC has been based on arguably more 'traditional' infringements of fundamental rights, which are part of the enumerated inhumane acts under the *Rome Statute*.[263] However, it will be the judicial function of the Court to determine which rights are considered 'fundamental' in the context of persecution on a case-by-case basis.[264]

Therefore, the crime of persecution may encompass a wide variety of acts or omissions if such conduct resulted in the severe deprivation (on discriminatory grounds) of a fundamental human right. In the context of this study, the fundamental right to freedom of religion or belief, and the recognition and protection of religious identity, are essential elements of human rights.[265]

---

[261] *Tadić (Trial Judgement)* par 697.
[262] Cassese *ICL: Cases and Commentary* (2011) 186.
[263] Brady & Liss *Evolution of Persecution* (2014) 547.
[264] Brady & Liss *Evolution of Persecution* (2014) 547.
[265] Despite the close relation between religious identity and religious freedom rights, religious persecution is not premised on the violation of religious freedom rights specifically. However, because the intersection between religious persecution and deprivations of religious freedom is undeniable and often inseparable, the denial

3.5 The Relationship Between Persecution and Other International Crimes

Based on the preceding discussion it is clear that persecution, as an underlying inhumane act of crimes against humanity, constitutes an international core crime. However, its 'umbrella' character links it with a wide range of international crimes.[266] As Cassese adequately states:

> Persecution is the crime of violating a person's 'fundamental rights' with a discriminatory purpose... [and therefore] has the capacity to capture within a single charge a wide range of atrocities committed against a population.[267]

The purpose of this section is to briefly emphasise the relationship and interaction between persecution and other international crimes.

3.5.1 Persecution and war crimes

The post-Second World War jurisprudence has relied upon both underlying acts that amount to crimes against humanity and war crimes.[268] The reliance on war crimes as underlying acts or omissions grounding persecution convictions include acts such as deportation, slave labour and extermination.[269] In *Tadić*, the Trial Chamber found that acts which form the basis of a charge of war crimes can also additionally be charged as crimes against humanity of persecution, provided the definitional elements and conditions of applicability are satisfied.[270] Thus, acts committed against a civilian population in the context of an armed conflict amounting to war crimes can also constitute persecution.

3.5.2 Persecution and ethnic cleansing

The wars in Yugoslavia were predominantly fought between ethnic groups for the purpose of self-determination. Therefore, the crimes committed during the disintegration of the Federal Republic of Yugoslavia provided

---

or deprivation of religious freedom rights is often the precursor to religious persecution. Consequently, the right to freedom and religion or belief will be discussed in more detail in Appendix B.

[266] *Kordić (Trial Judgement)* par 192.
[267] Cassese, A. et al. *ICL: Cases and Commentary* (2011) 184.
[268] Brady & Liss *Evolution of Persecution* (2014) 467–468.
[269] Brady & Liss *Evolution of Persecution* (2014) 468.
[270] *Tadić (Trial Judgement)* par 700–701.

the particular historic background from which the term 'ethnic cleansing' entered international diplomatic parlance and official UN vocabulary.[271] Ethnic cleansing has been defined as:

> ...a purposeful policy designed by one ethnic or religious group to remove by violent and terror-inspiring means the civilian population of another ethnic or religious group from certain geographic areas.[272]

Although the origin of the term is unclear, it appears to resemble the expression 'racial hygiene', used by National Socialists.[273] The acts perpetrated as part of a policy of ethnic cleansing are systematically similar to the effect of genocide. The primary objective of a genocidal policy is the intent to destroy, in whole or in part, a specific national, ethnical, racial or religious group. Conversely, the *actus reus* of ethnic cleansing is committed with an intentional policy to target and permanently remove an identifiable group in order to establish homogenous lands.[274]

Clearly, 'removal' in the context of ethnic cleansing can be achieved through measures of extermination, similar to genocide. The term 'ethnic' is not used in a strict sense.[275] Most definitions of 'ethnic cleansing' comprise the systematic purge of various identifiable civilian groups, including ethnicity, religion, race, nationality, linguistic minorities, and indigenous people.[276] Ethnic cleansing is therefore inherently discriminatory, and directed against an identifiable civilian group:[277]

> At the most general level... ethnic cleansing can be understood as the expulsion of an 'undesirable' population from a given territory due to religious or ethnic discrimination, political, strategic or ideological considerations, or a combination of these.[278]

Ethnic cleansing may be achieved by any of a number of methods including, but not limited to, genocidal acts. For the purposes of the ICTY prose-

---

[271] Geiss, R. *Ethnic Cleansing. Max Planck Encyclopedia on Public International law*, Wolfrum, R. (ed). Heidelberg: Oxford University Press (2011), par 1.
[272] UN Security Council, *Report of the Commission of Experts Established Pursuant to United Nations Security Council Resolution 780* (1992), 27 May 1994 (S/1994/674), par 130.
[273] Geiss *Ethnic Cleansing* (2011) 681.
[274] Geiss *Ethnic Cleansing* (2011) 683.
[275] Geiss *Ethnic Cleansing* (2011) 682.
[276] Geiss *Ethnic Cleansing* (2011) 682.
[277] Geiss *Ethnic Cleansing* (2011) 686.
[278] Bell-Fialkoff, A. *A brief history of Ethnic Cleansing*. https://www.foreignaffairs.com/articles/1993-06-01/brief-history-ethnic-cleansing. Accessed 15/01/2019.

cutions, ethnic cleansing was not considered a separate crime, but was entirely encapsulated under the premise of the crime against humanity of persecution on political, racial or religious grounds.[279] For instance, during the Yugoslavian wars, the large-scale killing of Bosnian Muslims at Srebrenica in Bosnia formed the basis for the prosecution of the leadership of the Bosnian-Serb Army. Bosnian Muslim men were discriminately targeted and persecuted based on their religious identity, with the aim of deliberately removing them from the geographical area, by violent and terror-inspiring means.

In the context of the ICC, Article 7(1)(d) of the *Rome Statute* provides for deportation or forcible transfer of a population as an underlying act of crimes against humanity.[280] In terms of Article 7(2)(d), 'deportation or forcible transfer of population' means forced displacement of the persons concerned by expulsion or other coercive acts from the area in which they are lawfully present, without grounds permitted under international law. This seems to capture the notion of 'ethnic cleansing'. However, some commentators believe that deportation or forcible transfer of a population cannot be viewed as encapsulating ethnic cleansing:

> The very essence of ethnic cleansing being the intention to render an area ethnically homogenous, the mere intention to displace, without the intention to displace the targeted group permanently, would not seem to suffice for ethnic cleansing.[281]

A precise definition of 'ethnic cleansing' has not yet crystallised, however "there can be no doubt that ethnic cleansing violates fundamental prescriptions of international law",[282] and results in severe deprivations of fundamental human rights on a discriminatory basis.[283] Consequently, the notion of ethnic cleansing is clearly encapsulated by the conceptualisation of 'grievous persecution' in terms of the *Rome Statute*.

3.5.3 Persecution and genocide

At the outset, the most crucial *nexus* between persecution and genocide may be found in the origins of the crime of genocide itself. Polish lawyer Raphael

---

[279] Acquaviva & Pocar *Crimes Against Humanity* (2011) 5.
[280] Introduction to art 7, par 3 of the *ICC Elements of Crimes*.
[281] Geiss *Ethnic Cleansing* (2011) par 25.
[282] Geiss *Ethnic Cleansing* (2011) 685.
[283] UN General Assembly, *Vienna Declaration and Programme of Action*, 12 July 1993, A/CONF.157/23, par 28.

Lemkin coined the term 'genocide' during World War II to label the Holocaust policy of anti-Semitism, a system of methodical State-sponsored systematic mass extermination of millions of European Jews.[284] At the Nuremberg trials, Nazi war criminals were held individually criminally liable for crimes against peace, war crimes and crimes against humanity. Genocide only gained autonomous significance as a specific crime in 1948 with the adoption of the *Genocide Convention* and was not considered a separate crime in terms of the Nuremberg Charter. According to Fournet and Pigorier:

> ...it seems that the drafters of the IMT Charter preferred to use their more legitimate and justifiable judicial creation of 'crimes against humanity' and extend it to include genocide under what they chose to label 'persecutions'.[285]

The Holocaust policy entailed the persecution and extermination (genocide) of those with a 'Jewish identity'. The furious onslaught aimed at eliminating any trace of 'Jewishness', or any sign of 'Jewish spirit' reveals the inescapable fact that the persecutions were a necessary step directly leading to the systematic extermination of Jews in the occupied territories. In essence, in considering the crime of persecutions as a crime against humanity, the law of Nuremberg effectively conceived genocide into positive international law.[286]

However, the relation between the two crimes does not stop there, as the jurisprudence of the international criminal tribunals "have at times operated a quasi-merger between persecutions and genocide".[287] The tribunal in *Kupreškić*, explained that:

> [P]ersecution as a crime against humanity is an offence belonging to the same genus as genocide. Both persecution and genocide are crimes perpetrated against persons that belong to a particular group and who are targeted because of such belonging. [...] Thus, it can be said that, from the viewpoint of mens rea, genocide is an extreme and most inhuman form of persecution. To put it differently, when persecution escalates to the extreme form of wilful and deliberate acts designed to destroy a group or part of a group, it can be held that such persecution amounts to genocide.[288]

---

[284] See Ferguson, N. *The War of the World: History's Age of Hatred*. Penguin UK (2012). and also Lemkin, R. *Axis Rule in Occupied Europe: Laws of Occupation, Analysis of Government, Proposals for Redress*. Carnegie Endowment for International Peace, Division of International Law (1944), pg 79–95.
[285] Fournet & Pigorier *Only One Step Away From Genocide* (2010) 721.
[286] Fournet & Pigorier *Only One Step Away From Genocide* (2010) 721.
[287] Fournet & Pigorier *Only One Step Away From Genocide* (2010) 718.
[288] *Kupreškić et al. (Trial Judgement)* 636.

What distinguishes these two crimes is their respective mental elements (*mens rea*). Genocide consists of the special intent (*dolus specialis*) to destroy, in whole or in part, a protected group, as such. Although persecution also requires a particular *dolus specialis*, this *mens rea* is satisfied by a mere discriminatory intent and the consequent severe deprivation of fundamental rights. Thus, when persecution escalates to the extreme form of wilful and deliberate acts intended to destroy a group or substantial part thereof, it can be said that such a discriminatory intent has escalated into a genocidal policy. Therefore, genocidal acts may be described as the most abhorrent manifestation of persecution.

3.6 Conclusion

'Grievous persecution' was contextualised as an underlying inhumane act of crimes against humanity in terms of the *Rome Statute*, i. e. the intentional and severe deprivation of fundamental rights of a group or collectivity based on a discriminatory intent. In this regard, the auxiliary relationship between international criminal law and the protection of human rights was highlighted. "International criminal law intervenes on the side of humanity"[289] in instances where internationalised crimes constitute severe human rights infringements. It was shown that a primary function of international criminal law is the direct protection and enforcement of human rights norms, as most international crimes have a detrimental consequence on human rights. International criminal responsibility constitutes the highest level of protection that specific human rights can achieve under international law through the suppression of offences, such as persecution, that result in deprivations of human rights. As a result, the emblematic nature of persecution served a functional role in defining the parameters and normative insights of international criminal law, especially in terms of its relation to the protection of fundamental human rights.[290] Although the precise scope of protection of human rights through international criminal law requires greater clarity, the legal threshold of the core crimes represents serious and obvious infringements of fundamental human rights on a considerable level.

Occasionally, the lack of precision regarding the persecution rubric under international criminal law causes a problematic relation with other acts or crimes of international concern. Based on their shared genesis, per-

---

[289] Werle & Jessberger *Principles of International Criminal Law* (2014) par 143.
[290] Brady & Liss *Evolution of Persecution* (2014) 430.

secution is closely intertwined with genocide and ethnic cleansing. However, for purposes of this study, persecution constitutes one of the enumerated inhumane acts of crimes against humanity. In the context of crimes against humanity, the nature and gravity of persecution are evidence of consistent and systematic inhumanity on the greatest scale.[291] As with all the enumerated inhumane acts of crimes against humanity, the conditions of applicability must be satisfied and thus forms part of the definitional requirements for 'grievous persecution'. As such, this chapter serves as a prelude that contextualises the later conceptualisation of 'grievous religious persecution' in Chapter Six.

In the context of the *Rome Statute*, the persecutory conduct, when considered cumulatively and in context, must have resulted in a severe deprivation of *fundamental* principles of human dignity, equality or freedom.[292] However, considering that persecution does not necessarily entail a physical element, a serious form of discrimination may suffice as a severe deprivation of the fundamental right to equality and non-discrimination. Aside from the universally recognised fundamental rights and freedoms in terms of customary international law, the ICC will have to assess whether 'other' human rights amount to 'fundamental rights' on a case-by-case basis. An exhaustive list of 'fundamental rights' is therefore unnecessary.

Essentially, 'grievous persecution' was conceptualised as a mass *discriminatory crime* resulting in severe deprivations of fundamental human rights. As a result, the persecutor must have acted with a conscious and preconceived discriminatory mindset to target a person or persons by reason of their identity, which identity must be based on the grounds listed in the *Rome Statute*. In other words, the identity element associated with the discriminatory intent is a key component in understanding and identifying the ground of persecution. Consequently, the identity element and the role of identity in the context of characterising persecution will form the basis of the next chapter. While this chapter has provided a basic conceptualisation of persecution in its generic sense, the identity element is the aspect that determines the relevant mode or ground of persecution. Specific to the context of this book, the subsequent question is: What is a religious identity and what is its role in classifying the ground of persecution as religiously orientated?

---

[291] *IMT Judgment* (1946) 247.
[292] *Duch (Appeal judgement)* par 257.

Chapter Four: The Role of Religious Identity in Determining the Grounds of Persecution

4.1 Introduction

In the context of international criminal law and its *nexus* to the protection of human rights, a 'religious group' is considered a 'protected group',[1] and an adherent's resultant 'religious identity' is a 'protected ground' of human existence.[2] The criminalisation of religious persecution as a crime against humanity in the *Rome Statute* is aimed at protecting individuals and groups against human rights deprivations and mass-scale atrocities because of their 'religious identity'. However, religious persecution is not the only ground of persecution criminalised by the *Rome Statute*.[3]

The grounds of persecution are based on the identifying factor (prohibited ground) of the targeted person or group 'by reason' of which they were targeted. These identifying factors constitute aspects that form part of one's personal and/or collective identity, and are protected as significant issues of human life and dignity in terms of international law. In other words, the ground of persecution, or the multiplicity thereof, is based on

---

[1] A religious group is considered a protected group in terms of Art 2 of the UNGA, *Convention on the Prevention and Punishment of the Crime of Genocide*, 9 December 1948 (*Genocide Convention*); and Art 6 of the *Rome Statute of the International Criminal Court*, Doc. A/CONF.183/9 of 17 July 1998 *in force* 1 July 2002 (2002).

[2] 'Religion' is a protected ground in terms of the '*International Bill of Rights*' (which includes the *Universal Declaration of Human Rights* (adopted in 1948), the *International Covenant on Civil and Political Rights* (ICCPR, 1966) with its two Optional Protocols and the *International Covenant on Economic, Social and Cultural Rights* (ICESCR, 1966); the UN General Assembly, *Declaration on the Elimination of All Forms of Intolerance and of Discrimination Based on Religion or Belief*, UNGA Res 36/55, 73rd plenary meeting, 25 November 1981 (*Religious Discrimination Declaration*); and in the context of persecution, Art 7(1)(h) of the *Rome Statute*.

[3] In terms of a broad generic understanding of persecution, the following grounds of persecution are considered to be identifiable protected grounds in terms of the *Rome Statute*: political, racial, national, ethnic, cultural, religious, gender, or other grounds that are universally recognized as impermissible under international law.

a protected aspect of the victim's identity, which made him or her the target of the persecutor's discriminatory intent.[4] Therefore, understanding the victim's identity and how a specific aspect of his identity relates to the perpetrator's discriminatory mindset, will help to classify the relevant ground of persecution. Characterising the grounds of persecution and how they intersect with religious persecution may prove to be vital in proposing the intended taxonomy.

However, the conception of 'identity', as an essential part of human dignity, relates to aspects of the human identity that comprise various complex, intertwined and interlinking factors, alongside religion. Therefore, classifying the nature of persecution in a given situation is often complicated by the inseparability of multiple aspects of the victim's identity. As a result, the complexity of human identity often makes it difficult to recognise the primary basis upon which the perpetrator discriminately identified and targeted his victims. Consequently, religion is usually not the only ground of persecution in a specific situation.

Nevertheless, individuals or groups of individuals, in various places throughout the world, are continually being persecuted on the basis of their religious identity, or lack of thereof.[5] Religion or belief is one of the fundamental elements in a person's conception of life, which gives individuals a sense of identity and belonging, and configures personal ethics and public morals.[6]

> Religious Freedom is perhaps the most personal of human rights, as it goes to the very core of being a human being. Yet limitations, abuse, and persecution are a daily occurrence.[7]

In the context of *religious* persecution, the international legal standards applicable to the right to freedom of 'thought, conscience and religion or belief' plays a pivotal interpretive role. It is pertinent in (1) defining the parameters of protection of religious freedom in order to gauge potential

---

[4] Art 7(2)(g), read together with Art 7(1)(h) of the *Rome Statute*. It should be noted that the use of the terms 'intent' and 'intention', as used throughout this book, are concomitantly similar expressions which refer to a form of culpability or fault which may be defined as 'the blameworthy state of mind' of a criminally responsible person who performs an unlawful act with the will to perform such act or cause such consequence while knowing that this conduct is unlawful.

[5] Thames, H. et al. *International Religious Freedom Advocacy: A guide to Organizations, Law and NGO's*. Baylor University Press (2009) pg 10–11.

[6] Preamble par 4 of the *Religious Discrimination Declaration* (1981).

[7] Thames et al. *International Religious Freedom Advocacy* (2009) 1.

infringements, such as religious persecution; (2) recognising and contextualising equality on the basis of religion and the protection against religious discrimination as the core element of the notion of 'religious persecution'; and (3) formulating what constitutes a 'religious identity' as a deep existential view, as an identifying element, and as a way of life. As such, this chapter focusses on the role that 'religion' and 'religious identity' may have in the context of religious discrimination and persecution, and the habitual deprivations of religious freedom rights.[8] Bielefeldt explains that:

> ...[F]reedom of religion or belief institutionalizes due respect for all human beings as potential holders of profound, identity-shaping convictions and conviction-based practices.[9]

At this point, it is advisable to readers unacquainted with the right to freedom of religion or belief in international human rights law, to first read Appendix B for an overview of the topic.

In instances where the religious identity of the victim constitutes the primary basis of discrimination 'by reason of' which he or she was targeted, it is this aspect of identity that determines the ground of persecution as religion-based.

Therefore, classifying a situation as *religious* persecution will require an appreciation of the nature and importance of religious identity, the influence that religious freedom has in forming and protecting a religious identity, and how such an identity becomes the object of perception and discrimination. Consequently, in the context of persecution, this chapter will seek to understand the importance of a religious identity as a deep or profound existential view, as a vital element in a person's conception of identity, as a source of moral guidance and behavior, and as a fundamental aspect of human freedom. Therefore, an assessment of the role that an individual or collective religious identity has in a given situation is essential in determining the ground of persecution. However, before examining the role of religious identity, it is necessary to conceptualise the notion of 'religion'.

---

[8] The phrases 'religious freedom', 'freedom of religion' or otherwise will have contextually similar meanings that must be interpreted in terms of international human rights law. Religious freedom refers to the right to freedom of thought, conscience, and religion or belief – art 18 of the *UDHR* and *ICCPR*.

[9] Bielefeldt, H. *Freedom of Religion or Belief: Thematic Reports of the UN Special Rapporteur 2010 – 2016.* Religious Freedom Series of the International Institute for Religious Freedom, Vol 3, 2nd and extended edition, Bonn. (2017) pg 200.

4.2 Religion and Persecution

Although the full extent of 'religion as a fundamental human right' is discussed in Appendix B, it is necessary to provide a basic characterisation of two significant aspects in this regard, viz. 'religion' and 'religious persecution', in order to facilitate a constructive progression of thought.

In this section, a doctrine of 'religion' is formulated for purposes of this study. It should be noted that a detailed philosophical or theological discussion of 'religion' falls outside the scope of this study. Thereafter, a *preliminary* characterisation and definition of religious persecution will also be provided in order to facilitate a constructive progression of argument.[10]

4.2.1 A doctrine of 'religion'

All aspects of the notion of 'religion' are philosophically unique and fundamental elements that depict humanity's existential cognisance of their existence, identity and conception of life. Therefore, it is a vital aspect of an adherent's way of life and how they relate, either completely or partially, to the world.[11] Despite many noble attempts, no consensus has emerged on a universally accepted definition of 'religion'.[12] Inevitably, definitions may be contextual acceptable, but varies from discipline to discipline and may therefore, not be functional in another context. However, a defining religion serves an important interpretive role in law, and failing to realize a legal definition of religion has certain inherent risks.[13] Deagon argues that a definition of religion is of central importance

> "to creating the constitutional space for freedom of religion, for it is religion which receives protections in constitutional law and international law, and

---

[10] It should be noted that this conceptualisation of religious persecution is not limited to an international criminal law perspective specifically. In Chapter Six, the proposed taxonomy will provide a formal definition and characterisation of 'grievous religious persecution'.

[11] Par 8 of the UN High Commissioner for Refugees (UNHCR), *Guidelines on International Protection No. 6: Religion-Based Refugee Claims under Article 1A(2) of the 1951 Convention and/or the 1967 Protocol relating to the Status of Refugees*, 28 April 2004, HCR/GIP/04/06. (*UNCHR: Religion-Based Refugee Claims*).

[12] Par 4 of the *UNCHR: Religion-Based Refugee Claims* (2004).

[13] For a discussion in this regard, see Barker, R. *The Scientology case: Defining religion for the world?* (Not yet published). Used with the author's permission.

the definition of religion in freedom of religion will determine the scope of that freedom".[14]

After noting certain challenges to defining religion, he proposes that religion is "a set of systematic beliefs in relation to a transcendent being, thing, or principle".[15] Generally, the judiciary have either found it notoriously difficult to provide a legal definition of religion or have studiously avoided such a attempts.[16] While the judicial approach, "I know it when I see it" may be pragmatic,[17] "legal certainty demands that a term essential to a myriad of legal rights and privileges be defined".[18]

In the context of this book, 'religion' is best understood in the context of the right to freedom of religion or belief. The right to freedom of religion or belief protects believers, whether individual or communitarian, not beliefs.[19] On the one hand, this implies that in terms of human rights law, neither a 'religion', *per se*, nor the ideas and doctrines that may be imparted from such a religion, are protected against ridicule and criticism. On the other hand, it implies that religious freedom, guaranteed as a fundamental right in what has been termed the *International Bill of Rights*,[20] protects the dimensional elements and core values of religious freedom, i. e. the *forum internum* or freedom to have a religion of choice, and the *forum externum* or freedom to manifest such a religion.[21] These aspects of religious freedom are distinctive yet connected values to which an individual is entitled from birth.

'Religion' as a fundamental human freedom under international human rights law, encapsulates the human inclination towards "freedom of thoughts on all matters, personal conviction and the commitment to reli-

---

[14] Deagon, A. *Towards a Constitutional Definition of Religion: Challenges and Prospects*. From Babie, P.T., Rochow, N.G. & Scharffs, B.G. (eds). *Freedom of Religion or Belief: Creating the Constitutional Space for Fundamental Freedoms*. Edward Elgar Publishing (2020), pg 92.
[15] Deagon *Towards a Constitutional Definition of Religion* (2020) 92–108.
[16] Barker *The Scientology case: Defining religion for the world?*
[17] *Jacobellis v Ohio*, 378 US 184, 197 (Stewart J).
[18] Barker *The Scientology case: Defining religion for the world?* Referring to Durham, W.C. & Scharffs, B.G. *Law and Religion: National, International and Comparative Perspectives*. Wolters Kluwer. (2010), pg 40.
[19] Bielefeldt, H., Ghanea, N. & Michael Wiener M. *Freedom of Religion or Belief: An International Law Commentary*. Oxford University Press. (2016), pg 11.
[20] Art 18 of the *UDHR* and Art 18 of the *ICCPR*.
[21] This is discussed in Appendix B.

gion or belief, whether manifested individually or in community with others".[22] Thus, the perception of a religious identity is completely dependent on the recognition and protection of religious freedom as a fundamental human right under international human rights law.[23] General Comment No. 22 relating to Article 18 of the *International Covenant on Civil and Political Rights (ICCPR)* states that the right to freedom of religion or belief includes:

> ... theistic, non-theistic and atheistic beliefs, as well as the right not to profess any religion or belief. The terms belief and religion are to be broadly construed [and their application should not be limited] to traditional religions or to religions and beliefs with institutional characteristics or practices analogous to those of traditional religions.[24]

In other words, 'religion' is an umbrella term that encapsulates not only aspects of religion in the traditional sense of belief, but other aspects derived from the inner-self, including belief, thought and conscience. Each of these elements are philosophically unique denotations of conviction, inherently linked to the notion of 'religion'.[25]

'Thought' and 'conscience' do not necessarily relate to a spiritual predisposition, and are essentially preferences that pertain to a value-system.[26]

'Belief' may be interpreted as a person's religious belief or similar philosophical belief or conviction "about the divine or ultimate reality or the spiritual destiny of humankind".[27] It may also include views that attain "a

---

[22] UN Human Rights Committee, *General Comment No. 22: The Right to Freedom of Thought, Conscience, and Religion in terms of Article 18 of the ICCPR.* CCPR/C/21/Rev.1/Add.4, 30 July, par 1. (*UNHRC: General Comment No. 22*)

[23] Walter, C. *Religion or Belief, Freedom of, International Protection. Max Planck Encyclopedia on Public International law*, Wolfrum, R. (ed). Heidelberg: Oxford University Press (2009) pg 864. See Art 18 common to the *UDHR* and the *ICCPR*.

[24] Par 2 of the *UNHRC: General Comment No. 22*.

[25] Par 2 of *General Comment No. 22* states that religious freedom includes... theistic, non-theistic and atheistic beliefs, as well as the right not to profess any religion or belief. The terms belief and religion are to be broadly construed [and their application should not be limited] to traditional religions or to religions and beliefs with institutional characteristics or practices analogous to those of traditional religions.

[26] Council of Europe, *Freedom of thought, conscience and religion: A guide to the implementation of Article 9 of the European Convention on Human Rights*, Human rights handbooks, No. 9 (2007), pg 12.

[27] Par 6 of the *UNCHR: Religion-Based Refugee Claims* (2004).

4. The Role of Religious Identity in Determining the Grounds of Persecution 113

coherent view on fundamental problems",[28] provided it exhibits "a certain level of cogency, seriousness, cohesion and importance".[29] Thus, not every opinion can be claimed as a serious 'belief'.[30]

Bielefeldt et al. warn against the 'pitfalls of trivialisation' if the right to freedom of religion is used to protect all sort of trivial interest,[31] for example, followers of a 'Star Wars' religion, or those who worship the 'big spaghetti monster'. Consequently, the European Court of Human Rights qualified a 'belief' for the purposes of the application of the right to religious freedom, as a conviction regarding "weighty and substantial aspect of human life and behaviour"[32] to such an extent that such a belief may be deemed worthy of protection in a democratic society. Importantly, States should not have *carte blanche* to decide what is a genuine religious belief and what is not.[33]

Based on the preceding interpretation, 'religion' should be viewed as an encapsulating term that is broadly inclusive of all deeply held philosophically unique denotations of personal or existential conviction. 'Religion' thus represents deep existential views, which may either relate to: (1) a spiritual predisposition, i. e. religious beliefs such as monotheistic faiths, non-religious beliefs such as atheism,[34] or a general belief system such as the Church of Scientology;[35] or (2) a personal and elementary preference that pertain to a value-system derived from deep personal thoughts and conscience,[36] such as secularity.[37] Bielefeldt notes that:

---

[28] Swedish Mission Council: *What freedom of religion involves and when it can be limited. A quick guide to religious freedom* (2010), pg 5.
[29] *Campbell and Cosans v. United Kingdom*, judgment of 25 February 1982, App. Nos. 7511/76, 7743/76, Eur. Ct. H.R. (1982), pg 13.
[30] Bielefeldt, H. *Misperceptions of Freedom of Religion or Belief*. Human Rights Quarterly, Volume 35, Number 1, pp. 33-68 (Article). Published by The Johns Hopkins University Press (2013), pg 39.
[31] Bielefeldt et al. *FORB: An International Law Commentary* (2016) 19-20.
[32] *Campbell* (ECtHR Judgment) (1982) 13.
[33] Discussion of the Human Rights Committee's draft general comment no. 22 on 24 July 1992, CCPR/C/SR.1166, par 48.
[34] Council of Europe *Freedom of thought, conscience and religion* (2007) 11-12.
[35] See Urban, H. B. *The Church of Scientology: A History of a New Religion*. Princeton University Press. (2011). See also Kent, S. A. *Scientology - Is this a Religion?* Marburg Journal of Religion 4 (1): 1-23 (1999).
[36] Council of Europe *Freedom of thought, conscience and religion* (2007) 11-12.
[37] For example post-religious 'secular' belief systems such as the 'Secular Society' founded by George Holyoake, which subscribes to the motto that 'Science is the Available Providence of Man' – Holyoake, G.J. *English Secularism: A Confession of Belief*.

"... religions or beliefs, whatever their precise content, generally relate to people's deep and existential convictions and concomitant individual and communitarian ethical or ritualistic practices".[38]

As such, a common definitional misconception regarding 'religion or belief' is to equate such notions with the necessity to believe in an existential or supernatural entity.[39]

Regardless of which criteria are applied to define 'religion' and 'belief', such criteria must "remain open and for this reason fairly formal so as to allow for the inclusion of different manifestations of these existential convictions and ritualistic or ethical practices".[40] 'Religion' must be viewed in its broadest sense and should not be easily limited, otherwise one runs the risk of excluding some people from its legal protection.[41] Regardless of their nature, all deep existential views are equally and non-discriminately protected grounds of religious freedom.[42] This protection relates to members of all religious communities, whether large or small, including, *inter alia*, religious minorities and minorities within minorities (for example, so-called 'sects' or 'cults'), conservatives and liberals, converts or re-converts, dissenters or other critical voices, and women.

Ultimately, religious freedom implies a concomitant individual and communitarian fundamental human right and the commitment to a certain deep existential way of life, indispensable to religious identity. As such, a 'religious identity' relates to the invariable derivative effect of the freedom to have and maifest a chosen profound, identity-shaping existential view. Consequently, an expansive interpretation of 'religion' implies a broad understanding and protection of an adherent's resultant 'religious identity', which in turn expands a conceptualisation of 'religious' persecution.

The Open Court Publishing Company, Chicago (1896), pg 35. See Spartacus Educational: https://spartacus-educational.com/PRholyoak.htm. Accessed 24/01/2019. See also Bielefeldt et al. *FORB: An International Law Commentary* (2016) 357–358.

[38] Bielefeldt *Misperceptions of FORB* (2013) 39.

[39] See for example Institute on Religion and Public Policy (ed.): *Know your rights: What is Religious Freedom?* Alexandria, Virginia, USA, (September 2014) 3.

[40] Bielefeldt *Misperceptions of FORB* (2013) 40.

[41] Bielefeldt et al. *FORB: An International Law Commentary* (2016) 20.

[42] Bielefeldt *Misperceptions of FORB* (2013) 38.

4.2.2 A preliminary characterisation of religious persecution

As mentioned, a broad understanding of 'religion' justifies an expansive interpretation of *religious* identity and *religious* persecution. Essentially, religious persecution or "persecution for reasons of religion" should be understood as a form or mode of persecution in terms of which the persecutor intentionally and discrimi nately directed his/her conduct at certain individuals or a group of individuals, 'by reason of' their religious identity.[43] Thus, the victims are chosen 'by reason of' their deep existential identity, or lack thereof.

'Religious persecution' denote religion as being the discriminatory ground of persecution, "with its common characteristic being the denial of the human rights and fundamental freedoms to which every individual is entitled without distinction".[44] Thus, it may be considered as a serious form of religious discrimination that results in the severe deprivation of fundamental rights, including the right to equality and non-discrimination on the basis of religion.

For purposes of this preliminary characterisation it is important to clarify the conceptual interrelation between religious persecution and deprivations of religious freedom. Religious persecution is often understood and equated with the denial of the right to freedom of religion or belief.[45] Such an interpretation of religious persecution is indicative of a misconception regarding the nature of persecution. Religious persecution need not necessarily limit or deprive a believer's ability to hold or practice their belief or faith.[46] In other words, the classification of religious persecution is not a quintessential derivative of the deprivation of the right to

---

[43] Par 72 of the UN High Commissioner for Refugees (UNHCR), *Handbook and Guidelines on Procedures and Criteria for Determining Refugee Status under the 1951 Convention and the 1967 Protocol Relating to the Status of Refugees*, December 2011, HCR/1P/4/ENG/REV. 3.

[44] UN General Assembly, *Report of the International Law Commission on the work of its 48th session: resolution / adopted by the General Assembly.*, 30 January 1997, A/RES/51/160. Par 11.

[45] "Persecution in the religious sense *always* involves a severe violation of the human right to religious freedom". – University of Notre Dame – Under Caesar's Sword: Christian Response to Persecution. *In Response to Persecution: Findings of the Under Caesar's Sword Project on Global Christian Communities.* Report released on April 20, 2017 in Washington D.C, pg 9. http://ucs.nd.edu/report/. Accessed 19/02/2018. Emphasis added.

[46] Tieszen, C.L. *Re-Examining Religious Persecution: Constructing a Theological Framework for Understanding Persecution.* Religious Freedom Series, Vol 1 (2008), pg 42-44. See also The *Bad Urach Statement* published as part of the compendium on the *Bad*

freedom of thought, conscience, religion or belief specifically. The persecutor targets those with a specific religious identity; whether such an 'attack' infringes upon religious freedom is inconsequential for the purposes of its classification as religious persecution. However, such a particularity is often academic as the denial or deprivation of religious freedom rights is frequently the precursor to religious persecution. The denial or deprivation of religious freedom rights thus serves as the proverbial canary in the coal mine, forewarning the denial of other fundamental liberties, which almost surely follow.[47]

The quintessential nature of religious persecution requires discriminatory practices based on ideologies that formally or factually effect unequal treatment between adherents of different religions or beliefs. Consequently, any severe deprivation of any fundamental human rights may be contextualised as religious persecution, provided such deprivations were directed at an individual or group 'by reason' of their religious identity or lack thereof.

However, the justification or motivation for persecution based on religious identity is hardly ever the sole factor or only impulse for persecution.[48] Therefore, it is common to find an intersectionality between other protected grounds and religious identity, which will be discussed below.

A further common mis-perception about religious persecution is to equate religious discriminatory intent with religiously motivated persecution. In this regard, the motive or reason for committing persecution should be differentiated from the discriminatory intent to target victims based on their religious identity, regardless of the reason or motive. This will be discussed in more detail in Chapter Five.

A final consideration in a preliminary characterisation of religious persecution, is the means employed to enforce persecution and the subsequent effect on the victim's experience of persecution. The means employed to enforce persecutory actions often have distinct effects on the persecuted. In this regard, the *World Watch List Methodology* distinguishes

---

Urach Consultation: *Suffering, persecution and martyrdom – Theological reflections*. Edited by Sauer, C. & Howell, R. Religious Freedom Series: Suffering, Persecution and Martyrdom. Vol 2. Kempton Park: AcadSA Publishing / Bonn: VKW (2010), pg 41.

[47] Abrams, E. *The Persecution of Christians as a Worldwide Phenomenon*. Testimony at the U.S. Commission on International Religious Freedom before the Subcommittee on Africa, Global Health, Global Human Rights, and International Organizations of the House Foreign Affairs Committee, 11 February 2014, pg 1. It should be noted that for this book, it will be assumed that severe deprivations of religious freedom constitute 'grievous religious persecution'.

[48] Tieszen *Re-Examining Religious Persecution* (2008) 41.

two main experiences of persecution: (1) 'squeeze' (the inward pressure that believers experience in all areas of life) and (2) 'smash' (the outwardly invasive expression of persecution through violence).[49]

Incidents and evidence of 'smashing' or violence through various motivational triggers, attributed to either State involvement or societal intolerance, are easier to track and assess, may be less intricate, and thus more readily contextualised as religious persecution. In the context of 'grievous religious persecution', instances of 'smash' may be similar in nature to physical 'persecution atrocities' evident from either 'inhumane-type' conduct or non-enumerated acts of a physical nature. These 'persecution atrocities' cause great suffering and include deprivation of physical freedom, serious damage to property, serious injury to body and/or to mental or physical health, or other forms of physical hostility or threats. For example, religious extremism by the Islamic militant group, *Boko Haram* in Nigeria, provides a clear and obvious attempt to 'smash' dissenting religious identities.[50]

However, contrary to popular belief, it is often the 'squeeze' or restrictive pressure that constitutes gross or blatant denials, on discriminatory grounds, of religious freedom. This is because "the degree of persecution can be so intense, and so all-pervasive, it actually results in fewer incidents of [physical acts of] persecution, since acts of public witness and defiance are so rare"[51]. In some instances, persecutors prefer to employ measures that 'squeeze' religious identities, rather than violent smashes, in the belief that it is a more successful form of persecution.[52] In the context of 'grievous religious persecution', physical acts of violence are not a prerequisite. In this regard, discriminatory policies that result in 'squeezing' the rights and freedoms of adherents that belong to a certain religious identity may be inherently inhumane in nature if their cumulative effect satisfies the requisite intensity threshold. Persecution in the form of a restrictive 'squeeze' is thus similar in nature to 'iniquitous persecution'. 'Iniquitous persecution' or 'squeeze' refers to discriminatory measures that place increasing pressure on religious adherents to witness their faith. As such, it may include discriminatory policies or restrictive laws, practices, or omis-

---

[49] Open Doors Analytical. *World Watch List Methodology*. November 2017, pg 17–18. Available at: http://opendoorsanalytical.org/world-watch-list-methodology-latest-edition-november-2017/. Accessed 09/01/2019.
[50] *World Watch List Methodology* (2017) 18.
[51] *World Watch List Methodology* (2017) 18.
[52] *World Watch List Methodology* (2017) 18.

sions, which are offensive to humanity, whether based on its inherent discriminatory nature or its cumulative effect. The intense restrictions on human rights and freedoms in North Korea may prove a typical example of an extreme degree of persecution through 'squeeze'. The persecution 'squeeze' is evident as a lack of religious pluralism and freedom, especially regarding the manifestation of diverging deep existential views.

There may even be situations where these two experiences of persecution may overlap; such is the case in areas in northern Iraq and Syria, where the group *Da'esh* (Islamic State) exercise *de facto* control. In Appendix C it is shown that *Da'esh* is or was an active participant in violent armed attacks ('smash') against certain religious groups, inspired and motivated by religious ideology. Furthermore, *Da'esh* religious rights and freedoms through the enforcement of their own brand of *Sharia* law ('squeeze'). For example, *Da'esh* forces forced dissident believers to either convert to Islam, pay special taxes, leave the region, or face summary execution.[53] These two forms of persecutive experiences may overlap when those victims are publicly reprimanded for choosing or exercising their dissenting beliefs. Such penalties are often very violent, such as beheadings and beatings, intended to instil an aura of control over, and fear within, the broader public.

At this point it should already be clear that the complexities and diversity of religious identity perpetuate the difficulty in defining persecution. However, a preliminary description of religious persecution may be formulated as follows:

> Religious persecution is the unjustified infliction of persecutory conduct resulting in sufficiently severe harm, which may not necessarily prevent or limit religious freedom rights, and is based on the persecutor's discriminatory intention that is primarily directed at a specific individual or group because of their religious identity.[54]

4.3 The Notion of Identity and the Role of Religion or Belief in Forming Personal Identity

In this section the notion of identity is discussed, then the role of religion in forming identity is presented.

---

[53] UN Office of the High Commissioner for Human Rights (OHCHR), Report of the Independent International Commission of Inquiry on the Syrian Arab Republic (IICISAR). *Rule of Terror: Living under ISIS in Syria*, 14 November 2014, par 24.

[54] Paraphrasing the definition of Tieszen, C.L. *Towards Redefining Persecution*. Religious Freedom Series: Suffering, Persecution and Martyrdom, Vol 2. (2010) 168.

4.3.1 Personal identity

At the core of human identity is the fact that we are some form of living organism, capable of conscience and choice. The journey and development of a personal identity and discovering one's true self is surely one of the most complex psychological, sociological and philosophical anomalies one may experience. Palmer summarises a philosophy on identity as follows:

> By identity I mean an evolving nexus where all the forces that constitute my life converge in the mystery of self: my genetic makeup, the nature of the man and woman who gave me life, the culture in which I was raised, people who have sustained me and people who have done me harm, the good and ill I have done to others, and to myself, the experience of love and suffering – and much, much more.[55]

The sociological notion of identity formulates personal identity along personal, physical and social qualities that differentiate and define the true self as a continuous, unique and connected entity. As a human rights philosopher, Bielefeldt notes that:

> Human rights, when viewed from a universal perspective, force us to face the most demanding of all dialectics: the dialectics of identity and otherness, of 'self' and 'other'. They teach us, in the most direct way, that we are, at one and the same time, the same and different.[56]

A person's self-identity or self-conception is based on qualities, beliefs, aspects of personality, physical appearances, and expressions that make him yet her unique, or qualitatively different from others. Regarding his observations in the Middle East, Andrews notes that:

> The sense of identity and belonging comes from a variety of factors, including family, wider family, tribe, ethnicity, religious affiliation, employment/career, as well as nationality.[57]

---

[55] Palmer, P. J. *The heart of a teacher: Identity and integrity in teaching.* (2008) Essay of edited excerpts from Palmer, P.J. *The Courage to Teach: Exploring the Inner Landscape of a Teacher's Life.* Jossey-Bass Publishers. (1997), pg 5.

[56] Par 119 of the UN Commission on Human Rights, *Report submitted by the Special Rapporteur on freedom of religion or belief, in accordance with Commission on Human Rights resolution 2002/40*, 15 January 2003, E/CN.4/2003/66. (*Report submitted by the Special Rapporteur on freedom of religion*).

[57] Andrews, J. *Identity Crisis: Religious Registration in the Middle East.* Gilead Books Publishing (2016), pg 23.

A person may be identified in terms of his or her social standing and affiliation with certain identifiable groups, whether through self-identification or the perception of others. The formation of identity is thus largely based on internal and external conception, perception, and depiction. 'Identity' and the forming of an identity is a complex phenomenon that exhibits both subjective and objective criteria. Various 'self-identifiers' (or 'communal-identifiers') may co-exist, complicating the perception of identity and consequently the classification of the ground/s of persecution, including, *inter alia*, ethnicity, nationality, political or cultural grounds. An appropriate example would be the 'Jewish identity',[58] which is clearly illustrative of the intersection and inseparability of religion with race, nationality and ethnicity.[59]

Consequently, identity formation is at the core of the development of the distinct personality of an individual. It can be regarded as an ever-evolving characterisation of co-existing 'identifiers' by which a person is recognised, known or perceived. As such, identity is at the core of being human and human dignity, which requires widespread respect and protection of human rights in order to "freely develop, change, or defend one's individual or communitarian identity".[60]

In the midst of all the forces that constitute one's conception of self, 'identity' is a moving intersection of the inner and outer forces that make up the true self, converging in the irreducible mystery of being human.[61] 'Identity' is, therefore, a complex and adaptable phenomenon based on multiple 'identifiers' (identifying factors) that differentiate and define the true self as a continuous, unique and connected entity. Thus, establishing a clear and identifiable religious identity may be complicated, especially considering that many of these 'identifiers' intersect with religion.

---

[58] The 'Jewish identity' is based on an indistinguishable joining of common beliefs, rituals, traditions, ethnicity, language, nationality, ancestry and race.
[59] "The anti-Jewish policy was formulated in Point 4 of the Party Programme which declared 'Only a member of the race can be a citizen. A member of the race can only be one who is of German blood, without consideration of creed. Consequently, no Jew can be a member of the race'". – *The Trial of German Major War Criminals, Proceedings of the International Military Tribunal Sitting at Nuremberg, Germany*. International Military Tribunal, Judgment of 1 October 1946, pg 75.
[60] Bielefeldt *Misperceptions of FORB* (2013) 44–45.
[61] Palmer *Identity and integrity in teaching* (2008) 5.

4.3.2 The role of religion in forming an identity

Considering that 'religion' is broadly construed to encapsulate all aspects of religious freedom,[62] a 'religious identity' constitutes an inherent and consequential element of the enjoyment of such freedoms. In other words, 'religious identity' is the inevitable consequential effect of the freedom to change, develop, reconsider, configure, and externally manifest a chosen deep existential view.[63] Consequently, the use and understanding of the term 'religious identity' include all aspects of religious freedom, and not only as an aspect of identity, *per se*.

For many people a religious identity constitute a vital part of their daily lives, their conception of life, the backbone of their personal and communitarian identities, their engagement with society in general, and their world-view.[64] Consequently, the concept of 'religious identity' may involve one or more of the following elements: religion as a belief, religion as an identifying element, and religion as a way of life.

4.3.2.1 Religion as a belief

'Religion as a belief' entails that a religious identity forms part of a deep personal conviction, which constitutes an essential part of the daily lives of adherents. In this sense, an adherent's religious identity refers to the nature and choice of his deep existential conviction. Depending on the etymological interpretation, a 'religious identity' may encompass various manifestations of belief.[65] For instance, the fundamental religious idea of Islam is that a Muslim believer accepts surrender to the will of *Allah*, viewed as the sole God—creator, sustainer, and restorer of the world.[66]

---

[62] Par 1 of the *UNHRC: General Comment No. 22*.
[63] Bielefeldt *FORB: Thematic Reports* (2017) 341.
[64] Bielefeldt *et al. FORB: An International Law Commentary* (2016) 11.
[65] This may include, *inter alia*: conscious knowledge and ethical standards, the practice of good deeds or manifestations of tenets, an enlightened persuasion and conviction, a sense of community (e. g. *ubuntu*), harmonious and peaceful co-existence, faithfulness and trust in the metaphysical aspects of divinity, the paradoxes or transcendence of life, submission to the higher authority or commandments of an enlightened or celestial being, and perhaps ultimately, the acceptance of the mystery of life itself.
[66] https://www.britannica.com/topic/Islam. Accessed 28/07/2019.

Importantly, the nature of free will and choice inextricably links the positive and negative components of freedom.[67] In other words, the freedom to choose a religious identity also includes the freedom to abstain from such a choice or the right not to profess any religion or belief; so-called 'freedom from religion'.[68] For example, Atheism is the critique and denial of metaphysical beliefs and the existence of deities.[69]

4.3.2.2 Religion as an identifying element

Freedom of religion or belief "facilitates the free search and development of faith-related identities in the broadest sense of the word".[70] Therefore, a religious or belief-identity is one of the most vital elements that make up individual or communitarian identities.[71] However, it is important to remember that an individual's religious or belief conviction, although essential, is one of many complex factors that influence a person's identity.[72]

Normally, the formation of a 'religious identity' also includes a collective affiliation and commitment to a religion or belief "that observes or is bound together by common beliefs, rituals, traditions, ethnicity, nationality, or ancestry".[73] This will be discussed in more detail below.

A 'religious identity' may be established when the individual freely identifies with, or has a sense of belonging to, a particular religious group or belief-based community.[74] However, the perception of others may also impute a person with a certain religious identity.

> It may not be necessary ... for an individual (or a group) to declare that he or she belongs to a religion, is of a particular religious faith, or adheres to religious practices, where the persecutor imputes or attributes this religion, faith or practice to the individual or group ...[75]

This means that others may form a perception of a person's religious identity, not merely by what that person declares his identity to be, but often more importantly, how the person behaves or through the manifestation

---

[67] Bielefeldt *Misperceptions of FORB* (2013) 49–50.
[68] Bielefeldt *Misperceptions of FORB* (2013) 47.
[69] https://www.britannica.com/topic/atheism. Accesed 28/07/2019.
[70] Bielefeldt *et al. FORB: An International Law Commentary* (2016) 11.
[71] Council of Europe *Freedom of thought, conscience and religion* (2007) 12.
[72] Tieszen *Towards Redefining Persecution* (2010) 163.
[73] Par 6 of the *UNCHR: Religion-Based Refugee Claims* (2004).
[74] Par 6 of the *UNCHR: Religion-Based Refugee Claims* (2004).
[75] Par 9 of the *UNCHR: Religion-Based Refugee Claims* (2004).

of that person's religious identity. Furthermore, a person may also be designated with a religious identity in a formal sense, for example through religious registration requirements.[76] Consequently, a person's religious identity is not a matter of fact, but a matter of subjective or objective perception.[77]

Religion may thus serve as an identifying factor (identifier) through which an adherent self-identifies or is identified by others to hold a certain identifiable religious identity.[78] For example, a person who holds the religious conviction of Buddhism, is identified as a Buddist, while an adherent of the teachings of Confucius (Confucianism) is identified as a Confucian, or being a Hindu, a Buddhist, or a Bahá'í.

In the context of persecution, 'religious identity' entails the common feature according to which victims were singled out by the perpetrator.[79] In such instances, the adherent is associated with a certain concomitant individual or collective religious identity, which makes him the discriminate target of persecution, for example, cases motivated by Islamophobia, anti-Semitism and Christianophobia.[80] The identity element is the important link between the persecutory conduct and the discriminatory intent to target a victim based on his or her religious identity. This means that a person becomes the target of persecution because of his/her actual or perceived relation to the targeted religious identity.

4.3.2.3 *Religion as a way of life*

As mentioned, 'religious identity' is not limited to identity semantics *per se*, but include religious doctrine that may influence or even prescribe a believer's way of life. Thus, religion may serve as a gauge for behaviour, which may guide many aspects of personal decision-making and influence the conception of, *inter alia*, ethics, morality, and even legal justifiability or wrongfulness.

In other words, the adherence or commitment to a religious identity and the concomitant and communitarian ethical or ritualistic practices it

---

[76] Andrews *Identity Crisis* (2016) 24.
[77] Bielefeldt *Misperceptions of FORB* (2013) 44.
[78] Bielefeldt *FORB: Thematic Reports* (2017) 91.
[79] Ambos, K. & Wirth, S. *The Current Law of Crimes Against Humanity: An Analysis of UNTAET Regulation 15/2000.* Crim LF, 13 (2002). pg 76.
[80] Par 4 of the *Elimination of all forms of intolerance and of discrimination based on religion or belief*: resolution / adopted by the General Assembly, 16 March 2009, A/RES/63/181. (*UNGA Res. Discrimination based on Religion*).

entails, may influence or even dictate an adherent's way of life, and how they relate to others.[81] As Marshall put it:

> Since religious freedom involves the freedom to live out one's religion, it is also a question of what people's faith leads them to be and to do, so that their actions rather than their identity can become the object of others' rage. (sic!)[82]

While the formation of one's 'religious identity' should always be open to transformation, evolution and choice,[83] it should be noted that "freedom of conscience [including thought, religion or belief] and freedom of choice are not the same; where conscience dictates, choice decides".[84] In other words, choice is essential in deriving at, adapting, or contemplating one's existing religious identity, but once such a decision has been made, most beliefs impose certain divine directives on adherents, which may, unfortunately, be based on radical or fundamentalist interpretations of religious texts and teachings by religious leaders. Therefore, while the adherence to a religious identity generally contributes to a positive sense of moral behaviour,[85] it may also be the root cause of manifestations of intolerance, discrimination and persecution in instances where a religious ideology negatively motivates interaction.[86] In this regard, the com-

---

[81] Par 8 of the *UNCHR: Religion-Based Refugee Claims* (2004).
[82] Marshall, P. *Persecution of Christians in the Contemporary World*. International Bulletin of Missionary Research (1998), pg 5.
[83] Bielefeldt *Misperceptions of FORB* (2013) 44. Bielefeldt warns that the clarity of a person's identity should always be considered as an adaptable personal agenda of deep existential thought based on the crucial component of free choice around which the right to freedom of religion or belief is conceptualised. To do otherwise may negate the freedom of choice accompanying religious or belief-based identity and harbours the risk of marginalising the elements that constitute a person's or a group's identity.
[84] Sandel, M. *Democracy's Discontent: America in Search of a Public Philosophy*. Harvard University Press (1998), pg 66.
[85] In a religious pluralist society, diverging religious identities may co-exist peacefully, without harbouring negative intra-perceptions.
[86] Societal and religious rifts are not limited to hostility directed against adherents or communities of different faiths (interreligious), but may also include differences within the same religion but between different denominations, or amongst members of the same denomination (intra-religious or intra-denominational) – *UN Rapporteur's Digest on Freedom of Religion or Belief: Excerpts of the Reports from 1986 to 2011 by the Special Rapporteur on Freedom of Religion or Belief Arranged by Topics of the Framework for Communications*. Geneva, (2011), pg 75. Available at:

mitment to a religious identity may motivate action and even persecution, especially in a situation of perceived threats to one's own religious identity.[87]

The commitment to a religious identity may influence a person's perception of various aspects of life, including their perception about others' religious identities. In a religious pluralist society, diverging religious identities may co-exist peacefully, without harbouring negative intra-perceptions. However, in other societies there may be certain pre-existing perceptions about a religious identity, which may be interpreted in such a way that it cultivates a supposed threat to one's familiar religious experience or fears of a decline in religious morals.[88] In this way, a diverging religious identity may be considered as inferior or dangerous, which may justify intolerance, polarisation and dehumanisation of that particular religious identity. Alternatively, a diverging religious identity may be perceived as a perilous sect, when such a religious group is viewed as a threat to its interests or security, which justifies the suppression, prohibition and criminalisation of such a religious identity.

Furthermore, the commitment to a religious identity may also influence a person's perception of religious persecution, whether from the victim's perspective or the persecutor's perspective.[89] In this regard, the commitment to a religious identity may motivate action and even persecution, especially in a situation of perceived threats to one's own religious identity.

In summary, a religious identity, along with other multiple intersecting 'identifiers' (identifying factors), is an essential ingredient in a person's conception of individual identity dynamics. Consequently, the formation of personal identity may be complex and is always in a state of autonomous flux based on the crucial components of human dignity and freedom of

---

https://www.ohchr.org/Documents/Issues/Religion/RapporteursDigestFreedomReligionBelief.pdf. Accessed 09/08/2016.
It should be note that such discriminatory tendencies based on religion may also be State-impose, especially in situations where States adhere to an official religious identity – Bielefeldt et al. FORB: An International Law Commentary (2016) 315.

[87] In societies based on religious exclusivity, religious monism, or totalitarianism, there may be certain pre-existing perceptions about diverging religious identity, which may justify intolerance, polarization, and even persecution of that particular religious identity.

[88] Bielefeldt FORB: Thematic Reports (2017) 185.

[89] Such a subjective perception is true from both the victim and persecutor's point of view.

choice.⁹⁰ A 'religious identity' is the by-product of holding and enjoying a chosen existential view as an invariable and inherent consequence of the fundamental right to religious freedom. Based on the broad interpretation of 'religion' in international human rights law, the scope of a 'religious identity' should not be limited to a narrow interpretation of identity semantics. Consequently, 'religious identity' should be broadly interpreted as inclusive of any deep existential view that impacts on an adherent's: conception of life (i. e. religion as a belief); part of his or her personal identity and sense of belonging (i. e. religion as an identifying element); and engagement with society in general (i. e. religion as a way of life).⁹¹ A religious identity, along with other identifying factors, is an essential ingredient in a person's conception of individual and collective identity dynamics, and should always be considered as a freely adaptable personal agenda of deep existential thought.

Consequently, 'religious identity' should be broadly interpreted as inclusive of an existential belief that impacts on an adherent's way of life and interaction with others, and not merely an aspect that makes up part of his or her personal identity, *per se*.⁹² It should also be recalled that the crucial components of human dignity and freedom of choice inextricably links the positive and negative counterparts of identity and consequently, a person's "religious identity" should always be interpreted as either embracing a certain religious identity or lacking a certain religious identity, i.e. not accepting, abstaining from, or rejecting. Therefore, in the context of the discussion regarding persecution, reference is continually made to religious identity or lack thereof.

4.4 Collective Religious Identity

In addition to the unique identity aspects of the individual, a person may also have a sense of collective identity or belonging, which come from a variety of factors, including, *inter alia*, family and extended family ties, professional and career related associations, and affiliations based tribal, national, ethnical or religious backgrounds.⁹³ This sense of belonging imply that multiple individuals associate together based on a shared 'collective identity'. Therefore, in this section the group aspects will be considered:

---

⁹⁰ Bielefeldt *Misperceptions of FORB* (2013) 44.
⁹¹ Stefanus Alliance International: *Freedom of Religion or Belief for everyone*. Oslo (2012), pg 6.
⁹² Stefanus Alliance International (2012) 6.
⁹³ Andrews *Identity Crisis* (2016) 23.

group identity as a ground of persecution, the nature of a collective religious identity, and how religious persecution relates to it.

4.4.1 Group identity and persecution

Although persecutory acts are committed against individuals, such individuals are most often targeted based on their affiliation to a specific 'identifiable' group. 'Identifiability' is closely related to the question of the victim's identity, and whether an aspect of his or her identity made him or her the identifiable target of the persecutor's discriminatory persecutory conduct. In the context of the *Rome Statute*, the persecutory conduct must be sufficiently tethered to an identifiable group or collectivity by reason of their identity, which must be on one or more of the protected grounds.

In terms of the *Rome Statute*, a 'group' seems to imply a single or specific group, whereas a 'collectivity' may include the combination of a number of groups that are being attacked.[94] For example, in North Korea, religious freedom simply does not exist and religious groups are, *per se*, illegal.[95] As a result, religious people have been consistently and thoroughly persecuted. Effectively, all religious groups in North Korea, constituting a 'collectivity', are targeted. The collective identifier based on which the victim group is chosen, encapsulates the nature of the discriminatory intent and subsequently determines the ground of persecution.

4.4.2 The nature of a collective religious identity

Certain collective identities are based on a 'collective consciousness', which is based on a "set of shared beliefs, ideas and moral attitudes which operate as a unifying force within society",[96] and may be referred to as a 'collective religious identity'. The collective identity of a religious group is based on adherents or members who share the same religion,

---

[94] Brady, H. & Liss, R. *The Evolution of Persecution as a Crime Against Humanity*, in *Historical Origins of International Criminal Law: Volume 3*, Bergsmo, M. et al. (eds). Torkel Opsahl Academic EPublisher, Brussels (2014), pg 550.

[95] Storms, R. A. *Korea, North*. Encyclopedia of Law and Religion. General Editor Robbers, G. First published online (2015), pg 8. http://dx.doi.org/10.1163/2405-9749_elr_COM_00000055. Accessed 23/11/2018.

[96] Jary, D. & Jary, J. *Collins Dictionary of Sociology. Collins Dictionary of Series. Collins Internet-Linked Dictionary of Series.* Published by Collins, 3rd edition. (2005), pg 93. The term was introduced by the French sociologist Émile Durkheim in his doctoral dissertation, *The Division of Labour in Society* in 1893.

denomination, mode of worship or common beliefs.[97] In terms of Article 18 common to the *Universal Declaration of Human Rights (UDHR)* and the *International Covenant on Civil and Political Rights (ICCPR)*, freedom of religion or belief has an explicit community dimension in order for certain dimensions of religious freedom to have practical relevance.[98]

Associating with a religious group or with a collective religious identity recognises every person's right to have and manifest their religion or belief of choice in association with others, making them part of a defined and protected religious community.[99] A belief community's identity may be as diverse as that of an individual. Therefore, a 'collective religious identity' will include the adherence to any profound and substantial existential view. Although many spiritual belief systems are conceived by a 'founding myth', the origins and nature of collective religious identities are irrelevant for the purposes of this study.[100]

A 'religious group' is considered a 'protected group' in international law, implying protection for members to an identifiable religious community, whether they belong to the targeted group in an objective sense or were perceived as such by their persecutors.[101] In line with the extensive interpretation of 'religion', a 'religious group' is broadly construed, provided they are united by a single deep existential view,[102]

---

[97] *Prosecutor v Clément Kayishema and Obed Ruzindana (Trial Judgement)*, Case No. ICTR-95-1-T, 21 May 1999, par 98.

[98] Bielefeldt et al. *FORB: An International Law Commentary* (2016) 22.

[99] The *forum internum* or internal freedom or dimension guarantees that everyone has the right to freedom of thought, conscience and religion, which includes the freedom to have, retain or maintain; change, replace or convert; choose; or adopt a religion or belief and amounts to an absolute right that cannot be limited or derogated from. The *forum externum* or external freedom or dimension guarantees the freedom that everyone, either alone or in community with others, in public or private, can manifest his/her religion or belief in teaching, practice, worship and observance, which can be restricted in conformity with the criteria spelled out in article 18(3) of the ICCPR. This is discussed in more detail in Appendix B.

[100] A 'founding myth' denotes the origins of the belief, presented as a sacred narrative that communicated the truth of life and the world to believers. A founding myth may be used to legitimise the belief in order to maintain the *status quo* for fear that the belief will otherwise crumble. As such, the traditions of belief become important criteria for acceptance and faithfulness – Neusner, J. *World Religions in America*. Westminster John Knox Press, 4th edition. (2009), pg 256.

[101] Schabas, W. *Genocide. Max Planck Encyclopedia on Public International law*, Wolfrum, R. (ed). Heidelberg: Oxford University Press (2011) par 24.

[102] Lippman, M. *The 1948 Convention on the Prevention and Punishment of the Crime of Genocide: Forty-Five Years Later*. TICLJ Vol. 8 No. 1 (1994), pg 29.

whether theistic, non-theistic, polytheistic, atheistic, agnostic, sceptic, or unconcerned.[103]

4.4.3 Religious persecution and a collective religious identity

The persecutor, at the time of committing the persecutory acts, must have realised or must have subjectively believed that the targeted group had a certain collective religious identity or that the individual victims targeted, belonged to such a religious group. If the religious group itself is the object of the persecutory conduct, it is important that the group of individuals share, or are perceived to share, a common spiritual affiliation or collective religious identity. In this regard, 'by reason of the identity of the group or collectivity' should be broadly construed to include situations where the adherent: (1) actually belong, or has a sense of belonging to (or associate, support or identify with),[104] a religious identity in an objective sense (actual religious identity); (2) is perceived to have a religious identity based on the perception of others, or in the mind of the perpetrator (perceived religious identity);[105] or (3) is designated with a religious identity based on religious registration requirements (assigned religious identity).[106]

Persecutory conduct may be directed at a specific religious group because of their 'religious identity', or at any diverging collective religious identity because they either lacked a certain identity, did not conform to a particular identity, or opposed a certain identity. This will be discussed in more detail below.

In summary, a collective religious identity may be established by a group of individuals who are united by a single deep existential view. Unfortunately, the affiliation with some forms of collective religious identity bears the inherent risk of religious exclusivity in the name of religion. While such collective religious identities are inclined towards engaging in religious discrimination and persecution, religious minority groups most of-

---

[103] Bielefeldt *Misperceptions of FORB* (2013) 38.
[104] May also include actual or perceived membership, support or identification to a targeted religious identity – Byron, C. *War Crimes and Crimes Against Humanity in the Rome Statute of the International Criminal Court*. Manchester University Press (2009), pg 230.
[105] Schabas, W. *Genocide. Max Planck Encyclopedia on Public International law*, Wolfrum, R. (ed). Heidelberg: Oxford University Press (2011) par 24.
[106] Andrews *Identity Crisis* (2016) 24.

ten experience the greatest brunt of such measures. Although the international standards on freedom from religious discrimination provide such freedoms to everyone, exceptional protection is required by, and provided for, adherents to non-predominant or dissident religions or beliefs, including members of emerging or religious minorities.[107]

The quintessential discriminatory nature of persecution is directed towards a specific group or collectivity, but the persecutory acts are nevertheless committed against individuals, provided that the targeted individual is affiliated with the collective religious identity, "either based on objective criteria or in the mind of the accused".[108]

4.5 Identity and the Protected Grounds of Persecution

Religious persecution is not the only mode or ground of persecution criminalised by the *Rome Statute*.[109] In this regard, the ICTY in *Tadic* noted that:

> Although there is no definitive list of persecutory grounds in customary international law, it is a common feature that whatever grounds are listed are alternatives, one only is sufficient to constitute persecution.[110]

The grounds of persecution are based on the identifying factor (aspect of identity) by reason of which the person or group was targeted. As mentioned, these identifying factors are complex, interrelated and multifaceted and include, *inter alia*, race, ethnicity, nationality, gender, culture, religion and political affiliations. Therefore, this 'identity element' must be "interpreted in a broad sense referring to the common feature according to which the victims were singled out by the perpetrators".[111] The identity of, or affiliation to, a certain protected aspect of identity becomes the basis of the perpetrator's discrimination and persecution.

---

[107] Van Boven, T. *Racial and Religious Discrimination. Max Planck Encyclopedia on Public International law*, Wolfrum, R. (ed). Heidelberg: Oxford University Press (2009), pg 614.

[108] Triffterer, O., & Ambos K. *Commentary on the Rome Statute of the International Criminal Court: Observers' Notes, Article by Article*. Beck Publishers, 2nd edition (2008), pg 217.

[109] In terms of a broad generic understanding of persecution, the following grounds of persecution are considered to be identifiable protected grounds in terms of the *Rome Statute*: political, racial, national, ethnic, cultural, religious, gender, or other grounds that are universally recognized as impermissible under international law.

[110] *Prosecutor v Duško Tadić (Trial Judgement)*, Case No. IT-94-1-T, 7 May 1997, par 712.

[111] Ambos & Wirth *The Current Law of Crimes Against Humanity* (2002) 76.

4. The Role of Religious Identity in Determining the Grounds of Persecution

Consequently, if a protected aspect of identity becomes the basis for discrimination and persecution, such an identifying factor may determine the ground of persecution.

However, the complexity, multiplicity and intersectionality of diverse individual and collective identifying factors, means that is it often difficult to clearly establish the primary grounds of persecution. These aspects will be discussed in three parts in the section that follows. First, a classification of the grounds of persecution based on the identity element will be attempted, second, the multiplicity and complexity of identity will be outlined, and finally, the intersectionality of the grounds of persecution with religion will be examined.

4.5.1 Distinguishing the grounds of persecution with the use of the identity element

The grounds of persecution are based on the 'identity' of the targeted person or group, implying that the "decisive reason to choose a particular victim must have been the impermissible ground".[112] Therefore, the ground of persecution signifies the primacy of a specific aspect of the victim's identity as the basis of the perpetrator's discriminatory mindset.[113] In other words, the ground of persecution is established by assessing the identity of the targeted group, or lack thereof, and whether such an identity constituted the decisive basis upon which the perpetrator discriminately chose such particular victims. For instance, if a government decides to discriminately, unjustifiably and intentionally restrict the freedom of speech of members of a specific political opposition party, such a restriction may constitute persecution on political grounds, depending on the circumstances.[114]

Therefore, the subjective discriminatory mindset of the perpetrator is essential in determining: (1) whether there was, in fact, discrimination, which is a prerequisite for criminal culpability; and (2) crucial in establishing the relevant ground of persecution.[115] However, establishing the nature of the discriminatory mindset of the perpetrator is not always forthright as it may often be difficult to distinguish the persecutor's motive for

---

[112] Ambos & Wirth *The Current Law of Crimes Against Humanity* (2002) 82.
[113] Acquaviva, G and Pocar, F. *Crimes Against Humanity. Max Planck Encyclopedia on Public International law*, Wolfrum, R. (ed). Heidelberg: Oxford University Press (2011), par 16.
[114] The *Bad Urach Statement* (2010) 38.
[115] Acquaviva & Pocar *Crimes Against Humanity* (2011) par 16.

persecution from his discriminatory intent to persecute a certain person or group. This distinction will be clarified in Chapter Five.

Essentially, religious discriminatory intent means that the victim is targeted based on his religious identity or lack thereof, regardless of the root cause or the persecutor's motives. However, a person or group's identity is always based on multiple identifying and intersecting factors, which complicate an unqualified determination of the grounds of persecution.

4.5.2 The multiplicity and complexity of identity

A person can never be identified through a solitary 'identifier', as identity always involves a complex interplay of subjective and objective identifying criteria. As a result, this complexity and constantly evolving multiplicity of indistinguishable 'identifiers' obscure the classification of the ground of persecution. In the context of this study, such a predicament implies that a victim's "religious identity is not the sole factor used in determining a type of persecution", thus religion is rarely, if ever, the only basis for persecution.[116] Singling out one ground of persecution is therefore not always possible.

Arguably, there may be instances where religious identity can be identified as the solitary ground for discrimination and persecution. In reference to violations of religious freedom, 'ChinaAid' labelled[117] the 'crackdown' by Chinese authorities a historical, massive case of pure religious persecution, showing that Xi's regime has "no interest in respecting its citizens' freedom of religion or belief".[118]

The multiplicity of identifying factors may further be complicated by various other factors, such as the motivational triggers for persecution,[119] political and diplomatic discourse, false narratives proclaimed by

---

[116] Tieszen *Re-Examining Religious Persecution* (2008) 41.
[117] Bob Fu, the leader of 'ChinaAid', an international non-profit Christian human rights organisation.
[118] Radio Free Asia. *China Jails Six Protestants in Yunnan Amid Massive Crackdown on 'Evil Cult'*. 18 January 2018. https://www.rfa.org/english/news/china/protestants-01182018110902.html. Accessed 31/01/2018. Chinese authorities in the southwestern province of Yunnan, recently found six Protestant church followers guilty of "using an evil cult to organize [in order] to undermine law enforcement". The Three Grades of Servants church, which has been designated as a dangerous cult by the ruling Chinese Communist Party, is being targeted as an evil cult second only to the Buddhism and qigong-based Falungong.
[119] 'Motivational triggers' refer to the root causes or motives of religious persecution, which may not necessarily be anti-religious or religiously motivated in itself.

4. The Role of Religious Identity in Determining the Grounds of Persecution

the media, community leaders or otherwise, and the mischaracterisation of instances of persecution.[120] Such factors trivialize persecutions to the extent that persecutors violently pursue their religious agenda in the shadow of political rhetoric, acting with impunity.

The complexity and multiplicity of indistinguishable 'identifiers' obscure the identification of persons as having an identifiable religious identity. However, even in such situations it may still be possible to recognise which aspect of identity constitutes the primary basis of the persecutor's discriminatory intent.

4.5.3 Intersectionality of grounds of persecution with religion

The multiplicity of identifiers is not the only complication in the classification of religious persecution. In many instances this multiplicity of identifiers intersect to the extent that they become indistinguishable.[121] The often indistinguishable intersection of these 'identifiers' with religion complicates an assessment of a person's identity and thus the determination of a clear ground of persecution. The intersectionality between race,

---

[120] It may be argued that the religiously motivated attacks and persecution by *Boko Haram* are obscured as civil unrest in Nigeria. Consequently, religious persecution and civil conflict overlap to the extent that religious discrimination and persecution is 'eclipsed', rendered almost invisible by the mischaracterisation of the situation as civil conflict. "[P]ersecution eclipse minimises, overlooks or denies the suffering of a victim of persecution; encourages a causal analysis that provides vicarious justifications for the perpetrators' actions; shifts the focus of interrogation from religious freedom violations to conflict analysis; and embraces an instrumental view of conflict in which religion assumes an insignificant place in the analysis." Anonymous author. *Nigeria: Persecution or Civil Unrest?* Full report annexed to World Watch Unit (WWU) of Open Doors International (ODI), *Is conflict in Nigeria really about persecution of Christians by radical Muslims?* June 24, 2013. Available at: https://www.worldwatchmonitor.org/old-site-imgs-pdfs/2576904.pdf. Accessed 03/12/2018. See Jubilee Campaign. *Jubilee Campaign Engages the International Criminal Court at The Hague*. http://jubileecampaign.org/iccmay21/. Accessed 06/06/2012. See also Office of the Prosecutor of the International Criminal Court, *Report on Preliminary Examination activities*, 13 December 2011, pg 12.

[121] In instances where a group's only common 'identifier' is clearly their collective religious identity, persecution is more readily identifiable as the appropriate ground of persecution. However, as explained above, certain groups' identity is historically based on a multiplicity of 'identifiers' that often intersect with religion or belief.

culture, nationality, politics, ethnicity, and religion undoubtedly exist.[122] Bielefeldt notes that:

> [R]eligion can be used as a proxy for a person's or a group's ethnicity, resulting in overlapping ethnic, racial, and religious identities, at times to a degree of becoming indistinguishable. This includes possible overlaps in the respective grounds of discrimination.[123]

Therefore, persecution is ordinarily a multi-layered intersection of various protected grounds, which refer to the complex interplay, and occasional indistinguishability, of multiple aspects of individual and sometimes communitarian identity.[124]

In the discussion that follows, the intersectionality of each of the other listed grounds of persecution with religion will be briefly illustrated with reference to related examples.

4.5.3.1 Ethnicity and religion

The notion of ethnicity closely intersects with race, culture, nationality, language and religion.[125] In the context of discrimination based on ethnicity, the notion of 'ethnic cleansing' comes to mind, as discussed previously. The etymology of the term 'ethnic cleansing' closely resembles the expression 'racial hygiene'.[126] For these reasons it would be difficult to find persecution solely on ethnic grounds. Nevertheless, ethnic persecution could be considered as the targeting of those "whose identity as such is distinctive in terms of common cultural traditions or heritage".[127]

Regarding the intersection with religious identity, we often find that an ethnic group's members are unified by a common religious background. In instances where ethno-religious communities possess a distinct identity

---

[122] Bielefeldt *Misperceptions of FORB* (2013) 45.
[123] Bielefeldt *Misperceptions of FORB* (2013) 44–45.
[124] Kadayifci-Orellana, S. A. Ethno-Religious Conflicts: Exploring the Role of Religion in Conflict Resolution. The SAGE Handbook of Conflict Resolution. Bercovitch, J. et al. (eds), SAGE, London (2008), pg 264–280. See also Fox, J. *Ethnoreligious Conflict in the Late Twentieth Century: A General Theory*. Lexington Books (2002), pg 25.
[125] Grosby, S. *The verdict of history: The inexpungeable tie of primordialityhuth – A response to Eller and Coughlan*. Ethnic and Racial Studies Review, Vol. 17. (1994), pg 168. See *Kayishema (Trial Judgement)* par 513, and Geiss *Ethnic Cleansing* (2011) 681.
[126] Geiss *Ethnic Cleansing* (2011) 681.
[127] The *Genocide Convention Implementation Act* of 1987 (Proxmire Act), par 1093(5). A similar definition is found in *Prosecutor v Jean-Paul Akayesu (Trial Judgement)*, Case No. ICTR-96-4-T, 2 September 1998, par 513.

arising from a complex interplay of ethnicity, religion, customs and traditions,[128] members may define their religious identity as a multiplicity of inseparable identifying factors. For instance, in Iran (an Islamic State), ethnic Persians are by definition Muslim, therefore only Armenians and Assyrians can be Christian. By definition, ethnic Persian Christians are apostates.[129]

Religion and ethnicity are also difficult to distinguish in the context of 'ethno-religious conflicts'. 'Ethno-religious conflicts' should be understood as conflicts that involve "… groups where religion is an integral part of social and cultural life, and religious institutions are representative, possess moral legitimacy, and mobilisation potential".[130] In the scope of 'ethno-religious conflicts', religious discrimination does not exist in isolation insofar as the persecutory acts are not underlined by a discriminatory intent solely based on religion. Nevertheless, the crimes committed may be regarded as religious persecution when one or more of the parties involved is characterised by religious homogeneity and was targeted on such an identification, regardless of other related cultural identities.

Therefore, it may still be possible to distinguish between religious persecution and ethnic persecution. For example, although some argue that "ethnic groups and nationalities exist because there are traditions of belief",[131] others conclude that in the context of Rwanda:

> Religious people of various convictions made up parts of both sides, and so the nature and motivation of this persecution situation cannot be understood in religious terms.[132]

Consequently, it seems objectively evident that the predominant factor in the Rwandan genocide was ethnicity.[133]

---

[128] UN Report, *United Nations World Conference against Racism, Racial Discrimination, Xenophobia and Related Intolerance*, Declaration, 31 August to 8 September 2001, UN DocA/CONF.189/12, par 67.

[129] Open Doors Analytical / World Watch Research Unit. *World Watch List 2018: Compilation Volume 3 – Persecution Dynamics for Countries Ranking 1-25*. January, 2018, pg 93. http://opendoorsanalytical.org/wp-content/uploads/2018/01/WWL-2018-Compilation-3-Persecution-Dynamics-of-countries-ranking-1-25-WWR.pdf. Accessed 28/01/2019.

[130] Kadayifci-Orellana *Ethno-Religious Conflicts* (2008) 264.

[131] Grosby *The verdict of history* (1994) 168.

[132] Tieszen *Re-Examining Religious Persecution* (2008) 163.

[133] Human Rights Watch Briefing Paper. *The Rwandan Genocide: How It Was Prepared*. April 2006. http://www.hrw.org/legacy/backgrounder/africa/rwanda0406/rwanda0406.pdf. Accessed 14/02/2016.

Although it may be possible on an academic level to differentiate between the different notions of ethnicity, race and religion,[134] the definitive factor remains on which grounds the perpetrator identified and targeted the victims in a subjective sense.

4.5.3.2 Race and religion

The notion of 'race' has no universally accepted definition,[135] and is generally considered as a social construct rather than a biological fact:

> It is erroneous to assume that humanity is made up of a variety of races. Race is not so much a biological phenomenon as a social myth.[136]

In essence, the notion of 'race' has become virtually obsolete,[137] with the international community "[s]trongly rejecting any doctrine of racial superiority, along with theories which attempt to determine the existence of so-called distinct human races".[138] Consequently, it is difficult to conceptualise 'race' separately from other identifying factors, such as ancestry, nationality, or ethnicity.[139] In this regard, the *United Nations World Conference against Racism* recognised that racial discrimination and intolerance:

> [O]ccur on the grounds of race, colour, descent or national or ethnic origin and that victims can suffer multiple or aggravated forms of discrimination

---

[134] "[R]eligions and beliefs typically include intellectual ideas—for instance, ideas of a metaphysical or of a practical nature—which can become objects of reflection, communication, and critical comment. They may even be exposed to systematic theological, philosophical, ethical, or jurisprudential argumentation. In fact, the possibility of critical communication constitutes an indispensable part of freedom of religion or belief. In this regard, religion and belief clearly have a different epistemological status than ethnicity or race". – Bielefeldt *Misperceptions of FORB* (2013) 45.

[135] Triffterer, O., & Ambos K. *Commentary on the Rome Statute of the International Criminal Court: Observers' Notes, Article by Article*. Beck Publishers, 2nd edition (2008), par 65. Art 1 of the UNGA *International Convention on the Elimination of All Forms of Racial Discrimination*, 21 December 1965, pg 195, defined racism and racial discrimination as "any distinction, exclusion, restriction or preference based on race, colour, descent, or national or ethnic origin".

[136] Van Boven *Racial and Religious Discrimination* (2009) 608.

[137] Schabas, W. *Genocide in International Law*. Cambridge University Press. (2000) 122-123, in Byron *War Crimes and Crimes Against Humanity* (2009) 231.

[138] Preamble of the *UN World Conference against Racism* (2001).

[139] Art 1 of the UNGA *International Convention on the Elimination of All Forms of Racial Discrimination* (1965) 195.

based on other related grounds such as sex, language, religion, political or other opinion, social origin, property, birth or other status[140]

This intersection of identifying factors with 'race' has been confirmed in the jurisprudence of the *International Criminal Tribunal of Rwanda (ICTR)*. In *Akayesu*, the tribunal identified a racial group based on hereditary physical attributes frequently related to a geographical area, irrespective of linguistic, cultural or religious factors.[141] Therefore, the notion of 'race' is based on the multiplicity of inseparable identifying 'racial factors', which requires a broad interpretation of a 'racial' identity and 'racial persecution'.[142]

A suitable example that illustrates the intersection between racial and religious discrimination is the Nazi persecution of the 'Jewish identity', which is based on an indistinguishable joining of religious beliefs and practices, ethnicity, ancestry and race. The Nazis' anti-Semitic policy was based on a multiplicity of religious anti-Semitism (anti-Judaism) and racial or other forms of anti-Semitism. Consequently, the exact ground of persecution of the Jews has remained an aspect of debate.[143]

4.5.3.3 Political grounds and religion

Political grounds might constitute one of the few grounds of persecution that one may demarcate with relative certainty. A political affiliation or identity is based on membership of a particular political party or adherence to a particular political or constitutional ideology.[144] Consequently, the victim of political persecution is targeted on the basis of his affiliation to a political party's beliefs and political ideology.[145] However, regarding the intersection with religion, there are various political parties who base their political ideology on certain religious beliefs. In addition, unlike most other religions, Islam is also meant to be a political ideology

---

[140] General Issue 2 of the *UN World Conference against Racism* (2001).
[141] *Akayesu (Trial Judgement)* par 514.
[142] Triffterer & Ambos *Commentary on the Rome Statute* (2008) par 65.
[143] *IMT Judgment* (1946) 75.
[144] Triffterer & Ambos *Commentary on the Rome Statute* (2008) par 64. However, it may also concern public affairs in general, such as foreign policy, environment and health. A victim persecuted on political grounds would therefore refer to "at least the existence of a difference of opinion concerning these issues as a reason for committing the acts concerned".
[145] *Kayishema (Trial Judgement)* par 130.

wherein religious leaders wield enormous political power.[146] The Bosnian genocide may serve as an appropriate example. The Trial Chamber in *Tadić* found that the accused committed multiple acts of persecution with the motive of furthering national homogeneity, and directed such actions specifically at Muslims and non-Serbs while exhibiting a discriminatory basis for his actions on religious and political grounds.[147]

4.5.3.4 Nationality and religion

National grounds refers to "a collection of people who are perceived to share a legal bond based on common citizenship..."[148] In the *Nottebohm Case*, the *International Court of Justice (ICJ)* applied the principle of effective nationality, in terms of which a national must prove a meaningful or genuine connection to the State in question for purposes of obtaining a legal recognition as a citizen.[149]

However, national grounds might be considered to be broader than citizenship and include attributes of a group which regards itself as deriving from the same nationality, even though the members of the group are located in more than one State.[150] Because of the conceptual differences in culture, religion, ethnicity, sovereignty, territoriality and statehood, the conceptualisation of 'nationality' does not have a universally accepted understanding. For example, in Arabic, nation or '*millah*' means "a distinct community of people sharing a language, culture and religion, and people living in a loosely defined area".[151] Therefore, it is difficult to separate 'nationality' from the other grounds of persecution.

Persecution based on nationality may thus refer to persecution targeting nationals of a particular State, who are affiliated by citizenship, irrespective of their cultural, religious or ethnic origins;[152] as well as those who are not citizens of a particular State, but who are affiliated with a common historic nationality language, culture, religion or ancestry, regardless of citizenship.

---

[146] Mahmoudi, S. *Islamic approach to international law*. Max Planck Encyclopedia on Public International law, Wolfrum, R. (ed). Heidelberg: Oxford University Press (2011), pg 388.
[147] *Tadić (Trial Judgement)* par 714.
[148] *Akayesu (Trial Judgement)* par 512.
[149] *Nottebohm Case (Liechtenstein v. Guatemala); Second Phase*, International Court of Justice (ICJ), 6 April 1955.
[150] Triffterer & Ambos *Commentary on the Rome Statute* (2008) par 66.
[151] Andrews *Identity Crisis* (2016) 58.
[152] Byron *War Crimes and Crimes Against Humanity* (2009) 231.

4. The Role of Religious Identity in Determining the Grounds of Persecution 139

A telling example of the intersection between religion and nationality concerns instances of religious nationalism. Religious nationalism relates to occurrences where official State ideology uses religion in rhetoric on national and cultural identity, in order to promote national homogeneity,[153] which obscures the distinction between national and religious identity.[154] The 'Burmanization policy' in Burma,[155] or atheistic nationalism (communism) in North Korea,[156] may be illustrative of religious nationalism.[157]

4.5.3.5 Cultural grounds and religion

The term 'cultural' also lacks a universally accepted definition.[158] According to Hsueh-Hua Chen:

> Cultural identity refers to identification with, or sense of belonging to, a particular group based on various cultural categories, including nationality, ethnicity, race, gender, and religion. Cultural identity is constructed and maintained through the process of sharing collective knowledge such as traditions, heritage, language, aesthetics, norms and customs.[159]

Therefore, cultural persecution relates to the targeting of persons or groups that are affiliated with a particular identifiable cultural homogeneity. However, based on Hsueh-Hua Chen's understanding, it is seemingly impossible to separate a 'cultural identity' from some of the 'cultural categories' upon which such an identity is based.[160] Nonetheless, some 'cultural categories', such as customs, arts, social institutions, and language may be more easily distinguishable. As such, one of the most evident forms

---

[153] Bielefeldt *FORB: Thematic Reports* (2017) 346.
[154] As part of protecting national heritage, 'foreign' religions are deemed dangerous or destructive to national cohesion. – Bielefeldt *FORB: Thematic Reports* (2017) 347.
[155] Minority cultures, histories and socio-political aspirations are subsumed into an homogenizing national identity derived from the Burman historical tradition – Ashley South as quoted in Horton, G. *Dying Alive – A Legal Assessment of Human Rights Violations in Burma*, a report co – funded by the Netherlands Ministry for Development Co-operation. Images Asia (2005), par 5.5.
[156] *World Watch List Methodology* (2017) 4. This term will be explained in more detail in Chapter Five.
[157] For other examples see Open Doors *World Watch List 2018*.
[158] Triffterer & Ambos *Commentary on the Rome Statute* (2008) 219.
[159] Hsueh-Hua Chen, V. *Cultural identity: Key Concepts in Intercultural Dialogue*, No. 22, 2014. https://centerforinterculturaldialogue.files.wordpress.com/2014/07/key-concept-cultural-identity.pdf. Accessed 04/11/2017.
[160] Hsueh-Hua Chen *Cultural identity* (2014).

of cultural persecution is the destruction of cultural heritage, which ranges from built heritage (including religious buildings, museums, monuments, and archaeological sites), to works of art, customs, music, fashion and other traditions within a particular culture.[161]

The intersection of cultural persecution with religion may be evident in instances of tribal antagonism,[162] or the destruction of cultural heritage. For example, the destruction of a pair of monumental statues, known as the Buddhas of Bamiyan, is a clear blend of cultural persecution and extreme religious intolerance. The ancient statues were carved into the side of a cliff in the Bamyan valley, in the Hazarajat region of central Afghanistan.[163] These statues were destroyed by the Taliban, who declared them heretical idols.[164]

4.5.3.6 Gender and religion

The term 'gender' has a specific meaning under the *Rome Statute* that differs from the accepted descriptions of sex and gender. Byron explains that the conventional understanding of 'sex' refers to biological differences, while 'gender' refers to the social differences between men and women.[165] However, Article 7(3) of the *Rome Statute* defines 'gender' as the two sexes, male and female, within the context of society, and does not indicate any meaning different from the above. Accordingly, 'gender' seems to reflect an "unsuccessful attempt to combine the different concepts of 'sex' and 'gender'".[166]

---

[161] UNESCO – *What is meant by "cultural heritage"?* https://web.archive.org/web/20160316203151/http://www.unesco.org/new/en/culture/themes/illicit-trafficking-of-cultural-property/unesco-database-of-national-cultural-heritage-laws/frequently-asked-questions/definition-of-the-cultural-heritage/. Accessed 29/01/2018.

[162] Tribal or Ethnic antagonism is a category used in the World Watch List Methodology on persecution of Christians by the NGO Open Doors. It is defined as an attempt to force the continuing influence of age-old norms and values shaped in a tribal or ethnic context, and which takes the form of traditional religious beliefs or something similar – *World Watch List Methodology* (2017) 13. The motivational triggers of persecution will be discussed in Chapter Five.

[163] Morgan, K. W. (editor). *The Path of the Buddha: Buddhism Interpreted by Buddhists.* Motilal Banarsidass Publisher (1956), pg 43–44.

[164] Rathje, W. L. *Why the Taliban are destroying Buddhas.* 22 March 2001. USAtoday.com: https://usatoday30.usatoday.com/news/science/archaeology/2001-03-22-afghan-buddhas.htm. Accessed 29/01/2018.

[165] Byron *War Crimes and Crimes Against Humanity* (2009) 232.

[166] Askin, K. D. *Crimes within the jurisdiction of the International Criminal Court.* 10 CLF 33 (1999), pg 47.

4. The Role of Religious Identity in Determining the Grounds of Persecution 141

> This definition acknowledges the social construction of gender, and the accompanying roles, behaviours, activities, and attributes assigned to women and men, and to girls and boys.[167]

In the interim, gender-based persecution in terms of the *Rome Statute* is superficially limited to discrimination against an identifiable gender identity, male and female, and does not include discrimination based on sexual orientation.[168] It could be argued that gender-persecution would include individuals of intersex (hermaphrodites), i.e. individuals who are born with any of several variations in their biological characteristics that "do not fit the typical definitions for male or female bodies".[169] However, it remains unclear whether gender-based persecution would include discrimination based on sexual orientation, such as homosexuals, bisexuals or transsexuals.[170] Nevertheless, such categories will certainly be included under 'other grounds that are universally recognised as impermissible under international law'.[171]

Many human rights infringements stem from stereotypical gender roles which are motivated or justified by religion or belief.[172] Consequently, many women suffer from a multiplicity of discrimination and persecution on the grounds of the intersectionality between religion and gender.[173]

---

[167] Office of the Prosecutor of the International Criminal Court, *Policy Paper on Sexual and Gender-Based Crimes*, June 2014, pg 3. https://www.icc-cpi.int/iccdocs/otp/otp-policy-paper-on-sexual-and-gender-based-crimes--june-2014.pdf. Accessed 14/02/2017.
[168] Art 7(3) of the *Rome Statute*.
[169] UN Office of the High Commissioner for Human Rights (OHCHR), *Free & Equal Campaign Fact Sheet: Intersex*. 4 March 2016. https://www.unfe.org/wp-content/uploads/2017/05/UNFE-Intersex.pdf. Accessed 07/12/2018.
[170] Byron *War Crimes and Crimes Against Humanity* (2009) 233.
[171] Art 7(1)(h) of the *Rome Statute*.
[172] Bielefeldt *FORB: Thematic Reports* (2017) 155–156.
[173] Bielefeldt *FORB: Thematic Reports* (2017) 156. "Women in such communities often face multiple forms of discrimination and violence, including restrictions on freedom of dress and movement, employment and legal discrimination, false charges, reprisals for conversion, sexual harassment, forced marriage, kidnapping, rape and other forms of sexual violence, including human trafficking". – The *Marcham Conference on Women and Persecution: Message to the Global Church on the Double Vulnerability of Women due to Gender and Religion*, 2016, published in Johnson, T. K. (editor). *Global Declarations on Freedom of Religion or Belief and Human Rights*. The WEA Global Issues Series, Vol 18. Verlag für Kultur und Wissenschaft Culture and Science Publ. Bonn (2017) 115. See also Andrews *Identity Crisis* (2016) 197.

The kidnapping of the Chibok schoolgirls in 2014 is a chilling example of the intersection between religion and gender. Female students from the Government Secondary School in the town of Chibok, primarily a Christian village, in Borno State, Nigeria, were kidnapped by *Boko Haram*.[174] As a terrorist organisation motivated by an religious extremist ideology, *Boko Haram* opposes the education of women, especially 'Western'-based education.[175] Unfortunately, this extremist religious ideology opposing female education and gender-based discrimination is not unique to Nigeria, nor specific to the religion of Islam.[176] In Appendix C it is explained that the rape, sexual violence and sexual enslavement of the Yazidi women and girls by *Da'esh* in northern Iraq constitute one of the most abhorrent contemporary examples of the aggravated nature of intersecting religious and gender-based persecutory atrocities.[177] Other cruel and harmful practices against females include genital mutilation, forced marriages, widow burning, enforced 'sacred prostitution', and honour killings.[178]

4.5.3.7 'Other' grounds of persecution

Included amongst the protected grounds for persecution in terms of Article 7(1)(h) of the *Rome Statute* is an open-ended form or ground of persecution, namely persecution against any identifiable group or collectivity on 'other grounds that are universally recognised as impermissible under international law'. Universally recognised grounds may be interpreted as referring to aspects of human rights law that have become part of customary international law.[179] Such 'other grounds' may include discrimination based on mental or physical disability, pregnancy, marital status, social status or origin, sexual orientation, or even age.

---

[174] Hill, J. N. C. *Boko Haram, the Chibok Abductions and Nigeria's Counterterrorism Strategy.* Combating Terrorism Center – CTC Sentinel, July 2014, Vol 7, Issue 7, pg 15. https://ctc.usma.edu/app/uploads/2014/07/CTCSentinel-Vol7Iss75.pdf. Accessed 14/02/2017.

[175] Duthiers, V. *et al. Boko Haram: Why terror group kidnaps schoolgirls, and what happens next.* CNN International, 2 May 2 2014. https://edition.cnn.com/2014/04/24/world/africa/nigeria-kidnapping-answers/index.html. Accessed 29/01/2018.

[176] Hill *Boko Haram, the Chibok Abductions and Nigeria's Counterterrorism Strategy* (2014) 15–16.

[177] For a study of gender-based persecution by *Da'esh* see Chertoff, E. *Prosecuting Gender-Based Persecution: The Islamic State at the ICC.* The Yale Law Journal (2017).

[178] Bielefeldt *et al. FORB: An International Law Commentary* (2016) 29.

[179] Triffterer & Ambos *Commentary on the Rome Statute* (2008) par 71.

4. The Role of Religious Identity in Determining the Grounds of Persecution

It is important that whatever the precise nature of 'other grounds', the group or members thereof must be universally identifiable with a common affiliation with such an identity, whether through self-conception or in the mind of the accused. Furthermore, the perceived ground must be worthy of protection under international law, and the perpetrator must have targeted the person or group based on such a protected ground.

Some of the most common grounds that might be included in terms of this category and also intersect with religion, are marital status and sexual orientation. With the emergence of human rights and equality, religion-related aspects of 'morality', such as polygamy within a marriage or the sexual orientation of homosexuality, have become difficult topics within religious communities. Furthermore, the effect of religious registration has particularly discriminatory consequences based on gender, marital status, and religious identity.

In this context, it is often women who suffer from a multiplicity of discrimination. For example, in some Middle Eastern countries where religious registration is applied, the inequality between the choices and consequences of marriage for men and women are vast.[180] In Jordan, women may only marry within their religious communities, or in the case of Islam, such a woman must convert to her husband's Muslim religion.[181] If a woman is to marry a Muslim man, her registration status will automatically change to Muslim, hence in some instances, Muslim men are encouraged to marry non-Muslim women in order to facilitate such conversions.[182] Such government restrictions have had profound consequences on the legitimacy of some marriages and the matrimonial property system available to others.

Persecution in the form of government restrictions on legal marital options, the changing of one's religion and related conversion issues raise serious risks and profound legal consequences. These not only include legal penalties, but also social hostility and ostracism. The limitation on women to marry only within their registered religious community is compounded by inequality, and clearly intersects with marital status and religion.

In summary, the persecutor's intention to discriminate against an identifiable aspect of the victim's identity (identifying element) is instrumental in recognising the ground of persecution. However, most of the specific

---

[180] Andrews *Identity Crisis* (2016) 197.
[181] Andrews *Identity Crisis* (2016) 197.
[182] Andrews *Identity Crisis* (2016) 197.

protected grounds in terms of the *Rome Statute* are plagued by a lack of succinct legal description or unanimity. Furthermore, given the complex nature and inseparable multiplicity of such identifying grounds in some instances, it is often very difficult to determine a particular ground upon which their common identity as an identifiable group is based.[183]

Nevertheless, the definitive factor in determining the contextual ground of persecution is not whether the victims belong to a specific identifiable group in an objective sense, but rather how the persecutors perceived their identity.[184] In other words, in the mind of the persecutor, on what basis was the group or collectivity discriminately targeted? Therefore, religious persecution will remain an accurate classification of the context of persecutory conduct if the victim was subjectively identified by the persecutor to be affiliated with a certain 'religious identity' (or lack thereof), which protected ground constituted the primary basis of discrimination, and based on which the victim was targeted (regardless of other related identifiers).[185]

In terms of the *Rome Statute*, the protected grounds should be considered as alternatives; one is sufficient to constitute persecution.[186] Furthermore, a determination of the ground of persecution is not mutually exclusive. This begs the question, is it legally necessary in the context of the *Rome Statute*, to determine an exact ground or grounds of persecution for the purposes of legality relating to the discriminatory intent?

---

[183] Kadayifci-Orellana *Ethno-Religious Conflicts* (2008) 264–280. See also Fox *Ethnoreligious Conflict in the Late Twentieth Century* (2002) 25.

[184] Schabas *Genocide* (2011) par 24.

[185] This is possible because ethnicity, race and religion may, to some extent, contain some characteristic differences. "[R]eligions and beliefs typically include intellectual ideas—for instance, ideas of a metaphysical or of a practical nature—which can become objects of reflection, communication, and critical comment. They may even be exposed to systematic theological, philosophical, ethical, or jurisprudential argumentation. In fact, the possibility of critical communication constitutes an indispensable part of freedom of religion or belief. In this regard, religion and belief clearly have a different epistemological status than ethnicity or race." – Bielefeldt *Misperceptions of FORB* (2013) 45.

[186] *Tadić (Trial Judgement)* par 712.

4.6 The Primacy of 'Religious Identity' as the Basis of Discrimination in the Context of Religious Persecution

The grounds of persecution are based on the 'identity' of the targeted person or group, implying that the "decisive reason to choose a particular victim must have been the impermissible ground".[187]

It was explained that the persecutor's intention to discriminate against an identifiable aspect of the victim's identity is instrumental in recognising the ground of persecution. Therefore, the ground of persecution signifies that a specific aspect of the victim's identity constitutes the decisive reason by reason of which the perpetrator discriminately chose that particular victim. Therefore, the ground of persecution signifies the primacy of a specific aspect of the victim's identity as the basis of the perpetrator's discriminatory mindset.[188] In other words, the ground of persecution is established by assessing the identity, or lack thereof, of the targeted group and whether such an identity constituted the decisive basis upon which the perpetrator discriminately chose such particular victims.

This implies that in the context of determining whether religion constitutes the applicable ground of persecution, a 'religious identity' has two important purposes, which will be discussed next: (1) 'religious identity' as the basis of discrimination, and (2) 'religious identity' as the primary or predominant basis of such discrimination.

4.6.1 'Religious identity' as the basis of discrimination in the context of religious persecution

As stated, the subjective discriminatory mindset of the perpetrator and how it relates to the victim's identity is a key component in determining the ground of persecution, but is also a prerequisite for criminal culpability as part of the definitional element of the crime of persecution. Religious discriminatory intent, as a part of the definitional elements of crimes against humanity of persecution, is discussed in detail in Chapter Six. However, in order to facilitate a methodical progression of thought, a few aspects regarding religious discrimination are clarified below.

The expression 'religious discrimination' entails differential treatment based on religious identity, deliberately resulting in the infringement or

---

[187] Ambos & Wirth *The Current Law of Crimes Against Humanity* (2002) 82.
[188] Acquaviva & Pocar *Crimes Against Humanity* (2011) par 16.

denial of the recognition, enjoyment or exercise of human rights and fundamental freedoms on an equal basis.[189] This description in the *Religious Discrimination Declaration* provides a clear indication of the inherent and often indivisible *nexus* between religious discrimination and the deprivation of religious freedom rights.

Normally, the same religious discriminatory ideology that deliberately infringes on the right to equality on the basis of religious identity, also deprives such victims of the recognition, enjoyment or exercise of the fundamental right to freedom of religion or belief.[190] Consequently, it has been recognised that discrimination against communities because of their religious identities may have a particularly detrimental effect on the enjoyment of religious freedom.[191]

As mentioned, discrimination based on a person's belief orientation or religious identity is also the core characteristic that contextualises religious persecution. As Bielefeldt *et al.* notes:

> The impetus for the 'distinction, exclusion, restriction or preference' (based on religious identity) may be grounded in the sense of superiority of the perpetrator, or the religion or belief violation may be based on broader or intersectional prejudices regarding the victim.[192]

In itself, the existence of religious discrimination constitutes a denial of equality on the basis of religion. However, it may also may escalate into actions that entail "consequences of a substantially prejudicial nature for the person concerned".[193] Consequently, religious discrimination in its ex-

---

[189] Art 2(2) of the *Religious Discrimination Declaration* (1981).

[190] Other worrying patterns resulting from religious discrimination include, *inter alia*, the targeting of places of worship and other religious buildings or properties; negative stereotyping of religion with religious extremism, which leads to *de facto* differentiation in State policies, legislation and practices intended to combat terrorism; discriminatory application of domestic registration procedures for religious communities, especially minority or emerging religious movements or indigenous peoples; undue State interference in religious teaching and dissemination of related publications, for example when the authorities censor, monitor and write sermons or prosecute religious leaders; restrictions imposed on different forms of religious expression, for example, the wearing of distinctive clothing or displaying religious symbols; and the inequitable denunciation of human rights abuses based on either the religious or belief affiliations of the victim or the perpetrator, rather than the act itself – *Rapporteur's Digest on Freedom of Religion or Belief* (2011) 55–56.

[191] UN *World Conference against Racism* (2001) par 59.

[192] Bielefeldt et al. FORB: An International Law Commentary (2016) 314.

[193] Par 17 of the *UNCHR: Religion-Based Refugee Claims* (2004).

4. The Role of Religious Identity in Determining the Grounds of Persecution 147

treme and systematic form outrages the conscience of mankind and endangers the foundations of freedom, justice and peace in the world.[194] In other words, the effect of religious discrimination may constitute deprivations of human rights on an equal basis, but may further escalate into situations constituting crimes against humanity ('grievous religious persecution'), and even genocide,[195] which is the "ultimate and most evil corollary of racial and religious discrimination".[196]

In the context of 'grievous religious persecution', the *Rome Statute* requires only that the individuals must be targeted 'by reason of' the identity of the group or collectivity. The element of 'by reason of' may be determined objectively or based on the persecutor's perception and is therefore, a broader threshold than membership or participation. Consequently, "those persons who were not part of the group, and yet were targeted because of their association with or support of the group, would also be protected".[197] In other words, the persecutor acts with religious discriminatory intent if he targets his victims 'by reason of' their religious identity, whether such an identity is based on actual or perceived membership in, support of, or identification with, the targeted religious group.[198] Thus, it is "the perpetrator who defines the victim group while the targeted victims have no influence on the definition of their status".[199] Consequently, there is 'discrimination in fact' and in consequence where the victims are discriminated against by reason of their identity or perceived identity in the mind of the perpetrator, not the subjective perception of the victim.

Considering that it is the persecutor's discriminatory mindset that defines the victim group, it was mentioned in Chapter Three that 'by reason of' should be interpreted with dual effect:

1. The group or collectivity may be defined in a positive manner ('specific religious discriminatory intention'), *vis a vis* the identity of the group to be targeted (e. g. Hindus or Shia Muslims). In other words, a 'specific religious discriminatory intent' targets specific victims

---

[194] Art 11 of the United Nations, *Final Act of the International Conference on Human Rights, Tehran*, 13 May 1968.
[195] Art 2 of the *Genocide Convention*.
[196] Van Boven, T. *Racial and Religious Discrimination. Max Planck Encyclopedia on Public International law*, Wolfrum, R. (ed). Heidelberg: Oxford University Press (2009), pg 609.
[197] Byron *War Crimes and Crimes Against Humanity* (2009) 230.
[198] Brady & Liss *Evolution of Persecution* (2014) 533.
[199] *Naletilic and Martinovic* (*Trial Judgement*) par 636.

because they have, or are perceived to have, a certain religious identity, therefore the discriminatory intention is narrowly applied.
2. The group or collectivity might also be identifiable by the accused as those *not* belonging to a particular religious persuasion, or *not* having the same religious identity as the accused.[200] In other words, the religious discrimination is defined in a negative manner targeting any person/s from a non-acceptant or dissenting religion or belief (e. g. all non-Christians, or anyone who does not believe in Allah). Such a discriminatory mindset consists of a non-specific 'negative discriminatory intent'. In this sense, those persecuted may also have been chosen and targeted because they either lacked a certain religious identity, did not conform to the persecutor's religious ideology, or otherwise opposed or criticised the persecutor's religious identity.

Thus, the victims of religious persecution may include a person, identifiable group or collectivity that was targeted 'by reason of' their religious identity, or lack thereof (negative discriminatory intent), either based on objective criteria or in the mind of the accused. However, it is essential to determine or prove that the persecutor had a specific or negative religious discriminatory intent.

4.6.2 The primacy of a religious identity

Once it is established that the group was identifiable, whether objectively or in the mind of the accused, on the basis of their religious identity, it must be established that 'religion' constitutes the discriminatory basis upon which the persecutor chose his victim's. In other words, establishing that the victims may be, or subjectively was, identified as being part of the identifiable religious group, is only the first step in identifying the ground of persecution. The second step is to establish whether the group's identity constituted the primary reason for their persecution, based on the persecutor's discriminatory mindset (identity element). As Marshall notes:

> [R]eligious persecution is persecution that stems, at least in part, from the fact that the targeted people are believers of a particular religion.[201]

---

[200] Triffterer & Ambos *Commentary on the Rome Statute* (2008) 217
[201] Marshall *Persecution of Christians in the Contemporary World* (1998) 4.

4. The Role of Religious Identity in Determining the Grounds of Persecution 149

In other words, what epitomizes *religious* persecution is the primacy of religious identity as the leading or predominant factor 'by reason of' which the victims were specifically chosen, albeit *not* necessarily the only basis.[202] It is thus clear that "religious people who are persecuted are not necessarily the victims of religious persecution"[203] if such victims were not primarily targeted 'by reason of' their religious identity. In essence, this means that a person's religious identity (or lack thereof) makes him the specific target of discrimination and persecution.

In order to assess the *nexus* between the victim's religious identity and the persecutory conduct, the question is whether the victim's religious identity was the primary factor that made him the target of discrimination and persecution. This *nexus* is essentially a question of 'factual causation', in terms of which we may apply an 'assimilated version' of the *conditio sine qua non theory*.[204] If one is to ignore the victim's religious identity, does the basis of discrimination and persecution also disappear? If the persecution of an individual or group will cease to exist if such a person or group's religious affiliations (including perceived affiliations, or lack thereof) are removed, then religion will constitute the primary basis for such persecutory conduct. However, if religious factors are removed and such a person or group would remain the target of persecutory conduct, then religion may amount to an auxiliary factor, but not the primary impetus.

In summary, discrimination based on a person's religious identity is the core aspect that determines or contextualises persecutory acts as religious persecution. In the context of persecution, religious discriminatory intent may be defined as the conscious, preconceived, and deliberate targeting[205] of a person or identifiable group or collectivity based primarily (but not necessarily exclusively)[206] on their actual or perceived religious identity, or lack thereof (negative discriminatory intent). Nevertheless, a persecutor's reasons or motives is irrelevant to the classification of the mode of persecution.[207]

The primacy of religious identity, as the prevailing source of the perpetrator's discriminatory mindset, distinguishes religious persecution from other grounds of persecution. Therefore, even though a person's

---

[202] Tieszen *Towards Redefining Persecution* (2010) 163.
[203] Tieszen *Re-Examining Religious Persecution* (2008) 42.
[204] Marshall *Persecution of Christians in the Contemporary World* (1998) 2.
[205] *Prosecutor v. Radoslav Brdjanin (Appeal Judgement)*, Case No. IT-99-36-A ICTY, 3 April 2007, par 996.
[206] Tieszen *Towards Redefining Persecution* (2010) 164.
[207] The motives or root causes of religious persecution is discussed in Chapter Five.

identity is comprised of multiple intersecting identifying factors, it is objectively possible to classify a persecutory situation as religious persecution by evaluating the persecutor's discriminatory intent. Establishing a victim's religious identity and whether such an identity was the primary cause of persecution, are thus essential components in identifying the ground or mode of persecution.

4.7 Conclusion

Globally, religion or religious identity remains the basis for intolerance, discrimination and persecution.[208] However, religion is not the only mode or ground of persecution criminalised by the *Rome Statute*. Therefore, religious persecution must be recognised and differentiated from other forms of persecution. In this regard, an assessment of the role that the victim's religious identity has in relation to the persecutor's discriminatory intent in a given situation, is essential in order to determine the mode of persecution. Such a conception requires an appreciation of the nature and importance of religious identity from various perspectives, the influence that the right to freedom of religion or belief has in forming a religious identity, and how such an identity becomes the object of perception and discrimination.

A person's religion, or deep existential view, becomes part of their identifying label, whether in a person's own mind or that of others, or in terms of social standing.[209] This fundamental right to one's individual or communitarian identity is a core aspect of protection against discrimination and unequal treatment under international human rights law. In relation hereto, the discriminatory nature of persecution signifies that a person is reduced to their identification or an identifying element, and deliberately targeted for discriminatory treatment. In determining the mode of persecution, or the multiplicity thereof, religious persecution is distinguishable based on the primacy of the victim's religious identity, which made him or her the target of the persecutor's discriminatory intent.[210] Consequently, the perpetrator's discriminatory mindset and his

---

[208] Thames *et al. International Religious Freedom Advocacy* (2009) 10-11. Reliable statistics on the number of those persecuted because of their religion, or of those murdered for their faith, are hard to produce because of the absence of a unified definition and because of the multidimensional nature and motivations of acts constituting persecution.

[209] Andrews *Identity Crisis* (2016) 23.

[210] Art 7(2)(g) read with art 7(1)(h) of the *Rome Statute*.

subjective perception about the victim's religious identity is the most crucial elements in establishing the ground of persecution. In the context of religious persecution, this means that a person's religion is not only a crucial component in forming a personal and communitarian identity, but is also the primary identifying factor upon which that person is discriminately targeted. In order to assess the *nexus* between the victim's religious identity and the persecutory conduct, the point at issue is whether the victim's religious identity was the primary factor that made him or her the target of discrimination and persecution. The required *nexus* is satisfied if the perpetrator, at the time of committing the persecutory acts, specifically targeted the victim based on his/her actual, perceived, or assigned religious identity. Such a discriminatory intent may be directed at a person, identifiable group or collectivity with a particular religious identity ('specific religious discriminatory intention'), or that lack an accepted religious identity ('negative religious discriminatory intention'), either based on objective criteria or in the mind of the accused, provided that such a religious discriminatory intent constituted the primary (not necessarily exclusive) basis for targeting those victims. Based on this reasoning, it may be possible to identify 'religious identity' as the specific ground of persecution in a given situation, provided that it is possible to acquire proof of a religious discriminatory intent on the part of the persecutor; and that the discriminatory intent is sufficiently tethered to the victim's identifiable religious identity, or lack thereof.

The consequential effect of religious persecution manifests in different forms. In this regard, religious persecution is experienced, either as a 'squeeze' that deprives the victims of their freedom of choice and/or enjoyment of religious freedom rights, or as a physical and violent 'smash' directed at dissident believers or adherents to perceived morally fallacious existential convictions, or a combination of both. In the context of 'grievous religious persecution', these manifestations may result in severe deprivations of fundamental human rights, which are therefore termed:

- 'iniquitous persecution', referring to restrictive discriminatory measures that place increasing pressure on religious adherents to witness their faith, and are offensive to humanity, whether based on its inherent nature or its cumulative effect; and
- 'persecution atrocities', referring to various physical acts, which are inhumane in nature or in terms of its cumulative effect.

International human rights law provides equal rights and protection for those who exercise a religious choice, as well as those who actually belong, or are perceived to belong (support, associate or identify with), a collective religious identity. In the context of religion, a collective religious identity may be denominational (religious group), or may be so extensive as to include all denominations within the religion as a whole. This implies that persecutory conduct may be directed at:

1. individuals because of their concomitant religious identity or lack thereof;
2. a specific religious denomination because of their 'collective religious identity' or lack thereof;
3. a collectivity of differing religious identities in a specific setting or area; or
4. a collectivity of differing denominational identities within the constructs of a broader religion ('broad collective religious identity').

In Chapter Six, this understanding of the role of religion, religious identity and religious freedom, will form a core consideration in conceptualising 'grievous religious persecution'. However, preceding this conceptualisation, a common mis-perception about religious persecution must be clarified. Whilst most religious identities impose a commitment to a belief and the exercise of religious behaviours that contribute to a positive sense of moral behaviour, other religious identities may be the root cause of manifestations of intolerance, discrimination and persecution in instances where a religious ideology negatively motivates interaction. In this regard, Chapter Five will differentiate, where applicable, between religiously motivated persecution (persecution in the name of religion), and religious persecution (persecution on the basis of religious identity).

Chapter Five: 'Motive' and its Effect on the Classification of Religious Persecution

5.1 Introduction

The scattered spectrum of concurrent contextual understandings of 'persecution', discussed in Chapter Two, results in the conflicting use of terminology. Consequently, the indiscriminate use of terminology regarding religion and persecution makes it much more difficult to advocate on behalf of the persecuted, and to persuade and motivate the various stakeholders into action.[1] Thames argues that:

> [T]he word persecution is often carelessly thrown around without thought as to its true [contextual] meaning. This overuse only cheapens the term and lessens the impact when describing an actual situation of persecution.[2]

Therefore, preceding the conceptualisation of 'grievous religious persecution' in Chapter Six, this chapter will clarify an important misperception regarding religious persecution in the context of international criminal law, viz. equating religious discriminatory intent with religiously motivated persecution. In this regard, the motive or reason for committing persecution should be differentiated from the discriminatory intent to target victims based on their religious identity, regardless of the reason or motive.

The misconception of 'motive' in the context of persecution, stems largely from the hybrid nature of international criminal law, mixing international law with principles that derive from national criminal law. These principles predominantly emerged from the two major global legal systems or legal 'traditions', namely the common law or adversarial system, and the civil law or inquisitorial system.[3] The International Criminal Court itself is

---

[1] Thames, H. et al. *International Religious Freedom Advocacy: A guide to Organizations, Law and NGO's*. Baylor University Press (2009), pg 6.
[2] Thames et al. *International Religious Freedom Advocacy* (2009) pg 6.
[3] Zgonec-Rožej, M. (Principal author). *International Criminal Law Manual*. International Bar Association (IBA) (2013), pg 25.

"common-law orientated, but at all thresholds a civil-law corrective instrument is implanted".[4] In a practical sense, this 'concoction' of legal traditions and terminology may give rise to certain misperceptions regarding persecution. This 'concoction' has unfortunately resulted in the inaccurate use and understanding of the term 'motive' in the context of persecution. 'Motive', used in civil law legal systems, describes the cause or reason that induced the perpetrator's actions, but does not equate to intent.[5]

However, establishing the nature of the discriminatory mindset of the perpetrator is not always forthright, and sometimes it may be difficult to distinguish the *persecutor's motive for persecution* from his *discriminatory intent to persecute* a certain person or group. Consequently, this chapter will differentiate between 'religious persecution' and 'religiously motivated persecution'. In addition, the root causes or motivational triggers for persecution will be discussed.

5.2 Distinguishing Religiously Motivated Persecution from Religious Persecution in International Criminal Law

In the same way that the determination of religious intolerance and discrimination can be made regardless of the motive of the actor,[6] so too is the motive for persecution inconsequential for the purposes of characterising religious persecution. In other words, the accused's motive for committing 'grievous religious persecution' is in principle legally irrelevant to the question of his culpability or guilt.[7]

In the sections below, the persecutor's motive for persecution is distinguished from his *discriminatory intent to persecute* a certain person or group.

---

[4] Orie, A. *Accusatorial v Inquisitorial Approach in International Criminal Proceedings Prior to the Establishment of the ICC and in the Proceedings Before the ICC* in Cassese, A. et al. (eds) II *The Rome Statute of the International Criminal Court: A Commentary* (OUP, Oxford 2002) 1439, 1442–1456. The legal principles governing international proceedings at the ICC are contained in the Assembly of States Parties to the Rome Statute of the International Criminal Court, *Rules of Procedure and Evidence*, ICC-ASP/1/3, at 10, and Corr. 1 (2002), U.N. Doc. PCNICC/2000/1/Add.1 (2000) [*ICC Rules of Procedure and Evidence*].

[5] Garner, B. A. *Blacks Law Dictionary*. Abridged Eight Edition. Thomson / West Publishers (2005), pg 855.

[6] Bielefeldt, H., Ghanea, N. & Michael Wiener M. *Freedom of Religion or Belief: An International Law Commentary*. Oxford University Press. (2016), pg 314.

[7] *Prosecutor v Dragoljub Kunarac, Radomir Kovac and Zoran Vukovic (Appeal Judgment)*, Case No. IT-96-23 & IT-96-23/1-A, ICTY, 12 June 2002, par 103.

5. 'Motive' and its Effect on the Classification of Religious Persecution

In other words, a distinction is made between persecution that is intentionally directed at a religious identity (*religious persecution*), and persecution that is motivated by a religious identity (*religiously motivated persecution*), but do not intentionally directed at a religious identity.

5.2.1 Religious discriminatory intent and persecution (persecution 'by reason of' religious identity)

'Grievous religious persecution' requires an additional, *sui generis*, element of culpability, *viz*. a conscious religious discriminatory mindset,[8] in terms of which a perpetrator targets a specific individual or group 'by reason of' their religious identity.[9] Religious discriminatory intent was defined as the conscious, preconceived, and deliberate targeting[10] of a person or identifiable group or collectivity based primarily (but not necessarily exclusively)[11] on their actual or perceived religious identity, or lack thereof, for reasons or motives peculiar to the perpetrator.[12] It is this subjective element (*mens rea*) to categorise, differentiate and target

---

[8] Cassese, A. (ed.), *The Oxford Companion to International Criminal Justice*. Oxford University Press (2009), pg 453. This additional element of culpability constitutes a higher standard of criminal intent, similar to *dolus specialis* or intent in the narrow sense of 'purpose' or 'aim' – Brady, H. & Liss, R. *The Evolution of Persecution as a Crime Against Humanity*, in *Historical Origins of International Criminal Law: Volume 3*, Bergsmo, M. *et al* (eds). Torkel Opsahl Academic EPublisher, Brussels (2014), pg 553.

[9] Tieszen, C.L. *Towards Redefining Persecution*. Religious Freedom Series: Suffering, Persecution and Martyrdom. Vol 2. (2010), pg 164. *Appeal Judgement (Kaing Guek Eav alias Duch)*, Case File 001/18-07-2007/ECCC/SC, Extraordinary Chambers in the Courts of Cambodia, 3 February 2012, paras 226, 240, 267 and 278. See also *Prosecutor v Milomir Stakić (Trial Judgement)*, Case No. IT-97-24-T, 31 July 2003, par 738. Intention or intent thus implies that a person means to engage in the conduct, or cause a prohibited consequence, or is aware that it will occur in the ordinary course of events.

[10] *Prosecutor v. Radoslav Brdjanin (Appeal Judgement)*, IT-99-36-A, ICTY, 3 April 2007, par 996, in Byron, C. *War Crimes and Crimes Against Humanity in the Rome Statute of the International Criminal Court*. Manchester University Press (2009), pg 229.

[11] Tieszen *Towards Redefining Persecution* (2010) 164.

[12] The accused's motive for committing 'grievous religious persecution' is in principle legally irrelevant to the question of his culpability or guilt – *Prosecutor v Dragoljub Kunarac, Radomir Kovac and Zoran Vukovic (Appeal Judgment)*, Case No. IT-96-23 & IT-96-23/1-A, ICTY, 12 June 2002, par 103. Although the root causes of religious persecution are often anti-religious or religiously motivated, a persecutor's motivations are *sui generis* in each case, and may be complex, manifold and interrelated.

victims based on their religious identity, which epitomizes religious persecution. Therefore, if a persecuted victim was targeted primarily because of his religious identity (or lack thereof), the persecutor's motive for such conduct is immaterial.

In the context of religious persecution, the question is not why the persecutor is doing what he is doing, but rather *who* he is doing it to. This means that the victim was targeted 'by reason of' his/her religious identity, regardless of the root cause or the persecutor's motives.

5.2.2 Religiously motivated persecution (persecution in the name of religion)

Persecution in the name of religion or belief (religiously motivated persecution) is committed and motivated in the name of the persecutor's self-righteous religious identity, which relates to the misuse of religious freedom for ends inconsistent with international human rights principles. Thus, the persecutor is motivated by his own religious doctrine or ideology, resulting in the propagation of fear, hatred, dehumanisation, discrimination and violence. The emphasis is on *why* the persecutor did what he did; what motivated him? Consequently, religiously motivated persecution is concerned with the perpetrator's motive for committing persecutory conduct. Considering that the interpretation of religious doctrine requires human intervention,[13] it would be more accurate to say that the persecutor's 'religious motive' is based on a narrow-minded and fundamentalist interpretation of religious doctrine, resulting in the persecutor adopting an extremist and anti-pluralistic view. Thus, persecution is committed and justified in the name of the persecutor's self-righteous religious identity (religiously motivated persecution). In most instances, the persecutor's fundamentalist interpretation and commitment to his or her chosen religious identity causes a misperception about the rightfulness of inflicting harm unto others. Consequently, the persecutor may view himself as the defender of the collective cause, belief, and/or identity. The persecutor may therewith believe that he is acting in the common good, by addressing the object of concern, perceived objects of fear, or whatever other peculiar reason.[14] At an organisational

---

[13] Bielefeldt, H. *Freedom of Religion or Belief: Thematic Reports of the UN Special Rapporteur 2010-2016*. Religious Freedom Series of the International Institute for Religious Freedom, Vol 3, 2nd and extended edition, Bonn (2017), pg 195.

[14] Recent examples of discrimination and related violence in the name of religion or belief include, *inter alia*: riots and attacks on places of worship perpetrated by

5.2.3 Instances of entanglement and disentanglement

As an important watershed between motive and intent in the context of religious persecution, it was mentioned that a religious identity might have a polarising effect.

On the one hand, the perpetrator's religious identity may provide the motive or basis for discrimination, serving as the root cause or trigger that cultivates fear, resentment, discontent, exclusivity and supremacy.[15] Religion as the '*motivator*' for discrimination (religiously motivated discrimination) is referred to as "discrimination and violence in the name of religion or belief, i. e., based on or arrogated to religious tenets of the perpetrator".[16] In this case, the adherence to a religious identity may provide the justification for, or constitute the root cause of, manifestations of

---

members of a group who sought to impose their interpretation of religious law on all other individuals in that region; an alleged instance of blasphemy where certain political and religious groups threatened to seal off a whole city and attack a religious minority unless the police arrested five members of this religious minority; two members of a religious minority were killed after the perpetrator had requested to see the victims' identity cards, which state the religious affiliation of the bearer; and a new criminal code was adopted for one religious community, effectively legalising marital rape – UN Rapporteur's Digest on Freedom of Religion or Belief: Excerpts of the Reports from 1986 to 2011 by the Special Rapporteur on Freedom of Religion or Belief Arranged by Topics of the Framework for Communications. Geneva, March 2011, pg 57. Available at: https://www.ohchr.org/Documents/Issues/Religion/RapporteursDigestFreedomReligionBelief.pdf. Accessed 09/08/2016.

[15] Although not the only reason, it is clear that one of the leading reasons or motives for religious discrimination and persecution is based on the perpetrator's sense of religious or ideological superiority. In this regard, the perpetrator's religious identity is based on an ideology of religious supremacy, in terms of which only one particular religion or belief system is true. Accordingly, this superior 'truth claim' becomes the impetus that motivates intolerance, discrimination, and persecution of religious identities perceived to be inferior. In other words, the impetus for the discrimination is based on prejudice towards the victim's religious identity, or lack thereof.

[16] Par 33 of the UN General Assembly, *Report of the Special Rapporteur on freedom of religion or belief, Asma Jahangir*. A/HRC/13/40, 21 December 2009.

intolerance, discrimination, and persecution.[17] Discrimination and violence in the name of religion or belief may be religiously motivated, but is not necessarily directed at other non-acceptant or dissenting religious identity. Thus, the intended targets of religiously motivated discrimination may be diverse and is not limited to discrimination 'by reason of' the victim's religious identity.

On the other hand, the victim's religious identity, whether actual or perceived, may constitute the *'identifier'* of discriminatory intent. In other words, the emphasis is on *who* the persecutor targets. In this context, the victim or victim group is deliberately, consciously and discriminately targeted because of their religious identity. In such instances, the persecutor's motive for such persecutory conduct may be based on any number of motivational triggers, which may not necessarily be anti-religious or motivated by religion. This implies that the persecutor's intention for persecution directly intersects with the need to target persons or groups based on their religious identity; the motive is irrelevant. A topical example is the 2019 terrorist attack of two Mosques in Christchurch, New Zealand. In that case, the attackers justified their extreme violence in defence of their ideology of white supremacy and fascism, while directing their discriminatory intent at Muslim communities in retaliation of attacks in Europe perpetrated by Muslim extremists. In other words, their actions were directed at a specific religious identity, yet their justification thereof was not religiously motivated.

Bielefeldt *et al.* argue that these two aspects of 'religious discrimination' build on the references in the *Religious Discrimination Declaration*, in terms of which the former may be referred to as 'manifestations of *intolerance*', whereas the latter may be understood as the 'existence of *discrimination* in matters of religion or belief'.[18] Nevertheless, for the purposes of this paper, 'religious discrimination' may include either or both of these strands.

5.2.3.1 Disentanglement: cases of distinguishability of religiously motivated persecution

Discriminatory intent should not be confused with the motivational triggers (root causes or motives) of persecution. The concept of motivational

---

[17] See the UN General Assembly, *Declaration on the Elimination of All Forms of Intolerance and of Discrimination Based on Religion or Belief*, UNGA Res 36/55, 73rd plenary meeting, 25 November 1981 (*Religious Discrimination Declaration*).
[18] Bielefeldt *et al. FORB: An International Law Commentary* (2016) 330.

triggers of religious persecution explores the root causes or motives why, in certain circumstances, a concomitant individual or collective religious identity was targeted. Religious identities are targeted for all sorts of reasons or motives, such as greed, power, or a cause. Thus, a persecutor's motivations are *sui generis* in each case and may be complex, manifold and interrelated. Nonetheless, the root causes of religious persecution are often anti-religious or religiously motivated, in which case the distinction between 'intent' and 'motive' is essential.

In instances of religiously motivated persecution, the persecutor's own religious identity is motivating him to persecute others, yet his persecutory conduct may be directed at any collective cause, belief, and/or identity that threaten his self-righteous aspirations. This means that the victim group is not necessarily targeted 'by reason of' their religious identity, in which case the relevant ground of persecution will depend on the group or identity that is discriminately targeted, such as persecution based on political grounds, age, sexual orientation, profession, or ethnicity. Thus, religiously motivated persecution may very well intersect with any of the grounds of persecution.[19] In such instances, religiously motivated persecution is distinguishable from, and does *not* constitute, religious persecution.[20] The distinction is essentially a matter of separating the persecutor's 'religious motive' – i. e. the cause that moved him to commit the persecutory conduct – from a deliberate discriminatory mindset to target victims based on their religious identities.

Therefore, persecution in the name of a religious identity (religiously motivated persecution) is often distinguishable from religious persecution,[21] especially in circumstances where the persecutor's aspirations or purpose is inspired by his religious identity, yet his discriminatory intent is not directed at adherents who have or lack a certain religious identity. Consequently, religiously motivated violence and discrimination may

---

[19] Bielefeldt *FORB: Thematic Reports* (2017) 250–251. The categories, person's or groups that are the most vulnerable targets or generally affected by discrimination and related violence in the name of religion or belief, include dissident religious minorities; homosexuals; children in public schools who are forced to receive religious instruction that is contrary to the child or parents' religious convictions; conversely, children that are indoctrinated with religious intolerance; laws that discriminate against women; converts and their families; and individuals who live in countries where they are forced to disclose their religion or belief in official documents.

[20] UN General Assembly, *Elimination of all forms of religious intolerance*, A/73/362, 5 September 2018, par 23–27.

[21] UNGA A/73/362 (2018) par 23–27.

constitute persecution, but the ground of persecution is not automatically based on religion.

5.2.3.2 Entanglement: cases of indistinguishability

Persecution in the name of a religion may amount to religious persecution if the religiously motivated persecutor specifically targets his victims based on their religious identity, or lack thereof. In such cases, the root cause of persecution remains the persecutor's self-righteous religious ideology, and his persecutory conduct is discriminately directed at specific victims because of their religious identity. It is thus impossible to differentiate the motive for religious persecution from the discriminatory intent to persecute on religious grounds. In such cases, the motive and the discriminatory intent is aligned. Consequently, in instances where the persecutor's religious motive and religious discriminatory intent may be intertwined, a distinction between motive and intent is artificial or superfluous.

In instances where a perpetrator commits religious persecution in the name of a religious identity (religiously motivated persecution based on religious identity), the perpetrator's discriminatory parameters differentiate between his own religious identity and that of others. Consequently, the persecutor does not necessarily target a specific religious identity, but may target *any* religious identities dissimilar to his own (negative discriminatory intent), which poses a threat to the attainment or maintenance of the persecutor's overall purpose. Generally, religious persecution committed by religiously motivated persecutors are "likely to target religious groups that are different from their own because they see that religious identity as part of a threat to their own identity or legitimacy".[22]

Although such persecution disproportionately targets religious nonconformists, members of religious minorities or converts, it also affects followers of the very same religion in whose name such acts are perpetrated, especially critics who actively oppose the abuse of their religion for the justification of violence.[23] Concealing and justifying persecution with

---

[22] Par 6 of the UN High Commissioner for Refugees (UNHCR), *Guidelines on International Protection No. 6: Religion-Based Refugee Claims under Article 1A(2) of the 1951 Convention and/or the 1967 Protocol relating to the Status of Refugees*, 28 April 2004, HCR/GIP/04/06.

[23] Bielefeldt *FORB: Thematic Reports* (2017) 250–251. The categories, person's or groups that are the most vulnerable targets or generally affected by discrimination and related violence in the name of religion or belief, include dissident religious minorities; homosexuals; children in public schools who are forced to receive religious instruction that is contrary to the child or parents' religious

religious rhetoric, therefore, has dire consequence for those who bear an associative religious identity. This is particularly evident in situations where militant religious extremist actions, that amount to acts of terrorism, are equated with a broader collective religious identity as a whole,[24] such as the identification of the Islamic faith with religious extremism.[25]

Consequently, religiously motivated persecution will only be considered 'religious persecution', if those persecuted were primarily identified, targeted and persecuted based on their religious identity.

5.3   Motivational Triggers of Religious Persecution

The 'motivational triggers', also referred to as the "persecution engines",[26] refer to the root causes or motives of persecution. The motivational triggers are concerned with the perpetrator's motive or purpose for committing the persecutory conduct. It is often assumed that the root cause for all religious persecution lies in religious intolerance, that is, "an attitude of narrow-mindedness that does not accommodate any interreligious or intrareligious diversity".[27] Although religious intolerance is one of the most instrumental causes and motivations for religious persecution, there are numerous others, which may be complex and interrelated.[28]

Habitually, our first response to a traumatic experience, such as religious persecution, is to ask "why?". Why did this happen to me, to us, to him or her, or them? Why did the perpetrator do this? The concept of motivational triggers of religious persecution explores the root causes why, in certain circumstances, a concomitant individual or collective religious identity becomes the target of persecution.

---

convictions; conversely, children that are indoctrinated with religious intolerance; laws that discriminate against women; converts and their families; and individuals who live in countries where they are forced to disclose their religion or belief in official documents.

[24] Par 13 of the UN General Assembly, *Elimination of all forms of intolerance and of discrimination based on religion or belief: resolution / adopted by the General Assembly*, 16 March 2009, A/RES/63/181.

[25] Par 96 of the UN Commission on Human Rights, *Report submitted by the Special Rapporteur on freedom of religion or belief, in accordance with Commission on Human Rights resolution 2002/40*, 15 January 2003, E/CN.4/2003/66.

[26] Open Doors Analytical. *World Watch List Methodology*. November 2017, pg 8. Available at: http://opendoorsanalytical.org/world-watch-list-methodology-latest-edition-november-2017/. Accessed 09/01/2019.

[27] Bielefeldt *FORB: Thematic Reports* (2017) 345.

[28] Bielefeldt *FORB: Thematic Reports* (2017) 345.

The complexity of religious persecution and its correlation with other grounds of persecution mean that the causes and motivations for religious persecution may differ from place to place, time to time, and from religion to religion. A comprehensive analysis of the motives behind State-induced violations or societal abuses of religious freedom may result in a multiplicity and intersectionality of religious identity with other grounds of persecution.[29] Consequently, it is impossible to comprehensively list all possible root causes of persecution. Therefore, the following observations remain non-exhaustive. It will also become clear that the various impulses or motivations of religious persecution rarely occur independently; they are complex, intertwined and not mutually exclusive.

In the discussion that follows, the motivational triggers will be grouped together based on the nature of the persecutory motivation.[30] The following root causes or impulses will be discussed, most of which include sub-cate-

---

[29] Bielefeldt *FORB: Thematic Reports* (2017) 356–357.

[30] There are various conceptual approaches to classify the motivational triggers of religious persecution. For the purpose of this study, the most useful approaches were found in the following sources:

(1) The *World Watch List Methodology* statement of *Open Doors Analytical*. The World Watch List Methodology was developed by the World Watch Research unit of Open Doors and is dedicated to monitoring and reporting on the persecution of Christians. In their methodology, they differentiate between exclusivist impulse, secularist impulse and exploitative impulse. In some instances, the motivational triggers that where only relevant to the persecution of Christians, were excluded or amended, if possible.

(2) The thematic report of the UN Special Rapporteur of freedom of religion or belief, Heiner Bielefeldt in[30] Bielefeldt *FORB: Thematic Reports* (2017) 338–364. Bielefeldt, in the context of his work as former Special Rapporteur on religion or belief, discusses the broad range of violations of freedom of religion or belief, their root causes and variables. This assessment is broadly developed in the context of violations or abuses of the right to freedom of religion or belief, used to the extent that they are applicable to religious persecution. The root causes provide a non-exhaustive list of factors that result in, or contribute to, deprivations of religious freedom. These include intolerant interpretations of religions or beliefs (referred to in this study as the religious antagonist impulse), utilising religion for demarking national identity, exercising excessive political control, failing and failed States, and social power imbalances and other variables. Given the context of the thematic report, most of the identified root causes stem from State responsibility for human rights obligations related to freedom of religion or belief. Thereafter, a discussion on the patterns of deprivations differentiates between violations by State actors and abuses by non-State actors. Identified patterns of State-induced violations include criminal law sanctions, bureaucratic harassment and burdensome administrative stipulations, discriminatory structures in family laws, violations in the context of school education, State-

gories indicating the various motivational triggers: religious antagonist impulse, exclusivist impulse, secularist impulse, and exploitative impulse.

5.3.1 Religious antagonist impulse

The religious antagonist or 'religious fanaticism' impulse is based purely on religious intolerance, which can be interreligious or intra-religious. This religious discriminatory impulse may, therefore, be separated from the other impulses based on the difference in its core motivation. While all the impulses display some or other forms of ideological protectionism, not all the impulses are religiously motivated or anti-religious. Some form of self-preservation or the attainment of dominance and control generally motivates the exclusivist, secularist and exploitative impulses, which often directly intersect with religious identity. Conversely, the antagonist impulse is motivated by religious protectionism and fanaticism specifically, "where a given individual or group believes that he or it possesses the absolute truth and wishes to impose it on others",[31] which results in an anti-pluralistic world-view.

---

     induced discrimination and stigmatization. Abuses by non-State actors and societal restrictions include terrorism, extremism, vigilantism and social ostracism. The thematic reports are further supplemented by Bielefeldt et al. *FORB: An International Law Commentary* (2016).

(3) Additional reports, which include include: United States Commission on International Religious Freedom, *Annual Report of the U.S. Commission on International Religious Freedom*. April 2018. https://www.uscirf.gov/sites/default/files/2018USCIRFAR.pdf. Accessed 20/12/2018. This report does not focus or discuss the various possible motivational triggers for persecution, but in its discussion regarding country specific situation, it often mentions the motivation behind State violations or societal abuses. Therefore, this report is mostly used to reference certain examples in the context of certain States, to illustrate the motivational triggers. The same may be said of Robbers, G. & Durham, W. C. (Editors). *Encyclopedia of Law and Religion Online*. In *Encyclopedia of Law and Religion Online*. Leiden, The Netherlands: Brill | Nijhoff. https://brill.com/view/db/elro. Accessed 25/01/2019. This publication is a study of religion-state relations, and as such generally outlines the measures States use, based on a country specific context, to restrict, outlaw or violate the right to freedom of religion or belief on its inhabitants. Boyd-MacMillan, R. *Faith That Endures: The Essential Guide to the Persecuted Church*. Sovereign World (2008), pg 123–142. This book is limited to describing persecution from a Christian perspective.

31 Par 80 of the UN General Assembly, *Elimination of all forms of religious intolerance, Interim report by the Special Rapporteur of the Commission on Human Rights on the elimination of all forms of intolerance and of discrimination based on religion or belief.* A/55/280, 8 September 2000.

Consequently, the antagonist impulse is directed towards dissident religious identities, is always religiously motivated, and includes religious intolerance, religious extremism and related violence committed in the name of religion or belief. In such situations, the persecutor's religiously motivated intolerance overlaps with the discriminatory intent to target the victim because of his religious identity, or lack thereof.

It can, therefore, be said that the root cause of the antagonist impulse is violence and hostility towards a diverging religious identity, which constitutes religious discrimination and persecution. The antagonist impulse may very well intersect with other persecutive impulses. However, collective religious intolerance remains the primary motive of the persecutor, whether directed at those with a specific religious identity or those who lack a certain religious identity. In other words, the discriminatory intent to target certain religious identities constitutes the primary motive for persecution.

Conversely, the other impulses are motivated by various self-serving interests or ideologies, with a consequential effect on other religious identities. Here, the primary aim is not necessarily religiously motivated, but the persecutor resorts to aspects of religious discrimination and persecution in order to attain or maintain the integrity of his or her ideological interests, power or motives. In other words, in the context of the other impulses, the motive for persecution is usually distinguishable from the discriminatory intent to target the specific religious identity.

Hereafter, the most important elements of the religious antagonist impulse will be analysed.

5.3.1.1 *Religious antagonism results in collective religious hatred*

The religious antagonist impulse is religiously motivated persecution with its primary motive rooted in the name of the perpetrator's religion, which results in collective religious hatred. Collective religious hatred may be understood as "any joint manifestations of intense and irrational emotions of opprobrium, enmity and animosity towards a specific target group or individual that are proclaimed in the name of a particular religion or belief".[32]

---

[32] Bielefeldt *FORB: Thematic Reports* (2017) 193–194.

5. 'Motive' and its Effect on the Classification of Religious Persecution

5.3.1.2 Religious antagonism is driven by religious protectionism

Religious protectionism provides justification for collective hatred, violence and hostility for a number of possible reasons. For example: defending the persecutor's religious-related 'truth claims', scriptures, practices, or identity against perceived or imagined threats to their own identity or legitimacy,[33] retribution for perceived defamations of the persecutor's religious ideology, or the enforcement of an official or State religion.

5.3.1.3 A religious antagonist impulse is usually aggravated by political factors

Manifestations of collective hatred may be aggravated by various political factors. Firstly, endemic corruption undermines the authority of the State, shaping societal interaction to the extent that diversity cannot be sustained and persons and communities revert to an introspective mentality of self-preservation.[34] Secondly, an authoritarian political atmosphere inhibits freedom of speech, debate and criticism, resulting in misconceptions and suspicion between groups and individuals.[35] Thirdly, lack of trust in the rule of law and fair functioning of public institutions, which provide a climate for denial and impunity for serious infringements of international human rights law.[36] Finally, narrow identity politics harness religion for the purposes of national identity politics, causing political and communal religious marginalisation, labelling certain religious identities the subjects of prejudice and misconception.[37]

5.3.1.4 A religious antagonist impulse is usually directed at religious dissidents

Persecution in the name of religion severely affects religious dissidents, members of religious minorities and converts.[38] Conversely, such persecution may adversely cause reactive religious discrimination and persecution elsewhere, affecting followers from the religion in whose name such acts were perpetrated. Furthermore, those from within the same religion

---

[33] Bielefeldt *FORB: Thematic Reports* (2017) 194.
[34] Bielefeldt *FORB: Thematic Reports* (2017) 214.
[35] Bielefeldt *FORB: Thematic Reports* (2017) 214.
[36] Bielefeldt *FORB: Thematic Reports* (2017) 274.
[37] Bielefeldt *FORB: Thematic Reports* (2017) 214–215.
[38] Bielefeldt *FORB: Thematic Reports* (2017) 250.

who oppose or criticise such "abuse of their religion for the justification of violence, bear an increased risk of being accused of 'betrayal' or 'blasphemy' and having retaliatory penalties inflicted upon themselves".[39]

5.3.1.5 Religious antagonism is often the breeding ground for religious fundamentalism, extremism and related terrorism

The most distinguishable motivational trigger of persecution in terms of the antagonist impulse is religious extremism and terrorism committed in the name of religion or belief. Religious extremism and related terrorism are usually not confined to religious motivations. Typically, such terrorist groups operate in the name of religion, and in areas that lack good governance, which provides impunity for serious infringements of international human rights law.[40] Therefore, in instances where religious extremism, terrorism, vigilantism and social ostracism occur, the exploitative impulse may also be prevalent through organised crime and corruption, aspirations of ideological legitimacy and exclusivity, as well as political control.

The *raison d'être* of religious terror groups is based on intolerant and narrow-minded religious interpretations, which result in intra-religious as well as interreligious discrimination, "thereby creating a climate of fear in which no one can enjoy their freedom of religion or belief".[41] Unfortunately, the intersectional character of extremism and terrorism with religious identity makes it difficult to understand the numerous motivations of this form of religious persecution, yet the root cause remains religiously motivated.

5.3.2 Exclusivist impulse

The exclusivist impulse is based on the exclusivity or the superiority of a group's identity.[42] In the context of religious persecution, this exclusivity usually contains a strong religious or ideological presence, and is therefore based on the doctrine that only one particular religion or belief system is true.[43] The exclusivists may even "arrogate to themselves the authority to act as guardians of the purity of religious doctrines against so-called 'unbelievers', 'heretics' and people demonstrating religiously 'deviant' behaviour".[44]

---

[39] Bielefeldt *FORB: Thematic Reports* (2017) 251.
[40] Bielefeldt *FORB: Thematic Reports* (2017) 357.
[41] Bielefeldt *FORB: Thematic Reports* (2017) 357–358.
[42] *World Watch List Methodology* (2017) 9.
[43] *World Watch List Methodology* (2017) 9.
[44] Bielefeldt *FORB: Thematic Reports* (2017) 346.

5. 'Motive' and its Effect on the Classification of Religious Persecution

The exclusivist impulse may also be indicative of collective religious hatred, whether based on societal or national religious polarisation. In such instances, religious discrimination and intolerance are common, whether by the State or non-State actors, and are motivated by an identity ideology based on the racial, ethnic or religious supremacy of the persecutor. The exclusivist impulse is therefore not restricted to purely religious motivations, but may be indicative of other forms of ideological protectionism based on other interlinking aspects of identity.

The impulse is driven by an indoctrination of superiority of 'us' versus the inferiority of 'them'.[45] It is preached throughout such societies, which stereotypes dissident religious groups ('infidels') as dangerous, inferior or morally corrupt. This indoctrination is propagated over the course of years and even decades, which systematically desensitises the 'superior society' to impairments of the equality or human dignity of the 'inferior group' and inevitably 'legitimises' or justifies hostile attitudes towards these dissident religions and their adherents.

> It is considered permissible to deal with such a person in bizarre, amoral ways that would never be allowed in one's own group without compromising one's own moral standards.[46]

An appropriate example of such an exclusivist ideology may be found in the context of the Holocaust, as discussed in the judgement of the International Military Tribunal (outlined next).[47] The anti-Jewish policy preached a doctrine that disseminated hatred of the Jews, and consequently, the Jews were victims of public ridicule and contempt. With the Nazi party's seizure of power, the persecution of the Jews intensified. Initially, a series of discriminatory laws were passed, which effectively marginalised, differentiated and completely excluded Jews from German life. Gradually, the indoctrination allowed the exclusivists to make terrible utterances, which systematically desensitised public opinion against severe injustice, hatred and even pogroms against Jews. The combination of such publicly accepted supremacy, together with violent social and governmental hostility, paved the way for a system of ideological nationalism. It excluded certain religious and political groups and other individuals or groups with

---

[45] *World Watch List Methodology* (2017) 9.
[46] *World Watch List Methodology* (2017) 9.
[47] *The Trial of German Major War Criminals, Proceedings of the International Military Tribunal Sitting at Nuremberg, Germany*. International Military Tribunal, Judgment of 1 October 1946, pg 75–79.

perceived morally fallacious beliefs or characteristics, for example, homosexuals. An anti-Semitic policy was adopted that resulted in: the creation of ghettoes on an extensive scale in order to erase the presence of Jews from the visible German society; the imposition of civic and economic disadvantages, including resource and opportunity limitation; and the sponsoring of an extensive rearmament programme in anticipation of an aggressive war against non-conforming States. The 'Jewish question' became a factor in German Foreign Policy and described 'Jewry' as a problem of most urgent concern. This resulted in attempts to resolve the 'Jewish problem' with the adoption of certain anti-Semitic policies, and ultimately the enforcement of 'the final solution' of the Jewish question in all of Europe.[48] This 'final solution' meant the systematic extermination of Jews in concentration camps through a planned and systematic persecution of the Jewish population in the occupied territories. The policy of persecution, repression and murder of civilians of Jewish identity in Germany, was established beyond all doubt as an ideology based on exclusiveness. It resulted in consistent and systematic inhumanity on the greatest scale, which amounted, *inter alia*, to crimes against humanity of persecution and genocide. Consequently, the Nazi's exclusivist nationalist impulse paved the way for discrimination and persecution.

It should not be overlooked that the exclusivist impulse (and the subsequent inclination towards intolerant interpretations religious pluralism) "does not directly originate from religions themselves, but always presupposes the intervention of human beings".[49] Bielefeldt explains:

> Although there may be differences between inclinations towards open-mindedness and tolerance in various traditions, there is scope for interpretation in all of them. Thus, human beings themselves are ultimately responsible for open-minded or narrow-minded interpretations, which actually exist side by side in virtually all religious and philosophical traditions.[50]

Governments, religious leaders and religious adherents may all contribute to the climate within which different faiths and denominations must co-exist, whether through amicable or hateful interactions.[51] Therefore, religious pluralism is a precondition for overcoming 'fatalistic misunderstandings'

---

[48] See in this regard: Fest, J. C. *The Face of the Third Reich*. Published by Pelican (1979), and also Dawidowicz, L. S. *The War Against the Jews, 1933-1945*. Open Road Media (2010).
[49] Bielefeldt *FORB: Thematic Reports* (2017) 345.
[50] Bielefeldt *FORB: Thematic Reports* (2017) 345.
[51] Bielefeldt *FORB: Thematic Reports* (2017) 346.

that equate a certain religious identity with exclusivist and intolerant behaviour, while considering other religious identities as inferior.[52] Furthermore, open-minded interpretations of religious doctrines and religious pluralism should not be misconstrued as surrendering an established or mainstream *boni mores*. In instances where intolerant interpretations of a religion or belief result in discriminatory and persecutory behaviour towards a dissident religious identity in one State, such intolerance may trigger an interreligious reprisal in another State.

Intolerant interpretations of a religion may further undermine the majority or official religion itself. Based on personal experience, Bielefeldt points out that 'theocratic'[53] regimes "typically stifle any serious intellectual debate on religious issues and thus often create a climate of bigotry and hypocrisy".[54] Consequently, believers from within the established religion are often amongst the strongest opposition against a theocratic regime, "since they may feel that such governmental 'guardianship' merely leads to superficial conformism, which actually undermines any persuasiveness and attractiveness of their religion".[55] In States or religious communities where an exclusivist impulse exists, such intolerant behaviour may not only have a far-reaching effect on dissident religious groups, but may also have a destabilising impact on such a religion in other parts of the world, as well as weakening the reputation and legitimacy of specific 'truth claims' of the religion within its own quarters.

The religious exclusivist impulse is inclined towards absolute, exclusive power to the detriment of 'others'.[56] Consequently, dissident religious identities are forced, through acts of intolerance or violence, to endure certain 'hardships' or conform to the perceived superior ideology.[57]

The motivational triggers of persecution directly related to the exclusivist impulse are religious nationalism, tribal antagonism and denominational bigotry, as explained next.

---

[52] Bielefeldt *FORB: Thematic Reports* (2017) 346.
[53] The Oxford English Dictionary defines a theocracy or theocratic regime as: "A system of government in which priests rule in the name of God or a god". Many historic examples of such regimes exist. Contemporarily, an appropriate example is Iran, which has been described as a "theocratic republic" – US Central Intelligence Agency, *World Fact Book* / Middle East / Iran. https://www.cia.gov/library/publications/the-world-factbook/geos/ir.html. Accessed 09/01/2019.
[54] Bielefeldt *FORB: Thematic Reports* (2017) 346.
[55] Bielefeldt *FORB: Thematic Reports* (2017) 346.
[56] *World Watch List Methodology* (2017) 9.
[57] *World Watch List Methodology* (2017) 9.

5.3.2.1 Intra-religious or denominational bigotry

Intra-religious bigotry may amount to the condemnation of a religious ideology other than that of the persecutor, or the belief that the persecutor's denominational interpretation is the only legitimate or dominant expression. In other words, persecuting adherents of the same religion, but from different denominational backgrounds in an attempt to ensure it remains the only legitimate or dominant expression of that religion in the area.[58] For example, in Ethiopia, the Ethiopian Orthodox Church (EOC) used to be the State religion. Those who left their ranks to join other religious denominations or sects were subjected to severe persecution by the Ethiopian Orthodox anti-reformist movement, in an attempt to curtail the development of non-Orthodox churches and the restriction of the expansion of Protestant Christianity.[59]

5.3.2.2 Tribal antagonism

Tribal or Ethnic antagonism describes the persecution situation where communities are forced to adhere to age-old indigenous customs, norms and values, established by tribes or ethnic groups in the form of traditional religion or something similar.[60] Consequently, there is a very distinct interplay between religious factors with other identity factors, especially ethnicity, culture and nationality.[61]

For example, in Afghanistan, tribal and age-old values are deeply entrenched in society and any converts that embrace something new and possibly foreign, are either pressured to reconvert or may be looked upon as a traitor and excluded from the community.[62]

5.3.2.3 Religious nationalism

Religious nationalism constitutes an attempt to enforce a dominant or State religion. This motivational trigger describes the situation where

---

[58] *World Watch List Methodology* (2017) 13.
[59] *World Watch List Methodology* (2017) 13.
[60] *World Watch List Methodology* (2017) 13.
[61] "The scope of this 'ethnic movement' is mainly subnational (part of territory of country) but can involve the crossing of national borders depending on the regional spread of the ethnic people groups" – *World Watch List Methodology* (2017) 13.
[62] Open Doors Analytical / World Watch Research Unit. *World Watch List 2018: Compilation Volume 3 – Persecution Dynamics for Countries Ranking 1–25.* January, 2018, pg 15.

5. 'Motive' and its Effect on the Classification of Religious Persecution

countries or communities are being forced, whether gradually and systematically or abruptly, under the control of one particular religion.[63]

Religious nationalism is a clear example of how official State ideology uses religion in rhetoric on national and cultural identity, in order to promote national homogeneity,[64] which obscures the distinction between national and religious identity.[65] As part of protecting national heritage, 'foreign' religions are deemed dangerous or destructive to national cohesion.[66] Obviously, this may result in a government's tacit approval of hostile stereotypes and religious discrimination, which may encourage nationalist groups or even direct State participation in acts of persecution against members of dissident religious identities. The 'Burmanization policy' in Burma,[67] or atheistic nationalism in North Korea,[68] may be illustrative of religious nationalism.[69]

5.3.3 Secularist impulse

'Doctrinal secularism' or simply 'secularism', in the sense of a comprehensive official creed or belief system (i. e. a 'non-religious identity'), is distinguishable from 'constitutional secularity' or simply 'secularity' in the sense of a neutral and pluralist framework capable of accommodating or cooperating with a broad range of religions or beliefs.[70] Secularity infers inclusiveness, epitomising open-mindedness with regard to religious pluralism.[71] In this regard, a constitutional secular State functions on the basis of neutrality in order to

---

[63] *World Watch List Methodology* (2017) 12-13.
[64] Bielefeldt *FORB: Thematic Reports* (2017) 346.
[65] As part of protecting national heritage, 'foreign' religions are deemed dangerous or destructive to national cohesion. - Bielefeldt *FORB: Thematic Reports* (2017) 347.
[66] Bielefeldt *FORB: Thematic Reports* (2017) 347.
[67] Minority cultures, histories and socio-political aspirations are subsumed into an homogenising national identity derived from the Burman historical tradition - Ashley South as quoted Horton, G. *Dying Alive - A Legal Assessment of Human Rights Violations in Burma*, a report co-funded by the Netherlands Ministry for Development Co-operation. Images Asia (2005), par 5.5.
[68] USCIRF *Annual Report on International Religious Freedom* (2018) 58.
[69] Some other examples may include India, Laos, and Nepal - *World Watch List 2018: Persecution Dynamics for Countries Ranking 1-25* (2018).
[70] Durham, W.C. Jr. *Religious Freedom in a Worldwide Setting: Comparative Reflections*. Universal Rights in a World of Diversity: The Case of Religious Freedom. Glendon, M. A. & Zacher, H. F. (eds). The Pontifical Academy of Social Sciences (2012), pg 368 and Bielefeldt et al. *FORB: An International Law Commentary* (2016), pg 358.
[71] Bielefeldt et al. *FORB: An International Law Commentary* (2016) 35.

accommodate equality on the basis of religion or belief.[72] However, in the context of 'secularism' a privileged ideology exists under the auspices of a 'secular' State.[73] Therefore, secularism infers exclusiveness that provides a pretext for tight political restrictions in this field.[74]

In this section, a secularist impulse and secularist intolerance, or similar derivatives, must be understood as referring to 'doctrinal secularism' or a formal State ideology based on secularism that guides State or organisational activities based on its ideological priority over external manifestation of religious pluralism.[75] It has been explained that an official State belief ideology conceals serious risks of discrimination to those people or groups that do not adhere to the dominant ideology, "which is always somehow anti-religious or sceptical of organized religion".[76] The aim of a superior doctrinal ideology, similar to the exclusivist impulse, often relates to the attainment of absolute, elite power.[77]

The main motivational triggers of persecution relating to the secularist impulse, are secularist intolerance, and communist and post-communist oppression.

5.3.3.1 Secularist intolerance

Secularist intolerance[78] attempts to eradicate religion from the public domain, therefore limiting religious freedom rights to private observance.[79] In the context of religious freedom, secularist intolerance seeks to transform societies into the shape of a modern, radically secularist moral belief.[80] Religious groups that resist such publicly endorsed worldviews encounter persecutory opposition.[81]

---

[72] Bielefeldt *Misperceptions of FORB* (2013) 56.
[73] Bielefeldt *FORB: Thematic Reports* (2017) 347.
[74] Bielefeldt et al. *FORB: An International Law Commentary* (2016) 35.
[75] Bielefeldt *Misperceptions of FORB* (2013) 55–56.
[76] *World Watch List Methodology* (2017) 9.
[77] *World Watch List Methodology* (2017) 9.
[78] Holyoake *English Secularism: A Confession of Belief.* (1896). "Secularism is a code of duty pertaining to this life, founded on considerations purely human, and intended mainly for those who find theology indefinite or inadequate, unreliable or unbelievable. Its essential principles are: (1) The improvement of this life by material means. (2) That science is the available Providence of man. (3) That it is good to do good. Whether there be other good or not, the good of the present life is good, and it is good to seek that good". (Page number unavailable).
[79] *World Watch List Methodology* (2017) 14.

A topical situation is when such secularist moral beliefs relate to norms and values about sexuality, marriage and related issues, which are contradictory to certain religious morals. In some countries, the conflict arises when children from such religious groups are exposed to compulsory sexual education based on gender ideology (including LGBTI insights) in nursery and primary schools, which contradicts their religious upbringing.

5.3.3.2 Communist oppression

Communism can be regarded as the constitutional order or authoritarian ideology that places restrictions on certain human rights, and which controls the exercise of religious freedom rights through a system of registration and oversight based on communist views.[82] The main reason for exercising excessive political control in relation to religious freedom is "to prevent religious communities from running their own affairs independently for fear that this might in the long run erode the control of the State over society".[83] Therefore, communist and post-communist oppression may closely link to dictatorial or authoritarian paranoia, as well as the exclusivist impulse.

For example, the Socialist Republic of Vietnam is ruled by a communist party, which functions predominantly in the communist way, and is not a real democracy.[84] Vietnam monitors and exercises a high level of pressure on all ethnic and religious minorities as a result of fear and suspicion.[85] This became very apparent when Heiner Bielefeldt, as the UN Special Rapporteur on freedom of religion and belief at the time, was prevented from travelling to scheduled visits to meet with members of religious minorities during his visit to Vietnam in July 2014; despite an official invitation.[86]

---

[80] *World Watch List Methodology* (2017) 14.
[81] *World Watch List Methodology* (2017) 14. When religious individuals or institutions try to resist this new ethic, they are opposed by (i) non-discrimination legislation, (ii) attacks on parental rights in the area of education, (iii) the censorship of religious symbols in the public square, (iv) the use of various manifestations of "hate" speech laws to limit the freedom of expression, and (v) registration laws.
[82] *World Watch List Methodology* (2017) 14.
[83] Bielefeldt *FORB: Thematic Reports* (2017) 347.
[84] USCIRF *Annual Report on International Religious Freedom* (2018) 122-128. See also Cuba 148.
[85] USCIRF *Annual Report on International Religious Freedom* (2018) 122. See also *World Watch List 2018: Persecution Dynamics for Countries Ranking 1-25* (2018) 160-161.
[86] Introduction par 3 of the UN Human Rights Council, *Report of the Special Rapporteur on freedom of religion or belief, Addendum: Mission to Viet Nam (21 to 31 July 2014)*, 30

5.3.4 Exploitative impulse

The exploitative impulse relates to plain greed, through the unfair and manipulative use of political or military power in the attainment of personal wealth and resources.[87] However, the use of power is only a means to an end:

> While in the context of the exclusivist and secularist impulses power is actively sought as token of the supremacy of one's religion or ideology, the exploitative impulse needs power to safeguard its interests.[88]

It will become clear that the motivational triggers associated with the exploitative impulse are not aimed primarily at targeting religious communities, but the attainment of personal gain. It is only when religion, religious communities, or the consequences of a pluralist viewpoint based on religious freedom opposes the attainment of such wealth, that the exploitative impulse motivates religious persecution. The motivational triggers of persecution related to the exploitative impulse are organised corruption and crime, and dictatorial paranoia.

5.3.4.1 Organised corruption and crime

In countries characterised by systemic political maladministration, corruption, cronyism and ethnocentrism, massive breaches of fundamental human rights occur.[89] The decline in State control over traditional branches of authority and territory, societal fragmentation, and impunity, typically results in immoral societal groups filling the power vacuum, including mafia-like organisations, self-appointed vigilante groups, warlords, and even terrorist organisations, some of which commit violence in the name of religion.[90]

January 2015, A/HRC/28/66/Add.2. The Special Rapporteur also had serious concerns regarding the privacy and confidentiality of some meetings and sources of information had been seriously compromised. "He experienced first-hand and received credible information that some individuals with whom he wanted to meet had been heavily surveilled, warned, intimidated, harassed or prevented from travelling by the police. Even those who successfully met with him were not free from different degrees of police surveillance or questioning".

[87] *World Watch List Methodology* (2017) 10.
[88] *World Watch List Methodology* (2017) 10.
[89] Bielefeldt *FORB: Thematic Reports* (2017) 349.
[90] Bielefeldt *FORB: Thematic Reports* (2017) 349.

These factions may be involved with organised crime and corruption for financial, political and/or ideological self-enrichment, while the government's inability to enforce justice results in impunity and anarchy.[91] The exploitative impulse of organised corruption and crime are therefore not characteristically intolerant to religion in particular. The perpetrator/s attempt "to create a climate of impunity, anarchy and corruption as a means for self-enrichment"[92] and thereby limit or infringe upon, *inter alia*, religious freedom and related rights.

Organised criminal syndicates often rely on manipulating other actors into achieving their goals. As such, two main branches exist: (1) corruption within State structures, which allows syndicates to illegally co-opt government officials, and (2) aspirations of self-enrichment or simply financial upliftment, which corrupt members of society into joining criminal syndicates.

In Mexico, for example, the development of more liberal legislation in combination with organised corruption and crime have effectively reduced the freedom to express one's faith in the public sphere.[93] In Latin American countries such as Colombia, criminal syndicates that engage in drug and human trafficking, use violence to keep the opposing religious community under control, while also co-opting politicians and the security apparatus of the State.[94]

It should, however, not be ignored that organised corruption within State structures is not dependent upon the involvement of organised crime syndicates, and may therefore constitute a separate branch in terms of the exploitative impulse. Organised corruption of government officials and State structures may closely intersect with dictatorial or authoritarian paranoia.

5.3.4.2 *Dictatorial or authoritarian paranoia*

Dictatorial or authoritarian paranoia is based on the exercise of political power or control by a dominant political party or leader, in terms of which the maintenance of power is paramount. The primary motive is a "lust for power and the benefits it brings",[95] and the focus is therefore not specifically on religious identities.

---

[91] *World Watch List Methodology* (2017) 15.
[92] *World Watch List Methodology* (2017) 15.
[93] *World Watch List 2018: Persecution Dynamics for Countries Ranking 1-25* (2018) 107.
[94] *World Watch List Methodology* (2017) 15.
[95] *World Watch List Methodology* (2017) 14.

Although religious orthodoxy versus heterodoxy may not be the main interest of many authoritarian governments, unorthodox religious groups or denominations may be perceived to challenge the authoritarian government's monopoly on the control of society. In an attempt to curtail critical thought against government rule, such authoritarian governments may, for example, impose far-reaching control measures on freedom of speech and public communication that inevitably encroach on religious freedom and other human rights.

Even though North Korea is still run according to communist traditions and administrative customs, the enforced indoctrination of the personality cult around the Kim family and the incumbent leader, Kim Jong Un, is best categorised as dictatorial paranoia.[96]

> The North Korean government's approach toward religion and belief is among the most hostile and repressive in the world. The regime exerts absolute influence over the handful of state-controlled houses of worship permitted to exist, creating a facade of religious life in North Korea. In practice, the North Korean regime treats religion as a threat, particularly faiths associated with the West, such as Christianity, and is known to arrest, torture, imprison, and even execute religious believers.[97]

North Korea's political system is based on a cult-like ideology, described in two parts: 'Juche', which basically preaches that man is self-reliant; and 'Kimilsungism', which refers to worshipping the leaders from the Kim personality or family cult.[98] In terms of this personality cult, the people of North Korea live under a system of strict social control, which leaves absolutely no room for any religious choice.

In summary, religious persecution may not necessarily be anti-religious or religiously motivated in nature. Therefore, discrimination and persecution based on the victim or victim group's religious identity may not be the primary motive of the persecutor, or may prove to be a direct, yet incidental result thereof. Consequently, religious persecution may derive from a multiplicity of interrelated causes and motivations, which are com-

---

[96] *World Watch List 2018: Persecution Dynamics for Countries Ranking 1–25* (2018) 4.
[97] USCIRF *Annual Report on International Religious Freedom* (2018) 58.
[98] USCIRF *Annual Report on International Religious Freedom* (2018) 59, and Open Doors Analytical / World Watch Research Unit. *World Watch List 2016: Long version of all 50 country persecution dynamics*. January, 2016, pg 3–4. http://opendoorsanalytical.org/wp-content/uploads/2014/10/WWL-2016-Compilation-2-Long-profiles-Edition-2016-02-01.pdf. Accessed 12/08/2016.

plex, non-exhaustive, and often inseparable. In the context of the exclusivist and secularist impulses of persecution, the ideologies motivating societal or governmental bigotry may be found in the motivational triggers of religious persecution related to religious nationalism, tribal antagonism, denominational protectionism, formal secularist State ideology and the prescriptive ideology of communism. In terms of the exclusivist and secularist impulses of persecution, political or religious dominance and control is actively pursued in order to attain religious or ideological supremacy. The exploitative impulse includes dictatorial paranoia as a motivational trigger of persecution, which is often obsessed with the manipulative use of political or military power in order to oppress and restrict religious freedom in the attainment and safeguarding of its financial interests. On the contrary, the religious antagonist impulse is religiously motivated and justified, resulting in collective religious hatred. Religious extremism and related terrorism may be indicative of this impulse driven by religious protectionism based on the persecutor's religious ideology.

Although such root causes of religious persecution are often anti-religious or religiously motivated, a persecutor's motivations are *sui generis* in each case and may be complex, manifold and interrelated.

5.4 Conclusion

In the context of 'grievous religious persecution' the reason why a persecutor targets a religious identity is irrelevant to the classification of ground of persecution. If the persecutor intended to discriminate based on the victim's religious identity, his or her motive for such persecutory conduct is irrelevant. Therefore, persecution committed 'in the name of religion' (religiously motivated persecution) is, under certain circumstances, distinguishable from religious persecution. Religiously motivated persecution is concerned with the perpetrator's motive or purpose, which is based on his/her religious orientation. Religious persecution, on the other hand, is concerned with the perpetrator's discriminatory intent, which is primarily directed at victims because of their religious identity or lack thereof. It is, therefore, important to distinguish the motive or aim for the commission of persecutory conduct from the religious discriminatory intent to direct the persecutory conduct at a specific religious identity. Consequently, persecution in the name of religion will only be considered 'religious persecution', if those persecuted were primarily identified, targeted and persecuted based on their religious identity.

As a result, knowledge of the amalgamated nature of international criminal law and its effect on the use of correct terminology is essential in clearly distinguishing religious persecution from other grounds of persecution, or from instances where religion motivates persecution, but the persecutory conduct does not necessarily target victims on the basis of their religious identities.

It is, therefore, important to correctly distinguish between the motive for the commission of persecutory conduct and the discriminatory intent to direct the persecutory conduct at a specific group. In this regard, the correct terminology is also essential. Nonetheless, it could be argued that understanding a persecutor's motive for persecution may, under certain circumstances, assist in determining how he/she perceived the victim's identity (identifying element), which in turn, constitute an essential aspect in classifying the relevant ground of persecution.

Chapter Six: A Taxanomy of Crimes Against Humanity of Religious Persecution

6.1 Introduction

Due to their scale, severity, and discriminatory intent, certain forms of religious persecution are so heinous that such conduct may be justifiably categorised as crimes of serious concern to the international order and outrage the conscience of mankind. However, despite the persistent recognition expressed by the inclusion of 'grievous persecution' as an enumerated inhumane act of crimes against humanity, such universal acceptance and recognition have been void of substantive or practical clarity, definitional coherence and distinct characterisation. Consequently, such legal uncertainty and judicial unease may be responsible, at least in part, for the international criminal justice systems' perceived reluctance to enforce prosecution measures based on 'grievous persecution'. In order to argue for the individual criminal accountability of actors responsible for 'grievous persecution', such deficiencies were addressed in Chapter Three, which established a legal framework of 'grievous persecution' in its generic sense. Chapter Six will integrate the preceding framework with the acquired understanding of the role of religious identity in order to definitively conceptualise 'grievous religious persecution' or crime against humanity of religious persecution in terms of the *Rome Statute*.[1]

Thus, Chapter Six addresses the primary aim of the book, *viz.* to lift the veil on the obscure notion of religious persecution by proposing a justifiable, comprehensively formulated and pragmatically verified conceptualisation in the context of international criminal law. This conceptualisation or taxonomy will comprise a focussed discussion of the definitional elements of 'grievous religious persecution', including the different forms of persecutory conduct, the *mens rea* requirement, the intensity threshold, and the conditions of applicability for crimes against humanity.

---

[1] Art 7(2)(g) read together with Art 7(1)(h) of the *Rome Statute of the International Criminal Court*, Doc. A/CONF.183/9 of 17 July 1998 *in force* 1 July 2002 (2002)(*Rome Statute*).

In order to guard against the careless and indiscriminate overuse of the term 'persecution', this chapter will conclude with an attempt at the arduous task of defining crimes against humanity of religious persecution in the context of the *Rome Statute*. It should be noted that the conceptualisation below may contain various aspects that have already been discussed previously. However, in the interest of a thorough and definitive conceptualisation, some of those considerations will be repeated below.

6.2 Proposed Taxonomy of Crimes Against Humanity of Religious Persecution ('Grievous Religious Persecution')

The aim of the taxonomy is to formally and directly address the primary legal problem identified in this paper, *viz.* the substantive ambiguity of the crime of persecution. The taxonomy functions as a substantive synopsis of the legal preconditions for establishing the ICC's subject-matter jurisdiction over conduct constituting crimes against humanity of religious persecution. The taxonomy of 'grievous religious persecution' comprises two parts. The first part involves a systematic analysis of the unique definitional elements and the second part consists of a proposed definition.

6.2.1 Substantive elements of 'grievous religious persecution'

According to the conditions of applicability,[2] persecution may amount to an enumerated inhumane act of crimes against humanity if: (1) the *chapeau* elements are satisfied, which establish the contextual framework,[3] and (2) certain *sui generis* definitional requirements or elements of persecution are also satisfied. These elements may be divided into three main categories: (1) the *actus reus*, i. e. the required material elements or criminally liable conduct, (2) the *mens rea*, i. e. the required mental elements or subjective mindset of the perpetrator, and (3) the required threshold of severity. In the discussion below, the *chapeau* elements of crimes against humanity will

---

[2] Art 7(2)(g) and Art 7(1)(h) of the *Rome Statute*, read with the ICC, *Elements of Crimes*, 2011, Official Records of the Review Conference of the Rome Statute of the International Criminal Court, Kampala, 31 May–11 June 2010 (International Criminal Court publication, RC/11). (*ICC Elements of Crimes*).

[3] Cassese, A. *et al. International Criminal Law: Cases and Commentary.* Oxford University Press (2011), pg 179.

6. A Taxanomy of Crimes Against Humanity of Religious Persecution

be integrated amongst the other categories of definitional elements of 'grievous religious persecution'.[4]

6.2.1.1 The actus reus of religious persecution

The *actus reus* (as it is known in Anglo-American legal systems), or criminally liable conduct, as it relates to religious persecution, essentially refers to conduct that discriminates on the basis of religious identity, and which results, separately or cumulatively, in the severe deprivation of fundamental rights contrary to international law.[5] In defining the objective element (*actus reus*) of religious persecution, the following elements may be identified:

- underlying conduct or practice which discriminates in fact (persecutory conduct);
- which results in the severe deprivation of a fundamental right laid down in international customary or treaty law (causation requirement);
- was committed in connection with any other acts of an inhumane nature or any other jurisdictionally relevant international crime (connection requirement); and
- constitutes part of a pattern of widespread or systematic crimes directed against a civilian population targeted by reason of their religious identity (participation context).

a) Underlying religious persecutory conduct or practice

Persecutory conduct must be understood as voluntary (will-controlled) and discriminatory human conduct, which may either consist of a 'positive act'

---

[4] The *chapeau* elements for crimes against humanity comprise of: an attack, which is committed as part of a widespread or systematic practice; directed against any civilian population; and in terms of which the perpetrator's attack was committed with intent and knowledge; pursuant to or in furtherance of a State or organizational policy to commit such attack – Introduction par to Art 7, *ICC Elements of Crimes* (2011), as well as elements 5 and 6 of Art 7(1)(h). It should be noted that although the participation context and the contextual threshold are discussed separately, they essentially comprise of the same elements serving two functions.

[5] *Prosecutor v Miroslav Kvočka et al. (Trial Judgement)*, Case No. IT-98-30/1-T, 2 November 2001, par 186. See also *Appeal Judgement (Kaing Guek Eav alias Duch)*, Case File 001/18-07-2007/ECCC/SC, Extraordinary Chambers in the Courts of Cambodia, 3 February 2012, paras 226, 240, 267 and 278.

or a 'failure to act' (omission).⁶ However, there is "a limit to the acts which can constitute persecution".⁷ Persecutory conduct must be directed discriminately and must result, separately or cumulatively, in a deprivation of fundamental rights to the extent that it is equal in gravity to the enumerated 'inhumane-type' conduct or are otherwise 'offensive to humanity'.⁸ Problematically, persecutory conduct is not based on a specific list of prohibited acts, but may encompass any inhumane act or conduct of an inhumane nature,⁹ or a serious form of discrimination¹⁰ to the extent that it may be termed inhumane or offensive to humanity,¹¹ whether based on its inherent nature or its cumulative effect.¹² Consequently, persecution may understood most simply as a materially defined crime or result crime in terms of which a specific condition or consequence is prohibited, viz. the severe deprivation of a fundamental right on a discriminatory basis. Therefore, a comprehensive list of persecutory conduct is unattainable. Nevertheless, the following forms of persecutory conduct may be identified:

1. The commission of one or more of the enumerated inhumane acts of crimes against humanity on a discriminatory basis. 'Inhumane-type' acts are generally physical acts and inherently inhumane in nature, i. e. on their own they are sufficiently serious to constitute persecution, even if only one act is committed. This category would include all the other enumerated inhumane acts of crimes against humanity, including 'other inhumane acts',¹³ provided the common element of discrimination in regard to the enjoyment of a basic or fundamental right is present.¹⁴ Thus, an 'inhumane act' or an act of an inhumane nature includes any conduct of which its nature and gravity are similar to any of the underlying acts constituting crimes

---

⁶ *Prosecutor v Dario Kordić, Mario Cerkez (Trial Judgement)*, Case No. IT-95-14/2-T, 26 February 2001, par 694; and *Prosecutor v Tihomir Blaškić (Trial Judgement)*, Case No. IT-95-14-T, ICTY, 3 March 2000, par 556.
⁷ *Prosecutor v Duško Tadić (Trial Judgement)*, Case No. IT-94-1-T, ICTY, 7 May 1997, par 707.
⁸ Duch *(Appeal Judgement)* par 257. See also Ambos, K. & Wirth, S. *The Current Law of Crimes Against Humanity: An Analysis of UNTAET Regulation 15/2000.* Crim LF, 13 (2002), pg 79.
⁹ *Tadić (Trial Judgement)* par 699.
¹⁰ *Tadić (Trial Judgement)* par 697.
¹¹ Implicit in the use of the phrase 'inhumane act' or 'conduct of an inhumane nature', is the severe infringement of a fundamental right.
¹² Ambos & Wirth *The Current Law of Crimes Against Humanity* (2002) 76.
¹³ Art 7(1)(k) of the *Rome Statute*.

against humanity. For example, the application for an arrest warrant against Laurent Koudou Gbagbo, relied on separate charges of murder and rape as the underlying acts of persecution.[15]
2. The commission of a range of other physical acts, other than the enumerated inhumane acts (that are not inherently inhumane in nature), provided they are committed on a discriminatory basis and their cumulative effect satisfies the severity threshold. Such physical 'other-type' acts may include known felonious conduct or acts that are not inherently criminal.[16] For example, the unlawful and intentional arrest and detention of members of a specific religious group.[17]
3. A deliberate failure to take action ('persecutory omission') under circumstances where there is a legal duty upon the *de facto* authority to perform a certain type of positive act, provided the common element of discrimination is present and their cumulative effect satisfies the severity threshold. For example, if the State abdicates in its responsibility to control social hostility discriminately directed at a certain religious community through the deliberate inaction of responsible office bearers.
4. The enforcement of a severe discriminatory ideology or policy that is either inherently inhumane in nature, or may be considered to offend humanity based on its cumulative effect.[18] For example, only followers of the official State religion can publicly manifest their religious convictions.

Therefore, underlying persecutory conduct may be summarised as a sufficiently serious 'inhumane act' which discriminates in fact, or the substantially serious effect of a course of discriminatory conduct or practices, provided it results in the severe deprivation of a fundamental human right.

---

[14] *Tadić (Trial Judgement)* par 697. See also Cassese *et al. ICL: Cases and Commentary* (2011) 184. If the underlying persecutory conduct is based on an enumerated inhumane act or crime, the prosecution must prove the definitional elements of the underlying act.

[15] *Prosecutor v Laurent Koudou Gbagbo* (ICC) Case No ICC-02/11-01/11, Public redacted version of 'Decision on the Prosecutor's Application Pursuant to Article 58 for a warrant of arrest against Laurent Koudou Gbagbo' (30 November 2011).

[16] *Kvočka (Trial Judgement)* par 186.

[17] For a non-exhaustive list see Triffterer, O. & Ambos, K. *Commentary on the Rome Statute of the International Criminal Court: Observers' Notes, Article by Article.* Beck Publishers, 2nd edition (2008), pg 260-261.

[18] *Tadić (Trial Judgement)* par 697.

b) Causation of severe deprivation of a fundamental right (causation requirement)

The persecutory act or its cumulative effect must result in the intentional[19] and severe deprivation of a fundamental right laid down in international customary or treaty law, which is similar to the standard of a 'gross and blatant denial of fundamental rights' required by the *ad hoc* tribunals.[20] The deprivation of a fundamental right refers to an unjustifiable violation or infringement of international human rights principles. The consequential effect of which, not each individual underlying act, must be of sufficient gravity to be considered 'severe'.[21]

c) Connection requirement

The underlying persecutory conduct must be objectively (clearly and obviously) linked to a separate enumerated inhumane *act*, or any jurisdictionally relevant international *crime* (war crimes, genocide or crimes of aggression), which may also serve to satisfy the 'broader attack' requirement.[22] An objective contextual link entails a clear and obvious connection if the act or crime supports the purpose of the persecution or *vice versa*. In practice, the connection requirement establishes three possible scenarios:

1. If the underlying persecutory conduct is based on the cumulative effect of multiple 'other acts' or an act that is not an enumerated inhumane act, such conduct must be connected to a separate enumerated inhumane act, or any jurisdictionally relevant crime (provided the requirements for those crimes are also satisfied).[23]

---

[19] The word 'intentional' requires that the act of deprivation must have been committed intentionally, but should not be construed as to require that the perpetrator intended to deprive human rights specifically.

[20] Brady, H. & Liss, R. *The Evolution of Persecution as a Crime Against Humanity*, in Historical Origins of International Criminal Law: Volume 3, Bergsmo, M. et al (eds). Torkel Opsahl Academic EPublisher, Brussels (2014), pg 545.

[21] Ambos & Wirth *The Current Law of Crimes Against Humanity* (2002) 79. The 'severity' aspect of the deprivation will be considered separately under the intensity requirement.

[22] The connection requirement confirms that persecution can be based on 'inhumane-type' or 'other-type' conduct and must thus be interpreted to be a merely jurisdictional requirement (objective conditions of punishability) – Ambos & Wirth *The Current Law of Crimes Against Humanity* (2002) 74.

[23] Ambos & Wirth *The Current Law of Crimes Against Humanity* (2002) 82.

6. A Taxonomy of Crimes Against Humanity of Religious Persecution

2. If an enumerated inhumane act forms the basis for the persecutory conduct (i. e. an aggravated form of an inhumane act),[24] a further connection to yet another inhumane act is not required and need only be linked to a single inhumane *act* (not part of a widespread and systematic attack consisting of other enumerated inhumane acts).[25] In this case, persecutory conduct does not pertain to conduct unique unto itself, but is incidental to, or dependent upon, the commission of other enumerated inhumane acts within the jurisdiction of the ICC, committed with the relevant *dolus specialis*.
3. If the persecutory conduct itself is sufficiently widespread or systematic, the persecutory acts themselves can satisfy the context element, provided such acts are connected by a collective religious discriminatory intent.[26]

d) Participation context

In terms of the *chapeau* elements, the 'participation context' clarifies the accused's requisite participation in, or commission of, persecutory conduct, which must be sufficiently linked to a 'broader attack'.[27] The course of persecutory conduct must be widespread or systematic, not the individual persecutory acts of the accused, provided his actions form part of the broader attack.[28] Thus, the persecutory conduct must not constitute isolated and random acts or omissions.

A course of persecutory conduct may constitute religious persecution if such an 'attack' is based on a pattern of persecution against a civilian group with an identifiable religious identity,[29] implemented by way of an asserted policy, plan or ideology based on, or has the effect of, discriminating on the basis of religion which may be inferred from the circumstances. A course of

---

[24] Persecution may be considered as a multi-layered or heightened crime against humanity, requiring a specific *mens rea* in addition to the contextual intent required of all underlying crimes – Fournet, C., & Pégorier. 'Only One Step Away From Genocide': The Crime of Persecution in International Criminal Law. International Criminal Law Review, Vol. 10, Issue 5, pages 713–738. Marthinus Nijhoff Publishers (2010), pg 716.
[25] Ambos & Wirth *The Current Law of Crimes Against Humanity* (2002) 72.
[26] Triffterer & Ambos *Commentary on the Rome Statute* (2008) 221.
[27] Triffterer & Ambos *Commentary on the Rome Statute* (2008) 176.
[28] Triffterer & Ambos *Commentary on the Rome Statute* (2008) 176.
[29] The use of the phrase 'directed against a civilian population' indicates that persecution, in the ambit of crimes against humanity, is not relevant in circumstances where for example a combatant group is targeted based on a specific aspect of their identity. However, in such circumstances, the commission of war crimes may be satisfied.

religious discriminatory practices may itself constitute an 'attack', provided the contextual threshold is satisfied.

6.2.1.2 The mens rea of religious persecution

The mental element (*mens rea*) is what is unique about crime against humanity of persecution, as it requires a *dolus specialis* in addition to the contextual intent required of all underlying crimes.[30]

In the interest of clarity and simplicity of reference, the persecutor's required subjective mindset must consist of:[31]

- the contextual knowledge by the persecutor that his conduct may be contextualised as part of a broader attack (contextual knowledge);
- the intent to commit the underlying act/s (persecutive intent); and
- the conscious and preconceived discriminatory intent to target a group or collectivity by reason of their religious identity (religious discriminatory intent).

a) Contextual knowledge

The contextual mental element of religious persecution indicates that the persecutor's conduct must form part of a broader attack. Thus, contextual knowledge require that the persecutor was:[32] (1) aware of a pattern of widespread or systematic discriminatory practices (broader attack), (2) aware that it was directed against a civilian population based on their collective religious identity, and (3) intended, or at least realised, the risk that his persecutory conduct may objectively form part of that attack or pattern of persecution.[33] Such contextual knowledge may be actual or inferred from the circumstances.[34]

---

[30] Fournet & Pigorier *Only One Step Away From Genocide* (2010) 716.
[31] Cassese et al. *ICL: Cases and Commentary* (2011) 184–188. See also *Prosecutor v Duško Tadić aka "Dule"* (*Sentencing Judgement*), Case No. IT-94-1-T, ICTY, 14 July 1997, par 697. Therefore, as far as intention in the form of *mens rea* is concerned, it is submitted that three categories of intent must be proven to qualify acts of persecution as crimes against humanity.
[32] *ICC Elements of Crimes*, Art 7(1)(h) par 6.
[33] Therefore, a *dolus eventualis* standard is sufficient with regard to the contextual element – Ambos & Wirth *The Current Law of Crimes Against Humanity* (2002) 40 and 86. See also *Situation in the Democratic Republic of the Congo, in the case of the Prosecutor v Thomas Lubanga Dyilo*, Case No ICC-01/04-01/06, Decision on the Confirmation of Charges, ICC, 14 March 2012, paras 351–355.

b) Persecutive intent

'Persecutive intent' relates to the deliberate commission of persecutory acts or omissions.[35] Persecutive intent requires that the persecutor must have meant to engage in the persecutory conduct that had discriminatory consequences, or acted while reconciled to the knowledge that such a result will occur in the ordinary course of events. Persecutive intent is only required if the persecutory conduct is based on physical acts.[36]

Considering that a severe form of discrimination may inherently constitute a deprivation of a fundamental right, it is accepted that the persecutor need not have intended to severely deprive the victims of their fundamental rights in addition to a religious discriminatory intent.[37]

c) Religious discriminatory intent

'Grievous religious persecution' requires an additional, *sui generis*, element of culpability, viz. a conscious religious discriminatory mindset.[38] Religious discriminatory intent refers to the conscious, preconceived, and deliberate targeting[39] of a person or identifiable group or collectivity based primarily (but not necessarily exclusively)[40] on their actual or perceived religious identity, or lack thereof, for reasons or motives peculiar to the perpetrator. Therefore, the persecutory conduct must have been directed at certain victims 'by reason of' their religious identity (including actual or perceived membership, support or identification), or lack thereof.

---

[34] Triffterer & Ambos *Commentary on the Rome Statute* (2008) 182.
[35] Art 7(1) of the *Rome Statute*, read with the *ICC Elements of Crimes* (2011).
[36] Persecutive intent is not specifically required under all circumstances, especially considering that the specific discriminatory intent encapsulated by persecution activates the 'unless otherwise provided' proviso in Art 30 of the Statute.
[37] Triffterer & Ambos *Commentary on the Rome Statute* (2008) 257–258. Therefore, the deprivation of fundamental rights need not constitute the purpose or aim of the conduct (material element), and consequently, such a result need not have been committed with any form of criminal culpability.
[38] Cassese, A. (ed.), *The Oxford Companion to International Criminal Justice*. Oxford University Press (2009), pg 453. This additional element of culpability constitutes a higher standard of criminal intent, similar to *dolus specialis* or intent in the narrow sense of 'purpose' or 'aim' – Brady & Liss *The Evolution of Persecution* (2014) 553.
[39] *Prosecutor v. Radoslav Brdjanin (Appeal Judgement)*, IT-99-36-A, ICTY, 3 April 2007, par 996, in Byron, C. *War Crimes and Crimes Against Humanity in the Rome Statute of the International Criminal Court*. Manchester University Press (2009), pg 229.
[40] Tieszen, C.L. *Towards Redefining Persecution*. Religious Freedom Series: Suffering, Persecution and Martyrdom. Vol 2. (2010), pg 164.

Persecution of a religious identity may be defined both in a positive manner ('specific religious discriminatory intention'), *vis a vis* the identity of the group to be targeted, (e. g. Hindus or Shia Muslims);[41] and in a negative manner (a non-specific 'negative religious discriminatory intention'),[42] i. e. any person/s not belonging to a particular religious persuasion, (e. g. all non-Christians, or anyone who does not believe in 'Allah').[43] Thus, the victims of religious persecution may include a person, identifiable group or collectivity that was targeted *primarily* on their religious identity, or lack thereof, either based on objective criteria or in the mind of the accused. It is, therefore, essential to determine or prove that the persecutor had a specific or negative religious discriminatory intent.

A religious discriminatory intent may be proven by way of direct evidence (direct discriminatory intent),[44] or may be inferred from the circumstances (inferred discriminatory intent)[45] that provide *prima facie* proof of an apparent pattern of religious discrimination,[46] to the extent that such

---

[41] Therefore, the persecutor forms a discriminatory mindset in relation to a specific religious identity, and directs the persecutory conduct at persons, groups or the collectivity that embody such an identity.

[42] *Tadic (Trial Judgement)* par 714; *Blaškić (Trial Judgement)* par 236; *Kvočka (Trial Judgement)* par 195.

[43] Byron *War Crimes and Crimes Against Humanity* (2009) 229–230. In such instances, those persecuted are chosen and targeted because they either lacked a specific accepted religious identity, did not conform to the persecutor's religious ideology, or otherwise opposed or criticized the persecutor's religious identity, wherefore the perpetrator's discriminatory intention is broadly applied.

[44] Brady & Liss *Evolution of Persecution* (2014) 536. For example where an explicit or systemised policy of conscious and religious discrimination existed within by a structured group, or in instances where a *de facto* authority subscribes to a deliberate policy of passive toleration consciously aimed at encouraging such religious discrimination and persecution. However, the existence of such a policy cannot be inferred solely from the absence of governmental or organizational action – *ICC Elements of Crimes*, Art 7, Introduction, footnote 6.

[45] Brady & Liss *Evolution of Persecution* (2014) 536. This does not mean that a discriminatory intent may be automatically inferred directly from the general discriminatory nature of the persecutory conduct – *Prosecutor v Milorad Krnojelac (Appeal Judgement)*, Case No. ICTY-97-25-A, ICTY, 17 September 2003, par 184. Confirmed in *Blaškić (Appeal Judgement)* par 164, and *Prosecutor v Dario Kordić, Mario Cerkez (Appeal Judgement)*, Case No. IT-95-14/2-A, ICTY, 17 December 2004, par 110.

[46] *Gbagbo Arrest Warrant* (2011) par 204. See also *Prosecutor v Ahmad Harun and Al Kushayb, Decision on the Prosecution Application under Article 58(7) of the Statute*, 27 April 2007 (ICC-02/05-01/07-1), pg 74.

inference is the only reasonable conclusion to be drawn.[47] Alternatively, a religious discriminatory intent may also be inferred from the persecutor's active participation and association with an explicit religious discriminatory policy by a *de facto* authority (discriminatory policy).[48]

6.2.1.3 The threshold of severity for religious persecution

The Court's jurisdiction is limited to persecutory conduct that have reached a certain level or grade of severity before it will constitute 'grievous religious persecution'. Though persecution may be perpetrated by a variety of regimes and actors, and manifest in varying degrees of severity,[49] the scope of 'grievous religious persecution' is limited to a consistent pattern of inhumanity (contextual threshold),[50] which conduct, separately or cumulatively, must result in a *severe* deprivation of *fundamental* human rights (intensity threshold).[51] Thus, the threshold of severity for 'grievous religious persecution' is based on:

1. the contextual threshold of the attack or pattern of persecution (internationalising factor); and
2. the intensity threshold consequential to the persecutory conduct or its cumulative effect.

a) Contextual threshold (international element)

The contextual threshold of severity serves to distinguish isolated or sporadic discrimination and related acts, from a discriminatory policy or a consistent pattern of persecution, which constitutes 'grievous persecution'.[52] Therefore, the contextual threshold requires that the religious persecution

---

[47] *Krnojelac (Appeal Judgement)* par 186 and 202. The context may include the systematic nature of the crimes committed against a specific religious identity, and the general discriminatory attitude of the perpetrator as seen through his behaviour. – *Prosecutor v Miroslav Kvočka et al. (Appeal Judgement)*, Case No. IT-98-30/1-A, ICTY, 28 February 2005, par 460.
[48] Chertoff, E. *Prosecuting Gender-Based Persecution: The Islamic State at the ICC*. The Yale Law Journal (2017), pg 1107.
[49] University of Notre Dame – Under Caesar's Sword: Christian Response to Persecution. *In Response to Persecution: Findings of the Under Caesar's Sword Project on Global Christian Communities*. Report released on April 20, 2017 in Washington D.C. http://ucs.nd.edu/report/. Accessed 19/02/2018, pg 10.
[50] Chertoff *Prosecuting Gender-Based Persecution* (2017) 1065–1066.
[51] Art 7(2)(g) of the *Rome Statute*.
[52] Triffterer & Ambos *Commentary on the Rome Statute* (2008) 176.

was carried out in a systematic manner or on a mass scale (or was part of an 'attack' of a widespread or systematic nature), actively promoted, encouraged, or tolerated (through deliberate inaction), by way of an asserted policy, plan or ideology by a *de facto* authority (which need not be publicised),[53] and directed against a civilian population targeted by reason of their identifiable religious identity.

b) Intensity threshold

The intensity threshold relates to the consequential gravity or material effect of the persecutory conduct.[54] In the context of the *Rome Statute*, the crux in analysing the intensity threshold lies in determining whether or not the persecutory conduct, when considered cumulatively and in context, resulted in a *severe* deprivation of *fundamental* rights.[55] Therefore, not every denial or infringement of a human right is sufficient to qualify as 'grievous religious persecution'.[56] The threshold requirement may be summarised with the following elements:

bi) Fundamental human rights

The human rights which are deprived must be of a *fundamental* nature, i. e. elementary and inalienable rights.[57] The 'fundamental' nature of a right may be inferred from the minimum norms and values that are universally considered as an essential necessity for an existence worthy of human dignity.[58] In addition, the connection requirement provides a framework of

---

[53] Ambos & Wirth *The Current Law of Crimes Against Humanity* (2002) 26–27.
[54] Triffterer & Ambos *Commentary on the Rome Statute* (2008) 257.
[55] Duch (*Appeal judgement*) par 257. This threshold is similar to the 'gross or blatant denial of fundamental rights' standard required by the *ad hoc* tribunals – Brady & Liss *The Evolution of Persecution* (2014) 545.
[56] Ambos & Wirth *The Current Law of Crimes Against Humanity* (2002) 74.
[57] Blaškić (*Trial Judgement*) par 220.
[58] The defined parameters for the definition of human dignity can be construed from the international standards on human rights, such as those laid down in the UN General Assembly, *Universal Declaration of Human Rights,* 10 December 1948, Resolution 217 A (III) (*UDHR*). In essence, *fundamental* rights encapsulates certain higher norms of customary international law and have the character of *jus cogens*, and are thus non-derogable rights. It may, therefore, be "possible to identify a set of fundamental rights appertaining to any human being, the gross infringement of which may amount, depending on the surrounding circumstances, to a crime against humanity" – *Kupreškić* (*Trial Judgement*) par 617 and 621. However, consid-

6. A Taxonomy of Crimes Against Humanity of Religious Persecution

inhumane-type acts or crimes, all of which result in severe deprivations of fundamental rights.[59] From this it is possible to infer which rights may be considered *ejusdem generis* (of the same kind), and consequently 'fundamental', based on the nature of the deprivation of human dignity and inhumanity incidental to jurisdictionally relevant mass atrocity crimes and inhumane acts.

Although 'grievous religious persecution' is often understood and equated with the denial of the right to freedom of thought, conscience, religion or belief,[60] this is not a definitional prerequisite. Nonetheless, the denial or deprivation of religious freedom rights often serve as the proverbial canary in the coal mine, forewarning the denial of other fundamental liberties, which almost surely follow.[61] Considering that religion is one of the essential elements in an adherent's conception of life and inner consciousness, which may influence their sense of personal or collective identity and belonging, and guide their way of life and interaction with others,[62] religious freedom is considered a *fundamental* human right.[63] In addition, equality on the basis of religion, as an interrelated aspect of human dignity and religious freedom, is also considered a fundamental right.[64]

---

ering the deliberately flexible nature of the crime of persecution and the complexity of the notion of human dignity, the "explicit inclusion of particular fundamental rights could be interpreted as the implicit exclusion of other rights", which would not be in the interests of justice – Cassese *et al. ICL: Cases and Commentary* (2011) 187.

[59] Ambos & Wirth *The Current Law of Crimes Against Humanity* (2002) 74.

[60] See for example *Under Caesar's Sword: Christian Response to Persecution* (2017) 9.

[61] Abrams, E. *The Persecution of Christians as a Worldwide Phenomenon*. Testimony at the U.S. Commission on International Religious Freedom, 11 February 2014, pg 1.

[62] Preamble par 4 of the UN General Assembly, *Declaration on the Elimination of All Forms of Intolerance and of Discrimination Based on Religion or Belief*, UNGA Res 36/55, 73rd plenary meeting, 25 November 1981 (*Religious Discrimination Declaration*). See also Bielefeldt, H., Ghanea, N. & Wiener, M. *Freedom of Religion or Belief: An International Law Commentary*. Oxford University Press (2016), pg 11.

[63] Par 1 of UN Human Rights Committee, *CCPR General Comment No. 22: Article 18 (Freedom of Thought, Conscience or Religion)*, 30 July 1993, CCPR/C/21/Rev.1/Add.4.

[64] Art 3 of the *Religious Discrimination Declaration* (1981) – "[D]iscrimination between human beings based on grounds of religion or belief constitutes an affront to human dignity... and shall be condemned as a violation of human rights and fundamental freedoms...".

bii) Severe deprivation

The nature and gravity of the deprivation must be *severe* or substantial. 'Severe'[65] establishes the level or threshold of severity. Severity refers to the nature and gravity of the infringement of fundamental rights, not the character of the persecutory conduct as such.[66] The level of gravity required to classify acts of persecution as crimes against humanity is established when "the overall consequence ... offend humanity in such a way that they may be termed inhumane".[67] Thus, 'severity' may be based on a sufficiently harmful isolated incident, or may be based on the cumulative harmful effect of a range of actions. The inferred *ejusdem generis* of inhumane acts or other jurisdictionally relevant crimes mentioned above, may also assist in assessing what will constitute as a 'severe deprivation' for purposes of criminal responsibility. Generally, the deprivation of fundamental rights must be so severe as to be considered similar in nature to other enumerated inhumane acts or core crimes.

Nevertheless, it will be the function of the Court to assess, on a case-by-case basis, whether the deprivation of a certain human right, when considered in context, may be considered as a sufficiently *severe* deprivation of a *fundamental* right.

In the case of religious persecution the inherent and often indivisible link between religious discrimination, persecution, and the impairment of the enjoyment of religious freedom rights is clear.[68] Religious discriminatory intent invariably constitutes an infringement of the fundamental right to equality based on religion, and the subsequent conduct (or its effect) ordinarily deprives those persecuted of their religious freedom rights[69] because of their membership, affiliation or identification with a specific religion or belief.[70] The *severity* of a deprivation does require further proof to establish the legal threshold. In this regard, a different intensity threshold may be applicable to each of the dimensions of religious freedom, should the persecution entail such a deprivation:

---

[65] In terms of the *ICC Elements of Crimes* (2011), General Introduction, par 4, it is unnecessary that the perpetrator personally completed a particular value judgement pertaining to the mental elements of "inhumane" or "severe".
[66] Byron *War Crimes and Crimes Against Humanity* (2009) 230.
[67] Cassese et al. *ICL: Cases and Commentary* (2011) par 622.
[68] Par 2 of the UNGA Res. *Discrimination based on Religion* (2009).
[69] Cassese et al. *ICL: Cases and Commentary* (2011) 186.
[70] Brady & Liss *Evolution of Persecution* (2014) 430.

6. A Taxonomy of Crimes Against Humanity of Religious Persecution

- The absolute character of the *forum internum* (internal dimension) of a person's religious identity implies that any coercion, limitation or derogation thereof, inevitably constitutes a *severe* deprivation of a 'fundamental' human right.
- The *forum externum* or external manifestation of religious behaviour constitutes an integral part of the fundamental character of religious freedom. However, the freedom to give direct expression to one's chosen religious identity may be subject to certain legitimately justifiable limits, based on prescribed requirements.[71] However, if the nature and effect of restrictive measures are impermissible under international law, such limitations will entail a discriminatory control mechanism regarding religious freedom, providing *prima facie* evidence of a *severe* deprivation of a fundamental human right.

Considering that one of the basic principles of international human rights is that of the dignity and equality inherent in all human beings, equality on the basis of one's religious identity clearly constitutes a 'fundamental' right.[72] Consequently, "discrimination between human beings based on grounds of religion or belief constitutes an affront to human dignity... and shall be condemned as a violation of human rights and fundamental freedoms..."[73]

In conclusion, it is clear that the right to freedom of thought, conscience, religion or belief, including the right to equality based on religious identity, has a 'fundamental character' in international human rights law.[74] Therefore, if the religious persecutory conduct or its cumulative effect results in

---

[71] See art 18 of the UDHR and art 18 of the *ICCPR*. See also UN Human Rights Committee, *General Comment No. 22: The Right to Freedom of Thought, Conscience, and Religion in terms of Article 18 of the ICCPR*. CCPR/C/21/Rev.1/Add.4, 20 July 1993. Restrictions or limitations of international human rights refer to instances where States or governments are legitimately allowed to control the enjoyment or exercise of human rights, provided such restrictions meet certain legal criteria.

[72] Equality and non-discrimination is one of the architectural principles of human rights and aligns with the concept of normative universalism, in terms of which all members of the human family are endowed with inherent dignity which entitles them to equal treatment and enjoyment of rights – Bielefeldt, H. *Misperceptions of Freedom of Religion or Belief*. Human Rights Quarterly, Volume 35, Number 1, pg 33–68. The Johns Hopkins University Press (2013), pg 50.

[73] Art 3 of the *Religious Discrimination Declaration* (1981).

[74] Par 1 of *UNHRC General Comment No. 22*.

"seriously disadvantaging" the group or a part thereof[75] on the arbitrary basis of religious identity, both prongs of the intensity threshold have been satisfied.

6.2.2 Religious persecution taxonomy checklist

Within the broader proposed taxonomy framework, this section is intended to present the taxonomy as an abbreviated 'religious persecution taxonomy checklist', based on the definitional elements. This checklist will consist of a concise breakdown of the definitional elements of 'grievous religious persecution'. It will be presented as a flowchart, posing a series of sequential polar questions with the intention of establishing whether each of the definitional requirements for crimes against humanity of religious persecution had been met, or not. It is anticipated that the checklist will accurately, yet concisely, address each identified element of the taxonomy.

---

[75] Triffterer & Ambos *Commentary on the Rome Statute* (2008) 258.

6. A Taxonomy of Crimes Against Humanity of Religious Persecution

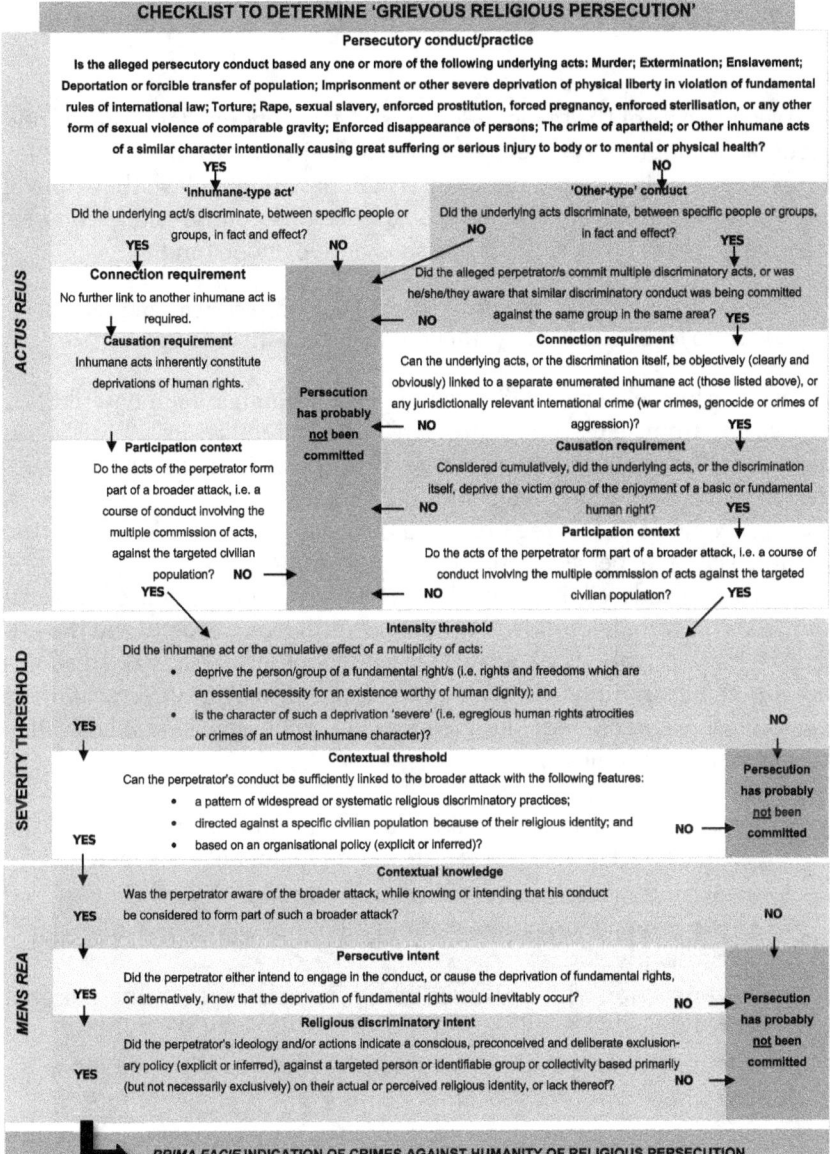

6.2.3 Defining crimes against humanity of religious persecution

The second part of the taxonomy consists of a proposed definition of religious persecution as a crime against humanity in terms of the *Rome Statute*. Despite its criminalisation under international criminal law, the crime of persecution is disadvantaged by the absence of a definitive and comprehensive definition for purposes of a substantive understanding.

> There is no universally accepted definition of 'persecution', and various attempts to formulate such a definition have met with little success.[76]

Indeed, a comprehensive definition of persecution has been described as everything from "elusive" to "protean".[77] The fateful reality of this *status quo* cannot be contested; however, as idealistic as it may seem, it is suggested that a comprehensive definition is attainable. Therefore, any positive contribution in this regard may improve the discourse regarding the criminalisation of persecution.

Having considered the general understanding of the crime of persecution, the role of religious identity based on religious freedom, and the human rights deprivations associated with religious intolerance and discrimination, the definitional elements of the crime of religious persecution or persecution based on 'religious identity' as a crime against humanity may be summarised as follows:

- The unjustifiable and deliberate infliction of an inhumane act, a course of persecutory acts or the enforcement of an ideology;
- which by its very nature, or based on its cumulative effect, resulted in the severe deprivation of one or more fundamental human rights of those targeted;
- in connection with any other inhumane acts or other international core crimes;
- committed with a conscious and preconceived discriminatory intent;

---

[76] Par 51 of the UN High Commissioner for Refugees (UNHCR), *Handbook and Guidelines on Procedures and Criteria for Determining Refugee Status under the 1951 Convention and the 1967 Protocol Relating to the Status of Refugees*, December 2011, HCR/1P/4/ENG/REV. 3.

[77] Rempell, S. *Defining Persecution*. Utah Law Review, Vol. 2013, No. 1 (2013), pg 3.

- to target an identifiable protected group or individuals belonging to such a group;
- primarily (not exclusively) based on their religious identity or lack thereof, or aimed at any irreconcilable religious identity or ideology, as contemplated by the perpetrator;
- regardless of whether the perpetrator's actions are religiously motivated or not;
- while the perpetrator/s knew or should have known that the conduct was part of, or intended the conduct to be part of, the widespread or systematic attack directed against the victim group; and
- regulated or enforced through an implied or explicit policy by a State or organisation, or under circumstances where the *de facto* authority tolerated or condoned a wide practice of atrocities.

Based on the preceding assessment, 'grievous religious persecution' may be defined as:

The deliberate and unjustifiable persecutory conduct by a persecutor based on an explicit or implied policy of conscious and intentional discrimination against a particular civilian group, primarily targeted by reason of their religious identity (irrespective of the persecutor's motive), which act or its cumulative effect, resulted in the severe deprivation of the fundamental human rights of those persecuted, is connected to any jurisdictionally relevant inhumane act or core crime, and knowingly forms part of a widespread or systematic attack.

6.3 Conclusion

The most detrimental human rights atrocities and deprivations require the international community to counteract impunity by resorting to the use of international prosecution systems in the pursuit of criminal accountability. The implementation of criminal prosecutions and punitive sanctions for religious persecution, may provide an assertive solution to curb and deter further human rights atrocities. The international legal order has confirmed 'grievous religious persecution' as a crime of international concern through its inclusion as one of the inhumane acts constituting crimes against humanity. Disconcertingly though, such a codified recognition of the 'significantly pernicious' nature of religious persecution has failed to materialise in consistent and reliable criminal prosecutions. Therefore, the aim was to clarify the legal framework for 'grievous religious persecution'.

In order to do so, this chapter built on the international criminal law framework of 'grievous persecution' established in Chapter Three. By integrating the acquired understanding of the role of religious identity into this legal framework, it was possible to systematically analyse each of the unique definitional elements of 'grievous religious persecution'. Based on this analysis it was possible to propose a comprehensive definition in the context of international criminal law. Together, these two aspects constitute a holistic and definitive conceptualisation of 'grievous religious persecution' in terms of the *Rome Statute*. In order to test its legal and practical applicability, Appendix C is dedicated to surmise the effectivity of the religious persecution checklist by applying it to factual evidence of an appropriate and contemporary case study.

The recommended conceptualisation is aimed at improving the legal semantics and discourse regarding religious persecution, hopefully addressing its substantive anomalies and lessening the judicial unease regarding its scope and application. It could be argued that the envisioned conceptualisation may provide greater legal certainty regarding the definitional elements of 'grievous religious persecution', which would strengthen the enforceability of, and resolve to pursue, international criminal prosecutions. However, depending on the nature, severity and surrounding circumstances, the enforcement of criminal prosecution measures for religious persecution may not always serve the interests of justice. Therefore, Chapter Seven considers some of the alternative responses to religious persecution.

Chapter Seven: Counteractive Responses to Religious Persecution

7.1 Introduction

Despite the fact that "religious freedom protections are well established at the international level",[1] the global prevalence of religious persecution constitutes a contemporary affront to human dignity, freedom and equality. Manifestations of intolerance, discrimination, and hostility against various communities because of their religious beliefs still prevail in many areas of the world,[2] and in particular limit people's right to freely practise their belief.[3] Accordingly, appropriate intervention measures or responses are required in order to counteract religious persecution.

Inconveniently, the persecution phenomena is based on a diversity of concurrent contextual understandings, conceptualisations and applications, including the legal and existential dimensions discussed earlier. As a result, it was discussed that a holistic view of the persecution phenomenon requires a multidimensional understanding. Consequently, an appropriate response to the persecution phenomena requires a similar holistic approach. This implies that an appropriate response to religious persecution should be conscious of a scattered spectrum of counteractive responses, the multiplicity of root causes or motives that may have triggered such occurrences, and which constitutes a suitable response in the given context.

Accordingly, this chapter will provide a non-exhaustive overview of some of the most related responses to persecution from various perspectives and stakeholders.[4] In other words, while this book advocates for the

---

[1]   Thames, K. H., Seiple, C. & Rowe, A. *International Religious Freedom Advocacy: A guide to Organizations, Law and NGO's.* Baylor University Press (2009), pg 1.

[2]   UN General Assembly, *Declaration on the Elimination of All Forms of Intolerance and of Discrimination Based on Religion or Belief*, UNGA Res 36/55, 73rd plenary meeting, 25 November 1981.

[3]   UN Report, *United Nations World Conference against Racism, Racial Discrimination, Xenophobia and Related Intolerance*, (2001), UN DocA/CONF.189/12, par 59.

[4]   The substance of this Chapter is simultaneously published in the International Journal for Religious Freedom as "Counteractive Responses to Religious Persecution: A Selective Contextualised Overview", Vol 10/1-2 (2017). Certain perspectives will not be considered, such as contributions by public and private media,

use of international prosecution mechanisms before the ICC in pursuit of criminal accountability for 'grievous religious persecution', it should be considered that other responses may be more appropriate in certain circumstances. In the discussion that follows, a broad perspective of the following will be considered: the response from the perspective of the religious community, a governmental response; and international humanitarian responses, including: religious freedom advocacy and human rights mechanisms.

In closing, this chapter will consider certain aspects related to international criminal prosecutions as a response to 'grievous religious persecution'. In this regard, the suitability of this response will be briefly assessed and certain legality concerns regarding a charge of persecution in the light of the legality principle will be deliberated. Finally, considering that religious persecution may be instigated by State or non-State actors, certain legal liability options are considered.

7.2 The Notion of Responses to Religious Persecution

An appropriate response, intended to deter, intervene and address incidents of religious persecution, is essential.[5] However, at the outset it seems fitting to observe that 'prevention is better than cure'. Thus, although adequate responses to persecution may remedy a certain situation; addressing the origins of such discriminatory mindsets is the only way in which to prevent reoccurrences:

> [P]ersecutions and such discrimination constitute a total disregard of the most elementary humanitarian principles and... give rise to serious and complex social problems requiring urgent remedies, which remedies will, needless to say, be entirely without effect unless the evil is attacked at its root.[6]

---

the role of neutral and pluralistic public and school education, and the appropriate response from civil society organisations.

[5] Bielefeldt, H. *Freedom of Religion or Belief: Thematic Reports of the UN Special Rapporteur 2010 - 2016.* Religious Freedom Series of the International Institute for Religious Freedom, Vol 3, 2nd edition, Bonn (2017), pg 209.

[6] UN General Assembly, *General committee: Resolution on persecution and discrimination: Request for the inclusion of an additional item in the agenda / from the delegation for Egypt.* A/BUR/51, 11 November 1946.

Manifestations of religious hatred, discrimination and religious persecution are not natural phenomena but are caused by human action and/or omission.[7] Consequently, humanity itself has the ability, and the shared responsibility, to address such manifestations. The full realisation of basic human rights requires that effective preventative measures be developed at the national, regional and global levels, in order to deter such manifestations. States and other stakeholders, including political- religious- and community leaders may prove to be the pivot around which the successful implementation of policies and counter-narratives intended to respond to manifestations of religious intolerance, hinges.[8] As a starting point, States are required to: (1) respect all human beings as holders of profound, identity-shaping convictions; (2) commit to an ideology of respectful non-identification in issues of religion; and (3) operate as a trustworthy guarantor of religious freedom for everyone.[9]

Even so, an appropriate response requires the effective cooperation of all relevant role-players, including: governments and its representatives, religious communities, civil society organisations, the media and other relevant stakeholders.[10] Coping strategies must present a fitting response through diplomatic, judicial and even combative measures. However, it should be borne in mind that even in extreme situations affecting national security, measures deemed necessary and that effectually restrict religious freedom, must comply with all the criteria laid down in respective international human rights instruments.[11]

A suitable entry point for the discussion on adequate responses to religious intolerance and persecution is to incorporate the *Rabat Plan of Action*.[12] This programme is the culmination of a series of regional expert workshops concerning the prohibition of advocacy of national, racial or religious hatred that constitutes incitement to real acts of discrimination, hostility or violence.[13] The main aim was to conduct a comprehensive assessment of the implementation of effective strategic responses to incite-

---

[7] Bielefeldt *FORB: Thematic Reports* (2017) 214.
[8] Bielefeldt *FORB: Thematic Reports* (2017) 215.
[9] Bielefeldt *FORB: Thematic Reports* (2017) 215.
[10] Bielefeldt *FORB: Thematic Reports* (2017) 275.
[11] Most notably, Art 18 of the UN General Assembly, *International Covenant on Civil and Political Rights*, 16 December 1966.
[12] Office of the UN High Commissioner for Human Rights: *Rabat Plan of Action on the prohibition of advocacy of national, racial or religious hatred that constitutes incitement to discrimination, hostility or violence*. Adopted on 5 October 2012 in Rabat, Morocco.
[13] Par 1 and 2 of the *Rabat Plan of Action*.

ment to hatred, both non-legal and legal in nature. Consequently, the intersectionality between freedom of expression and hate speech, especially in relation to religious issues, was a core motivation of the expert panel.[14] Although a comprehensive discussion of the outcomes of the *Rabat Plan of Action* fall outside the scope of this book, some of the conclusions and recommendations in the area of legislation, judicial infrastructure, and policy, may facilitate more effective and appropriate responses to religious discrimination and persecution. Therefore, some of these relevant responses has been incorporated into the discussion below.

7.3 Response from the Perspective of the Religious Community

From an anthropological view, the perspectives on, and consequent responses to, persecution, may differ from religion to religion, as well as in terms of temporal and territorial suitability. In-depth discussions of these various possible responses to persecution are too broad to consider fully. Instead, the religious communities' response to religious discrimination and persecution will be considered from internal and external perspectives. The internal perspective will consider the appropriate reaction by a religious community in whose name hostility, violence and persecution occur. The external perspective refers to the reaction to religious persecution by a persecuted religious community.

7.3.1 Internal response to persecution in the name of religion

An appropriate internal or introspective response from those religious groups in whose name religious persecution is being committed is very important. Arguably, the most important function of responding to persecution in this context is to distance the religion itself from such manifestations.[15] As Bielefeldt observes:

---

[14] Par 2 of the *Rabat Plan of Action*.
[15] Other appropriate responses, considering the gravity of such situations, could include immediate and public condemnation combined with, *inter alia*: allowing international and transboundary cooperation and investigation, considering the establishment of an *ad hoc* court or tribunals, referring the matter to the ICC in order to bring such perpetrators to justice, and requesting or allowing humanitarian intervention by the UN Security Council or responsive States where such situations have grown beyond the control of the *de facto* authority.

Perpetrators of violence typically represent comparatively small segments of the various religious communities to which they belong, while the large majority of believers are usually appalled to see violence perpetrated in the name of their religion. It is all the more important for the majorities and their leaders, who do not endorse the violence, to speak out against it.[16]

Religious distancing can only occur when the associated religious group "visibly and audibly reject advocacy of religious hatred that constitutes incitement to discrimination, hostility or violence [which] can have very practical effects in discouraging such advocacy, while at the same time showing solidarity and support for their targets".[17] In this regard, religiously motivated extremism is a prime example.

Although religious extremism is based on radical or fundamentalist interpretations of religious texts and teachings, religious persecution and other acts of terror cannot and should not be considered to be representative of a religious community as a whole.[18] Such a sentiment is specifically aimed at preventing interreligious or intra-religious retaliation, by separating the human rights abuses from their claimed religious affiliation. In considering that the actions of a religious extremist group do not speak on behalf of a religion,[19] a distinction is made between the extreme or fundamentalist interpretation of the terror group versus the nature of the religion in whose name they justify their actions. In the hearts and minds of those affected, the ideology of such a religious extremist group is impulsively associated with the religious foundation of the associated religion, resulting in negative stereotyping, hatred, hostility and reprisal, especially in other areas of the world where the associated religion constitutes a minority. In any instance, religious and community leaders must be ethically

---

[16] Bielefeldt *FORB: Thematic Reports* (2017) 267.

[17] Bielefeldt *FORB: Thematic Reports* (2017) 213.

[18] UN Security Council, *Security Council resolution 2170 (2014) [on threats to international peace and security caused by terrorist acts by Al-Qaida]*, 15 August 2014. However, it should be noted that there are some who maintain that it cannot be excluded that violence and hatred are core choices innate to the origins and development of some belief systems. They therefore reject as idealistic and wishful thinking a neat differentiation of extremist ideology and the supposed 'real nature' of a religion. Nonetheless, this does not detract from the need to prevent escalation and stereotyping.

[19] Statement by former President Barack Obama, Martha's Vineyard, Massachusetts on 20 August 2014. However, it is not a law of nature that the 'silent majority' is always against the persecutory acts of extremists. They could also be silently or publically applauding the acts of extremists while they themselves live peaceful lives. They may even provide financial support.

conscious and socially responsible, by: (1) refraining from using messages of intolerance or expressions which may incite violence, hostility or discrimination;[20] (2) strongly condemning such hatred and violence; and (3) distancing their beliefs and religious ideologies from such atrocities.[21]

Furthermore, the teaching of radical or fundamentalist ideology by religious leaders may hamper dialogue between and within religions, which may result in radical or extremist ideological interpretations. Unfortunately, radical and fundamentalist ideologies in the name of religion will continue as long as religious clerics and leaders publicly indoctrinate a radical literalist interpretation of an associated religion. For example, in countries like Saudi Arabia, Qatar and Turkey, such teachings is associated with Islam and results in extremist incitement to intolerance and hostility against dissenting religious groups.[22] To reiterate, it is the moral obligation of the majority not to remain silent.

7.3.2 External response to persecution from the religious victim groups perspective

From a broader sociological perspective, the experience of religious groups may differ greatly based on the nature and severity of religious persecution. Religious groups that are subjected to severe religious persecution, experience a relentless assault on their human dignity, equality, and basic freedoms.[23] Such persecuted communities either *remain* living in fear and *endure* such oppression and suffering, or they *flee* their homes as refugees in order to escape. In contrast, religious groups that are subjected to 'subsidiary forms' of persecution,[24] may have more response options available to them. Nevertheless, they suffer religious intolerance, threat of harm, and fear.

---

[20] Par 24 of the *Rabat Plan of Action*.
[21] Par 23 and 24 of the *Rabat Plan of Action*.
[22] Sookhdeo, P. *Editorial: The Two Faces of Islam*. (2014). Available at: https://barnabasfund.org/news/Editorial-The-Two-Faces-of-Islam. Accessed 09/02/2015.
[23] Par 2 of the UN Office of the High Commissioner for Human Rights (OHCHR), *Report of the Independent International Commission of Inquiry on the Syrian Arab Republic (IICISAR). Rule of Terror: Living under ISIS in Syria*, 14 November 2014.
[24] It should be made clear that using the phrase 'subsidiary forms of persecution' should in no way be construed as to diminish the harm associated with forms of persecution that may not satisfy the intensity threshold for 'grievous persecution'. The writer remains conscious of not depreciating the damaging physical and psychological effects such acts may have on individuals or communities.

Religious groups will differ in their response to religious discrimination and persecution, depending on their theological or ideological doctrine. However, for the sake of brevity, this book will be limited to a Christianity-based response to persecution, which should not be construed as a parochial choice or favouritism. Two important aspects affected this choice. In the first place, some estimate that nearly one-third of the world's population are Christians,[25] constituting the largest and most internationally widespread religious movement. In the second place, findings suggest that Christians have consistently endured the most religiously motivated harassment of any religious group.[26] In other words, the focus is justified because of the supposition that "Christians suffer the denial of religious freedom and heavy discrimination more than the members of any other religion".[27] Consequently, it may prove useful to briefly outline some observations about Christian responses to persecution:[28]

- The persecuted Christian community's response to persecution is based on their theology of suffering, church, and culture, which is cultivated by an expectation of persecution and a determination to rejoice in suffering. Such measures include intercession, prayer and solidarity.
- Christian communities most commonly adopt survival strategies, such as going underground, flight, and behavioural respect for repressive regimes. These strategies are the least proactive form of

---

[25] See Johnson, T. M. & Zurlo, G. A. (Eds.). *World Christian Database*. Leiden/Boston: Brill (2018).

[26] When assessed as per the number of countries in which each group is affected by restrictions of religious freedom and social hostilities – Pew Research Center. *Global Uptick in Government Restrictions on Religion in 2016*. (2018). Available at: https://www.pewforum.org/2018/06/21/global-uptick-in-government-restrictions-on-religion-in-2016/. Accessed 15/07/2018.

[27] Philpott, D. & Shah, T.S. (editors). *Under Caesar's Sword: How Christians Respond to Persecution*. Cambridge Studies in Law and Christianity. Cambridge University Press (2018), pg 4. See Pew Research Center. *Trends in Global Restrictions on Religion*. (2016), pg 20. Available at: https://www.pewforum.org/2016/06/23/trends-in-global-restrictions-on-religion/. Accessed 23/07/2016.

[28] University of Notre Dame – Under Caesar's Sword: Christian Response to Persecution. *In Response to Persecution: Findings of the Under Caesar's Sword Project on Global Christian Communities*, 20 April 2017. Available at: http://ucs.nd.edu/report/. Accessed 19/02/2018. Executive summary, pg 5, with an in-depth explanation of these findings from pg 34–44. See also Boyd-MacMillan *Faith That Endures. The essential guide to the persecuted church*. Lancaster: Sovereign World. (2008), pg 254–283.

opposition to persecution, and often involve creativity, determination, and courage.
- Strategies of association with sympathisers are the second most common response. In this regard, Christian communities seek to strengthen their resilience and secure their religious freedom by developing ties with other actors, including other Christian denominations or communities, non-Christian religions, and secular figures.
- Strategies of confrontation are the least common response and if used, are usually non-violent and, with very few exceptions, do not involve acts of extremism or terrorism. Rather, confrontation strategies serve to bear witness to the faith, expose (publicises) and end injustice, mobilise others to oppose injustice, and engage positively with the aim of replacing oppression with religious pluralism. In relatively open political systems, confrontation may take the form of legal intervention, even in countries where the rule of law has failed. Boyd-MacMillan suggests that there are three useful effects of taking the legal route: (1) it provides critical testimony for the exertion of political pressure from outside the country (although political pressure may also be achieved through other advocacy efforts), (2) the 'embarrassment effect' of ousting a State's lack of international commitment to the rule of law and human rights, rendering that State vulnerable to foreign criticism and the possibility of other political or economic consequences, and (3) an empowering effect for those persecuted that stand up for themselves. Other forms of confrontation include resistance from, or assistance to, the persecuted community, which involves methods that contravene legal norms and rules, such as smuggling Bibles to oppressed or 'underground' churches.
- Strategies adopted by persecuted Christian communities may also show intra-denominational differences. Protestant Evangelical and Pentecostal Christians are more likely to be persecuted. They are more likely to engage in strategies of survival or, on rare occasions, confrontation, and less likely to engage in strategies of association. On the other hand, mainline Protestants, Catholics, Orthodox Christians, or other Christians associated with ancient churches are less likely to be persecuted. In response to persecution, they are more likely to respond through strategies of association.

- The intensity or severity of persecution and the level of commitment by adherents only partly explains Christians' responses, implying that the level and type of persecution that Christian communities face do shape, enable, and constrain their responses.

Although some of the mentioned strategies of response have produced tangible results worthy of emulation, it should be remembered that the effectivity of each of these strategies is temporally, territorially and contextually sensitive. Often, the most effective approaches is considerate of the particular circumstance, the interests of the target society, and the persecuted community's theology regarding persecution.

7.4 Governmental Responses in Line with Human Rights Obligations

A governmental response to religious persecution include a wide spectrum of reactions through different branches of authority (judicial, executive and administrative) exercised on various levels, including international. These possible responses depend on seemingly endless factors, ranging from politics and policy, to law and religion. In terms of the focus this book, a governmental response should be in line with human rights obligations and responsibilities under national, regional and international law. In this regard, international human rights law has developed a comprehensive legal system that recognizes, protects and promotes fundamental human rights, especially religious freedom (which is discussed in detail in Appendix B).

Religious freedom forms part of the *genus* of civil and political rights that is at the core of human rights and was among the first to be recognized and codified as a fundamental human freedom.[29] Religious freedom is part of customary international law,[30] implying that such principles and values are binding upon all States regardless of formal recognition.[31] The

---

[29] Walter, C. *Religion or Belief, Freedom of, International Protection. Max Planck Encyclopedia on Public International law.* Wolfrum, R. (Ed.). Heidelberg: Oxford University Press (2009), pg 864.
[30] Par 8 of the UN Human Rights Committee, *General Comment No. 24: Issues relating to reservations made upon ratification or accession to the Covenant or the Optional Protocols thereto, or in relation to declarations under article 41 of the Covenant,* 12 May 2004, HRI/GEN/1/Rev.7.
[31] Sepúlveda, M. et al, *Human Rights Reference book.* University for Peace Publisher (2004), pg 23.

significance of religious freedom means that its recognition and protection is vital at domestic, regional and global levels.

> ...[F]reedom of thought, conscience and religion is one of the foundations of a 'democratic society'... [and as such is] one of the most vital elements that go to make up the identity of believers and their conception of life, but it is also a precious asset for atheists, agnostics, sceptics and the unconcerned. The pluralism indissociable from a democratic society, which has been dearly won over the centuries, depends on it.[32]

Consequently, religious freedom is an inherent right of all persons, which places upon States certain responsibilities regarding its protection. Generally, States have the duty to take effective measures to protect and promote religious freedom, equality and tolerance, and to prevent and eliminate discrimination on the grounds of religion or belief.[33] The scope of protection and legal obligations of States in this regard is extensive.[34] Consequently, based on the core international documents regarding religious freedom,[35] the following basic principles are applicable:[36]

1. Respect or recognize the normative status of fundamental human rights of all people, including religious freedom, which applies similarly to States and non-state actors as potential perpetrators;
2. Prevent and protect, on an equal basis, all of its population, whether nationals or not, against infringements of human rights, including religious freedom;

---

[32] Council of Europe, *Freedom of thought, conscience and religion: A guide to the implementation of Article 9 of the European Convention on Human Rights*, June 2007, Human rights handbooks, No. 9, pg 12.

[33] See UN General Assembly, *Resolution 103(I) Persecution and Discrimination*, 19 November 1946; Arts 2 and 7 of the *UDHR*, and Arts 2 and 3 of the *ICCPR*.

[34] For a more comprehensive analysis of State's obligations in relation to the right to freedom of religion or belief, see Bielefeldt, H., Ghanea, N. & Wiener, M. *Freedom of Religion or Belief: An International Law Commentary*. Oxford University Press (2016), pg 33 – 38, and also pg 8 of the *Rabat Plan of Action* regarding recommendations to States.

[35] The core international documents regarding religious freedom include: Art 18 of the *Universal Declaration of Human Rights* (UDHR); Art 18 of the *International Covenant on Civil and Political Rights* of 1966; the UN Human Rights Committee, *General Comment No. 22: The Right to Freedom of Thought, Conscience, and Religion in terms of Article 18 of the ICCPR*; the *Declaration on the Elimination of All Forms of Intolerance and of Discrimination Based on Religion or Belief of 1981* (Religious Discrimination Declaration); and the various reports of the UN Special Rapporteur on freedom of religion or belief.

[36] See also Bielefeldt *et al*. *FORB: An International Law Commentary* (2016) 33.

3. Enact constitutional and legislative reforms that bring domestic law in line with international law and, if applicable, regional human rights obligations;
4. Obligations on all spheres of government and at different levels to take all appropriate measures in compliance with their international obligations and with due regard to their respective legal systems to, *inter alia*:
   - Refrain from discriminatory practices or policies, whether they amount to formally prescribed (*de jure*) or actual (*de facto*) discrimination;[37]
   - Commit to a deliberate ideology of impartiality or 'respectful non-identification' in relation to all religions or beliefs in order to be equally fair, open and inclusive to all people living on the State's territory;[38]
   - Implement a consistent policy of non-discrimination that prohibits and condemns any discrimination on the grounds of religion or other beliefs as a serious violation of a fundamental human right;
   - Prevent and eliminate discrimination on the grounds of religion or belief in the recognition, exercise and enjoyment of human rights and fundamental freedoms, which again applies similarly to non-state actors as potential perpetrators;
   - Promote and encourage, through legislative, judicial, administrative, educative and other means, understanding, tolerance and respect in all matters relating to religious freedom in order to cultivate a general climate of societal openness and acceptance in which all citizens can actually enjoy their human rights;
   - Condemn any advocacy of religious intolerance or hatred that constitutes incitement to discrimination, hostility or violence;
   - Refrain from inciting violent stereotypes, discrimination and persecution, both nationally and in other countries;
   - Guarantee equality and effective protection before the law and in legal proceedings, including effective remedies for victims of

---

[37] *De jure* discrimination refers to discrimination enshrined in laws, while *de facto* discrimination results from the effect of laws, policies, and practices – Bielefeldt et al. *FORB: An International Law Commentary* (2016) 316.

[38] Bielefeldt, H. *Misperceptions of Freedom of Religion or Belief*. Human Rights Quarterly, Volume 35, Number 1, pp. 33-68 (Article). Johns Hopkins University Press (2013), pg 53.

discrimination at national, regional and international levels; and
- Exercise its criminal jurisdiction over those responsible for serious forms of religious discrimination and persecution, and if such infringements amount to international crimes, to apply the principle of *aut dedere aut judicare* (duty to extradite or prosecute) in regard to such persons.[39]

In the context of religious persecution, States are responsible to ensure that a culture of impunity does not exist within their territory. Participants who commit or who are complicit in acts of violence and persecution on the basis of religion must be brought to justice.[40] In this regard, States should consider enacting a penal code of international crimes, including crimes against humanity of religious persecution, into national law.[41]

7.5 International Humanitarian Responses

A decline in the territorial autonomy of States, and the increased awareness that mass atrocity crimes and gross human rights deprivations do not fall within the internal or exclusive affairs of States, constitute a significant and progressive development in international human rights politics and law.[42] Consequently, respect for, and protection and promotion of, human rights by States has become a matter of international concern.[43] Furthermore, following the transition from a State-centric approach to an individualistic approach, the recognition, protection and enforcement of human rights filtered into international criminal law.[44] As a result, the international community has created a number of appropriate responses to take direct action to stop *severe* human rights violations and provide early warning of developing human rights concerns, including violations and abuses of religious freedom.[45] These responses, which will be referred to as 'humanitarian responses to persecution', relate to actions or reactions aimed at saving human lives and the mitigation of human suffering, and

---

[39] See Bassiouni, M. C. & Wise, E.M. *Aut Dedere Aut Judicare. The Duty to Extradite or Prosecute in International Law.* Marthinus Nijhoff Publishers (1995).
[40] Bielefeldt *FORB: Thematic Reports* (2017) 275.
[41] For example, *Germany: Act to Introduce the Code of Crimes Against International Law* [Germany], 26 June 2002, Sec 7(10).
[42] Bielefeldt *FORB: Thematic Reports* (2017) 359.
[43] Bielefeldt *FORB: Thematic Reports* (2017) 360.
[44] Thames *et al. International Religious Freedom Advocacy* (2009) 7.
[45] Bielefeldt *FORB: Thematic Reports* (2017) 360.

include, *inter alia*: assistance to persecuted communities through humanitarian aid; asylum and refugee protection; and traditional international humanitarian law responses, including the use of force against acts or threats of aggression, self-determination, and humanitarian intervention.[46] Hereafter, religious freedom advocacy and human rights mechanisms will be considered as a specific humanitarian response.

7.5.1   Religious freedom advocacy

Considering the fundamental influence that religious freedom has in shaping a person's sense of belonging, identity, conception of life, and engagement with society, deprivations or impermissible restrictions of religious freedom transcend regular categories of harm.[47] Consequently, religious pluralism and religious freedom continuously depend on advocates and human rights defenders to ensure its normative development and protection.[48] Therefore, advocating for those persecuted on the basis of their religious identity are best assessed with an eye towards human rights protection. Such religious freedom advocacy efforts may take many forms and avenues, whether judicial, political or administrative. Unfortunately, a detailed discussion in this regard falls outside the scope of this book, and will be limited the observations below.[49]

Human rights defenders come in various forms, and serve as "indispensable counterparts to States in advancing freedom of religion or belief".[50] The term 'human rights defenders' generally refers to those persons who, individually or with others, act to promote or protect human rights through various efforts.[51] In relation hereto, some human rights defenders are specifically engaged in advocating on behalf of the religiously persecuted or simply in religious freedom advocacy.[52]

---

[46] Chapter VII of the *Charter of the United Nations*, 24 October 1945, 1 UNTS XVI.
[47] Rempell, S. *Defining Persecution*. Utah Law Review, Vol. 2013, No. 1 (2013), pg 24.
[48] Bielefeldt et al. *FORB: An International Law Commentary* (2016) 581.
[49] For a detailed discussion see Thames et al. *International Religious Freedom Advocacy* (2009) and Bielefeldt et al. *FORB: An International Law Commentary* (2016) 581–592.
[50] Bielefeldt et al. *FORB: An International Law Commentary* (2016) 582.
[51] Bielefeldt et al. *FORB: An International Law Commentary* (2016) 588.
[52] In this regard, the activities of the UN Human Rights Council's 'Special Rapporteur on the situation of human rights defenders' is not exclusively related to religious freedom, however its mandate often intersects with the work of the Special Rapporteur on freedom of religion or belief and human rights defenders working in this area, prompting regular cooperation – Bielefeldt et al. *FORB: An International Law Commentary* (2016) 584.

In a general sense, religious freedom advocacy refers to the efforts of all those individuals, institutions and even governments, operating at the international, regional, national, and local levels, tirelessly confronting oppression, discrimination and persecution on behalf of those persecuted for their religious identities.[53]

In a more formal sense,[54] religious freedom advocacy implies using certain official measures in order to act as a catalyst for change.[55] Such measures may include, *inter alia*: make use of legal protections and remedies in the domestic arena; petitioning and leveraging those who wield political influence regarding policy matters, whether governmental authorities, political leaders or international officials; collaborating with non-governmental organisations (NGOs), international institutions, and other concerned groups committed to religious freedom;[56] utilising individual human rights complaints measures at a regional and/or international level; and researching and reporting on compliance to monitoring bodies.[57] In such endeavours it is imperative that when advocating for policies that impact on religious freedom, such proposals must, *inter alia*, strive for universal religious pluralism, and appropriately prevent, and react to, incidents of religious discrimination and persecution.[58]

---

[53] For example through disseminating information, complaining or submitting proposals, and organising peaceful protests.

[54] As provided for in the UN General Assembly, *Declaration on the Right and Responsibility of Individuals, Groups and Organs of Society to Promote and Protect Universally Recognized Human Rights and Fundamental Freedoms : resolution / adopted by the General Assembly.* A/RES/53/144, 8 March 1999.

[55] Thames *et al. International Religious Freedom Advocacy* (2009) 5.

[56] Thames *et al. International Religious Freedom Advocacy* (2009) 4.

[57] Such monitoring bodies may include special oversight agencies or commissions, rapporteurs, ombudsmen, and even research centres. The efforts of such monitoring bodies may include systematic examination of countries or issues of serious concern for religious freedom, track governmental compliance to human rights obligations and issue reports, respond and raise concern regarding governmental violations, and provide education, awareness and dissemination of academic or public publications on human rights concerns or issues – Thames *et al. International Religious Freedom Advocacy* (2009) 3.

[58] Other aims include: building public trust, imparting an atmosphere of inclusiveness, and, furthering public discourse, freedom of speech, debate and critical thought on issues of religion or belief.

7.5.2 Human rights mechanisms

In terms of regional and international human rights instruments, complaint recourse mechanisms offer judicial recourse through international courts or quasi-judicial review systems, in pursuit of justice for the victims of human rights deprivations.[59] As a general course of action, a matter should only be escalated to a regional or international level if the situation is life-threatening, if the right to judicial remedies in the national legal system have been exhausted, or if domestic legal recourse has proven to be unsuitable in providing a proper response.[60] Similarly, international control mechanisms must be viewed as a last resort, should regional systems prove inadequate or if the country of concern fails in its legal duties.

At the international and regional level, there are various international human rights mechanisms, which deal, *inter alia*, with issues related to freedom of religion or belief.[61] Under the UN system, there are three main procedures for bringing complaints of violations of the provisions of the human rights treaties before such human rights treaty bodies: (1) individual complaints, (2) inter-State complaints, and (3) inquiries upon receipt of reliable information on serious, grave or systematic violations by a State party of the conventions the treaty body monitors.[62]

Furthermore, within the scope of the UN's Special Procedure mechanisms, the Human Rights Council mandate independent human rights experts to report and advise on human rights aspects from a thematic or country-specific perspective.[63] Religious freedom is one of the identified

---

[59] Thames *et al. International Religious Freedom Advocacy* (2009) 4.
[60] Thames *et al. International Religious Freedom Advocacy* (2009) 5.
[61] For a detailed discussion regarding these mechanisms, see Bielefeldt *et al. FORB: An International Law Commentary* (2016) 41–51.
[62] OHCHR website: http://www.ohchr.org/EN/HRBodies/TBPetitions/Pages/HRTBPetitions.aspx. Accessed 16/02/2018. The functions of two of the established committees are directly engaged with control recourse mechanisms regarding deprivations of religion freedom, and the elimination of religious discrimination. The *International Convention on the Elimination of All Forms of Racial Discrimination, the Committee on the Elimination of Racial Discrimination* (CERD) may consider individual petitions, inter-State complaints, or conduct inquiries regarding alleged infringements. Similar mechanisms are provided for in terms of the ICCPR, affording the *Committee on Economic, Social and Cultural Rights* (CESCR) the capacity to consider complaints regarding infringements of any of the relevant rights, including the right to freedom of thought, conscience, religion or belief.
[63] For more information visit the website of the UN Office of the High Commissioner for Human Rights (OHCHR) / Human Rights Bodies / Special Procedures:

themes. In this regard, the Special Rapporteur on freedom of religion or belief is an independent expert acting in his personal capacity without financial remuneration. In principle, the Special Rapporteur is mandated "to identify existing and emerging obstacles to the enjoyment of the right to freedom of religion or belief and present recommendations on ways and means to overcome such obstacles".[64]

7.6 International Criminal Prosecutions as a Response to 'Grievous Religious Persecution'

7.6.1 The suitability of international criminal prosecutions

In the context of religious persecution that result in *severe* human rights deprivations, the responses outlined above may be inadequate or insufficient to properly address injustice and impunity. In such instances, those who commit or are complicit in *'grievous religious persecution'*,[65] must be brought to justice.[66] The international community view such gross human rights violations as a global concern, justifying direct criminal intervention in some instances. In this regard, it was discussed that 'grievous religious persecution' is naturally positioned between the legal recognition, enforcement and protection of fundamental human rights in terms of international human rights law, and the suppression and punishment, under international criminal law, of individuals responsible for, *inter alia*, the commission of mass discriminatory crimes that result in severe deprivations of such fundamental values. The idea of humanity as the foundation

---

https://www.ohchr.org/en/hrbodies/sp/pages/welcomepage.aspx. Accessed 28/01/2019.

[64] Schirrmacher, T. *The United Nations Special Rapporteur on Freedom of Religion or Belief: An introduction to the role and the person* (2011) in Bielefeldt *FORB: Thematic Reports* (2017) 17. For a detailed analysis of this mandate, see the doctoral research by Michael Weiner – Wiener, M. *The Mandate of the Special Rapporteur on Freedom of Religion or Belief - Institutional, Procedural and Substantive Legal Issues*. Religion and Human Rights – An International Journal, Issue 1-2, Volume 2, Marthinus Nijhoff Publishers (2007), pg 3–17.

[65] 'Grievous religious persecution' is a term coined by the writer to refer to situations that satisfy the intensity threshold for crimes against humanity of religious persecution in terms of the *Rome Statute of the International Criminal Court*, Doc. A/CONF.183/9 of 17 July 1998 *in force* 1 July 2002 (2002)(*Rome Statute*). It serves to distinguish such extreme forms of persecution from other 'subsidiary' forms of persecution.

[66] Bielefeldt *FORB: Thematic Reports* (2017) 275.

7. Counteractive Responses to Religious Persecution

for human rights protection and of international criminal law is particularly influential on persecution, and developed the notion that persecution attacks, more directly than any other crime against humanity, the core aspects of humanity.[67] In essence, religious persecution attacks two fundamental features of 'humanness',[68] namely: the persecuted victim's individuality, and his/her ability to freely choose a religious identity, and in terms thereof, associate with others.[69]

However, despite the internationalised concern for 'grievous religious persecution', international courts and tribunals cannot prosecute all persons suspected of having perpetrated such crimes. In order to fully realise the utilisation of criminal prosecution mechanisms, the primary responsibility belong to the national legal order.

National prosecutions of international crimes are often preferable to international prosecution, for various political, sociological and practical reasons. National prosecutions is more directly grounded in justice for the affected people and circumvent the legitimacy concerns of the international law and the political pitfalls of international relations. Unfortunately, in many cases, it is the Government itself, through State organs or Government officials, who commit or participate, at least tacitly, in the commission of persecution and is effectively above national law.[70] In such instances the relevant national legal system may not be willing or in the position to properly prosecute mass atrocities or severe human rights deprivations.[71] Without the internationalisation of human rights protection in such cases, victims would remain unprotected and impunity would prevail. Accordingly, where national prosecutions fail to provide an effective and unprejudiced remedy, international prosecution systems are to be resorted to in the pursuit of criminal accountability for the protection of fundamental human rights and the punishment for 'grievous religious persecution'.[72]

---

[67] Brady, H. & Liss, R. *The Evolution of Persecution as a Crime Against Humanity*, in Historical Origins of International Criminal Law: Volume 3, Bergsmo, M. et al (eds). Torkel Opsahl Academic EPublisher, Brussels (2014), pg 430.

[68] Brady & Liss *Evolution of Persecution* (2014) 554.

[69] Luban, D. *A Theory of Crimes Against Humanity*. YJIL, Vol. 29 (2004), pg 116–117.

[70] Chertoff, E. *Prosecuting Gender-Based Persecution: The Islamic State at the ICC*. The Yale Law Journal (2017), pg 1066.

[71] Triffterer, O. & Ambos, K. *Commentary on the Rome Statute of the International Criminal Court: Observers' Notes, Article by Article*. Beck Publishers, second edition (2008), pg 24.

[72] Van Boven, T. *Racial and Religious Discrimination*. Max Planck Encyclopedia on Public International law. Wolfrum, R. (Ed.). Heidelberg: Oxford University Press (2009), par 22.

Although various human rights conventions explicitly authorise criminal prosecution for related violations,[73] individual criminal responsibility for international crimes remain a mechanism of last resort. However, in some instances, States choose to deal with crimes committed during a war or civil turmoil by seemingly opting for peace to the exclusion of justice. Such 'alternatives' to criminal prosecutions often include the granting of amnesties[74] and/or the establishment of Truth and Reconciliation Commissions.[75] While both alternatives might be an effective tool in the process of national reconciliation, both allow for immunity in law from criminal responsibility for gross human rights abuses. It is doubtful that utilising such alternatives exclusively can ever produce a lasting and meaningful peace,[76] especially in the context of ethnic, religious or political discrimination and persecution. Therefore, it is argued that "Peace and Justice go hand-in-hand".[77] In societies transforming themselves after a period of pervasive human rights abuses, the restoration of peaceful relations and national reconciliation can only truly be achieved by balancing the legal accountability of perpetrators with non-judicial mechanisms aimed at contributing to a sense of truth and justice, essential in the healing process of victims and witnesses.

Thus, in relation to occurrences of grievous religious persecution, international criminal prosecutions speaks to the right to judicial remedies

---

[73] In the context of religious persecution, see Par 9(b) of the UN General Assembly, *Elimination of all forms of intolerance and of discrimination based on religion or belief: resolution / adopted by the General Assembly*, 16 March 2009, A/RES/63/181.

[74] Amnesty laws have been defined as a "sovereign act of forgiveness for past offences" – Micaela Frulli, M. *Amnesty*. In Cassese, A. (Ed) *The Oxford Companion to International Criminal Justice*. Oxford University Press (2009), pg 243. Blanket amnesties are, at least 'in general', considered impermissible in international law for serious international crimes or gross human rights atrocities. Consequently, domestic amnesties do not prevent prosecution before international criminal courts or ad hoc tribunals.

[75] Truth and Reconciliation Commissions provides a forum where perpetrators are encouraged, through the incentive of immunity, to disclose the whole truth about their misdeeds, which the victims of repression seek so desperately – *Azanian People's Organization (AZAPO) and Others v President of the Republic of South Africa* (1996) 4 SA 562 (CC), par 17.

[76] Zgonec-Rožej, M. (Principal author). *International Criminal Law Manual*. International Bar Association (IBA) (2013), pg 357.

[77] Antonio Cassese, former President of the International Criminal Tribunal for the former Yugoslavia in November 1995, upon the conclusion of the Dayton Peace Agreement.

7. Counteractive Responses to Religious Persecution

for breaches of human rights[78] in order to: fight impunity and establish accountability for those most responsible for international crimes; render justice to the victims and give them a voice; deter further crimes;[79] and protect and encourage respect for fundamental human rights.[80] Thus, in relation to occurrences of 'grievous religious persecution', international criminal prosecution mechanisms constitute a justifiable and appropriate response to address severe and discriminatory deprivations of fundamental human rights, and may be complemented by other non-judicial measures intended to promote reconciliation and sustainable peace.

Unfortunately, international prosecutorial mechanisms are a legal and political minefield. As a result, the ultimate failure of the current system is a lack of resolve in addressing emerging patterns of human rights atrocities. In this regard, it is argued that the proposed conceptualisation in Chapter Six addresses the substantive ambiguities, which in turn, speak to such deficiencies. In addition, such an understanding will also make it possible to argue that 'grievous persecution' satisfies the 'fair warning' requirement in terms of the legality principle.

7.6.2 The principle of legality and a charge of persecution

The principle of legality, also known as *nullum crimen, nulla poena sine lege* ('no crime, no penalty without law'), is a fundamental concept which prescribes criteria for the legitimate application of criminal law.[81] The principle of legality requires that the type of conduct forming the basis of the charge must be recognised as a crime by the relevant legal order at the time of its commission, in order to hold a person criminally liable. The principle of legality imposes the following strict requirements:[82]

---

[78] Art 8 of the *UDHR*; Arts 2(3), 9(5) & 14(6) of the *ICCPR*; and Art 2(1) if the *ICESCR*.
[79] Zgonec-Rožej *International Criminal Law Manual* (2013) 77. Other aims include: to restore and maintain peace and security; to help in the process of reconciliation and peace-building; to provide for a historical record of events and crimes; to strengthen the rule of law; and to assist in reforming or setting up national judiciaries.
[80] Shelton, D. *Human Rights, Remedies. Max Planck Encyclopedia on Public International law.* Wolfrum, R. (Ed.). Heidelberg: Oxford University Press (2011), pg 1097.
[81] Zgonec-Rožej *International Criminal Law Manual* (2013) 240.
[82] Ambos, K. *Remarks on the General Part of International Criminal Law.* Journal of International Criminal Justice, Vol 4, Issue 4 (2006), pg 669-671. See also Zgonec-Rožej *International Criminal Law Manual* (2013) 241-246.

- the *nullum crimen* principle (individuals may only be held criminally responsible according to law);
- the *nulla poena* principle (punishment should be carried out in accordance with the law and must be proportional to the crime for which the perpetrator has been convicted);
- *Lex praevia* or the principle of non-retroactivity (the relevant proscription under law must have existed before the time of the commission of the act);
- *Lex certa* or the principle of specificity (the law must be certain);
- *Lex stricta* which bans analogy (the law must be interpreted strictly without the court having to stretch the meaning of the words and concepts in the definition), together with *favor rei* principle (interpretation in favour of the person being investigated, accused, prosecuted or convicted); and
- *Lex scripta* (the law must have existed in written form).

Article 22 of the *Rome Statute* encapsulates the principle of *nullum crimen sine lege*; the *favor rei* principle; the principle of specificity; as well as the ban on analogy. Furthermore, Article 23 confirms the principle of *nulla poena sine lege*.[83] Finally, Article 24 confirms the principle of non-retroactivity *ratione personae*.

It has been argued that these provisions in the *Rome Statute* "do not necessarily lead to the conclusion that the ICC's approach to legality will in fact be stricter than that applied by other international tribunals".[84] Whereas domestic criminal courts may apply the guarantees under the *nullum crimen, nulla poena sine lege* more stringently, the jurisprudence of the international courts and tribunals are likely to continue to interpret the various contours of the principle of legality purposively. The mentioned requirements imposed by the legality principle will not be considered mechanistically, as the core objective of the principle is the provision of 'fair warning'. 'Fair warning' implies that individuals should be able to "reasonably foresee the legal consequences of their actions... thereby providing fundamental protection against arbitrary prosecution and imprisonment"[85]. Therefore, the nature of international crimes thus validates an interpretation in line with natural law. Thus, even if one of these legal guarantees appear to have

---

[83] Art 22 of the *Rome Statute*.
[84] Zgonec-Rožej International Criminal Law Manual (2013) 243.
[85] Boot, M. *Genocide, Crimes Against Humanity, War Crimes: Nullum Crimen Sine Lege and the Subject Matter Jurisdiction of the International Criminal Court*. Volume 12 of School of Human Rights Research series, Published Intersentia nv (2002), pg 176, 611, 616.

7. Counteractive Responses to Religious Persecution

been infringed, it may not suffice as significant if the core objective of 'giving fair warning' was nonetheless satisfied.

The *sui generis* nature of persecution necessitates specific consideration of the legality principle.

> [P]ersecution as such is not known in the world's major criminal justice systems. [Therefore] the crime of persecution needs careful and sensitive development in the light of the principle of nullem crimen sine lege.[86]

The ICTY has acknowledged that neither international law nor international jurisprudence provides an exhaustive list of illegal acts encapsulated under the crime of persecution.[87] Therefore, in order to comply with the principle of legality, the Trial Chamber noted that the prosecution should not rely on a general charge of persecution, as this will not be in line with the legality principle, and must therefore charge the perpetrator with specific acts that constitute persecution.[88] Cassese concurs by stating that in order to "observe the principle of legality, the Prosecution must charge particular acts ... in sufficient detail for the accused to be able to fully prepare their defence".[89] The *Kvočka* Trial judgement interpreted these particular acts to include 'inhumane-type' and 'other-type' persecutory conduct, stating that:

> [j]ointly or severally, the acts alleged ... must amount to persecution, not that each discriminatory act alleged must individually be regarded as a violation of international law.[90]

Consequently, in the context of the *ad hoc* tribunals, the legality principle is respected even when each underlying act of persecution was not independently an autonomous crime.[91] It was thus considered that the underlying act or the cumulative effect of a range of acts must provide evidence

---

[86] *Prosecutor v Dario Kordić, Mario Cerkez (Trial Judgement)*, Case No. IT-95-14/2-T, 26 February 2001, par 694.
[87] *Kordić (Trial Judgement)* par 192.
[88] *Prosecutor v Kupreškić et al. (Trial Judgement)*, Case No. IT-95-16-T, 14 January 2000 in Cassese et al. *ICL: Cases and Commentary* (2011) 188. See also *Prosecutor v Vasiljević (Trial Judgment)*, Case No IT-98-32-T, ICTY, 29 November 2002, par 246; *Prosecutor v Milomir Stakić (Trial Judgement)*, Case No. IT-97-24-T, 31 July 2003, par 735; and *Prosecutor v Blagoje Simić et al. (Trial Judgement)*, IT-95-9-T, ICTY, 17 October 2003, par 50.
[89] Cassese et al. *ICL: Cases and Commentary* (2011) 188.
[90] *Prosecutor v Miroslav Kvočka et al. (Trial Judgement)*, Case No. IT-98-30/1-T, 2 November 2001, par 186.
[91] Brady & Liss *Evolution of Persecution* (2014) 512.

of persecution, which must have the same gravity as that of other inhumane acts.[92] The legality principle does not require that underlying acts be contained in separate charges, but may form part of the broader charge of persecution. However, an indictment on persecution must provide sufficient detail regarding the underlying acts upon which the charge is based, to the extent that it constitutes 'fair notice' to the accused in order to prepare his/her defence.[93]

It is not yet clear whether the ICC will follow a similar approach. However, it is doubtful that the interests of justice will be constrained by these concerns regarding legality, and it may therefore prove unnecessary to charge the perpetrator with specific acts that constitute persecution in terms of the *Rome Statute*. This is because the legality principle should not be interpreted formalistically to the extent that it constitutes an impediment on the core objective of individual criminal responsibility and human rights protection. Legality must ensure legal certainty regarding the foreseeability of what constitutes illegitimate actions or consequences.[94] Consequently, for international criminal law a natural law approach may be advocated in terms of which a norm must possess 'sufficient clarity' to the extent that the general nature of an offence, its criminal character, and its approximate gravity were foreseeable to the accused.[95]

A collective consideration of the elements of persecution, as set out in Chapter Six, provides empirical limitations to the application of the crime of persecution, appeasing the concerns regarding the legality principle. The following points may be highlighted:

First, the connection requirement was inserted into the *Rome Statute* out of concern about the elasticity of the concept of persecution, which may lead to prosecutions for crimes not envisaged as the most serious crimes of concern to the international community as a whole.[96] Several delegations to the Rome Conference were concerned that any discriminatory practices could be labelled 'persecution' and prosecuted by the ICC.[97] For concerned States, the connection requirement serves to restrict the ICC from intervening into certain domestic laws, policies or practices that

---

[92] *Krnojelac (Appeal Judgement)*, Separate Opinion of Judge Shahabuddeen, par 6-7.
[93] Brady & Liss *Evolution of Persecution* (2014) 531.
[94] Boot *Genocide, Crimes Against Humanity, War Crimes* (2002) 176, 611, 616.
[95] *Vasiljević (Trial Judgment)* par 201.
[96] Cryer, R. et al. *An Introduction to International Criminal Law and Procedure.* Cambridge University 214.
[97] Brady & Liss *Evolution of Persecution* (2014) 544.

7. Counteractive Responses to Religious Persecution

could potentially be labelled discriminatory, but which did not occur in the context of war crimes or crimes against humanity.[98]

The connection requirement reinforces the severity threshold for persecutory conduct by linking prosecutions of persecution to any underlying inhumane act constituting crimes against humanity or any jurisdictionally relevant crime.[99] If persecutory conduct is based on the commission of a specific inhumane act, the connection requirement and the legality principle would be considered satisfied. Furthermore, if persecutory conduct is based on the cumulative effect of 'other-type' conduct, the connection requirement serves to limit the scope of persecution to situations where at least one other recognised crime or inhumane act was also committed; this is to be expected in a situation warranting international prosecution.[100] Therefore, the connection requirement, read with the *chapeau* elements, limits the contextual application of persecution to situations equal in severity to other underlying crimes against humanity.

Second, the criminalisation of 'grievous persecution' is not concerned with the proscription of specific inhumane acts, but rather acts that are rendered serious by the discrimination they seek to instil within humankind.[101] Therefore, the emphasis regarding the legality of persecution should not revolve around the specificity of the persecutory conduct itself, but is satisfied by a sufficiently serious form of discrimination as the deprivation of the fundamental right to equality and non-discrimination. The nature of such discriminatory conduct indicates that it is inconceivable that a perpetrator could not have foreseen the "fundamental nature of the moral outrages committed".[102] Subsequently, for the purposes of 'fair warning', it is sufficient that the perpetrator acted with a discriminatory intent.

Third, the elevated threshold of severity in the *Rome Statute* eases the concern that nebulous discriminatory practices at the domestic level will be included under a charge of persecution. The severity threshold limits the application of persecution to the deprivation of 'fundamental rights'. Their impermissible restriction, deprivation or denial are therefore universally accepted as clear and obvious breaches of international human rights law. In addition, discriminatory conduct will only constitute 'grievous persecution' if the deprivation of such fundamental rights is considered severe or substantial.

---

[98] Brady & Liss *Evolution of Persecution* (2014) 544.
[99] Ambos & Wirth *The Current Law of Crimes Against Humanity* (2002) 73.
[100] Cryer et al. *International Criminal Law and Procedure* (2007) 214.
[101] *Blaškić (Trial Judgement)* par 227.
[102] Zgonec-Rožej *International Criminal Law Manual* (2013) 246.

Fourth, if the threshold of severity is satisfied by the cumulative effect of a range of 'other-type' conduct, which need not be autonomous criminal acts, it is inconceivable that it would require the perpetrator to have foreseen the unlawfulness of such conduct. Consequently, in such instances a perpetrator must act with the contextual knowledge that his actions may be objectively linked to the broader attack, pursuant to a discriminatory policy. Therefore, his deliberate and informed participation in a range of discriminatory conduct provides 'sufficient clarity' regarding the general offensive nature of such conduct.

Last, the persecutory conduct must be committed with a special discriminatory mindset or (*dolus specialis*), i. e. the accused must have consciously and deliberately discriminated between persons based on their identity. The *mens rea* for persecution indicates that it is a heightened form of crimes against humanity, which constitutes an additional element for its qualification.[103] By implication, such a specific discriminatory intent, coupled with actual discriminatory results, provides a *prima facie* indication of the deprivation of fundamental rights as an obvious consequence thereof.[104]

7.6.3 Legal liability for religious persecution

7.6.3.1 The participants in religious persecution

Religious persecution is perpetrated by a variety of regimes and participants, including State and non-State actors, or a combination of both,[105] and derived from various motivational factors.[106] Such forms of persecution may be interreligious, intra-religious (intra-denominational) or a combination of both.[107]

---

[103] Fournet & Pigorier *Only One Step Away From Genocide* (2010) 716
[104] Triffterer & Ambos *Commentary on the Rome Statute* (2008) 257–258.
[105] Open Doors Analytical. *World Watch List Methodology*. November 2017, pg 16–17. Available at: http://opendoorsanalytical.org/world-watch-list-methodology-latest-edition-november-2017/. Accessed 09/01/2018. This methodology is based on the work of Ron Boyd-Macmillan, the Strategy Director of Open Doors and published in Boyd-MacMillan, R. *Faith That Endures: The Essential Guide to the Persecuted Church*. Published by Fleming H. Revell (2006). Open Doors has been monitoring the worldwide persecution of Christians since the 1970s and has over time developed a comprehensive methodology that provides credibility, transparency, objectivity and scientific quality to their annual World Watch List publication. It is independently audited by the International Institute for Religious Freedom (IIRF).

7. Counteractive Responses to Religious Persecution

The methodology statement of the *World Watch List* on the persecution of Christians distinguishes twelve categories or 'drivers' (actors) of religious persecution:[108]

1. governments, government officials and leaders in all branches and levels of authority, for example, teachers, police officials, political functionaries such as ministers and heads of State;
2. ethnic group leaders, such as tribal chiefs;
3. religious leaders at various levels of engagement, for example, Imams, Rabbis, senior Buddhist Monks, Pastors, or Catholic Bishops. They may either be from:
   a) other religious identities in the context of interreligious persecution, or
   b) the same religious identity, but with a different denomination in the context of intra-religious persecution;
4. violent religious extremist groups acting in the name of religion, such as *Boko Haram* (Nigeria), *Hamas* (Palestinian Territories), or *Bodu Bala Sena* and the *Sinhala Ravaya* (Sri Lanka);
5. ideological pressure groups, such as gay rights organisations or pro-abortion activists;
6. normal citizens or communities from various parts of society, for example, students, neighbours, shopkeepers, mobs, or protestors;
7. members of the extended family, for example, direct family members who condemn religious conversion away from the traditional family religion;
8. political parties at any level of engagement, whether local or national. For example, the *Bharatiya Janata* Party in India, or the *Adalet ve Kalkınma Partisi* (Justice and Development Party) in Turkey;
9. revolutionaries or paramilitary groups, such as the Revolutionary Armed Forces of Colombia People's Army;
10. organised crime cartels or networks, such as the Yakuza groups of Japan, the Sicilian Mafia gangs, or Somali pirates; and
11. multilateral organisations (e. g. UN) and embassies in the context of secularity.

---

[106] Reimer, R. *Persecution, advocacy and mission at the beginning of the 21st century.* Sauer, C. (ed). Religious Freedom Series: Suffering, Persecution and Martyrdom. Vol 2 (2010), pg 335–337.
[107] Thames et al. International Religious Freedom Advocacy (2009) 12.
[108] *World Watch List Methodology* (2017) 16–17.

In his thematic reports for the UN, Professor Bielefeldt concludes that it is impossible to describe all types of incidents of violations or abuses of religious freedom, which may constitute religious persecution.[109] These incidents occur in different forms, and with different motives and root causes, but are ultimately committed by human actors, whether representing State authority, or societal or communal interests. In his report, he discusses many violations of religious freedom that directly originate from State agents,[110] even in democratic countries.[111] Furthermore, he found that many of the "most brutal abuses of freedom of religion or belief are currently perpetrated by non-State actors, such as terrorist groups or militant vigilante groups".[112] However, it should be clear that even if it is non-State actors carrying out acts of violence or deprivations of religious freedom, States are sometimes directly or indirectly complicit in such abuses by actively promoting, encouraging, or tolerating (through deliberate inaction), the actions of these actors for diverse motives. Most often, States abdicate in their responsibility to control the actions of non-State actors by creating an atmosphere of impunity within which such abuses are committed without consequences.[113] When abuses are not perpetrated by State agencies, the Government remains accountable for any violation of freedom of religion or belief occurring within its jurisdiction.[114]

In the context of international criminal law, 'grievous religious persecution' is perpetrated by a variety of participants or 'actors', and may be subdivided based on their role or involvement in the crime and their consequent criminal liability. The most important actors or participants include:

- The 'authors' or 'instigators', which are the architects and decision makers in the context of such breaches. Usually, they do not take a direct part in hostilities; therefore, their criminal liability is based on command responsibility, indirect perpetration ('perpetration by means'), or indirect co-perpetration.[115] These individuals are often considered as those persons 'most responsible'.

---

[109] Bielefeldt *FORB: Thematic Reports* (2017) 338–339, 357.
[110] Bielefeldt *FORB: Thematic Reports* (2017) 350–357.
[111] Sepúlveda et al. *Human Rights Reference book* (2004) 407.
[112] Bielefeldt *FORB: Thematic Reports* (2017) 357.
[113] Bielefeldt *FORB: Thematic Reports* (2017) 357–359.
[114] Bielefeldt *FORB: Thematic Reports* (2017) 359.
[115] Art 25(3)(a) of the *Rome Statute*.

- The 'triggermen', which are those directly or personally involved in the commission of the offence, or who in some other way participated therein. Their criminal responsibility is usually based on direct perpetration, but depending on the circumstances may also include command responsibility or perpetration through a group (i. e. liability based on the doctrine of common purpose or joint criminal enterprise, co-perpetration, and indirect co-perpetration).

As such, the liability of State and non-State actors will be discussed below and will be limited to 'grievous religious persecution'.

7.6.3.2 Liability of governments and State actors for 'grievous persecution'

Religious persecution that directly originates from State agents and targeting religious minorities or dissidents, includes various types of actions or inactions. Such conduct may be motivated by numerous factors, which may differ from country to country, and from time to time in the course of a country's development.[116]

It is important to note that although impermissible restrictions through laws, policies or administrative measures by governments on religious freedom may constitute 'grievous persecution', such governments are more likely to incur civil responsibility for an international wrongful act under international law. Criminal responsibility for government officials is thus usually not a measure of first resort. The most prominent reason is that States will not easily hold the Heads of foreign States criminally responsible based on the principle of State sovereignty. In such instances, the international community is more likely to enforce international sanctions against the transgressing State. This is likely to occur in instances where the religious persecution is based on a 'restrictive squeeze' or 'iniquitous persecution'.

This is not to say that 'grievous religious persecution' by *de facto* authorities will never result in the pursuit of criminal prosecution mechanisms against responsible actors. If the nature of the persecutory conduct is such that specific instigators may be singled out, those 'most responsible' may be held accountable, whether based on direct or indirect individual responsibility, command responsibility or common purpose. However, it is more likely that the international community will enforce individual criminal responsibility for 'grievous religious persecution' if the persecutory conduct is based on a 'violent smash' or 'persecution atrocities'.

---

[116] Bielefeldt *FORB: Thematic Reports* (2017) 356.

Consequently, if the persecutory conduct amounts to severe deprivations of fundamental human rights or the commission of international core crimes, such State-actors may be held individually and criminally responsible. The individual actor or agent acting on behalf of the government cannot hide behind official capacity or superior order as defences for crimes against humanity or genocide.[117]

International criminal law makes provision for the individual criminal accountability of natural persons who participate in international crimes,[118] but not States. However, it is generally accepted that "most of the acts prescribed by international criminal law as international crimes are regarded by international law as serious violations by States".[119] Consequently, it is possible that if "an agent of a State (an individual not acting in a private capacity) commits an international crime, the act in question may be attributable to the State, in which case that State may also be internationally responsible."[120] Such international responsibility refers to the civil liability of States for internationally wrongful acts.[121] In terms of Article 2 of the *Draft Articles on State Responsibility*, there is an internationally wrongful act of a State, whether an act or omission, which is attributable to the State under international law, and constitutes a breach of an international obligation of the State. In other words, the State may be held responsible for an internationally wrongful act if the commission of an international crime is attributable to the State (i. e. the perpetrators acted on behalf of, or with authority from, such a State in the commission of the crimes), which constitutes a breach of an international obligation of the State.[122]

Dual responsibility for international crimes will mean that alternative judicial proceedings may be instituted based on the commission of 'grievous religious persecution'.[123] On the one hand, it entails criminal

---

[117] Art 33 of the *Rome Statute*. See also Zgonec-Rožej *International Criminal Law Manual*. (2013) 322. This is explained in Appendix A.
[118] Art 25 of the *Rome Statute*.
[119] Zgonec-Rožej *International Criminal Law Manual* (2013) 36.
[120] Zgonec-Rožej *International Criminal Law Manual* (2013) 36.
[121] In this regard see the International Law Commission, *Draft Articles on Responsibility of States for Internationally Wrongful Acts*, November 2001, Supplement No. 10 (A/56/10), chp.IV.E.1. (UN Doc. A/CN.4/L.602/Rev.1).
[122] See Chapter II of the ILC's *Draft Articles on Responsibility of States for Internationally Wrongful Acts*.
[123] The Bosnian Genocide case provides a good illustration – The *Application of the Convention on the Prevention and Punishment of the Crime of Genocide (Bosnia and Herzegovina v. Serbia and Montenegro)*, Judgment, I.C.J. Reports (2007). The Bosnian genocide case related to Serbia's alleged involvement in the attempted extermination of the Bosniak (Bosnian Muslim) population of Bosnia and Herzegovina. At the

accountability of an individual agent of the State as a potential perpetrator under international criminal law, and, on the other hand, the international responsibility of a State for the commission of an internationally wrongful act.[124]

7.6.3.3 Liability of non-State actors for 'grievous persecution'

Societal bigotry and the subsequent religious persecution by non-State actors may be motivated by various intersecting reasons. Despite civil society's essential and dynamic role in promoting freedom of religion or belief,[125] non-State actors may also contribute to a societal rift because of the improper engagement in religious activities or the justification of their actions through religious ideology. Regardless of its source, such religious rifts may range in severity and practice, and may be interreligious, intrareligious, or a combination of both. Although not all forms of societal hostility will satisfy the severity threshold for 'grievous persecution', there may be certain situations that signify widespread or systematic deprivations of fundamental human rights.

Although the term 'non-State actor' may include private individuals, the nature of 'grievous religious persecution' dictate that criminal prosecutions will mostly be limited to members of various types of structured groups.[126] The characteristics of such a group are not essential. However,

---

same time the ICTY had jurisdiction to prosecute individuals responsible for the crime of genocide in that area. The ICJ found that although Serbia was neither directly responsible for the Srebrenica genocide, nor was complicit in it, Serbia had nonetheless committed a breach of the Genocide Convention by failing to prevent the genocide from occurring and for not cooperating with the ICTY in punishing the perpetrators of the genocide. See also Zgonec-Rožej *International Criminal Law Manual* (2013) 36; and Art 25(4) of the *Rome Statute*.

[124] Zgonec-Rožej *International Criminal Law Manual* (2013) 36.

[125] *UN Rapporteur's Digest on Freedom of Religion or Belief: Excerpts of the Reports from 1986 to 2011 by the Special Rapporteur on Freedom of Religion or Belief Arranged by Topics of the Framework for Communications.* Geneva, March 2011, pg 106.

[126] In the context of crimes against humanity, persecutory conduct must form part of a course of conduct pursuant to, or in furtherance of, a State or organisational policy. It is therefore generally accepted that for the purposes of the *Rome Statute*, the persecutory conduct must be linked to a State or organisational policy to commit such an attack – Ambos, K. & Wirth, S. *The Current Law of Crimes Against Humanity: An Analysis of UNTAET Regulation 15/2000.* Crim LF, 13 (2002), pg 26–27. Consequently, a widespread or systematic attack on a specific religious group must be adopted by the responsible group and implemented by way of an asserted policy, plan or ideology. The essential purpose of the link to a declared or implicit policy

for the purposes of 'grievous persecution' the group's actions must establish a coordinated pattern capable of infringing basic human rights. Consequently, international crimes committed by non-State actors are usually endemic of systemised-criminality committed by large groups of people, such as terrorist networks.

Non-State persecutors may incur individual criminal responsibility, provided the accused personally engaged or participated in the persecutory conduct,[127] and such conduct constituted a significant contribution to the crime.[128] Individual criminal responsibility before international criminal tribunals will be limited to those perpetrators within the hostile group that are 'most responsible' for such international crimes.

It is also possible to hold all of the participating members of the group responsible based on the doctrine of common purpose. This implies that persecutory acts committed as part of a pattern of broader social hostility will only constitute 'grievous persecution' if the actors involved were united by an underlying policy, plan or ideology, or if they acted with a common purpose, which implies contextual knowledge. Therefore, in situations where the "persecutory act reaches the necessary gravity only when seen cumulatively with other conduct, the perpetrator must be aware of this other conduct".[129]

Traditionally, human rights obligations under international human rights law had been reserved for States. However, an evolving approach recognises the role of non-State actors in the international environment and the necessity to expect them to fulfil certain human rights obligations under specific circumstances:[130]

> [U]nder certain circumstances, in particular where an armed group with an identifiable political structure exercises significant control over territory and population, non-State actors are obliged to respect international human rights. [Similarly,] gross violations of human rights and serious violations of humanitarian law could entail individual criminal responsibility, including

---

is to clarify the context within which certain criminal conduct attains an international character. The policy achieves this aim by requiring that the underlying crimes must form part of a course of conduct, rather than isolated events. Such a course of conduct is of serious concern as it relates to actions or omissions by an authoritative and legally responsible group.

[127] *Prosecutor v Duško Tadić (Appeal Judgement)*, Case No. IT-94-1-A, 15 July 1999, par 186.
[128] *Prosecutor v. Radoslav Brdjanin (Appeal Judgement)*, IT-99-36-A, ICTY, 3 April 2007, par 427.
[129] Ambos & Wirth *The Current Law of Crimes Against Humanity* (2002) 87.
[130] Bielefeldt *FORB: Thematic Reports* (2017) 265.

for members and leaders of non-State armed groups and private military contractors.[131]

Therefore, non-State armed groups with (or arguably even without) effective control over a territory are obliged to respect international human rights, and may incur individual criminal responsibility for human rights abuses, such as persecution committed in the name of religion.[132] In the context of an internal armed conflict, a non-State armed group's obligation may also include obligations under international humanitarian law as generally contained in the *Geneva Conventions*.[133]

Although there is no general definition of 'non-State actors', nor consensus on their human rights obligations,[134] a non-State group or organisation exercising effective control over a territory may, under certain circumstances, incur international responsibility for crimes against humanity of religious persecution in the same way as States and State actors. Furthermore, , some human rights obligations may apply to non-State armed groups with (or arguably even without) effective control over a territory,[135] while at the same time the most responsible participants of such crimes may incur individual criminal responsibility in terms of the *Rome Statute*.

Religious persecution by non-State actors may establish international responsibility for both the actors as well as the *de facto* authority or government if that State directly or indirectly supports these actors for whatever motive or reason.[136] This is because a government "remains accountable for any violation of freedom of religion or belief occurring within its jurisdiction",[137] whether committed by State or non-State actors. As Bielefeldt explains:

> [I]n situations in which abuses are mainly committed by non-State actors, Governments still bear a responsibility for not being willing – or not being fully able – to provide effective protection for individuals and groups whose rights are being violated.[138]

---

[131] Par 16 of the UN Committee on the Elimination of Discrimination Against Women (CEDAW), *General recommendation No. 30 on women in conflict prevention, conflict and post-conflict situations*, 1 November 2013, CEDAW/C/GC/30.
[132] Bielefeldt *FORB: Thematic Reports* (2017) 265.
[133] Bielefeldt *FORB: Thematic Reports* (2017) 266.
[134] Bielefeldt *FORB: Thematic Reports* (2017) 357.
[135] Bielefeldt *FORB: Thematic Reports* (2017) 265.
[136] Bielefeldt *FORB: Thematic Reports* (2017) 357.
[137] Bielefeldt *FORB: Thematic Reports* (2017) 359.
[138] Bielefeldt *FORB: Thematic Reports* (2017) 339.

Therefore, a form of indirect support may refer to instances where a government overlooks religious persecution or discrimination committed by non-State actors in the area under its control. The government's failure to take action could be considered a deliberate policy of passive tolerance, consciously aimed at encouraging such an attack. In other words, a deliberate omission by the State to address religious persecution or discrimination committed by non-State actors may constitute an underlying policy for purposes of crimes against humanity. However, the existence of such a policy cannot be inferred solely from the absence of governmental or organisational action.[139]

7.7 Conclusion

Appropriately and effectively responding to religious persecution is dependent on various contributing factors, including the nature of the victim group, the nature of the relevant concerned role-players, the nature and severity of harm, and other surrounding circumstances. Remaining conscious of the underlying systemic root causes of religious persecution and the surrounding circumstances in each case, dictates that a fitting response at a given time requires careful consideration. Subsequently, a few such responses were considered.

First, an introspective response by believers sincerely and unequivocally denouncing the justification of religious persecution as manifestations of devotion in the name of their religion.[140] It is crucial for the majorities and their leaders, who do not endorse persecution in the name of their religion, to publically condemn it. Appropriately distancing a religion from discriminatory or extremist religious ideologies show solidarity and support for those persecuted, and may prove pivotal in preventing interreligious or even intra-religious stigmatisation, hatred and reprisals against members of associated religious groups.

Second, response strategies useful to persecuted religious communities based on documented observations about Christian responses to persecution. A religious response to persecution by those persecuted will depend on that religious community's theology of suffering, persecution and martyrdom. In response to extensive and consistent persecution, persecuted

---

[139] International Criminal Court (ICC), *Elements of Crimes*, 2011, Official Records of the Review Conference of the Rome Statute of the International Criminal Court, Kampala, 31 May–11 June 2010 (International Criminal Court publication, RC/11), art 7, Introduction, footnote 6. (*ICC Elements of Crimes*).
[140] Bielefeldt *FORB: Thematic Reports* (2017) 213.

7. Counteractive Responses to Religious Persecution

Christian communities have adopted some theologically based strategies of response that have produced tangible results and are worthy of measured emulation. These approaches was used as a strategic model to illustrate a predominantly non-violent and non-extremist response to persecution.

Third, a governmental response in line with human rights obligations. In the context of religious persecution, States have the duty to take effective measures to protect and promote religious freedom, equality and tolerance, and counteract impunity by bringing persecutors to justice.

Last but not least, humanitarian responses to religious persecution based on the internationalised concern for severe deprivations of human rights, including freedom of religion or belief. In this regard, religious freedom advocacy efforts broadly entail identifying existing and emerging obstacles to the enjoyment of religious freedom and utilizing legal, political, co-operative, or international control mechanisms to overcome such obstacles. In addition, it was concluded that the most appropriate response to significantly 'pernicious' human rights deprivations require the use of criminal prosecution systems in the pursuit of criminal accountability. Although national prosecutions of international crimes are often preferable, international criminal prosecution mechanisms constitute a justifiable and appropriate response to 'grievous religious persecution' should the relevant national prosecution system prove unwilling or unable to properly prosecute those responsible. Disconcertingly, the criminalisation of religious persecution has failed to materialise in consistent and reliable criminal prosecutions. However, despite the nebulous nature of persecution, the application and prosecution for 'grievous persecution' is adequately limited in terms of the *Rome Statute* to the extent that it provides the accused with 'sufficient clarity' in order to satisfy the legality principle. The general discriminatory nature of the offence implies that the effect of any underlying persecutory conduct connected to the broader attack acquires a criminal or depriving character. The inevitability of severe deprivations of fundamental rights is an obvious consequence of a severe discriminatory act, or the cumulative effect of a range of acts, providing clear foreseeability to the accused regarding the required approximate gravity of 'grievous persecution'.

Individual criminal responsibility for religious persecution will be limited to those 'most responsible', based on their significant contribution to, or participation in, the commission of the crime. This may include State and non-State actors. While a list of non-State actors is not limited to any form of organised structure or leadership, the *chapeau* elements necessitate an underlying policy, plan or ideology, which is more common in a structured group. Thus, the members of the non-State group may be held responsible as co-perpetrators acting with a common purpose, while the instigators may be held liable in terms of command responsibility. On the other hand, dual responsibility is activated for the commission of core crimes by agents acting on behalf of a *de facto* authority. Dual responsibility for international crimes entail both individual criminal responsibility of the individual responsible under international criminal law, and may also give rise to State responsibility for internationally wrongful acts.

Advocating on behalf of those who are persecuted on the basis of their religious identity, require utilising any conceivable intervention, whether judicial, political, conscientious, or otherwise. Most importantly, a fitting response to religious persecution is dependant upon situational awareness and respect for the wishes of the affected religious group. While certain strategies of response may produce tangible results worthy of measured emulation, counteractive responses should not be mindlessly reproduced and applied to other occurences of religious persecution. Responding decisively and sensibly to religious persecution reiterates the significance of religious freedom and acknowledges the severe impact that religious discrimination and related persecution may have on human dignity, freedom and equality. A meaningful response may serve to counteract the detrimental impact of religious persecution and demonstrates solidarity with those who have been persecuted.

Chapter Eight: Conclusions

8.1 Introduction

The primary aim of this book was to lessen the legal vagueness surrounding religious persecution as a crime against humanity. It was argued that greater legal certainty regarding the definitional elements of religious persecution would strengthen the resolve of international judicial bodies to pursue accountability for such mass discriminatory crimes. During the course of this study, three broad themes emerged:

- The first theme entailed an understanding of the broader legal framework within which our understanding of persecution in its generic sense would be assessed.
- The second theme channelled the initial expansive discussion regarding persecution into a more focussed view on the role that religious identity and freedom of religion or belief may have in categorising the ground of persecution.
- The third theme conceptualised 'grievous religious persecution' by proposing a legal taxonomy of religion-related persecution, supplemented by a pragmatic case study in Appendix C.

8.2 The Persecution Phenomenon in International Criminal Law

Initially, it was shown that although the words 'persecute' and the act of 'persecution' have come to acquire a universally accepted meaning, a consensual definition has remained elusive.[1] Unfortunately, the careless overuse of the term 'persecution' has reduced its impact when describing an actual situation of persecution,[2] making it much more difficult to advocate on behalf of the persecuted, and to encourage an appropriate response.[3]

---

[1] Bassiouni, M. C. *Crimes Against Humanity in International Criminal Law*. Martinus Nijhoff: Dordrecht (1992), pg 317.
[2] Thames, H. et al. *International Religious Freedom Advocacy: A guide to Organizations, Law and NGO's*. Baylor University Press (2009), pg 6.
[3] Thames et al. *International Religious Freedom Advocacy* (2009) 6.

An understanding of persecution may range from a theological, sociological and psychological perspective, to a human rights protection context under refugee and international law, which exacerbates its opacity. It was demonstrated that although each of these contextual uses of 'persecution' differ significantly, in some or other way each of these contextual uses contributes to the overall conception of the term for purposes of this study. Despite these different contextual uses of the term 'persecution', discrimination and unequal treatment persist as the core element of the notion of 'persecution'.

Ultimately, the 'persecution' rubric for the purposes of this study was restricted to an international criminal law perspective. In order to differentiate this understanding of persecution from other 'subsidiary' forms, it was suggested that the prefix 'grievous' should be used. This notion would thus serve as an indication of 'persecution' that satisfies the severity threshold for prosecution under international criminal law, whether such persecutory conduct consisted of 'persecution atrocities' (violent 'smash') or 'iniquitous persecution' (impermissible restrictive 'squeeze').

This contextual understanding of 'grievous persecution' was supplemented by the overview of the basic principles of international criminal law in Appendix A. In this regard, it was established that the nature of 'grievous persecution' has been a primary concern of the international community since the acceptance that certain fundamental notions of humanity should govern the conduct of States.[4] Consequently, widespread or systematic discrimination warrant persecution's proscription as an enumerated inhumane act of crimes against humanity in terms of the *Rome Statute*.

At the core of this proscription is the fundamental proposition of this book: Religious discrimination and persecution remain "a major human rights issue of national and international concern, [accordingly] international prosecution systems, as provided by the International Criminal Court (ICC), are to be resorted to in pursuit of criminal accountability".[5]

As its primary aim, international criminal law protects society against the most harmful breaches of fundamental values of the international legal community by imposing individual criminal accountability

---

[4] Brady, H. & Liss, R. *The Evolution of Persecution as a Crime Against Humanity*, in *Historical Origins of International Criminal Law: Volume 3*, Bergsmo, M. *et al.* (eds). Torkel Opsahl Academic EPublisher, Brussels (2014), pg 433.

[5] Van Boven, T. *Racial and Religious Discrimination*. Max Planck Encyclopedia on Public International law, Wolfrum, R. (ed). Heidelberg: Oxford University Press (2009), par 22.

and punishment for the responsible perpetrators.[6] Such accountability before international criminal forums is restricted to those who bear the greatest responsibility for such crimes. The principle of personal accountability before the ICC includes direct perpetrators and command responsibility, as well as collective modes of participation, such as 'co-perpetration' (common purpose) or indirect perpetration.[7]

While individual criminal responsibility may be limited to natural persons who commit crimes within the jurisdiction of the Court, the commission of international crimes may also give rise to State responsibility for internationally wrongful acts if the perpetrator acted on behalf of, or under instruction from, such an authority in the commission of the crimes.[8] Consequently, gross violations of human rights, such as 'grievous persecution' by perpetrators of a *de facto* authority, could entail dual responsibility, *viz.* individual criminal responsibility for the perpetrators and civil liability of the responsible authority.

Several aspects have an important bearing on the enforcement of individual criminal responsibility before the ICC, most notably jurisdictional threshold questions and considerations of the legality principle for persecution. In this regard, the national judiciary acts as the primary enforcer of the international *ius puniendi* in terms of the *Rome Statute*, also considering that 'grievous persecution' establishes universal jurisdiction over such acts at the national level. The ICC's complementary jurisdiction will be limited to instances where one of the three 'trigger mechanisms' is activated,[9] and the relevant domestic criminal courts have failed or were unable or unwilling to prosecute persons responsible for international core crimes.

The criminalisation of persecution raises some important concerns regarding pleading and legality. It was explained that the principle of legality prescribes criteria for the legitimate application of criminal law, while ensuring certain basic human rights standards regarding due process. The

---

[6] Cassese, A. *International Criminal Law*. Oxford University Press, 1st edition (2003) pg. 20.

[7] Ambos, K. *Modes of Participation*. Oxford Bibliographies (2013). http://www.oxford bibliographies.com/view/document/obo-9780199796953/obo-9780199796953-00 68.xml. Accessed 08/09/2017. For a more detailed discussion in this regard, see Appendix A.

[8] International Law Commission, *Draft Articles on Responsibility of States for Internationally Wrongful Acts*, November 2001, Supplement No. 10 (A/56/10), chp.IV.E.1. (UN Doc. A/CN.4/L.602/Rev.1).

[9] Triffterer, O., & Ambos K. *Commentary on the Rome Statute of the International Criminal Court: Observers' Notes, Article by Article*. 2nd edition. (2008), pg 581.

core objective of the principle is ensuring that an individual may reasonably foresee the legal consequences of their actions (fair warning). Because of its nebulous ('umbrella crime') nature, an exhaustive list of illegal acts encapsulated under the crime of persecution does not exist.[10] It was argued that the drafters of the *Rome Statute* successfully delineated the definition and description of persecution to the extent that the legality concern is sufficiently addressed. Some of the most important empirical limitations in the Statute include:

- a clear contextual threshold, which requires that the persecutory conduct must form part of an attack of a widespread or systematic nature against a targeted civilian population because of an aspect of their identity, and pursuant to an organisational policy;
- a *nexus* between the persecutory conduct or its cumulative effect and the causation of severe deprivation of fundamental rights on a discriminatory basis (severity threshold); and
- the reintroduction and reinvention of the 'connection requirement', necessitating that the persecutory conduct must be objectively linked to other inhumane acts or any other jurisdictionally relevant crime.

Essentially this means that regardless of the nature of the underlying acts of persecution, whether 'inhumane-type' or 'other-type' conduct, the Prosecutor may indict an accused based on a general charge of persecution, provided its general nature of depriving fundamental rights, its discriminatory character, and its approximate gravity within the context of a broader 'attack', were foreseeable to the accused.[11]

'Severe deprivation of fundamental rights', as referenced in the *Rome Statute*, may comprise of crimes that threaten the maintenance of international peace and security, and conduct that severely infringe upon internationally recognised fundamental human rights. Consequently, it was considered that in terms of persecution's dual nature, international criminal prosecution systems provide the most adequate enforcement mechanism, which simultaneously addresses impunity and accountability in the criminal context while also serving to protect and encourage respect for

---

[10] *Prosecutor v Dario Kordić, Mario Cerkez* (Trial Judgement), Case No. IT-95-14/2-T, 26 February 2001, par 192.
[11] *Prosecutor v Mitar Vasiljević (Trial Judgement)*, IT-98-32-T, International Criminal Tribunal for the former Yugoslavia (ICTY), 29 November 2002, par 201.

fundamental human rights. Therefore, the proscription of 'grievous persecution' emphasises the auxiliary function of international criminal law, which is to intervene on the side of humanity in instances where internationalised crimes constitute severe human rights infringements.[12] Considering that the nature and legal threshold of the core crimes, including persecution, represent extreme and obvious infringements of fundamental human rights, the relationship between international criminal law and human rights protection is clear.

The quintessential nature of 'grievous persecution' means that a perpetrator severely infringes upon the fundamental human rights of persons because of their identity. This discriminatory nature of persecutory conduct also implies that the nature and severity of the discrimination itself may constitute the deprivation or denial of the fundamental right to equal treatment. Brady and Liss capture this phenomenon perfectly when they state:

> Whatever the grounds upon which the individual is targeted, the harm of the offence goes, in essence, to the heart of what it is to be human – that is, the combination of a person's very individuality and his or her ability to associate and identify with others; the crime of persecution simultaneously reduces a person to their identification with or membership in a group, and attacks the group itself. The crime of persecution as a crime against humanity is really aimed at protecting these fundamental features of humankind, of 'humanness'.[13]

8.3 Establishing the Role of 'Religion' in Religion-Based Persecution

In the context of international criminal law and its *nexus* to the protection of human rights, a 'religious group' is considered a 'protected group' and the consequent 'religious identity' is a protected ground of identity. As such, the criminalisation of 'grievous religious persecution' is aimed at protecting individuals and groups against human rights infringements based on their 'religious identity'. It was explained that in order to classify a situation as religious persecution, the conception of a religious identity is essential. Such a conception requires an appreciation of the nature and importance of religious identity, the influence that religious freedom has

---

[12] Werle, G. & Jessberger, F. *Principles of International Criminal Law.* Oxford University Press (2014), par 143.
[13] Brady & Liss *Evolution of Persecution* (2014) 554.

in forming a religious identity, and how such an identity becomes the object of perception and discrimination. The inherent problem is that persecution on the basis of religion is not the only mode or ground of persecution criminalised by the *Rome Statute*. Therefore, the purpose of the second theme was to recognise and differentiate *religious* persecution from other forms of persecution. In this regard, an assessment of the role that an individual or collective religious identity has in a given situation is essential in order to determine the mode of persecution.

A person's identity comprises a broad range of identifying elements, based on which a person is able to self-identify his individuality and assume a collective identity in association with others.

'Identity' is a complex and adaptable phenomenon based on multiple 'identifiers' that differentiate and define the true self as a continuous, unique and connected entity. The complexity and constantly evolving multiplicity of indistinguishable 'identifiers' obscure the classification of the mode of persecution.

Establishing a clear and identifiable identity may, therefore, be complex, especially considering that many of these 'identifiers' intersect. The intersection of these 'identifiers' with religion further complicates an assessment of a person's identity and the classification of a situation as religious persecution. In regards to the specific protected grounds listed in the *Rome Statute*, it became clear that most of these grounds are plagued by a lack of succinct legal description. It was also disconcerting to find that some victims experience intensified persecution based on the compounding effect of multiple intersecting grounds. For example, many women suffer from a multiplicity of discrimination and persecution on the grounds of the intersectionality between religion and gender.[14]

Essentially, it is human nature that a person's identity becomes their identifying label, whether in a person's own mind or that of others, or in terms of social standing.[15] This fundamental right to "freely develop, change, or defend one's individual or communitarian identity"[16] is a core aspect of protection against discrimination and unequal treatment under international human rights law. The grounds of persecution are based on the identifying factor (prohibited ground) of the targeted person or group.

---

[14] Bielefeldt, H. *Freedom of Religion or Belief: Thematic Reports of the UN Special Rapporteur 2010 - 2016*. Religious Freedom Series of the International Institute for Religious Freedom, Vol 3, 2nd and extended edition, Bonn (2017), pg 156.
[15] Andrews, J. *Identity Crisis: Religious Registration in the Middle East*. Gilead Books Publishing (2016), pg 23.
[16] Bielefeldt *Misperceptions of FORB* (2013) 44–45.

8. Conclusions and Recommendations

Therefore, the aspects that make up one's personal and/or collective identity are protected as significant aspects of human life and dignity in terms of international law. The discriminatory nature of persecution signifies that a person is reduced to their identification or an identifying element, and deliberately targeted for discriminatory treatment. Therefore, the ground of persecution, or the multiplicity thereof, is based on an aspect of the victim's identity, which made him or her the target of the persecutor's discriminatory intent.[17]

However, because the complex interplay of subjective and objective identifying criteria makes it nearly impossible to identify a person based on a single ground, the mode of persecution is contextualised by the persecutor's subjective perception of the victim's identity. In other words, the ground of persecution signifies the primacy of a specific aspect of the victim's identity as the decisive reason for choosing that particular victim, which must have been based on one or more of the impermissible grounds (identifying elements). As a result, the ground of persecution is established by assessing the identity of the targeted group, or lack thereof, and whether such an identity constituted the decisive basis upon which the perpetrator discriminately chose those particular victims. The perpetrator's discriminatory mindset and his subjective perception about the victim or victim group's identity is the most crucial element in establishing the ground of persecution and whether there was factual discrimination.

Understanding the victim's identity and how a specific aspect of his identity relates to the perpetrator's discriminatory mindset is critical in classifying the relevant ground of persecution.

8.3.1 'Religious identity'

The notion of a 'religious identity' should be understood in the context of human rights protection, specifically the right to religious freedom. Within the context of international human rights law, religious freedom is guaranteed as a fundamental human right, which entails the protection of both religious dimensions. The *forum internum* or internal dimension guarantees everyone's right to *have* freedom of thought, conscience and religion or belief. It includes the associated freedom to retain or maintain, change, replace or convert, choose, or adopt a religion or belief. Internal religious freedom constitutes an absolute and unconditional right to hold any deep existential view, which cannot be limited or derogated from. The

---

[17] Art 7(2)(g) read together with Art 7(1)(h) of the *Rome Statute of the International Criminal Court*, Doc. A/CONF.183/9 of 17 July 1998 *in force* 1 July 2002 (2002).

forum externum or external dimension guarantees everyone's freedom to manifest their religion or belief, either alone or in community with others, in public or private. The freedom to manifest a religion or belief in teaching, practice, worship and observance, may be restricted in conformity with the criteria spelled out in Article 18(3) of the *International Covenant on Civil and Political Rights (ICCPR)*. These dimensional elements of religious freedom include other associated rights and freedoms, referred to as the normative core values of religious freedom. These distinctive yet connected values constitute a set of minimum standards in regards to the scope of protection of religious freedoms to which everyone is entitled from birth.[18]

All aspects of the elusive notion of 'religion' are philosophically unique and fundamental elements that depict humanity's existential cognisance of their existence, identity, and 'conception of life'. As a result, they are a vital aspect of an adherent's way of life and how they relate, either completely or partially, to the world.[19] In human rights law, the term 'religion' is to be broadly construed to include the "freedom of thoughts on all matters, personal conviction and the commitment to religion or belief, whether manifested individually or in community with others".[20] Fundamentally, 'religion' is an umbrella term that encapsulates not only aspects of religion in the traditional sense of belief, but other aspects derived from the inner-self, including thought and conscience. Consequently, a 'religion' denotes an existential circadian viewpoint that is either based on a spiritual predisposition, a personal conviction or pertains to a value-system. As a result, the notion of 'religion' is broadly construed as a 'deep existential view' and includes theistic, non-theistic, polytheistic and atheistic beliefs, as well as the right not to profess any religion or belief. Importantly, all profoundly held existential views are equally and non-discriminately protected grounds of the right to freedom of religion or belief.[21]

By implication, the 'religious identity' of a person or group is the quintessential by-product of the belief in and practice of any deep existential

---

[18] A more detailed discussion in this regard may be found in Appendix B.
[19] Par 8 of the UN High Commissioner for Refugees (UNHCR), *Guidelines on International Protection No. 6: Religion-Based Refugee Claims under Article 1A(2) of the 1951 Convention and/or the 1967 Protocol relating to the Status of Refugees*, 28 April 2004, HCR/GIP/04/06.
[20] Par 1 of the UN Human Rights Committee, *General Comment No. 22: The Right to Freedom of Thought, Conscience, and Religion in terms of Article 18 of the ICCPR.* CCPR/C/21/Rev.1/Add.4, 30 July.
[21] Bielefeldt *Misperceptions of FORB* (2013) 38.

8. Conclusions and Recommendations

view. Therefore, within the context of religious freedom, all profound, identity-shaping convictions or existential views may be protected as elements of a person's 'religious identity'. In addition, 'religious identity' should also be interpreted as inclusive of the negative element of freedom of identity, i. e. the freedom to refrain from holding a certain existential view. Such a religious identity may be held and manifested individually or in community with others (collective religious identity), and in public or private, which is protected as an invariable and inherent consequence of religious freedom. Normally, the formation of such a 'religious identity' may occur when the adherent

- actually belongs, or has a sense of belonging to (or associate, support or identify with), a religious identity in an objective sense (actual religious identity);
- is perceived to have a religious identity based on the perception of others, or in the mind of the perpetrator (perceived religious identity); or
- is designated with a religious identity based on religious registration requirements (assigned religious identity).

A 'religious identity' may thus serve as an indication of an individual's membership to, or identification with, or sense of belonging to, or acceptance into, a religious community. A person's religious identity is therefore not a matter of fact, but a matter of subjective or objective perception, and is always subject to transformation, evolution and choice.[22]

The fundamental character of religious freedom implies that a religious identity is an essential element of human existence. A person's 'religious identity' may thus have a number of important functions and consequences:

- A religious identity may influence an adherent's sense of personal or collective identity and belonging (i. e. religion as an identifying element), e. g. being a Hindu, a Scientologist, an atheist, etc. In the context of religious persecution, this means that a victim's religious identity becomes the identifying factor upon which he or she is discriminately targeted, e. g. by Islamophobia, anti-Semitism or Christianophobia.

---

[22] Bielefeldt *Misperceptions of FORB* (2013) 44.

- A religious identity may inspire an adherent's conception of life and inner consciousness (i. e. religion as a belief – deep existential view).
- A religious identity may affect concomitant individual or communitarian ideologies and practices, which may influence or even dictate an adherent's way of life and how they relate to, interact with or perceive others (i. e. religion as a way of life).

In terms of this latter consequence of religious identity, a religious ideology may, unfortunately, be the root cause of discrimination and persecution. In such instances, a religious belief or identity may serve as the justification or motivation for targeting and persecuting other non-accepting or dissenting religious identities. Persecution in the name of a religious identity (religiously motivated persecution) is concerned with the perpetrator's motive or purpose. In such instances, the perpetrator's religious identity provides the motivation or justification for persecuting others, which may or may not be directed at individuals or groups 'by reason of' their religious identity.

Importantly, persecution in the name of a religious identity (religiously motivated persecution) is distinguishable from religious persecution. The latter form is concerned with the perpetrator's subjective mindset, which is specifically and discriminately directed at a specific person or group based on their religious identity. There may be various root causes why a persecutor targets a specific religious identity, but religious persecution is concerned with the discriminatory nature of the conduct, not the motive thereof. In the context of religious persecution, the question is not why the persecutor is doing what he is doing, but rather who he is doing it to.

Consequently, religiously motivated persecution will only amount to religious persecution if the persecutors' actions were not only motivated by their self-righteous religious ideology, but were also predominantly and deliberately directed at specific targets based on the victims' religious identity. Therefore, a religious identity is the identifying element of religious persecution, but may also be the root cause or motivation that triggers persecution. It is, therefore, important to correctly distinguish the motive for the commission of persecutory conduct from the discriminatory intent to direct the persecutory conduct at a specific group. However, in some instances understanding the motive for persecution may assist in identifying the persecutor's subjective perception about the victim's identity.

8.3.2 The role of religious identity in determining the 'mode of persecution' as a crime against humanity

It is clear from the assessment that 'religion' in the context of the right to freedom of religion or belief is 'a particularly controversial right'.[23] Despite the presumption that the universally accepted nature of religious freedom and a societal decline in religiosity in preference to secularism has curtailed occurrences of religious persecution, religion or religious identity has remained the basis for intolerance, discrimination and persecution in various places throughout the world.[24] Such misperceptions regarding religion and 'religious persecution' trigger misnomers of persecution, which trivialise the fundamental status of religious freedom and underrates the necessity for enforcing prosecution mechanisms for 'grievous religious persecution'. Furthermore, the rise of fundamentalism, religious extremism and religion-related terrorism has proven that the assumption of the redundancy of religious freedom and the criminalisation of religious persecution, is not contemporaneous.

Religious persecution is a form of persecution in terms of which the 'religious identity' of those persecuted constitutes the primary or predominant reason for their suffering. The *Rome Statute* requires only that the individuals must be targeted by reason of the identity of the group or collectivity. The required *nexus* is satisfied if the perpetrator, at the time of committing the persecutory acts, specifically targeted the victim based on his/her actual, perceived, or assigned religious identity.

The primacy of the persecutor's discriminatory mindset, based on the victim's religious identity, is the core aspect that determines or contextualises persecutory acts as religious persecution. Importantly, the subjective perception of the victim is largely irrelevant in this regard. Religious discriminatory intent refers to the conscious, preconceived, and deliberate differentiation of a person or identifiable group or collectivity based on their actual or perceived religious identity.

Persecution of a religious identity may be defined both in a positive manner ('specific religious discriminatory intention'), *vis a vis* the identity of the group to be targeted, and in a negative manner ('negative religious

---

[23] Bielefeldt *Misperceptions of FORB* (2013) 34.
[24] Thames *et al. International Religious Freedom Advocacy* (2009) 10–11. Reliable statistics on the number of those persecuted because of their religion, or of those murdered for their faith, are hard to produce because of the absence of a unified definition and because of the multidimensional nature and motivations of acts constituting persecution.

discriminatory intention'), any person/s from a non-acceptant or dissenting religion or belief. Thus, the victims of religious persecution may include a person, identifiable group or collectivity that was targeted primarily (but not necessarily exclusively)[25] on their religious identity, or lack thereof (negative discriminatory intent), either based on objective criteria or in the mind of the accused.

Establishing a victim's religious identity and whether such an identity was the primary cause of persecution are thus essential components in identifying the nature of persecution as religion-based. Therefore, proof of a religious discriminatory intention is of significant importance. Such a discriminatory intent may be proven based on:

- direct evidence (direct discriminatory intent), e. g. a religious discriminatory ideology in the case of *Da'esh*;
- inferences from the surrounding circumstances (inferred discriminatory intent), which provide *prima facie* proof that deliberate religious discrimination is the only reasonable conclusion; or
- the persecutor's active participation in, and association with, an implied or explicit religious discriminatory policy by a *de facto* authority (discriminatory policy).

In the context of 'grievous religious persecution', a religious discriminatory intent implies that the victim suffers a severe deprivation of fundamental rights, primarily because of his or her religious identity. In essence, this suggests that the deprivation of religious freedom rights in association with one's religious identity is a *prima facie* indicator of religious persecution. However, despite this inherent and indivisible *nexus*, it is not a prerequisite that religious persecutory conduct limits or deprives a believer's ability to have or practice their belief or faith. Nonetheless, deprivations of religious freedom rights are often a typical derivative of, or precursor to, religious persecution.

Religious persecution will remain an accurate classification of the context of persecutory conduct if the victim's 'religious identity' was the primary basis for discrimination; even if the victim was characterised by a perceived religious homogeneity in the mind of the persecutor, and was targeted on such identification, regardless of other related identifiers. Based on this reasoning, it may be possible to identify 'religious identity' as the specific ground of persecution in a given situation.

---

[25] Tieszen, C.L. *Towards Redefining Persecution*. Religious Freedom Series: Suffering, Persecution and Martyrdom. Vol 2. (2010), pg 164.

8.4 Proposing and Endorsing the Conceptualisation

The contextual delineation of persecution to crimes against humanity, and the identification of the role of religious identity in characterising the nature of persecution made it possible to propose a legally justifiable taxonomy of 'grievous religious persecution' and practically apply such a taxonomy to a relevant case subject.

8.4.1 The taxonomy of 'grievous religious persecution' as a crime against humanity

The aim of the taxonomy was to formally and directly address the primary legal problem identified in this study, *viz.* the substantive ambiguity of the crime of persecution. The taxonomy functions as a substantive synopsis of the legal preconditions for establishing the ICC's subject-matter jurisdiction over conduct constituting crimes against humanity of religious persecution.

The taxonomy of crimes against humanity of religious persecution comprise two parts. The first part involved a systematic analysis of the unique definitional elements of 'grievous religious persecution', which were divided into three main categories: the *actus reus*, i. e. the required material elements or criminally liable conduct; the *mens rea*, i. e. the required mental elements or subjective mindset of the perpetrator; and the required threshold of severity. These definitional elements may be summarised as follows:

1. The *actus reus* of 'grievous religious persecution'
   - underlying religious persecutory conduct may consist of a physical 'inhumane act', or the substantially serious effect of a course of discriminatory acts or policies of an 'inhumane nature';
   - such persecutory conduct must have caused the severe deprivation of a fundamental right, whether separately or cumulatively;
   - such persecutory conduct must be objectively linked to any enumerated inhumane act, or any jurisdictionally relevant international crime; and
   - such persecutory conduct must be sufficiently linked to the broader attack. A course of religiously discriminatory practices may itself constitute the attack, provided the contextual threshold is satisfied.

2. The *mens rea* of 'grievous religious persecution'
   The mental element for religious persecution is satisfied if the persecutor committed the persecutory conduct and at the same time:
   – was aware of a pattern of religious discriminatory practices (broader attack) and the risk that his conduct may be objectively linked therewith;
   – deliberately meant to engage in the persecutory conduct (persecutive intent); and
   – discriminately and consciously targeted his victim/s based primarily on their actual or perceived religious identity.

3. The required threshold of severity
   Religious persecutory conduct will only amount to 'grievous religious persecution' if:
   – the religious persecution was carried out in a systematic manner or on a mass scale (or was part of an 'attack' of a widespread or systematic nature), directed against a civilian population with an identifiable religious identity, based on an implied or explicit policy of a *de facto* authority; and
   – the persecutory act, or the cumulative effect of a course of religiously discriminate practices, resulted in the *severe* deprivation (a 'gross and blatant denial') of *fundamental* rights. 'Fundamental rights' are established by either serious atrocities against elementary principles of humanity (fundamental human rights), or crimes of an utmost inhumane character which violate international norms.

The second part of the taxonomy consisted of a proposed definition of religious persecution as a crime against humanity in terms of the *Rome Statute*. The proposed definition may be summarised as: deliberate persecutory conduct, connected to any jurisdictionally relevant inhumane act or crime, based on a policy of conscious and intentional religious discrimination, which resulted in the severe deprivation of fundamental human rights, committed in the knowledge that such conduct forms part of a widespread or systematic attack.

8.4.2 Testing the taxonomy in a case study

In order to facilitate a pragmatic approach to the proposed taxonomy, the definitional elements of 'grievous religious persecution' were summarised as an abbreviated checklist and presented as a flowchart, containing a series

8. Conclusions and Recommendations

of sequential questions pertaining to the identified definitional elements of 'grievous religious persecution'. This religious persecution taxonomy checklist was then applied to a relevant case study in order to analyse its practical efficiency. This case study is available below, under Appendix C, but a brief summary of the case study is provided below.

The global trend of rising fear of Islamic extremism and religiously motivated persecution stood out as a significant case subject from the outset. It was found that religious extremists exploit their collective religious identity, usually on a denominational level, as the motivation and justification for persecution, which may or may not entail religious persecution. Unfortunately, it became clear that when such Islamic extremist groups proclaim to act in the name of the entire religion, their actions adversely affect those who bear an associative religious identity as a counter-reaction to religiously motivated persecution, i. e. Islamophobia.[26]

In the context of the case study, the scope of Islamic extremism was confined to the actions of the group *Da'esh*, which, based on a strong body of evidence, had committed systematic and mass atrocity crimes and human rights deprivations against religious minorities and dissident religious denominations in the areas under its control at the time. After making some important preliminary observations regarding the group's origins, religious ideology and pattern of offences, a number of significant conclusions could be made about *Da'esh's* accountability for 'grievous religious persecution':

- During the time of the commission of the conduct, the organised armed group exercised effective control over territory, acting under responsible command with a cohesive organisational structure. This aspect is especially relevant in terms of command responsibility.
- This formal organisational structure, combined with its unified ideological policy, clearly constitutes an organisational policy.
- The group's doctrinally motivated ideology is based on a widely repudiated misinterpretation of the Islamic religion, 'divinely sanctioned' and enforced by their self-proclaimed caliph.

---

[26] "[B]y misusing religious motivations for their choices and acts, foreign fighters actually do harm to the religious communities which they claim to belong to and fight for". – par 7 of the Council of Europe, Parliamentary Assembly, *Resolution 2190 (2017) – Prosecuting and punishing the crimes against humanity or even possible genocide committed by Daesh*. Text adopted by the Assembly on 12 October 2017 (34th Sitting).

- This fundamentalist and extremist ideology provides religious justification and motivation for the group's overall goals and resulted in the group employing specific discriminatory Islamic practices.
- Their organisational policy propagated their religious superiority and exclusivity, meaning that the individual acts and crimes by *Da'esh* fighters are clearly connected to the organisational policy and overall goal, which was aimed at eradicating religious pluralism and creating a homogenous religious region in northern Iraq and Syria.
- This ideology is substantiated by the systematic, near-identical treatment of certain civilian groups, which demonstrates a common purpose (i. e. collective participation in terms of the *Rome Statute*).
- The perceived 'sanctity' of their common purpose provided its fighters with the necessary 'religious incentive' to willingly commit egregious abuses, crimes and atrocities against specific groups based on their religious identity, or lack thereof. This provides explicit and implicit evidence of a conscious, preconceived and deliberate religious discriminatory intent at an organisational level, shared by all the *Da'esh* fighters, (i. e. satisfying the *dolus specialis* requirement of religious persecution).
- The nature of the violent acts provides clear evidence of 'religious persecution atrocities', while the cumulative effect of the systematic denial of fundamental human rights and freedoms constitutes 'iniquitous religious persecution' (*actus reus* of persecution).
- The group intended to advance their political, religious or ideological causes through committing acts that would result in the 'religious cleansing' of the region under their *de facto* control, in order to create a pure State of Islam (caliphate), i. e. religiously motivated persecution.
- Their systematic and widespread attack on specific religious identities, regarded as infidels or heretics, showed a clear pattern of sectarian atrocities and severe deprivations of fundamental rights, pursuant to their 'divine' organisational ideology, thus clearly satisfying the required intensity threshold.
- Therefore, *Da'esh's* conduct indicates a manifest pattern of religious discrimination and violent conduct on a colossal scale, which provides conclusive proof of religious persecution committed in the name of a religion. In relation to certain religious groups, such as the Yazidi and Christian communities, it was argued that *Da'esh's*

religious discriminatory intent to destroy these groups might have escalated their actions into *prima facie* genocide by religious persecution.

In terms of the primary objective of this study, the most significant conclusion was that the 'taxonomy checklist' provided an adequate framework with which to assess crimes against humanity of religious persecution. However, this does not equate to a determination by an independent and competent court.

8.4.3   Anticipated outcomes of the conceptualisation

The recommended taxonomy is envisioned to be used as a functional 'law-based barometer' to assess factual evidence of contemporary situations of alleged religious persecution in order to ascertain whether or not such situations could be designated as crimes against humanity. Although the proposed taxonomy may not be elevated beyond reasonably merited criticism, it does serve as a holistic, multidisciplinary approach, in understanding crimes against humanity of religious persecution. It is believed that if the proposed conceptualisation proves effective and generally acceptable, it may have various practical applications, such as:

- improve the legal semantics and discourse regarding religious persecution
- create greater legal certainty regarding the scope and application of persecution in the context of international criminal justice;
- lessen judicial and political unease;
- positively influence political and diplomatic rhetoric in order to improve advocacy efforts on behalf of those persecuted;
- provide a practical legal framework that provides greater credibility, objectivity and legal accuracy to the efforts of those advocating for the religiously persecuted, whether through monitoring, supporting, researching, reporting, or otherwise;
- improve criminal accountability for religious persecution by justifying the use of international criminal prosecution systems; which will ultimately
- function as a deterring factor to help curb religious intolerant hostilities and sectarian violence; and
- address the existing impunity for 'grievous religious persecution' and related human rights deprivations.

8.5 Limitations and Future Research

After having critically evaluated this study, two final aspects require consideration before concluding the discussion. In the following section, the limitations of the conceptualisation and suggestions for further research are briefly considered.

8.5.1 Limitations of the proposed conceptualisation

The first instance includes limitations on the scope of application of the research because of structural or institutional constraints, indicative to the public international law system; many of which have already been mentioned. One such example is the consensual nature of the *Rome Statute* of the ICC, which places far-reaching restrictions on the admissibility and jurisdiction of the Court in dealing with situations of 'grievous persecution'. Another is the lack of uniform State practice in recognising, protecting and promoting universally accepted human rights, as well as the lack of a global or unified determination to deter, prevent, and punish severe human rights infringements. In this regard, the ultimate failure of the current system is a lack of resolve in addressing emerging patterns of human rights infringements or atrocities. Consequently, while the proposed taxonomy may serve to advance the cause of criminalising and enforcing prosecution mechanisms for 'grievous persecution', the *ex post facto* attainment of justice may fulfil the right to know the truth and provide a measure of satisfaction for the victims and their families, but fails to serve as a preventative measures.

Second, the nature of this study and the context within which it is situated, inevitable limit the study to a hypothetical proposition, despite support suggesting that the taxonomy checklist may provide for a pragmatic application. In the context of the international legal theatre, legal pluralism will always challenge traditional or conventional legal rules. Consequently, despite a certain level of substantive credibility, it is conceivable that the proposed taxonomy will not be voluntarily accepted by all sectors of society or all governmental administrations, and may even be vigorously opposed by some. Therefore, considering that public international law is based primarily on consensual State acceptance and enforcement, it seems probable that, for the time being, the contribution of this study remains theoretical in nature.

Finally, delineating the scope of 'other-type' conduct remains problematic. Although it was argued that conditions of applicability for crimes against humanity of persecution are sufficiently clear in order to satisfy

8. Conclusions and Recommendations

the legality principle, the exact extent and nature of 'other-type' conduct remain an underdeveloped area of concern. While such an assessment fell outside the parameters of this study, it may well constitute a potential area for future studies. Finding and demarcating a legal description for the scattered spectrum of concurrent 'other-type' persecutory conduct may do more justice to a complex global reality. Other potential areas for further research will be considered next.

8.5.2 Potential for future studies

Considering that international human rights law and international criminal law are still in a relative state of 'infancy', various research contributions have the potential of developing these areas of law and the topic at hand. In relation to the context of this study, and in addition to the potential future topic mentioned, this section is limited to a few specific future topics.

First, during this study the nature and role of religion and a religious identity were discussed in some detail. However, it became clear that the other identity elements constituting acknowledged grounds of persecution are inadequately defined and ambiguous. Developing a better understanding of the discriminatory grounds of persecution may provide further clarity on the nature of the crime.

Second, considering that States have the primary responsibility regarding human rights obligations and enforcing prosecutions for international crimes, advocating for the inclusion of religious persecution under States' domestic legal systems will certainly elevate the status and recognition of this crime. However, it should be clear that what is advocated for in this regard is not merely enacting legislation implementing the *Rome Statute* into national law, but rather a penal code of international crimes, including crimes against humanity of persecution. For example, the German Code of Crimes against International Law establishes individual criminal responsibility for whoever, as part of a widespread or systematic attack directed against any civilian population,

> persecutes an identifiable group or collectivity by depriving such a group or collectivity of fundamental human rights, or by substantially restricting the same, on political, racial, national, ethnic, cultural or religious, gender or other grounds that are recognized as impermissible under the general rules of international law.[27]

---

[27] *Germany: Act to Introduce the Code of Crimes Against International Law* [Germany], 26 June 2002, sec 7(10). The Act also provides for minimum sentences based on persecution.

In this regard, national proscriptions of persecution need not be based on the same threshold of severity as under international criminal law, and may serve to deter and address societal intolerance, discrimination and persecution.

Third, the reciprocal *mens rea* requirement of discriminatory intent shared by 'grievous persecution' and genocide, implies close proximity between these crimes.

> [P]ersecution as a crime against humanity is an offence belonging to the same genus as genocide. Both persecution and genocide are crimes perpetrated against persons that belong to a particular group and who are targeted because of such belonging. [...] Thus, it can be said that, from the viewpoint of mens rea, genocide is an extreme and most inhuman form of persecution. To put it differently, when persecution escalates to the extreme form of wilful and deliberate acts designed to destroy a group or part of a group, it can be held that such persecution amounts to genocide.[28]

Therefore, in building on this study, a possible topic for future studies may include a clear differentiation between religious discriminatory intent constituting persecution, and instances where such intent has escalated into a genocidal intent based on religious identity.

Finally, the proposed taxonomy may have practical application and implication for the ILC's proposal for a *Convention on the Prevention and Punishment of Crimes Against Humanity*.[29] The ILC decided to include the subject 'crimes against humanity' into its long-term programme of work at its 66th session in 2014, and appointed Professor Sean D. Murphy as Special Rapporteur.[30] The text of the draft articles on crimes against humanity, adopted by the Commission,[31] is based on what the ILC Special Rapporteur on crimes against humanity regards as the most widely accepted formulation of

---

[28] *Prosecutor v Kupreškić et al. (Trial Judgement)*, Case No. IT-95-16-T, 14 January 2000, par 636.

[29] UN General Assembly, *Report of the International Law Commission, 69th session (1 May-2 June and 3 July-4 August 2017)*, 2017, A/72/10, pg 10.

[30] UN General Assembly, *Report of the International Law Commission, 66th session (5 May-6 June and 7 July-8 August 2014)*, 2014, Supplement No. 10, A/69/10.

[31] International Law Commission, *Draft articles on Prevention and Punishment of Crimes Against Humanity*. Adopted at its seventy-first session (2019) Available at: https://legal.un.org/ilc/texts/instruments/english/draft_articles/7_7_2019.pdf. Accessed: 12/06/2020.

8. Conclusions and Recommendations

crimes against humanity, that of Article 7 of the *Rome Statute*.[32] Therefore, "except for three non-substantive changes that are necessary given the different context in which the definition is being used",[33] the proposed draft article uses the exact same definition of 'crimes against humanity' as appears in Article 7 of the *Rome Statute*, including the crime of persecution. Consequently, any positive contribution towards conceptualising 'grievous persecution' may have actual application on the interpretation of such a crime in terms of the Draft Convention.[34] It is also noted that the first draft articles further supplement the second suggestion for future research mentioned, requiring States to take the necessary measures "to ensure that crimes against humanity constitute offences under its criminal law ... [and] to establish its jurisdiction over the offences covered".[35]

In summary, it is clear that despite the comparatively extensive nature of this study, there remain many underdeveloped areas or aspects of concern regarding the persecution phenomena. While some of these considerations might be addressed in future research, others might only be resolved through the course of judicial intervention.

8.6 Final Remarks

The international community has come to recognize the common danger posed by 'grievous religious persecution', constituting the flagrant disregard of basic human rights and particularly the right to religious freedom and equality on the basis of religion. In response, the nations of the world have banded together to prescribe acceptable norms of behavior through the legal recognition, enforcement and protection of fundamental human rights on the one hand, and the suppression and punishment of individuals responsible for severe deprivations of such fundamental values, on the

---

[32] UN General Assembly, *First report on crimes against humanity by Sean D. Murphy, Special Rapporteur*, at the 67th session (4 May-5 June and 6 July-7 August 2015), 2015, A/CN.4/680 and Corr.1.
[33] UNGA *First report on crimes against humanity* (2015) par 8.
[34] According to Professor Max Du Plessis, the most important contribution of the Draft Convention is the confirmation of the *jus cogens* nature of crimes against humanity and the consequential effect on universal jurisdiction for such crimes – oral presentation entitled: *A Delicate dance: Complementarity, domestic prosecutions and the Crimes against Humanity Convention*, at a policy seminar entitled: *Forging a Convention on Crimes against Humanity: the Way Forward*, held at the Holocaust and Genocide Centre, Johannesburg, on the 21st of February 2019.
[35] UNGA *Report of the ILC 69th session* (2017) Art 6(1) read with Art 7(1).

other. Though these aspirations have remained elusive in some instances, that circumstance cannot diminish the true progress that can be made if fundamentally optimistic endeavors, such as this one, advance advocacy for those religiously persecuted. As such, this conceptualisation of 'grievous religious persecution' could be a small, but significant contribution in the fulfillment of the timeless dream to free all people from sectarian violence, discrimination and persecution.

Appendix A: Overview of the Basic Principles of International Criminal Law

I   Introduction

The multidisciplinary nature of this study necessitates a general introductory survey of the basic principles of international criminal law to unacquainted readers. An elementary purpose of international criminal law is the direct protection and enforcement of legal and moral values regarded as fundamental to human existence. Furthermore, international prosecution mechanisms may be used as a procedural instrument to prosecute and punish persons responsible for international crimes. It may also serve to end impunity and act as a deterring factor in order to prevent and/or redress the contravention of human rights. Therefore, this appendix will provide an overview of the role and function of international criminal law and its relation to the crime of religious persecution.

The unimaginable human rights atrocities committed during the twentieth century galvanised 'internationalised' concern and direct criminalisation of gross and systematic human rights atrocities. The recognition and protection of human rights in such a way aimed to ensure that there would be no repetition of such horrid atrocities or, at least, if such crimes were committed they would not go unpunished.[1] In this way, most of the international community unified in a conscious determination to punish and deter the recurrence of international crimes by effectively prosecuting those responsible in a concerted effort to end impunity for severe human rights atrocities. However, despite international consensus regarding the need to repress international crimes and human rights atrocities, many such instances occur in the domestic sphere where the scope of national jurisdictional powers and mechanisms may often be biased or ineffective. This is especially prominent in countries where the government either participates in, or precipitates, such violations.[2] Despite the judicial influence that human rights law has had on domestic, regional and international legal systems, the effective implementation of the rule of law and

---

[1]   Zgonec-Rožej, M. (Principal author). *International Criminal Law Manual*. International Bar Association (IBA) (2013), pg 23.
[2]   Triffterer, O., & Ambos K. *Commentary on the Rome Statute of the International Criminal Court: Observers' Notes, Article by Article*. 2nd edition. (2008), pg 24.

recognition of human rights, remain elusive in some areas in the world. Therefore, the protection of human rights and the punishment for international crimes require a supranational dimension through an international control mechanism, such as international criminal law. International criminal law mechanisms are specifically aimed at the maintenance of international peace and security, and are permanently engaged to prevent and punish severe human rights infringements.[3]

2 The basic characteristics of international criminal law

2.1 An introduction to international criminal law

'International criminal law' *sensu stricto* as it will be used in the context of this study,[4] refers to a body of law which establishes individual criminal responsibility under international law in an attempt to protect the "fundamental values of the international legal community as a whole and articulates an *ius puniendi* of that community".[5] These fundamental values of the international legal community include the maintenance of international peace and security, and the protection of internationally recognised human rights.[6]

International criminal law is a body of international rules proscribing international crimes, as well as regulating the principles and procedures governing the investigation, prosecution and punishment of international crimes.[7] International criminal law is primarily aimed at imposing direct individual criminal responsibility and punishment for the authors or instigators of international crimes.[8] Simultaneously, States incur the obligation to take measures at the national level to end impunity for these crimes and contribute to the prevention of such crimes by exercising its criminal jurisdiction over those responsible for international crimes.[9]

---

[3] Triffterer & Ambos *Commentary on the Rome Statute* (2008) 23. See also Cassese, A. *International Criminal Law*. Oxford University Press, 1st edition (2003), pg 18.
[4] The concept of 'international criminal law' may have a number of different meanings within the context of domestic criminal law and transnational criminal law, or may infer aspects of international co-operation in criminal matters.
[5] Kreß, C. *International Criminal Law*. *Max Planck Encyclopedia on Public International Law*, Wolfrum, R. (ed). Heidelberg: Oxford University Press (2011), pg 3.
[6] Kreß *International Criminal Law* (2011) 3.
[7] Zgonec-Rožej *International Criminal Law Manual* (2013) 24.
[8] Art 25 of the *Rome Statute of the International Criminal*.
[9] Preamble of the *Rome Statute*.

International law lacks an international executive body that enforces criminal law, and therefore States are self-governing. Likewise, no international legislative body exists that can enact legislation in order to create a universally accepted criminal code for all international crimes. International courts and tribunals are established by treaty, which provides for and defines the international crimes over which they will have jurisdiction. Jurisdiction over international crimes is shared between international and domestic courts based on the principles of primary and complementary jurisdiction. The enforcement of international criminal law is therefore largely dependent upon consent, in terms of which members of the international community are generally only bound by the principles of international criminal law if they recognise such rules and principles as binding upon them.[10]

2.1.1 The development of international criminal law

Despite earlier propositions, it was not until after World War I that the League of Nations[11] considered the establishment of individual criminal responsibility under an international criminal judicial system.[12] Subsequently, the development of international criminal law was fuelled by three international events. Firstly, the principles that were laid down in the Nuremberg and subsequent Tokyo trials after World War II constituted the precedent for internationalised criminal proceedings. The United Nations (UN) General Assembly affirmed these principles, which found application in the jurisprudence of the war tribunals stemming from the Charter of the IMT at Nuremberg and Tokyo in later years.[13] The second event was the establishment of the *ad hoc* criminal tribunals created by the UN in the former Yugoslavia and Rwanda during the 1990s[14]. The jurisprudence flowing from these courts has cultivated international criminal law

---

[10] Kaul, H. *International Criminal Court (ICC)*. Max Planck Encyclopedia on Public International law, Wolfrum, R. (ed). Heidelberg: Oxford University Press (2011), par 7.
[11] League of Nations, *Covenant of the League of Nations*, 28 April 1919.
[12] Kreß *International Criminal Law* (2011) 4.
[13] UN General Assembly, *Resolution 95(1) on the Affirmation of the Principles of International Law Recognized by the Charter of the Nuremberg Tribunal*. 11 Dec. 1946. A/RES/95.
[14] UN Security Council, *Statute of the International Criminal Tribunal for the Former Yugoslavia* (as amended on 17 May 2002), 25 May 1993; and UN Security Council, *Statute of the International Criminal Tribunal for Rwanda* (as last amended on 13 October 2006), 8 November 1994.

and has added to the realisation of the necessity for a permanent international criminal court. Finally, the adoption of the Rome Statute of the International Criminal Court (Rome Statute) in 2002, established the first permanent and independent international criminal court. Yet, the universality of these principles remains contentious, as Kreß explains:

> The international consensus that perpetrators of crimes under international law should not go unpunished does not mean that there is universal agreement on the way the international criminal justice system should be devised.[15]

2.1.2 Substantive and procedural international criminal law

International criminal law not only criminalises conduct causing harm to others[16] but also conduct that creates an unacceptable risk of harm to others.[17] As such, international criminal law has a punitive as well as a preventative role in enforcing international peace and security as one of the main functions of the UN.[18] In order to achieve this aim, international criminal law comprises both a substantive as well as a procedural law element.

The rules prescribing the substantive and procedural law of international criminal law "can be created and developed in principle by all sources of the law of nations",[19] but are generally derived from treaties, customary law and general principles of criminal law.[20] In this regard, the Statutes and jurisprudence of the various international criminal courts and tribunals have been essential in the development of international criminal law. The provisions of international criminal law can be applied by international courts (such as the ICC) and internationalised courts (such

---

[15] Kreß *International Criminal Law* (2011) 7.
[16] For example, systematic and widespread murder, persecution or rape.
[17] Cassese *International Criminal Law* (2003) 22.
[18] Art 1 of the United Nations, *Charter of the United Nations*, 24 October 1945, 1 UNTS XVI (*UN Charter*).
[19] Triffterer & Ambos *Commentary on the Rome Statute* (2008) 22.
[20] As a subsection of public international law, the legal sources and hierarchy of international criminal law is derived from par 1 of Art 38 of the United Nations, *Statute of the International Court of Justice*, 18 April 1946, established in terms of Chapter XIV of the *Charter of the United Nations* (hereinafter ICJ Statute), which are: international conventions; international custom, as evidence of a general practice accepted as law; general principles of law recognised by the community of nations; judicial decisions and the teachings of the most highly qualified publicists as subsidiary means for the determination of rules of law.

as the *ad hoc* tribunals for Rwanda and Yugoslavia). If such provisions have been incorporated into the national legal system of a State and the proscription of criminal law has not been restricted to substantive law passed by the State, such national courts may also apply the provisions of international criminal law.[21]

Substantive international criminal law entails the proscription of conduct which amounts to international crimes, the subjective or mental elements of international crimes, the defences and circumstances which may excuse the accused from individual criminal liability, and the conditions under which States incur the obligation to prosecute and punish persons accused of international crimes.[22] Substantive international criminal law incorporates principles of national criminal law, human rights law, and international humanitarian law (law of armed conflict). Individual criminal accountability for international crimes may refer to the prohibition or the conditions for the criminal repression and punishment of acts that amount to violations of international humanitarian law. In this way, the crimes committed in the course of an international or an internal armed conflict refer to violations of international humanitarian law principles and is a direct insinuation of war crimes and crimes of aggression. On the other hand, individual criminal accountability may also ensue in instances where international crimes constitute severe international human rights atrocities.[23] Consequently, human rights violations by State actors or human rights abuses by non-State actors infer genocide or crimes against humanity, whether committed in peacetime or in time of armed conflict.[24]

The procedural element of international criminal law governs the procedural requirements before an international tribunal in prosecuting those responsible for international crimes. Procedural mechanisms include the various stages of the procedure, the organs that authorise prosecution, aspects of the law of evidence, and the protection of victims and

---

[21] Triffterer & Ambos *Commentary on the Rome Statute* (2008) 22.
[22] Cassese *International Criminal Law* (2003) 5.
[23] Zgonec-Rožej *International Criminal Law Manual* (2013) 25.
[24] Human rights violations include government transgressions of the rights guaranteed by national, regional, and international human rights laws and acts and omissions directly attributable to the State involving failure to implement legal obligations derived from human rights standards. Human rights abuses, on the other hand, "describes conduct inflicted by non-State actors" – UNHCHR Training manual, No 7, p. 10, in Horton, G. *Dying Alive – A Legal Assessment of Human Rights Violations in Burma*, a report co – funded by the Netherlands Ministry for Development Co-operation. Images Asia (2005), par 5.17 and 5.18.

witnesses.[25] The law of international criminal procedure is not based on a single unified criminal procedure act or treaty; there are consistent procedural rules that have emerged from the principles of due process in terms of human rights law, as well as from practice and jurisprudence of the international criminal tribunals.[26] In the context of international courts, the treaty within which they are contained usually provides for some basic procedural principles, further elaborated in the adoption of a specialised procedural document. In the case of the ICC, the Assembly of States parties adopted the *ICC Rules of Procedure and Evidence* by a two-thirds majority.[27]

Ultimately, international criminal law may be used as an enforcement mechanism to prosecute and punish persons responsible for infringements that constitute international crimes which inherently contravene principles of fundamental human rights. By doing so, criminal prosecution may serve as a deterring factor,[28] which compels respect for fundamental human rights and abstention from acts constituting severe human rights atrocities. However, international criminal law is

> bound by principles and limitations which are generally accepted as a decisive part of criminal law, like the principle of certainty, guilt, responsibility and liability, as well as those for legal justification, excuse and other defences, and the notion that sentences should be proportional to the gravity of harm caused by the act and to the guilt of the individual perpetrator.[29]

2.1.3   Jus cogens norms and obligations erga omnes

International law recognises that certain fundamental rules are higher in authority than the law stipulated in treaties or developed in customary international law.[30] The different categories of these fundamental rules are distinguished as either *jus cogens* norms or obligations *erga omnes* according

---

[25] Cassese *International Criminal Law* (2003) 5.
[26] Zgonec-Rožej *International Criminal Law Manual* (2013) 24.
[27] Art 51(1) and (2) of the *Rome Statute*. Assembly of States Parties to the *Rome Statute* of the International Criminal Court, *Rules of Procedure and Evidence*, ICC-ASP/1/3, at 10, and Corr. 1 (2002), U.N. Doc. PCNICC/2000/1/Add.1 (2000) (hereinafter *ICC Rules of Procedure and Evidence*).
[28] Triffterer & Ambos *Commentary on the Rome Statute* (2008) 24.
[29] Triffterer & Ambos *Commentary on the Rome Statute* (2008) 22–23.
[30] Thouvenin, J. et al. *The Fundamental Rules of the International Legal Order: Jus Cogens and Obligations Erga Omnes*. Leiden: Brill (2006), pg 21.

to the legal consequences attributed to them.[31] *Jus cogens* norms, or peremptory norms of general international law, are defined as norms accepted and recognised by the international community of States as a whole, from which no derogation is permitted. They can only be modified by a subsequent norm of general international law having the same character.[32] Thouvenin explains the role of *jus cogens* norms, stating that:

> ... the concept of jus cogens is founded on community interests and characterized by the prohibition against disposing over certain rights, be it to one's own disadvantage or to the detriment of others who are not in a position to provide effectively for their protection themselves, such as peoples, groups or individuals.[33]

Erga omnes obligations are generally considered as a concept of State responsibility, understood as obligations of a State towards the international community as a whole. These are therefore the concern of all States, and in terms of which all States could be held to have a legal interest.[34] An appropriate example is the obligation on States to proscribe certain conduct as punishable in their domestic penal system and to either prosecute the offenders found on their territory or to extradite them to States that are willing and able to prosecute.[35] The duty on States to criminalise, and to either investigate and prosecute or to extradite a suspect (*aut dedere aut judicare*),[36] forms the basis for the enforcement of international criminal law and may even be regarded as an obligation under customary international law.[37]

The primary rules which belong to *jus cogens* and *erga omnes* norms are virtually identical,[38] including, for example, the prohibition against acts of aggression, war crimes, genocide, crimes against humanity, the core elements of humanitarian law, and also the principles and rules concerning

---

[31] Thouvenin *The Fundamental Rules of the International Legal Order* (2006) 26.
[32] Thouvenin *The Fundamental Rules of the International Legal Order* (2006) 35.
[33] Thouvenin *The Fundamental Rules of the International Legal Order* (2006) 35.
[34] *Case concerning the Barcelona Traction, Light and Power Company, Limited (Belgium v. Spain);* Second Phase, International Court of Justice (ICJ), 5 February 1970, par 32–33.
[35] Zgonec-Rožej *International Criminal Law Manual* (2013) 37.
[36] The obligation of States to try or extradite persons responsible for committing international core crimes is an obligations *erga omnes*.
[37] Bassiouni, M. C. & Wise, E.M. *Aut Dedere Aut Judicare. The Duty to Extradite or Prosecute in International Law.* Marthinus Nijhoff Publishers (1995), pg 5.
[38] Frowein, J.A. *Ius cogens. Max Planck Encyclopedia on Public International law*, Wolfrum, R. (ed). Heidelberg: Oxford University Press (2009), par 10.

the basic rights of the human person.[39] The exclusion of traditional challenges to jurisdiction such as immunity and the principle of universal jurisdiction are consequences of the development of the concepts of *jus cogens* and *erga omnes*.[40] For the purposes of international criminal law it may be inferred that international crimes (which have a *jus cogens* character), may also constitute violations of obligations *erga omnes*, if such crimes were committed by, or imputable to, a State.[41]

2.2 Role and characteristics of the International Criminal Court

The ICC is the first permanent, treaty-based, international criminal court established to help end impunity for the perpetrators of the most serious crimes of concern to the international community. By their very commission, these crimes are serious and obvious infringements of fundamental human rights on a considerable level. The Court is a *sui generis* juristic entity, with a clearly demarcated subject-matter jurisdiction or *ratione materiae*.[42] The ICC "investigates and, where warranted, tries individuals charged with the gravest crimes of concern to the international community: genocide, war crimes, crimes against humanity and the crime of aggression".[43] These crimes oblige State parties to investigate, prosecute, or extradite those individuals who are accused of having committed such crimes, and to punish those individuals who violate these norms and values.[44] However, as a treaty-based institution, the ICC is not a truly universal court as its application is usually restricted to consensual jurisdiction through ratification under national law. This means that States have the primary duty to exercise their criminal jurisdiction over those responsible for international crimes, and the ICC

---

[39] *Barcelona Traction* (1970) par 34.
[40] Thouvenin *The Fundamental Rules of the International Legal Order* (2006) 23.
[41] Thouvenin *The Fundamental Rules of the International Legal Order* (2006) 26.
[42] The ICC is governed by an international treaty, the *Rome Statute*, and functions as a court of last resort, seeking to complement, not replace, national Courts. Although the Court is not an organ of the United Nations, there is a working relationship between certain functions of the UN and the Court – see art 2 of the *Rome Statute*.
[43] ICC website: https://www.icc-cpi.int/about#learnmore. Accessed 06/11/2018. See also *Rome Statute* Art 5.
[44] Bassiouni, M. C. *Introduction to International Criminal Law*. Leiden: Brill | Nijhoff (2012), pg 654.

shall have complementary jurisdiction to national criminal jurisdictions.[45] Therefore, the ICC is merely an extension of national jurisdictional systems and is not assigned more functions than what States themselves are capable of performing under international law. The ICC is thus a court of last resort and it can only exercise jurisdiction over crimes committed after the entry into force of the Statute, which was 1 July 2002 (temporal jurisdiction or *ratione temporis*).[46] The ICC may exercise jurisdiction over nationals of a State party who are accused of crimes, regardless of where the acts are perpetrated (personal jurisdiction or *ratione personae*),[47] and over crimes committed on the territory of State parties, regardless of the nationality of the offender (territorial jurisdiction or *ratione loci*).[48]

The ICC represents the international community's most concerted response to the unimaginable atrocities that deeply shock the conscience of humanity and serves as "the expression of collective action by states parties to a treaty that establishes an institution to carry out justice for certain international crimes".[49]

The functions of the ICC are not only important for State parties. In accordance with the *Rome Statute*, the ICC is established as an independent permanent institution in relationship with the UN system.[50] The most important aspects regarding the relationship between the ICC and the UN relates to jurisdictional triggers of the ICC. In this regard, the Court may exercise its jurisdiction with respect to the commission of a jurisdictionally relevant crime, if such a situation is referred to the Prosecutor by the United Nations Security Council (UNSC).[51]

---

[45] Preamble to the *Rome Statute*.
[46] Zgonec-Rožej *International Criminal Law Manual* (2013) 63. In terms of Art 11 of the *Rome Statute*, the Court will only have jurisdiction over crimes committed after the entry into force of the Statute with respect to States that become parties to the Statute subsequent to its entry into force.
[47] Art 12(2)(b) of the *Rome Statute*.
[48] Art 12(2)(a) of the *Rome Statute*.
[49] Bassiouni *Introduction to International Criminal Law* (2012) 655.
[50] Preamble of the *Negotiated Relationship Agreement Between the International Criminal Court and the United Nations*. ICC-ASP/3/Res.1. Adoption: 04.10.2004. Entry into Force: 22.07.2004. The mutual obligation of cooperation and coordination between the UN and the ICC provides for, *inter alia*: institutional relations (such as reciprocal representation, reports to the UN, and administrative cooperation); as well as judicial assistance (such as documentation and information, testimony of an official of the UN, assistance with investigations by the Prosecutor, privileges and immunities).

Article 21 of the *Rome Statute* provides that the hierarchy of primary sources of the Court are as follows: the *Rome Statute*, *Elements of Crimes* and its *Rules of Procedure and Evidence*; applicable treaties and principles and existing or developing rules of international law,[52] including the established principles of the international law of armed conflict; general principles of law derived by the Court from national laws of legal systems of the world, provided that those principles are not inconsistent with the Statute and with international law and internationally recognised norms and standards; and persuasive judicial precedents (the Court may apply principles and rules of law as interpreted in its previous decisions).

2.3. International crimes

International criminal law comprises international rules and principles that entail the proscription of international crimes. Ambos notes that the internationalisation of certain crimes as crimes of concern to the international community, primarily entails two rationales:

> Firstly, a crime can obtain an international character since it cannot be prosecuted effectively on a national level and there is a common interest of states to prosecute... [t]he second reason is the extreme gravity of certain crimes which is usually accompanied by the unwillingness or inability of national criminal systems to prosecute them.[53]

International crimes are understood as breaches of international rules, values or interests entailing the personal criminal liability of the individuals concerned.[54] There exists "no universally accepted definition of an international crime nor general criteria for determining the scope and the content of an international crime".[55] However, the preamble of the *Rome Statute* refers to unimaginable atrocities that deeply shock the conscience of humanity, and threaten the peace, security and well-being of the world.

---

[51] Art 13(b) of the *Rome Statute*. No investigation or prosecution may be commenced or proceeded under this Statute for a period of 12 months after the Security Council, in a resolution adopted under Chapter VII of the Charter of the UN, has requested the Court to that effect; that request may be renewed by the Council under the same conditions. – art 16 of the *Rome Statute*.
[52] Art 10 of the *Rome Statute*.
[53] Ambos, K. & Wirth, S. *The current law of crimes against humanity: an analysis of UNTAET Regulation 15/2000*. Criminal Law Forum, vol. 13 (2002), pg 13.
[54] Cassese *International Criminal Law* (2003) 5.
[55] Zgonec-Rožej *International Criminal Law Manual* (2013) 26.

Thus, 'international crimes' are referred to as such, based on the grave nature and global effect of their contravention. International crimes exhibit the following general characteristics:

1. International crimes threaten international peace and security and are therefore of concern to the international community as a whole.
2. These crimes are generally restricted to genocide, crimes against humanity, war crimes and aggression.
3. They are either derived from criminal norms emanating from customary international law or found in international treaties, without requiring the intermediate provision of domestic law.
4. Both treaty crimes and customary crimes are, by definition and practice, crimes that violate or threaten fundamental rights values or interests protected by international law.
5. They entail direct individual criminal responsibility for those who commit or are otherwise responsible for such acts.
6. International criminal law is a *jus cogens* norm and trumps any conflicting national laws as well as States' traditional rights to immunity *ratione materiae*, and is therefore binding upon all (or a great majority of States and individuals).
7. The commission of international core crimes establishes universal jurisdiction over such acts, subject to complementary (supplementary) jurisdiction, wherefore such crimes may be prosecuted before international or domestic criminal courts.
8. The proscription of international crimes is aimed principally at the suppression of human rights abuses and violations.[56]

Looking at the historical development of the codification of international law, the earliest customary international law crime was piracy, which today is codified in international law.[57] War crimes and crimes against humanity, which has a customary international law status, are codified in the

---

[56] As summarised in Zgonec-Rožej *International Criminal Law Manual* (2013) 27. See also Kreß *International Criminal Law* (2011) 4.
[57] Art 101 of the UN General Assembly, *Convention on the Law of the Sea*, 10 December 1982.

Rome Statute,⁵⁸ together with genocide⁵⁹ and torture.⁶⁰ Multilateral treaty crimes include, *inter alia*, apartheid,⁶¹ hijacking of aircraft,⁶² offences against the safety of maritime navigation⁶³, drug-trafficking⁶⁴ and international terrorism.⁶⁵ International criminal law may, therefore, be said to include the so-called 'core crimes', which fall within the jurisdiction of international courts and tribunals, as well as subsuming certain transnational crimes or so-called treaty crimes as underlying acts of the core crimes, such as persecution.⁶⁶

2.3.1 The international core crimes

The most serious crimes of concern to the international community⁶⁷ are the so-called core crimes of international criminal law *stricto sensu*,⁶⁸ and are the gravest of crimes in international law.⁶⁹ The international core crimes have reached the status of *jus cogens* norms, trump any conflicting

---

⁵⁸ Art 5(1) of the *Rome Statute*.
⁵⁹ UN General Assembly, *Convention on the Prevention and Punishment of the Crime of Genocide*, 9 December 1948, United Nations, Treaty Series, vol. 78, pg 277 (*Genocide Convention 1948*).
⁶⁰ UN General Assembly, *Convention against Torture and Other Cruel, Inhuman or Degrading Treatment or Punishment: resolution / adopted by the General Assembly*, 10 December 1984, A/RES/39/46, (hereafter referred to as the *Convention against Torture*).
⁶¹ UN General Assembly, *International Convention on the Suppression and Punishment of the Crime of Apartheid*, U.N Doc. A/Res/3068 (XXVIII), 30 November 1973, entered into force on 18 July 1976, (hereafter referred to as the *Apartheid Convention*).
⁶² UN General Assembly, Convention on Offences and Certain Other Acts Committed on Board Aircraft (1963) 704 U.N.T.S. 219.
⁶³ UN General Assembly, *Convention for the Suppression of Unlawful Acts Against the Safety of Maritime Navigation*, 10 March 1988, No. 29004.
⁶⁴ UN Economic and Social Council (ECOSOC), *United Nations Convention Against Illicit Traffic in Narcotic Drugs and Psychotropic Substances*, 19 December 1988.
⁶⁵ Organization of American States (OAS), Convention to Prevent and Punish the Acts of Terrorism Taking the Form of Crimes against Persons and Related Extortion that are of International Significance, 2 February 1971, OAS, Treaty Series, No. 37.
⁶⁶ Zgonec-Rožej *International Criminal Law Manual* (2013) 37.
⁶⁷ Preamble (4) and (9) and Art 5 of the *Rome Statute*.
⁶⁸ Werle, G. *Principles of International Criminal Law*. The Hague: TMC Asser Press (2005), pg 26.
⁶⁹ Preamble of UN General Assembly, *Convention on the Non-Applicability of Statutory Limitations to War Crimes and Crimes Against Humanity*, 26 November 1968, A/RES/2391(XXIII), (hereafter referred to as the *Convention on War Crimes and Crimes Against Humanity*).

national judicial systems, and supersede traditional limitations on admissibility.[70] This status attached to the core crimes recognises the preservation of peace and the protection of peoples and individuals as a higher value of international law,[71] especially in relation to their own State or government leadership. It is apparent that the international core crimes are norms of international law, accepted as such by the international community. Therefore, the criminalisation of the international core crimes is part of fundamental international law norms from which no derogation is ever permitted.

Historically speaking, the *Versailles Peace Treaty* in 1919 may be considered as containing the first references to what was the most serious of international crimes condemned by the international community, viz. violations of the sanctity of treaties, crimes against international morality, crimes against humanity, and the violations of the laws and customs of war.[72] The post World War II Charter of the IMT provided that war crimes, crimes against peace, and crimes against humanity entail individual criminal responsibility.[73] In the aftermath of the mass atrocities in Yugoslavia and Rwanda, the UN adopted resolutions by establishing the *ad hoc* tribunals that expanded the codification and function of the international core crimes.[74] The *Rome Statute* served to codify and crystallise the substantive definitions of the core crimes[75] "under general international law instead of creating new crimes under international conventional law".[76] In the section below, war crimes, genocide and crimes of aggression will be briefly discussed. Crimes against humanity forms part of the central theme of persecution and will thus be discussed separately below.

---

[70] Kreß *International Criminal Law* (2011) 4.
[71] Frowein *Ius cogens* (2009) par 6.
[72] Werle *Principles of International Criminal Law* (2005) 2-6.
[73] Werle *Principles of International Criminal Law* (2005) 6.
[74] UN Security Council, *Security Council resolution 955 (1994) [Establishment of the International Criminal Tribunal for Rwanda]*, 8 November 1994, S/RES/955 (1994). UN Security Council, *Security Council resolution 1660 (2006) [International Tribunal for the Prosecution of Persons Responsible for Serious Violations of International Humanitarian Law Committed in the Territory of the Former Yugoslavia since 1991]*, 28 February 2006, S/RES/1660 (2006).
[75] See Art 5 to 8 of the *Rome Statute*.
[76] Kreß *International Criminal Law* (2011) 3.

a) War crimes

Article 8 of the *Rome Statute* sets out approximately fifty offences, and defines war crimes by reference to serious violations of the laws and customs of war,[77] (which belong to the *corpus* of international humanitarian law of armed conflict)[78] or, whenever applicable, 'grave breaches' in terms of the Geneva Conventions.[79] 'War crimes' may be considered as an international crime during the course of an international or non-international armed conflict. War crimes comprise of 'grave breaches', which are "designed to protect military personnel who are no longer taking part in the fighting (i. e. wounded, shipwrecked and sick combatants) and people not actively involved in hostilities (i. e. civilians, medical and religious military personnel)".[80] War crimes also comprise serious violations of the laws and customs applicable in armed conflict that "establishes the rights and obligations of belligerents in the conduct of military operations, and limits the means (i. e. weapons) and methods (i. e. military tactics) of warfare".[81]

b) Genocide

Genocide, or the 'crime of crimes'[82] as it has also been called, is an international treaty crime under the *Genocide Convention*.[83] The Convention "seeks to prevent, to combat, and to criminalize – as an ultimate and most evil corollary of racial and religious discrimination – acts committed with intent to destroy, in whole or in part, a national, ethnical, racial or religious

---

[77] The Court shall have jurisdiction in respect of war crimes in particular when committed as part of a plan or policy or as part of a large-scale commission of such crime – Art 8(1) of the *Rome Statute*.
[78] Cassese *International Criminal Law* (2003) 47.
[79] The Geneva Conventions include the International Committee of the Red Cross (ICRC), *Geneva Convention for the Amelioration of the Condition of the Wounded and Sick in Armed Forces in the Field* (First Geneva Convention), 12 August 1949, 75 UNTS 31; *Geneva Convention for the Amelioration of the Condition of Wounded, Sick and Shipwrecked Members of Armed Forces at Sea* (Second Geneva Convention), 12 August 1949, 75 UNTS 85; *Geneva Convention Relative to the Treatment of Prisoners of War* (Third Geneva Convention), 12 August 1949, 75 UNTS 135; *Geneva Convention Relative to the Protection of Civilian Persons in Time of War* (Fourth Geneva Convention), 12 August 1949, 75 UNTS 287.
[80] Zgonec-Rožej *International Criminal Law Manual* (2013) 85.
[81] Zgonec-Rožej *International Criminal Law Manual* (2013) 85.
[82] *Prosecutor v Jean Kambanda* (Judgement and Sentence), Case No. ICTR 97-23-S, 4 September 1998, par 16.
[83] *Genocide Convention* (1948).

group".[84] Genocide is a denial of the right of existence of an entire human group based on national, ethnical, racial or religious grounds with intent to destroy such a group by means of acts such as mass murder or enforcing such measures that will lead to the large-scale physical or psychological destruction of the group.

c) Crimes of aggression

The concept of crimes of aggression means the planning, preparation, initiation or execution, by a person in a position to exercise control over or direct the political or military action of a State, of an act of aggression which, by its character, gravity and scale, constitutes a manifest violation of the Charter of the UN. An act of aggression is understood as the use of armed force by a State against the sovereignty, territorial integrity or political independence of another State, or in any other manner inconsistent with the Charter of the UN.[85]

2.3.2   The elements of crimes under the Rome Statute

Considering that this study is focussed on crimes against humanity, this section is not intended to provide an analysis of the individual elements of each of the core crimes, as such. The aim is to provide a general explanation of the framework that is followed throughout the *Rome Statute* and the *ICC Elements of Crimes*.[86]

The *ICC Elements of Crimes*[87] is a document outlining conduct which amounts to core crimes, the mental elements of such crimes, and the contextual framework within which such acts must be committed. Therefore, the *ICC Elements of Crimes* provides greater certainty and clarity regarding

---

[84] Van Boven, T. *Racial and Religious Discrimination. Max Planck Encyclopedia on Public International law*, Wolfrum, R. (ed). Heidelberg: Oxford University Press (2009), pg 609.

[85] Art 8 of the *Rome Statute*. Although the Special Working Group on the Crime of Aggression has elaborated on proposals for a provision on the crime of aggression, the Court's jurisdiction over crimes of aggression is yet to be activated, subject to ratification or acceptance, and shall only enter into force in accordance with art 121, par 5.

[86] International Criminal Court (ICC), *Elements of Crimes*, 2011, Official Records of the Review Conference of the *Rome Statute* of the International Criminal Court, Kampala, 31 May-11 June 2010 (International Criminal Court publication, RC/11) (hereinafter referred to as *ICC Elements of Crimes*).

[87] Under Art 9 of the *Rome Statute*.

the content of each crime.[88] The *ICC Elements of Crimes* assist the Court in the interpretation and application of the crimes under its jurisdiction and is reflective of the primary rules of international law.[89] The majority of the Rome Diplomatic Conference "were concerned at the prospect of unduly restricting judicial discretion and felt that it would be unacceptable to make the elements binding".[90] Consequently, the *ICC Elements of Crimes* serves as a primary source of applicable law, yet it is not binding on the Court.

The point of departure regarding an understanding of the *ICC Elements of Crimes* is the general introduction, in which certain crucial issues that arise in all crimes are dealt with. The elements of crimes are generally structured in accordance with the following principles:

a) As the elements of crimes focus on the conduct, consequences and circumstances associated with each crime (material elements or *actus reus*), they are generally listed in that order.
b) Generally, Article 30 discusses the requisite mental element (*mens rea*) applicable to all crimes, however, when required a particular mental element (*dolus specialis*) is listed after the affected conduct, consequence or circumstance.
c) Contextual circumstances are listed last (*chapeau* elements).

In order to convict the accused, the Court must be convinced of the guilt of the accused beyond reasonable doubt.[91] Accordingly, in order to secure a conviction, the Prosecution must invariably prove the following key elements:

a) Material element (*actus reus*)

Actus reus (as it is known in Anglo-American legal systems), or criminally liable conduct, refers to the general concept which encompasses conduct, compliance with the definitional elements of each particular crime (and thus the necessary conduct), as well as unlawfulness.[92] In terms of this basic understanding, the principle of legality requires that an accused can only be convicted of an offence if that person's conduct falls within the

---

[88] Dörmann, K. et al. *Elements of War Crimes under the Rome Statute of the International Criminal Court: Sources and Commentary*. Cambridge University Press (2003), pg 8.
[89] Zgonec-Rožej *International Criminal Law Manual* (2013) 105.
[90] Dörmann *Elements of War Crimes* (2003) 8.
[91] Art 66(3) of the *Rome Statute*.
[92] Snyman, C.R. *Criminal law*. LexisNexis, 6th edition (2014), pg 74.

ambit of a specific type of conduct set out in the definitional elements of the relevant crime. Such conduct must also have occurred in circumstances which are contrary to the *boni mores* (legal convictions of society). Within this concept, 'criminal conduct' can consist of: (1) the proscription of the commission of a particular type of act, regardless of its consequences (so-called formally defined crimes or conduct crimes); or (2) the prohibition of any conduct which causes a specific condition or effect (so-called materially defined crimes or result crimes).

The 'material elements' in terms of the *Rome Statute* thus include three types of non-mental elements (conduct, consequence and circumstance).[93] Contextual circumstance will be discussed separately later. However, it should be noted that such contextual requirements form part of the material elements of the crimes and must therefore be committed with intent and knowledge regarding 'condcut'. While it may be relatively easy to list the core crimes, it is more difficult to encapsulate the 'conduct' that defines them. In this sense, the core crimes are usually not defined as separate criminally liable conduct, but are qualified based on the commission of one or more underlying act, committed in definitional circumstances that qualify such conduct as core crimes. The underlying act can be compared to a crime under domestic criminal law, such as rape, which in itself contains certain definitional requirements to constitute a criminal offence; whether based on the nature of the act or its prohibited consequences. Such a criminal offence may constitute a core crime, provided the necessary prerequisites of applicability are satisfied. It is also generally accepted that any underlying act must be committed with its own *mens rea* and *actus reus*, including any specific requirements accompanying the offence, such as discriminatory intent in the case of persecution.

The requirement of 'unlawfulness' found in the Statute or in other parts of international law, particularly international humanitarian law, is generally not specified in the elements of crimes and is thus inferred from general principles of criminal law.[94] It is also assumed that there are no constraints on the principle of legality in this regard.[95]

---

[93] *ICC Elements of Crimes*, General Introduction par 7.
[94] *ICC Elements of Crimes*, General Introduction par 6.
[95] "The principle of legality aims at preventing the prosecution and punishment of an individual for acts which he reasonably believed to be lawful at the time of their commission" See Kittichaisaree K. *International Criminal Law*. Oxford University Press (2001), pg 43.

b) Mental element (*Mens rea* or guilty mind of the accused)

In order to establish that a person is guilty of a crime within the Rome Statute, it must be shown that the perpetrator possessed the necessary mental element of the crime at the time of the commission of the prohibited act or consequence. Article 30 of the Rome Statute essentially establishes the default position regarding the requisite mental element pertaining to all crimes under its jurisdiction.[96]

> Unless otherwise provided, a person shall be criminally responsible and liable for punishment for a crime within the jurisdiction of the Court only if the material elements are committed with intent and knowledge.[97]

In terms of the mental element, a person has intent where: in relation to conduct, that person means to engage in the conduct; or in relation to a consequence, that person means to cause that consequence or is aware that it will occur in the ordinary course of events.

In relation to formally defined crimes (conduct crimes), the accused must have intended to engage in the conduct (*dolus directus*).[98] Such conduct must consist of a voluntary (willing) human act. Although not explicitly provided for, it seems likely that certain offences within the jurisdiction of the Court may also be committed by omission when considering the history and jurisprudence of the particular offence in international law and principles drawn from national legal systems.[99] It will be argued that persecution may, under certain circumstances, be committed through the omission of a *de facto* authority regarding certain obligations *erga omnes*.

In relation to materially defined crimes (result crimes), the aim or objective of the accused must have been to cause the prohibited result or consequence (*dolus directus*); or where the accused aimed to achieve another result, but foresaw such a consequence inevitably occurring (*dolus*

---

[96] Art 30 read with par two of the General Introduction of the *ICC Elements of Crimes* details the manner in which Art 30 of the *Rome Statute* (the mental element), is to be applied.

[97] Art 30(1) of the *Rome Statute*. The existence of intent and knowledge can be inferred from relevant facts and circumstances.

[98] Please note that the use of the terms 'intent' and 'intention', as used throughout this paper, are concomitantly similar expressions which refer to a form of culpability or fault. These terms may be defined as 'the blameworthy state of mind' of a criminally responsible person that performs an unlawful act with the will to perform such act or cause such consequence while knowing that this conduct is unlawful.

[99] Art 21 of the *Rome Statute*.

indirectus) in the ordinary course of events (or as a prerequisite or necessary side effect of the desired objective). The phrase 'will occur in the ordinary course of events' used in the *Rome Statute* appears to allow for a lower threshold required for the foreseeability of a particular prohibited result. However, it leaves little room for an interpretation which includes *dolus eventualis* within the concept of intent as a kind of constructive intention.[100]

'Knowledge' means awareness that a circumstance exists or a consequence will occur in the ordinary course of events.[101] Although this understanding of 'knowledge' seems ambiguous, 'awareness that a circumstance exists' is relevant to the mental element in circumstances where the offence requires awareness of a particular circumstance in addition to the intent to act.[102] In regards to crimes against humanity, the *International Criminal Tribunal for the Former Yugoslavia* (ICTY) has stated that: "[t]he perpetrator must have intended to commit the underlying offence, combined with knowledge of the broader context in which the offence occurs".[103] In criminal law, the term 'knowledge' is also commonly understood to refer to a cognitive appreciation of the unlawfulness or unjustifiability of the prohibited act or result.[104] In this sense, 'knowledge' could be interpreted to mean awareness by the perpetrator that a circumstance exists or a consequence will occur in the ordinary course of events which precludes any justification for his actions, i. e. wrongfulness.

Where no reference is made in the *ICC Elements of Crimes* to a mental element for any particular conduct, consequence or circumstance listed, it is understood that the relevant mental element contained in Article 30 applies, i. e. intent, knowledge, or both. With respect to mental elements associated with elements involving a value judgement, such as those using the terms 'inhumane' or 'severe', it is not necessary that the perpetrator personally completed a particular value judgement, unless otherwise indicated.[105]

---

[100] Ambos, K. *General Principles of Criminal Law in the Rome Statute*. Crim LF, 10 (1999) 22. The threshold of *dolus eventualis* entails the concept of recklessness, but not that of negligence or gross negligence.
[101] "Know" and "knowingly" shall be construed accordingly.
[102] Byron, C. *War Crimes and Crimes Against Humanity in the Rome Statute of the International Criminal Court.* Manchester University Press (2009), pg 8.
[103] *Prosecutor v Tihomir Blaškić (Trial Judgement)*, Case No. IT-95-14-T, 3 March 2000, par 220.
[104] Snyman *Criminal law* (2014) 197–198.
[105] *ICC Elements of Crimes*, General Introduction par 4.

c) *Chapeau* requirements (contextual requirements)

The core crimes are founded on the commission of underlying criminally liable conduct in circumstances or based on the extreme gravity of certain crimes, which qualifies such conduct as serious crimes of international concern. The *chapeau* or contextual requirements refer to the conditions of applicability which must be satisfied in order to turn a specific underlying offence into a core crime. For example, murder may qualify as genocide if the conduct took place in the context of a manifest pattern of similar conduct directed against that group. The contextual requirements capture the essence of such crimes in order to establish the jurisdictional threshold of the Court.

2.4 Jurisdiction

International criminal law may be directly enforced through international criminal jurisdictions, such as the *ad hoc* tribunals or the ICC, or may be enforced indirectly through States.[106]

2.4.1 Primary and universal jurisdiction of national courts

As a direct consequence of the responsibility on States to prevent, and to either investigate and prosecute or to extradite a suspect responsible for acts constituting international crimes, such State obligations restrict the jurisdiction of the ICC. Therefore, "the national judiciary acts as the fiduciary of the international *ius puniendi*",[107] in terms of which States have the primary duty to exercise its criminal jurisdiction over those responsible for international crimes, or alternatively to extradite such persons to a State that is willing and able to exercise jurisdiction.[108]

> Thus, for international criminal justice truly to be achieved, national courts must be in a position to prosecute the great majority of offenders.[109]

The exercise of domestic jurisdiction for international crimes will mean that a State is asserting a form of sovereignty based on aspects of territoriality, active nationality, passive nationality, or based on the 'protective'

---

[106] Kreß *International Criminal Law* (2011) 4.
[107] Kreß *International Criminal Law* (2011) 4.
[108] Zgonec-Rožej *International Criminal Law Manual* (2013) 333.
[109] Zgonec-Rožej *International Criminal Law Manual* (2013) 333.

principle.¹¹⁰ In the context of this study, these traditional forms of jurisdiction will not be considered. However, it is important to note that the primacy of jurisdiction is not always provided to States, as is the case with the two *ad hoc* international tribunals. The relevant Statutes provide for the primary jurisdiction of the *ad hoc* tribunals, in concurrence with national courts.¹¹¹

In terms of the *Rome Statute*, it is the duty of every State to exercise its criminal jurisdiction over those responsible for international crimes,¹¹² thus charging States with the primary but also universal duty to exercise jurisdiction. Universal jurisdiction is "based solely on the nature of the crime, without regard to where the crime was committed, the nationality of the alleged or convicted perpetrator, the nationality of the victim, or any other connection to the State exercising such jurisdiction".¹¹³

> ... the prevalent view, which is consistent with current State practice, is that States have the right to assert universal jurisdiction over genocide, war crimes, crimes against humanity and torture.¹¹⁴

Universal jurisdiction over an international crime may be triggered when two criteria are satisfied: firstly, the crime must be one of a *jus cogens* nature; and secondly, the commission of the crime is so serious and on such a scale that it can justly be regarded as an attack on the international legal order.¹¹⁵ The reason for this is that *jus cogens* offences may be punished by any State because the offenders are "common enemies of all mankind and all nations have an equal interest in their apprehension and prosecution".¹¹⁶ Therefore, the international community as a whole is entrusted with the obligation to prosecute and punish any person for such international crimes. By its very nature, the exercise of universal jurisdiction is

---

[110] Zgonec-Rožej *International Criminal Law Manual* (2013) 334.
[111] Art 8(2) *ICTR* and art 9(2) of the *ICTY*.
[112] Art 1 of the *Rome Statute*.
[113] 'Principle 1 – Fundamentals of Universal Jurisdiction' in *The Princeton Principles on Universal Jurisdiction* (Princeton Project on Universal Jurisdiction, 2001) (Routledge, Oxford 2001) 28, in Zgonec-Rožej *International Criminal Law Manual* (2013) 339.
[114] Zgonec-Rožej *International Criminal Law Manual* (2013) 338.
[115] Jones, J. R. W.D. *Immunity and 'Double criminality': General Augusto Pinochet before the House of Lords'* in Sienho Yee and Wang Tieya (eds) *International Law in the Post-Cold War World* (Routledge, London 2001), pg 264, in Zgonec-Rožej *International Criminal Law Manual* (2013) 362.
[116] *Demanjuk v Petrovsky* (1985) 603 F. Supp. 1468; 776 F. 2d. 571.

highly politicised and is therefore only preferred as a 'default jurisdiction'.[117] Consequently, it is generally accepted that

> unless the territorial State or State of nationality is unable or unwilling to carry out proceedings, much in line with the principle of complementarity that limits the operation of the ICC, other States should not assert jurisdiction based on universality.[118]

Universal jurisdiction does, however, provide an important preventative measure in cases where an impunity gap for international crimes may otherwise arise, wherefore universal jurisdiction for international crimes must be considered to be a viable and realistic option.[119] As mentioned, the *Rome Statute* implicitly enforces the exercise of universal jurisdiction in terms of the core crimes, but is explicit on conferring the priority in the exercise of jurisdiction over crimes within the jurisdiction of the Court to national criminal jurisdictions.

2.4.2 Complementary jurisdiction of the ICC

Complementarity implies that the ICC is a 'court of last resort', and may only exercise it's jurisdiction in a subsidiary manner (complementary) to that of national jurisdictions.[120] In terms of the *Rome Statute*, the principle of complementary jurisdiction means that the Court can neither infringe upon national sovereignty nor override national legal systems capable and willing to carry out their international legal obligations.[121] The ICC will, therefore, only investigate and prosecute where national courts have failed or are unwilling or unable to undertake *bona fide* prosecutions.[122] In this regard, the principle of complementarity requires a comprehensive test regarding the adequacy of national criminal jurisdictions. This assessment of adequacy "involves an obligation on States parties to establish their jurisdiction over the ICC crimes to the extent required for the purpose of national prosecution".[123] In other words, the principle of

---

[117] Cassese, A. *Is the Bell Tolling For Universality? A Plea For A Sensible Notion of Universal Jurisdiction*. 1 J Int'l Crim Justice (2003), pg 595.
[118] Zgonec-Rožej *International Criminal Law Manual* (2013) 339.
[119] Zgonec-Rožej *International Criminal Law Manual* (2013) 346.
[120] Preamble of the *Rome Statute*.
[121] Bassiouni *Introduction to International Criminal Law* (2012) 655.
[122] Art 17 of the *Rome Statute*.
[123] Kleffner, J. K. *The Impact of Complementarity on National Implementation of Substantive International Criminal Law*. 1 J Int'l Crim Justice (2003), in Zgonec-Rožej *International Criminal Law Manual* (2013) 350.

complementarity is not absolute. The 'assessment of adequacy' must determine whether the relevant State has affected domestic legislation in order to give effect to their *aut dedere aut judicare* obligation.

> ... a purposive evaluation of the ICC Statute leads to the conclusion that unless States do implement the substantive law of the ICC Statute in their national legislation, the ICC will be unable to perform its complementary function effectively [and the Court] will become a court of first (and only) instance for the prosecution of international crimes instead of the subsidiary court it is envisaged to be.[124]

It is clear that the ICC may not exercise its jurisdiction over a particular case if a State (whether State party or non-party State) is willing and able to conduct a proper and fair trial.[125] Therefore, Court will only exercise its complementary jurisdiction when one of the three 'trigger mechanisms'[126] are activated:

- when a State party refers a matter to the Court[127] in circumstances where the accused is a national of a State party,[128] or the alleged crime took place on the territory of a State party;[129]
- a situation is referred to the Court by the UN Security Council;[130] or
- the Prosecutor initiates an investigation *proprio motu* on the basis of information on crimes within the Court's jurisdiction.[131]

It seems unfortunate that the *Rome Statute* does not provide for the alleged victims of crimes (or non-governmental organisations acting on their behalf), to refer a case to the ICC.[132] Whereas the UN Human Rights Treaty

---

[124] Zgonec-Rožcj *International Criminal Law Manual* (2013) 350.
[125] Cassese *International Criminal Law* (2003) 15.
[126] Triffterer & Ambos *Commentary on the Rome Statute* (2008) 581.
[127] Art 14 of the *Rome Statute*.
[128] Art 12(2)(b) of the *Rome Statute*.
[129] Art 12(2)(a) of the *Rome Statute*.
[130] Art 13(b) of the *Rome Statute*.
[131] Art 15 read with Art 13(c) of the *Rome Statute*. The prosecutor is authorised to initiate an investigation on the basis of information he has received, after which he must state a conclusion on whether a reasonable basis to proceed exist. If the Prosecutor concludes that there is a reasonable basis to proceed with an investigation, he or she shall submit to the Pre-Trial Chamber a request for authorisation of an investigation, together with any supporting material collected.
[132] Zgonec-Rožej *International Criminal Law Manual* (2013) 422. Although the Prosecutor may use such evidence to initiate an investigation *proprio motu* on the basis of

Bodies make provision for an individual complaints system in order to monitor the core international human rights treaties, the Prosecutor may only use the information and allegations from individual complaints as evidence.

The functions of the ICC may affect non-member States by regulating State parties' relationship obligations to non-member States.[133] As a result of the consensual nature of the ICC's jurisdiction, non-member States are usually not subject to the exercise of the Court's jurisdiction. However, there are four exceptions to this rule. The first exception is where the UNSC refers the matter to the ICC. A referral by the UNSC "can enlarge the scope of activity of the ICC in that it can refer situations ... even if the concerned States are not parties to the *Rome Statute*".[134] The second is where a non-member State accepts the exercise of jurisdiction by the Court 'with respects to the crimes in question' on an *ad hoc* basis in terms of Article 12(3). The third exception is in the case where a State party refers a situation to the Court. Kaul concludes that:

> Consistent with the concept of the international legal interest in the liability for international crimes and its fundamental value for the international community, there is no requirement of reciprocity or of a specific interest in the matter.[135]

Therefore, no territorial or personal jurisdictional link is required, provided the referring State possesses the relevant information. In such instances, the Court may investigate the matter regardless of the current whereabouts or nationality of the accused, and regardless of whether or not the relevant State is a party to the Statute. Finally, the Prosecutor may initiate an investigation *proprio motu* in accordance with Article 15, provided the other prerequisites for jurisdiction and admissibility are met.

In conclusion, in order to put an end to impunity for the perpetrators of core crimes, and to contribute to the prevention of breaches of human rights, national criminal jurisdictions have the primary responsibility to prevent, investigate, prosecute and punish such perpetrators. The exercise of universal jurisdiction by States flows directly from this obligation on States to prosecute and punish, or at least extradite, persons responsible

---

information on crimes within the Court's jurisdiction, no provision is made for individuals to approach the Office of the Prosecutor.
[133] Bassiouni *Introduction to International Criminal Law* (2012) 655.
[134] Kaul *International Criminal Court* (2011) par 74.
[135] Kaul *International Criminal Court* (2011) par 72.

for international crimes.[136] Based on the principle of complementarity, national prosecutions of international crimes are preferable to international prosecution for a number of reasons.[137] However, in instances where domestic criminal courts fail to satisfy the adequacy assessment in Article 17, the ICC may exercise jurisdiction, provided one of the jurisdictional triggers is activated. It is thus clear that in instances where the crimes committed are of concern to the international community, the variants of jurisdictional triggers will ultimately prevent a complete ban on prosecution by the Court.

3. The contextual framework of crimes against humanity in terms of the Rome Statute

The criminalisation of acts as 'crimes against humanity' originated from the idea that there exist some elementary principles of humanity under a universal standard of human dignity, freedom and equality, which should be adhered to in all circumstances. It is generally accepted that the Martens Clause was the first formal recognition of "the laws of humanity and the requirements of the public conscience".[138] The subsequent 1907 Hague Convention reaffirmed that the human person remains under the protection of the principles of humanity and the dictates of the public conscience, arguing that "existing State practices derived from those values and principles [are] deemed to constitute the 'laws of humanity'".[139] However, the notion of 'crimes against humanity' was used for the first time in the Declaration of 28 May 1915, denouncing the Armenian massacre by the Turkish Government during World War I.[140] In 1919, the notion resurfaced at the *Preliminary Peace Conference of the Versailles Peace Treaty* in regards to the responsibilities relating to World War I. It was submitted to the Versailles Conference that the criminal accountability of

---

[136] Werle *Principles of International Criminal Law* (2005) 60.

[137] Such as: aspects of politics and foreign policy involved in international adjudication, sociological reasons, the vast commission of international crimes and the impracticality of prosecutions before a single court, the greater recognition and legitimacy provided by domestic courts, and direct democratic accountability – Zgonec-Rožej *International Criminal Law Manual* (2013) 333.

[138] *Convention (II) with Respect to the Laws and Customs of War on Land and its annex: Regulations concerning the Laws and Customs of War on Land.* The Hague, 29 July 1899.

[139] Bassiouni, M. C. *Crimes Against Humanity*. http://www.crimesofwar.org/a-z-guide/crimes-against-humanity/#sthash.xfVy1loq.dpuf. Accessed 27/02/2013.

[140] Ambos, K. *Treatise on International Criminal Law: Volume II: The Crimes and Sentencing.* (2014), pg 46.

individuals during the war should extend to "offences against the laws of humanity".[141] However, no consensus could be reached regarding a definition for crimes against the laws of humanity as a universal standard of humanity was unattainable. Although the *Treaty of Versailles* was the first treaty to codify individual criminal responsibility for crimes of international law,[142] crimes against the laws of humanity at that stage would have amounted to breaches of moral and not positive law, thus discarding the principle of legality.[143]

It was not until the Nuremberg trials, following the Second World War, that 'crimes against humanity' became a distinct and identifiable crime used in a courtroom setting. It was clear that the atrocities committed by Nazi Germany not only pertained to those found in traditional warfare, such as violations of the laws and customs of war, but that some of the most egregious violations ascribed to the Third Reich were acts of an utmost inhumane character based on political, religious and racial discrimination and intolerance. The signing of the Declaration of St James in 1942 established the UN War Crimes Commission, with the aim of documenting atrocities amounting to war crimes and crimes against humanity. This sculpted the foundation for the *International Military Tribunal* to prosecute major war criminals.[144] Consequently, the Charters of Nuremberg and Tokyo[145] included crimes against humanity in Articles 6(c) and 5(c), respectively.[146] An important feature in the Charter's terminology of crimes against humanity is the phrase 'whether or not in breach of the domestic law of the country where perpetrated', which essentially circumvented the problem of legality indicative of this newly conceived crime. *Control Council*

---

[141] *Report presented to the Preliminary Peace Conference by the Commission on the Responsibility of Authors of the War and on the Enforcement of Penalties*, in *Carnegie Endowment for International procedure, Division of International Law*, Pamphlet No. 32.
[142] Ambos *Treatise on International Criminal Law* (2013) 3.
[143] Bassiouni *Crimes Against Humanity*.
[144] Ambos *Treatise on International Criminal Law* (2013) 4.
[145] United Nations, *Charter of the International Military Tribunal for the Far East*, 19 January 1946.
[146] Art 6(c) of the United Nations, *Charter of the International Military Tribunal*, 8 August 1945 (Nuremberg Charter), defined crimes against humanity as: "...murder, extermination, enslavement, deportation, and other inhumane acts committed against any civilian population, before or during the war; or persecutions on political, racial or religious grounds in execution of or in connection with any crime within the jurisdiction of the Tribunal, whether or not in violation of the domestic law of the country where perpetrated".

Law No. 10 formed the basis of a second series of prosecutions of Nazi leaders.[147] Importantly, the omission of the 'connection' requirement (found in Article 6 of the Nuremberg Charter) permitted individual criminal responsibility for acts committed by the German Government against German nationals.[148] Crimes against humanity could, therefore, be committed against persons of the same nationality as the perpetrator.

The UN General Assembly affirmed the principles of Nuremberg and upheld the prosecution for crimes against humanity on 1 December 1946.[149] The 'Nuremberg Law', codified by the ILC, expounded that "individual criminal responsibility... through participation... with regards to international crimes... is neither opposed by interstate-arranged impunity... nor – in principle – by acting in an official capacity... nor by grounds of command".[150] This would effectively confirm the crime under international law and also excluded certain defences found under domestic criminal justice.

The violations of international humanitarian law and human rights atrocities of the late twentieth century triggered the re-emergence and further evolution of the *chapeau* elements of crimes against humanity. The establishment of the two UN *ad hoc* tribunals for Yugoslavia and Rwanda developed individual criminal responsibility for the listed acts of crimes against humanity, *inter alia*. Article 5 of the ICTY Statute established the ICTY's temporal and territorial jurisdiction over crimes against humanity "committed in armed conflict, whether international or internal in character, and directed against any civilian population".[151] Article 1 of the ICTR

---

[147] *Control Council Law No. 10*, pg 5. It added imprisonment, torture and rape to the list of acts comprising crimes against humanity. The definition of crimes against humanity under the IMT for the Far East mirrored the expanded list of crimes in terms of *Control Council Law No. 10*, but differed from the Nuremberg Charter by omitting the words 'before or during the war', thus negating the requirement that acts of crimes against humanity had to be connected to the war – See Ambos *Treatise on International Criminal Law* (2013) 6.

[148] US Military Tribunal Sitting in Nuremberg, *US v. Altstötter et al.* (Justice Trial), Judgement of 3–4 December 1947, discussed in Cassese *ICL: Cases and Commentary* (2011) 161.

[149] *Nuremberg Principles* (1946). Although this affirmation by the UN is not a binding source of law, is does "constitute evidence of state practice and state understanding as to the law" – Shaw, M.N., *International law*. Cambridge University Press, Sixth edition. (2008), pg 115.

[150] Ambos *Treatise on International Criminal Law* (2013) 10.

[151] The Statutes of the *ICTY* (Art 5) and *ICTR* (Art 3) enumerates the same acts as punishable as "crimes against humanity" and include: (a) murder; (b) extermination;

Statute echoes the ICTY's restricted temporal and territorial application, but the ICTR's jurisdiction is not limited to acts committed during an armed conflict. Article 3 of the ICTR states that the tribunal shall have the power to prosecute persons responsible for the listed acts of crimes against humanity when such crimes are "committed as part of a widespread or systematic attack against any civilian population on national, political, ethnic, racial or religious grounds".

Two years after the adoption of the ICTR Statute, the ILC issued a draft code that included a definition of crimes against humanity that was based on negotiation and consensus. Article 18 stated that a crime against humanity means any of the listed acts, "when committed in a systematic manner or on a large scale and instigated or directed by a government or by any organization or group...".[152] Accordingly, the draft code required that acts constituting crimes against humanity must either be part of a governmental or organisational policy, and based on a widespread or systematic practice of atrocities.[153] In addition, a number of subject-specific Statutes contributed to the list of acts that constitute crimes against humanity, including apartheid[154] and the enforced disappearance of persons.[155]

The *Rome Statute* is, for the time being, the most advanced, comprehensive, and widely accepted codification of crimes against humanity. Article 7 provides for the contextual (*chapeau*) elements of crimes against humanity,[156] which will be discussed below. The *Rome Statute* does not require a *nexus* to an armed conflict and is therefore applicable during peacetime or armed conflict.

(c) enslavement; (d) deportation; (e) imprisonment; (f) torture; (g) rape; (h) persecutions on political, racial and religious grounds; (i) other inhumane acts.

[152] International Law Commission, *Draft Code of Offences against the Peace and Security of Mankind with commentaries 1996*, Yearbook of the International Law Commission, 1996, Vol. II, Part Two, par 50. http://www.legaltools.org/doc/5e4532/. Accessed 13/02/2019. (Hereinafter referred to as the *1996 ILC Draft Code, with commentary*).

[153] The manifestation of a policy or a plan drawn up or inspired by State authorities could be regarded as being indicative of a systematic practice.

[154] UNGA *Apartheid Convention* (1976).

[155] *Inter-American Convention on the Forced Disappearance of Persons*, entered into force 28 March 1996, 14861 UN Treaty Collection 1015; and the *UN Declaration on the Protection of All Persons from Forced Disappearance*, 18 December 1992, UN Doc. A/Res/47/133 47 U.N GAOR Supp. (No. 49), at 207.

[156] The contextual elements are regarded as the link that connects the specific listed act with the broader context of the attack. Schabas W. A. *An Introduction to the International Criminal Court.* Cambridge University Press, 3rd edition (2007), pg 104.

Appendix A

3.1 The notion of crimes against humanity

Crimes against humanity refer to serious human rights atrocities or crimes "committed against a civilian population on a massive scale, or repeatedly over time".[157] In *Erdemovic*, the ICTY elaborated on the nature of crimes against humanity as serious inhumane acts of violence "...that by their extent and gravity go beyond the limits tolerable to the international community, which must perforce demand their punishment... [and] [i]t is therefore the concept of humanity as victim which essentially characterises crimes against humanity".[158] The *Rome Statute Explanatory Memorandum* states that crimes against humanity:

> ...are not isolated or sporadic events, but are part either of a government policy (although the perpetrators need not identify themselves with this policy) or of a wide practice of atrocities tolerated or condoned by a government or a de facto authority...[159]

The proscription of crimes against humanity "provides a mechanism to put individual crimes into a broader context, and to designate for particular condemnation (and more serious punishment) crimes that are part of a larger, organised and planned attack on civilians".[160] For that reason, crimes against humanity "encompass criminal conduct acknowledged by customary international law"[161] as the "most serious of crimes of concern to the international community as a whole".[162] Accordingly, when interpreting crimes against humanity in terms of the *Rome Statute*, customary international law should be considered.[163]

International concern for crimes against humanity provides States with the right to assert universal jurisdiction over such crimes. Accordingly, "perpetrators of crimes against humanity, whatever their status or

---

[157] Cassese et al. *ICL: Cases and Commentary* (2011) 154.
[158] *Prosecutor v Drazen Erdemovic (Sentencing Judgement)*, Case No. IT-96-22-T, ICTY, 29 November 1996, par 28.
[159] Horton *Dying Alive* (2005) par 12.52.
[160] Cassese et al. *ICL: Cases and Commentary* (2011) 154.
[161] Pikis, G. M. *The Rome Statute for the International Criminal Court: Analysis of the Statute, the Rules of Procedure and Evidence, the Regulations of the Court and Supplementary Instruments* (2010), pg 62. See also Acquaviva, G. & Pocar, F. *Crimes Against Humanity. Max Planck Encyclopedia on Public International law*, Wolfrum, R. (ed). Heidelberg: Oxford University Press (2011), par 21.
[162] Art 5 of the *Rome Statute*.
[163] Triffterer & Ambos *Commentary on the Rome Statute* (2008) 169.

immunity within their domestic systems, are subject to universal jurisdiction by any State and are protected by no statute of limitation".[164] Universal jurisdiction over crimes against humanity implies that "all States can exercise their jurisdiction in prosecuting a perpetrator irrespective of where the crime was committed",[165] or alternatively a State holding an alleged perpetrator may extradite the individual in terms of the *aut dedere aut iudicare* principle. Consequently, the international community, as a whole, is obligated to prosecute and punish any person, as enemies of all humankind (*hostis humani generis*), for their participation in such conduct.[166] Furthermore, the prohibition of crimes against humanity constitutes *jus cogens* norms (non-derogable rules of international law).

'Crimes against humanity' is a distinct, albeit extensively defined crime, comprising various underlying inhumane acts. Despite the broad range of underlying acts, 'crimes against humanity' covers actions that share a set of common features. They are mass "atrocity crimes"[167] violating fundamental rights by deliberately targeting a civilian population as part of a policy or plan, committed either repeatedly; or against a substantial quantity of individuals from such a group; or in circumstances where such an 'attack' takes place over a vast area.

3.2. Conditions of applicability of crimes against humanity

At the outset, it is sensible to provide a basic analysis of crimes against humanity and its conditions of applicability pertaining to all the enumerated underlying offences. In terms of the *Rome Statute*, the conditions of applicability of crimes against humanity can be divided into two categories:

1. the contextual or *chapeau* requirements; and
2. definitional elements of the underlying conduct, i. e. the physical act or consequences (*actus reus*), and mental (*mens rea*) elements relating to specific or so-called underlying offences (enumerated inhumane acts).[168]

---

[164] Acquaviva & Pocar *Crimes Against Humanity* (2011) par 21.
[165] Bassiouni *Crimes Against Humanity*.
[166] Zgonec-Rožej *International Criminal Law Manual* (2013) 338.
[167] Justice Richard Goldstone, speaking at a policy seminar *"Forging a Convention on Crimes Against Humanity: The Way Forward"*. Holocaust and Genocide Centre Johannesburg, 21 February 2019.
[168] Zgonec-Rožej *International Criminal Law Manual* (2013) 137.

In order to establish the context of specific acts under the auspices of crimes against humanity, Article 7(1) read together with Article 7(2) of the *Rome Statute* lists a number of specific underlying inhumane acts or omissions.[169] This constitute crimes against humanity if committed as part of a widespread or systematic attack.[170]

Based on the principles of legality and individual criminal responsibility, the Court's jurisdiction will be limited to conduct that was committed within a certain legal context and threshold. Each of the underlying offences is based on certain inherent definitional elements that may constitute a punishable crime under municipal or international law, but may fall short of corroborating a charge of crimes against humanity if such acts are unsuccessful in satisfying the contextual requirements. Therefore, in addition to the unique definitional requirements for each of the enumerated inhumane acts, the *chapeau* element must also satisfied. Consequently, the *chapeau* elements place an additional requirement for the prosecution of acts as crimes against humanity, and serve three important functions:

1. they describe the requisite knowledge or awareness by the accused of the broader context within which the enumerated inhumane acts must be committed (contextual knowledge);[171]
2. they clarify the requisite participation in the widespread or systematic attack against a civilian population (participation context); and
3. they establish the minimum threshold of severity for the enumerated inhumane acts, thus serving as an internationalising factor that distinguishes isolated or sporadic acts of cruelty from a consistent pattern of inhumanity (contextual threshold/international element).

Thus, crimes against humanity comprise the following *chapeau* elements: (1) the commission of any of the underlying inhumane acts, (2) as part of 'an attack', (3) pursuant to or in furtherance of an 'organisational policy', (4) which attack must be committed, either on a 'widespread' scale, or

---

[169] State or organisational action can, in exceptional circumstances, be implemented by a deliberate failure to take action, which is consciously aimed at encouraging such attack. The existence of such a policy cannot be inferred solely from the absence of governmental or organisational action. *ICC Elements of Crimes*, Introduction, Art 7, fn 6.
[170] Cassese *et al. ICL: Cases and Commentary* (2011) 179.
[171] *Tihomir Blaškić (Trial Judgement)* par 220.

'systematically', (5) 'directed against any civilian population', and (6) in terms of which the perpetrator acted with 'intent and knowledge' of the overall policy.[172]

3.2.1 'Any of the following acts' (enumerated inhumane acts)

'Crimes against humanity' is not a crime defined as a distinguishable form of criminal conduct, but refers to a range of acts of a very serious inhumane nature, committed as part of a widespread or systematic attack against any civilian population.[173] The accused must have committed at least one of the acts enumerated in Article 7(1) of the *Rome Statute*, in the circumstances outlined in the *chapeau* elements.[174]

Even a single act against a single victim can qualify as a crime against humanity if the act formed part of a widespread or systematic attack, or if the act had a widespread effect.[175]

The use of the word 'any' implies that any of the listed inhumane acts in Article 7(1) may, in themselves, constitute crimes against humanity.[176] The nature of the underlying acts constituting crimes against humanity includes serious atrocities, inhumane acts of violence, and gross or systematic deprivations of fundamental human rights.

In terms of Article 30 of the *Rome Statute*, it is generally accepted that any underlying act must be committed with its own *mens rea* and *actus reus*, including any unique requirements accompanying the offence, such as a

---

[172] Art 7(1) of the *Rome Statute*, read with art 7 Introduction to 'Crimes against humanity' – *ICC Elements of Crimes*.
[173] Report of the Secretary-General pursuant to paragraph 2 of Security Council resolution 808 (1993) and Annex thereto, U.N. Doc. S/25704, par 48.
[174] The underlying acts of crimes against humanity in terms of the *Rome Statute*, include: (a) Murder; (b) Extermination; (c) Enslavement; (d) Deportation or forcible transfer of population; (e) Imprisonment or other severe deprivation of physical liberty in violation of fundamental rules of international law; (f) Torture; (g) Rape, sexual slavery, enforced prostitution, forced pregnancy, enforced sterilization, or any other form of sexual violence of comparable gravity; (h) Persecution against any identifiable group or collectivity on political, racial, national, ethnic, cultural, religious, gender as defined in paragraph 3, or other grounds that are universally recognised as impermissible under international law, in connection with any act referred to in this paragraph or any crime within the jurisdiction of the Court; (i) Enforced disappearance of persons; (j) The crime of apartheid; (k) Other inhumane acts of a similar character intentionally causing great suffering, or serious injury to body or to mental or physical health.
[175] Zgonec-Rožej *International Criminal Law Manual* (2013) 145.
[176] Triffterer & Ambos *Commentary on the Rome Statute* (2008) 174.

specific intent or act. Article 7(2) of the ICC Statute, together with the *ICC Elements of Crimes,* contains descriptions of most of the listed crimes in an attempt to clarify the physical and mental elements of the particular offences. In the context of this study, it is immaterial to elaborate on the definitional elements of all the inhumane acts of crimes against humanity.

3.2.2. 'Committed as part of a[n] ... attack'

For the purposes of crimes against humanity, an 'attack' does not have the same meaning as in the context of the law of war crimes.[177] An 'attack' does not require violent force, only the severe mistreatment of the civilian population.[178] Acts may constitute crimes against humanity if committed as part of an attack, however, the acts could constitute the attack itself.[179] Based on the Appeal Chamber decision in *Kunarac,* it is clear that 'an attack' encompasses the following five elements:

1. there must be an attack;
2. the acts of the perpetrator must be part of the attack;
3. the attack must be directed against a civilian population;
4. the attack must be widespread or systematic; and
5. the perpetrator must know that his acts constitute part of a pattern of widespread or systematic crimes directed against a civilian population and know that his acts fit into such a pattern.[180]

In terms of the *Rome Statute,* an 'attack' is defined in Article 7(2)(a) as "a course of conduct involving the multiple commission of acts against any civilian population, pursuant to or in furtherance of a State or organisational policy to commit such attack".[181] 'Multiple commission of acts' implies more than a few isolated incidents of listed acts, but rather numerous acts committed in the context of repeated breaches of the same listed acts, or the commission of different types of acts within the same context. The requirement of 'multiple' should be differentiated from 'widespread' in that, although both terms refer to the measurement of scale or severity, 'multiple' has a lower threshold than 'widespread'. Accordingly, the attack must also constitute multiple offences (a minimum threshold) that may

---

[177] Zgonec-Rožej *International Criminal Law Manual* (2013) 138.
[178] *Prosecutor v Dragoljub Kunarac, Radomir Kovac and Zoran Vukovic (Trial Judgment),* Case No. IT-96-23-T & IT-96-23/1-T, 22 February 2001, par 416.
[179] Triffterer & Ambos *Commentary on the Rome Statute* (2008) 174.
[180] Cassese *et al. ICL: Cases and Commentary* (2011) 181.
[181] Triffterer & Ambos *Commentary on the Rome Statute* (2008) 235.

either be of a widespread or systematic nature.¹⁸² Thus, crimes against humanity require a course of conduct involving the multiple commission of the listed acts and therefore a single act will not suffice as an 'attack' unless the act itself is of a widespread nature¹⁸³. However, if a broader attack pursuant to or in furtherance of a State or organisational policy to commit such attack exist, an accused may be charged with a crime against humanity based on that single specific act committed in connection with or in the context of the broader attack. Therefore, it has been accepted that a single specific act by a perpetrator may trigger his individual criminal responsibility for crimes against humanity.¹⁸⁴ Cassese explains:

> A perpetrator need only commit a single specific crime to be charged with a crime against humanity, but must do so in the context of a widespread or systematic attack and with awareness of the link between his act and the larger attack.¹⁸⁵

The wording of the *chapeau* of Article 7(1) of the *Rome Statute* provides that the enumerated inhumane acts must be "committed *as part* of a widespread or systematic attack directed against any civilian population" (emphasis added).¹⁸⁶ This means that the individual criminal act of the perpetrator must be committed within a broader setting of specified circumstances (the attack). In order to establish that the inhumane act is objectively part of the attack, the question is whether the individual inhumane act would be less dangerous for the particular victim, had the attack not existed.¹⁸⁷ In other words, within the context of the broader attack, the individual inhumane act of the perpetrator elevated the particular victim's general risk to become a victim, into an aggravated risk.¹⁸⁸ An individual's acts may be regarded as being part of an attack if there is a "sufficient nexus between the unlawful acts of the accused and the attack".¹⁸⁹ The nature of the perpetrator's actions needs to resemble the broader attack in terms of its temporal dimensions or character, provided that his actions

---

[182] Cryer, R. et al. *An Introduction to International Criminal Law and Procedure*. Cambridge University Press (2007), 195.
[183] Zgonec-Rožej *International Criminal Law Manual* (2013) 145.
[184] *Prosecutor v Duško Tadić (Sentencing Judgement)*, Case No. IT-94-1-T, ICTY, 14 July 1997, par 649. *Prosecutor v Kupreškić et al. (Trial Judgement)*, Case No. IT-95-16-T, 14 January 2000, pg 550.
[185] Cassese et al. *ICL: Cases and Commentary* (2011) 154.
[186] Ambos & Wirth *The Current Law of Crimes Against Humanity* (2002) 2.
[187] Ambos & Wirth *The Current Law of Crimes Against Humanity* (2002) 86.
[188] Ambos & Wirth *The Current Law of Crimes Against Humanity* (2002) 36.
[189] Triffterer & Ambos *Commentary on the Rome Statute* (2008) 176.

are not unrelated to the attack, i. e. isolated and random conduct of an individual acting alone.[190] The connection, if any, between the accused and the organisation or government responsible for the broader attack, is a relevant indication. Triffterer and Ambos provide the following *indicia* that may prove such a *nexus*:

> ...similarities between the accused's acts and the acts occurring within the attack; the nature of the events and circumstances surrounding the accused's acts; the temporal and geographical proximity of the accused's acts with the attack; and, the nature and extent of the accused's knowledge of the attack when the accused commits the acts.[191]

The factual circumstances of each case will require proof that a sufficient *nexus* between the unlawful act and the broader attack exist to warrant a charge of crimes against humanity.[192] Therefore, it is generally not required that an underlying act must rise to a certain threshold of severity apart from that required in terms of the definitional elements of the crime itself.

3.2.3. A policy to commit such an attack

In terms of Article 7(2)(a) of the *Rome Statute*, the enumerated inhumane acts must form part of the 'attack', "pursuant to or in furtherance of a State or organisational policy to commit such attack",[193] which requires that the State or organisation must have actively promoted or encouraged such an attack against a civilian population.

The term 'State' is self-explanatory. It includes all branches of authority and at all levels of governmental authority.[194] The use of the term 'organisational' implies that the entity behind the attack may also include a group capable of exercising *de facto* control over, or capable to move freely,

---

[190] Triffterer & Ambos *Commentary on the Rome Statute* (2008) 176.
[191] Triffterer & Ambos *Commentary on the Rome Statute* (2008) 176.
[192] Triffterer & Ambos *Commentary on the Rome Statute* (2008) 176.
[193] ICC *Elements of Crimes*, art 7, Introduction, par 3. The jurisprudence of the ICTY has rejected the policy requirement for crimes against humanity – *Prosecutor v Dragoljub Kunarac, Radomir Kovac and Zoran Vukovic (Appeal Judgment)*, Case No. IT-96-23 & IT-96-23/1-A, 12 June 2002, par 98; See also *Blaškić (Trial Judgement)* paras 203-204.
[194] *Decision Pursuant to Article 15 of the Rome Statute on the Authorisation of an Investigation into the Situation in the Republic of Kenya*, Pre-Trial Chamber II, 31 March 2010, par 89.

within a defined territory.[195] The ICC Pre-trial Chamber noted that an 'organisation' includes any entity capable of committing widespread or systematic attacks against a civilian population, to the extent that it results in the infringement of basic human values.[196] Therefore, an 'organisational policy' is not limited to the policies of State-like organisations, but may include any group or organisation, provided the group displays sone form of organisational structure and follow a regular pattern or show a common purpose.[197]

The use of the term 'actively', generally excludes a policy inferred solely from the absence of governmental or organisational action, unless such an omission amounts to a deliberate policy of passive tolerance.[198] Consequently, in exceptional circumstances, an 'organisational policy' may include a deliberate failure to take action, which is consciously aimed at encouraging such an attack.[199]

Therefore, crimes against humanity "must be sponsored by a State, Government or entity holding *de facto* authority over a territory, be a part of the policy of such an authority, or at least, be tolerated by such an authority".[200] Ambos argues that the policy element is indicative of a widespread or systematic attack against any civilian population:

> [B]oth a systematic and a widespread attack require some kind of link with a state or a de facto power in a certain territory by means of the policy of this entity. The policy in the case of a systematic attack would be to provide at least certain guidance regarding the prospective victims in order to coordinate the activities of the single perpetrators. A systematic attack thus requires active conduct from the side of the entity behind the policy... whether the conduct suffices to trigger and direct the attack. A widespread attack which is not at the same time systematic must be one that lacks any guidance or organisation. The policy behind such an attack may be one of mere

---

[195] *Prosecutor v Duško Tadić (Trial Judgement)*, Case No. IT-94-1-T, 7 May 1997, par 654.
[196] *Situation in the Republic of Kenya*, Pre-Trial Chamber II, 31 March 2010, par 90.
[197] *Prosecutor v Germain Katanga & Mathieu Ngudjolo Chui* (ICC) Case No ICC-01/04-01/07, Decision on the Confirmation of Charges (30 September 2008), par 396.
[198] ICC Elements of Crimes, art 7, Introduction, pg 5, fn 6: "A policy which has a civilian population as the object of the attack would be implemented by State or organizational action. Such a policy may, in exceptional circumstances, be implemented by a deliberate failure to take action, which is consciously aimed at encouraging such attack. The existence of such a policy cannot be inferred solely from the absence of governmental or organizational action".
[199] Zgonec-Rožej *International Criminal Law Manual* (2013) 138.
[200] Horton *Dying Alive* (2005) par 12.59.

deliberate inaction (toleration). Such a policy, however, can only exist if the entity in question is able and, moreover, legally obligated to intervene.[201]

The policy element therefore serves to distinguish crimes that do not include an international character from crimes which are of concern to the international community.

Ambos provides the following synopsis of the policy element:[202]

- the entity behind the policy must be the State or organisation which exercises *de facto* control;
- the outcome of the policy must be to commit a multiplicity of inhumane acts against a civilian population;
- there are no formalities regarding the policy, it may be adopted as a declared or implicit policy of a State or organisation, and need not be declared expressly or stated clearly and precisely;
- the implementation of the policy during a systematic attack requires active conduct by the *de facto* authority, such as the active identification of possible victims that provides guidance to the perpetrators; and
- the policy regarding a widespread attack can be implemented by deliberate non-interference, provided the *de facto* authority is under a legal obligation to interfere and must be able to do so.

3.2.4. 'Widespread or systematic attack'

The threshold for the 'attack' is satisfied "either by their magnitude and savagery or by their large number or by the fact that a similar pattern was applied at different times and places".[203] In other words, the 'attack' must have been carried out in a systematic manner or on a large scale.[204] 'Widespread or systematic', which is indicative of contemporary customary international law,[205] is used in the *Rome Statute*. In order to establish whether

---

[201] Ambos & Wirth *The Current Law of Crimes Against Humanity* (2002) 34.
[202] Ambos & Wirth *The Current Law of Crimes Against Humanity* (2002) 85.
[203] United Nations War Crimes Commission, *History of the United Nations War Crimes Commission and the Development of the Laws of War* (London: United Nations War Crimes Commission by His Majesty's Stationery Office, 1948). Available at http://www.unwcc.org/wp-content/uploads/2014/11/UNWCC-history-contents.pdf. Accessed 02/07/2016.
[204] *1996 ILC Draft Code, with commentary (1996)*. The *1996 ILC Draft Code* replaced the qualifier "mass" with a less restrictive term "large-scale".
[205] *Tadić (Trial Judgement)* par 646.

the attack was indeed widespread or systematic in nature, the adjudication will have to take place on the merits of each case.[206]

The course of conduct, not the individual acts of the accused, must be widespread or systematic.[207] Accordingly, it is not required that each act occurring within the context of the broader attack be widespread or systematic, provided the broader attack itself satisfies the contextual threshold.[208]

'Widespread' refers to prohibited conduct that is spread over a wide area, amounts to a large-scale attack, or is committed against a multitude of targeted people.[209] In *Jean-Paul Akayesu*, the tribunal explained:

> The concept of widespread' may be defined as massive, frequent, large scale action, carried out collectively with considerable seriousness and directed against a multiplicity of victims.[210]

'Systematic' is indicative of an attack committed in a methodical, organised and planned manner.[211] A 'systematic' attack is endemic of a thor-

---

[206] Triffterer & Ambos *Commentary on the Rome Statute* (2008) 179.

[207] *Kunarac (Appeal Judgment)* par 96; *Blaškić (Appeal Judgement)* par 101. In order to establish whether the attack was indeed widespread or systematic in nature, the following factors may be considered, *inter alia*: "the number of criminal acts; the existence of criminal patterns; the logistics and financial resources involved; the number of victims; the existence of public statements or political views underpinning the events; the existence of a plan or policy targeting a specific group of individuals; the means and methods used in the attack; the inescapability of the attack; the foreseeability of the criminal occurrences; the involvement of political or military authorities; temporally and geographically repeated and coordinated military operations which all led to the same result or consequences; alteration of the ethnic, religious, or racial composition of the population; the establishment and implementation of autonomous political or military structures at any level of authority in a given territory; adoption of various discriminatory measures". Mettraux G, *International Crimes and the Ad Hoc Tribunals*. Oxford University Press (2006), pg 171.

[208] Triffterer & Ambos *Commentary on the Rome Statute* (2008) 176.

[209] *Prosecutor v Dario Kordić, Mario Cerkez (Appeal Judgement)*, Case No. IT-95-14/2-A, ICTY, 17 December 2004, par 94. *Prosecutor v Kayishema and Ruzindana (Trial Judgement)*, Case No. ICTR-95-1-T, 21 May 1999, par 123. See also *Prosecutor v Ahmad Harun and Al Kushayb, Decision on the Prosecution Application under Article 58(7) of the Statute*, 27 April 2007 (ICC-02/05-01/07-1), par 61–63.

[210] *Prosecutor v Jean-Paul Akayesu (Trial Judgement)*, Case No. ICTR-96-4-T, 2 September 1998, par 580.

[211] "A systematic attack means an attack carried out pursuant to a preconceived policy or plan" – *Kayishema (Trial Judgement)*, par 123. In *Blaškić (Trial Judgement)* par

oughly organised policy or system, or at least a tacit acceptance or acquiescence, of a State or organisational policy to commit the acts[212] and the "improbability of their random occurrence".[213] The ICTR has defined the concept of 'systematic' as "thoroughly organised and following a regular pattern on the basis of a common policy".[214]

3.2.5. 'Attack directed against any civilian population'

The attack must be 'directed against' a civilian population, i. e. the civilian population must be the primary object of the attack. In case of doubt whether a person is a civilian, there is a rebuttable presumption that the person is a civilian.[215]

> The essence of crimes against humanity is that a population is targeted precisely because of its civilian character... [and therefore, the] presence of others who may or may not also be targets is irrelevant.[216]

The acts or crimes must be directed against any civilian population. A specific discriminatory intent need not be proven (except in the case of persecution).[217] Therefore, it is the civilian population in general that becomes the victim of crimes against humanity and not a specific or identifiable group as is the case with the crime of genocide.

An attack against a civilian population need not be very large in scale to meet the requirements of severity.[218] The word 'population' does not

---

203 the ICTY concluded that the element of "systematic" possesses the following four elements: The existence of a political objective, a plan pursuant to which the attack is perpetrated or an ideology, in the broad sense of the word, that is, to destroy, persecute or weaken a community; The perpetration of a criminal act on a very large scale against a group of civilians or repeated and continuous commission of inhumane acts linked to one another; The preparation and use of significant public or private resources, whether military or other; The implication of high level political and/or military authorities in the definition and establishment of the methodical plan.

[212] Cassese et al. ICL: Cases and Commentary (2011) 168.
[213] Harun (Decision on the Prosecution Application under Article 58(7) of the Statute), par 61-63.
[214] Akayesu (Trial Judgement) par 580.
[215] Art 50 of the International Committee of the Red Cross (ICRC), Protocol Additional to the Geneva Conventions of 12 August 1949, and relating to the Protection of Victims of International Armed Conflicts (Protocol I), 8 June 1977, 1125 UNTS 3.
[216] Zgonec-Rožej International Criminal Law Manual (2013) 140.
[217] Horton Dying Alive (2005) par 12.52.
[218] Mettraux International Crimes and the Ad Hoc Tribunals (2006) 156.

require the intent to target or subject the entire population of the geographical region to the widespread or systematic attack.[219] In *Kunarac*, the tribunal found that:

It is sufficient to show that enough individuals were targeted in the course of the attack, or that they were targeted in such a way... that the attack was in fact directed against a civilian 'population', rather than against a limited and randomly selected number of individuals.[220]

3.2.6. 'With knowledge of the attack'

The perpetrator must have committed the specific act or underlying offence with knowledge of the course of conduct of a widespread or systematic nature, directed against the civilian population. Accordingly, the perpetrator must have acted while aware of the broader context within which such acts were committed.[221] In other words, "the perpetrator must know that there is an attack on a civilian population and that he or she knows that his or her acts are part of that attack".[222] Without this awareness on the part of the perpetrator, his acts will be considered as unrelated to the broader attack.

The general mental element for crimes against humanity requires that the "perpetrator knew that the conduct was part of or intended the conduct to be part of a widespread or systematic attack against a civilian population"[223], but "should not be interpreted as requiring proof that the perpetrator had knowledge of all characteristics of the attack or the precise details of the plan or policy of the State or organization".[224] Knowledge of the attack and the perpetrator's awareness of his participation therein may be inferred from circumstantial evidence.[225] Where such "knowledge is established beyond reasonable doubt, the accused's motive for participating in the attack is in principle legally irrelevant to the question of his guilt".[226]

In terms of the mental element, a person has intent where: in relation to prohibited conduct, the accused must have intended to engage in the

---

[219] *Kunarac (Appeal Judgment)* par 90.
[220] *Kunarac (Appeal Judgment)* par 90.
[221] *Blaškić (Trial Judgement)* par 220.
[222] Triffterer & Ambos *Commentary on the Rome Statute* (2008) 182.
[223] *ICC Elements of Crimes*, contextual element common to all crimes against humanity in Art 7.
[224] *ICC Elements of Crimes*, Introduction par 2 on pg 5.
[225] Mettraux *International Crimes and the Ad Hoc Tribunals* (2006) 15.
[226] *Kunarac (Appeal Judgment)* par 103.

conduct; in relation to a prohibited consequence, the accused must have intended to cause the prohibited result, or was aware that it will occur in the ordinary course of events.[227]

3.2.7. Contextual threshold of applicability (international element)

Article 17(1)(d) states that the Court shall determine that a case is inadmissible if such a case is not of sufficient gravity to justify further action by the Court, thus limiting the Court's jurisdiction to the most serious crimes of concern to the international community as a whole.[228] Collectively, the *chapeau* elements serve this purpose in the context of crimes against humanity. Consequently, the Court's jurisdiction is limited to offences that are unimaginable atrocities and deeply shock the conscience of humanity, which threaten the peace, security and well-being of the world (international element).[229] In other words, inhumane acts that may be contextualised as crimes against humanity may be distinguished from ordinary crimes under domestic law, based on its 'international element',[230] or so-called 'context element'.[231] Ambos argues that "the rationale of the context element can be summarised as the protection of human rights against the most serious and most dangerous violations".[232]

In terms of the *ICC Elements of Crimes*, Article 7 must be strictly construed, considering that crimes against humanity are:

> among the most serious crimes of concern to the international community as a whole, warrant and entail individual criminal responsibility, and require conduct which is impermissible under generally applicable international law, as recognized by the principal legal systems of the world.[233]

---

[227] Art 30(2) & (3) of the *Rome Statute* 2. For the purposes of this study, a person has intent where: (a) In relation to conduct, that person means to engage in the conduct; (b) In relation to a consequence, that person means to cause that consequence or is aware that it will occur in the ordinary course of events. 3. For the purposes of this study, "knowledge" means awareness that a circumstance exists or a consequence will occur in the ordinary course of events. "Know" and "knowingly" shall be construed accordingly.

[228] Art 5 of the *Rome Statute* – Crimes within the jurisdiction of the ICC is limited to (a) The crime of genocide; (b) Crimes against humanity; (c) War crimes; and (d) The crime of aggression.

[229] Preamble of the *Rome Statute*.

[230] Ambos & Wirth *The Current Law of Crimes Against Humanity* (2002) 2.

[231] Ambos & Wirth *The Current Law of Crimes Against Humanity* (2002) 2.

[232] Ambos & Wirth *The Current Law of Crimes Against Humanity* (2002) 15.

[233] *ICC Elements of Crimes*, Art 7, Introduction, par 1.

The internationalising element means that a pattern of crimes committed in the domestic setting has escalated into an 'attack', triggering international concern. Thus, the context within or scale with which such offences have been committed warrants international intervention.

> One ought to look at these atrocities or acts in their context and verify whether they may be regarded as part of an overall policy or a consistent pattern of an inhumanity, or whether they instead constitute isolated or sporadic acts of cruelty and wickedness.[234]

Although the *chapeau* elements should be read together in considering whether the contextual threshold of severity has been met, in practice the requirement of 'widespread or systematic' is the most widely accepted 'internationalising factor or element'.[235] The requirement of a 'widespread or systematic attack' distinguishes crimes against humanity from isolated or unconnected crimes against civilians that will generally fall only under national jurisdictions.[236] In other words, isolated crimes, which are not part of a policy of a widespread or systematic attack, cannot be categorised as a crime against humanity.

4   Individual criminal responsibility

As alluded to, international criminal law is based on the criminal accountability of those individuals responsible for international crimes. A breach of international criminal law establishes the individual criminal responsibility of the person concerned once the principle of legality has been satisfied. Therefore, the perpetrator is held personally liable for his unlawful criminal actions. In its renowned assertion, the IMT noted that:

> Crimes against international law are committed by men, not by abstract entities, and only by punishing individuals who commit such crimes can the provisions of international law be enforced.[237]

---

[234] Horton *Dying Alive* (2005) par 12.52.
[235] Triffterer & Ambos *Commentary on the Rome Statute* (2008) 170.
[236] Zgonec-Rožej *International Criminal Law Manual* (2013) 139.
[237] *The Trial of German Major War Criminals, Proceedings of the International Military Tribunal Sitting at Nuremberg, Germany*. International Military Tribunal, Judgment of 1 October 1946, pg 41.

In the context of the *Rome Statute*, individual criminal responsibility for the core crimes is directly established under Article 25.[238] In terms of this article, the Court's jurisdiction is restricted to natural persons who shall be held individually criminally responsible and liable for punishment for their participation in the commission of the core crimes of the Statute. Individual criminal responsibility is therefore not limited to only those who directly commit such crimes (direct perpetrators).[239] The codification of the components of individual criminal responsibility in terms of Article 25 is a testimony to the growth of international criminal law as a fundamental aspect of international law. Individual criminal responsibility under the Statute is not subject to any statute of limitations, but is limited in terms of jurisdiction, based on the principle of complementarity,[240] *ratione personae*,[241] *ratione temporis*,[242] *ratione loci*[243] and *ratione materiae*.[244]

The individual is clearly identified as the subject of international criminal law and therefore only human beings can incur individual criminal responsibility for the core crimes.[245] While States may incur responsibility for internationally unlawful acts, there is no criminal responsibility of legal persons or State criminal responsibility under contemporaneous international law.[246]

The doctrine of individual criminal responsibility for international crimes forms part of a larger body of law known as the 'general principles' of criminal law, which reinforces the guarantees of efficacy and fairness in international criminal law.[247] In this regard, the principles of legality and double jeopardy are cardinal protections under international law, both from an international human rights perspective, as well as an essential procedural guarantee of fairness in criminal law.[248] A brief overview of these principles is thus necessary. However, the *sui generis* nature of persecution necessitates specific consideration of the legality principle and will be discussed separately in Chapter Seven.

---

[238] Kreß *International Criminal Law* (2011) 3.
[239] Participation or the forms of individual criminal responsibility will be discussed below.
[240] Art 1 of the *Rome Statute*.
[241] Art 12(2)(b) of the *Rome Statute*.
[242] Art 11 and 29 of the *Rome Statute*.
[243] Art 12(2)(a) of the *Rome Statute*.
[244] Art 5 of the *Rome Statute*.
[245] Kreß *International Criminal Law* (2011) 4.
[246] Kreß *International Criminal Law* (2011) 4.
[247] Zgonec-Rožej *International Criminal Law Manual* (2013) 239.
[248] Zgonec-Rožej *International Criminal Law Manual* (2013) 247.

4.1 The principle of *ne bis in idem*

The *ne bis in idem principle*[249] (also known as the rule against double jeopardy or the *autrefois acquit/ autrefois convict* principle) provides that no one shall be tried or punished more than once for the same crime.[250] In the context on international criminal adjudications, the *ne bis in idem* principle is particularly important given the intersection of jurisdictional powers.

> While it constitutes a valuable protection against arbitrary and malicious prosecution ... its significance may be even greater in ... the international legal order – where various bodies may be able to exercise jurisdiction in a particular case but are not necessarily bound to defer to one another's findings.[251]

Concerning the principle of *ne bis in idem,* Article 20 of the *Rome Statute* states that:

- no person shall be tried before the Court with respect to conduct or a core crime which formed the basis of crimes for which the person has been convicted or acquitted by the Court; and
- no person who has been tried by another court for core crimes shall be tried by the Court with respect to the same conduct unless the proceedings in the other court:
  – were for the purpose of shielding the person concerned from criminal responsibility for crimes within the jurisdiction of the Court; or
  – otherwise were not conducted independently or impartially in accordance with the norms of due process recognised by international law and were conducted in a manner which, in the circumstances, was inconsistent with an intent to bring the person concerned to justice.

In the context of the ICC, the wording in Article 20 seems to provide for an interpretation conundrum in that such prosecutions will only be considered 'final' or foreclosed for the purpose of *ne bis in idem* for a 'crime' covered by Article 5.[252] It may be argued that it is not foreclosed for a

---

[249] In civil law countries double jeopardy is often referred to as *non bis in idem*.
[250] Zgonec-Rožej International/ Criminal Law Manual (2013) 247.
[251] Zgonec-Rožej *International Criminal Law Manual* (2013) 248.
[252] Cassese, A. et al. *International Criminal Law: Cases and Commentary.* Oxford University Press (2011), pg 107.

subsequent prosecution before a national court for the same acts on a different charge.[253] For example, a person may be tried before a national court for an 'ordinary' crime, such a murder, instead of genocide or crimes against humanity. Conversely, it seems probable, based on the primacy of national jurisdiction, that the ICC will be barred from prosecution in the event that there had previously been a national prosecution based on the same underlying conduct, even for an 'ordinary' crime, provided that the relevant 'conduct' was prosecuted in a fair or proper manner.[254]

4.2 Forms of individual criminal responsibility

Similar to the forms or modes of criminal responsibility found in domestic criminal law, international law recognises not only the direct perpetrator of international crimes, but also other types of participants. Article 25 of the *Rome Statute* specifies the various forms of individual criminal responsibility under the Court's jurisdiction and provides that a person shall be criminally responsible and liable for punishment for a crime within the jurisdiction of the Court if that person:

- commits such a crime, whether as an individual (direct perpetrator), jointly with another (co-perpetrators), or through another person (vicarious or indirect perpetrator), regardless of whether that other person is criminally responsible;
- orders, solicits or induces the commission of such a crime which, in fact, occurs or is attempted;
- facilitate the commission of such a crime, aids, abets or otherwise assists in its commission or its attempted commission, including providing the means for its commission (the accomplice or accessory after the fact);
- in any other way contributes to the commission or attempted commission of such a crime by a group of persons acting with a common purpose;
- attempts to commit such a crime by taking action that commences its execution by means of a substantial step, but the crime does not occur because of circumstances independent of the person's intentions. However, a person who abandons the effort to commit the crime or otherwise prevents the completion of the crime shall not

---

[253] Cassese *et al. ICL: Cases and Commentary* (2011) 107.
[254] Zgonec-Rožej *International Criminal Law Manual* (2013) 250.

be liable for punishment under this Statute for the attempt to commit that crime if that person completely and voluntarily gave up the criminal purpose;
- conspires to commit genocide, and direct and public incitement to commit genocide;[255] and
- incurs vicarious liability in the form of command responsibility for crimes within the jurisdiction of the Court committed by forces under the military commander's effective authority and control, or as a result of his or her failure to exercise proper control over such forces.[256]

In the subsequent sections, the most important forms of individual criminal responsibility for the purposes of this book are considered.

4.2.1. Direct and individual perpetration

Direct and individual perpetration refers to a situation where the perpetrator's "conduct, the circumstances in which it takes place... and the culpability with which it is carried out are such that he satisfies all the requirements for liability contained in the definition of the crime".[257] Thus, a perpetrator's involvement requires that his conduct, the circumstances and his culpability must be in line with the requirements of the specific offence.

In international criminal law, a perpetrator may be considered to have committed an international crime personally "when he or she physically perpetrates the relevant criminal act or engenders a culpable omission in violation of a rule of criminal law".[258] In this context, 'perpetrate' or 'commit' are used interchangeably and the reference to 'physical' should be interpreted to connote 'direct' and 'personal' (i.e. individual) involvement in the commission of the offence, and therefore does not include only direct physical involvement.[259] In *Tadic*, the Appeal Chamber held that "nobody may be held criminally responsible for acts or transactions in which [they] have not personally engaged or in some other way participated".[260]

---

[255] Other forms of incomplete crimes are rarely used in international criminal law as they may be less suitable for serious crimes.
[256] Art 28 of the *Rome Statute*.
[257] Snyman *Criminal law* (2014) 252.
[258] Kunarac (Trial Judgment), par 390.
[259] Zgonec-Rožej *International Criminal Law Manual* (2013) 264.
[260] *Prosecutor v Duško Tadić* (Appeal Judgement), Case No. IT-94-1-A, 15 July 1999, par 186.

Direct involvement requires that the perpetrator's deliberate conduct formed an 'integral' part of the *actus reus* of the offence charged.[261] In the context of direct or individual perpetration before the ICC, the Prosecution must establish the following elements:

1. the deliberate conduct of the accused formed an 'integral' part of the *actus reus* of the offence charged;
2. the accused 'intended' the offence, or acted while reconciled to the knowledge of the substantial likelihood that his actions would result in that offence coming to pass; and
3. the accused possessed any specific intent required regarding the particular underlying offence.[262]

For a culpable omission as a crime under international law, the jurisprudence of *ad hoc* tribunals found that the accused may be considered to have perpetrated the crime if he failed to act in circumstances where there was a positive legal duty to act at the relevant time.[263] No reference is made to the liability for an offence based on an omission in terms of the *Rome Statute*. However, in this regard a 'reading-in' of relevant principles of customary international law may be justified to fill a gap in the law, as permitted by Article 21.[264]

4.2.2. Perpetration through a group

International crimes are usually endemic in systemised-criminality committed by large groups of people, such as terrorist networks, pirate groups, governments and military agencies responsible for the commission of war crimes, or paramilitary groups responsible for crimes against humanity. Unfortunately, international courts can only hold those who bear the greatest responsibility, accountable. Ambos explains:

> Given limited personal and other resources, the prosecution policy of international tribunals focuses on the 'most responsible' for international crimes.[265]

---

[261] Zgonec-Rožej *International Criminal Law Manual* (2013) 265.
[262] Zgonec-Rožej *International Criminal Law Manual* (2013) 266.
[263] *Prosecutor v. Radoslav Brdjanin (Appeal Judgement)*, IT-99-36-A, International Criminal Tribunal for the former Yugoslavia (ICTY), 3 April 2007, par 274.
[264] Zgonec-Rožej *International Criminal Law Manual* (2013) 265.
[265] Ambos, K. *Modes of Participation*. Oxford Bibliographies (2013). http://www.oxford bibliographies.com/view/document/obo-9780199796953/obo-9780199796953-0068.xml. Accessed 08/09/2017.

Criminal accountability for perpetration as part of a group requires a meaningful link between the personal conduct of the accused and the criminal offence with which he is charged.[266] To attribute individual responsibility to an accused who is 'most responsible' for international crimes, often requires proof of both the direct perpetrator's conduct in conjunction with that of the accused. The main legal ingredient in this regard is the principle of personal culpability. It is thus required that an accused can only be held criminally responsible for acts in which he personally engaged or in some other way participated,[267] and such conduct must constitute a significant contribution to the crime.[268]

Consequently, the international community has created special rules regarding the modes of participation that will help prosecutors to prove international crimes in a situation where it will be very difficult to do so under the ordinary forms of criminal liability found in domestic penal codes. In terms of Article 25 of the *Rome Statute,* such collective modes of participation are: (1) 'co-perpetration',[269] i. e. commission of the offence jointly with another (similar to joint criminal enterprise under the ICTY and International Criminal Tribunal for Rwanda (ICTR)); (2) indirect perpetration or perpetration by means, i. e. commission of an offence through another person; and (3) command responsibility.[270]

In terms of Article 25, criminal accountability for joint criminal action or perpetration through a group shall require an intentional contribution to the commission of the offence. In this regard, a person's intentional contribution must consist of furthering the criminal activity or criminal purpose of the group (where such activity or purpose involves the commission of crimes within the jurisdiction of the Court) to the extent that is has "a direct and substantial effect on the commission of the illegal act".[271] Furthermore, the accused must at least know (or be

---

[266] Zgonec-Rožej *International Criminal Law Manual* (2013) 256.
[267] *Tadić* (Appeal Judgement), par 186.
[268] *Brdjanin* (Appeal Judgement), par 427.
[269] The ICC Pre-Trial Chamber defined 'co-perpetration' in the following terms: "Co-perpetration is based on joint control over the crime. It involves the division of essential tasks between two or more persons, acting in a concerted manner, for the purposes of commiting that crime. The fulfillment of the essential task(s) can be carried out by the co-perpetrators physically or they may be executed through another person". - *Prosecutor v Germain Katanga & Mathieu Ngudjolo Chui* (ICC) Case No ICC-01/04-01/07, Decision on the Confirmation of Charges (30 September 2008), par 521.
[270] Ambos *Modes of Participation* (2013).
[271] *Tadić* (Trial Judgement) par 674.

aware of the substantial likelihood) that his acts will render assistance to the criminal consequence.[272]

Regardless of which mode of responsibility may be applicable to hold a perpetrator responsible as part of a group of co-perpetrators, each member of the group whose conduct satisfies the principle of criminal responsibility, as set out above, shall incur equal criminal responsibility. However, appropriate sentencing will be considered on an individualised basis to take account of personal circumstances.[273]

4.2.3. Command or superior responsibility

As mentioned, international prosecution mechanisms are compelled to focus their efforts on those 'most responsible' for international crimes, such as the senior political and military leaders of the *de facto* authority.[274] However, given their status or rank, such high-ranking officials are usually not directly responsible for 'pulling the trigger', but may be responsible for exercising control over or ordering others to do so.[275] Consequently, a military commander who condones an environment of lawlessness through his failure to exercise proper control over such forces may incur criminal responsibility.[276] The responsibility of commanders and other superiors is the "primary mechanism through which superiors can be held responsible for failing to prevent or punish crimes committed by their subordinates".[277] Consequently, "certain eligible superiors may be held responsible for offences committed by their subordinates, even though the superior made no personal contribution to the criminal activity at all".[278] In terms of Article 28, the law of superior responsibility before the ICC differs from that applicable before the *ad hoc* tribunals.[279] The criminal responsibility of military commanders requires proof of a *nexus* between the personal conduct of the accused and the criminal offence with which they are

---

[272] Zgonec-Rožej *International Criminal Law Manual* (2013) 255.
[273] Zgonec-Rožej *International Criminal Law Manual* (2013) 265.
[274] Ambos *Modes of Participation* (2013).
[275] Responsibility of commanders and other superiors is not a form of vicarious liability because their liability is predicated on their own culpable failure – Zgonec-Rožej *International Criminal Law Manual* (2013) 284.
[276] Art 28 of the *Rome Statute*.
[277] Van Sliedregt, E. *Article 28 of the ICC Statute: Mode of Liability and/or Separate Offense?* New Criminal Law Review: An International and Interdisciplinary Journal, vol. 12, no. 3, (2009), pg 420.
[278] Zgonec-Rožej *International Criminal Law Manual* (2013) 283.
[279] Zgonec-Rožej *International Criminal Law Manual* (2013) 291.

charged. In order to establish command responsibility before the ICC, four elements must be satisfied:[280]

1. there must be a 'superior-subordinate' relationship between the accused and the person who committed the crime;
2. the accused failed to exercise proper control over his subordinates;
3. the accused knew (actual knowledge) or had reason to know (constructive knowledge) that his subordinate was committing, was about to, or had committed a crime under international law (mental element);[281] and
4. the accused failed to take the necessary and reasonable measures to prevent the subordinate from committing the anticipated crimes and/or to punish the subordinate for the crime (physical element).

The personal criminal responsibility of military commanders and other superiors is thus based on a legitimate attribution of criminal responsibility 'up' the chain of causation.[282]

---

[280] Zgonec-Rožej *International Criminal Law Manual* (2013) 257, 284–285 & 292. The Prosecution must invariably prove the following key elements: (1) the commission of the *chapeau* elements or conditions of applicability of the crime(s) charged with in terms of the Statute; (2) the general and definitional elements of the underlying offence(s) completed – but not necessarily by the accused, including any specific requirements for such an offence, such as discrimination; (3) legitimate attribution of criminal responsibility based on a nexus between the personal conduct of the accused and the criminal offence with which they are charged, which requires proof that the commander acted with the necessary *actus reus* (guilty conduct, usually a failure to exercise proper control in order to condemn, prevent or punish crimes committed by their subordinates); and *mens rea* (guilty mind, the commander knew or should have known) that his subordinate was committing or was about to or had committed a crime under international law.

[281] Zgonec-Rožej *International Criminal Law Manual* (2013) 257. The threshold of *dolus eventualis* entails the concept of recklessness, but not that of negligence or gross negligence. Whereas, the form of culpability required usually for the criminal responsibility of the underlying act is direct or indirect intent, the legitimate attribution of criminal responsibility for commanders simply requires, at minimum, *dolus eventualis*.

[282] Zgonec-Rožej *International Criminal Law Manual* (2013) 255–256.

5 Grounds for contesting criminal responsibility

Excluding criminal responsibility is generally based on raising a defence, thus offering a justification or excuse in order to avoid liability. The criminal defences in terms of the *Rome Statute* will form the primary consideration of this section. It is, however, important to note that there are two additional ways to contest a prosecution: (1) to challenge the Court's jurisdiction in some manner (i. e. attacking the Court's right to try the accused for particular conduct, a particular event or a particular person), and (2) to challenge the Prosecution's proof of the elements of the crime as specified in the indictment (i. e. an attack on the Prosecution's case), normally by raising reasonable doubt and/or proposing an alternative theory of events.[283] A 'challenge of proof' of the elements may also be considered as a defence of criminal liability, but it is more accurately considered an absence of proof.[284] In this sense a challenge to proof may be considered as the duty of the defence council to raise reasonable doubt in the case of the prosecution, by offering various forms of explanations or defences, such as: an alibi, proof of consent for crimes where consent is a definitional element or a mistake of law or fact.[285]

5.1. Immunity in international criminal proceedings

An immunity challenge to jurisdiction argues that a particular person, by virtue of his or her occupation or status, falls into a protected category in terms of which a particular judicial authority may not exercise jurisdiction over him or her.[286] The principles of immunity are based on the sovereignty of statehood under international law and the protection of State agents and certain officials in terms of which such protected persons are exempt from the exercise of territorial jurisdiction of a foreign State.[287]

> It should be pointed out that immunity operates as a procedural bar to the foreign jurisdiction to entertain a case and the appropriate authorities of the official's State of nationality may waive it. This is because immunity is a right of the State rather than a right of the individual.[288]

---

[283] Zgonec-Rožej *International Criminal Law Manual* (2013) 294.
[284] Zgonec-Rožej *International Criminal Law Manual* (2013) 294.
[285] Art 32 of the *Rome Statute*.
[286] Zgonec-Rožej *International Criminal Law Manual* (2013) 295.
[287] Dugard, J. *International Law: A South African Perspective*. 3rd edition (2005), pg 238.
[288] Zgonec-Rožej *International Criminal Law Manual* (2013) 295.

Protection of a person under immunity includes not only a challenge to the exercise of jurisdiction for the purposes of adjudication, but will also prohibit other measures such as extradition and surrender.[289]

In the scope of human rights, immunity may arise in two situations: firstly, in the course of the principle to extradite or punish, where a foreign State wishes to exercise territorial jurisdiction for the purposes of criminal proceedings for international crimes; and secondly, in civil proceedings before a foreign court for compensation resulting from an international crime or serious human rights violations.[290] In such proceedings, a distinction must be made between immunity *ratione personae* and immunity *ratione materiae*.

Immunity *ratione personae* (personal immunity or 'procedural' immunities) attaches to a person *ex officio* and protects the person of certain individuals essential to the State's administration.[291] Immunity *ratione personae* attaches to certain senior State officials, such as Heads of State and Ministers of Foreign Affairs, and remains in force only while they remain in office. In this regard, foreign courts are barred from prosecuting such persons while they remain in office, regardless of whether the act was carried out as part of the official functions or in a personal capacity attached directly to the person by virtue of his or her position.[292] Thus, immunity *ratione personae* is absolute; however, the subsequent departure from office will withdraw immunity over such persons. Although immunity *ratione personae* for incumbent State officials before national courts is still consistently practised, even with regards to international crimes, international courts and tribunals may indict and charge incumbent high State officials suspected of core crimes under their jurisdiction.[293]

State officials are also entitled to immunity *ratione materiae* (functional immunity or 'subject-matter' immunity), which relates to acts performed in an official capacity and protects the carrying out of 'official business' for the State.[294] Immunity *ratione materiae* "attaches only to the official acts of State officials and is determined by the nature of the acts in question rather than by the position of the person performing them".[295] Therefore, State officials leaving office may still enjoy immunity *ratione materiae* because of the importance of their decision-making in the national sphere.

---

[289] Zgonec-Rožej *International Criminal Law Manual* (2013) 295.
[290] Dugard *International Law* (2005) 250.
[291] Zgonec-Rožej *International Criminal Law Manual* (2013) 295.
[292] Zgonec-Rožej *International Criminal Law Manual* (2013) 298.
[293] Zgonec-Rožej *International Criminal Law Manual* (2013) 298.
[294] Werle *Principles of International Criminal Law* (2005) 173.
[295] Zgonec-Rožej *International Criminal Law Manual* (2013) 295.

Immunity *ratione materiae* protects individuals only insofar as their actions are genuinely 'official' as a matter of State sovereignty and will not include private criminal acts committed by State officials. Immunity *ratione materiae* attaches on the basis of representation, whereby the official was acting on behalf of the State or under the authority of the government in exercising certain functions.

However, with the emergence of human rights obligations under international law, some "human rights norms enjoy such a high status that their violation, even by State officials, constitute an international crime".[296] As such, a customary international rule has evolved rendering immunity *ratione materiae* inapplicable to the international core crimes.[297] Therefore, the commission of acts constituting international core crimes cannot be considered as 'official acts'. It has also been found that "a state cannot assert immunity *ratione materiae* in relation to a criminal prosecution for torture in as much as torture is a breach of *jus cogens* under international law".[298]

In terms of Article 27 of the *Rome Statute*, the defence of official capacity before the ICC is specifically excluded.[299] Therefore, immunity *ratione materiae* is excluded as a challenge to the jurisdiction of the Court over a particular person and can never constitute a challenge to jurisdiction over the 'official acts' of a particular person. The exclusion of immunity *ratione materiae* is applicable to cases before the ICC itself or the domestic court of a State party. It seems as though the provision 'shall not bar the *Court* from exercising its jurisdiction' provides for the exclusion of immunity *ratione personae* as a challenge to jurisdiction over the official capacity of a particular person, only in regards to proceedings before the 'the Court' (ICC) and

---

[296] Dugard *International Law* (2005) 249-250.
[297] Frulli, M. *Immunities of Persons from Jurisdiction* in Antonio Cassese (ed), *The Oxford Companion to International Criminal Justice*, OUP, Oxford (2009), pg 368.
[298] *Jones v Ministry of Interior Al-Mamlaka Al Arabiya as Saudiya (The Kingdom of Saudi Arabia) & another* (2004) EWCA Civil 1394, paras 123-4. See also *R v Bow Street Metropolitan Stipendiary Magistrate: Ex parte Pinochet Ugarte* 2 All ER 97 (1999).
[299] Art 27 of the *Rome Statute*: This Statute shall apply equally to all persons without any distinction based on official capacity. In particular, official capacity as a Head of State or Government, a member of a Government or parliament, an elected representative or a government official shall in no case exempt a person from criminal responsibility under this Statute. Nor shall it, in and of itself, constitute a ground for reduction of sentence. Immunities or special procedural rules which may attach to the official capacity of a person, whether under national or international law, shall not bar the Court from exercising its jurisdiction over such a person.

not domestic jurisdictions.[300] It should also be noted in this regard that Article 98(1) of the *Rome Statute* qualifies the scope of Article 27.[301]

> ICC cannot compel a State party to surrender an official of a State not party to the Statute in violation of its obligations under international law with regard to immunities vis-à-vis the State not party concerned.[302]

5.2. Defences for excluding criminal responsibility

Raising a defence against criminal responsibility is the rebuttal of a criminal charge and often amounts to an admission that the acts constituting the alleged crime have been committed but does not constitute a confession. However, such admissions are made with the intention to exclude the defendant from criminal liability. Generally, such defences consist of offering either: (1) a justification for such actions; (2) a denial that the act was wrongful, transforming what would otherwise be an unlawful action into a rightful one (e. g. self-defence); or (3) an explanation that will otherwise excuse the responsibility of the defendant for the wrongful act (e. g. mental incapacity). The following defences, set out in the *Rome Statute*, expressly provides for the 'exclusion' of criminal responsibility:

- Age: Article 26 excludes the Court's jurisdiction in regards to persons under the age of eighteen years.
- Mental incapacity: Article 31(1)(a) states that individual responsibility is precluded when the person suffers from a mental disease or defect that destroys that person's capacity to appreciate the unlawfulness or

---

[300] *Prosecutor v Omar Hassan Ahmad Al Bashir* (ICC) Case No ICC-02/05-01/09-1, Decision on the Prosecution's Application for a Warrant of Arrest against Omar Hassan Ahmad Al Bashir, Public Redacted Version (4 March 2009) par 40.

[301] If the Court seeks to exercise its jurisdiction over a person who is alleged to be criminally responsible for a crime within the jurisdiction of the Court, and if, in the circumstances, such a person enjoys (according to the Convention on the Privileges and Immunities and the relevant rules of international law), any privileges and immunities as necessary for the independent exercise of his or her work for the UN, the UN undertakes to cooperate fully with the Court, and to take all necessary measures to allow the Court to exercise its jurisdiction. In particular, such measures include waiving any privileges and immunities in accordance with the Convention on the Privileges and Immunities of the UN and the relevant rules of international law. See art 19 of the *Negotiated Relationship Agreement Between the International Criminal Court and the United Nations*. ICC-ASP/3/Res.1. Adoption: 04/10/2004. Entry into Force: 22/07/2004.

[302] Zgonec-Rožej *International Criminal Law Manual* (2013) 301.

illegal nature of his or her conduct, or capacity to control his or her conduct to conform to the requirements of law.
- Intoxication: Article 31(1)(b) states that individual responsibility is precluded when the person is in a state of intoxication that destroys that person's capacity to appreciate the unlawfulness or nature of his or her conduct, or capacity to control his or her conduct to conform to the requirements of law, unless the person has become voluntarily intoxicated under such circumstances that the person knew, or disregarded the risk, that, as a result of the intoxication, he or she was likely to engage in conduct constituting a crime within the jurisdiction of the Court.
- Private defence (defence of the self, another, or certain property): Article 31(1)(c) imposes a two-part test: (a) the act must be in response to an 'imminent and unlawful use of force' against an attack on a 'protected' person or property; (b) the act of defence must be 'proportionate to the degree of danger'.[303]
- Duress (necessity): Article 31(1)(d) states that individual responsibility is precluded when the conduct which is alleged to constitute a crime within the jurisdiction of the Court has been caused by duress resulting from a threat of imminent death or of continuing or imminent serious bodily harm against that person or another person, and the person acts necessarily and reasonably to avoid this threat; provided such acts are proportional to the threat of harm or danger. Such a threat may either be made by other persons or constituted by other circumstances beyond that person's control.
- Superior order: Article 33 provides for the 'qualified exclusion' of criminal responsibility on the basis of superior orders. The fact that a crime within the jurisdiction of the Court has been committed pursuant to an order of a government or of a superior, whether military or civilian, shall not relieve that person of criminal responsibility unless:
  a) the person was under a legal obligation to obey orders of the government or the superior in question;
  b) the person did not know that the order was unlawful; and
  c) the order was not manifestly unlawful (however, as a matter of law, orders to commit genocide or crimes against humanity are automatically considered to be manifestly unlawful, therefore confining the application of the defence to war crimes).[304]

---

[303] *Kordić (Appeal Judgement)* par 451.
[304] Zgonec-Rožej *International Criminal Law Manual* (2013) 322.

Additionally, it may be possible for the Court to accept other defences from international law in accordance with the mechanism provided for in Article 21 of the *Rome Statute*.[305] The most notable defences which may exist in customary law, but do not receive express consideration in the ICC Statute, are military necessity, *tu quoque* and reprisals.[306]

6. Principles of Criminal procedure before the ICC

A detailed discussion of the principles of criminal procedure before the ICC falls outside the scope of this study. Accordingly, the following few remarks will suffice. International criminal procedure before the international courts and tribunals is unique in nature, which "while not purely adversarial, is predominantly inspired by the common law, adversarial tradition".[307] The ICC itself is also "common-law orientated, but at all thresholds a civil-law corrective instrument is implanted".[308] The legal principles governing international proceedings at the ICC are contained in the *ICC Rules of Procedure and Evidence*. The Assembly of States parties, established by the *Rome Statute*, was responsible for drafting and adopting the *ICC Rules of Procedure and Evidence*, voting with a two-thirds majority.[309] Rigorous rules apply for amending the *ICC Rules of Procedure and Evidence*, which undoubtedly enhances the legitimacy, stability and transparency of the rules.[310]

Since the legal principles governing proceedings before the ICC are entirely contained in the *ICC Rules of Procedure and Evidence*, it is sufficient to briefly mention some of the general principles governing international

---

[305] Art 31(3) of the *Rome Statute*.
[306] In this regard, see the discussion in Zgonec-Rožej *International Criminal Law Manual* (2013) 322–327.
[307] Zgonec-Rožej *International Criminal Law Manual* (2013) 407.
[308] Orie, A. *Accusatorial v Inquisitorial Approach in International Criminal Proceedings Prior to the Establishment of the ICC and in the Proceedings Before the ICC* in Cassese, A. et al. (eds) II *The Rome Statute of the International Criminal Court: A Commentary* (OUP, Oxford 2002) 1439, 1442–1456.
[309] Art 51 of the *Rome Statute*.
[310] Zgonec-Rožej *International Criminal Law Manual* (2013) 408. Any amendments to the *ICC Rules of Procedure and Evidence* may be proposed by any State party; the judges acting by an absolute majority; or the Prosecutor, but such amendments shall only enter into force upon its adoption by a two-thirds majority of the members of the Assembly of States Parties. See Art 51(2) of the *Rome Statute*. It is also possible for the judges of the Court, acting with a two-thirds majority, to draw up provisional rules to be applied in urgent cases where the rules do not provide for a specific situation before the Court. See Art 51(3) of the *Rome Statute*.

proceedings before the international courts and tribunals. These general principles regarding due process include universal international human rights standards designed to protect defendants in criminal proceedings, and include the following main principles:

- Everyone shall be entitled to a fair and public hearing by a competent, independent and impartial tribunal established by law,[311] including, *inter alia*: the right to be informed of charges brought against the accused; the right to legal assistance; the right to remain silent; the right of the accused to be present during the trial; the right to be heard (*audi alteram partem*); and the right to expeditious proceedings.[312]
- Everyone shall be presumed innocent until proved guilty before the Court in accordance with the applicable law. The onus is on the Prosecutor to prove the guilt of the accused beyond reasonable doubt.[313]

The stages of proceedings before the ICC are as follows: preliminary situation analysis,[314] investigation,[315] securing the attendance of the accused at the trial (the issuance of either a warrant of arrest[316] or summons to appear),[317] first appearance and initial proceedings,[318]

---

[311] Art 14(1) of the UN General Assembly, *International Covenant on Civil and Political Rights*, 16 December 1966.
[312] Art 67 of the *Rome Statute*.
[313] Art 66 of the *Rome Statute*.
[314] Art 53(1) of the *Rome Statute*.
[315] The Court will only initiate an investigation when the Court's right to exercise complementary jurisdiction has been triggered. See Art 53 of the *Rome Statute*. If the Pre-Trial Chamber, upon examination of the request and the supporting material, considers that there is a reasonable basis to proceed with an investigation, and that the case appears to fall within the jurisdiction of the Court, it shall authorise the commencement of the investigation. The Prosecutor is in charge of the criminal investigation, in terms of which he or she will have a number of powers and functions – See Arts 15, 54, 56 and 57 of the *Rome Statute*.
[316] If the Pre-Trial Chamber it is satisfied that there are reasonable grounds to believe that the person has committed a crime within the jurisdiction of the Court, and the arrest of the person appears necessary. Pursuant to the provisions of Art 58(2). See also Art 59.
[317] Art 58(7) – Summons may be used as an alternative to seeking a warrant of arrest, provided a summons is sufficient to ensure the person's appearance.
[318] Art 60 – At initial proceedings, the Pre-Trial Chamber shall satisfy itself that the person has been informed of the crimes which he or she is alleged to have committed, and of his or her rights under the Statute.

confirmation hearing,[319] trial,[320] appeal,[321] and revision proceedings (if applicable).[322]

7. Conclusion

The atrocities committed during the twentieth century galvanised international efforts to recognise humanity's basic entitlement to fundamental human rights and the subsequent necessity to repress international crimes, as a primary cause of such human rights infringements. International criminal law is a hybrid branch of public international law, derived from national criminal law, international humanitarian law, and human rights law.[323]

In terms of the aspects of procedural criminal law, the principles regulating the international proceedings are essential in providing both due process as a universal international human rights standard for a fair and just trial, and to regulate a procedure conducive to the attainment of criminal justice and the protection of victims and witnesses.

Substantive international criminal law serves to (1) criminalise acts prohibited under international law; (2) set out the subjective elements required for such acts to be regarded as prohibited; (3) provide for the possible circumstances under which persons accused of such crimes may be excused from criminal liability; and (4) clarify the modes of responsibility possible under international law.

The notion of 'international crimes' is understood as breaches of international rules, signifying a universal interest in repressing these crimes through criminalisation, prevention and punishment. International crimes, therefore, often constitute a breach of a *jus cogens* norm

---

[319] Art 61 – A hearing by the Pre-Trial Chamber for the confirmation of the charges may be held *in absentia* of the accused.

[320] Art 62 to 76 – Trial Chamber shall be responsible for the conduct of subsequent proceedings. Such proceedings include, *inter alia*, the plea stage, the leading of evidence and examination of witnesses by both prosecution and defence, closing arguments, the decision by the Trial Chamber, sentencing and punishment.

[321] Art 81, 82 and 83 – In this regard, the Prosecutor or the convicted person may make an appeal on any of the following grounds: procedural error, error of fact, error of law, or on the ground of disproportion between the crime and the sentence. In addition to these grounds of appeal, the convicted person, or the Prosecutor on that person's behalf, may appeal on any other ground that affects the fairness or reliability of the proceedings or decision.

[322] Art 84 of the *Rome Statute*.

[323] Cassese *International Criminal Law* (2003) 19.

under international law establishing liability for such acts as universally binding. Therefore, international criminal law "aims at protecting society against the most harmful transgressions of legal standards of behaviour perpetrated by individuals".[324] Establishing individual criminal responsibility under international law for the commission of international crimes aims to protect the fundamental values of the international legal community as a whole. Such fundamental rules or values of international law include: (1) crimes that threaten the maintenance of international peace and security; and (2) crimes that constitute unimaginable human rights atrocities that deeply shock the conscience of humanity (i. e. crimes that severely infringe upon internationally recognised human rights).

The proscription of breaches of international values aimed at the suppression of human rights deprivations entails the personal criminal liability for the individual/s responsible as well as binding obligations upon States. International law imposes the obligation upon States to proscribe certain conduct as punishable in their domestic penal system and to either prosecute the offenders found on their territory or to extradite them to States that are willing and able to prosecute.

Individual criminal responsibility before international criminal courts and tribunals is generally restricted to the perpetrator who is 'most responsible' for international crimes. Consequently, individual criminal responsibility is focussed on those who committed, or are otherwise responsible for, such acts. However, attributing individual criminal responsibility for international crimes should only occur when there is a certain degree of personal culpability. It is, however, clear that those 'most responsible' for international offences are often high on the chain of causality. In this regard, it was explained that Article 25 of the *Rome Statute* not only provides for direct and individual criminal responsibility, but may also criminalise other forms of participation, including co-perpetration, vicarious liability of military commanders or high-ranking leaders, and participation as part of a group acting with a common purpose.

Although the notion of 'international crime' lacks universal consensus, it is generally accepted that the prevention and punishment of international crimes include the so-called 'core crimes'. By their nature, the international core crimes are crimes of concern to the international community as a whole, therefore establishing universal jurisdiction over such acts at the national level. Consequently, it is the duty of every State to exercise its criminal jurisdiction over those responsible for international crimes. States are entrusted with the obligation to proscribe certain conduct as

---

[324] Cassese *International Criminal Law* (2003) 20.

punishable under their domestic penal system, and to either: prosecute the offenders found on their territory, or to extradite them to States that are willing and able to prosecute. In this regard, the jurisdiction of the ICC functions merely as a stop-gap, functioning on a complementarity basis to that of national criminal jurisdictions. Except in instances where the Court's jurisdictional triggers are activated, the primacy of national criminal jurisdiction means that a situation will only be admissible before the ICC in instances where domestic criminal courts have failed or were unable or unwilling to bring those responsible to justice. Despite the judicial influence that human rights law has had on domestic, regional and international legal systems, many human rights atrocities still occur within the domestic arena, often because of a lack of recognition of human rights or as a result of biased or ineffective national jurisdictional powers and mechanisms. Therefore, the effective implementation, recognition and protection of fundamental human rights require a supranational control mechanism. Individual criminal prosecution before international criminal courts thus signify a generally accepted course through which basic human rights may be protected and enforced in cases where national judicial systems are ineffective.

Appendix B: Freedom of Religion or Belief in the Context of Religious Persecution

1 Introduction

International criminal law in conjunction with human rights law, primarily seek to protect the religious identity of an adherent or religious group in relation to the right to freedom of religion or belief. This establishes the foundation for the individual criminal responsibility of 'authors' or 'instigators' responsible for severe deprivations of fundamental rights 'by reason of' religion.

The principles of international human rights law provide legal protection for the pluralist scope of normative conviction, as well as the pragmatic expression or manifestation of such convictions. Understanding the exact nature of the dimensions and normative core values of religious freedom, and the extent of its protection, is essential in defining a 'religious identity' and may also assist in differentiating between subsidiary and grievous deprivations for the purposes of the intensity threshold of 'grievous religious persecution'. For these and other reasons, it is imperative to examine the international legal standards applicable to the right to freedom of thought, conscience, religion or belief, including the right to equality on the basis of religion.

Thus, this appendix will first survey the international human rights standards. Thereafter, it will expound the normative core values of the right to freedom of religion or belief. A third consideration is the varied use of the term 'recognition' in the context of religious freedom. The fourth aspect of discussion explains the intersection and relation of religious freedom with other human rights. The final two sections deal with frequent patterns of deprivations of the right to freedom of religion or belief, as well as differentiating between the different intensities of such deprivations.

2 Applicable international human rights standards of religious freedom

Initially, it should be considered what 'religious freedom' entails. In human rights law, the freedom of 'thought, conscience and religion or belief' is considered to be inherently inclusive of 'religion' as a 'protected ground',[1] and furthermore, faith-based ideologies or deep existential views are indicative elements shaping the 'religious identity' of a person, as part of a 'protected group'.[2] As explained in Chapter Four, 'thought, conscience, religion or belief' are distinctive yet interrelated convictions that depict humanity's existential cognisance of its existence, identity and conception of life, and consequently signify a vital aspect of an adherent's way of life.[3] The use of the terms 'religion' or 'religious freedom' thus constitutes 'umbrella terms', which are inclusive of all deep existential views and consequent 'religious identities'. It is therefore clear that "[f]reedom of religion or belief is a multifaceted right".[4]

Considering that the notions of 'religious freedom' and 'religious identity' have already received significant attention, the rest of this section will focus on the applicable international human rights standards of religious freedom.

---

[1] 'Religion' is a protected ground in terms of the 'International Bill of Rights' (which includes the *Universal Declaration of Human Rights* (adopted in 1948), and the *International Covenant on Economic, Social and Cultural Rights* (ICESCR, 1966); the UN General Assembly, *Declaration on the Elimination of All Forms of Intolerance and of Discrimination Based on Religion or Belief*, UNGA Res 36/55, 73rd plenary meeting, 25 November 1981 (Religious Discrimination Declaration); and in the context of persecution, art 7(1)(h) of the *Rome Statute of the International Criminal Court*, Doc. A/CONF.183/9 of 17 July 1998 in force 1 July 2002 (*Rome Statute*).

[2] A religious group is considered a protected group in terms of art 2 of the UN General Assembly, *Convention on the Prevention and Punishment of the Crime of Genocide*, 9 December 1948, United Nations, Treaty Series, vol. 78, pg 277, (Genocide Convention); and art 6 of the *Rome Statute*.

[3] Par 8 of the UN High Commissioner for Refugees (UNHCR), *Guidelines on International Protection No. 6: Religion-Based Refugee Claims under Article 1A(2) of the 1951 Convention and/or the 1967 Protocol relating to the Status of Refugees*, 28 April 2004, HCR/GIP/04/06. (*UNCHR: Religion-Based Refugee Claims*).

[4] Bielefeldt, H. *Freedom of Religion or Belief: Thematic Reports of the UN Special Rapporteur 2010 - 2016*. Religious Freedom Series of the International Institute for Religious Freedom, Vol 3, 2nd and extended edition, Bonn (2017) pg 341.

Religious freedom forms part of the *genus* of civil and political rights that is at the core of human rights and was amongst the first to be recognised and codified as fundamental human rights.[5] Most principles of religious freedom have become part of customary international law, implying that States need not consent to its rules in order to be bound.[6] The significance of religious freedom means that its recognition and protection is vital at domestic, regional and global levels.

> ...freedom of thought, conscience and religion is one of the foundations of a 'democratic society'... [and as such is] one of the most vital elements that go to make up the identity of believers and their conception of life, but it is also a precious asset for atheists, agnostics, sceptics and the unconcerned. The pluralism indissociable from a democratic society, which has been dearly won over the centuries, depends on it.[7]

Consequently, religious freedom is an inherent right of all persons, which places certain responsibilities on States regarding its protection. As Bielefeldt points out:

> Protecting every human being's freedom of choice is a perfectly appropriate manner to institutionalize, in the specific sphere of human rights law, respect for human beings as potential holders of deep, existential convictions that themselves necessarily remain beyond the realm of legal enforcement.[8]

As a result, international human rights law has developed a comprehensive legal system that recognises, protects and promotes fundamental human rights,[9] especially religious freedom. The core international documents regarding the right to freedom of religion or belief include:

---

[5] Walter *Religion or Belief* (2008) 864.
[6] The UDHR has the status of customary international law. De Baets, A. *The impact of the Universal Declaration of Human Rights on the study of history*. History and Theory, Vol. 48 (2009) 20. The United Nations, *Statute of the International Court of Justice*, 18 April 1946, established in terms of Chapter XIV of the *Charter of the UN (ICJ Statute)*, defines customary international law in art 38(1)(b) as "...as evidence of a general practice accepted as law".
[7] Council of Europe, *Freedom of thought, conscience and religion: A guide to the implementation of Article 9 of the European Convention on Human Rights*, Human rights handbooks, No. 9 (2007) 12.
[8] Bielefeldt, H. *Misperceptions of Freedom of Religion or Belief*. Human Rights Quarterly, Volume 35, Number 1, pg 33–68. The Johns Hopkins University Press (2013), pg 47.
[9] Respecting human rights entails avoiding human rights abuse and violations. Protecting human rights implies taking an active role in order to ensure that neither

- Article 18 of the Universal Declaration of Human Rights (UDHR);
- Article 18 of the International Covenant on Civil and Political Rights (ICCPR);
- UN Human Rights Committee, General Comment No. 22: The Right to Freedom of Thought, Conscience, and Religion in terms of Article 18 of the ICCPR;
- Declaration on the Elimination of All Forms of Intolerance and of Discrimination Based on Religion or Belief (Religious Discrimination Declaration); and
- Reports of the UN Special Rapporteur on freedom of religion or belief.

The adoption of the UDHR in 1948 echoed the culmination of the struggle for religious freedom over many centuries into a pluralist legal codification. Article 18 declares that "[e]veryone shall have the right to freedom of thought, conscience and religion". The ICCPR broadened the scope of human rights in 1966 and finally gave legal effect to the protection of a citizen's freedom from unjustified infringement by the government or other external influences. Furthermore, it safeguards the citizen's ability to participate in the civil and political life of the State without discrimination or repression on various grounds, including religion.

The Human Rights Committee has been authorised to make definitive interpretations of the rights articulated in the ICCPR, which are referred to as 'General Comments'. The UN Human Rights Committee provided normative substance to the right to freedom of thought, conscience and religion or belief in terms of Article 18 of the ICCPR under *General Comment No. 22* in 1993. The explanatory contribution of the General Comment is significant and provides, *inter alia*, for a broad interpretation of 'religion' and clarity in regards to the framework for legitimate restrictions of religious freedom rights.

After a lengthy process, the UNGA adopted the *Religious Discrimination Declaration* in 1981. The declaration was intended to articulate the strong position of the UN against religious discrimination and religious intolerance. Also of importance is the extent of manifesting one's beliefs in Article 6. Although the *Religious Discrimination Declaration* does not have

---

the State nor anyone else within their territory, disrespect the rights of its inhabitants. Promoting human rights requires an active participation in teaching about and encouraging respect and protection of human rights.

binding force, the most fundamental principles of religious freedom contained therein are considered customary international law.[10]

The office of the UN Special Rapporteur on freedom of religion or belief was established in 1986 with the adoption of the resolution on the *Implementation of the Declaration on the Elimination of All Forms of Intolerance and of Discrimination Based on Religion or Belief*.[11] Under the authority of the UN Human Rights Council, the Special Rapporteur was given the responsibility to deal with individual situations, to conduct fact-finding country visits and to report serious cases of infringements of religious freedom to the UN.

There are numerous other international documents that all contain clauses concerning the freedom to exercise religion, the extent of religious freedom, the prohibition of discrimination on religious grounds, as well as the obligations placed on States.[12] In addition, all regional conventions on human rights contain provisions regarding the freedom of thought and religion.[13] However, during this discussion, the focus will be on the aforementioned core international instruments. In terms of these standard-setting documents, the provisions of the right to freedom of religion or belief may be summarised as follows:

- The conception of 'religion or belief' is inclusive of the freedom of thought and conscience.
- Religious freedom includes the freedom to have or to adopt a religion or belief of choice (*forum internum*), which is protected against any coercion that would impair one's freedom of choice in this regard.
- Religious freedom also includes the freedom to manifest one's deep existential view in worship, observance, practice and teaching, whether individually or in community with others, in public

---

[10] Walter *Religion or Belief* (2008) 867.
[11] UN Commission on Human Rights, *Implementation of the Declaration on the Elimination of All Forms of Intolerance and of Discrimination Based on Religion or Belief*, 10 March 1986, E/CN.4/RES/1986/20.
[12] For a detailed discussion see Sepúlveda, M. et al, *Human Rights Reference book*. University for Peace Publisher (2004), 203–207.
[13] Art 9 of the Council of Europe, *European Convention for the Protection of Human Rights and Fundamental Freedoms, as amended by Protocols Nos. 11 and 14*, 4 November 1950, ETS 5, (*European Convention on Human Rights*); art 12 of the Organization of American States (OAS), *American Convention on Human Rights, "Pact of San Jose", Costa Rica*, 22 November 1969; and art 8 of the Organization of African Unity (OAU), *African Charter on Human and Peoples' Rights ("Banjul Charter")*, 27 June 1981, CAB/LEG/67/3 rev. 5, 21 I.L.M. 58 (1982).

or private (*forum externum*). This external dimension of religious freedom may only be limited in terms of strict requirements.
- Religious freedom includes various normative core values, such as the protection of parents and guardians to ensure the religious and moral education of their children in conformity with their own convictions.

Essentially, religious freedom constitutes a core fundamental human right, and one of the foundations of a democratic society. The reason for this is that religion is one of the fundamental elements in a person's conception of life, which gives individuals a sense of identity and belonging, and configures personal ethics and public morals.[14] The profound existential nature of religion may unfortunately also be the cause of manifestations of intolerance and the basis of discrimination and persecution in matters of religion or belief. As a result, the disregard and infringement of the right to freedom of thought, conscience and religion or belief have brought, directly or indirectly, conflicts and great suffering to mankind.[15] However, freedom of religion may also serve as an instrument for the regulation of conflicts, especially in a culturally diverse society.[16]

Religious freedom is primarily concerned with the protection of the individual against impairments of his or her religious rights and freedoms. However, considering that religious freedom also contains an associative element, some aspects exercised in community with others are also protected as collective freedoms. It is, however, essential to remember that human rights law and the freedoms enshrined in the *UDHR* and *ICCPR* are not intended to protect any religion, nor the ideas and doctrines that may be imparted from such a religion against ridicule and criticism.[17]

In summary, 'religious freedom' is an 'umbrella' right that protects all forms of deep existential views. It constitutes a core element of human society and therefore necessitates international legal protection. Its fundamental character means that it has received legal recognition, protection and enforcement in the most prominent international human rights instruments. It is also true that freedom of religion or belief has been exposed to criticism, scepticism and objection, whether from a 'traditionalist' or 'liberalist' point of view.[18]

---

[14] Preamble par 4 of the *Religious Discrimination Declaration* (1981).
[15] Preamble of the *Religious Discrimination Declaration* (1981).
[16] Walter *Religion or Belief* (2008) 871.
[17] Bielefeldt, H., Ghanea, N. & Michael Wiener M. *Freedom of Religion or Belief: An International Law Commentary*. Oxford University Press. (2016), pg 12.
[18] Bielefeldt et al. *FORB: An International Law Commentary* (2016) 1-2.

Appendix B

3 The normative core values of the right to freedom of religion or belief

Within its broad understanding, religious freedom provides protection for both the choice of deep existential conviction, as well as the pragmatic manifestation thereof, which encapsulates a range of core values or elements. Therefore, 'religious freedom' includes legal protection for a broad range of rights and freedoms, which comprise internal and external freedoms or dimensions.

The *forum internum* or internal freedom or dimension of religious freedom refers to the internal and private realm of the individual's freedom of conviction. The *forum internum* includes the right to freedom to have, retain or maintain, change, replace or convert, choose, or adopt thoughts on all matters, personal convictions and the commitment to a religion or belief. The right to choose one's religion or belief, whatever the form, amounts to an absolute right that does not permit any limitation,[19] derogation,[20] or reservation,[21] and with which the State has no right to interfere.[22] The *forum internum* does not contain public or outer manifestations of religious practice, but simply the choice regarding one's deep existential views. Therefore, an individual has an absolute and unconditional right to hold any profound, identity-shaping religion or belief conviction, and such a freedom may not be limited under any circumstances. A natural consequence regarding the absolute freedom to hold any religious belief is that no one may be compelled to reveal adherence or non-adherence to a religion or belief.

---

[19] Sepúlveda *et al. Human Rights Reference book* (2004) 203.
[20] Art 4(2) of the ICCPR.
[21] "Reservations that offend peremptory norms would not be compatible with the object and purpose of the Covenant... Accordingly, provisions in the Covenant that represent customary international law (and a fortiori when they have the character of peremptory norms) may not be the subject of reservations. Accordingly, a State may not... deny freedom of thought, conscience and religion" – UN Human Rights Committee, *General Comment No. 24: Issues relating to reservations made upon ratification or accession to the Covenant or the Optional Protocols thereto, or in relation to declarations under article 41 of the Covenant*, par 8. From the UN International Human Rights Instruments, Compilation of General Comments and General Recommendations Adopted by Human Rights Treaty Bodies, 12 May 2004, HRI/GEN/1/Rev.7.
[22] *UN Rapporteur's Digest on Freedom of Religion or Belief: Excerpts of the Reports from 1986 to 2011 by the Special Rapporteur on Freedom of Religion or Belief Arranged by Topics of the Framework for Communications.* Geneva (2011), pg 42.

The *forum externum* or external dimension of religious freedom guarantees the freedom that everyone, either alone or in community with others, in public or private, may manifest their religion or belief in teaching, practice, worship and observance. The *forum externum* refers to the external manifestation of religious practice or behaviour, whether exercised individually or in community with fellow believers. In this regard, the *forum externum* relates to religious behaviour of an individual or a group, which seems to require some form of outwardly visible practice or manifestation. These external manifestations may be restricted in conformity with the criteria spelled out in Article 18(3) of the *ICCPR*, which will be discussed below.

These rights and freedoms are associated with the internal and external dimensions of religious freedom as the normative core values of the right to freedom of religion or belief. These core values may be described as the elements of the right to freedom of religion or belief,[23] and constitute a set of minimum standards in regards to its scope of protection.[24] The core values of religious freedom have developed over time through the interpretation of the core international documents referred to earlier, as well as relevant regional sources.[25] These normative core values of religious freedom include:

- the freedom to have, choose, change or leave a religion or belief;
- the right to manifest one's belief, either publicly or in private, through teaching, practice, worship, and observance;
- the freedom from coercion;
- the right to conversion, i. e. the right to change a religion and to try to convince others to change their religion; including the right to disseminate religious convictions and missionary activities;
- freedom from discrimination on the basis of religious conviction;
- freedom from derogation;
- freedom from impermissible restrictions or limitations on the right to freedom of religion or belief;
- the right and freedom of parents and children regarding religion or belief;[26] and

---

[23] *Rapporteur's Digest on Freedom of Religion or Belief* (2011) 5.
[24] Lindholm *Freedom of Religion or Belief from a Human Rights Perspective* (2015) 8.
[25] Art 9 of the *European Convention on Human Rights*; art 12 of the *American Convention on Human Rights*; and art 8 of the *Banjul Charter*.
[26] Art 18(4) of the *ICCPR* and art 13(3) of the *ICESCR* confirms this right of parents in the context of religious freedom and religious education and requires States to

Appendix B

- the right to conscientious objection.[27]

These core values will be briefly discussed in the next section. However, for the sake of brevity, the two latter values will not be considered.

3.1 Freedom to choose a religion or belief

At its core, the right to freedom of religion or belief is concerned with the freedom of human beings to search for an ultimate meaning in life, to choose their own path concerning religious and belief-related issues, and to come up with their own results (or no results) in such endeavours.[28]

The right to 'have' a religion or belief in terms of Article 18 of the UDHR is an indispensable core freedom.[29] Paragraph 5 of the *United Nations Human Rights Committee (UNHRC) General Comment No. 22* states that:

> [T]he freedom to "have or to adopt" a religion or belief necessarily entails the freedom to choose a religion or belief, including the right to replace one's current religion or belief with another or to adopt atheistic views, as well as the right to retain one's religion or belief.

---

guarantee "respect for the liberty of parents and, when applicable, legal guardians to ensure the religious and moral education of their children in conformity with their own convictions".

[27] The right of everyone to have conscientious objections to military service as a legitimate exercise of the right to freedom of thought, conscience and religion has also been evaluated or confirmed in Resolutions 1984/93, 1989/59, 1991/65, 1993/84, 1995/83 and 1998/77 of the UNCHR. The notion of 'conscientious objection' can be defined as dissention regarding the irreconcilable moral or ethical imposition between an imperative rule or law and adherence to a genuinely held religious or belief-based convictions. The Human Rights Committee in its *General Comment No. 22* makes provision for the right of everyone to have conscientious objections to military service as a legitimate exercise of the right to freedom of thought, conscience and religion inasmuch as the obligation to use lethal force may seriously conflict with the freedom of conscience and the right to manifest one's religion or belief for those "who genuinely hold religious or other beliefs that forbid the performance of military service". Other forms of conscientious objection that are recognised by some States, but which fall short of constituting widespread State practice or an entitlement under the premise of religious freedom, include matters relating to issues of morality in certain healthcare practices such as abortion, contraception and euthanasia. See Bielefeldt et al. *FORB: An International Law Commentary* (2016) 258.

[28] Bielefeldt et al. *FORB: An International Law Commentary* (2016) 56.

[29] This terminology is restated in art 18 of the *ICCPR*, art 1(1) of the *Religious Discrimination Declaration* (1981), and par 3 and 5 of the *UNHRC General Comment No. 22*.

The right to freedom of choice regarding one's religion or belief orientation lays the foundation of normative universalism in that all human beings are inherently entitled to have whatever deep existential view they may choose without interference. Furthermore, it is important to keep in mind that the nature of free will and choice in terms of human rights law inextricably links the positive and negative components of freedom, because "one is not free to do something unless he is also free not to do it".[30] In other words, the freedom to choose a religion or belief also includes the freedom to abstain from such a choice or the right not to profess any religion or belief; so-called 'freedom from religion'.[31]

Article 18 of the UDHR interprets the freedom to have a religion of choice, to also include the freedom to change such a religion or belief freely. The right to 'change' is expressed in Article 18 of the ICCPR as the "freedom to have or to adopt a religion or belief of his choice".[32] The freedom to 'adopt' has been interpreted as "the right to replace one's current religion or belief with another or to adopt atheistic views, as well as the right to retain one's religion or belief".[33] To 'adopt' may also be understood to involve the freedom to supplement one's existing view with an additional belief, or to embrace a completely different position on religion or belief.[34] All of these aspects relate to the internal dimension of religious freedom and may therefore not be limited or derogated from.[35]

> [A]ccording to universally accepted international standards, the right to freedom of religion or belief includes the right to adopt a religion of one's choice, the right to change religion and the right to maintain a religion... [and that] these aspects of the right to freedom of religion or belief have an absolute character and are not subject to any limitation whatsoever.[36]

Therefore, the freedom of choice is an essential aspect of internal religious freedom, whether such a choice relates to retaining, maintaining, changing, replacing, renouncing, adding or adopting one's deep existential views.

---

[30] Bielefeldt *Misperceptions of FORB* (2013) 49–50.
[31] Bielefeldt *Misperceptions of FORB* (2013) 47.
[32] The term 'adopt' is also used in the UNHRC General Comment No. 22 par 5.
[33] UNHRC General Comment No. 22 par 5.
[34] Bielefeldt et al. *FORB: An International Law Commentary* (2016) 56.
[35] UNHRC General Comment No. 22 par 3.
[36] *Rapporteur's Digest on Freedom of Religion or Belief* (2011) 8.

3.2. Right to manifest one's belief, either publicly or in private, through teaching, practice, worship, and observance

Choosing and having a religious identity is not enough; any deep existential conviction will inevitably lead to practical manifestations of concomitant individual and communitarian ethical or ritualistic practices in various ways.[37] Therefore, in order to do justice to religious freedom, Article 18 of the UDHR and Article 18(1) of the ICCPR provides for the freedom to manifest a religion or belief in worship, observance, practice and teaching, whether individually or in community with others and in public or private.[38] In other words, the international human rights standards make provision for the freedom to choose a religion (*forum internum*), but also the freedom to practice or manifest such a religion or belief, which relates to the external manifestation or *forum externum* dimension of religious freedom. Although the degree of legal protection of these two dimensions differs, they are usually deeply interwoven and should always be seen in conjunction.[39]

Unlike the unconditional nature of the *forum internum*, the freedom to practice or manifest a religion may be legitimately restricted or limited. Article 18(3) of the ICCPR states that the right to manifest a religion or belief "may be subject only to such limitations as are prescribed by law and are necessary to protect public safety, order, health, or morals or the fundamental rights and freedoms of others".[40]

The term 'manifestation' has been interpreted to imply "a perception on the part of adherents that a course of activity is in some manner prescribed or required"[41] in compliance with their chosen existential conviction, or "acts which are intimately linked to these attitudes, such as acts of worship or devotion which are aspects of the practice of a religion or a belief in a generally recognized form".[42] Therefore, the freedom to manifest religion or belief in worship, observance, practice and teaching seem to suggest some form of outwardly visible

---

[37] Bielefeldt *et al. FORB: An International Law Commentary* (2016) 93.
[38] See also Art 1(1), 1(3) and 6 of the *Religious Discrimination Declaration* (1981), and par 4, 7 and 8 of the *UNHRC General Comment No. 22*.
[39] Bielefeldt *et al. FORB: An International Law Commentary* (2016) 93.
[40] Confirmed *verbatim* in Art 1 of the *Religious Discrimination Declaration* (1981).
[41] Council of Europe *Freedom of thought, conscience and religion* (2007) 15.
[42] *C v United Kingdom* [1983] 37 DR 142 at par 144, as discussed in Walter *Religion or Belief* (2008) 868.

demeanour or behaviour, which may be referred to as 'religious behaviour' or behaviour in compliance with religious or belief convictions. Regarding the scope of freedom to manifest religion or belief, the *Study of Discrimination in the Matter of Religious Rights and Practices* in 1959 concluded that it might safely be assumed that "the intention was to embrace all possible manifestations of religion or belief within the terms 'teaching, practice, worship and observance'".[43] Therefore, the elaboration on the broad range of acts in Article 6 of the *Religious Discrimination Declaration*[44] and paragraph 4 of the *UNHRC's General Comment No. 22*,[45] does not constitute an exhaustive list of manifestations.[46] In fact, the initial draft version of this general comment also included an explanation that the "various means of giving expression to religion or belief are not mutually exclusive and do not leave a choice to authorities as to which of these manifestations [of] religion or belief is to be guaranteed".[47] In the face of religious diversity in interpretations of manifestations of religion, it is clear that the various elements of religious manifestations

---

[43] Office of the United Nations High Commissioner for Human Rights. *Study of discrimination in the matter of religious rights and practices*, by Arcot Krishnaswami, Special Rapporteur of the Sub-Commission on Prevention of Discrimination and Protection of Minorities. E/CN.4/Sub.2/200/Rev.1 (1960), pg 17.

[44] Art 6 provides for the following manifestations of religion or belief through worship, observance, practice and teaching that have been internationally recognised: to worship or assemble in connection with a religion or belief, and to establish and maintain places for these purposes; to establish and maintain appropriate charitable or humanitarian institutions; to make, acquire and use to an adequate extent the necessary articles and materials related to the rites or customs of a religion or belief; to write, issue and disseminate relevant publications in these areas; to teach a religion or belief in places suitable for these purposes; to solicit and receive voluntary financial and other contributions from individuals and institutions; to train, appoint, elect or designate by succession appropriate leaders called for by the requirements and standards of any religion or belief; to observe days of rest and to celebrate holidays and ceremonies in accordance with the precepts of one's religion or belief; and to establish and maintain communications with individuals and communities in matters of religion and belief at the national and international levels.

[45] *UNHRC General Comment No. 22* par 4. See also art 6 of the *Religious Discrimination Declaration* (1981).

[46] A discussion of the scope of the various elements of the right to manifest one's religion or belief 'in worship, observance, practice and teaching' falls outside the ambit of this study. However, it may be noted that no agreed, precise definition exist, because these elements largely overlap – Bielefeldt et al. *FORB: An International Law Commentary* (2016) 97.

[47] UN Docs. CCPR/C/45/CRP.2 (1992), par 4 (second sentence).

are to be viewed as a 'conceptual continuum', without a hierarchy between these four elements.[48] Inevitably, such religious diversity depicts that a clear differentiation between the various elements of religious manifestations is theological, rather than a legal concern. In this regard, Bielefeldt et al. advise that it is not the role of State agencies, domestic courts or international bodies to determine what constitutes as religious manifestations. The "insistence on having a clear overview of manifestations often stems from the authorities' interest to narrow down the scope of freedom of religion or belief in order to exercise control and oversight".[49] More accurately, the deeply personal nature of religious freedom dictates that it is ultimately the individual's freedom to interpret their own understandings and priorities of what constitutes a religious manifestation within the conception of their own deep existential views.[50]

However, the freedom to manifest a religion or belief does not relate to every act motivated by or influenced by religion or belief,[51] and will only pertain to 'religious behaviour' which is central or integral to the expression of a religion or belief; it will not protect 'religious behaviour' that is merely inspired or encouraged by such conviction.[52] Furthermore, the freedom to exercise 'religious behaviour' cannot be used as the justification for manifestations that "amount to propaganda for war or advocacy of national, racial or religious hatred that constitutes incitement to discrimination, hostility or violence".[53]

The freedom to manifest a belief entitles a person to give expression to his or her personal convictions in terms of the right to religious freedom and is therefore an integral part of the core values of religious freedom. Freedom to manifest, including its many associated freedoms, gives pragmatic realisation to the freedom of a chosen deep existential view and the external commitment to such a belief. Although the manifestation of religious freedom may be legitimately restricted or limited within certain parameters, impermissible restrictions may, under certain circumstances, amount to religious persecution.

---

[48] Bielefeldt et al. FORB: An International Law Commentary (2016) 97–98.
[49] Bielefeldt et al. FORB: An International Law Commentary (2016) 98.
[50] Bielefeldt et al. FORB: An International Law Commentary (2016) 98.
[51] Arrowsmith v The United Kingdom, 7050/75, Council of Europe: European Commission on Human Rights, 5 December 1978, 19 DR 5, par 71.
[52] Council of Europe Freedom of thought, conscience and religion (2007) 15.
[53] UNHRC General Comment No. 22 par 7.

3.3. Freedom from coercion

Freedom of choice is "essentially a natural right emanating from creation"[54] and is thus a fundamental human right. In this regard, the freedom of choice may be "impaired by measures that force people to act or refrain from acting in a manner contrary to their religious beliefs".[55] Thus, the right to choose a religious identity and the commitment to its way of life requires the freedom to make a voluntary, non-coerced decision. Consequently, the prohibition of coercion, which would impair a person's freedom to have or to adopt a religion or belief of her/his choice,[56] is an unconditional norm within international human rights law, regardless of the nature of such a deep existential view.[57]

Coercion or compulsion in the sphere of religious freedom refers to the forceful persuasion of a person regarding the choice to have, maintain or change a belief, and thus affects the internal dimension of religious freedom. Therefore, the right not to be compelled or coerced to have, choose, change or leave a religious identity constitutes an absolute right.[58] It is "fundamental to human identity that one should not be compelled to hide, change or renounce this in order to avoid persecution".[59] Article 18(2) of the *ICCPR* bars coercion that would impair a person's freedom to have or to adopt a religion or belief of his or her choice.[60]

International human rights law prohibits coercion to change one's religion, which should be broadly interpreted to include all forms of coercion, intimidation or compulsion, whether by State or non-State actors.[61] Coercive measures by States are thus impermissible, which may include: pressure applied by a State, policies aiming at facilitating religious conversions, physical force, torture or cruel, inhuman or

---

[54] The *Bad Urach Statement* published as part of the compendium on the *Bad Urach Consultation: Suffering, persecution and martyrdom – Theological reflections*. Edited by Sauer, C. & Howell, R. Religious Freedom Series: Suffering, Persecution and Martyrdom. Vol 2. (2010), Kempton Park: AcadSA Publishing / Bonn: VKW 2010, pg 38.
[55] Durham, W.C., et al. *Law and Religion: National, International, and Comparative Perspectives*. Aspen Elective Series, 3rd edition (2010) 248.
[56] Bielefeldt et al. *FORB: An International Law Commentary* (2016) 75.
[57] UNHRC General Comment No. 22 par 5.
[58] Bielefeldt *FORB: Thematic Reports* (2017) 48.
[59] Par 12 of the *UNCHR: Religion-Based Refugee Claims* (2004).
[60] Restated *verbatim* in Art 1(2) of the *Religious Discrimination Declaration* (1981).
[61] *Rapporteur's Digest on Freedom of Religion or Belief* (2011) 12–13. See also Bielefeldt *Misperceptions of FORB* (2013) 47.

degrading treatment or punishment,[62] the use of penal sanctions,[63] State-sponsored incentives or material benefits to convert or reconvert, or policies that may limit access to medical care, education and/or employment in order to influence people's choice of religion.[64]

Coercive measures by States are most evident in cases where a States adheres to an official religious identity. Bielefeldt warns States about the dangers of conforming to an official religion and the associated risk of coercion.

> [The] autonomy of religious institutions falls within the forum externum dimension of freedom of religion or belief which, if the need arises, can be restricted..., while threats or acts of coercion against a person may affect the forum internum dimension of freedom of religion or belief, which has an unconditional status. In other words, respect by the State for the autonomy of religious institutions can never supersede the responsibility of the State to prevent or prosecute threats or acts of coercion against persons (e. g., internal critics or dissidents), depending on the circumstances of the specific case.[65]

The State is obliged to provide protection against coercive measures, including protection for newly established or religious minority communities and vulnerable groups. This includes situations where non-State actors are responsible for coersive measures.

Coercive actions by non-State actors or third parties, such as private individuals or organisations, may include resorting to means of improper propagation of religious views, coercive persuasion, or by directly exploiting situations of particular vulnerability to try to convert others.[66] The right to change, replace or leave a religion or belief inherently also includes conversion,[67] which will be discussed in more detail in the section that follows. In this regard, it should be noted that the right to freedom of conversion has a dualistic application. On the one hand it establishes the freedom from, or protection against, forced or coerced conversions, while on the other hand, it allows the right to try to convert others through non-coercive means.[68]

---

[62] Art 1 of the UNGA *Convention against Torture* 1984.
[63] UNHRC *General Comment No. 22* par 5. Other forceful persuasive measures may include: undue influence, physical violence or threats thereof, psychological harm, discrimination, criminal penalties, or more subtle forms of illegal influence.
[64] *Rapporteur's Digest on Freedom of Religion or Belief* (2011) 12–13.
[65] Bielefeldt *FORB: Thematic Reports* (2017) 182.
[66] Bielefeldt *FORB: Thematic Reports* (2017) 110.
[67] Bielefeldt *FORB: Thematic Reports* (2017) 110.
[68] Bielefeldt *FORB: Thematic Reports* (2017) 109.

An interesting question is whether the unconditional prohibition of coercion in Article 18(2) only relates to the *forum internum*, or whether it may also include coercion that would impair a person's freedom to choose the manner in which he or she gives expression to their religion or belief.[69] Bielefeldt *et al.* argues that what Article 18(2)

> specifically prohibits is not any kind of impact on the forum internum, but more narrowly 'coercion' of such a nature that it would actually 'impair' the affected person's 'freedom to have or to adopt a religion or belief of his choice'.[70]

3.4. Right to conversion – the right to adopt, change or renounce one's religion

The right to freedom of conversion is intrinsically provided for in terms of a person's freedom to have, adopt, change, or renounce a religion or belief, which is coherent with the universal nature of human rights.[71] Indeed, Bielefeldt *et al.* state, "without this particular element, freedom of religion or belief would lose its character as a human right that aims at empowering human beings".[72] Understood within the freedom to choose a religion, human beings should have the freedom to reconsider their inherited or existing faith, to express personal doubts and, depending on their own decision, to retain and maintain their current existential view. They may also adopt an additional view, change, abandon, or renounce their previous faith and adopt a different existential view, or not profess any religion or belief whatsoever.[73]

The broader international normative framework regarding the right to change a religion implies the following legal features: (a) the right to change in the narrow sense of changing one's own religion, (b) the right not to be forced to change, (c) the right to persuade others in a non-coercive manner, and (d) the rights of parents and children in the context of a conversion.[74] The multifaceted nature of the right to freedom of conversion implies that

---

[69] See discussion regarding the interrelatedness of the *forum internum* and the *forum externum* – Bielefeldt *et al. FORB: An International Law Commentary* (2016) 82–85.

[70] Bielefeldt *et al. FORB: An International Law Commentary* (2016) 82–85 (own emphasis added).

[71] The right to 'change' one's religion or belief is specifically provided for in terms of art 18 of the *UDHR* and art 9 of the *ECHR*.

[72] Bielefeldt *et al. FORB: An International Law Commentary* (2016) 56.

[73] Bielefeldt *et al. FORB: An International Law Commentary* (2016) 56.

[74] Bielefeldt *et al. FORB: An International Law Commentary* (2016) 63.

it cannot exist in isolation. In other words, the freedom of conversion cannot truly exist without a pluralist approach that embraces the right to non-coercive proselytism.[75] Therefore, the right to propagate and disseminate one's religious beliefs, including communicative elements relating to the freedom of expression, are essential components without which neither the freedom to retain nor the freedom to change can truly be equated with free choice. This multifaceted approach implies that the right to freedom of conversion protects both the individual who has taken the decision to convert, or not to convert, as well as those who engage in activities to proselytise their existential views with the aim of converting others.[76] Consequently, the right to freedom of conversion relates to the convert's fundamental right to freedom of religion or belief, as well as the balancing of the opposing rights of the religious 'persuader' against those of the addressee of such attempts at religious conversion. Although this interpretation of the right to freedom of conversion constitutes the international human rights standard, its application is by no means consensual amongst all States or religions.[77] As a result, the right to freedom of conversion remains a very controversial issue in the debate and drafting of international instruments.[78] Unsurprisingly, the conversion issue "has become a human rights problem of great concern which occurs in various parts of the world and seems to stem from different motives".[79] Bielefeldt advises that:

> Religious leaders and opinion makers should become aware that not only is conversion to their own religion or belief protected, but the decision to replace one's current religion or belief with a different one is too.[80]

---

[75] For the purposes of this study and regardless of any religious affiliation or connotation, the terms 'proselytism' or to 'proselytise' will refer to the propagation or dissemination of religion or beliefs with the aim of trying to convert others by means of non-coercive persuasion and may include, *inter alia*, the exercise of any of the freedoms provided for in terms of art 6 of the *Religious Discrimination Declaration* in pursuit of such an objective. 'Proselytism' seems to represent a more secular description of activities that may differ based on religious orientation, for example 'evangelism' within the sphere of Christianity. Colloquially, terms such as 'outreach', 'bearing witness', "*da'wa*" (the call), 'invitation', or 'missionary work' are more often used, but may be contextually restrictive.

[76] *Rapporteur's Digest on Freedom of Religion or Belief* (2011) 10.

[77] For a detailed discussion regarding the international human rights framework on the right to conversion, see Bielefeldt *FORB: Thematic Reports* (2017) 110–132.

[78] Walter *Religion or Belief* (2008) 868. See also Bielefeldt *et al. FORB: An International Law Commentary* (2016) 55.

[79] Bielefeldt *FORB: Thematic Reports* (2017) 108–109.

[80] *Rapporteur's Digest on Freedom of Religion or Belief* (2011) 57.

The UN Special Rapporteur on freedom of religion or belief has reported on numerous violations and breaches of this aspect of religious freedom, which are "unacceptable and still occur too often" in contemporary society.[81]

> In quite a number of countries individuals who have converted away from the mainstream religions, or who would like to do so, live in an atmosphere of permanent hostility, discrimination, and intimidation. They are exposed to multiple violations and abuses perpetrated by State agencies or non-State actors or – indeed quite often – a combination of both.[82]

Based on observations made by the Special Rapporteurs on freedom of religion or belief in their country visits and when dealing with thematic reports on conversion,[83] the following non-exhaustive typology of the phenomena outlines four broad types of situations regarding such contraventions of the right to conversion:

- Situations where State agents try to convert, reconvert or prevent the conversion of persons by violence or threats thereof, depriving them of their liberty, torturing and ill-treating them or threatening to dismiss them from their jobs. In some countries State officials targeted dissident believers, often of minority religious communities, to renounce their religion and join a State-approved religion.
- Situations where religious conversion is prohibited by law as 'apostasy', and punished through imprisonment, and sometimes the death penalty. Where conversion is not actually prohibited by law, administrative requirements such as registration and obtaining official documentation can also make it difficult to change one's religion or belief and may lead to harassment or threats by State and religious officials.
- Situations where members of majority religious groups seek to convert or reconvert members of religious minorities, most often through attempts aimed at forced conversions.
- Situations where so-called 'unethical' conversions have been reported, such as the promise of material benefit or by taking advantage of the vulnerable situation of the person whose conversion is sought. Such conversions are often facilitated through law

---

[81] *Rapporteur's Digest on Freedom of Religion or Belief* (2011) 8.
[82] Bielefeldt et al. *FORB: An International Law Commentary* (2016) 58.
[83] *Rapporteur's Digest on Freedom of Religion or Belief* (2011) 8. See also Bielefeldt et al. *FORB: An International Law Commentary* (2016) 58–62.

and vague legal jargon, and the acts facilitating such conversion may constitute a criminal offence.

Clearly, the right to freedom of conversion is an essential element of religious freedom. It is used as an overarching freedom that includes the following sub-categories, which will be discussed next:

- the right to conversion in the sense of changing one's religion or belief;
- the right not to be forced to convert; and
- the right to try to convert others using non-coercive persuasion or proselytism, including missionary work, propagating a religious belief, and the right to disseminate religious convictions.[84]

3.4.1. The right to conversion in the sense of changing one's religion or belief

The freedom to change one's religion or belief is expressly included in Article 18 of the *UDHR* as an indispensable component of freedom of religion or belief, which includes the right to change to, from, or between, religious identities.[85] It guarantees the 'freedom to have or adopt a religion or belief of his choice'. Article 1 of the *Religious Discrimination Declaration* refers to everyone's 'freedom to have a religion or whatever belief of his choice'. In its *General Comment No. 22* the UNHRC uses the verb 'replace' in connection with the freedom of choice.[86] Regardless of such differences in the use of official terminology, "the word 'choice' does not make any sense unless it includes the possibility of changing one's orientation and adherence".[87]

The right to conversion forms part of the internal dimension of the individual's religious freedom and is therefore an absolute right that does not permit any limitations, derogations or coercive measures that would impair a person's freedom of choice in this regard.[88]

> [T]he right to change one's religion or belief thus demands apodictic respect, since any violation would amount to a direct negation of the due respect for everyone's human dignity.[89]

---

[84] Bielefeldt *FORB: Thematic Reports* (2017) 109.
[85] Bielefeldt *et al. FORB: An International Law Commentary* (2016) 63.
[86] *UNHRC General Comment No. 22* par 5.
[87] Bielefeldt *et al. FORB: An International Law Commentary* (2016) 63.
[88] Bielefeldt *et al. FORB: An International Law Commentary* (2016) 64.
[89] Bielefeldt *et al. FORB: An International Law Commentary* (2016) 64.

The universal and absolute nature of this dimension of the freedom of conversion requires absolute protection, whether such interferences emanate from societal prejudices or State policies and practices.[90] States, as the primary addressees of human rights obligations, are obligated to respect everyone's right to conversion, to protect all persons within their jurisdiction against exploitation, infringements or coercion, and provide safeguards against reprisals targeting converts.[91] It is thus disconcerting that some States enact anti-conversion laws by essentially criminalising acts that amount to conversions under the auspices of 'apostasy', 'heresy', 'blasphemy' or 'insult to/of a religion', which warrants severe criminal sanctions, including the death penalty in extreme cases.[92] Such judicial measures are a direct violation of the absolute and unconditional internal freedom to change or adopt a religion or belief of choice.

3.4.2. The right not to be forced to convert

As an established right to freedom, the right to change always means voluntary conversion.[93] The right not to be forced to convert is the negative corollary of the right to change, which includes the freedom not to change, provided such a choice remains an unrestricted one. Consequently, the freedom not to convert implies the freedom against forced conversion, which also forms part of the internal dimension of religious freedom.[94] Therefore, the right not to be forced to convert is guaranteed unconditionally, regardless of whether such forced conversions emanate from State policies or non-State actors or third parties.[95] In guaranteeing the right to conversion, the State must also ensure protection for everyone's right to change or retain their chosen religion and provide safeguards against possible coercion to convert or reconvert against their will, including actions by non-State actors and also governmental institutions and authorities.[96]

---

[90] Bielefeldt *et al. FORB: An International Law Commentary* (2016) 65.
[91] Bielefeldt *FORB: Thematic Reports* (2017) 111.
[92] Bielefeldt *FORB: Thematic Reports* (2017) 117.
[93] Bielefeldt *et al. FORB: An International Law Commentary* (2016) 65.
[94] Bielefeldt *et al. FORB: An International Law Commentary* (2016) 66.
[95] Bielefeldt *FORB: Thematic Reports* (2017) 119.
[96] Bielefeldt *FORB: Thematic Reports* (2017) 112.

3.4.3. The right to try to convert others 'non-coercively'

Bielefeldt *et al.* explain that the verb 'to convert' may be interpreted as providing for its intransitive use, i. e. the act of changing one's own religious identity, as well as its transitive use, i. e. act of inducing others to change their religious identity.[97] Consequently, the right to propagate or disseminate one's religion or beliefs with the aim of trying to convince others to change their religion is closely related to the question of conversion.[98] Whether in its intransitive or transitive form, 'to convert' must remain a voluntary action. However, whereas the decision to convert or not to convert falls within the internal dimension of religious freedom, 'missionary activities' aimed at converting others fall within the scope of the external dimension of religious freedom. Therefore, from the intransitive viewpoint, the aim is to provide for the unconditional right to freedom of choice regarding conversion and protection against forced conversion measures. Conversely, from the transitive viewpoint, the aim is to provide for the freedom to propagate, disseminate and express one's religious beliefs with the intention of converting others, while providing legal safeguards against coercive conversion measures.

As a secular description of attempted conversion measures, 'proselytism' or to 'proselytise', provides for the right to engage in non-coercive activities in order to persuade others to convert. Consequently, the right to proselytise through non-coercive means constitutes a manifestation of religious freedom, which may be exercised either individually or in community with others and in public or private.[99] As such, the right to proselytise may be lawfully restricted in terms of Article 18(3) of the *ICCPR*. Such activities may not be exercised in a way that propagates war or the advocacy of national, racial or religious hatred that constitutes incitement to discrimination, hostility or violence.[100] States should apply restrictions on proselytism with circumspect.[101] The justification for legitimate aims in this regard usually relates to safeguarding public order or morals, and also protecting the basic human rights and freedoms of others. Restrictive measures limiting acts motivated by proselytism should be applied strictly

---

[97] Bielefeldt *et al. FORB: An International Law Commentary* (2016) 66.
[98] Walter *Religion or Belief* (2008) 868.
[99] In par 4 its *General Comment No. 22* the Human Rights Committee states that "the practice and teaching of religion or belief includes acts integral to the conduct by religious groups of their basic affairs, [... and] the freedom to prepare and distribute religious texts or publications".
[100] Art 20(2) of the *ICCPR*.
[101] Walter *Religion or Belief* (2008) 868.

in order to protect vulnerable groups such as minors, subordinates[102] and religious minorities.[103] States must be mindful that the international human rights standards protecting persons against coercion also applies to the restrictive measures imposed by States to restrict missionary activities. Therefore, a general prohibition on conversion or a law prohibiting non-coercive proselytism would amount to a disproportional and unnecessary restriction on religious freedom and may "constitute a State policy aiming at influencing individual's desire to have or adopt a religion or belief and is therefore not acceptable under human rights law".[104]

The right to proselytise through non-coercive means "is accepted as a legitimate expression of religion or belief and therefore enjoys the protection afforded by article 18 [and article 19] of *ICCPR* and other relevant international instruments".[105] The right to freedom of expression protects the collective or individual freedom to seek, receive, and impart information and ideas of all kinds through any chosen media. Therefore, the right to freedom of expression may include communicative outreach activities aimed at persuading others to convert, which serves to reinforce the right to freedom of conversion.[106]

In regards to communicative freedoms relating to the right to proselytise, the *Religious Discrimination Declaration* recognises the following freedoms: (1) to write, issue and disseminate relevant publications in these areas; (2) to teach a religion or belief in places suitable for these purposes; and (3) to establish and maintain communications with individuals and communities in matters of religion and belief at national and international levels.[107]

In terms of regional human rights protection, Article 9 of the *ECHR* ensures the right to proselytise through non-coercive means with the aim of trying to convince others to change their religion, under the premise of 'teaching' on religion or belief. In *Kokkinakis v Greece*, the European Court on Human Rights addressed the balancing of legal restrictions regarding proselytism against the right to manifest a

---

[102] See *Larissis and Others v. Greece*, European Court of Human Rights, Reports 1998-I, judgement of 24 February 1998.
[103] States that restrict missionary or other outreach activities in order to protect vulnerable groups against exploitation or coercion, bear the burden to justify such limitations and must provide clear empirical evidence that such activities amount to exploitation or coercion – Bielefeldt *FORB: Thematic Reports* (2017) 114–120.
[104] *Rapporteur's Digest on Freedom of Religion or Belief* (2011) 9.
[105] *Rapporteur's Digest on Freedom of Religion or Belief* (2011) 33.
[106] Bielefeldt *FORB: Thematic Reports* (2017) 113.
[107] Art 6(d), (e) & (i) of the *Religious Discrimination Declaration*.

religion.[108] The Court provided an important distinction between 'improper proselytism' and 'non-coercive proselytism', stating that:

> ... [A] distinction has to be made between bearing... witness and improper proselytism. The former corresponds to true evangelism... as an essential mission and a responsibility of... [believers and religious communities]. The latter represents a corruption or deformation of it. It may... take the form of activities offering material or social advantages with a view to gaining new members... or exerting improper pressure on people in distress or in need; it may even entail the use of violence or brainwashing; more generally, it is not compatible with respect for the freedom of thought, conscience and religion of others.[109]

Proselytism, or similar activities, must be done in a respectful manner that does not amount to coercion aimed at religious conversion. Coercive proselytism constitutes a human rights violation, and other forms of 'improper proselytism' may cause a disturbance in religious tolerance, resulting in religious discrimination and persecution.[110] In such instances, the State has the obligation to ensure religious freedom for everyone on its territory and under its jurisdiction, regardless of their religious beliefs.[111] Conversely, non-coercive proselytism

> cannot be considered a violation of the freedom of religion and belief of others if all involved parties are adults able to reason on their own and if there is no relation of dependency or hierarchy between the missionaries and the objects of the missionary activities.[112]

In summary, the right to freedom of conversion is a multi-layered dimension of religious freedom. It provides for the freedom to choose whether or not to convert, as well as the right to attempt to convert others through non-coercive means. Importantly, legal measures or restrictions cannot be

---

[108] *Kokkinakis v. Greece*, App No. 3/1992/348/421, Council of Europe: European Court of Human Rights, 19 April 1993.
[109] *Kokkinakis* (1993) par 48. For a more in-depth study on the dangers of aspects such as undue influence, brainwashing and unethical hypnosis in the scope of religion, see the work of Steven Hassan, who is a former cult member of the Unification Church of the United States ('Moonies'), author, clinical professional, and founding director of the Freedom of Mind Resource Center. https://freedomofmind.com/about-us/steven-hassan/. Accessed 20/12/2018.
[110] *Rapporteur's Digest on Freedom of Religion or Belief* (2011) 33.
[111] *Rapporteur's Digest on Freedom of Religion or Belief* (2011) 9.
[112] *Rapporteur's Digest on Freedom of Religion or Belief* (2011) 33.

used to facilitate undue conversions, or prevent against conversions from the mainstream or official religion by excluding non-coercive proselytism.

3.5. Freedom from discrimination and the right to equality

Equality[113] is one of the 'architectonic principles' of human rights and aligns with the concept of normative universalism,[114] in terms of which all members of the human family are endowed with inherent dignity, which entitles them to equal treatment and enjoyment of rights.[115] The principle of equality thus filters through all human rights and freedoms and can be said to be applicable in all spheres of government, all circles of society, and in the everyday life of all persons. The freedom from discrimination requires equal respect and equal concern for everyone's rights and freedoms, but non-discrimination is not upheld merely with 'identical treatment'. There may be instances where differential treatment is actually necessary to attenuate or suppress conditions that perpetuate discrimination.[116] Non-discrimination "primarily requires systematic endeavours to eliminate all forms of discrimination, including on grounds of religion or belief",[117] for example, reasonable accommodation.[118] Indeed, Article 2 of the UDHR states that "[e]veryone is entitled to all the rights and freedoms

---

[113] "'Equality' as a human rights principle can never mean mere sameness or uniformity; it must be conceptualized as a diversity-friendly equality" – Bielefeldt *et al. FORB: An International Law Commentary* (2016) 323.

[114] Bielefeldt *et al. FORB: An International Law Commentary* (2016) 24.

[115] Bielefeldt *Misperceptions of FORB* (2013) 50.

[116] "[F]air and non-discriminatory treatment may still accommodate and at times even necessitate 'different treatment', depending on relevant circumstances" – Bielefeldt *et al. FORB: An International Law Commentary* (2016) 323. "Such measures [to achieve substantive equality] are legitimate to the extent that they represent reasonable, objective and proportional means to redress *de facto* discrimination" – par 8 and 9 of the UN Committee on Economic, Social and Cultural Rights (CESCR), *General comment No. 20: Non-discrimination in economic, social and cultural rights (art. 2, para. 2, of the ICESCR).* E/C.12/GC/20, 2 July 2009. (*CESR General Comment No. 20*).

[117] Bielefeldt *FORB: Thematic Reports* (2017) 140.

[118] "Reasonable accommodation aims at relaxing generally applicable rules in order to guarantee a more substantive equality in which the specificities of everyone are taken into account" – Caceres, G. *Reasonable Accommodation as a Tool to Manage Religious Diversity in the Workplace: What About the "Transposability" of an American Concept in the French Secular Context?* From Alidadi, K. *et al.* (eds), A Test of Faith?: Religious Diversity and Accommodation in the European Workplace. Ashgate Publishing, Ltd. (2012), pg 284.

set forth in this Declaration, without distinction of a kind, such as... religion". Some argue that religious discrimination is 'one of the oldest forms of discrimination'.[119]

The right to freedom of religion or belief not only prohibits undue infringements into a person's religious freedom, it also prohibits religious discrimination, i. e. the denial of equality on the basis of religion.[120] In other words, the right to freedom of religion or belief is "not only a right to freedom, but also a right to equality and non-discrimination".[121] Bielefeldt *et al.* observe that:

> Without taking account of equality, rights of freedom would amount to the privileges of the happy few and without regard to freedom, the principle of equality could lead to uniformity or 'sameness'.[122]

It was explained that religious discrimination might have two strands. On the one hand, religion may be the 'motivator' for discrimination which flows from the perpetrator's religious identity, referred to as "discrimination and violence in the name of religion or belief, i. e., based on or arrogated to religious tenets of the perpetrator".[123] On the other hand, the victim's religious orientation, whether actual or perceived, may constitute the 'identifier' of the discriminatory ground. In such cases, the victim is targeted because of his religious identity, in which case the perpetrator's religious identity or motive is irrelevant. Bielefeldt *et al.* argue that these two aspects of 'religious discrimination' build on the references in the *Religious Discrimination Declaration*, in terms of which the former may be referred to as 'manifestations of *intolerance*', whereas the latter may be understood as the 'existence of *discrimination* in matters of religion or belief'.[124] Nevertheless, for the purposes of this study, 'religious discrimination' may include either or both of these strands.

Discrimination on prohibited grounds may be direct or indirect and can originate from the State or from non-State actors. Direct religious discrimination occurs when an individual is treated less favourably than another person in a similar situation on the basis of religion or belief, or in

---

[119] Nowak, M. *UN Covenant on Civil and Political Rights: CCPR Commentary.* Published by N. P. Engel, 2nd revised edition (2005), pg 51.
[120] Bielefeldt *et al. FORB: An International Law Commentary* (2016) 311.
[121] Bielefeldt *et al. FORB: An International Law Commentary* (2016) 24.
[122] Bielefeldt *et al. FORB: An International Law Commentary* (2016) 311.
[123] Par 33 of the UN General Assembly, *Report of the Special Rapporteur on freedom of religion or belief, Asma Jahangir.* A/HRC/13/40, 21 December 2009.
[124] Bielefeldt *et al. FORB: An International Law Commentary* (2016) 330.

relation to freedom of religion or belief. It may also include detrimental acts or omissions on the basis of religion or belief, where there is no comparable similar situation.[125] Indirect religious discrimination refers to laws, policies or practices which appear neutral at face value, but have a disproportionate impact on the exercise of rights as distinguished on the basis of religion or belief or in relation to freedom of religion or belief.[126] Although mostly not openly targeting a specific religious community, the rules may have a religious discriminatory effect in practice.[127]

The definition of religious discrimination in Article 2(2) of the *Religious Discrimination Declaration* provides us with the only definition in international human rights instruments of non-discrimination on the basis of religion or belief. It states that religious discrimination and intolerance based on religion or belief "*means any distinction, exclusion, restriction or preference based on religion or belief and having as its purpose or as its effect nullification or impairment of the recognition, enjoyment or exercise of human rights and fundamental freedoms on an equal basis*".[128] It conceptualises close similarities with religious persecution. In this sense, both concepts are based on intolerance and discrimination based on religion or belief, having as its purpose or as its effect, the nullification or impairment of the recognition, enjoyment or exercise of human rights and fundamental freedoms on an equal basis. Consequently, it was established that 'grievous religious persecution' constitutes a severe form of religious discrimination if the purpose or effect of the discriminatory conduct results in a severe deprivation of fundamental rights. It is therefore the primacy of 'religious identity' as the basis of the perpetrator's discriminatory intent which establishes a *nexus* with religious persecution.

Similar to religious persecution, religious discrimination is not contextualised by the nature of the rights that are infringed (i. e. the right to freedom of religion or belief), but rather the basis upon which the distinction, exclusion, restriction or preference occurs, namely religious identity.[129] Therefore, the 'human rights and fundamental freedoms' referred to in the definition may include an infringement of the exercise of a person's civil and political rights or in the enjoyment of economic, social and cultural rights on the grounds that such a person belongs, or does not belong, to a certain religion or belief.[130] However, it has already been

---

[125] Paraphrasing par 10(a) of the *CESR General Comment No. 20* (2009).
[126] Paraphrasing par 10(b) of the *CESR General Comment No. 20* (2009).
[127] Bielefeldt *et al*. *FORB: An International Law Commentary* (2016) 322.
[128] Art 2(2) of the *Religious Discrimination Declaration*.
[129] Bielefeldt *et al*. *FORB: An International Law Commentary* (2016) 314.

established that religious discrimination and persecution may have a particularly detrimental effect on the enjoyment of the right to freedom of religion or belief.[131] Consequently, discrimination against communities because of their religious identities is inherently and indivisibly linked to religious persecution and the deprivation of religious freedom. In other words, it is almost inevitable that victims of religious discrimination and persecution will experience a denial, deprivation or infringement of the recognition, enjoyment or exercise of the fundamental right to religious freedom.

In the subsections that follow, the international standards on equality on non-discrimination on the basis of religion, and the principle of 'respectful non-identification' by the State regarding religion are considered. Discrimination committed by States, *de facto* authorities, and societal non-State actors is also differentiated.

3.5.1. *International human rights standards regarding religious discrimination*

International human rights instruments categorically insist upon equality and non-discrimination on the grounds of religion or belief, and are therefore expounded in a range of international human rights instruments.[132] However, an overview of all the international standards on religious equality and non-discrimination falls outside the scope of this study. Instead, attention is placed on the most comprehensive standard-setting international instrument focussed and concerned with discrimination on grounds of religion or belief, viz. the *Religious Discrimination Declaration* of 1981.

The most fundamental principles laid down in the *Religious Discrimination Declaration* must be considered part of customary international law constituting peremptory rules of a *jus cogens* nature.[133] The *Religious Discrimination Declaration* states that "[n]o one shall be subject to discrimination by any

---

[130] Van Boven, T. *Racial and Religious Discrimination*. Max Planck Encyclopedia on Public International law, Wolfrum, R. (ed). Heidelberg: Oxford University Press (2009), pg 613.

[131] Par 59 of the UN Report, *United Nations World Conference against Racism, Racial Discrimination, Xenophobia and Related Intolerance*, Declaration, 31 August to 8 September 2001, UN DocA/CONF.189/12. (2001). (*UN World Conference against Racism*).

[132] For a comprehensive list of the principal provisions on religious discrimination see Bielefeldt *et al. FORB: An International Law Commentary* (2016) 309-311.

[133] The *Religious Discrimination Declaration* could be regarded as the most extensive standard-setting document on freedom from religious discrimination – Van Boven *Racial and Religious Discrimination* (2009) 613.

State, institution, group of persons, or person on the grounds of religion or other belief".[134] It also confirms that "discrimination between human beings based on grounds of religion or belief constitutes an affront to human dignity ... and shall be condemned as a violation of human rights and fundamental freedoms".[135] Furthermore, "the right to freedom of thought, conscience and religion applies equally to all people, regardless of their religions or beliefs, and without any discrimination as to their equal protection by the law".[136]

The *Religious Discrimination Declaration* provides protection against discrimination by the State or government, whether formal or factual discrimination. Formal discrimination refers to discrimination enshrined in laws, whereas factual discrimination pertains to the effects of laws, policies or practices.[137] Bielefeldt states that:

> The principle of non-discrimination thus prohibits both unjustified distinctions when similar situations are treated differently and unjustified comparisons when different situations are treated in the same manner.[138]

It is important to note that the principle of non-discrimination is not absolute. Reasonable and objective differential treatment, distinction, exclusion, restriction or preference may not amount to unlawful discrimination.[139] Differential treatment will

> constitute discrimination if the criteria for such differentiation, judged in the light of the objectives and purposes of the Convention, are not applied pursuant to a legitimate aim, and are not proportional to the achievement of this aim.[140]

However, such differentiation between religious groups will only be allowed in terms of the external dimensions of religious freedom rights and in compliance with the legal framework set out in Article 18(3) of the *ICCPR*.

---

[134] Art 2(1) of the *Religious Discrimination Declaration* (1981).
[135] Art 3 of the *Religious Discrimination Declaration* (1981).
[136] Par 2 of the UNGA *Res. Discrimination based on Religion*. (2009).
[137] *Rapporteur's Digest on Freedom of Religion or Belief* (2011) 54.
[138] *Rapporteur's Digest on Freedom of Religion or Belief* (2011) 53.
[139] Van Boven *Racial and Religious Discrimination* (2009) 611.
[140] *Report of the Committee on the Elimination of Racial Discrimination.* General Assembly Official Records: Forty-Fifth Session, Supplement No. 18 (A/52/18), chap. VII, par 4.

3.5.2. The principle of 'respectful non-identification' by the State regarding religion

In order to guarantee religious freedom for everyone, States should not identify themselves with a particular religion (or particular types of religions), and maintain an open framework in which religious pluralism may develop freely and without discrimination.[141] The consequence of a State or official religion or belief system may differ in terms of its practical implications for different religious groups. However, it may ultimately result in favourable treatment for preferred religious groups and/or discriminatory policies against undesirable religious identities.[142] For example:

> In some extreme cases, only followers of the official state religion can publicly manifest their religious convictions. Some states render citizenship or public positions dependent upon adherence to the state religion.[143]

Consequently, the requirement of equality or non-discrimination has an important ideological implication for a State or government in that it requires 'neutrality' or impartiality *vis-à-vis* issues of religion or belief.[144] The duty of a State to remain neutral regarding issues of religion or belief requires that the State refrains from taking part in religious disputes or favouring certain religious or secular groups over others.[145] The principle of neutrality also has a significant corollary implication on the concept of the 'State religion', and the situation of religious minorities.[146]

The principle of State neutrality requires the realisation of freedom of religion or belief for all and must be implemented in a non-discriminatory manner.[147] However, State neutrality should not be mistaken as a proxy for non-commitment by States in regards to issues of religion or belief. Therefore, Bielefeldt argues that an ideology of 'respectful non-identification' by

---

[141] Bielefeldt *et al. FORB: An International Law Commentary* (2016) 34.
[142] Bielefeldt *et al. FORB: An International Law Commentary* (2016) 34.
[143] Bielefeldt *FORB: Thematic Reports* (2017) 99.
[144] For example, in the case of *Metropolitan Church of Bessarabia v. Moldova*, App no. 45701/99, ECtHR 2001-XII, the European Court of Human Rights stated that "in exercising its regulatory power... in its relations with the various religions, denominations and beliefs, the State has a duty to remain neutral and impartial" – par 116.
[145] Bielefeldt *et al. FORB: An International Law Commentary* (2016) 351-352.
[146] Bielefeldt *Misperceptions of FORB* (2013) 52.
[147] Bielefeldt *Misperceptions of FORB* (2013) 52-53.

the State regarding religion or belief may better encapsulate the international human rights expectations on States in this regard.[148]

> In the area of freedom of religion or belief, non-discrimination... implies a policy of deliberate "non-identification" of the state with any particular religion or belief in order to be equally fair, open and inclusive to all people living on the state's territory. Neither should the government use (or rather abuse) religion as a source of its own political legitimacy, nor should it privilege one particular tradition...[149]

Therefore, the principle of 'respectful non-identification' by the State regarding religion or belief has an important auxiliary function in support of the right to religious freedom and serves as a standard-setting objective for such States to "consistently act in a fair, inclusive and non-discriminatory manner *vis-à-vis* the existing or emerging religious and philosophical diversity in society".[150] Consequently, 'respectful non-identification' in issues of religion presents two opposing challenges to the State:

> As the formal guarantor of human rights, the state is supposed to actively protect and promote freedom of religion or belief while, at the same time, exercising a specific self-restraint in order to respect freedom and equality of all in their different convictions.[151]

International human rights law does not prescribe how the 'church-State relationship' should function.[152] Religion or belief has "played an indispensable role in the evolution of nation States and communities at every level",[153] and historically, the intersection between law, State and religion have been intertwined. In this regard, Bielefeldt *et al.* note that:

> Authority was vested in religions long before the emergence of the nation State and, once nation States emerged, they often developed their identity, grew and survived largely through negotiating with and drawing on religious authority and religious leaders. Traces of this symbiotic relationship – whether overtly or more implicitly – continues, in some form or another, in many States to the present day.[154]

---

[148] Bielefeldt *Misperceptions of FORB* (2013) 53.
[149] Bielefeldt *Misperceptions of FORB* (2013) 53.
[150] Bielefeldt *Misperceptions of FORB* (2013) 53.
[151] Bielefeldt *Misperceptions of FORB* (2013) 67.
[152] Bielefeldt *et al. FORB: An International Law Commentary* (2016) 34.
[153] Bielefeldt *et al. FORB: An International Law Commentary* (2016) 338.
[154] Bielefeldt *et al. FORB: An International Law Commentary* (2016) 338.

Contemporarily, the 'symbiotic relationship' between religion and the State raises serious human rights concerns, most notably a lack of freedom to choose a religious identity resulting from *de jure* or *de facto* discrimination.[155] However, different State-religion relationships may deeply affect other religious communities in various ways, including the legal, the political, the social, and the cultural spheres of life.[156] Essentially, an official belief ideology protects or promotes a particular religious identity, not a pluralist freedom of religion or belief.[157] Despite obvious concerns regarding tendencies of particularisation,[158] the notion of an official or 'State religion' is not prohibited.[159] However, in its *General Comment No. 22*, the UNHRC notes that:

> The fact that a religion is recognized as a State religion or that it is established as official or traditional or that its followers comprise the majority of the population, shall not result in any impairment of the enjoyment of any of the rights ... nor in any discrimination against adherents to other religions or non-believers [nor against persons who do not accept the official ideology or who oppose it].[160]

In other words, the UNHRC cautions that an official religion may inherently provide preferential treatment or privileges to pre-selected religions, while imposing different forms of restrictions or exclusions against members of non-traditional or unknown beliefs.[161] As a result, a State or official religion conceals serious risks of discrimination against newly established or minority religions.[162] The burden of proof is on the State to show that when a set of beliefs is treated as official ideology, whether in law or practice, this does not result in any impairment of the rights and freedoms in the *ICCPR*, nor in discrimination against persons who do not accept the official ideology or who oppose it.[163]

In consideration of the concerns regarding an official religion, some States have separated religion from political and legal interference and

---

[155] Bielefeldt et al. *FORB: An International Law Commentary* (2016) 338.
[156] For a discussion on a range of concerns raised by the Special Rapporteurs of religion or belief regarding official or State religions in particular States, see Bielefeldt et al. *FORB: An International Law Commentary* (2016) 343–353.
[157] Bielefeldt et al. *FORB: An International Law Commentary* (2016) 342.
[158] Bielefeldt et al. *FORB: An International Law Commentary* (2016) 18, 350–351.
[159] Bielefeldt et al. *FORB: An International Law Commentary* (2016) 342.
[160] *UNHRC General Comment No. 22* par 9–10.
[161] Bielefeldt et al. *FORB: An International Law Commentary* (2016) 18.
[162] Bielefeldt *Misperceptions of FORB* (2013) 54.
[163] Bielefeldt et al. *FORB: An International Law Commentary* (2016) 342.

have no established religion, such as Brazil, the Netherlands, South Africa, China and India.[164] However, the mere declaration of secularity in law does not guarantee full respect and protection for the human rights of all on an equal basis.[165] As a result, Bielefeldt argues that "every state is governed by some sort of belief system, on the basis of which the government will explicitly or implicitly differentiate adherents and non-adherents".[166] Thus, to a varied extent, all States exhibit some form of official belief or secularist statehood.[167]

The conflicting interpretations of the term 'secular' (including its derivatives, such as 'secularity' and 'secularism') has been subjected to very different, frequently conflicting, interpretations. Durham differentiates between 'secularism' as an ideological position and 'secularity' as a neutral framework of religious pluralism.[168] Based on this understanding, Bielefeldt et al. refer to the former as 'doctrinal secularism' and the latter as 'constitutional secularity'.[169] Consequently, they argue that a moral secularist understanding ('constitutional secularity' or a political secularist State)[170] may best preserve the principle of neutrality regarding religion or belief in the sense that political secularism "sees itself as operating in the service of a non-discriminatory implementation of freedom of religion

---

[164] Thames, K. H. et al. *International Religious Freedom Advocacy: A guide to Organizations, Law and NGO's*. Baylor University Press (2009), pg 10.

[165] Bielefeldt et al. *FORB: An International Law Commentary* (2016) 351.

[166] Bielefeldt *Misperceptions of FORB* (2013) 55.

[167] In its most fundamental form, a 'Secularist State' refers to a State governed by atheists and agnostics.

[168] Durham, W.C. Jr. *Religious Freedom in a Worldwide Setting: Comparative Reflections*. Universal Rights in a World of Diversity: The Case of Religious Freedom. Glendon, M. A. and Zacher, H. F. (eds), The Pontifical Academy of Social Sciences (2012) 368. "By "secularism", I mean an ideological position that is committed to promoting a secular order as an end in itself. [...] By 'secularity', I mean an approach to religion-state relations that avoids identification of the state with any particular religion or ideology (including secularism itself) and that provides a neutral framework capable of accommodating or cooperating with a broad range of religions or beliefs".

[169] Bielefeldt et al. *FORB: An International Law Commentary* (2016) 358.

[170] Political secularism can be distinguished from doctrinal secularism or a formal secular State ideology because "...doctrinal secularism, once guiding state activities, may claim an ideological priority over freedom of religion or belief, [whereas] the secular state in the understanding of political secularism sees itself as operating in the service of a non-discriminatory implementation of freedom of religion or belief for everyone". From Bielefeldt *Misperceptions of FORB* (2013) 55-56. See also Bielefeldt et al. *FORB: An International Law Commentary* (2016) 358.

or belief for everyone".[171] This is in contrast with 'doctrinal secularism' (in the sense of a comprehensive secular belief system), which may invoke an ideological superiority and exclusivity over religious freedom, resulting in a decline of religious pluralism.[172] In this regard, Bielefeldt *et al.* explain that:

> [T]he term secularity can indicate a policy of deliberate non-commitment in this area [religious pluralism]. Moreover, it can even become a proxy for antireligious attitudes which, if adopted as a State policy, have detrimental effects on the enjoyment of freedom of religion or belief for everyone.[173]

Therefore, it is theoretically possible for a State that proscribes to a moral secularist understanding (political secularity), rather than a doctrinal secular ideology, to refrain from explicitly or implicitly differentiating between adherents and non-adherents of any religious identity. In such instances, adhering to the principle of 'respectful non-identification' by the State provides for a non-discriminatory implementation of religious freedom for everyone.

However, although it may be theoretically possible for the government in a politically secular State to achieve belief-based neutrality, religion constitutes one of the numerous factors that motivate State ideology, law and policy. Therefore, such a non-discriminatory implementation of religious freedom for everyone may well remain an optimistic philosophy in many countries. Indeed, a more factual assertion remains the assumption that all States adhere to some form of ideology, which ultimately differentiates between individuals based on adherence or non-adherence to the mainstream views, whether religious or otherwise. As a result, such differentiation regarding religious identity may result in various degrees of religious discrimination, including discrimination of a structural or indirect nature.[174]

3.5.3. *Discrimination committed by States, de facto authorities, and societal non-State actors*

Religious discrimination can be very forthright, for instance, the use of criminal law provisions to shield a hegemonic religion against proselytism, imposing burdensome registration procedures on minorities or new

---

[171] Bielefeldt *Misperceptions of FORB* (2013) 56.
[172] Bielefeldt *et al. FORB: An International Law Commentary* (2016) 36.
[173] Bielefeldt *et al. FORB: An International Law Commentary* (2016) 35.
[174] Bielefeldt *Misperceptions of FORB* (2013) 59.

religious communities while providing preferential treatment to official or national religions.[175] However, contemporarily, religious discrimination has taken on more subtle forms, which require "a more sensitive approach to less visible forms of discrimination, such as indirect and structural discrimination in various sectors of the society, including in relation to freedom of religion or belief".[176] Therefore, religious discrimination may result from State restrictions, exclusions, or limitations of rights, or the actions of various non-State actors, although these actors are not equivalent in power or responsibility.[177]

Below, State-imposed discrimination, the growing concern regarding discrimination committed by *de facto* authorities, and the significance of societal discrimination are considered.

3.5.3.1. *State-imposed discrimination*

State-imposed religious discrimination relates to a State's restrictions on freedom of religion or belief and related discrimination. Bielefeldt *et al.* explain that

> This type of 'vertical discrimination' is carried out by State agents targeting individual(s) on grounds of their religion or belief, or is discrimination that results from State agents acting in the name of a particular religion, thus discriminating against those not following that hegemonic faith.[178]

As mentioned, contemporary human rights treaties unanimously contain clauses concerning religious freedom and the prohibition of discrimination on religious grounds.[179] Generally, the primary emphasis is on States' responsibility to take effective measures to protect and promote religious equality and tolerance, and to prevent and eliminate discrimination on the grounds of religion or belief.[180] However, the scope of protection and legal obligations in regards to religious discrimination is extensive.

---

[175] Bielefeldt *et al. FORB: An International Law Commentary* (2016) 311–312.
[176] Bielefeldt *et al. FORB: An International Law Commentary* (2016) 312.
[177] Bielefeldt *et al. FORB: An International Law Commentary* (2016) 315.
[178] Bielefeldt *et al. FORB: An International Law Commentary* (2016) 315.
[179] Art 18 and 2 of the *UDHR* (1948); Arts 18 and 2(1) of the *ICCPR* (1966); Arts 9 and 14 of the *European Convention on Human Rights*; arts 12 and 1(1) of the *American Convention on Human Rights*; arts 8 and 2 of the *Banjul Charter*; and arts 30 and 4 of the League of Arab States, *Arab Charter on Human Rights*, May 22, 2004, entered into force March 15, 2008.
[180] See UN General Assembly, *Resolution 103(I) Persecution and Discrimination*, 19 November 1946; arts 2 and 7 of the *UDHR*, and arts 2 and 3 of the *ICCPR*.

Although legislation plays an important role in guaranteeing religious freedom on an equal basis for all, the impact of State-induced discrimination on the enjoyment of rights can be profound, whether as a result of legal provisions or through its practical effect.[181]

3.5.3.2. Discrimination perpetrated by de facto authorities

In States where the government has lost 'effective control' over its territory or parts thereof, *de facto* authorities may fill the power vacuum. In this context, the Special Rapporteur has determined that 'effective control' means that a "non-State armed group has consolidated its control and authority over a territory to such an extent that it can exclude the State from governing the territory on a more than temporary basis".[182] In the context of religious freedom and discrimination, a number of reports and communications have referred to human rights violations committed by *de facto* authorities in the name of religion, including for example, the *Taliban*,[183] *Hezbollah*,[184] *Al-Shabaab*,[185] *Da'esh*,[186] and *Boko Haram*.[187] Bielefeldt *et al.* point out that:

---

[181] Bielefeldt *et al. FORB: An International Law Commentary* (2016) 316–317. "Discrimination enshrined in the law or the effect thereof, may be tantamount to unequal citizenship and adversely affect free movement, choice of employment, participation in public life, the eligibility to hold high posts or 'sensitive posts', the right to marry, the possibility of obtaining ID cards, access to education, equal enjoyment with regards to family life, divorce, custody, and inheritance for millions around the world. Policies or practices affect the enjoyment of numerous rights too and, either alone or in combination with de jure discrimination, lead to extensive discrimination".

[182] UN General Assembly, *Report of the Special Rapporteur on Freedom of Religion or Belief, Heiner Bielefeldt.* A/HRC/28/66, 29 December 2014, par 55.

[183] Par 27 and 30 of the UN General Assembly, *Elimination of all forms of religious intolerance*, Interim report of the Special Rapporteur of the Commission on Human Rights on the elimination of all forms of intolerance and of discrimination based on religion or belief, A/56/253, 31 July 2001.

[184] Par 19 of the UN General Assembly, *Implementation of General Assembly Resolution 60/251 of 15 March 2006 entitled "Human Rights Council".* A/HRC/2/7, 2 October 2006.

[185] Par 31 of the UN General Assembly, *Report of the independent expert on the situation of human rights in Somalia, Shamsul Bari.* A/HRC/18/48, 29 August 2011.

[186] See Appendix C.

[187] UN General Assembly, *Resolution adopted by the Human Rights Council S-23/1: Atrocities committed by the terrorist group Boko Haram and its effects on human rights in the affected States.* A/HRC/RES/S-23/1, 21 May 2015, and UN General Assembly, *Report*

Such recommendations by international human rights mechanisms imply that certain non-State actors, due to the direct impact of their acts on rights-holders, actually also have human rights obligations, obviously alongside the State which remains a duty bearer too.[188]

Thus, it is argued that even non-State armed groups that lack 'effective control' over a territory are obliged to respect international human rights, and may incur individual criminal responsibility for human rights abuses.[189]

3.5.3.3. Discrimination by societal non-State actors

Although this section deals with religious discrimination by societal non-State actors, it should not be ignored that the responsibility of non-State actors does not absolve the State of its responsibility or liability.[190] Furthermore, non-State actors may incur individual criminal responsibility for religious discrimination that amounts to human rights abuses.[191]

The list of actors responsible for social hostilities is more extensive than State-actors and may include, *inter alia*: ethnic group leaders, religious leaders at any level from local to national, religious extremist movements and terror cells, political parties whether regional or national, revolutionaries or paramilitary groups, organised crime cartels or networks, multilateral organisations, and even ordinary citizens (people from broader society) motivated by any number of reasons.[192]

Societal and religious rifts are not limited to hostility directed against adherents or communities of different faiths (interreligious), but may also include differences within the same religion but between different denominations, or amongst members of the same denomination (intra-religious or intra-denominational).[193]

---

of the United Nations High Commissioner for Human Rights: Violations and abuses committed by Boko Haram and the impact on human rights in the countries affected. A/HRC/30/67, 9 December 2015.

[188] Bielefeldt et al. *FORB: An International Law Commentary* (2016) 319.
[189] Bielefeldt *FORB: Thematic Reports* (2017) 265.
[190] Bielefeldt et al. *FORB: An International Law Commentary* (2016) 320.
[191] The liability aspects of State and non-State actors will be discussed in Chapter Seven.
[192] Open Doors Analytical. *World Watch List Methodology*. November 2017, pg 16–17. Available at: http://opendoorsanalytical.org/world-watch-list-methodology-latest-edition-november-2017/. Accessed 09/01/2019.
[193] *Rapporteur's Digest on Freedom of Religion or Belief* (2011) 75.

3.5.4. Discrimination against religious minorities

State practice towards existing and emerging religions varies throughout the world.[194] Religious minorities are regarded and treated as a particularly vulnerable group that deserves special protection under international human rights law.

> In those States in which ethnic, religious or linguistic minorities exist, persons belonging to such minorities shall not be denied the right, in community with the other members of their group, to enjoy their own culture, to profess and practice their own religion, or to use their own language.[195]

Religious minorities are afforded the same rights and freedoms in regard to religion or belief as the members of majority religions or State religions. Their status as a religious minority is protected against any impairment of the enjoyment of their rights, as well as any discrimination against adherents of emerging or new religions, including persons who do not accept the official ideology or who oppose it.[196] States thus have a specific obligation under international law regarding the rights of minority groups.[197] Such obligations will even be applicable in instances where non-State entities, such as religious extremist groups, are responsible for abuses of religious freedom rights against religious minorities, which will require the State to bring such perpetrators to justice.[198]

Instances of religious persecution against a collective religious identity is a global occurrence and is not limited to specific religions, whether as perpetrators or persecutors. Although people with diverse religious identities "may be exposed to anti-minority victimisation when living in a minority situation, certain religious communities have a particularly long-lasting history of discrimination, harassment and even persecution".[199] Consequently, in different regions of the world, minority religious groups

---

[194] Thames *et al. International Religious Freedom Advocacy* (2009) 10.
[195] Art 27 of the *ICCPR*.
[196] UNHRC General Comment No. 22 par 2, 5, 9 & 10.
[197] See *inter alia*, Art 27 of the *ICCPR*; UN Human Rights Committee (HRC), *CCPR General Comment No. 23: Article 27 (Rights of Minorities)*, 8 April 1994, CCPR/C/21/Rev.1/Add.5; art 30 of the UN General Assembly, *Convention on the Rights of the Child*, 20 November 1989, United Nations, Treaty Series, vol. 1577; and the UN General Assembly, *Declaration on the Rights of Persons Belonging to National or Ethnic, Religious and Linguistic Minorities*, 20 December 1993, A/RES/48/138.
[198] *Rapporteur's Digest on Freedom of Religion or Belief* (2011) 82.
[199] Bielefeldt *FORB: Thematic Reports* (2017) 136.

are the object of suspicion, prejudices and derogatory stereotyping because of their religion or belief. They are subjected to serious limitations, violations and abuses of their right to freedom of belief, *inter alia*.[200]

The collective religious identity of minority beliefs deserves special protection under international human rights law and such religious communities are regarded and treated as a particularly vulnerable group.[201] Religious minorities are afforded the same rights and freedoms in regards to religion or belief as those adherents to majority religions or State religions. In addition, their status as religious minorities is protected against any impairment of the enjoyment of their rights, as well as any discrimination against adherents of emerging or new religions, including persons who do not accept the official ideology or those who oppose it.[202]

In fact, the *ICCPR* guarantees equal enjoyment and protection of all the rights contained therein, regardless of a person's religious or minority status.[203] Furthermore, States have specific obligations under international law relating to the rights of minority groups,[204] including to guarantee the right to freedom of religion and the practice of religion. Nonetheless, religious minorities and emerging religions face various forms of discrimination and intolerance, both from society and through policies, legislation and State practice.[205]

---

[200] *Rapporteur's Digest on Freedom of Religion or Belief* (2011) 84.

[201] "In those States in which ethnic, religious or linguistic minorities exist, persons belonging to such minorities shall not be denied the right, in community with the other members of their group, to enjoy their own culture, to profess and practice their own religion, or to use their own language". – Art 27 of the *ICCPR*.

[202] Par 2, 5, 9 & 10 of the *UNHRC: General Comment No. 22*.

[203] Art 2 of the *ICCPR*.

[204] See *inter alia*, Art 27 of the *ICCPR*; UN Human Rights Committee (HRC), *CCPR General Comment No. 23: Article 27 (Rights of Minorities)*, 8 April 1994, CCPR/C/21/Rev.1/Add.5; art 30 of the UN General Assembly, *Convention on the Rights of the Child*, 20 November 1989, United Nations, Treaty Series, vol. 1577; and the UN General Assembly, *Declaration on the Rights of Persons Belonging to National or Ethnic, Religious and Linguistic Minorities*, 20 December 1993, A/RES/48/138.

[205] "Religious minorities are also subject to direct and indirect limitations on the manifestation of their religious identity or belief, as shown by the destruction of Tibetan Buddhist places of worship and the expulsion of nuns and monks from monasteries in China; the occupation and partial destruction of a property belonging to the Armenian Patriarchate in Israel; the closure of places of worship of religious minorities in Eritrea; threats to close Baptist places of worship in the Republic of Moldova and those of the Protestant communities in Turkey; and the prevention or non-recognition of conscientious objection, leading to the imprisonment of Jehovah's Witnesses, in the Republic of Korea". – *Report submitted by the Special Rapporteur on freedom of religion* (2003) par 132.

The plight of religious minority groups affected by discriminatory laws or societal hostility may be regarded as an instance of particularly severe discrimination. Such vulnerable groups are not only discriminated against based on the grounds of their religious or belief affiliations, but also on the grounds of their status as a minority group. According to Bielefeldt, such situations of intensified discrimination may be referred to as a form of 'aggravated discrimination':

> [W]hen the right to freedom of religion and the right to belong to an ethnic group or to a minority are infringed in the case of a single person or group of persons, the violation is not just a superimposition or ordinary addition of offences or discriminations. It is not just a question of multiple offences. The combination of the two offences creates a new, more serious, offence – an aggravated discrimination – which, while of varying intensity, is by its very nature a separate concept.[206]

In summary, religious discrimination in general, and religious discrimination against minority religions in particular, remains a major human rights issue.[207] Although the international standards on freedom from religious discrimination provide such freedoms to everyone, exceptional protection is required by and provided for adherents to non-predominant or dissident religions or beliefs, including members of emerging or religious minorities.[208] Manifestations of intolerance, and the existence of discrimination in matters of religion or belief are still evident worldwide and constitute serious deprivations of, and impairments to, the full enjoyment of religious freedom rights – denying the axiomatic truth of normative universalism of human rights.[209] It is evident from the countless international documents dealing with the subject, that the prevention of, and protection against, religious discrimination, is a political, socio-economic and human rights priority for the international community as a whole. Violations and breaches of the right to equality, especially on the grounds of religion or belief, are regarded as serious infringements of universal human dignity.[210]

> [I]t is in the higher interest of humanity to put an immediate end to religious and so-called racial persecution and discrimination.[211]

---

[206] *Rapporteur's Digest on Freedom of Religion or Belief* (2011) 50.
[207] Preamble of the *Religious Discrimination Declaration* (1981).
[208] Van Boven *Racial and Religious Discrimination* (2009) 614.
[209] Preamble of the *UN World Conference against Racism* (2001).
[210] *Rapporteur's Digest on Freedom of Religion or Belief* (2011) 53.
[211] UN General Assembly, *Resolution 103(I) Persecution and Discrimination*, 19 November 1946.

3.6. Principle of non-derogability and religious freedom

Some international human rights documents allow States to take temporary measures derogating some of their obligations under exceptional circumstances.[212] Derogation measures imply the temporary suspension of the right to exercise certain derogable rights for the purpose and to the extent that such measures are strictly required by the exigencies of an exceptional situation.[213] Article 4(1) of the *ICCPR*[214] provides that States may take measures derogating from their obligations in terms of the *ICCPR* in times of public emergency, which threatens the life of the nation. Two fundamental conditions must be met before a State may implement derogation measures. Firstly, the situation must amount to a public emergency, and secondly, the *de facto* authority must have officially proclaimed a State of emergency in compliance with its domestic legislation.[215] Should the situation dictate the need for temporarily derogating from certain obligations, the measures employed should be limited 'to the extent strictly required by the exigencies of the situation', which "relates to the duration, geographical coverage and material scope of the state of emergency and any measures of derogation resorted to because of the emergency".[216] An important consequence of the obligation to limit any derogations to those strictly required by the exigencies of the situation reflects the principle of proportionality; States can only derogate from certain rights to the extent that it is justifiably required for the restoration of a state of normalcy.

Conversely, derogating from certain categories of rights or specific derogating measures can never become necessary to serve the purpose of restoring law and order.[217] A State may not take discriminatory derogating measures on a number of grounds, including religion.[218] Article 4(2) explicitly prescribes that States may make no derogation regarding their

---

[212] Sepúlveda *et al. Human Rights Reference book* (2004) 45.
[213] Par 2 of UN Human Rights Committee, *General comment No. 29: Article 4: Derogations during a state of emergency*. From the UN International Human Rights Instruments, *Compilation of General Comments and General Recommendations Adopted by Human Rights Treaty Bodies* , 12 May 2004, HRI/GEN/1/Rev.7. (*UNHRC: General Comment No. 29*).
[214] See also Art 15(2) of the *ECHR* and Art 27(2) of the *ACHR*.
[215] Par 2 of the *UNHRC: General Comment No. 29*.
[216] Par 4 of the *UNHRC: General Comment No. 29*.
[217] Par 11 of the *UNHRC: General Comment No. 29*.
[218] Par 1 of the UN Human Rights Committee (HRC), *CCPR General Comment No. 5: Article 4 (Derogations)*, 31 July 1981.

obligations in terms of the right to freedom of religion or belief.[219] The right to freedom of religion or belief is therefore included amongst an exclusive group of rights that are non-derogable.[220] The non-derogable nature of religious freedom may be interpreted as a recognition of the peremptory nature of the fundamental right ensured in treaty law.[221] The principle of non-derogation is applicable to both the internal and external dimensions of religious freedom.[222]

However, the *ICCPR* does permit derogation measures *in re* the right to freedom of assembly in terms of Article 21. Essentially this entitles a State to limit the possibility of manifesting one's religious belief in community with others during a state of emergency. Such limitations on the freedom of assembly must, however, be implemented universally and cannot specifically limit the gathering of religious communities or a specific religious community under the auspices of derogation.

The qualification that a right is non-derogable does not mean that no limitations or restrictions would ever be justified, because the permissibility of restrictions is mostly unrelated to the issue of derogability.[223] The right to freedom of religion in terms of Article 18 of the *ICCPR* is a good example of a non-derogable right that contains a specific clause on restrictions. Religious freedom in its entirety is always a non-derogable right, however the external freedom to manifest a religion or belief may be limited in times of serious public emergencies, provided that a restriction is justified in terms of Article 18(3) of the *ICCPR*.[224] The reason for such a distinction between restrictions and derogating measures is based on the more extensive nature of derogations in relation to legal measures that impose restrictions.

Religious freedom is a fundamental right that is not susceptible to derogation, even in times of emergency or because of national security concerns. Therefore, no individual can be deprived of this right. States should also be very clear in their understanding of the principle of non-derogation and the application of restrictions on the freedom to manifest a religion.

---

[219] Bielefeldt *et al. FORB: An International Law Commentary* (2016) 543–550.
[220] Sepúlveda *et al. Human Rights Reference book* (2004) 46.
[221] Par 11 of the *UNHRC: General Comment No. 29*.
[222] Bielefeldt *et al. FORB: An International Law Commentary* (2016) 544–545.
[223] Par 7 of the *UNHRC: General Comment No. 29*.
[224] Par 7 of the *UNHRC: General Comment No. 29*.

3.7. Freedom from impermissible restrictions or limitations on the right to freedom of religion or belief

Restrictions or limitations of human rights refer to instances where States or Governments are lawfully allowed to control the enjoyment or exercise of certain human rights.

> ...[R]estrictions must be used only to establish the proper limits of the protected right and not as an excuse for undermining the right itself or destroying it altogether. In general, there must be a proportionate relationship between the restriction of the right as such and the reason for the restriction.[225]

'Restrictions' should thus be distinguished from impermissible denials or infringements of religious freedom. Consequently, for the purposes of this study the terms 'restrictions' or 'limitations' of religious freedom will refer to legitimate restrictive margins as provided for in terms of international human rights law. On the other hand, unjustifiable or impermissible restrictions of religious freedom constitute an infringement of such human rights.

3.7.1. Requirements of permissible restrictions

Various national, regional and international instruments dealing with human rights contain provisions allowing for either general or subject-specific restrictions of the human rights contained in that document. Therefore, not all human rights are treated equally in terms of permissibility of restriction, and it is generally accepted that most rights and freedoms may only be limited "the rights of others, by the security of all, and by the just demands of the general welfare, in a democratic society".[226] Therefore, only some specific rights, which are regarded as fundamental rights and freedoms, are considered 'absolute' or non-restrictive in terms of international instruments and/or customary international law. Essentially, a restriction or limitation on the free exercise of human rights must comprise the following principles: it must be legally established, non-discriminatory, proportional, compatible with the nature of the rights, imposed for a legitimate reason, and designed to further general welfare.[227]

The *ICCPR* states that no State, group, or person has

---

[225] Sepúlveda *et al. Human Rights Reference book* (2004) 43.
[226] Art 32(2) of the *American Convention on Human Rights* (1969).
[227] Sepúlveda *et al. Human Rights Reference book* (2004) 44.

Appendix B

the right to engage in any activity or perform any act aimed at the destruction of any of the rights and freedoms recognized herein or at their limitation to a greater extent than is provided for in the present Covenant.[228]

The Covenant does not provide a general limitation clause applicable to all human rights contained therein and instead opts for specific limitation clauses, as is the case regarding the right to freedom of religion or belief.

In addition to the general requirements for legitimate restrictions in international human rights law, any restriction or limitation on the right to freedom of religion must meet all of the following requirements in terms of Article 18(3) of the *ICCPR*:[229]

- Established by law – restrictions can only be permissible if they are legally prescribed. However, whether such a legal subscription amounts to discrimination based on religion or otherwise remains a separate question.
- Necessary and justified by the protection of a strictly limited set of well-defined public interests – restrictions must be essential to pursue one of the legitimate aims (and the burden of proof rests on the party who wishes to enforce such restrictions) exhaustively listed in Article 18(3). An example of legitimate aims in the context of religious freedom is the protection of the basic human rights and freedoms of others against harmful religious manifestations or practices.
- Proportional – restrictive measures must be limited to minimum interference as a last resort. It must be applied in a manner that would vitiate the rights guaranteed in Article 18 and must be enacted in a strictly non-discriminatory manner.

3.7.2. *Restrictions and the dimensions of religious freedom*

As mentioned, it is accepted that the strongest rationale for interference with, or restriction (limitation) of rights, relates to the protection of the

---

[228] Art 5(1) of the *ICCPR*.
[229] See also Art 1(3) of the *Religious Discrimination Declaration* (1981); par 12 of the UN Commission on Human Rights, *Resolution 2005/40 on Elimination of All Forms of Intolerance and of Discrimination Based on Religion or Belief*, 19 April 2005, E/CN.4/RES/2005/40; and UNHRC General Comment No. 22 par 8. For a more detailed discussion regarding these requirements in the context of the *forum externum*, see Bielefeldt *et al. FORB: An International Law Commentary* (2016) 559–565.

rights and freedoms of others, i. e. limitations should strive to strike a balance between two competing interests.[230] Importantly, Article 29 of the *UDHR* provides for legitimate limitations in the exercise of rights and freedoms. Therefore, Bielefeldt *et al.* explain that:

> This formulation clarifies that it is not the 'claiming' or 'holding' of rights and freedoms which is subject to limitations, but their 'exercise'. This distinction is also clear from the structure of rights such as freedom of opinion and expression and freedom of religion or belief. In some rights, there is a clear distinction between the 'having' aspect (forum internum) and its expression or manifestation (forum externum). The former cannot be limited but the latter can.[231]

Therefore, the criteria of permissible restrictions are not applied similarly to both dimensions of religious freedom. Accordingly, the legal framework for the limitation of religious freedom rights is largely depended upon the understanding of these two dimensions of religious freedom.

As explained, the *forum internum* or the internal freedom to choose and have a religious identity, enjoys the status of an absolute guarantee under international human rights law. In this regard, no derogation or limitation is ever permitted.[232] It is submitted that the internal dimension should include religious activities intended to give effect to a person's deep existential convictions, provided such activities do not contain an outwardly visible manifestation of the individual's existential views.[233] The reason for such an argument is that some forms of religious behaviour through worship, observance and practice may not necessarily require an external, public or communicative manifestation, *per se*. Nevertheless, such internal religious acts may directly relate to a person's inner convictions regarding his or her religious identity and give personal expression to such a conviction. For instance, to 'worship' does not necessarily require any outward practice or manifestation in community with others. Meanwhile, the notion of 'observance'

---

[230] Bielefeldt *et al. FORB: An International Law Commentary* (2016) 553.
[231] Bielefeldt *et al. FORB: An International Law Commentary* (2016) 553.
[232] *Rapporteur's Digest on Freedom of Religion or Belief* (2011) 37. See also UNHRC General Comment No. 22 par 3 read with par 8.
[233] While not expressly supporting this argument, Bielefeldt's discussion regarding the interrelatedness of the *forum internum* and the *forum externum*, raises interesting questions regarding the exact practical separation of these domains within religious life – Bielefeldt *et al. FORB: An International Law Commentary* (2016) 82-85.

refers to all those prescriptions that are inevitably connected with a religion or belief and protects both the right to perform certain acts and the right to refrain from doing certain things.[234]

'Observance' can therefore relate to the commitment to adhere to an internal conviction. For example, actions such as quiet meditation on issues of faith may be considered as a form of worship, and the personal resolve to refrain from certain 'sinful' conduct may be regarded as the observance of a personal conviction through the internal refusal to engage in such conduct.

Other outwardly visible manifestations of religious freedom (religious behaviour) are subject to certain restrictions. The exercise of religious behaviour or manifestations may, in certain circumstances, be limited or restricted in adherence to Article 18(3) of the *ICCPR*, and further elaborated in *UNHRC General Comment No. 22*.[235] When interpreting Article 18(3) and considering the absence of any further restrictions, *UNHRC General Comment No. 22* requires a strict interpretation. Therefore, restrictions are not allowed on grounds that are not specified in the Covenant, nor may such limitations be applied for purposes other than those for which they were prescribed. Additionally, the restriction must be directly related and proportionate to the specific need on which they are predicated. Restrictions or limitations must amount to equal protection for all and may not be imposed for discriminatory purposes or applied in a discriminatory manner.[236] Permissible restrictions or limitations could include, *inter alia*: measures to prevent criminal activities (for example, ritual killings), harmful traditional practices (for example female genital mutilation),[237] limitations on religious practices injurious to the best interests of the child,[238] or, to a certain extent, the ceremonial use of plants and drugs, and the ritual slaughter of animals.[239] When applying legitimate restrictions, States must remain neutral and act with substantive equality on religious matters and apply any restrictive measures with strict scrutiny.[240]

---

[234] De Jong, C. D. *The freedom of thought, conscience and religion or belief in the United Nations (1946-1992)*. Volume 5, School of Human Rights Research series. Published by Intersentia (2000).
[235] Art 18(3) of the *ICCPR*; Art 1(3) of the *UNGA Res. Discrimination based on Religion* (2009); and Art 29(2) of the *UDHR*.
[236] *UNHRC General Comment No. 22* par 8.
[237] It may be argued that such practices are more obviously based on cultural traditions than religious beliefs. See *Rapporteur's Digest on Freedom of Religion or Belief* (2011) 78-79.
[238] Par 13 of the *UNCHR: Religion-Based Refugee Claims* (2004).
[239] Bielefeldt et al. *FORB: An International Law Commentary* (2016) 112-115.
[240] Bielefeldt et al. *FORB: An International Law Commentary* (2016) 567-568.

A further important limitation measure is contemplated in Article 20(2) of the *ICCPR* and elaborated on in *UNHRC General Comment No. 22*:

> According to article 20, no manifestation of religions or beliefs may amount to propaganda for war or advocacy of national, racial or religious hatred that constitutes incitement to discrimination, hostility or violence.

Article 20(2) constitutes an important safeguard against possible infringements triggered by the manifestation of religious behaviour, which aims to protect legitimate causes. However, Article 20(2) does not create the right to be protected from incitement on religious grounds.[241] It refers to such instances where the exercise of the freedom to manifest religion or belief, either individually or in community with others, amounts to incitement to discrimination, hostility or violence, requiring restrictive measures by the State. Importantly, "this provision does not demand a prohibition of sharp or even hostile speech in general; instead it concentrates on such forms of hatred advocacy that constitute 'incitement' to real acts of discrimination, hostility or violence".[242] The reason for this is that the freedom of religion protects primarily the individual, and the collective rights of the community to some extent, but does not protect a religion or a religious identity, *per se*.

In summary, Article 18 of the ICCPR makes it clear that the right to have or to adopt a religion or belief of one's choice is not subject to derogation, coercion or limitations. The general assumption is that the freedom to manifest one's religion or belief may be subject to legitimate limitations pursuant to Article 18(3) of the ICCPR, which "allows for restrictions only in very exceptional cases" and the "test of legality of a prohibition of any act motivated by belief or religion is [...] extremely strict".[243] However, the external dimension of religious freedom is not subject to derogation measures or coercion.

---

[241] Onley, R. B., *Defending the freedom of expression – The danger and failure of the Organization for Islamic Cooperation's campaign for global anti-blasphemy laws*. IJRF, Vol 7, Issue 1/2 (2014), pg 45.

[242] Bielefeldt *FORB: Thematic Reports* (2017) 210.

[243] Par 62 and 63 of the UN General Assembly, *Elimination of all forms of religious intolerance: Report of the Special Rapporteur of the Commission on Human Rights on freedom of religion or belief, Asma Jahangir*. A/60/399, 30 September 2005.

4 'Recognition' of a religion and a religious group

In the context of the right to freedom of religion or belief, 'recognition' may have a number of different connotations, which require distinction. These include 'recognition' of the person's status as a bearer of human rights, 'recognition' of the person's chosen religious identity as an accepted or acknowledged religious option, and registration procedures for the 'recognition' of legal personality of a religion or a religious group.

4.1. 'Recognition' of the individual's status as a bearer of human rights

'Recognition' may be understood as referring to the "axiomatic status of human dignity" that forms the foundation upon which the entire notion of human rights is based. The preamble of the UDHR acknowledges such an understanding and confirms that "…recognition of the inherent dignity and of the equal and inalienable rights of all members of the human family is the foundation of freedom, justice, and peace in the world".[244] Thus, in this context 'recognition' refers to the acknowledgement of the universalistic nature of human rights to which all human beings are inherently entitled, simply because they are human and deserve equality, dignity and respect.[245] Therefore, the right to freedom of religion is an inherent and inalienable birthright, and is not a privilege reliant on the 'recognition' by a government. The State, as the primary addressee of correlative human rights obligations, is compelled to respect, protect and enforce the inalienable entitlement that all human beings have to religious freedom. It does not presuppose a State's formal recognition or acceptance of the capacity of human beings to be the bearers of human rights and duties.[246] Human beings are endowed with fundamental rights simply because they are human. Such an understanding of the inherent, universal right to fundamental freedoms directly links to the internal dimension of religious freedom.

4.2. 'Recognition' of religious options

Alternatively, 'recognition' in the context of religious freedom is also understood to refer to the acknowledgement of the acceptability of a religion or a religious group. Many religious communities the world over face daily

---

[244] Bielefeldt *FORB: Thematic Reports* (2017) 87.
[245] Bielefeldt *FORB: Thematic Reports* (2017) 87.
[246] Bielefeldt *FORB: Thematic Reports* (2017) 88.

obstacles because they are not officially recognised by the State.[247] In this context, the realisation and implementation of religious freedom rights are not depended upon the 'recognition' of the person's chosen 'religion or belief' as an accepted or acknowledged option by the government or State. The reason for this is that religious freedom rights do not protect a religion or religious values, *per se*, nor the practices, 'truth claims', doctrines or ideas contained within a religion.[248] It protects the individual's right and freedom to whichever chosen deep existential views such an individual may hold. An individual has an absolute right of freedom of choice regarding religion or belief and therefore such a freedom cannot be curtailed by non-recognition of a chosen conviction. Consequently, a deep existential view need not be 'recognised' or accepted by States or society in order to constitute a 'legitimate' religious option.

Whether the State or other entities choose not to 'recognise' such a religious identity, does not automatically limit a person's freedom to choose such a religious identity for him or herself. Consequently, non-recognition by a State does not spontaneously infringe on a person's freedom of choice, unless the refusal to recognise constitutes an impermissible interference with the right of a religious group to freedom of religion. In other words, if non-recognition of a religious group formally or factually discriminates against those religious groups. Thus, a State policy of non-recognition may effectively coerce non-believers or dissident believers to recant their beliefs and compel them to adhere to the official belief policy. For example:

> Eritrea only recognizes three Christian denominations (Eritrean Orthodox, Lutherans, and Catholics) as well as Islam, while excluding for instance Jehovah's Witnesses who, given their conscientious objection to military service, frequently face political harassment and persecution.[249]

Even if certain religious identities are not officially recognised or defined by the State's legal provisions, the inclination towards an official or State religion may still privilege those religious communities or identities to which they feel a certain historical or cultural attachment, with a discriminatory and detrimental impact on other communities.[250] However, restrictive tendencies and associated prejudices "may be even more pronounced in the

---

[247] Bielefeldt *et al. FORB: An International Law Commentary* (2016) 224.
[248] Bielefeldt *et al. FORB: An International Law Commentary* (2016) 12.
[249] Bielefeldt *Misperceptions of FORB* (2013) 36–37. For more examples of official religious options imposed by governments, see Bielefeldt *et al. FORB: An International Law Commentary* (2016) 224.
[250] Bielefeldt *et al. FORB: An International Law Commentary* (2016) 224.

day-to-day practice of administrative bodies, public schools, or law enforcement agencies".[251] Consequently, the Commission on Human Rights urged States to "review, whenever relevant, existing registration practices in order to ensure the right of all persons to manifest their religion or belief, alone or in community with others and in public or in private".[252]

Though a person is still 'free' to choose a non-recognised religious identity, non-recognition may, *inter alia*, limit an individual's external religious freedom to manifest a religion. Bielefeldt points out that:

> Although members of other denominations are not per se excluded from the enjoyment of freedom of religion or belief, they may encounter discriminatory treatment, a danger that particularly affects small communities often stigmatized as 'sects' or 'cults'.[253]

For example, in the case of *Metropolitan Church of Bessarabia v. Moldova*, the European Court of Human Rights (ECtHR) considered the refusal of the Moldavian Government to recognise a religious group which had split from a recognised religious group. The ECtHR found that "...the refusal to recognise the applicant church had such consequences for the applicants' freedom of religion that it could not be regarded as proportionate to the legitimate aim pursued".[254] Therefore, it constituted interference with the right of that church and the other applicants to freedom of religion in terms of the *ECHR*. The refusal to recognise the applicant church effectively limited the right of the religious group to manifest their religion collectively within a distinctive church, and to have the right of access to a court to defend their rights and protect their property, given that only denominations recognised by the State enjoyed legal protection.[255] It should be noted that 'recognition' in the context of this case should be distinguished, at least in part, from the formal recognition procedures with the aim of obtaining legal subjectivity status, which will be discussed next.

In terms of Article 18(3) of the *ICCPR*, States are not allowed to restrict freedom of choice, which is part of the internal dimension of religious freedom. A person is, and should always be, free to choose any religious identity, which in practice is not always the case. The recognition of religious

---

[251] Bielefeldt *et al. FORB: An International Law Commentary* (2016) 224.
[252] Par 4(c) of the UN Commission on Human Rights, *Resolution 2005/40 on Elimination of All Forms of Intolerance and of Discrimination Based on Religion or Belief*, 19 April 2005, E/CN.4/RES/2005/40.
[253] Bielefeldt *Misperceptions of FORB* (2013) 37.
[254] ECtHR *Metropolitan Church of Bessarabia* (2001) 3.
[255] ECtHR *Metropolitan Church of Bessarabia* (2001) 3.

options is evident in anti-universalistic policies regarding the treatment of religious diversity, which lead to discrimination against newly established religions, or against groups that represent religious minorities.[256] Bielefeldt condones the recognition of religious options as an impermissible deprivation of the freedom of religious choice, stating that:

> [A]ttempts to limit the enjoyment of freedom of religion or belief to particular lists of legitimate religious options factually deny the universalistic character of this human right.[257]

The *ECtHR* found that the "autonomous existence of religious communities is indispensable for pluralism in a democratic society".[258] Therefore, a predefined list of legitimate religious options is an unacceptable interpretation of the human rights perspective on religious freedom. As such, a limitation along these lines contradicts the foundational concept of normative universalism and effectively opens the door for marginalisation, discrimination and persecution.[259]

Although religious freedom presupposes the full embrace of diversity, such freedoms "cannot give carte blanche for violating the rights of others, even if such violations are committed in the name of religion".[260] Therefore, not all behaviour or manifestations of religion are beyond legitimate restriction. Accordingly, Article 18(3) of the *ICCPR* provides that a State may justifiably limit the external manifestation of religious behaviour for a legitimate cause. Detrimental religious practices are often committed in the name of religions or beliefs, and such manifestations may be legitimately restricted in terms of Article 18(3) of the *ICCPR*. Therefore, non-recognition may provide a legitimate means through which States can restrict the manifestation of religious behaviour in order to protect the rights of others or important public interests. However, such measures must be applied fairly and equally, and must be based on clear, empirical evidence of harmful religious manifestations or practices emanating from a religion or a religious group. Importantly, non-recognition as a restrictive measure should not be utilised to limit legitimate religious options, but would be considered permissible if it objectively intended to restrict harmful religious manifestations.

---

[256] Bielefeldt *Misperceptions of FORB* (2013) 36.
[257] Bielefeldt *Misperceptions of FORB* (2013) 67.
[258] *Hasan and Chaush v Bulgaria (GC)*, App no 30985/96, ECtHR 2000-XI, (26 October 2000), par 62.
[259] Bielefeldt *Misperceptions of FORB* (2013) 37.
[260] Bielefeldt et al. *FORB: An International Law Commentary* (2016) 12.

4.3. Registration procedures for the recognition of legal personality

On this final level, the term 'recognition' is used to describe formal registration procedures or practices in order for a religious group to obtain a certain legal status.[261] Consequently, those religious communities which fail to obtain registration status or which prefer to operate without registration by the State, are sometimes called 'non-recognised' religions.[262] Bielefeldt et al. argue that such registration procedures "obscure the insight that the entire system of human rights is based on the 'recognition of the inherent dignity' of all human beings".[263] There are various practical reasons why a religious group may choose to acquire such a recognised status, such as those mentioned earlier in the *Moldavian case* before the ECtHR.[264] Therefore, in such instances the non-recognition of certain religions or religious groups results in an inability to acquire legal subjectivity coupled with registration. Bielefeldt et al. explain that:

> While 'registration' may prima facie appear to be a merely technical theme of less political significance, the issue is actually a source of major human rights problems in the area of freedom of religion or belief. Quite a number of States assume that only members of 'registered' religious communities should be allowed to fully practise their freedom of religion or belief.[265]

It is therefore important that such registration procedures do not constitute a precondition for practising one's religion, and should be limited to the acquisition of legal subjectivity of those religious groups that choose to do so.[266]

> [L]egal procedures pertaining to religious or belief-based groups and places of worship are not a prerequisite for the exercise of the right to manifest one's religion or belief... [and if] legally required, [such procedures] should be non-discriminatory in order to contribute to the effective protection of the right of all persons to practise their religion or belief either individually or in community with others and in public or private.[267]

---

[261] Legal or registration procedures for the recognition of legal personality are a common administrative and judicial practice in legal systems around the world – Bielefeldt *FORB: Thematic Reports* (2017) 91.
[262] Bielefeldt et al. *FORB: An International Law Commentary* (2016) 231.
[263] Bielefeldt et al. *FORB: An International Law Commentary* (2016) 223.
[264] ECtHR *Metropolitan Church of Bessarabia* (2001) 3.
[265] Bielefeldt et al. *FORB: An International Law Commentary* (2016) 223.
[266] Bielefeldt *FORB: Thematic Reports* (2017) 91.
[267] Par 6 & 7 of the UNGA Res. *Discrimination based on Religion* (2009).

Therefore, non-recognition of a religion cannot be considered as a legitimate restrictive measure if it is implemented as a coercive registration scheme in order to be recognised as a valid religious option and subsequently escape restrictive measures. Thus, a person's freedom to manifest his religion or belief may be legitimately restricted through non-recognition for the purpose of limiting public exposure to detrimental religious practices associated with such a religion or belief. However, the freedom to manifest one's religion cannot be legitimately restricted as a result of non-recognition emanating from compulsory registration policies. Legal or registration requirements for religious groups may thus serve a legitimate administrative and judicial function, provided such procedures are not indirectly used to restrict legitimate religious options or the manifestation of religious freedom.

In summary, the realisation and implementation of religious freedom rights are not dependent upon 'recognition' of the person's status as a bearer of human rights, and a State or government can never restrict this right by not recognising a person's legal capacity. Furthermore, the choice of existential view should not be dependent upon the 'recognition' of such a chosen religious identity as an accepted or acknowledged option by the government or State. Although, while non-recognition of a religion or religious group may serve a legitimate restrictive purpose to limit public exposure to detrimental religious practices committed in the name of a religion or belief, it cannot be used as a method to restrict or limit people from starting or choosing a newly established or minority religion. Finally, registration procedures should be confined to obtaining legal subjectivity and should never be a precondition for the recognition of a 'religion' or a religious group.[268] Consequently, "in order to preserve the integrity of the human rights approach and to make sure that the status of freedom of religion or belief is not put at the mercy of (more or less accommodating) State agencies", it is advisable not to use the term 'recognition' in the context of registration procedures or practices.[269]

---

[268] For a comprehensive discussion regarding registrations issues, see Bielefeldt et al. *FORB: An International Law Commentary* (2016) 223–232.

[269] Bielefeldt et al. *FORB: An International Law Commentary* (2016) 231.

5 Intersection of freedom of religion or belief with other human rights

The right to freedom of thought, conscience and religion or belief belongs to the category of civil rights which some have argued are justiciable in the event of a deprivation of such rights.[270] Religious freedom is a basic human right without which no human being can lead a dignified existence.[271] Although international human rights law is mostly concerned with the protection and development of the individual (individual rights), some human rights may also be exercised and protected on a collective basis.[272] Consequently, religious freedom is a fundamental human right that provides individuals and religious groups with the freedom to have and exercise their religious identity, whether individually or in association with others, publicly or privately.[273] However, human rights are not isolated and independent rights. Therefore, the full realisation of religious freedom cannot occur unless other related rights receive equal recognition and protection. As the UNCHR declared in the outcome document of the 1993 *Vienna World Conference on Human Rights*:

> All human rights are universal, indivisible, interrelated and interdependent.[274]

Consequently, accepted human rights norms subscribe to the view that all human rights are of equal importance, in the sense that both civil and political rights, and economic, social and cultural rights are of paramount importance for the full realisation of an existence worthy of human dignity and for the attainment of the sincere aspirations of every individual.[275] The 'indivisibility' of human rights represents a holistic understanding of human rights, in terms of which human beings are intricate and multidimensional creatures, capable of existential thought, emotion and reason. In order to keep the entire human rights agenda intact, human rights interests are best understood in the context of a collection of essential and inseparable or amalgamated human rights.[276]

---

[270] Sepúlveda *et al. Human Rights Reference book* (2004) 9.
[271] Sepúlveda *et al. Human Rights Reference book* (2004) 11–12.
[272] Sepúlveda *et al. Human Rights Reference book* (2004) 12.
[273] Art 18(1) of the *ICCPR*.
[274] UN General Assembly, *Vienna Declaration and Programme of Action*, 12 July 1993, A/CONF.157/23.
[275] Sepúlveda *et al. Human Rights Reference book* (2004) 10.
[276] Bielefeldt *Misperceptions of FORB* (2013) 60.

It means that taking away one human rights would not only leave us with a specific gap; it would seriously affect and damage the entire system of human rights.[277]

A holistic understanding of the indivisibility of human rights also has practical significance in cases of serious conflicts between competing human rights interests, which obviously also include possible clashes between religious freedom and other human rights interests.[278]

The *sui generis* nature of the right to freedom of religion or belief requires that international norms aimed at the protection of religious rights and freedoms must also ensure and protect other indivisible, interrelated and interdependent substantive human rights that fulfil an indispensable auxiliary function in the realisation of religious freedom.[279] For instance, the intersection of the right to life and religion, "gives rise to a range of multifaceted issues, most of which bear no direct relationship to freedom of religion or belief itself".[280] When discussing this intersection certain moral questions are raised, such as the debate regarding abortion, suicide, and the death penalty.

Therefore, religious freedom intersects with various other human rights, which makes these rights indivisible, interrelated and interdependent. Thames illustrates this point:

> The multifaceted and interdependent nature of... [religious freedom] can be seen in several ways: to meet collectively for worship or religious education, the freedom of association must be respected; to allow the sharing of religious views, which is often a part of a belief system, speech freedoms must be enjoyed; to provide for some type of community legal status, laws must not discriminate on religious grounds; to maintain or own a place of worship, property rights must be respected; to obtain sacred books and disseminate religious publications, media freedoms must be protected.[281]

Some of these intersections will briefly be considered in the following section, including due process, freedom of expression, privacy, gender equality, and certain collective participation rights.

---

[277] Bielefeldt *et al. FORB: An International Law Commentary* (2016) 29.
[278] Bielefeldt *Misperceptions of FORB* (2013) 60.
[279] Thames *et al. International Religious Freedom Advocacy* (2009) 9.
[280] Bielefeldt *et al. FORB: An International Law Commentary* (2016) 508.
[281] Thames *et al. International Religious Freedom Advocacy* (2009) 9.

5.1. Freedom of religion or belief and due process

The first intersection with religious freedom is the right to due process and equality before the law. Broadly speaking, "due process refers to the right to be treated fairly, efficiently and effectively by the administration of justice".[282] The right to due process is universally applicable to all legal proceedings, whether under national, regional or international jurisdictional spheres, including adjudication for deprivations of human rights.[283] Due process is a collective term that incorporates a number of rules applicable to the administration of justice in order to guarantee fundamental fairness and justice. The *International Bill of Rights* provides for the following due process rules, *inter alia*, in regards to legal proceedings in the determination of rights and obligations:

- recognition of legal subjectivity and capacity in legal proceedings (Article 6);
- equality and equal protection of the law, including protection against discrimination and incitement to such discrimination (Article 7);
- the right to effective remedies for deprivations of human rights (Article 8) and the duty on States to ensure such effective remedies (Article 2(3)(a) of the *ICCPR*);
- the right to a fair and public hearing, including the right to be heard (*audi alteram partem*), by an independent and impartial tribunal (Article 10), and the duty on States to ensure such competent processes (Article 2(3)(b) and (c) of the *ICCPR*);
- the right to be presumed innocent until proven guilty (Article 11(1)); and
- the principle of legality (Article 11(2)).

The intersection of the principles of due process with religious freedom is evident in situations where individuals or religious groups seek legal protection of their rights. In considering the due process rules, religious freedom applies equally to all people, regardless of their religious identity and without any discrimination as to their equal protection by the law.[284] Consequently, the international obligations of States to ensure adequate and effective guarantees of religious freedom include, *inter alia*:

---

[282] Sepúlveda *et al. Human Rights Reference book* (2004) 187.
[283] Sepúlveda *et al. Human Rights Reference book* (2004) 187.
[284] Par 2 of the *UNGA Res. Discrimination based on Religion* (2009).

- providing effective remedies in cases where religious freedom was infringed;
- ensuring that no one within their jurisdiction is deprived of the right to life, liberty or security of person because of their religion or belief;
- that no-one is subjected to torture or other cruel, inhuman or degrading treatment or punishment, or arbitrary arrest or detention on the grounds of their beliefs; and
- bringing to justice all perpetrators of deprivations of religious freedom rights.[285]

5.2. Freedom of religion or belief and freedom of expression

The next intersection of religious freedom is with the right to freedom of expression in terms of Article 19 of the *ICCPR*.[286] Freedom of expression "is a right without which other rights are difficult to acquire and defend".[287] The freedom of expression and freedom of religion or belief positively assume and mutually enforce and empower one another, "since freedom of expression presupposes respect for the deep convictions that human beings hold".[288] As explained by the Special Rapporteur at the time, Heiner Bielefeldt:

> the right to freedom of religion or belief itself encompasses various forms of freely chosen communication, including the freedom to communicate within one's own religious or belief group, to share one's conviction with others, to broaden one's horizons by communicating with people of different convictions, to cherish and develop contacts across State

---

[285] Par 9(a) & (b) of the *UNGA Res. Discrimination based on Religion* (2009).
[286] Art 19: (1) Everyone shall have the right to hold opinions without interference; (2) Everyone shall have the right to freedom of expression; this right shall include freedom to seek, receive, and impart information and ideas of all kinds, regardless of frontiers, either orally, in writing or in print, in the form of art, or through any other media of his choice; (3) The exercise of the rights provided for in paragraph 2 of this article carries with it special duties and responsibilities. It may therefore be subject to certain restrictions, but these shall only be such as are provided by law and are necessary: (a) For respect of the rights or reputations of others; (b) For the protection of national security or of public order (*ordre public*), or of public health or morals.
[287] Sepúlveda *et al. Human Rights Reference book* (2004) 197.
[288] Bielefeldt *Misperceptions of FORB* (2013) 62.

boundaries, to receive and spread information about religious or belief issues and to try to persuade others by means of peaceful communication.[289]

The freedom of expression and the freedom of religion intersects with a shared common goal of safeguarding communicative freedom, and may therefore be viewed as "neighbouring rights".[290] The right to freedom of expression is fundamental in holding religious beliefs, inasmuch as thoughts and views may remain imperceptible if not expressed, and convictions about religion or belief are a valuable element of a person's conception of life only if he or she can profess them, either individually or in community with others.[291] The freedom to manifest religion or belief contains a broad range of acts exercised either individually or in community with others, thereby giving direct expression to belief.[292] Bielefeldt et al. state that "no component of 'manifesting' freedom of religion or belief is conceivable without some sort of communication".[293]

The *Rabat Plan of Action*[294] places great emphasis on the realisation of the right to freedom of expression in order to uphold a climate of free communication and public discourse by tolerating different perspectives or dissenting viewpoints regarding religion.[295] Consequently, freedom of expression and religion not only intersect, but are mutually indispensable and interdependent human rights:

> [The] freedom to exercise or not one's religion or belief cannot exist if the freedom of expression is not respected as free public discourse depends on

---

[289] Par 24 of the UN General Assembly, *Elimination of all forms of religious intolerance*, Interim report of the Special Rapporteur on freedom of religion or belief, A/66/156, 18 July 2011. The right to establish and maintain communications arguably also applies to missionary activities or proselytism – Bielefeldt et al. FORB: An International Law Commentary (2016) 239.
[290] Bielefeldt et al. FORB: An International Law Commentary (2016) 29–30.
[291] Sepúlveda et al. Human Rights Reference book (2004) 203.
[292] UNHRC General Comment No. 22 par 4.
[293] Bielefeldt et al. FORB: An International Law Commentary (2016) 233.
[294] Office of the United Nations High Commissioner for Human Rights: *Rabat Plan of Action on the prohibition of advocacy of national, racial or religious hatred that constitutes incitement to discrimination, hostility or violence*. Conclusions and recommendations emanating from the four regional expert workshops organised by OHCHR, in 2011, and adopted by experts in Rabat, Morocco on 5 October 2012. http://www.ohchr.org/Documents/Issues/Opinion/SeminarRabat/Rabat_draft_outcome.pdf. Accessed 27/09/2016.
[295] Bielefeldt *FORB: Thematic Reports* (2017) 210.

respect for the diversity of deep convictions which people may have. Likewise, freedom of expression is essential to creating an environment in which a constructive discussion about religious matters could be held.[296]

According to Article 19 of the *ICCPR*, any restrictions on freedom of expression are connected to a very high threshold, similar to the external manifestation of religious freedom. Some limitations on the right to freedom of expression may be necessary, in the sense that completely unrestricted freedom of expression may lead to the severe infringement of the rights of others. For example, in extreme incidents of hate speech directed against some religious communities, unrestricted free speech may lead to hatred advocacy that constitute 'incitement' to discrimination, hostility or violence.[297] Subsequently, it may cause adherents of the targeted religious communities to refrain from publicly professing and manifesting their religion or belief.[298] Conversely, despite the intersection between religious freedom and the right to freedom of expression, international legal standards do not protect the right to have a religion or belief that is free from criticism or ridicule as a permissible restriction on either of those two rights.[299] The limitation of freedom of expression cannot be utilised merely to 'combat defamation of religions'. Bielefeldt *et al.* note that religious freedom is "sometimes invoked to request protection for religious feelings against offensive speech acts, thus apparently limiting the scope of freedom of expression".[300] For example, in Pakistan ill-defined blasphemy offences disproportionately affect religious minorities, religious dissenters, critics, agnostics or atheists, which may lead to a death sentence.[301]

Freedom of religion or belief and freedom of expression are thus interdependent, interrelated and mutually reinforcing safeguards of communicative freedoms relating to religion or belief. It includes those recognised in the *Religious Discrimination Declaration*,[302] as well as protection for the freedom to disagree and criticise religious leaders, religious doctrine and tenets of faith.

---

[296] Par 10 of the *OHCHR: Rabat Plan of Action* (2012).
[297] Art 20(2) of the *ICCPR*. See also par 14 of the *OHCHR: Rabat Plan of Action* (2012).
[298] Bielefeldt *Misperceptions of FORB* (2013) 61.
[299] *Rapporteur's Digest on Freedom of Religion or Belief* (2011) 91.
[300] Bielefeldt *et al. FORB: An International Law Commentary* (2016) 29.
[301] Bielefeldt *et al. FORB: An International Law Commentary* (2016) 30.
[302] Art 6(d), (e) & (i) of the *Religious Discrimination Declaration*.

5.3. Freedom of religion or belief and privacy

Everyone has the right to security of person[303] and "no one shall be subjected to arbitrary or unlawful interference with his privacy... [and] everyone has the right to the protection of the law against such interference or attacks".[304] The right to respect privacy is a natural consequence of the foundations of human rights based on the universal principles of dignity and liberty of the individual as a self-autonomous being.[305] Aspects of the individual's right to privacy extend to the home, the family and communication, and include, *inter alia*, a person's intimacy, identity, good name, reputation, gender, honour, dignity, appearance, feelings, sexual orientation and personal convictions.[306] A person's right to privacy will be protected as long as his/her actions do not interfere with the rights and freedoms of others and may thus be limited by the State under certain circumstances.[307] An unlawful interference on the right to privacy occurs when a State unduly restricts, penalises, or prohibits actions that essentially only concern the individual.[308] Restrictions on personal liberty and freedom of movement may also constitute restraints or deprivations of privacy, such as unlawful arrest and imprisonment, arbitrary searches and seizures, and even slavery.[309]

Religious freedom may also intersect with the right to privacy. In the sphere of the internal dimension of religious freedom, the right to privacy protects a believer's right not to be compelled to reveal his/her thoughts and adherence or non-adherence to a religion or belief. Sepúlveda explains this intersection as follows:

> The guarantee of the value of freedom of thought and religion implies that one cannot be subjected to a treatment intended to change one's process of thinking, be forced to express thoughts, to change opinion, or to divulge a religious conviction; thus, the right to freedom of thought, conscience, religion, belief and opinion is closely associated with the right to privacy. No sanction may be imposed holding any view, or on the change of a religion or conviction; and the freedom of thought and religion protects against indoctrination by the state.[310]

---

[303] Art 3 of the *UDHR*.
[304] Art 17 of the *ICCPR*.
[305] Art 1 of the *UDHR*.
[306] Sepúlveda *et al. Human Rights Reference book* (2004) 249.
[307] Sepúlveda *et al. Human Rights Reference book* (2004) 249.
[308] Sepúlveda *et al. Human Rights Reference book* (2004) 249.
[309] Rempell *Defining Persecution* (2013) 11.
[310] Sepúlveda *Human Rights Reference book* (2004) 203.

Infringements of the right not to be compelled to reveal one's convictions include situations where a person is obligated to reveal his/her religious conviction in a public forum, such as on ID-cards or other required government forms, which in turn may be used to discriminate.[311]

5.4. Freedom of religion or belief and gender issues

In the past, the notion of gender equality was viewed narrowly. However, a holistic approach to human rights now also includes aspects such as sexual orientation and gender identity. Consequently, the promotion of equal treatment and the elimination of gender-related discrimination in society leads to a conflicting intersection with "traditional, anti-egalitarian understandings of gender relations frequently (although not exclusively) defended in the name of various religions".[312] Within various religious structures, positions of religious authority are exclusively reserved for men. This exclusivity of men in the context of religion is also evident in the context of patriarchal family structures deeply rooted in traditional religious interpretations of gender roles.[313] Another example is the denial of appropriate school education for girls as a result of religious doctrine. Consequently, the enforcement of traditionalist views of gender roles in certain religious communities negatively affect women in a number of different ways. Importantly, it may be reiterated here that Article 18 of the *UDHR* and *ICCPR* provides for "a right to freedom, it does not protect religious traditions per se, but instead empowers human beings to find their various ways within, without or beyond those traditions".[314]

Therefore, it seems as though gender equality and religious freedom are 'abstract antagonisms' of each other, in terms of which any concession in favour of the one, negatively impacts the other.[315] Bielefeldt *et al.* argue that this is a misperception about religious freedom and freedom of expression, in the sense that these rights protect all forms of thought, conscience, religion or belief, including those of liberals, conservatives, feminists and traditionalists.[316] In other words, in conjunction with freedom of expression and opinion, typically marginalised gender groups may actually utilise the right to freedom of religion or belief to protect their

---

[311] Bielefeldt *et al. FORB: An International Law Commentary* (2016) 316.
[312] Bielefeldt *et al. FORB: An International Law Commentary* (2016) 31.
[313] Bielefeldt *et al. FORB: An International Law Commentary* (2016) 29.
[314] Bielefeldt *et al. FORB: An International Law Commentary* (2016) 31.
[315] Bielefeldt *et al. FORB: An International Law Commentary* (2016) 31.
[316] Bielefeldt *et al. FORB: An International Law Commentary* (2016) 31.

personal and elementary preference that pertains to a value-system derived from deep personal thoughts and convictions.

Although religious freedom and gender equality are habitually at the opposite ends of the proverbial tightrope, it does not mean that the two rights cannot operate on a mutually accommodating manner. It is clear that religious freedom cannot be invoked to justify cruel and harmful practices in the name of religion, whereas gender equality cannot be used to fragment deeply personal or existential convictions or beliefs into a hollow indistinguishable secular view, deprived of religious pluralism and the essential right to believe or not to believe in certain 'things'.

5.5. Freedom of religion or belief and the freedom of collective participation

International human rights law provides for the right to freedom of peaceful assembly and association for everyone, including protection against coercion to belong to an association.[317] The *ICCPR* further elaborates and ensures the right of peaceful assembly[318] and the right to freedom of association with others.[319] The right to collective participation through association and peaceful assembly exist as interdependent, interrelated and mutually reinforcing rights. The functioning of collective rights is essential for a plural democratic society and may be intricately linked with other rights; such as the right to employment and religious freedom.[320]

The freedom of association allows an individual the freedom to choose whether or not to form, and/or join, an association of whatever nature.[321] The freedom of association can be described as "the right of the individual to join with others in a voluntary and lasting way for the common achievement of a legal goal".[322] The freedom of association implies a mutual relationship of rights for both the individual and the group, in the sense that an individual has the right to freely associate with a group, but only insofar as such an association is satisfied to freely allow membership to such an individual.[323]

---

[317] Art 20 of the *UDHR*.
[318] Art 21 of the *ICCPR*.
[319] Art 22 of the *ICCPR*.
[320] Sepúlveda *Human Rights Reference book* (2004) 299.
[321] Sepúlveda *Human Rights Reference book* (2004) 302.
[322] Inter-American Court, *Compulsory Membership in an Association Prescribed by Law for the Practice of Journalism* (Arts. 13 and 29 *American Convention on Human Rights*). Advisory Opinion OC-5/85, November 13, 1985. Series A No. 5, paras 39-40.
[323] Sepúlveda *Human Rights Reference book* (2004) 303.

The right to freedom of assembly and association are fundamental to practising one's religion or belief in community with others. The freedom to manifest a religion or belief in association with others has distinct collective participation components, such as collective worship, observance and practice. Collective rights in relation to religious freedom include: (1) the right to freely associate and congregate with a religious or belief-based group with the intention of exercising any of the listed behavioural freedoms in Article 6 of the *Religious Discrimination Declaration*, and (2) the right not to associate with such a group or any group for such purposes.

The external manifestation of religious freedom and collective participation rights require a similar high threshold for restrictive measures in limiting such rights.[324] An example of restrictive measures that may cut along the lines of a limitation of both the freedom of belief and the freedom of association, is the requirement to register as a religious association in order to establish legal personality. As mentioned, States may require associations to register in order to attain legal status, but such registration requirements cannot be legally used as a precondition to the exercise of the right of a group to associate and assemble.[325] Consequently, compulsory governmental registration processes that require registration as a precondition for the right to manifest one's religion in community with others amounts to a deprivation of both religious freedom rights as well as collective participation rights.[326]

Such collective religious associations have a right to function peacefully, free from arbitrary State interference. This right puts a duty on States to remain neutral in its relations with all religious identities.[327]

In summary, it may be reiterated that the programmatic profile of human rights law is based on the fundamental core principle that "[a]ll human beings are born free and equal in dignity and rights [and] are endowed with reason and conscience".[328] To the extent that all human rights are universal, indivisible, interrelated and interdependent, it has been shown that the multifaceted and interdependent nature of religious freedom can only be fully implemented and realised when it is protected with other interrelated human rights. Together, these rights positively assume and mutually enforce each other, as well as empower individuals to fully realise

---

[324] Art 18(3), 21 & 22(3) of the *ICCPR*. See also the *UNHRC General Comment No. 22* par 8.
[325] Bielefeldt *FORB: Thematic Reports* (2017) 91.
[326] Bielefeldt *FORB: Thematic Reports* (2017) 91.
[327] *Hasan and Chaush* ECtHR (2000) par 62.
[328] Art 1 of the *UDHR*.

Appendix B

their human dignity in the exercise of universal human rights. To this extent, it has also become clear that deprivations of the right to freedom of religion or belief are often "highly intertwined with and threaten other civil political rights, such as the right to life, privacy, assembly and expression, as well as social, economic and cultural rights".[329]

6 Patterns of deprivations of religious freedom

Deprivations of the right to freedom of religion or belief may be committed by States or non-State actors or entities, or quite frequently a combination of both. Such measures are diverse in form, effect and motivation. Therefore, the discussion that follows will be restricted to some of the most notable patterns of systematic violations and abuses of religious freedom that may constitute religious persecution. It should be recalled that for the purposes of this study, human rights violations refer to deprivations of rights directly attributable to the State, including the failure to protect in instances where a positive duty existed. On the other hand, human rights abuses refer to deprivations of rights inflicted by non-State actors.

Often, deprivations are the result of religious discrimination, and in extreme cases, result in religious persecution or even religious genocide. However, the discussion that follows is not specifically focussed on providing a non-exhaustive typology of patterns of deprivations of religious freedom, nor is it intended to scale the required threshold of severity of these deprivations for purposes of 'grievous persecution'.

6.1. Governmental restrictions and violations by State actors

Religious persecution by State actors are usually triggered by governmental or national religious bigotry, but may also result from any of the other motivational triggers. Government restrictions refer to measures employed by a *de facto* authority, which amount to a denial or deprivation of religious freedom rights. Government restrictions are evident as disproportional restrictions through government laws, policies or coercive actions or forces that restrict religious beliefs and practices through measures aimed at banning particular faiths, prohibiting conversion, limiting preaching or giving preferential treatment to one or more religious

---

[329] Stefanus Alliance International: *Freedom of Religion or Belief for everyone*. Oslo (2012), pg 6.

groups.³³⁰ It is also a deliberate failure to take action under circumstances where there is a positive legal duty upon the government.

The nature and extent of infringements on religious freedom by governments largely depend on how States relate to and regulate religious pluralism:

> [S]ome Governments narrowly focus on individualistic and private dimensions of freedom of religion or belief while paying inadequate attention to community-related, institutional and infrastructural aspects of religious life. By contrast, other Governments place all the emphasis on recognizing collective religious identities, thus missing the crucial element of personal freedom even though it figures in the title of freedom of religion or belief.³³¹

Ordinarily, religious persecutions by governments are identifiable as widespread patterns or systematic violations of religious freedom, committed by State agencies.³³² However, a comprehensive listing of the various measures by governments that violate religious freedom is not feasible. Following is a brief discussion of the most noteworthy violations by governments. These include criminal law sanctions, bureaucratic harassment and burdensome administrative stipulations, discriminatory structures in family law, violations in the context of the right of parents regarding religion or belief and school education, and State-induced discrimination and stigmatisation.

6.1.1. Criminal law sanctions

Domestic laws that provide for restrictions of various aspects of religious freedom, especially regarding the external dimension, often include criminal offences and penalties for perceived non-compliance. Such criminal offences and penalties generally target dissidents, critics, converts, non-believers or persons belonging to religious minorities.³³³

In some States, criminal sanctions formally prohibit apostasy, while others ban missionary activities through anti-proselytism laws. Anti-apostasy and anti-proselytism laws "have in common a tendency to prohibit

---

[330] Pew Research Center. *Trends in Global Restrictions on Religion.* 23 June 2016, pg 6. http://www.pewforum.org/2016/06/23/trends-in-global-restrictions-on-religion/#fnref-25807-1. Accessed 28/09/2016. See also Pew Research Center. *Global Uptick in Government Restrictions.* (2018).
[331] Bielefeldt *FORB: Thematic Reports* (2017) 339.
[332] Bielefeldt *FORB: Thematic Reports* (2017) 350–351.
[333] Bielefeldt *FORB: Thematic Reports* (2017) 351.

changes away from hegemonic religions, which typically receive privileged treatment".[334]

Another form of criminal sanction, which is often used to 'protect' official religions, is anti-blasphemy laws.

> What constitutes an offence of 'blasphemy' frequently remains merely vaguely circumscribed, thus giving Governments carte blanche to apply such laws in an arbitrary and discriminatory manner.[335]

There are other criminal offences and penalties which do not directly exhibit an intention to curb religious dissidence or criticism, but may nonetheless have such consequences in practice. One such example is the arbitrary application of overly broad anti-hatred or hate speech laws.[336] There are also restrictions on religious freedom, which, although *prima facie* 'neutral' in form, may become persecutory in nature if applied arbitrarily. Such examples include criminalising alleged acts of eroding national security, or the non-recognition of religious groups in the 'interest' of public safety and security.

6.1.2. Bureaucratic harassment and burdensome administrative stipulations

Human rights violations often come in the form of excessive political, economic or administrative bureaucracy.

> Arguably the most widespread pattern of State-induced violations of freedom of religion or belief relates to harassment by an uncooperative bureaucracy that may treat people belonging to certain religious communities with contempt, hostility or suspicion.[337]

A highly problematic form of such bureaucratic harassment and burdensome administrative stipulations is the requirements for registration. It was explained that registration in the context of religion may take the form of personal religious registration (i. e. every person is identified with a particular faith, making them part of a religion-based community), or acquiring legal personality status by religious groups coupled with registration procedures.

---

[334] Bielefeldt *FORB: Thematic Reports* (2017) 351.
[335] Bielefeldt *FORB: Thematic Reports* (2017) 351.
[336] Bielefeldt *FORB: Thematic Reports* (2017) 352.
[337] Bielefeldt *FORB: Thematic Reports* (2017) 353.

In regards to personal religious registration, the freedom to choose or change a religious identity is unnecessarily complicated by the administrative processes involved, constituting an obvious impediment on the freedom of changing or adopting a belief, which is in line with the internal dimension of religious freedom.

The latter form of registration often require religious communities to register and obtain official status with the relevant authorities as a precondition to practising their religion or belief. Such governmental registration requirements thus amount to limitations on the external dimension of religious freedom rights, in which case such limitations must, in form and practice, conform to the requirements set out in Article 18(3) of ICCPR. Furthermore, such registration requirements must be reasonably accommodating,[338] accessible, non-coercive, quick, transparent, fair, inclusive, non-discriminatory,[339] not unnecessarily bureaucratic, do not contain extensive formal preconditions, and should allow the applicant the right to information, reasons and remedies for adverse registration outcomes.[340]

Although registration may have beneficial practical and legal effects for those religious communities wishing to obtain such a legal personality status, such processes should never be a compulsory prerequisite for the recognition of a 'religion' or a religious group, nor become a precondition for the communitarian enjoyment of freedom of religion or belief.[341]

Consequently, unreasonable or arbitrary governmental registration requirements that deny appropriate legal personality status to religious groups, or unreasonable stipulations connected with such a status, constitute violations of freedom of religion or belief, which may amount to religious persecution.[342]

6.1.3. Discriminatory structures in family law

Even though most domestic jurisdictions have diverged law from religion, the family laws and customary laws in many countries and communities still reflect traditional religious hegemonies.[343] Religious family values, rites and customs play an indispensable part within religious communities, especially in regards to the raising and religious education of children

---

[338] Sepúlveda *Human Rights Reference book* (2004) 303.
[339] Bielefeldt *FORB: Thematic Reports* (2017) 102.
[340] Bielefeldt *FORB: Thematic Reports* (2017) 95.
[341] Bielefeldt *FORB: Thematic Reports* (2017) 353.
[342] Bielefeldt *FORB: Thematic Reports* (2017) 353.
[343] Bielefeldt *FORB: Thematic Reports* (2017) 354.

within family and communal structures. However, it may become highly troublesome when a government enacts and enforces laws based on a particular religion or denomination.

State-enforced 'denominational family laws' may have serious repercussions on family-related aspects such as marriage and divorce, child-rearing and related topics such as care, access or contact, guardianship and maintenance, inheritance and other areas of family life.[344] It was also explained that such issues "frequently reflect and reinforce inequalities between men and women",[345] and result in infringements on gender equality, the enforcement of legal penalties, and consequently structural and social hostility.

It is therefore clear that State-enforced 'denominational family laws' give rise to a number of serious concerns under freedom of religion or belief, and are usually compounded by the intersection with gender. In this regard, Jonathan Andrews' account of the story of an Egyptian woman named Martha is a telling example of the severe impact that State-enforced 'denominational family laws' may have, compounded by gender. In that instance, such measures denied them the legitimacy of their marriage, the legal custody of their children, and forced them into hiding.[346]

6.1.4. Violations in the context of the right of parents regarding religious education

Incidental to the intersection between family law and freedom of religion or belief is the unequivocal right of parents or legal guardians to raise and educate their children in accordance with their own beliefs.[347] The *ICCPR* and the *ICESCR* confirm this right of parents in the context of religious freedom and religious education. States are required to guarantee "respect for the liberty of parents and, when applicable, legal guardians to ensure the religious and moral education of their children in conformity with their own convictions".[348]

The rights and freedom of parents in relation to religious freedom incorporates two fundamental rights of parents, namely their right to raise

---

[344] Bielefeldt *FORB: Thematic Reports* (2017) 354.
[345] Bielefeldt *FORB: Thematic Reports* (2017) 354.
[346] Andrews, J. *Identity Crisis: Religious Registration in the Middle East.* Gilead Books Publishing. (2016), pg 108.
[347] Art 18(4) of the *ICCPR*. For a detailed discussion, see Bielefeldt *et al. FORB: An International Law Commentary* (2016) 204-222.
[348] Art 18(4) of the *ICCPR* and Art 13(3) of the *ICESCR*.

children within a certain religion or belief, and their right to ensure the religious and moral education of their children in conformity with their own views. Both these fundamental rights of parents in regards to the religious upbringing and education of their children inherently entail an element of free choice exercised by the parent on behalf of the child and thus form part of the internal dimension of religious freedom.[349] The ECtHR has found that a State is forbidden to pursue an aim of indoctrination that might be considered as not respecting the parents' religious and philosophical convictions.[350]

Conversely, the liberty of parents to ensure that their children receive a religious and moral education of their choice relates to the freedom to manifest a religion, either individually or in community with others and in public or private, through teaching.[351] Therefore, the religious and moral education of a child will customarily take on a collective public dimension through teaching, which allows for permissible restrictions. Teaching in subjects such as the general history of religions and ethics is permitted in public schools if it is presented in a neutral and objective way. However, "instruction in a particular religion or belief is inconsistent with article 18(4) unless provision is made for non-discriminatory exemptions or alternatives that would accommodate the wishes of parents and guardians".[352] The public school system, as an extension of State authority, must therefore respect religious and belief diversity in which case States should pursue an ideology of 'respectful non-identification'. These restrictions on exclusive religious teaching in schools are not imposed on private denominational schools.[353]

Importantly, the best interests of the child remain the guiding principle.[354] Consequently, this provision may be interpreted to suggest that parents' right to freedom to raise children within a certain religion or belief in conformity with their own convictions, may well be subject to some form of limitation which may affect religious freedom. Article 5(5) of the

---

[349] *UNHRC General Comment No. 22* par 8.
[350] *Kjeldsen, Busk, Madsen and Pederson v. Denmark*, Application Nos. 5095/71, 5920/72, 5926/72, Judgement of 7 December 1976, par 53.
[351] *UNHRC General Comment No. 22* par 6.
[352] *UNHRC General Comment No. 22* par 6. "Whenever religious ceremonies, such as public prayers or acts of collective worship, are performed in school, and in particular during regular school hours, safeguards are needed to ensure that no child feels compelled to participate in such ceremonies against his or her free will or the will of his or her parents. The same caveat applies to religious instruction in schools".
– Bielefeldt *FORB: Thematic Reports* (2017) 355.
[353] *Rapporteur's Digest on Freedom of Religion or Belief* (2011) 36.
[354] Art 3 of the *UNGA Convention on the Rights of the Child* (1989).

Religious Discrimination Declaration states that "practices of a religion or belief in which a child is brought up must not be injurious to his physical or mental health or to his full development".[355] The freedom of choice exercised by the parent on behalf of the child regarding religious and moral education should be done in a manner which is consistent with the evolving capacity of the child.[356] This acknowledges that the child will acquire the freedom at some point, in accordance with his or her age and maturity, to make personal choices in matters of religion or belief.[357]

In countries with a State or official religion, students belonging to religious minorities are occasionally pressured or even forcibly exposed to religious instruction against their will. Such practices may possibly constitute coercion that impairs the freedom to have or to adopt a religion or belief of choice.[358] Additionally, the compulsory status of public schools that adhere to a majority belief, regularly exposes children to peer pressure and bullying, a problem that disproportionately affects children from minorities.[359]

6.1.5. State-induced discrimination and stigmatisation

The patterns of systematic violations committed by State agencies mentioned earlier are often found concomitantly, creating an environment of State-induced bigotry "in which members of religious minorities, followers of non-traditional religious movements, individual dissidents, critics, converts, agnostics, atheists and others may suffer systematic discrimination, marginalization and exclusion".[360] Such circumstances may lead to multiple and intersectional forms of discrimination with religion.

'Religion' or a religious identity may be the primary motivator of governmental restrictions or bigotry when it views a particular religious group as a threat to its interests or security, or in circumstances where a government has adopted a State religion or official belief ideology.

> [Some] Governments privilege one particular religion or belief – or one particular type of religion – by promoting it as part of the national heritage, thereby ignoring the principles of equality and non-discrimination.[361]

---

[355] Art 5(5) of the *Religious Discrimination Declaration*.
[356] Art 14(2) of *UNGA Convention on the Rights of the Child* (1989).
[357] *Rapporteur's Digest on Freedom of Religion or Belief* (2011) 36.
[358] *Rapporteur's Digest on Freedom of Religion or Belief* (2011) 36.
[359] Bielefeldt *FORB: Thematic Reports* (2017) 355.
[360] Bielefeldt *FORB: Thematic Reports* (2017) 356.
[361] Bielefeldt *FORB: Thematic Reports* (2017) 339.

A State-religion relationship primarily results in discrimination against 'other' religious communities.[362] Discrimination in this regard may be "direct or indirect, unintended or intentional, *de facto* or *de jure*, vertical or horizontal discrimination and intolerance".[363]

In some instances, discrimination against religious groups takes on specific forms based on governmental ideologies and motives. Governmental religious bigotry usually entails restrictive or prohibitive legal measures and subsequent penalties and punishment, but may also take the form of outright hostility and violence. A Pew research project concluded that in 31% of countries, the government prohibits worship or religious practices of one or more religious groups as a general policy.[364] In 22% of countries, the conversion from one religion to another is limited by the State. In 30% of countries, the national government displayed hostility involving physical violence towards minority or 'non-approved' religious groups. It was also found that in 9% of countries, the national government attempted to eliminate an entire religious group's presence in the country, which arguably constitutes a genocidal policy or attempted genocide based on religious grounds. In 52% of countries, governmental authorities used force towards religious groups (ranging in frequency and severity), that resulted in individuals being killed, physically abused, imprisoned, detained or displaced from their homes, or having their personal or religious property damaged or destroyed. This research shows a relatively high degree of discriminatory interference in religious choice throughout the 197 countries which were coded.

6.2. Social or societal hostility and religious persecution

Abuses of religious freedom by non-State actors include acts of religious hostility by private individuals, organisations or groups in society, which manifest as religion-related armed conflict or terrorism, mob or sectarian violence, harassment for religious reasons or other religion-related intimidation or abuse.[365] Such abuses are often perpetrated in circumstances

---

[362] Bielefeldt *et al. FORB: An International Law Commentary* (2016) 339.
[363] Bielefeldt *et al. FORB: An International Law Commentary* (2016) 342.
[364] Pew *Global Uptick in Government Restrictions* (2018) 67-80. Pew Research Center uses two 10-point indexes – the Government Restrictions Index (GRI) and the Social Hostilities Index (SHI) – to rate 198 countries and self-governing territories on their levels of restrictions. This report analyses changes in restrictions on an annual basis.
[365] Pew *Global Uptick in Government Restrictions* (2018) 4.

that allow for impunity, "thus indicating direct or indirect State involvement or even a human rights protection vacuum".[366]

Bielefeldt argues that grave abuses of religious freedom often occur in societal settings that lack interreligious or intra-religious diversity.[367] The referenced Pew research project concluded that in 80% of countries there were social hostility in the form of crimes, malicious acts, or violence that were motivated by religious hatred or bias.[368] Such societal hostilities may include a variety of actions, ranging in severity. These include social ostracism, religious-biased crimes, religion-related armed conflict or terrorism, systematic mob violence, efforts to stop particular religious groups from growing or operating, harassment or other religion-related intimidation, damage to property, displacements, physical assaults, and killings.[369]

In summary, deprivations or restrictions of religious freedom may be instigated through violations by State actors or abuses by non-State actors, or a combination of both. It is impossible to describe all forms of deprivations of religious freedom through governmental restrictions or omissions and social hostility, especially considering that such measures may differ contextually and in severity. Therefore, while governments and other *de facto* authorities remain primarily responsible to recognise, protect and enforce their human rights obligations, not all deprivations of religious freedom rights will satisfy the required intensity threshold for 'grievous persecution'. However, this section was not aimed at assessing the required threshold of severity for each of the mentioned patterns of deprivations of religious freedom. Although these patterns of deprivations of religious freedom may provide proof of a religious discriminatory ideology, in certain instances such patterns will only amount to 'grievous religious persecution' if they are committed on a widespread or systematic basis and result in the severe deprivation of the right to freedom of religion or belief. Thus, in each of the illustrated patterns, such violations or abuses, when considered cumulatively, may have the potential to satisfy the definitional requirements for persecution as a crime against humanity.

---

[366] Bielefeldt *FORB: Thematic Reports* (2017) 144.
[367] Bielefeldt *FORB: Thematic Reports* (2017) 358.
[368] Pew *Global Uptick in Government Restrictions* (2018) 81–88.
[369] Pew *Global Uptick in Government Restrictions* (2018) 4. See also Bielefeldt *Freedom of Religion or Belief: Thematic Reports* (2017) 358.

7 Varying intensities of deprivations of religious freedom

In the preceding sections of this appendix, many references were made and examples provided of various forms and intensities of violations and abuses of religious freedom. It is, however, unfeasible to "provide a 'global map' of existing infringements of freedom of religion or belief".[370] Therefore, the non-exhaustive typology set out in this section is aimed at distinguishing severe deprivations of religious freedom (possibly constituting grievous religious persecution), from other 'subsidiary' forms of deprivations of religious freedom.[371] Consequently, these various forms or manifestations of deprivations of religious freedom, ranging from harassment or intimidation, repression, restrictions or limitations, religious discrimination, to persecution do not generally satisfy the definitional requirements of 'grievous religious persecution'. Consequently, not all deprivations of religious freedom satisfy the intensity threshold or contextual requirement.

Adherents or non-adherents to religious convictions experience various pressures or difficulties in all areas of life, including their own personal convictions, family life and communal life. In reality, such deprivations may occur in a diversity of pernicious forms, which range in severity from persecution to repression to harassment to limitations to discrimination.

Harassment or intimidation often take the form of intra-religious verbal assaults, but may also target a specific religious group with physical assaults, arrest and detentions, desecration of holy sites, and discrimination against religious groups in employment, education and housing.[372] Generally, incidents of harassment or intimidation intended to silence non-adherents or dissident religions are not evidence of a widespread policy or systematic occurrences.[373]

'Repression' does not entail violent force, but may "describe situations in which believers are prohibited from meeting publicly, religious practice is made illegal, and proselytizing is banned".[374]

---

[370] Bielefeldt *FORB: Thematic Reports* (2017) 338.
[371] Section 3(13)(A) of the United States of America: *International Religious Freedom Act of 1998*, Pub. L. 105–292, 27 October 1998, provides a useful guide as to which conduct may amount to a deprivations of religious freedom.
[372] Pew *Trends in Global Restrictions on Religion* (2016) 20.
[373] Thames et al. *International Religious Freedom Advocacy* (2009) 12.
[374] Thames et al. *International Religious Freedom Advocacy* (2009) 12.

As already discussed, restrictions or limitations may also amount to violations of religious freedom rights if such restrictive measures do not comply with the criteria set out in Article 18(3) of the *ICCPR*. Disproportional restrictions often intersect with other related human rights, such as freedom of expression and freedom of association and assembly. On the other hand, if such unnecessary restrictive measures are intended to discriminate against a person or group based on their religious or belief affiliations, the effect of such limitations may also amount to religious discrimination and persecution.

As mentioned, religious discrimination and intolerance based on religion or belief is defined by Article 2(2) of the *Religious Discrimination Declaration*.[375]

Religious intolerance seems to refer to instances where societal prejudice or religious polarisation results in the refusal to tolerate practices, persons or beliefs on religious grounds. Conversely, religious discrimination refers to instances where such societal prejudice or religious polarisation results in differentiating between persons or groups, and devaluing them because of their religious identity, or lack thereof. However, religious discrimination implies not only a general intolerance based on religion, but discrimination in fact or in law. In other words, the discriminatory practices or ideologies result in unequal treatment between adherents and non-adherents of different religions or beliefs.

Religious discrimination or intolerance are often visible pertaining to issues such as conscientious objections, the enforcement and punishment of *mala fide* blasphemy laws and infringements of 'hate speech', and legal sanctions against missionary activities which are out-rightly branded as improper proselytism.

Thus, while intolerance may be regarded as a prejudicial mentality, discrimination pertains to actual prejudice, whether in practice or policy. Religious discrimination in its most extreme and systematic form constitutes a crime that ranks amongst the most serious crimes of concern to the international community, notably 'crimes against humanity of religious persecution' in terms of the *Rome Statute* of the *ICC*.[376] However, discriminatory intent does not spontaneously constitute persecution and requires the consequent severe deprivation of fundamental human rights.[377]

---

[375] "*...means any distinction, exclusion, restriction or preference based on religion or belief and having as its purpose or as its effect nullification or impairment of the recognition, enjoyment or exercise of human rights and fundamental freedoms on an equal basis*".

[376] General Issue 28 of the *UN World Conference against Racism* (2001).

[377] Par 53 of the UN High Commissioner for Refugees (UNHCR), *Handbook and Guidelines on Procedures and Criteria for Determining Refugee Status under the 1951 Convention*

The persecution of persons for the exercise of their religious beliefs may amount to a deprivation of various human rights, including the right to freedom of religion, equality, privacy, expression, thought, collective participation and choice. As discussed, these are all inalienable and interrelated human rights that are acknowledged as part of customary international law, protected by various international treaties.[378] Importantly, it should be recalled that 'grievous religious persecution' requires the severe deprivation of any of these fundamental human rights, not specifically religious freedom.

Religious persecution may be considered as the most severe form of religious intolerance and may amount to severe infringements of religious freedom. Although persecution may also encompass acts with varying levels of severity, 'grievous persecution' is limited to the most serious deprivations of religious freedom, such as a prohibition on free religious activities or even restrictions regarding permissible beliefs.[379]

In summary, deprivations of religious freedom may occur in various forms, ranging in source, motivation, and severity. Regardless of the 'subsidiary' nature of some infringements of religious freedom, all such deprivations constitute a serious affront to human dignity and place an obstacle on the full and holistic development of individuals. Impunity for deprivations of human rights, especially the fundamental right to religious freedom, is a serious constraint on democratic freedom, a fair and equitable justice system, and societal and national stability.[380]

8 Conclusion

Religious freedom belongs to a *genus* of fundamental human rights, which is rooted in the heart of identity, morality, freedom, and dignity. It is enshrined and protected by, *inter alia*, the core international documents regarding religious freedom. The right to freedom of religion or belief serves to empower human beings, individually and in community with others, who wish to have and enjoy their chosen religious identity and shape their lives in conformity with such convictions.[381]

---

and the 1967 Protocol Relating to the Status of Refugees, December 2011, HCR/1P/4/ENG/REV. 3.
[378] Sepúlveda Human Rights Reference book (2004) 203.
[379] Thames et al. International Religious Freedom Advocacy (2009) 11.
[380] General Issue 82 of the UN World Conference against Racism (2001).
[381] Bielefeldt FORB: Thematic Reports (2017) 339–340.

Religious freedom is a multifaceted human freedom, and consequently, infringements of religious freedom include breaches on dimensional elements, core values and the denial of equality on the basis of religion or belief (religious discrimination).

A State or *de facto* authority should never restrict this right by not recognising a person's legal capacity. Furthermore, the 'recognition' of a religion or religious group should never be a precondition to freely exercising their religious freedom rights. Registration procedures in regard to religions or religious groups should be confined to purposes of attaining legal personality status for those associations who wish to do so. Otherwise, the refusal of a government to recognise a religion may effectively limit the right of the religious group to manifest their religion collectively.

The individual's right to freedom of religion or belief entails a negative obligation on States to refrain from policies, in all spheres of government, which may limit or prohibit the free enjoyment of this right. It also entails a positive obligation on the State to ensure religious freedom for the persons on its territory and under its jurisdiction, as well as to protect persons from interferences with their religious freedom rights. Furthermore, States have a responsibility to respect, protect and promote the normative core values of the right to freedom of religion or belief. These core values constitute the minimum standards that should be protected *in re* religious freedom.

The internal dimension of religious freedom constitutes an absolute right to freedom of thought, personal conviction and the commitment to religion or belief. Such internal rights and freedoms include:

- the freedom of choice to have or adopt a religion or belief, including the right not to adhere to any belief and to profess no religion;
- the freedom to retain and maintain a belief;
- the freedom to establish a new religion;
- the freedom to leave, change or replace one's existing belief, including the right not to be forced to convert;
- the liberty of parents and legal guardians to raise their children within a certain religion or belief and to ensure the religious and moral education of the child in conformity with their own convictions; and
- the right not to be compelled to reveal one's thoughts and adherence or non-adherence to a religion or belief.

These absolute personal rights and freedoms may be enjoyed without any coercion, limitation or derogation, and apply equally to adherents of all deep existential views, including those of a non-religious nature.

The right to manifest one's religious identity, either individually or in community with others, and in public or private, refers to the external manifestation of religion or belief. The external dimension of religious freedom ensures protection for the pragmatic realisation of religious behaviour which gives direct expression to belief. However, this manifestation of religious behaviour is not protected unconditionally and may be subject to limitations that are proportional, prescribed by law and are necessary to protect public safety, order, health, or morals or the fundamental rights and freedoms of others. Restrictive measures cannot be enforced to preserve a religion, nor the ideologies and convictions that examplify such a religion against ridicule and criticism.

Freedom from coercion is also applicable to the manifestation of religious freedom rights in the sense that Article 18(1) of the *ICCPR* bars coercion which would impair a person's freedom to choose the manner in which he/she may give expression to their religion or belief.

The principle of non-discrimination in international human rights law requires States or Governments to systematically endeavour to eliminate all forms of religious discrimination. Consequently, States have a duty to prevent, combat and exercise its criminal jurisdiction over those responsible for gross and systematic human rights deprivations, committed on the grounds of religion or belief.

Human rights and fundamental freedoms are universal, interrelated, interdependent and indivisible, in the sense that the full realisation of the right to freedom of thought, conscience and religion or belief is impossible without the enjoyment of, *inter alia*:

- the freedom of collective participation to manifest one's convictions in association and assembly with other likeminded believers;
- the freedom to give direct expression to belief;
- the freedom from religious discrimination;
- the guarantee to fundamental due process in the administration of justice in attaining religious freedom;
- the right to communicative freedoms regarding aspects of religious discourse; and
- respect for the dignity and privacy of the individual's sovereign personal thought and existential conviction.

Deprivations of the right to freedom of religion or belief may differ in severity and occur in a diversity of pernicious forms, ranging from societal intolerance, violence, unjustified or discriminatory restrictions imposed by governments, disproportional and arbitrary legal prohibitions on religious freedom, or a predefined list of legitimate and protected religious or belief options.

It should be remembered that the multifaceted nature of religious freedom means that infringements on the right to freedom of religion or belief invariably and inherently include the denial of equality on the basis of religion or belief:

> Freedom of religion or belief does not only prohibit undue encroachments on the freedom of a person or a group of persons; it also prohibits discrimination – that is, the denial of equality – on the basis of religion or belief.[382]

In its extreme form, religious discrimination and persecution may escalate into severe deprivations of fundamental rights. Because of such deprivations, millions of people around the world enjoy religious freedom only to a limited extent.[383] Evidently, the intersection between religious persecution, religious discrimination, and deprivations of religious freedom is undeniable, inseparable and elementary. Therefore, religious discrimination and infringements of religious freedom rights concomitantly serve as the principal fundamental human rights infringed through acts of religious persecution, albeit that the denial of other rights and liberties may also form part of such a gross and systematic deprivations of human rights.

---

[382] Bielefeldt *FORB: Thematic Reports* (2017) 343.
[383] Sepúlveda *Human Rights Reference book* (2004) 203.

Appendix C: Assessing 'Grievous Religious Persecution' in the Context of the Atrocities Committed by *Da'esh*

1. Introduction

In order to successfully charge those responsible for religious persecution as a crime against humanity, a clear and justifiable legal framework is required, as proposed in Chapter Six. The purpose of this appendix is to put the proposed taxonomy into practice by assessing factual evidence of contemporary religious persecutions in the form of a case study. Finding the right case or situation is essential in this regard. Although it remains the function of a competent court to pronounce on 'grievous religious persecution', it will be argued that the context of religious extremism and terrorism that developed from the situation in northern Iraq and Syria is a suitable case study to test the proposed taxonomy.

Reports suggest that the group that calls itself the 'Islamic State'[1] or *Da'esh*,[2] as it is known in its Arabic language acronym, has systematically committed mass atrocity crimes and human rights deprivations against religious minorities and dissident religious denominations in areas formerly under its control. *Da'esh* has systematically targeted non-Arab and non-Sunni Muslim communities based on their religious identities or lack thereof, including Assyrian Christians, Turkmen Shia, Shabak Shia,

---

[1] Differentiate from Islamic State as a type of government, in which the primary basis for government is *Sharia* law. In the current sphere of political systems, many Muslim countries have incorporated Islam, in whole or in part, as their State religion.
[2] During its evolution, the group has undergone several name changes, including Islamic State of Iraq and the Levant (ISIL), the Islamic State of Iraq and Syria or the Islamic State of Iraq and al-Sham (ISIS), and finally rebranded itself as the so-called 'Islamic State' (IS). The acronym 'IS' is clearly linguistically undesirable. Furthermore, governments and Muslim leaders worldwide have rejected its claim to statehood or the concept of it being a caliphate and of it being named 'Islamic State'. In order to avoid inadvertently legitimizing their ideological assault on the very concept of an Islamic state or Caliphate, the group will be referred to by its Arabic acronym '*Da'esh*' (short for *al-Dawla al-Islamiya fi al-Iraq wa al-Sham*) in the course of this case study, or alternatively as the 'group' or 'armed group' where appropriate.

Yazidis, Kakai and Sabean Mandaeans.³ As a result of a global outcry against the crimes committed in the region and the presence of various military powers, a strong body of evidence provides factual support for potential charges against those most responsible in terms of the group's leadership structure. Preliminary information thus suggests that the armed group's treatment of non-conforming religious identities presents a typical case of grievous religious persecution.

Initially, the basis and context for choosing religious extremism will be explained. Thereafter, the origins and evolution of *Da'esh* will be traced and two very important aspects will be considered. The first relates to understanding the ideological foundation of the group, and the second entails an analysis of the scope or pattern of crimes, atrocities and human rights breaches committed by the group in northern Iraq and Syria.

In order to advocate for the prosecution of *Da'esh* commanders and fighters, their actions must be substantiated as constituting religious persecution in the context of crimes against humanity. Consequently, the mass atrocity crimes and human rights deprivations committed by *Da'esh* will be applied to the 'religious persecution checklist' proposed in Chapter Six.

It should be noted that the following discussion regarding Islamic law and tradition should in no way be construed as a claim to scholarly expertise in this field. This discussion is merely an attempt at using some secondary literature for sketching a rudimentary picture and for extracting information that is relevant for legal prosecution of crimes before an international court of law.⁴

2. The Global Trend of Fear Relating to Religious Extremism

Contemporarily, non-State actors, such as religious extremist networks, terrorist organisations and militant vigilante groups, are perpetrating many of the most brutal abuses of religious freedom.⁵ In the context of this

---

[3] Amnesty International, *Ethnic cleansing on a historic scale: Islamic State's systematic targeting of minorities in Northern Iraq*. 2 September 2014, Index number: MDE 14/011/2014, pg 4. https://www.amnesty.org/en/documents/MDE14/011/2014/en/. Accessed 08/01/2015.

[4] It should also be noted that this case study was finalized in June 2018 and may not accurately reflect events or reports thereafter.

[5] Bielefeldt, H. *Freedom of Religion or Belief: Thematic Reports of the UN Special Rapporteur 2010 - 2016*. Religious Freedom Series of the International Institute for Religious Freedom, Vol 3, 2nd and extended edition, Bonn (2017), pg 357.

case study, the focus is on religious extremism and related terrorism committed in the name of religion, specifically Islamic extremism. However, it should be noted that while religious extremism is primarily motivated by religious ideology, terrorism is not limited to perpetrators who are motivated by their religious ideology, but may also include "terrorist acts carried out by individuals or groups with a nonreligious identity that deliberately target religious groups or individuals, such as clergy".[6]

During the discussion that follows, the nature of religious extremism, the relation between religious ideology and extremism, and the adverse effect of religious extremism on associated religious communities are considered. Finally, it will be explained that the rising trend of fear relating to Islamic extremism, has become the leading cause of religiously motivated persecution and has resulted in a global deterioration of religious tolerance towards Muslims.

2.1. The nature of religious extremism

Though there may be various root causes for religious intolerance, "[m]ost justifications for religious extremism are fundamentalist in nature, based squarely on religious doctrine, strictly interpreted".[7] Such intolerant and narrow-minded interpretations of religious doctrine may result in adherents adopting an extremist view, which often advocates, glorifies and justifies violence and other human rights abuses in the name of religion.

> The phrase 'religious extremism' describes faith-based actions that are deliberate attempts to cause harm to other people... Religious tolerance, multiculturalism and equality are the particular targets of extremists. Their own religion provides guidance that trumps any secular law or any concept of human rights.[8]

The hazard of religious extremism is inherent in all collective religious or belief movements.[9] However,

---

[6] Pew Research Center. *Trends in Global Restrictions on Religion*. 23 June 2016. http://www.pewforum.org/2016/06/23/trends-in-global-restrictions-on-religion/#fnref-25807-1. Accessed 28/09/2016.
[7] Crabtree, V. *Religious Extremism* (2017). The Human Truth Foundation website: http://www.humanreligions.info/extremism.html. Accessed 21/06/2018.
[8] Crabtree, V. *Religious Extremism* (2017). The Human Truth Foundation website: http://www.humanreligions.info/extremism.html. Accessed 21/06/2018.
[9] Crabtree *Religious Extremism* (2017) based on Hoffer, E. *The True Believer: Thoughts on the Nature of Mass Movements*. HarperCollins (1951).

the horrific spectres of oppression and violent coercion have resulted mostly from Abrahamic monotheistic religions such as Judaism, Christianity (mostly in the past) and Islam (particularly prone to it at present), and to a lesser extent from other traditional religions such as Hinduism, especially as a result of battles against multiculturalism.[10]

Consequently, the origin of religious extremist ideologies is generally as old as the religious scripture from which the fundamentalist doctrine is derived. Some religious orthodox or religiously motivated fundamentalist groups are inclined to religious extremism and religion-related terrorism in "premeditated, politically motivated violence perpetrated against non-combatants".[11] Such groups use religion as a justification or motivation for their actions, which may include religion-related terrorism carried out by subnational groups, for example, the Nigeria-based Islamist group, *Boko Haram*.[12]

2.2. Religious motivation and extremism

Militant religious extremism is usually politically inspired and motivated by religious ideology. The subsequent discrimination and persecution compound several persecutory motivations and results in a complex phenomenon that interlinks religion with ethnicity, nationality, cultural identity, racial origin, and historical backgrounds. This results in a multiplicity of the grounds of persecution and religiously motivated violence.

Religious extremism is usually perpetrated against members of dissident religious communities by subnational groups or clandestine agents bearing an identifiable religious ideology.[13] However, in most instances States are directly or indirectly involved.

> The main problem in a number of countries stems from the State's failure in combating terrorism or violence of non-State actors, while certain State agencies in other countries support such violence directly or indirectly.[14]

Consequently, the acts of religious extremism are an appropriate example of religiously motivated persecution. Religious extremists exploit their collective religious identity, whether on a denominational level or

---

[10] Crabtree *Religious Extremism* (2017).
[11] Pew *Trends in Global Restrictions on Religion* (2016) 41.
[12] Pew *Trends in Global Restrictions on Religion* (2016) 9.
[13] Pew *Trends in Global Restrictions on Religion* (2016) 41.
[14] Bielefeldt *FORB: Thematic Reports* (2017) 250.

inclusive of an entire religion as a whole, as the justification for persecution.[15] In other words, in most instances religious extremism illustrates the intersection of religiously motivated persecution that is directed at victims based on their religious identity (religious persecution).

2.3. The adverse effect of religious extremism on associated religious communities

Militant religious extremist groups are often inclined to extremism and religion-related terrorism that have some identifiable religious ideology or religious motivation.[16] As such, they motivate, justify and even glorify their actions concerning an established religion, which may have an adverse effect on the concerned religion or religious community as a whole.[17] Therefore, religious extremism and religion-related terrorism not only entail a risk of severe human rights abuses against targeted religious identities, but may also incite fear, hatred, discrimination and persecutory reprisals against members of the religious communities which are equated with such extremist religious groups.[18]

The nature of extremism in any religion, whether lingering dormant or pursued vigorously, secretly or explicitly, is such that it may lead to negative stereotyping and societal polarisation. Militant religious fundamentalism or extremism may have severe antagonistic consequences of religious polarisation and may ultimately impact on the victims', as well as members of the associated religion's enjoyment of human rights:

---

[15] "[R]eligion-related terrorism includes acts carried out by subnational groups that use religion as a justification or motivation for their actions, such as the Nigeria-based Islamist group *Boko Haram*; al-Qaida in the Islamic Maghreb (AQIM); and the Islamic State, the militant group also known as ISIS or ISIL. Religion-related terrorism also includes terrorist acts carried out by individuals or groups with a non-religious identity that deliberately target religious groups or individuals, such as clergy" – Pew *Trends in Global Restrictions on Religion* (2016) 9.
[16] Pew *Trends in Global Restrictions on Religion* (2016) 41.
[17] It should be mentioned that although religion-related terrorism is generally carried out by subnational groups that use religion as a justification or motivation for their actions, such acts may also be carried out by individuals or groups who do not bear an identifiable religious identity, that deliberately target certain groups or individuals, because of their religious identity – See Pew *Trends in Global Restrictions on Religion* (2016) 9.
[18] UN *Rapporteur's Digest on Freedom of Religion or Belief* (2011) 75.

[R]eligious extremism acts as a cancer in a religious group of any denomination and... it affects the members of that religious group just as much as those of other [targeted] religious groups.[19]

The ensuing detrimental effect of religiously motivated persecution is particularly severe in situations where religious extremists are equated with a religion or religious community as a whole. Consequently, UN resolutions and communications have diverged terrorism from religious affiliations:

[N]o religion should be equated with terrorism, as this may have adverse consequences on the enjoyment of the right to freedom of religion or belief of all members of the religious communities concerned.[20]

Widespread and deliberate generalisations of religious identity cultivate a climate of mistrust and suspicion, which results in intolerant and discriminatory mindsets and may bring about religious persecution and subsequent counter-reactions. Therefore, it was explained in Chapter Six that a crucial consideration in curbing or preventing negative religious polarisation resulting from religion-related terrorism, is dependent upon the reactions of the religious community allegedly affiliated to such terrorist factions. However, the difficulty in eradicating the propagation of extremist and fanatical perceptions in order to overcome the distrust between opposing members of religiously diverse communities is often further strained by the interlinked nature of religion with ethnicity, nationality, cultural identity, racial origin, and political or historical backgrounds. Nonetheless, the denunciation of any affiliation that may implicate the concerned religious community with such behaviour is of primary importance.

---

[19] UN Commission on Human Rights, *Report of the Special Rapporteur on the implementation of the Declaration on the elimination of all forms of intolerance and of discrimination based on religion belief*, 15 December 1995, E/CN.4/1996/95, par 45.

[20] Par 13 of the UNGA *Res. Discrimination based on Religion.* (2009). Other such resolutions include, *inter alia*: UN Security Council, *resolution 2161 (2014) [on threats to international peace and security caused by terrorist acts by Al-Qaida]*, 17 June 2014, S/RES/2161 (2014); UN Security Council, *Security Council resolution 2170 (2014) [on threats to international peace and security caused by terrorist acts by Al-Qaida]* , 15 August 2014, and UN Security Council, *Security Council resolution 2354 (2017) [on implementation of the Comprehensive International Framework to Counter Terrorist Narratives]*, 24 May 2017, S/RES/2354 (2017).

2.4. The rising trend of fear relating to Islamic extremism

Modern-day terror-orientated Islamic extremism originated after the fall of the Ottoman Empire during World War I, which "protected the roots of Islam and acted as the last Caliphate of Islam".[21] It should be noted that within an Islamic context, there is no distinction between religion and State. Consequently, any confrontation with an Islamic State is inevitably interpreted as an 'attack' or criticism of the Islamic faith. Therefore, the demise of the Ottoman Empire prompted a return to Islamic fundamentalism based on an extremist or radical ideology aimed at restoring the tarnished prestige of Islam.[22] Subsequent provocations of Islamic radicalisation included, *inter alia*: the Six Day War of 1967 (in terms of which Egypt, Lebanon, Syria, Jordan, and Iraq declared a military *jihad*[23] against Israel in order to liberate Palestine); the Iranian Islamic revolution; the Soviet invasion of Afghanistan, and the subsequent anti-Soviet *mujahedeen* war (which started in the late 1970's); the United States-led coalition against Iraq in response to Iraq's invasion and annexation of Kuwait (the Gulf War); and the United States' invasion of Afghanistan and war on the Taliban, consequent to the coordinated terrorist attacks by *al-Qaeda* on 11 September 2001.

Despite early warning signs of a rise in militant extremist violence in the name of religion, and repeated appeals by the Special Rapporteur on freedom of religion or belief for the need to combat religious extremism, "such warnings did not have the desired effect in good time".[24] In the context of the terrorist attacks by *al-Qaeda*, the UN Security Council declared "that acts of international terrorism constitute one of the most serious threats to international peace and security in the twenty-first century".[25] Since then, the global trend of militant Islamic extremism and religion-related terrorism has become more diffuse, with an increase in various parts of the world.[26]

---

[21] Hume. J. *Balance of Powers: Syria*. (2014). http://numun.org/blog/wp-content/uploads/2014/02/BOP-Syria-Committee-Dossier.pdf. Accessed 08/01/2015.

[22] Hume Balance of Powers: Syria (2014) 8–9.

[23] The notion of '*jihad*' will be explained below.

[24] *Report submitted by the Special Rapporteur on freedom of religion or belief in re Examination of the consequences of the events of 11 September 2001 as regards tolerance and non-discrimination*. Outcome of the 2001 International Consultative Conference, 14 March 2002, E/CN.4/2002/73, pg 2.

[25] UN Security Council, *Security Council resolution 1377 (2001) [threats to international peace and security caused by terrorist acts]*, 12 November 2001, S/RES/1377 (2001), pg 2.

[26] UN Security Council, *Security Council resolution 2368 (2017) [threats to international peace and security caused by terrorist acts]*, 20 July 2017, S/RES/2368 (2017). See also

The rising trend of fear relating to Islamic extremism stands out as the leading cause of a global deterioration of religious tolerance and the increase in religious persecution.[27] Islamic extremists' self-styled caliphates[28] have expanded their spheres of operation across international borders through religion-related terrorism; this serves as the cause of fear resulting in a global sentiment of insecurity and helplessness against fundamentalist *jihadists*.

In reaction to this fundamental and deadly terror threat, much of the international community is more fearful than ever before about the effects of Islamic extremism; responses included either boosting nationalism as a counter force or tightening regulations and increasing surveillance over all religious expression. Consequently, religious freedom and restrictions on the manifestation thereof have been placed under the spotlight of human rights concerns.

In line with the discussion, the magnitude and savagery of contemporary Islamic extremism have had a very detrimental effect on associated Islamic communities. In this regard, the identification of the Muslim faith with religious extremism has had a concerting counter-effect, resulting in serious cases of Islamophobia.[29]

> [Generalizing publications] lend credence to the idea of a war of religion, describing Muslims as sympathizers with, or even parties to, Islamic terrorism, inciting hatred and presenting Islam as a dangerous and archaic religion ...[30]

Consequently, the global trend of fear relating to Islamic extremism has led to the equation of the Islamic faith with religious extremism, which has

---

UN Security Council, *Security Council resolution 2178 (2014) [on threats to international peace and security caused by foreign terrorist fighters]*, 24 September 2014, S/RES/2178 (2014), pg 1.

[27] Pew *Trends in Global Restrictions on Religion* (2016). See also Open Doors Analytical / World Watch Research Unit. *World Watch List* (2016) 12–13.

[28] A caliphate (*khilafah* in Arab), meaning 'succession' is an Islamic State led by a supreme religious and political leader known as a caliph – i. e. "successor" – to Muhammad. It is as an Islamic system of government, considered by believers to be a divinely sanctioned religious monarchy that invests power in the hands of the caliph, a supreme religious and political leader and 'successor' to Muhammad, who has the sole authority to declare *jihad* and to interpret Islamic texts – Friedland, E. *Special Report: The Islamic State*. Report prepared by Clarion Project, 10 May 2015, pg 22. https://clarionproject.org/the-islamic-state-isis-isil/. Accessed 15/10/2018.

[29] UN Commission on Human Rights, *Report submitted by the Special Rapporteur on freedom of religion or belief, in accordance with Commission on Human Rights resolution 2002/40*, 15 January 2003, E/CN.4/2003/66, par 96.

[30] UNCHR *Resolution 2002/40* (2003) par 96.

resulted in 'Islamophobia' and consequent religious persecution of Muslim believers in some 'Western' countries where such terrorist attacks are prevalent.[31] Marshall observes that:

> Muslims in North America and elsewhere have a legitimate concern that raising the question of Islamic persecution of Christians can contribute to already present anti-Muslim and anti-Arab prejudice.[32]

Islamic extremism and religion-related terrorism have caused Muslims the world over to become more 'Islamic' out of fear that extremists may take over their areas or sleeper cells may awake in their region.[33] According to *World Watch Research*:

> Muslims are outwardly at least becoming more fundamentalist. Islamic State is radicalizing the population even in countries where it has no presence, but especially where is nearby... However, there is a countertrend as many Muslims search for a new identity as they turn away in disgust from extremism.[34]

It is primarily for this reason that the international community has heeded the warning to society not to equate any religion as such with religious extremism or religion-related terrorism.[35] In characterising the nature of the severe human rights abuses committed against minority religions and dissenting Muslims in Iraq and Syria, the UNSC exclaims that "terrorism, including the actions of ISIL [*Daesh*], cannot and should not be associated with any religion, nationality, or civilization".[36] In support of such an interpretation, Bielefeldt emphasises that "religious intolerance does not directly originate from religions themselves, but always presupposes the intervention of human beings".[37] Essentially this means that although the extremist ideology of *Da'esh* is based on a fundamentalist interpretation of Islamic scripture, their terrorist actions, crimes and human rights abuses

---

[31] UNCHR *Resolution 2002/40* (2003) par 96.
[32] Marshall, P. *Persecution of Christians in the Contemporary World*. International Bulletin of Missionary Research, Vol. 22 issue 1 (1998), pg 2.
[33] Open Doors Analytical / World Watch Research Unit. *World Watch List 2016: Compilation 2 - Long version of all 50 country persecution dynamics*, January, 2016, pg 13. http://opendoorsanalytical.org/wp-content/uploads/2014/10/WWL-2016-Compilation-2-Long-profiles-Edition-2016-02-01.pdf. Accessed 12/08/2016.
[34] World Watch Research Unit. *World Watch List* (2016) 13.
[35] Par 13 of the *UNGA Res. Discrimination based on Religion* (2009).
[36] UNSC *Resolution 2170* (2014) 1.
[37] Bielefeldt *FORB: Thematic Reports* (2017) 345.

"speaks for no religion".[38] Others maintain that there are actually concurrent, competing interpretations of Islam and that Islamic extremists may, with some right, claim the example of their ultimate model, Muhammad, as much as others do. Of course, this should in no way be construed as condoning the acts of terrorism, or blaming such actions on a religion, *per se*. Consequently, it is suggested that the concern is not fundamentalism, *per se*, in the sense of returning to the origins or roots of a religion; the threat comes from the core of such ancient roots and how such a fundamentalist approach may be misused to indoctrinate others and achieve an ulterior, political, religious, or other motives.

In conclusion, it has been shown that religious extremism has an adversely detrimental effect on both the victims of such intolerant violence as well as for those associated with the religion in whose name such acts are committed. Contemporarily, Islamic extremism and related terrorism have been the source of global fear, violence and hatred. At the foreground of such recent Islamic extremism are the extremist ideology and actions of the group called *Da'esh*.

3. The Evolution of *Da'esh*

The declaration of an Islamic caliphate and the subsequent enforcement of an extremist Islamic ideology, sectarian violence, and extensive human rights abuses at the hands of Islamic extremists in northern Iraq and Syria, have been at the forefront of international human rights concern in recent years. It is clear that a course of conduct that constitutes gross human rights abuses, especially the mass-killing, forced displacement and other forms of persecution against religious minorities, may be attributed to Islamic extremists in that area. It has led to destabilisation in the region, threatening regional and international peace and security.[39] The two main groups responsible for the atrocities in northern Iraq and Syria are the Al-Nusrah Front for the People of the Levant (ANF) and *Da'esh*. The latter group will form the topic of discussion for this case study. In the discussion, the following aspects will be considered: the emergence and evolution of the

---

[38] Statement by President Barack Obama, Martha's Vineyard, Massachusetts on 20 August 2014. http://www.whitehouse.gov/the-press-office/2014/08/20/statement-president. 22/08/2014.

[39] UN Security Council, *Security Council resolution 2379 (2017)* [*on establishment of an Investigative Team to Support Domestic Efforts to Hold the Islamic State in Iraq and the Levant Accountable for Its Actions in Iraq*], 21 September 2017, S/RES/2379 (2017).

Appendix C

armed group, the nature of its organisational structure, its sources of funding, armaments and propaganda, and the international response with the emphasis on seeking justice.

3.1. The emergence of *Da'esh*

Da'esh originated from a Jordanian-led extremist group '*Jamaat al-Tahwid wa-i-Jihad*' (JTWJ), founded by Abu Musab al-Zarqawi in 1999.[40] Under Zarqawi's leadership, JTWJ was a prominent insurgency force against the 2003 invasion of Iraq by a United States-led coalition that overthrew the authoritarian government of Saddam Hussein.[41] JTWJ officially pledged allegiance to *al-Qaeda* core in 2004 and became commonly known as *al-Qaeda* in Iraq (AQI), participating in the Iraq War.[42] Although technically subordinate to *al-Qaeda* core, Zarqawi's fighters acted with practical autonomy, developing its own ultraviolent brand of *jihad*, engaging in a variety of terrorist attacks, including mass casualty attacks against civilians using suicide bombings and improvised explosive devices (IEDs).[43] Consequently, the group and all its subsequent formations have been listed as a terrorist organisation on the UN Security Council Sanction List.[44]

Before Zarqawi's demise in 2006, he subsumed several smaller Iraqi *jihadi* factions with the focus on developing the infrastructure necessary to enforce *Sharia* law (Islamic religious law) at State level in Iraq, prompting a name change to the Islamic State in Iraq (ISI).[45] ISI's concerted efforts to gain territory and enforce *Sharia* in the desert region of Anbar province

---

[40] Friedland Clarion project *Special Report: The Islamic State* (2015) 7.
[41] Friedland Clarion project *Special Report: The Islamic State* (2015) 7.
[42] Friedland Clarion project *Special Report: The Islamic State* (2015) 7. Their formal name was 'Al-Qaeda in the Land of the Two Rivers' (the Tigris and the Euphrates).
[43] UN Security Council, *Letter dated 13 November 2014 from the Chair of the Security Council Committee pursuant to resolutions 1267 (1999) and 1989 (2011) concerning Al-Qaida and associated individuals and entities addressed to the President of the Security Council*, 14 November 2014, S/2014/815. (2014), par 11.
[44] UN Security Council, *Security Council resolution 2253 (2015) [on renaming of Al-Qaida Sanctions Committee as "1267/1989/2253 ISIL (Da'esh) and Al-Qaida Sanctions Committee" and the Al-Qaida Sanctions List as "ISIL (Da'esh) and Al-Qaida Sanctions List" and on extension of the mandate the Office of the Ombudsperson for a period of 24 months from the date of expiration of its current mandate in Dec. 2017]*, 17 December 2015, S/RES/2253 (2015). *Da'esh* has also been classified a terrorist organisation by the European Union and its member States, the United States, Russia, India, Turkey, Saudi Arabia and many other countries.
[45] Friedland Clarion project *Special Report: The Islamic State* (2015) 8–9.

met with opposition by the local population, which led to ISI being dispelled from the region.[46]

In 2010, Abu Bakr al-Baghdadi assumed control of ISI in pursuit of the group's first goal, which was to establish a State based on extremist ideology covering Sunny majority parts of Iraq.[47] The group's consequent rapid ascension in Iraq was mostly due to the unstable and violent environment after a protracted armed conflict following the invasion of Iraq in 2003.[48] Their initial goal of *de facto* control in Iraq increased with the group extending its operations into the Syrian Arab Republic in 2013. However, rather than focussing "on defeating the regime of Bashar al-Assad, they focussed on building their Islamic state".[49] This prompted yet another name change to the Islamic State in Iraq and Syria (ISIS) or Islamic State of Iraq and al-Shame (the Levant – ISIL).[50] Following an internal power struggle regarding the group's *jihadist* efforts in Syria, *al-Qaeda* command publicly repudiated ISIL.[51]

During the course of 2013 and 2014, ISIL seized and consolidated territory in Syria, establishing its stronghold with total control in Raqqa.[52] Meanwhile in Iraq, ISIS took parts of Fallujah in January 2014,[53] and Mosul, Iraq's second largest city, in early June.[54] The fall of Mosul to ISIS marked a major step in its organisational development and allowed easier movement between Syria and Iraq. Their control of much of the Iraqi/Syrian border bolstered their propaganda and facilitated the flow of foreign terrorist fighters.[55]

---

[46] Friedland Clarion project *Special Report: The Islamic State* (2015) 9.
[47] UNSC S/2014/815 (2014) par 11.
[48] UN Human Rights Council, *Report of the Office of the United Nations High Commissioner for Human Rights on the human rights situation in Iraq in the light of abuses committed by the so-called Islamic State in Iraq and the Levant and associated groups*, 13 March 2015, A/HRC/28/18.
[49] Friedland Clarion project *Special Report: The Islamic State* (2015) 6.
[50] Friedland Clarion project *Special Report: The Islamic State* (2015) 10.
[51] Dettmer, J. *Al-Qaeda Denounces Syrian Jihadis*. The Daily Beast, 2 March 2014. https://www.thedailybeast.com/al-qaeda-denounces-syrian-jihadis. Accessed 12/10/2018.
[52] Friedland Clarion project *Special Report: The Islamic State* (2015) 11.
[53] Al-Jazeera news. *Iraq government loses control of Fallujah.* (4 January 2014). https://www.aljazeera.com/news/middleeast/2014/01/iraq-government-loses-control-fallujah-20141414625597514.html. Accessed 12/10/2018.
[54] Al-Salhy, S. & Arango, T. *Sunni Militants Drive Iraqi Army Out of Mosul.* The New York Times, 10 June 2014. https://www.nytimes.com/2014/06/11/world/middleeast/militants-in-mosul.html. Accessed 12/10/2018.
[55] UNSC S/2014/815 (2014) par 14.

Appendix C

On June 29, 2014, the first day of Ramadan, ISIS formalised its *de facto* authority by declaring its intention of secession. Under the leadership of Abu Bakr al-Baghdadi, whom it referred to as Caliph Ibrahim (a would-be successor to Mohammed), ISIS claimed the territories under its control in Iraq and Syria as part of an Islamic caliphate. With the proclamation of a pure State of Islam, the group ascended above a territorial claim and consequently referred to itself as *Dawla al-Islamiya (Da'esh)*, or the Islamic State. These events were significant in the context of *Sharia* law, considering that no Muslim group or organisation is authorised to wage military *jihad* unless it wields political authority in an independent piece of land.[56] As the self-proclaimed supreme religious leader of the entire Muslim community, al-Baghdadi claimed authority over, and allegiance of, the entire Muslim world.[57] Despite its claim to statehood being rejected throughout the international community and mainstream Muslim groups, several *jihadist* groups swore their allegiance to Abu Bakr al-Baghdadi,[58] with the most notable perhaps being *Boko Haram*, based in Nigeria.[59] Throughout the following months, *Da'esh* emerged as the "world's most committed and fanatical radical organization".[60] The report of the *Analytical Support and Sanctions Monitoring Team* stated that:

> the scale of the threat posed by [Da'esh] is qualitatively and quantitatively different because of the nexus between the funding of ISIL and its control over significant population and territory and the thousands of foreign terrorist fighters... that have joined.[61]

Consequently, the armed group quickly became a global threat to international peace and security based on its terrorist acts, its violent extremist ideology, its continued gross, systematic and widespread attacks directed against civilians, its violations of international humanitarian law and

---

[56] Ghamidi, J.A. *The Islamic Law of Jihad*. Studying Islam website: http://www.studying-islam.org/articletext.aspx?id=771. Accessed 20/08/2014.
[57] Friedland Clarion project *Special Report: The Islamic State* (2015) 11.
[58] Friedland Clarion project *Special Report: The Islamic State* (2015) 23.
[59] On 7 March 2015, *Boko Haram* swore formal allegiance to ISIL, giving ISIL an official presence in Nigeria, Niger, Chad and Cameroon. – Elbagir, N. et al. *Boko Haram purportedly pledges allegiance to ISIS*. CNN, 9 March 2015. https://edition.cnn.com/2015/03/07/africa/nigeria-boko-haram-isis/. Accessed 12/10/2018.
[60] World News – RT International. *All you need to know about ISIS and what is happening in Iraq*. (2 July 2015). https://www.rt.com/news/166836-isis-isil-al-qaeda-iraq/. Accessed 12/10/2018.
[61] UNSC S/2014/815 (2014) 5.

abuses of human rights, particularly those committed against women and children, and including those motivated by religious or ethnic grounds.[62]

3.2. Military and leadership structures

Da'esh started to become a self-sufficient and sophisticated military organisation in control of increasing swathes of populated areas in Syria and Iraq.[63] At the time, it functioned under responsible command and had a hierarchical structure with a central command under the supreme and absolute leadership of al-Baghdadi.[64] Baghdadi's immediate two deputies were responsible for the areas under control in Syria and Iraq, respectively.[65] *Da'esh's* top structure tasked to run the caliphate were dominated by foreign fighters.[66] It included a cabinet of advisors, ministers and military commanders, each with specific areas of responsibility.[67] It depended on a network of regional and local emirs and military commanders to enforce strict discipline amongst its ranks and ensure full territorial control.[68] The expansion of its territories required support and dependence upon its centralised military leadership in coordinating large redeployments of fighters and equipment to different frontlines.[69]

The armed group was fully committed to exercising effective control over the areas under its control. It spent considerable energy and resources on building the institutions and infrastructure of statehood in order to provide services to the population.[70] In the conquered northeastern Syrian city of Raqqa, the group established its *de facto* capital.[71] Each of its regions had a governor responsible for administration,[72] operating a

---

[62] UNSC *Resolution 2379* (2017) 1.
[63] OHCHR *Rule of Terror* (2014) 2–3.
[64] Council of Europe, Committee on Legal Affairs and Human Rights report to the Parliamentary Assembly, presented by the Rapporteur, Omtzigt, P. *Prosecuting and punishing the crimes against humanity or even possible genocide committed by Daesh.* Doc. 14167, Reference 4251 of 25 November 2016, pg 6.
[65] Friedland Clarion project *Special Report: The Islamic State* (2015) 18.
[66] Friedland Clarion project *Special Report: The Islamic State* (2015) 17.
[67] "Treasury, transport, security and prisoners all have their own ministry and there is also a minister in charge of looking after the needs of foreign *jihadi* fighters". – Friedland Clarion project *Special Report: The Islamic State* (2015) 18.
[68] OHCHR *Rule of Terror* (2014) par 13.
[69] OHCHR *Rule of Terror* (2014) par 13.
[70] Friedland Clarion project *Special Report: The Islamic State* (2015) 18.
[71] Friedland Clarion project *Special Report: The Islamic State* (2015) 18.
[72] Friedland Clarion project *Special Report: The Islamic State* (2015) 18.

primitive administrative system with morality and general police, courts, and bodies to manage recruitment, tribal relations and education, as well as some basic services made possible by its financial resources.[73]

3.3. Resources and funding

Da'esh boasted a diversity of funding streams, which it used to finance terrorist activities and armed assaults directly and on a daily basis. The territorial gains in Iraq greatly increased its resources and allowed the group to expand further into eastern Syria, where the protracted conflict and consequent power vacuum provided further funding opportunities.[74] It seized considerable assets from the areas that it conquered, as well as "benefits from a substantial continuing revenue flow gained from a range of sources, including the sale of crude oil, kidnapping for ransom, extortion and... donations".[75] Other revenue streams included the looting and sale of antiquities, the sale of wheat, the trafficking of women and children,[76] bank robbery,[77] and 'taxation' through the payment of *jizya*.[78] Over time, *Da'esh* became the world's wealthiest terrorist organisation.[79] The declaration of a caliphate and the group's 'spectacular' military successes attracted further foreign financial and material support, including foreign fighters.[80] In addition to its 'romanticised propaganda', the availability of vast resources allowed *Da'esh* to pay fighters generously, further attracting recruits.[81]

> The group's ideology and financial capabilities found resonance among socially and economically desperate communities. Locally, it exploited the gradual empowerment of the most radical armed groups and the existing social fragmentations along sectarian and tribal lines to secure a new network of alliances among local and external supporters.[82]

---

[73] Council of Europe *Omtzigt report on Da'esh crimes* (2016) 6.
[74] Council of Europe *Omtzigt report on Da'esh crimes* (2016) 5.
[75] UNSC *S/2014/815* (2014) par 52.
[76] UNSC *S/2014/815* (2014) 20.
[77] Council of Europe *Omtzigt report on Da'esh crimes* (2016) 5.
[78] Author unknown, *Convert, pay tax, or die, Islamic State warns Christians*. The Guardian. Reuters. http://www.theguardian.com/world/2014/jul/18/isis-islamic-state-issue-ultimatum-to-iraq-christians. Accessed 20/08/2014.
[79] Sources referred to in the UNSC *S/2014/815* (2014) 9 included: Macias, A. & Bender, J. *Here's how the world's richest terrorist group makes millions every day*. Business Insider, 27 August 2014; and Lock, H. *How ISIS became the wealthiest terror group in history*. The Independent, 15 September 2014.
[80] Council of Europe *Omtzigt report on Da'esh crimes* (2016) 6.
[81] Council of Europe *Omtzigt report on Da'esh crimes* (2016) 5.
[82] OHCHR *Rule of Terror* (2014) par 9.

3.4. Da'esh propaganda

The propaganda arm of *Da'esh* featured an effective use of modern communications, particularly social media and videos for the purposes of recruitment and fundraising.[83] This seems somewhat ironic and counter-intuitive for an organisation premised on a fundamentalist ideology that condemns any *bid'ah* (innovation) as un-Islamic. Nevertheless, their propaganda strategy employed distinct tactics,[84] with specific anticipated consequences:

> By publicising its brutality, the so-called ISIS seeks to convey its authority over its areas of control, to show its strength to attract recruits, and to threaten any individuals, groups or States that challenge its ideology.[85]

The intimidation strategy directed at civil society was intended to pacify the areas they control.[86] Their *modus operandi* was based on instigating a regime of fear and indoctrination by conducting public executions, a relentless assault on basic freedoms, and violent punishments in order to ensure the submission of communities under its control.[87] Religious and ethnic minorities and women felt the greatest impact of the armed group's discriminatory and inhumane treatment. It utilised the propaganda value of fear to discourage the sources of dissent with extreme violence.[88] The systematic targeting of activists, non-governmental organisation workers and journalists resulted in most of them fleeing from the region.[89]

Da'esh actively promoted their egregious violations, abuses and crimes through the dissemination of publications, photographs, social media, and video footage, which further served to humiliate victims and their families.[90] The widely disseminated violent images of executions, beheadings and stonings, served to attract many new recruits, from the region and beyond.[91]

---

[83] OHCHR *Rule of Terror* (2014) par 18.
[84] For a more detailed discussion of various propaganda tactics, see Human Rights Watch. *A Face and a Name: Civilian Victims of Insurgent Groups in Iraq*. 3 October 2005, E1709, pg 20–22. https://www.hrw.org/report/2005/10/02/face-and-name/civilian-victims-insurgent-groups-iraq. Accessed 06/04/2016.
[85] OHCHR *Rule of Terror* (2014) par 3.
[86] Friedland Clarion project *Special Report: The Islamic State* (2015) 19.
[87] OHCHR *Rule of Terror* (2014) 2–4.
[88] Friedland Clarion project *Special Report: The Islamic State* (2015) 19.
[89] OHCHR *Rule of Terror* (2014) par 19.
[90] OHCHR *Rule of Terror* (2014) par 2.
[91] OHCHR *Rule of Terror* (2014) par 18.

3.5. Arms and ammunition

At the height of its power, the armed group was particularly well-armed.[92] Apart from intercepting arms and material intended for moderate groups,[93] Da'esh had extensive supplies of heavy weapons seized from Iraqi armed forces and (to a lesser extent) the Syrian Arab Republic. Weapons and ammunition had also been smuggled primarily by routes that run through Turkey.[94] The internal conflicts in Iraq and Syria generated a significant rise in the demand for arms, resulting in an extensive economy of arms dealing, layered on top of existing traditions of weapon ownership amongst sections of the rural population.[95] The armed group's arsenal included an array of weaponry,[96] wielded by fighters "with experience in conventional warfare [and] who are well-versed on a range of weapons systems, including the use of tanks and artillery".[97]

3.6. In pursuit of justice for Da'esh offences

Initially, the international community seriously underestimated the threat posed by Da'esh, which allowed it to rapidly rise and expand before international intervention gained any momentum.[98] In response to its rapid territorial gains and the commission of acts that amounted to international crimes, multinational military intervention intensified. Subsequent to their loss of control of Mosul in July 2017, the group continued to lose territory to the various States and other military forces allied against it,[99] until it controlled no meaningful territory in Iraq by November 2017.

---

[92] UNSC S/2014/815 (2014) par 37.
[93] Council of Europe *Omtzigt report on Da'esh crimes* (2016) 5.
[94] UNSC S/2014/815 (2014) par 37.
[95] UNSC S/2014/815 (2014) par 38.
[96] Da'esh assets included light weapons, assault rifles, machine guns, heavy weapons, including possible man-portable air defence systems (MANPADS) (SA-7), field and anti-aircraft guns, mines, missiles, rockets, rocket launchers, artillery, aircraft, tanks (including T-55s and T-72s) and vehicles, including high-mobility multipurpose military vehicles, and other light and armoured vehicles to sustain highly mobile tactics – UNSC S/2014/815 (2014) par 41–42.
[97] Conflict Armament Research, *Islamic State weapons in Iraq and Syria: analysis of weapons and ammunition captured from Islamic State forces in Iraq and Syria*, dispatch from the field (London, September 2014) – in UNSC S/2014/815 (2014) par 37.
[98] Council of Europe *Omtzigt report on Da'esh crimes* (2016) 5.
[99] Iraqi and Syrian forces, supported by a US-led anti-ISIS coalition, Iran, and Russia (anti-ISIS forces) had been the primary role-players – Human Rights Watch. *Flawed Justice - Accountability for ISIS Crimes in Iraq*. 4 December 2017, pg 1.

On 9 December 2017, Iraq's Prime Minister Haider al-Abadi said that "Iraqi forces had driven the last remnants of Islamic State from the country, three years after the militant group captured about a third of Iraq's territory".[100] Consequently, at the end of 2017, *Da'esh* was 'territorially' defeated and the war in Iraq was declared over. On the 23rd of March 2019, the Syrian Democratic Forces announced that *Da'esh* had lost its final stronghold in Syria, bringing an end to the so-called caliphate declared in 2014.[101] Unfortunately, the group's existence has not been completely erased as it still maintains a scattered presence and sleeper cells across Syria and Iraq. *Al Jazeera* reports that:

> ISIL affiliates in Egypt's Sinai Peninsula, Afghanistan and other countries continue to pose a threat, and the group's ideology has inspired so-called lone-wolf attacks that had little if any connection to its leadership.[102]

With the fog of war lifting, the primary attention has shifted towards supporting the victims and bringing *Da'esh* fighters and leadership to justice for their atrocities. Contextually, this case study will focus on those crimes, atrocities and human rights breaches, which "had a common specific intention to destroy certain religious groups in the region".[103]

4. *Da'esh* Ideology

An essential aspect in assessing *Da'esh's* conduct is an understanding of the religious ideology that underpins the group's motives. Although the armed group's actions are motivated and justified by their repudiated interpretation of Islam, this case study and the related discussion is in no way an assimilation of the group's ideology with Islamic theology. It should be reiterated that the following discussion is not the writings of a scholar in

---

https://www.hrw.org/sites/default/files/report_pdf/iraq1217web.pdf. Accessed 15/10/2018.

[100] The Age. *Islamic State completely 'evicted' from Iraq, Iraqi PM says.* 10 December 2017. https://www.theage.com.au/world/islamic-state-completely-evicted-from-iraq-iraqi-pm-says-20171210-h01x2r.html. Accessed 12/10/2018.

[101] CNN website. *ISIS Fast Facts.* https://edition.cnn.com/2014/08/08/world/isis-fast-facts/index.html. Accessed 04/05/2019.

[102] Al-Jazeera news. *ISIL defeated in final Syria victory: SDF.* 23 March 2019. https://www.aljazeera.com/news/2019/03/isil-defeated-syria-sdf-announces-final-victory-190323061233685.html. Accessed 04/05/2019.

[103] Ochab, E. U. *Bringing Daesh To Justice – A Real Action At Last?* Forbes, 21 September 2017. https://www.forbes.com/sites/ewelinaochab/2017/09/21/bringing-daesh-to-justice-real-action-at-last/#1fc093c32622. Accessed 12/10/2018.

Appendix C

the field of Islamic studies, but rather a rudimentary discussion based on observations from relevant sources. These observations will include a short background on the inter-denominational hostility between Sunnis and Shias, the disagreement regarding the interpretation and legitimacy of *jihad*, and *Da'esh's* doctrinally motivated ideology based on an extremist interpretation of *Sharia* law.

4.1. Inter-denominational hostility between Sunnis and Shias

In the view of Muslim theology, the prophet Muhammad received his first divine revelations of Allah's message in Mecca, in or around the year 610 A.D. Since those early days, Islam was also meant to be a political ideology "connecting all those who profess the Islamic faith in a political community, the *umma*".[104] Islam, as a religious and political ideology, unified all its followers under a single 'nation' – the brotherhood of Muslims – with the ultimate goal that Islam would encompass the divine faith of all mankind to "bring the whole world under Islamic rule and to establish peace and order according to Islamic justice".[105]

However, at the time of prophet Muhammad's unexpected death (632 A.D.), the Muslim community (*umma*) was left "without a codified text of the Koran, without a completed compilation of tradition, without a systematic Islamic law set down in writing, and without a regulation of the succession in the leadership".[106] Consequently, during the early development of Islam immediately following the death of Muhammad, internal disagreements resulted in the rise of three major religious denominations within Islam: Sunnis, Shias (Shiites) and Kharijites.[107] These three traditional schools of thought in Islam differ in terms of their theological and jurisprudential interpretation of the primary sources of *Sharia* law, viz. the *Qur'an* (Koran) and the *Sunna* (sayings and tradition of the Prophet).[108] Within each of these traditional groups, further sub-

---

[104] Mahmoudi, S. *Islamic approach to international law. Max Planck Encyclopedia on Public International law*, Wolfrum, R. (ed), Max Planck Institute for Comparative Public Law and International Law, Heidelberg. Published by Oxford University Press (2011) 388.
[105] Mahmoudi *Islamic approach to international law* (2011) 388.
[106] Schirrmacher, C. *Islam: An Introduction*. Volume 6 of Global Issues Series, World Evangelical Alliance. Verlag für Kultur und Wissenschaft Culture and Science Publ. Bonn (2011), pg 51.
[107] Schirrmacher *Islam: An Introduction* (2011) 51–54.
[108] Mahmoudi *Islamic approach to international law* (2011) 388–389.

divisions emerged.¹⁰⁹ The Shia community constitutes a minority of approximately 10–15% of all Muslims worldwide, with Iran the only country in which the Shiite school of Islam is the State religion.¹¹⁰ Sunnis comprise the largest denomination of Islam worldwide. Within the Arab peninsula, the most notable countries where Sunni'ism constitutes the dominant religious denomination include Saudi Arabia, Egypt, Sudan, and Jordan. Relevantly, Syria has historically had a mosaic of diverse faiths, with the majority being Sunni Muslims, followed by Shia Muslims and other religious minorities. In Iraq, Shia communities constitute the dominant religious group followed by Sunni'ism, Christianity and Yazidism. Christine Schirrmacher notes that:

> As a rule, a rivalry exists between Sunnis and Shiites, indeed, in part, a bitter hostility. Both groups pray in most cases only in their own mosques, and consider some faith convictions of the other group as heresy.¹¹¹

This tension between Shias and Sunnis is probably most evident in the modern-day Kingdom of Saudi Arabia, where the State is deeply intertwined with the Saudi religious establishment's interpretation of Islam.¹¹² The Islamic State doctrine of Saudi Arabia is based on *Wahhabism*, the doctrine of Mohammed Ibn Abd al-Wahhab.¹¹³ Human Rights Watch has documented the Saudi-State's toleration of the incitement of hatred against Shia Muslims and others who do not conform to their views.¹¹⁴ Such 'anti-Shia' hate speech has had fatal consequences when extremist armed groups, including *Da'esh*, employ such sentiments to motivate and justify violence directed at Shia communities.

> ISIS has carried out attacks against six Shia mosques and religious buildings in Saudi Arabia's Eastern Province and Najran, killing over 40 individuals. ISIS press releases claiming these attacks stated that the attackers were targeting 'edifices of shirk' and rafidha, which is the same language used by Saudi religious scholars and Ministry of Education textbooks in describing

---

[109] Contemporarily, there are few remaining Kharijite-related groups and they will therefore not form part of this discussion.
[110] Schirrmacher *Islam: An Introduction* (2011) 53.
[111] Schirrmacher *Islam: An Introduction* (2011) 54.
[112] Human Rights Watch. *"They Are Not Our Brothers" Hate Speech by Saudi Officials.* September 2017, pg 11. https://www.hrw.org/report/2017/09/26/they-are-not-our-brothers/hate-speech-saudi-officials. Accessed 15/10/2018.
[113] Friedland Clarion project *Special Report: The Islamic State* (2015) 13.
[114] Human Rights Watch *"They Are Not Our Brothers"* (2017) 1.

Shia citizens... ISIS has employed similar justifications for attacking Shia civilians and religious sites in Kuwait, Lebanon, Syria, and Iraq.[115]

It is therefore clear that even within the Islamic faith, there are many interpretational differences between the different denominations that exist today, which often results in intra-denominational persecution.

4.2. Interpreting and justifying *jihad*

The exact meaning of the term *jihad* depends on context, but directly translated it means 'struggling' or 'striving' in the way of Allah.[116] The obedience of a call to *jihad* is an important religious duty for Muslims. A Muslim engaged in *jihad* is referred to as a *mujahid*, or *mujahideen* for plural.

There are two main dimensions of *jihad*. On the one hand, ṣabr or *jihād al-nafs* (the internal, spiritual struggle against the lower self) emphasises the internal dimension of *jihad*, which "refers to the practice of 'patient forbearance' by Muslims in the face of life's vicissitudes and toward those who wish them harm".[117] Thus, in the religious and ethical realm, *jihad* implies the human struggle and suffering associated with promoting what is right and preventing what is wrong in the eyes of Islam.

On the other hand, *qitāl* or *jihād al-sayf* (the physical combat with the sword) implies a form of self-defence through "a verbal and discursive struggle against those who reject the message of Islam".[118] This understanding of 'jihad' has resulted in the term being translated in the West as 'holy war'. Islamic jurists concur that *jihad* is a defensive act and constitutes the only legitimate form of warfare permissible under Islamic law.[119]

> Throughout Islamic history, wars against non-Muslims, even when motivated by political and secular concerns, were termed jihads to grant them religious legitimacy. During and since that time, Islamist extremists have used the rubric of jihad to justify violent attacks against Muslims whom they accuse of apostasy.[120]

---

[115] Human Rights Watch *"They Are Not Our Brothers"* (2017) 4.
[116] Mahmoudi *Islamic approach to international law* (2011) 391.
[117] Afsaruddin, A. *Jihad – Islam*. Encycloaedia Britannica, last updated on 15 January 2019. https://www.britannica.com/topic/jihad. Accessed 01/02/2019.
[118] Afsaruddin *Jihad* (2019).
[119] Mahmoudi *Islamic approach to international law* (2011) 391.
[120] Afsaruddin *Jihad* (2019).

In the context of a global fear of Islamic extremism, the lack of an unequivocal interpretation of what justifies a militant version of *jihad*[121] is a particularly problematic question of methodology.[122] An armed *jihad* is justified as a form of "defense against aggression against, the suppression of, and the threat to the Muslim '*umma*', the community, by its enemies".[123] Disconcertingly, what constitutes a 'threat' to, or 'suppression' of, the Muslim community is in the proverbial 'eye of the beholder'. As understood in the context of Islamic fundamentalism and extremism, '*jihad*' provides religious legitimacy to justify sectarian violence against opposing Muslim ideologies, unbelievers, and apostates and dissenters renouncing the authority of Islam.[124] Thus, an extremist interpretation of Islam is used to justify indiscriminate terror and suicide attacks, even against women and children, in the name of Islam.[125] Consequently, Celso notes that modern terror movements or extremists groups aim to:

> ...create an authentic Islam stripped of foreign liberal influence and modern jihadists believe they have divine sanction to engage in violence against apostate regimes. This includes killing all apostates and infidels that hinder the development of a purified ummah. Death is welcomed as an opportunity for martyrdom and slaughter of Islam's enemies becomes a moral imperative.[126]

Paul Berman's[127] interpretation of the work of the Muslim Brotherhood's theorist and inspiring source of *al-Qaeda*, Sayyid Qutb, concludes that modern military *jihadists* are committing irrational offences based on a "totalitarian Islamist state and the cleansing of pernicious Western influence".[128] Schirrmacher states that:

> the Western world is considered, on the basis of its social decay and its secularization, to be immoral and fundamentally inferior, since, with its humanly made laws, it is doomed to extinction.[129]

---

[121] For an assessment of what constitutes a legitimate *jihad* in terms of Islamic law, see Mahmoudi *Islamic approach to international law* (2011) 390–394.
[122] Schirrmacher *Islam: An Introduction* (2011) 45.
[123] Schirrmacher *Islam: An Introduction* (2011) 46.
[124] Mahmoudi *Islamic approach to international law* (2011) 391.
[125] Schirrmacher *Islam: An Introduction* (2011) 45.
[126] Celso, A.N. *Jihadist Organizational Failure and Regeneration: the Transcendental Role of Takfiri Violence*. (2014), pg 2. http://www.psa.ac.uk/sites/default/files/conference/papers/2014/PSU%20presentation.pdf. Accessed 08/01/2015.
[127] Berman, P. *Terror and Liberalism* (W.W. Norton: New York, 2003).
[128] Celso *Jihadist Organizational Failure and Regeneration* (2014) 2.
[129] Schirrmacher *Islam: An Introduction* (2011) 72.

Consequently, Islam has been designated as a potentially peaceful religion or a potentially belligerent religion, depending on the interpretation of the Koran's instructions concerning the dissemination and defence of Islam.[130] Thus, it seems the basis for *Islamophobia* lies not in the nature of the religion itself, but in the militant *jihad* ideology threat that reverberates from a literalist or fundamentalist interpretation of early Islamic sources.

4.3. Da'esh's interpretation of 'jihad'

Da'esh follows an extreme interpretation of the Koran known as *Salafist Jihadism*, a belief that *jihad* in the form of violence and terrorism is justified to realise political objectives, and "to carry out radical resistance to Western aggression against Muslim peoples".[131] *Salafist Jihadism* is a subsect movement within Sunni Islam that advocates a return to the traditions of the "devout ancestors" (the *salaf*).[132] Accordingly, they enforce a pure form of Islam practised by successors to the founder of Islam, and reject any later additions as *bid'ah* (innovation) and un-Islamic.[133] *Salafism*, sometimes referred to as *Wahhabism*, is a movement that began in Egypt, with shared ideological roots of those of the Muslim Brotherhood.[134] Its *jihadist* ideology was inspired by the ideological philosophies of prominent Islamic figures, such as Ibn Taymiyya, Abu Ala Maududi, Abdullah Azzam (the father of global *jihadism*), Sayyid Qutb, and Osama bin Laden.[135] Their contribution to *jihadism* was to term anything other than strict adherence to *Sharia*, including all contemporary Muslim regimes, as *jahiliyya* or un-Islamic. Therefore, this ideology is based on an austere and violent interpretation of Islam. Within such fundamentalist Islamic theology, religious freedom and pluralism are to be regarded as "the freedom to belong to the one true religion, Islam, or to turn towards it".[136] Consequently, such Islamic extremist ideologies have remained a source of religious intolerance and discrimination, denials and deprivations of religious freedom, and religiously motivated persecution.

---

[130] Schirrmacher *Islam: An Introduction* (2011) 46.
[131] Mahmoudi *Islamic approach to international law* (2011) 392.
[132] Human Rights Watch *"They Are Not Our Brothers"* (2017) 1.
[133] Friedland Clarion project *Special Report: The Islamic State* (2015) 6.
[134] Freidland Clarion project *Special Report: The Islamic State* (2015) 13. The terms '*Salafism*' and '*Wahhabism*' are often used interchangeably because of their very close connection.
[135] Friedland Clarion project *Special Report: The Islamic State* (2015) 14.
[136] Schirrmacher, C. *Apostasy: What do contemporary Muslim theologians teach about religious freedom?* IJRF, Vol 6, Issue 1/2 (2013), pg 190.

Da'esh is not only a militant terrorist group; it also has a political aim to pursue a broader regional and global agenda.[137] Consequently, the armed group sought to change the existing political order in the Middle East by establishing the caliphate, by consolidating and expanding its control of territory in Iraq, Syria and neighbouring Sunni countries, and by expelling any foreign influence, whether political, economic or ideological.[138]

The legitimacy for pursuing regional and global dominance was based on a widely repudiated misinterpretation of Islam,[139] adorning Caliph Ibrahim with the divine authority to interpret the Islamic texts, condemn dissenting versions, call all Muslims to *jihad* against *jahiliyyah*, and enforce a religious ideology characterised by extreme acts of violence and terrorism.[140] This divine authority also enables Da'esh leadership in employing the doctrine of *takfir*, which "allows them to proclaim as *takfir* (heretics) Muslims who deviate from their strictly defined interpretation of Islam, [the penalty for which is death]".[141] Therefore, although religious minorities have endured the worst of the human rights abuses, many Sunnis who reject the group's warped, sectarian extremist ideology have also been oppressed or murdered.[142]

> The killing of infidels by any method including martyrdom [suicide] operations has been sanctified by many scholars even if it means killing innocent Muslims. This legality has been agreed upon ... so as not to disrupt jihad. The shedding of Muslim blood ... is allowed in order to avoid the greater evil of disrupting jihad.[143]

Da'esh has "made calculated use of public brutality and indoctrination to ensure the submission of communities under its control"[144] in order to achieve a '*Da'esh-isation*' of the region.[145] It has enforced a violent and ruthless interpretation of *Sharia* law, which may be perceived as a religious

---

[137] Friedland Clarion project *Special Report: The Islamic State* (2015) 6.
[138] The Analytical Support and Sanctions Monitoring Team established pursuant to UN Security Council, *Security Council resolution 1526 (2004) [on improving implementation of measures imposed by paragraph 4 (b) of resolution 1267 (1999), paragraph 8 (c) of resolution 1333 (2000) and paragraphs 1 and 2 of Resolution 1390 (2002) on measures against Al-Qaida and the Taliban]*, 30 January 2004, S/RES/1526 (2004), par 6.
[139] Friedland Clarion project *Special Report: The Islamic State* (2015) 13–16.
[140] Friedland Clarion project *Special Report: The Islamic State* (2015) 6.
[141] Friedland Clarion project *Special Report: The Islamic State* (2015) 13.
[142] UNSC S/2014/815 (2014) par 23–26.
[143] Audio recording of Abu Mus'ab al-Zarqawi reported in HRW *A face and a name* (2005) 25.
[144] OHCHR *Rule of Terror* (2014) 2.

holy war against minority religions, as well as dissenting Muslims.[146] Its fighters are authorised to target civilians if they are in some way considered to be supporting the foreign military presence, Iraqi or Syrian forces, or their allies.[147] Dissident religious groups, such as Shia Muslims, Kurds and Christians, are by virtue of their religious identity legitimate targets as 'collaborators' of foreign intervention.[148] Individuals with a perceived 'Western' identity, are likewise justifiable targets. Therefore, the armed group's actions are exclusively motivated by religious ideology, and comprise a complex and multifaceted 'attack' on all dissenting religions or religious denominations, against democracy and fundamental human rights. However, any acts or manifestations of terrorism against civilians are criminal and unjustifiable regardless of their motivations or religious justification, whenever and by whomsoever committed.[149]

Da'esh and other insurgent groups are legally bound to respect international customary law, including international humanitarian law (regardless of their adversary's behaviour),[150] as well as aspects of international human rights law, whether they recognise such a law or not.[151] Attacks on civilians may be considered as war crimes during a time of war, or may be considered as crimes against humanity or genocide, if committed in peacetime. The *Da'esh* terrorist ideology encompasses a distorted narrative that is based on the misinterpretation and misrepresentation of Islam to justify violence and glorify its discriminatory crimes and atrocities as religiously sanctified.[152]

---

[145] Cockburn, P. *The Rise of Islamic State: ISIS and the New Sunni Revolution*. Verso, London (2015).

[146] Abi-Habib, M. *Iraq's Christian Minority Feels Militant Threat*. The Wall Street Journal. 20/08/2014. https://www.wsj.com/articles/iraqs-christian minority-feels-militant-threat-1403826576. Accessed 08/01/2015.

[147] HRW *A face and a name* (2005) 23.

[148] HRW *A face and a name* (2005) 24.

[149] UNSC *Resolution 2354* (2017) 1.

[150] HRW *A face and a name* (2005) 2. In terms of the laws of war, applicable to all armed forces during an international or internal conflict, civilians may never be the object of attack, and must distinguish between civilians and combatants, and attacks that cause civilian loss must be proportionate to the expected military gain. Attacks intended primarily to spread terror among the civilian population is also prohibited. For a more detailed discussion see Henckaerts, JM. & Doswald-Beck, L. *International Committee of the Red Cross (ICRC), Customary International Humanitarian Law*. (2005).

[151] HRW *A face and a name* (2005) 2.

[152] UNSC *Resolution 2354* (2017) 2.

5. The Pattern of Abuses, Atrocities and Crimes Committed by *Da'esh*

The range of reports documenting the atrocities and crimes by *Da'esh* is enormous.[153] Numerous international reports by international governmental organisations (IGOs)[154] and NGOs[155] alike have outlined the crimes

---

[153] These include various reports by the UN Office of the High Commissioner on Human Rights on the situation in Iraq – see OHCHR website: https://www.OHCHR.org/EN/Countries/MENARegion/Pages/IQIndex.aspx. Accessed 26/10/2018. See also the work of the United Nations Assistance Mission for Iraq (UNAMI), established in 2003 by UN Security Council, *Security Council resolution 1500 (2003) [on the situation between Iraq and Kuwait]*, 14 August 2003, S/RES/1500 (2003), at the request of the Government of Iraq, and expanded in 2007 with the adoption of UN Security Council, *Security Council resolution 1770 (2007) [on extension of the mandate of the UN Assistance Mission for Iraq (UNAMI)]*, 10 August 2007, S/RES/1770 (2007). UNAMI's mandate is to advise and assist the Government and people of Iraq on a number of issues. This includes advancing inclusive political dialogue and national reconciliation, assisting in the electoral process and in the planning for a national census, facilitating regional dialogue between Iraq and its neighbours, and promoting the protection of human rights and judicial and legal reforms. Other reports focus on the situation in Syria: See OHCHR website: https://www.OHCHR.org/EN/Countries/MENARegion/Pages/SYIndex.aspx. Accessed 26/10/2018.

[154] For example, the UNSC has been responsible for listing *Da'esh* as a terrorist organisation – UNSC *Resolution 2253 (2015)*, listed *Da'esh* (Islamic State of Iraq and the Levant) as a terrorist organization, which expanded on the UNSC *Resolution 1267 (1999)* Sanctions Committee's consolidated list. This includes a comprehensive international framework to counter terrorist narratives, in particular *Da'esh* – See UNSC *Resolution 2354 (2017)*; and the *Comprehensive international framework to counter terrorist narratives*. Annex to the Letter dated 26 April 2017 from the Chair of the Security Council Committee established pursuant to resolution UN Security Council, *Security Council resolution 1373 (2001) [on threats to international peace and security caused by terrorist acts]*, 28 September 2001, S/RES/1373 (2001). The UNSC, through the work of its various organs, was also responsible for establishing a Special Investigative Team to support domestic efforts to hold members of the group accountable for its actions – UNSC *Resolution 2379 (2017)*.

[155] Some of the most important NGOs that have conducted research and reports on the crimes committed by *Da'esh*, are Human Rights Watch (Human Rights Watch website – 'Daesh': https://www.hrw.org/publications?keyword=Daesh&date%5Bvalue%5D%5Byear%5D=&country%5B%5D=9637&country%5B%5D=9648. Accessed 26/10/2018.); Amnesty International (Amnesty International reports: 'Iraq': https://www.amnesty.org/en/countries/middle-east-and-north-africa/iraq/, and 'Syria': https://www.amnesty.org/en/countries/middle-east-and-north-africa/syria/. Accessed 26/10/2018.); Genocide Watch (Genocidewatch.net – 'ISIS': http://genocidewatch.net/category/updates/byissue/isis/, and new website – genocidewatch.com – 'ISIS/DAESH': http://www.genocidewatch.com/isis-daesh.

and atrocities committed by Da'esh. While some organisations have been specifically tasked with gathering and protecting evidence of Da'esh atrocities,[156] the information and evidence held by some of these organisations are confidential, only to be shared with judicial authorities who have jurisdiction over the relevant crimes and who are competent to prosecute them.

Based on reasonable inferences drawn from these reliable sources, this thesis will implicate Da'esh in the commission of serious international crimes.[157] However, throughout the course of this book, such references

---

Accessed 26/10/2018.); and Al-Jazeera Media Network (Al Jazeera website: https://www.aljazeera.com/. Accessed 26/10/2018.).

[156] The prolonged civil war in Syria also prompted the Human Rights Council to establish the 'Independent International Commission of Inquiry on the Syrian Arab Republic' (IICISAR) on 22 August 2011. The IICISAR was established pursuant to UN Office of the High Commissioner for Human Rights (OHCHR), *Independent International Commission of Inquiry*, established pursuant to UN Human Rights Council Resolutions S-17/1, 19/22 and 21/26, 20 December 2012. The Human Rights Council has repeatedly extended the Commission's mandate. It's mandate is to investigate all alleged violations of international human rights law since March 2011 in the Syrian Arab Republic, and to identify those most responsible with a view of ensuring that such perpetrators are held accountable – About the commission of inquiry: https://www.OHCHR.org/EN/HRBodies/HRC/IICISyria/Pages/AboutCoI.aspx. Accessed 26/10/2018. A further development in the context of Da'esh has been the establishment of the 'International, Impartial and Independent Mechanism to Assist in the Investigation and Prosecution of Those Responsible for the Most Serious Crimes under International Law Committed in the Syrian Arab Republic' (IIIM-SY). Established on 21 December 2016 with the adoption of the UN General Assembly Resolution 71/248. See also Report of the Secretary-General regarding the Implementation of the resolution establishing the International, Impartial and Independent Mechanism to Assist in the Investigation and Prosecution of Persons Responsible for the Most Serious Crimes under International Law Committed in the Syrian Arab Republic since March 2011, at the Seventy-first session, 19 January 2017, A/71/755. The IIIM-SY is an *ad hoc*, mechanism established by the UN General Assembly to ensure criminal accountability for those who have committed violations of international humanitarian law and international human rights law in Syria. A similar initiative is the Commission for International Justice and Accountability (CIJA), which is non-profit organisation committed to establishing the individual criminal responsibility of high-level perpetrators implicated in the violations committed during the conflict and post-conflict areas. The institution does not have a public profile, but the writer has engaged in email correspondence with the Founder and Director of CIJA, Bill Wiley. Email address: director@cijaonline.org.

[157] HRW *Flawed Justice* (2017) 15.

should be considered as theoretical allegations, which is not equivocal to the adjudication by a competent court of law.

Evidence suggests that Da'esh fighters have committed acts of terrorism, war crimes, numerous inhumane acts constituting crimes against humanity, ethnic cleansing, and possibly genocide.[158] These crimes and atrocities were committed regardless of the independence, sovereignty, or territorial integrity of Iraq and Syria, whose fate in this regard has been intertwined. Consequently, this study will disregard aspects of territoriality and consider these acts, crimes and human rights atrocities, whether committed before, during or after the relevant armed conflicts, collectively and cumulatively as part of a pattern of offences by Da'esh. Such an assessment may be justified by the exigencies of justice in bringing the offenders to justice for the full extent of their crimes, and the moral and legal duty owed to the victims of *Daesh's* atrocities.[159]

Therefore, this section aims to briefly outline this pattern of offences by scaling, contextualising, analysing and documenting the human rights abuses, crimes and atrocities committed by *Da'esh* in terms of international law. It should be mentioned that a discussion regarding terrorism, international humanitarian law and genocide falls outside the scope of this study. However, the discussion of these crimes in this context promotes a holistic impression of the pattern of offences, and will serve an important function when considering certain elements of the taxonomy checklist. Therefore, these acts or crimes will be considered to the extent that they are relevant to establish the pattern of offences by *Da'esh*.

5.1. Acts of terror and terrorism

Terrorism constitutes an international treaty crime. Although such treaties have been unable to define terrorism comprehensively, they have identified and banned various forms of terrorism.[160] The nature of the thematic conventions has prohibited specific acts as terror, rather than attempting to

---

[158] Amnesty International, *Amnesty International Report 2014/15: The State of the World's Human Rights*, 25 February 2015, Index number: POL 10/0001/2015, pg 40. https://www.amnesty.org/en/latest/research/2015/02/annual-report-201415/. Accessed 22/10/2018.

[159] Council of Europe *Omtzigt report on Da'esh crimes* (2016) 5.

[160] International terrorism conventions include sixteen universal instruments against international terrorism comprising thirteen thematic conventions and three amendments. They include the following: UNGA *Convention on Offences and Certain Other Acts Committed on Board Aircraft* (14 Sept 1963) 704 UNTS 219; *Convention for the Suppression of Unlawful Seizure of Aircraft* (16 Dec 1970) 860 UNTS 105;

criminalise 'terrorism' in its entirety.[161] The foremost contentious issue regarding the conceptualisation of 'terrorism' is whether the actions of 'freedom fighters' engaged in national liberation movements, could be classified as terrorism.[162] In this regard, the Islamic approach has been to condemn 'terrorism' as a breach of *Sharia* principles and fundamental human rights, but it does not regard actions by national liberation movements in the struggle against foreign aggression and colonialism or racist regimes, as terrorist acts.[163]

In a general sense, the UN has codified its non-binding understanding of 'terrorism' in its resolution on the *Global Counter-Terrorism Strategy*, stating that:

Convention for the Suppression of Unlawful Acts against the Safety of Civil Aviation (23 Sept 1971) 974 UNTS 177; *Convention on the Prevention and Punishment of Crimes against Internationally Protected Persons, including Diplomatic Agents* (14 Dec 1973) 1035 UNTS 167; *International Convention against the Taking of Hostages* (17 Dec 1979) 1316 UNTS 205; *Convention on the Physical Protection of Nuclear Material* (3 March 1980) 1456 UNTS 101; *Convention for the Suppression of Unlawful Acts against the Safety of Maritime Navigation* (10 March 1988) 1678 UNTS 221; *Protocol for the Suppression of Unlawful Acts against the Safety of Fixed Platforms Located on the Continental Shelf* (3 Oct 1988) 1678 UNTS 304; *Protocol for the Suppression of Unlawful Acts of Violence at Airports Serving International Civil Aviation, supplementary to the Convention for the Suppression of Unlawful Acts against the Safety of Civil Aviation* (24 Feb 1988) 27 ILM 627; *Convention on the Marking of Plastic Explosives for the Purpose of Detection* (1 March 1991) 30 ILM 721; *International Convention for the Suppression of Terrorist Bombings*, GA Res 52/164, UN Doc A/RES/52/164 (15 Dec 1997); *International Convention for the Suppression of the Financing of Terrorism*, GA Res 54/109, UN Doc A/RES/54/109 (9 Dec 1999); *International Convention for the Suppression of Acts of Nuclear Terrorism*, GA Res 59/290, UN Doc A/ RES/59/290 (13 April 2005). The three amendments adopted in 2005 are: *Amendments to the Convention on the Physical Protection of Nuclear Material; Protocol to the Convention for the Suppression of Unlawful Acts against the Safety of Maritime Navigation* (14 Oct 2005); *and Protocol to the Protocol for the Suppression of Unlawful Acts against the Safety of Fixed Platforms Located on the Continental Shelf.*

[161] Zgonec-Rožej, M. (Principal author). *International Criminal Law Manual.* International Bar Association (IBA) (2013), pg 222.

[162] The Islamic community has codified its own resolution on terrorism. The Organization of the Islamic Conference (OIC), *Convention of the Organisation of the Islamic Conference on Combating International Terrorism*, 1 July 1999, Annex to Resolution No: 59/26-P. Art 1 defines terrorism as "any act or threat of violence carried out with the aim of, among other things, imperilling people's honour, occupying or seizing public or private property, or threatening the stability, territorial integrity, political unity or sovereignty of a state".

[163] Mahmoudi *Islamic approach to international law* (2011) 404.

acts, methods and practices of terrorism in all its forms and manifestations are activities aimed at the destruction of human rights, fundamental freedoms and democracy, threatening territorial integrity, security of States and destabilizing legitimately constituted Governments.[164]

The Counter-Terrorism Strategy acknowledges that the commission of acts of terrorism is often motivated and justified by the ideological convictions of a religious extremist organisation, but stressed that "terrorism cannot and should not be associated with any religion, nationality, civilization or ethnic group".[165]

The international community has adopted and implemented various counter-terrorism strategies at the national, regional and international levels to enhance cooperation to prevent and combat terrorism, which includes domestic efforts to prosecute returning foreign terrorist fighters.[166] Although the national jurisdictional trigger mechanisms of these conventions differ,[167] they generally oblige State parties to criminalise the specific offences and provide penalties, and to either extradite the offender or to consider the case for prosecution (*aut dedere aut judicare*).[168]

Acts of international terrorism are not restricted to national jurisdictions and may constitute international crimes if they fall within one of the established categories of crimes against humanity or war crimes over which the ICC could exercise jurisdiction.[169] Terrorist acts are not specifically included as crimes against humanity or war crimes in terms of the *Rome Statute*. However, acknowledged forms of terrorism might

---

[164] UN General Assembly, *The United Nations Global Counter-Terrorism Strategy: resolution / adopted by the General Assembly*. 20 September 2006, A/RES/60/288, pg 2.
[165] UNGA *Global Counter-Terrorism Strategy* (2006) 2.
[166] UNSC *Resolution 2178* (2014) par 4. See also UNSC *Resolution 1373* (2001). Although there have even been national prosecutions of Da'esh fighters on the basis of participating in, or otherwise being a member of, a known terrorist organization, such prosecutions fall outside the scope of this study. See Worley, W. *At least 100 European Isis fighters 'to be prosecuted in Iraq, with most facing death penalty'*. Independent, 7 October 2017. https://www.independent.co.uk/news/world/middle-east/isis-foreign-fighters-iraq-prosecuted-death-penalty-families-mosul-a7987831.html. Accessed 18/10/2018.
[167] Zgonec-Rožej *International Criminal Law Manual* (2013) 222. Most general forms of jurisdiction is based on territoriality, active nationality, or even passive nationality.
[168] Zgonec-Rožej *International Criminal Law Manual* (2013) 222.
[169] Zgonec-Rožej *International Criminal Law Manual* (2013) 227. It may also happen that terrorism may constitute a 'discrete crime'. For a further discussion in this regard, see Zgonec-Rožej *International Criminal Law Manual* (2013) 228–229.

amount to war crimes if committed in times of international or non-international armed conflict.[170] Common acts of terrorism may amount to crimes against humanity if, in addition to the specific elements of the underlying act, the terrorist acts constitute part of a widespread or systematic attack directed against any civilian population, committed with contextual knowledge.[171]

The UNSC, prompted by "ongoing and multiple criminal terrorist acts aimed at causing the deaths of civilians and other victims, destruction of property and of cultural and religious sites, and greatly undermining stability"[172] in Iraq and Syria, unanimously confirmed *Da'esh* as a terrorist organisation whose actions are considered a threat to international peace and security. The UN designated the situation in northern Iraq and Syria with its highest level of emergency, citing the scale and complexity of the situation consequential of a humanitarian crisis.[173] *Da'esh* continues to be "directly or indirectly engaged in, preparing, planning, assisting in or fostering the doing of terrorist acts or advocates the doing of terrorist acts, involving threats to human life and serious damage to property".[174] It has engaged in a variety of 'traditional' terrorist attacks, including mass casualty attacks such as suicide bombings and the use of IEDs.[175] The UNSC emphasised that the terrorist acts committed by *Da'esh*, its violent extremist ideology, and its continued gross, systematic and widespread abuses of human rights directed against civilian populations because of their ethnic or

---

[170] Zgonec-Rožej *International Criminal Law Manual* (2013) 229–230. For example, indiscriminate attacks, attacks on civilians and civilian objects, and attacks on places of worship.

[171] Zgonec-Rožej *International Criminal Law Manual* (2013) 234.

[172] UNSC *Resolution 2170* (2014) 1.

[173] UN News Centre "Adopting resolution, Security Council approves sanctions against militants in Iraq, Syria" http://www.un.org/apps/news/story.asp?NewsID=48494#.U_br6WMdMuM. Accessed 22/08/2014.

[174] As assessed by the Australian Security Intelligence Organisation. https://www.nationalsecurity.gov.au/Listedterroristorganisations/Pages/IslamicState.aspx. Accessed 19/10/2018. The assessment concludes that in the course of pursuing its objectives, the group is known to have committed or threatened actions that: cause, or could cause, death, serious harm to persons, serious damage to property, endanger life (other than the life of the person taking the action), or create a serious risk to the health or safety of the public or a section of the public; are intended to have those effects; are done with the intention of advancing the Islamic State's political, religious or ideological causes; are done with the intention of intimidating the government of one or more foreign countries; and are done with the intention of intimidating the public or sections of the public.

[175] UNSC *S/2014/815* (2014) par 11.

political background, religion or belief, may constitute crimes against humanity.[176] It was also emphasised that individuals, groups, undertakings and entities associated with *Da'esh*, must be held accountable for such breaches.

5.2. War crimes committed in Iraq and Syria

War crimes refer to serious violations of international humanitarian law, including 'grave breaches' and other serious violations of the laws and customs applicable in international or non-international armed conflict.[177] Criminal responsibility for war crimes are especially relevant to military commanders or command responsibility, whether direct or imputed responsibility,[178] and whether they command regular armed forces or a non-State armed group. The conflicts in both Iraq and Syria are covered by these principles and *Da'esh's* direct involvement in both civil wars is clearly evident.

5.2.1. Da'esh's participation in the armed conflicts

In the case of Iraq,[179] internal armed tensions escalated into civil war following *Da'esh's* insurgency and conquest of major areas of northern Iraq.[180] *Da'esh* took advantage of the instability in the protracted Syrian civil war, following an attempted *coup d'etat* by the Free Syrian Army,[181] to create a territorial and political space in which to operate.[182] The nature of both

---

[176] UNSC *Resolution 2170* (2014) 3.
[177] For more information in this regard, see Appendix A.
[178] HRW *A face and a name* (2005) 29.
[179] Disaffection with the previous Government based on weak governance, sectarian divisions and ill-prepared security forces, were some of the major factors that allowed the armed group to advance and seize large swaths of territory in the country – UNSC *S/2014/815* (2014) par 8.
[180] *Amnesty International Report 2014/15* (2015) 191.
[181] Al Jazeera News. *Syria's civil war explained from the beginning.* 14 April 2018. https://www.aljazeera.com/news/2016/05/syria-civil-war-explained-160505084119966.html. Accessed 22/10/2018. The Syrian civil war started after hundreds of demonstrators, part of a wider wave of the 2011 'Arab Spring' protests, were killed and many more imprisoned by the Syrian government, led by President Bashar al-Assad. In July 2011 Syria slid into civil was as defectors from the military announced the formation of the Free Syrian Army, a rebel group aiming to overthrow the government.
[182] UNSC *S/2014/815* (2014) par 9.

Appendix C 425

these armed conflicts is rather complicated, with foreign backing and intervention on both sides.[183] Nevertheless, it should be noted that:

> The applicability of international humanitarian law is unrelated to the nature of the armed conflict; that is, whether the war is just or unjust, lawful or unlawful, international humanitarian law still applies.[184]

The rapid military advances in Syria and Iraq, combined with its summary killings of 'western' hostages and others, prompted an international military response through the Global Coalition against Da'esh.[185] The international coalition began air strikes and increased military support and training to Iraqi government forces and Kurdish Peshmerga forces fighting against Da'esh.[186] In both conflict zones, there have been accusations that all warring partisans have committed violations of international humanitarian law, including war crimes and gross abuses of human rights.[187] However, for the purposes of this study, the focus is on the conduct and criminal responsibility of Da'esh forces.

---

[183] Al Jazeera *Syria's civil war explained from the beginning* (2018). The Assad government has been supported by regional actors, such as the governments of majority-Shia Iran and Iraq, and Lebanon-based Hezbollah, as well as international actors, most prominently Russia. Anti-Assad groups include regional support from Sunni-majority countries, including Turkey, Qatar, and Saudi Arabia. Meanwhile, other actors have directed their efforts against specific terrorist groups involved in both sides of the hostilities, such as the international coalition, with the declared purpose of countering Da'esh, having conducted airstrikes against Da'esh as well as against government and pro-government targets.

[184] HRW *A face and a name* (2005) 23.

[185] An important initiative by a collaboration of State and non-State entity partners is the 'The Global Coalition against Da'esh', formed in September 2014 – *The Global Coalition against Da'esh website*. The Coalition's 79 members comprises of States and non-state actors, such as NATO and the European Union. http://theglobalcoalition.org/en/home/. Accessed 12/10/2018. The aim of the Global Coalition is to degrade and ultimately defeat the group through a multi-strategy approach, including: exposing the group's true nature, cutting off its financing and funding, dismantling its networks, countering its global ambitions, supporting stabilisation and the restoration in the region, and supporting anti-Da'esh military operations.

[186] *Amnesty International Report 2014/15* (2015) 192.

[187] Amnesty International, *Northern Iraq: Civilians in the line of fire*, 14 July 2014, MDE 14/007/2014. Regarding the situation in Syria, see *Amnesty International Report 2014/15* (2015) 192.

5.2.2. The responsibility of Da'esh under the principles of international humanitarian law

Some have argued that the armed group is not bound by the laws of war because they did not sign the Geneva Conventions or otherwise made legal commitments to abide by international law.[188] However, Da'esh is a cohesive and coordinated group functioning under responsible command with a hierarchical structure, able to "impose a policy on its members and ensure the co-ordinated implementation of decisions made by its leadership".[189] There are thus reasonable grounds to believe that the group possess the necessary chain of command and has carried out their attacks in accordance with organisational policy.[190] The Human Rights Watch categorically states that:

> While armed opposition groups such as insurgents in Iraq are not parties to the Geneva Conventions, it has long been recognized that such groups are bound by common article 3 and customary international humanitarian law. Recourse to competing principles such as 'the ends justifies the means' or other bodies of law, such as interpretations of Islamic law, have no legal bearing on whether or not international humanitarian law has been violated. Moreover, a failure by one party to a conflict to respect the laws of war does not relieve the other of its obligation to respect those laws. That obligation is absolute, not premised on reciprocity.[191]

The principles of international humanitarian law thus apply to the armed conflicts in Iraq and Syria, whether they are characterised as international or internal armed conflicts,[192] and regardless of whether those fighting are regular armies or non-State armed groups such as Da'esh.[193] Therefore, as an 'armed group', Da'esh has violated its obligations towards civilians and persons *hors de combat*, amounting to war crimes.[194] The pattern of war crimes committed by the armed group in the region is indicative of a widespread commission of international humanitarian law violations and war

---

[188] HRW *A face and a name* (2005) 26. See in this regard Bradley, M. M. *An analysis of the notions of 'organised armed groups' and 'intensity' in the law of non-international armed conflict.* LLD thesis at the University of Pretoria (2017).
[189] OHCHR *Rule of Terror* (2014) par 76.
[190] OHCHR *Rule of Terror* (2014) par 76.
[191] HRW *A face and a name* (2005) 28-29.
[192] HRW *A face and a name* (2005) 23.
[193] HRW *A face and a name* (2005) 118.
[194] OHCHR *Rule of Terror* (2014) par 74.

crimes.¹⁹⁵ The UN High Commissioner for Human Rights concluded in its report that, based on credible evidence, a pattern of abuses of international humanitarian law had been committed by members of the group.¹⁹⁶ The violations of international humanitarian law and related war crimes committed by *Da'esh*, were deliberate and calculated based on an endorsed organisational policy, and directed against the civilian population under their control.¹⁹⁷ The commanders and fighters of the armed group have acted wilfully, perpetrating various war crimes with the clear intent of attacking persons with awareness of their civilian or *hors de combat* status.¹⁹⁸

5.3. Possible genocide against the Yazidi community

During its occupation of large swaths of territory in northern Iraq and Syria, *Da'esh* fighters drove minority ethnic and religious groups from their ancestral homes, specifically targeting the Yazidi community. Genocide Watch believes that *Da'esh*, as a genocidal terrorist organisation, has also committed genocide against Christians, Shabak Shia, Turkmen, Kurds, Kakay, and other groups.¹⁹⁹ It is not the function of this section to establish or disprove the validity of ascribing the crimes committed by *Da'esh* against ethnic and religious minorities as genocide, also considering that

---

[195] OHCHR *Rule of Terror* (2014) par 77.
[196] It included the commission of the following in one or both of the conflict zones: "Members of ISIL may have committed war crimes by perpetrating murder, mutilation, cruel treatment and torture, outrages upon personal dignity, taking of hostages, the passing of sentences and the carrying out of executions without previous judgement pronounced by a regularly constituted court, directing attacks against the civilian population, directing attacks against buildings dedicated to religion or against historic monuments, pillaging a town or place, committing rape, sexual slavery and other forms of sexual violence, conscripting or enlisting children under the age of 15 years or using them to participate actively in hostilities, ordering the displacement of the civilian population or destroying or seizing the property of an adversary". – UNHRC A/HRC/28/18 (2015) par 78.
[197] OHCHR *Rule of Terror* (2014) par 78.
[198] OHCHR *Rule of Terror* (2014) par 78.
[199] Gregory Stanton, G. *ISIS is committing genocide*. Genocide Watch website. 10 September 2015 Genocide Watch website. http://genocidewatch.net/2015/09/10/isis-is-committing-genocide/. Accessed 22/10/2018; Genocide Watch, multiple articles: See specifically http://genocidewatch.net/2015/09/10/isis-is-committing-genocide/ and Yazda, *Working Against the Clock: Documenting Mass Graves of Yazidis Killed by the Islamic State*. https://www.academia.edu/37174833/Yazda_Mass_Grave_Report_03.08.2018. Accessed 11/03/2019. http://www.genocidewatch.com/single-post/2018/08/05/YAZDA-REPORT-Commemorating-the-Fourth-Anniversary-of-the-Yazidi-Genocide. Accessed 22/10/2018.

no national or international court has made a ruling in this regard. International mechanisms, State parliaments, NGOs and even scholars have rightly been cautious in commenting on whether the group has committed the specific crime of genocide.[200] However, there does seem to be consensus within the international community that the armed group has committed genocide against the Yazidi community.[201] Such authoritative international actors include the UN High Commissioner for Human Rights,[202] the UN Special Rapporteur on minority issues,[203] as well as specialised NGOs, such as the United States Holocaust Memorial Museum.[204] The following genocidal risk factors provide evidence of a genocidal policy:[205]

- the presence of illegal arms and armed elements;
- the motivation of *Da'esh's* leading actors;
- its motivation to target a group and separate it from the rest of the population;
- its use of exclusionary ideology and construction of identities in terms of "us" and "them";
- its depiction of a targeted group as unworthy or inferior to justify action against it;
- a permissive environment created by ongoing armed conflict that could facilitate access to weapons and the commission of genocide;

---

[200] Council of Europe *Omtzigt report on Da'esh crimes* (2016) par 10.

[201] Ochab, E. U. *Netherlands joins UN Security Council to shine light on IS genocide*. January 11, 2018, World Watch Monitor. https://www.worldwatchmonitor.org/2018/01/netherlands-joins-un-security-council-shine-light-genocide/. Accessed 22/10/2018. The United Nations, the European Parliament, the Council of Europe, Canada, the United States of America, France, Armenia, Australia, Scotland and the United Kingdom, have all recognized that the crimes committed by *Da'esh* against the Yazidis amount to genocide.

[202] UN Human Rights Council, Forum on Minority Issues. *Protecting minority rights to prevent or mitigate the impact of humanitarian crisis*, speech before the 9 Ninth session of the Forum on Minority Issues on *Minorities in situations of humanitarian crises*, 24 November 2016.

[203] *Statement of the Special Rapporteur on minority issues on conclusion of her official visit to Iraq, 27 February to 7 March 2016*. https://www.ohchr.org/EN/NewsEvents/Pages/DisplayNews.aspx?NewsID=17157&LangID=E. Accessed 22/10/2018.

[204] Kikoler, N. *'Our Generation is Gone': The Islamic State's Targeting of Iraqi Minorities in Ninewa*. Bearing Witness Trip report to the Simon-Skjodt Center for the Prevention of Genocide, United States Holocaust Memorial Museum, (2015). https://www.ushmm.org/m/pdfs/Iraq-Bearing-Witness-Report-111215.pdf. Accessed 22/10/2018.

[205] Council of Europe *Omtzigt report on Da'esh crimes* (2016) 8.

- evidence of *Da'esh's* intent to destroy, in whole or in part, a particular group;
- the nature of the atrocities committed, including the systematic rape of women which may be intended to transmit a new ethnic identity to the child or to cause humiliation and terror in order to fragment the group; and
- the targeted elimination of community leaders and/or men and/or women of a particular age group (the "future generation" or a military-age group).

Consequently, this discussion will focus specifically on the Yazidi genocide, with the aim of briefly outlining *Da'esh's* discriminatory and possibly genocidal intent, as this will serve an important function in later arguments regarding 'grievous religious persecution'.

An important observation is that although *Da'esh* has sought to subjugate civilians under its control and dominate every aspect of their lives through terror, indoctrination, and the systematic denial of basic human rights and freedoms,[206] the group "does not appear to have engaged in mass targeting of civilians, but its choice of targets".[207] It is therefore clear that *Da'esh* targets specific and identifiable protected groups, which constitutes a pattern of atrocities. In this regard, *Da'esh's* proclamation of a pure State of Islam is also significant. It was explained earlier that the *Da'esh* ideology is a warped, sectarian extremist interpretation of Islam, aimed at expelling or exterminating foreign influence.[208]

> Daesh targets religious minorities in Syria and Iraq as it wants to establish a purely Islamic State and so abolish religious pluralism in the region.[209]

Therefore, *Da'esh* acts targeted any deviant religious and ethnic identities in their territory with the intention of forcing such persons to either convert to Islam, leave the region, or face summary execution.[210]

---

[206] OHCHR *Rule of Terror* (2014) par 73–74.
[207] Amnesty International *Civilians in the line of fire* (2014) 4.
[208] UNSC S/2014/815 (2014) 6.
[209] Council of Europe *Omtzigt report on Da'esh crimes* (2016) 8.
[210] OHCHR *Rule of Terror* (2014) par 24.

> The Islamic State is carrying out despicable crimes and has transformed rural areas of Sinjar into blood-soaked killing fields in its brutal campaign to obliterate all trace of non-Arabs and non-Sunni Muslims.[211]

Declaring a caliphate provided a theological justification for committing various despicable atrocities, as well as for the enforcement of the Islamic doctrine of *takfir* against Muslims who deviate from their strictly defined interpretation of Islam.[212] The religious and ethnic purification of the region was intentional and calculated, based on *Da'esh's* ideological goal to uproot any diverging religious identities and those suspected of any form of dissent.[213] The result of this ideology has been a mass exodus of religious and ethnic minorities from the region.[214] It should be noted in this regard that although the Shia community make up the majority religious group in Iraq, its population constituted a minority in the region that *Da'esh* had targeted.

The attempts to create a religiously homogenous region, a '*Da'esh-isation*' of the region, through a policy of forced conversion or displacement, constitutes 'ethnic cleansing' or crimes against humanity of forced displacement in terms of Article 7(2)(d) of the *Rome Statute*, but does not necessarily prove genocidal intent. In order to substantiate a genocidal intent requires proof of the deliberate destruction of the group, in whole or in part. The corroborated report by the *Independent International Commission of Inquiry on the Syrian Arab Republic* (IICISAR) entitled "*They came to destroy: ISIS Crimes Against the Yazidis*", provides the most credible account of the genocide by *Da'esh* against the Yazidi community of Sinjar.[215] The discussion that follows will be predominantly based on and implicitly referencing this report. In this discussion, the factual background of Yazidi genocide in Sinjar will be considered, as well as a brief outline of

---

[211] Rovera, D. Amnesty International's Senior Crisis Response Adviser, quoted in Friedland Clarion project *Special Report: The Islamic State* (2015), pg 26.
[212] Friedland Clarion project *Special Report: The Islamic State* (2015) 26.
[213] Amnesty International, 'Punished for Daesh's Crimes' – *Displaced Iraqis Abused by Militias and Government Forces*, 18 October 2016, MDE 14/4962/2016, pg 15.
[214] Amnesty International *Civilians in the line of fire* (2014) 4. The employment of the Islamic practice of *takfir* (heretic), allows a caliph to declare a *fatwa*, thereby stripping or excommunicating a fellow Muslim or a Muslim community of their Islamic status, branding them as apostates or non-believers, and providing theological justification for indiscriminate violence and killing intra-Muslim – Celso *Jihadist Organizational Failure and Regeneration* (2014) 1.
[215] UN Human Rights Council, Report of the Independent International Commission of Inquiry on the Syrian Arab Republic (IICISAR). *"They came to destroy": ISIS Crimes Against the Yazidis*, 15 June 2016, A/HRC/32/CRP.2.

the methodical treatment of different sub-categories within the Yazidi community, based on aspects such as gender and age. The section concludes with the main findings and conclusions regarding the alleged genocide against the Yazidis.

5.3.1. Factual background of the alleged Yazidi genocide in Sinjar

In June 2014, ISIS seized Mosul, rattling the Sinjar region of Nineveh province in the northern region of Iraq. Its proximity to the Syrian border constituted an area of strategical importance to the group in its cross-border operations. The region's population, predominantly Yazidi,[216] with a smaller number of Arabs who followed Sunni Islam, lived there together in peace and diversity. The Yazidi community, a distinct ancient religious minority indigenous to northern Iraq, resided in various villages and especially Sinjar town, located in the area around Mount Shingal. The Yazidi faith, which creeds and practices span thousands of years, comprises a belief in one god and their theology mostly derives from ancient Iranian religious traditions, rather than 'divine' texts. They had been subjected to cycles of persecution, at least as far back as the Ottoman Empire. Contemporarily, the Yazidis have also experienced widespread discrimination based on their faith, being labelled as 'devil-worshipping pagans' (*mushrik*). Their adherents were publicly reviled as *infidels* (heathens) by *Da'esh*, which openly said it wants to eliminate the Yazidi religion.

In the early hours of 3 August 2014, hundreds of *Da'esh* fighters swept across Sinjar in a well organised and orchestrated attack, seizing towns and villages on all sides of Mount Sinjar. Apart from a few *ad hoc* groups of lightly armed, local Yazidi men, villages were left virtually defenceless. Consequently, by the time *Da'esh* entered Sinjar, there were few military objectives in the region. Therefore, the fighters focussed their attention on capturing Yazidis, most of whom were fleeing their homes in fear and panic.

Tens of thousands fled to Mount Sinjar, where they were besieged by *Da'esh* fighters on all sides, with no chance of escape. A humanitarian crisis quickly unfolded as *Da'esh* trapped thousands of Yazidis in the scorching heat, without water, food or medical care.[217] Despite some humanitarian aid, hundreds of Yazidis died on Mount Sinjar before they could be rescued.

---

[216] In Kurdish, referred to as Êzîdi or Êzdî.
[217] UN Security Council, *Security Council resolution 2258 (2015) [on the humanitarian situation in the Syrian Arab Republic and renewal for a period of 12 months of two decisions of*

The other Yazidis who stayed in their villages or who did not flee in time were rounded up by *Da'esh* fighters, nearly emptying all villages within 72 hours of the attack. The IICISAR report notes that this military operation was again particularly calculated and efficient:

> The conduct of ISIS fighters, on capturing thousands of Yazidis as they fled, cleaved closely to a set and evidently pre-determined pattern, with only minor deviations.[218]

5.3.2. Treatment of different sub-categories within the Yazidi community

Men and women were separated and forcibly transferred to temporary holding sites designated by operational commanders. Armed fighters, operating across a vast territory in the Sinjar region, systematically separated Yazidis into three distinct groups, each of which suffered distinct and systematic violations sanctioned under *Da'esh's* ideological framework.

Most Yazidi men and boys, aged approximately 12, who refused to convert to Islam were summarily executed. Other captives, including family members, were often forced to witness the victims being gunned-down or having their throats slit.

Da'esh's treatment of Yazidi women and girls was more torturous. It was documented that at least one group of older women, approximately 60 years and older, were mass murdered. However, unmarried girls over the age of nine were forcibly separated from their mothers and siblings.

> Once a Yazidi girl reaches the age of nine, ISIS takes the girl from her mother and sells her as a slave. When a Yazidi boy reaches seven years of age, he too is taken from his mother and sent to an ISIS training camp and from there on to battle.[219]

Girls and women were deemed property of *Da'esh* and were openly termed *sabaya* or slaves. Testimony to the rigid system and ideology governing *Da'esh's* handling of Yazidi women and girls as *khums* (spoils of war), mass rape of Yazidi women and girls did not occur. Sexual violence and slavery were tightly controlled in a manner prescribed and authorised by the armed group's ideology. Most of these women and girls were sold at slave

---

Security Council resolution 2165 (2014)], 22 December 2015, S/RES/2258 (2015). The resolution notes that 393,700 civilians were trapped in besieged areas.

[218] IICISAR *They came to destroy* (2016) par 29.
[219] IICISAR *They came to destroy* (2016) par 82.

markets, or *souk sabaya*, or as individual purchases to fighters, but were not allowed to be sold to non-*Da'esh* fighters. These Yazidi women and girls were subjected to brutal sexual violence, beatings, and daily rapes.

> Once ISIS sells a Yazidi woman and girl, the purchasing fighter receives complete rights of ownership and can resell, gift, or will his 'slave' as he wishes.[220]

The precise treatment of Yazidi women was part of *Da'esh's* broader discriminatory policy that showed evidence of a possible genocidal intent:

> The enslavement of Yazidi women was undertaken as part of ISIS's attack on civilian communities considered to be infidels. Their treatment in unlawful confinement and stated motivation behind their capture and enslavement demonstrates the intent of ISIS to forcibly impregnate and thereby affect the ethnic and religious composition of the group. Undertaken as part of a widespread and systematic attack, these acts amount to the crimes against humanity of enslavement, rape and sexual violence. The nature of attacks on the Yazidis, taken together with ISIS's public statements over social media, suggests a denial of this religious group's right to exist.[221]

Although understandably heavily traumatised by their ordeal, women and girls returning from captivity have been largely embraced by the Yazidi community, following clear statements by their religious leaders that survivors remain Yazidi and are to be accepted. Unfortunately, there has been a reluctance to accept babies conceived during captivity under *Da'esh* fighters.

The younger boys and girls were mostly allowed to stay with their mothers, who were forcibly displaced from site to site. The fate and treatment of young children held with their mothers depended on the fighter-owner that purchased them as a 'package'. These children were, directly or indirectly, exposed to the sexual violence and rape endured by their mothers. Whether living at a holding facility or a fighter-owners home, these children mostly suffered the same poor living conditions, including lack of food, water and proper healthcare.

---

[220] IICISAR *They came to destroy* (2016) par 62. Some reported that they were forced to take birth control, in the form of pills and injections, by their fighter-owners; others inevitably fell pregnant. Within this setting of fear, many Yazidi women and girls committed, or attempted to commit, suicide during their time in detention or attempted to escape, which was severely punished by organised gang-rapes or starvation.

[221] OHCHR *Rule of Terror* (2014) par 57.

5.3.3. Declarations and inferences on genocide against the Yazidi community

US Secretary of State John Kerry stated in August 2014 that: "ISIL's campaign of terror against the innocent, including Yezidi (sic) and Christian minorities, and its grotesque and targeted acts of violence bear all the warning signs and hallmarks of genocide".[222] Many have echoed these sentiments.[223]

Based on the legal analysis of genocide by the IICISAR, reported in "*They came to destroy: ISIS Crimes Against the Yazidis*", the following summary of their main findings is submitted:

- Although the Yazidis are often referred to as an ethno-religious group, there is no doubt that the Yazidis' identity is premised on their communal faith, which qualifies them as a protected religious group.
- Based on the factual information outlined earlier, the IICISAR has found that *Da'esh* has committed multiple prohibited acts of genocide against members of the Yazidi group.[224]
- *Da'esh* fighters focussed their attack and genocidal acts against individual Yazidis because of their Yazidi identity and affiliation to the Yazidi group,[225] an incremental step in the overall objective of destroying the group.
- The following aspects serve to prove *Da'esh's* intent to destroy, in whole or in part, the Yazidis:
  – direct genocidal intent to destroy the Yazidis of Sinjar, composing the majority of the world's Yazidi population, is evident from *Da'esh's* religious ideology, public statements and conduct;
  – Yazidis were branded as inferior and worthy of extinction;
  – indirect genocidal intent can also be inferred from: the physical targeting of the group or their property, the use of derogatory language towards members of the targeted group, the

---

[222] Report submitted to Secretary of State John Kerry by the Knights of Columbus and In Defense of Christians. *Genocide against Christians in the Middle East*. 9 March 2016, pg 6. http://www.stopthechristiangenocide.org/en/resources/Genocide-report.pdf. Accessed 31/01/2019.
[223] For some examples, see Knights of Columbus *Genocide against Christians in the Middle East* (2016) 6–10.
[224] For identified genocidal acts, see IICISAR *They came to destroy* (2016) par 202.
[225] Also stated in UNHRC *A/HRC/28/18* (2015) par 17.

methodical way of planning, the scale of atrocities committed, their general nature, and the deliberate and systematic separation of Yazidis from the rest of the population;
- the near-identical treatment of Yazidis by fighters across the region;
- the specifically mandated rules in dealing with a *mushrik* group,[226] evident from *Da'esh's* self-proclamations and ideology;
- differential, more unforgiving treatment than in relation to other religious minorities;[227]
- Yazidi shrines and temples in Sinjar were destroyed; and
- private homes were marked as belonging to Yazidis and looted.

- The Yazidi community of Sinjar has been devastated by the *Da'esh* attack, and no free Yazidis remain in the region. The 400,000-strong community had all been displaced, captured, or killed. This implies that a substantial part of the Yazidi community has been destroyed.
- Therefore, the IICISAR determined that *Da'esh* has committed the prohibited acts with the intent to destroy, in whole or in part, the Yazidis of Sinjar, and has thus committed the crime of genocide.[228]

It is reasonable to assert that the atrocities against the Yazidi population of Sinjar should be considered separately from those of other religious and ethnic minorities in the region. The genocidal acts "were committed against the Yazidis on discriminatory grounds based on their religion, and as such they also amount to the crime against humanity of persecution".[229] It is clear that the armed fighters acted in a systematic, premeditated and calculated manner in dealing with the Yazidi population. Their public statements and conduct clearly demonstrated their rigid obedience to the *Da'esh* ideology. These fighters had been so ideologically enslaved that they believed that by committing some of the most horrific crimes imaginable, they were bettering the society in which they lived.[230]

---

[226] A *mushrik* group refers to those who practice idolatry or polytheism, besides the singular Allah.
[227] Unlike the Jews and the Christians, there was no room for the *jizyah* payment [a tax to be paid to avoid conversion or death]. Also, their women could be enslaved according to the *Shariah*, unlike the female apostates.
[228] IICISAR *They came to destroy* (2016) par 165.
[229] IICISAR *They came to destroy* (2016) par 168.
[230] IICISAR *They came to destroy* (2016) par 204.

In conclusion, the intent to destroy the Yazidi's is evident from the existence of a manifest pattern of attacks against that religious community,[231] which has a protected status. Da'esh has, without a doubt, committed genocide against the Yazidi community of Sinjar.[232] They attempted to destroy the Yazidis in multiple ways, including mass murder, forcible transfer and displacement, forced conversion and indoctrination, and other measures aimed at erasing the ethnic and religious identity of the Yazidis.[233]

> Daesh is genocidal by self-proclamation, by ideology, and by actions – in what it says, what it believes, and what it does... Daesh kills Christians because they are Christians; Yazidis because they are Yazidis; Shia because they are Shia.[234]

5.4. Ethnic cleansing on a historic scale

In September 2014, Amnesty International reported that *Da'esh* had systematically targeted non-Arab and non-Sunni Muslim communities in the Nineveh province.[235] The report demonstrates that through the commission of war crimes and gross human rights abuses, *Da'esh* had pursued a policy of ethnic or religious cleansing against Assyrian Christians, Turkmen Shia, Shabak Shia, Yazidis, Kakai and Sabean Mandaeans:

> The group that calls itself the Islamic State (IS) has carried out ethnic cleansing on a historic scale in northern Iraq.[236]

Although the definition of ethnic cleansing has remained elusive and controversial, it has been described as a "purposeful policy designed by one ethnic or religious group to remove by violent and terror-inspiring means the civilian population of another ethnic or religious group from certain geographic areas".[237] The primary consideration underlying

---

[231] UNHRC A/HRC/28/18 (2015) par 17.
[232] IICISAR *They came to destroy* (2016) par 201.
[233] IICISAR *They came to destroy* (2016) par 202.
[234] *Remarks on Daesh and Genocide* by Secretary of State John Kerry, Washington DC, 17 March 2016. https://2009-2017.state.gov/secretary/remarks/2016/03/254782.htm. Accessed 24/10/2018.
[235] Amnesty International *Ethnic cleansing on a historic scale* (2014) 4.
[236] Amnesty International *Ethnic cleansing on a historic scale* (2014) 4.
[237] Report of the United Nations Commission of Experts Established Pursuant to Security Council Resolution 780 (1992), 27 May 1994, section III.B, (S/1994/674), pg 33, par 130. Amnesty International also subscribes to this definition in their report, see Amnesty International *Ethnic cleansing on a historic scale* (2014) 4, fn 2.

ethnic cleansing is the establishment of ethnically or religiously homogenous lands, which may be achieved through various means, but generally entail the extermination or forced removal and displacement of the unwanted group or identities from the region.[238]

There are no references to 'ethnic cleansing' in the *Rome Statute*. However, various forms of unlawful deportation or forced removal may constitute war crimes, if committed during the course of an armed conflict.[239] Alternatively, deportation or forcible transfer of a civilian population are considered inhumane acts of crimes against humanity,[240] provided such measures are achieved through the "forced displacement of the persons concerned by expulsion or other coercive acts from the area in which they are lawfully present, without grounds permitted under international law".[241]

Furthermore, there is international support for categorising ethnic cleansing as a form of cultural genocide.[242] The atrocities and human rights deprivations perpetrated as part of an abhorrent policy of 'ethnic cleansing' are systematically similar to the effect of genocide.[243] However, in *Blagojević*,[244] the ICTY concluded that ethnic cleansing is distinguishable from genocide in that displacement is not equivalent to destruction, implying that the "primary consideration underlining ethnic cleansing is the establishment of ethnically homogenous lands"[245] through forced displacement rather than the *dolus specialis* of genocide aimed at the physical-biological destruction of a protected group.[246]

---

[238] Geiss, R. *Ethnic Cleansing*. Max Planck Encyclopedia on Public International law, Wolfrum, R. (ed), Max Planck Institute for Comparative Public Law and International Law, Heidelberg. Published by Oxford University Press (2011), par 30.

[239] See Art 8 (2)(a)(vii), art 8 (2)(b)(viii), and art 8 (2)(e)(viii) of the *Rome Statute*.

[240] See art 7(1)(d) of the *Rome Statute*.

[241] Art 7(2)(d) of the *Rome Statute*.

[242] Schabas, W. *Genocide*. Max Planck Encyclopedia on Public International law, published by the Max Planck Institute for Comparative Public Law and International Law, Heidelberg and Oxford University Press. (2011), par 20.

[243] *Application of the Convention on the Prevention and Punishment of the Crime of Genocide (Bosnia and Herzegovina v. Serbia and Montenegro)*, Judgment, I.C.J. Reports (2007), par 190. ('Genocide case').

[244] *Prosecutor v Blagojević and Jokic (Appeal Judgment)*, Case No. IT-02-60-A, 9 May 2007, para 123.

[245] Schabas *Genocide* (2011) par 30.

[246] In other words, whether a particular situation of 'ethnic cleansing' constitutes genocide depends on whether the definitional elements of genocide under international law are satisfied, especially the intention to destroy the group, in whole or in part – *Genocide case* (2007) par 190.

In the context of the atrocities committed against the Yazidis, it was clear that *Da'esh* was not merely satisfied with removing the community from the region, but was intent on exterminating the group, thus constituting a genocidal policy. However, the same genocidal intent is not immediately evident from *Da'esh's* treatment of other religious minorities. Yet, based on the earlier discussion, *Da'esh* perceived their religious ideology as a divine authority with the aim of achieving a *'Da'esh-isation'* of the region.[247] Their subsequent proclamation of a pure State of Islam and the strict enforcement of their extremist interpretation of *Sharia* law provides *prima facie* evidence that the group was intent on creating religiously homogenous lands through a process of ethnic and religious cleansing.

Consequently, in the occupied areas, non-conforming religious and ethnic minorities were subjected to treatment aimed at systematically expelling them from the caliphate, forcing them to either assimilate or flee. These measures were undertaken as part of a policy of imposing discriminatory sanctions such as taxes or forced conversion, destroying religious sites and systematically expelling minority communities. Consequently, the report of the IICISAR concluded that:

> Evidence shows a manifest pattern of violent acts directed against certain groups with the intent to curtail and control their presence within ISIS areas.[248]

Navi Pillay, the UN High Commissioner for Human Rights, was quoted saying that *Da'esh* was:

> ...systematically targeting men, women and children based on their ethnic, religious or sectarian affiliation and ruthlessly carrying out widespread ethnic and religious cleansing in the areas under their control.[249]

However, for individual criminal responsibility, such discriminatory practices are better categorised under persecution. 'Ethnic cleansing' is closely related to crimes against humanity of persecution in that it constitutes severe deprivations of fundamental human rights, especially the deprivation of the right to liberty of movement[250] on a discriminatory

---

[247] Cockburn *The Rise of Islamic State* (2015).
[248] OHCHR *Rule of Terror* (2014) par 24.
[249] Harding, L. *ISIS accused of ethnic cleansing as story of Shia prison massacre emerges*. The Guardian. http://www.theguardian.com/world/2014/aug/25/isis-ethnic-cleansing-shia-prisoners-iraq-mosul. Accessed 17/02/2015.
[250] Art 12 of the UNGA, *ICCPR*, 16 December 1966, United Nations, Treaty Series, vol. 999, pg 171, states that: (1) Everyone lawfully within the territory of a State shall,

basis.²⁵¹ However, *prima facie* evidence of this so-called *'Da'esh-isation'* policy aimed at creating religiously homogenous lands through a process of religious cleansing, provides an even clearer indication of the armed group's discriminatory intentions and motives, as well as contributing towards a holistic conception of their pattern of offences.

5.5. Several inhumane acts of crimes against humanity

The reports available strongly suggest that the group has perpetrated numerous inhumane acts of crimes against humanity. However, this section is not intended to list and discuss the possible crimes against humanity that members of the group may have committed. Similarly, 'grievous persecution' will not be considered here as it forms the primary topic of discussion for the rest of the case study. The primary aim of highlighting the variety of inhumane acts committed by *Da'esh* is to supplement the evolving pattern of offences.

Da'esh propaganda gave careful consideration and formed an explicit ideological policy in terms of how different religious minorities should be treated in terms of its radical religious interpretation.²⁵² Consequently, this explicit ideological policy provided that particular religious groups were segregated from the rest of the civilian population and treated in a methodical manner throughout the occupied areas. *Da'esh* "systematically denied basic human rights and freedoms and in the context of its attack against the civilian population, has perpetrated crimes against humanity".²⁵³ Therefore, numerous reports provide credible evidence that corroborates the conclusion that *Da'esh* has perpetrated an array of inhumane acts as part of a widespread and systematic 'attack' directed against religious and ethnic minorities in Iraq and Syria, pursuant to, or in furtherance of, an organisational policy to commit such attacks.²⁵⁴ In 2014, IICISAR found that the group had committed the following enumerated inhumane

---

within that territory, have the right to liberty of movement and freedom to choose his residence. (2) Everyone shall be free to leave any country, including his own. (3) The above-mentioned rights shall not be subject to any restrictions except those which are provided by law, are necessary to protect national security, public order (ordre public), public health or morals or the rights and freedoms of others, and are consistent with the other rights recognised in the present Covenant. (4) No one shall be arbitrarily deprived of the right to enter his own country.

251 Geiss *Ethnic Cleansing* (2011), par 24.
252 Council of Europe *Omtzigt report on Da'esh crimes* (2016) 9.
253 OHCHR *Rule of Terror* (2014) par 74.
254 UNHRC *A/HRC/28/18* (2015) par 76.

acts as part of a widespread and systematic attack against the civilian population in Aleppo, Ar-Raqqah, Al-Hasakah and Dayr Az-Zawr governorates in Syria:

> murder and other inhumane acts, enslavement, rape, sexual slavery and violence, forcible displacement, enforced disappearance and torture.[255]

There are similar findings regarding attacks directed at Christian, Shia and Yazidi communities in Iraq.[256] The group had deliberately attacked civilians and civilian infrastructure, including pillaging, looting and destroying civilian homes.[257] The group destroyed and/or desecrated Christian, Yazidi and non-Sunni Muslim minority places of worship and other sites of religious or cultural significance.[258] It was further commented that indiscriminate attacks on the civilian population through suicide bombings claimed by *Da'esh* may also constitute crimes against humanity.[259] This means that *Da'esh* is responsible for committing virtually every established enumerated inhumane act of crimes against humanity, including some 'other inhumane acts', with the exception of the crime of apartheid.

The pattern of crimes against humanity committed by *Da'esh* is clearly and deliberately directed at civilian minorities. In most instances, *Da'esh* targeted such minorities because of their diverging or opposing religious views and their unwillingness to convert to the group's religious ideology. The enumerated inhumane acts were perpetrated and intended to discriminate between religious and ethnic minorities, thus constituting an aggravated form of crimes against humanity, namely persecution.

6. Charging Da'esh with 'Grievous Religious Persecution'

In consideration of this pattern of offences committed by *Da'esh*, attention is now focussed on 'grievous religious persecution'. The pattern of offences, coupled with the armed group's discriminatory religious ideology that motivated and justified such egregious crimes and atrocities against

---

[255] OHCHR *Rule of Terror* (2014) par 77.
[256] UNHRC *A/HRC/28/18* (2015) par 76. See also IICISAR *They came to destroy* (2016) par 168. In addition to those inhumane acts mentioned, imprisonment or other severe deprivation of physical liberty and persecution was also committed according to the report.
[257] Amnesty International *Punished for Daesh's Crimes* (2016) 15.
[258] Amnesty International *Punished for Daesh's Crimes* (2016) 15.
[259] HRW *A face and a name* (2005) 131.

Appendix C

particular religious minorities, provides the foundation for a claim of 'grievous *religious* persecution'. The assertion that Da'esh committed crimes against humanity of religious persecution will be determined on the basis of the proposed taxonomy of 'grievous religious persecution'. More specifically, the 'grievous religious persecution' checklist, contained in the flowchart presented in Chapter Six, will provide the structure for this discussion.

6.1. Applying the taxonomy checklist

Multiple sources provide reliable evidence about acts of violence perpetrated against civilians because of their affiliation or perceived affiliation to a non-conforming religious identity.[260] Therefore, the application of the 'grievous religious persecution' taxonomy checklist is based on the initial hypothesis that Da'esh has committed, or are otherwise responsible for, 'grievous religious persecution' against non-Arab and non-Sunni Muslim minorities, on the basis of their religion or belief, and must be held accountable.[261] Considering the conclusion that the crimes against the Yazidi community constitute genocide, this section will focus on the other religious minorities targeted by Da'esh, viz. Christians and non-Sunni Muslim minorities.

6.1.1. The actus reus of 'grievous religious persecution'

Da'esh must be charged with a specific underlying act of persecution, which may consist of either 'inhumane-type' conduct or the cumulative effect of 'other-type' conduct, or both.

6.1.1.1. Underlying religious persecutory conduct or practice

The proposed taxonomy checklist asks:

> Is the alleged persecutory conduct based any one or more inhumane acts of crimes against humanity, or other inhumane acts of a similar character intentionally causing great suffering, or serious injury to body or to mental or physical health? Alternatively, in the absence of 'inhumane-type' conduct, were there other underlying acts that discriminated between specific people or groups based in fact and effect? Supposing that either or both these

---

[260] UNHRC A/HRC/28/18 (2015) par 16. Such groups include: Yazidis, Christians, Turkmen, Sabea-Mandeans, Kaka'e, Shabak, Kurds and Shia Muslims.
[261] UNSC *Resolution 2170* (2014) 2.

questions were answered in the positive, did the underlying act/s discriminate between specific people or groups, in fact and effect?

As outlined, the group's conduct is based on a pattern of offences. Therefore, credible evidence supports the finding that *Da'esh* has committed enumerated inhumane acts of crimes against humanity on a discriminatory basis.[262]

The armed group has also committed 'other-type' acts, including discriminatory practices of persecution. Under their organisational or ideological policy, *Da'esh* imposed discriminatory practices against religious minorities with the intention to decrease and regulate the presence of non-conforming religious identities in the areas under its control.[263] Specific religious groups have been forced to either pay excessive taxes, assimilate or flee, to escape extermination. The commission of other crimes, atrocities and abuses have further victimised these communities, which led to the intended submission of the civilian population.[264] The armed group has sought to entrench its militant extremist ideology through indoctrination, coercion, fear and punishment in order to inhibit dissent or expedite forced assimilation or displacement.

Religious minority groups have also experienced a punitive and restrictive 'squeeze' on their basic rights and freedoms. In areas where the group exercised effective control, it systematically denied basic human rights and freedoms.[265] The group enforced its interpretation of *Sharia* summarily, inflicting harsh and discriminatory penalties against those who transgress or refuse to accept its self-proclaimed rule.[266]

---

[262] UNSC *Resolution 2170* (2014) 2–3. See also the following UN Security Council Resolutions: *Res. 2199 (2015)* [on threats to international peace and security caused by terrorist acts by Al-Qaida], 12 February 2015, S/RES/2199 (2015); *Res. 2233 (2015)* [on extension of the mandate of the UN Assistance Mission for Iraq (UNAMI) until 31 July 2016], 29 July 2015, S/RES/2233 (2015); *Res. 2249 (2015)* [on terrorist attacks perpetrated by ISIL also known as Da'esh], 20 November 2015, S/RES/2249 (2015); *Res. 2299 (2016)* [on extension of the mandate of the UN Assistance Mission for Iraq (UNAMI) until 31 July 2017], 25 July 2016, S/RES/2299 (2016); *Res. 2332 (2016)* [on the humanitarian situation in the Syrian Arab Republic and renewal of authorization of relief delivery and monitoring mechanism until 18 Jan. 2018], 21 December 2016, S/RES/2332 (2016); *Res. 2367 (2017)* [on extension of the mandate of the UN Assistance Mission for Iraq (UNAMI) until 31 July 2018], 14 July 2017, S/RES/2367 (2017); and UNSC *Resolution 2379* (2017).
[263] OHCHR *Rule of Terror* (2014) par 24.
[264] OHCHR *Rule of Terror* (2014) par 13.
[265] OHCHR *Rule of Terror* (2014) par 13.
[266] OHCHR *Rule of Terror* (2014) par 20.

In other words, it has been shown that Da'esh may be charged with specific underlying acts of persecution, including both 'inhumane-type' conduct and 'other-type' conduct.

6.1.1.2. Connection requirement

In terms of the taxonomy checklist, no further link to another inhumane act is required if the conduct is based on 'inhumane-type' acts. Regarding 'other-type' conduct, the taxonomy checklist asks: *Can the underlying acts, or the discrimination itself, be objectively (clearly and obviously) linked to a separate enumerated inhumane act, or any jurisdictionally relevant international crime?*

Considering the outlined pattern of offences, the 'other-type' underlying persecutory conduct committed by Da'esh is clearly linked to numerous inhumane acts, as well as jurisdictionally relevant international crimes, including war crimes and genocide. The mentioned 'inhumane-type' acts are aggravated because of their discriminatory nature, and therefore do not require such a connection, despite its obvious presence.

6.1.1.3. Causation requirement

In terms of the taxonomy checklist, proof of a causative link between the 'inhumane-type' conduct and the deprivation of human rights is not required, considering that by their inherent nature, 'inhumane-type' conduct inevitably constitute deprivations of human rights. Regarding 'other-type' conduct, the taxonomy checklist asks: *Considered cumulatively, did the underlying acts, or the discrimination itself, deprive the victim group of the enjoyment of a basic or fundamental human right?*

The armed group's persecutory conduct and/or its cumulative effect have resulted in the deprivation of fundamental rights laid down in international customary or treaty law. The commission of the 'inhumane-type' acts are, in and of themselves, abuses of international human rights.[267]

The outlined discriminatory practices may themselves constitute the causal link between the underlying conduct and the deprivation of fundamental rights. This may be evident from the group's treatment of Christians. Although Christians are historically sheltered as 'People of the Book', they nevertheless suffered serious deprivations of basic human

---

[267] IICISAR *They came to destroy* (2016) par 16. *In casu*, such rights include, *inter alia*: the right to life, liberty and security of person; the prohibition against slavery; and the prohibition against torture or cruel, inhuman or degrading treatment or punishment.

rights under *Da'esh's* religious onslaught.²⁶⁸ The discriminatory treatment of Christians under the *Da'esh* ideology will be assessed in more detail under religious discriminatory intent.

In other words, considered cumulatively, the presented pattern of offences provides a clear and obvious causative link between 'inhumane-type' and 'other-type' on the one hand, and the resulting deprivation of fundamental rights, on the other. In addition, it will be discussed under the section regarding religious discriminatory intent that the serious deprivation of the right to equality and equal treatment on the basis of religious identity, especially of Yazidi's and Christians, may itself constitute the causal link between the underlying conduct and the severe deprivation of fundamental rights.

6.1.1.4. Participation context

The taxonomy checklist asks: Do the acts of the perpetrator form part of a broader attack, i. e. a course of conduct involving the multiple commission of acts against the targeted civilian population? In addition, regarding 'other-type' conduct, the taxonomy checklist asks: Did the alleged perpetrator/s commit multiple discriminatory acts, or was he/she/they aware that similar discriminatory conduct was being committed against the same group in the same area?

The military offensives by *Da'esh* in northern Iraq and Syria were committed by individual *Da'esh* fighters in the course of executing official orders, acting towards a 'common purpose', thus constituting an 'attack' for the purposes of the *chapeau* elements.²⁶⁹ The abuses, crimes and atrocities committed by *Da'esh* against those under its *de facto* control have been deliberate and calculated, manifested through a coordinated campaign of spreading terror amongst the civilian population.²⁷⁰ Such a reign of terror, comprising of war crimes, genocide, crimes against humanity and terrorist acts, was intentionally committed in line with the group's ideological objectives. Therefore, the level of organisation, long-term vision, and character of its ranks and membership, indicate a cohesive and coordinated group, capable of perpetrating widespread and systematic crimes.²⁷¹ *Da'esh* fighters willingly and knowingly participated in the attack, committing some of the most horrific crimes imaginable.

---

[268] Council of Europe *Omtzigt report on Da'esh crimes* (2016) 9.
[269] OHCHR *Rule of Terror* (2014) par 75.
[270] OHCHR *Rule of Terror* (2014) par 13.
[271] OHCHR *Rule of Terror* (2014) par 75.

The same is true for the 'other-type' conduct. Da'esh's treatment of specific civilian groups was planned and calculated, based on an organisational policy that included discrimination, and denials or infringements on religious freedom, *inter alia*. On a structural and ideological level, all *Da'esh* fighters and commanders would have been aware that specific discriminatory practices and human rights deprivations were being committed by individual fighters in the area under *de facto* control based on their common religious ideology.

In other words, the methodical and near-identical treatment of specific civilian groups is a clear indication of an organisational or ideological policy that dictates to each fighter and commander the context and scope of their actions, which satisfies the contextual participation qualification for both the 'inhumane-type' and 'other-type conduct'.

6.1.2. Severity threshold for 'grievous religious persecution'

The severity threshold for 'grievous religious persecution' serves to limit the scope of the Court's jurisdiction to *severe* and discriminatory deprivations of *fundamental rights*, which form part of a broader 'attack'.

6.1.2.1. Intensity threshold

The taxonomy checklist asks: Did the inhumane act or the cumulative effect of a multiplicity of 'other-type' acts deprive the person/group of a fundamental right/s (i. e. rights and freedoms which are an essential necessity for an existence worthy of human dignity)? If so, is the character of such deprivations 'severe' (i. e. egregious human rights atrocities or crimes of an utmost inhumane character), when considered in an objective sense?

The 'inhumane-type' acts committed are, in and of themselves, serious abuses against elementary principles of fundamental human rights, and/or crimes of an utmost inhumane character, which violate international norms. Thus, the 'inhumane-type' conduct committed by *Da'esh* against religious minorities satisfies the intensity threshold, especially considering they were committed on a religious discriminatory basis, resulting in seriously disadvantaging the exercise of fundamental rights of those religious groups on an equal basis.[272]

The discriminatory basis of the 'other-type' conduct is also clearly indicative of deprivations that restrict the equal enjoyment of multiple human rights. However, in this context it is necessary to establish that the

---

[272] IICISAR *They came to destroy* (2016) par 16.

cumulative effect of the conduct offends humanity in the same way, or to a similar extent, as the 'inhumane-type' conduct, i. e. the 'severe' deprivation of 'fundamental' human rights.

Under the discussion on religious discriminatory intent, it will be shown that the nature and scope of *Da'esh's* doctrinally motivated discriminatory ideology and associated practices committed against Christians, and the consequences on the right to equality and equal treatment, surely suffice as a deprivation of a fundamental right. In areas under the armed group's control, civilians experienced a relentless assault and obstruction on the exercise of religious freedoms, the freedom of expression, assembly and association,[273] which are considered basic or fundamental rights. It has already been discussed that religious freedom is universally recognised as a fundamental human right in international law.[274] It was noted that the internal dimension of religious freedom is protected unconditionally, while the external dimension may be subject to certain permissible restrictions.[275] Through the imposition of forced conversion on diverging religious identities, *Da'esh* has deprived those affected of their right to freely choose, have, or adopt a religion or belief, which constitutes a severe deprivation of a fundamental human right. Furthermore, the destruction of churches, the imposition of discriminatory sanctions, the obstruction of freedom of assembly and association, forced displacement, and kidnapping of religious clerics have directly and indirectly resulted in the restriction on Christians and other groups to manifest their religious freedom.[276] The nature and consequence of these restrictions of religious freedom were not applied pursuant to a legitimate aim, established under law, non-discriminatory, proportional, compatible with the nature of the right, nor furthered general welfare. In other words, both dimensions of religious freedom were unlawfully deprived or restricted in the context of the *Da'esh* abuses on Christians.

When considered cumulatively, the nature of the obstructed rights and the discriminatory effect of the 'other-type' acts on the Christian communities are compellingly indicative of serious deprivations of fundamental human rights on an equal basis, thus also satisfying the intensity threshold.

---

[273] OHCHR *Rule of Terror* (2014) par 20, see also paras 74 and 77.
[274] Walter, C. *Religion or Belief, Freedom of, International Protection. Max Planck Encyclopedia on Public International law*, Wolfrum, R. (ed), Max Planck Institute for Comparative Public Law and International Law, Heidelberg. Published by Oxford University Press (2009), pg 864.
[275] See art 18(3) of the *ICCPR*.
[276] OHCHR *Rule of Terror* (2014) par 25.

6.1.2.2. Contextual threshold

The taxonomy checklist asks: *Can the perpetrators' conduct be sufficiently linked to the broader attack with the following features: a pattern of widespread or systematic religious discriminatory practices, directed against a specific civilian population because of their religious identity, and based on an organisational policy (explicit or inferred)?*

As mentioned, the participation context within which *Da'esh* fighters committed various atrocities can be sufficiently linked to a broader 'attack'. It has therefore been concluded that *Da'esh* has committed various 'inhuman-type' and 'other-type' acts as part of widespread and systematic attacks directed against religious minorities, pursuant to or in furtherance of an organisational policy of religious superiority, which satisfies the *chapeau* elements of crimes against humanity.[277]

a) A pattern of widespread and systematic religious discriminatory practices[278]

The brutal nature and overall scale of abuses outlined under the pattern of offences, linked with the number of victims affected, satisfies as a 'widespread' attack against the civilian population.[279] The attacks perpetrated by *Da'esh* involved the intentional and systematic targeting of members of religious communities in areas seized.[280] The attacks were evidence of a manifest pattern of violence and deprivations committed in a methodical, cohesive, organised and 'near-identical manner' across the region, with the intent to curtail and control their presence within those areas.[281] Consequently, their actions also constitute a 'systematic attack'.

b) Directed against a specific civilian population because of their religious identity

The systematic nature of the doctrinally motivated ideology, together with the demonstrated capacity and intent to deliberately apply measures of intimidation and terror to subdue civilians under its control, and the systematic and discriminatory denial of basic human rights and freedoms, is clearly evidence of a deliberate and calculated attack against the civilian

---

[277] UNHRC *A/HRC/28/18* (2015) par 78.
[278] UNSC *Resolution 2379* (2017). See also UNHRC *A/HRC/28/18* (2015) par 18.
[279] OHCHR *Rule of Terror* (2014) par 77.
[280] UNHRC *A/HRC/28/18* (2015) par 5.
[281] OHCHR *Rule of Terror* (2014) par 24.

population.²⁸² Importantly, the mass victimisation of civilians in occupied areas was directed at particular religious communities in order to establish a purely Islamic State and so abolish religious pluralism in the region.²⁸³

c) Based on an organisational policy

It has already been established that *Da'esh* functions under responsible command with the capacity to impose an organisational policy on its members, ensure the coordinated implementation of decisions made by its leadership, and exercise effective control over large swaths of land.²⁸⁴ The widespread pattern of offences, the methodically and systematic nature of their actions, and deliberate treatment of particular doctrinally motivated civilian targets provide reasonable grounds to conclude that the attacks were carried out in accordance with an organisational policy.²⁸⁵ A clear policy of 'religious cleansing' is evident from *Da'esh's* numerous declarations of doctrine and policy, before and during the commission of their exclusivist imposition of religious homogeneity.²⁸⁶

6.1.3. Mens rea of 'grievous religious persecution'

The armed group must have committed the persecutory conduct with a certain *mens rea* or subjective mindset.

6.1.3.1. Contextual knowledge

The taxonomy checklist asks: *Was the perpetrator aware of the broader attack, while knowing or intending that his conduct be considered to form part of such a broader attack?*

The armed group's methodical and widespread treatment of specific religious minorities based on an institutionalised discriminatory policy provides reasonable justification that all *Da'esh* fighters acted towards a collective ideological purpose and cause, indicative of shared contextual knowledge.²⁸⁷ *Da'esh's* public propaganda, especially on social media platforms, provided a clear testament of its motives and intentions. There can

---

[282] Amnesty International *Punished for Daesh's Crimes* (2016) 15, and OHCHR *Rule of Terror* (2014) par 45.
[283] Council of Europe *Omtzigt report on Da'esh crimes* (2016) 16.
[284] OHCHR *Rule of Terror* (2014) par 76.
[285] OHCHR *Rule of Terror* (2014) par 24 & 76.
[286] Council of Europe *Omtzigt report on Da'esh crimes* (2016) 3.
[287] OHCHR *Rule of Terror* (2014) par 13.

be no doubt that any individual that joined their ranks had received religious instruction on the group's ideological purpose and perceived religious legitimacy of engaging particular religious groups in a specific manner. In addition, fighters would have been trained and instructed on expected military targets and outcomes.

6.1.3.2. Persecutive intent

Considering that most of Da'esh's conduct is based on physical acts, the taxonomy checklist asks: *Did the perpetrator either intend to engage in the conduct or cause the deprivation of fundamental rights, or alternatively, knew that the deprivation of fundamental rights would inevitably occur?* Implied in this question, is also the requirement that those persecutory acts that are based on 'inhumane-type' conduct must also satisfy the inherent definitional requirements of such acts. Based on the quoted reports of Da'esh offences, and for the purposes of this study, it is reasonably concluded that those elements would be sufficiently satisfied if considered during criminal adjudication proceedings.

The group envisioned a long-term plan and had undertaken military operations towards their collective ideological goal.[288] The group's objectives, religious doctrine and its commission of egregious abuses were publicly documented, especially through its own propaganda campaigns. Consequently, its members knew they were expected to share the same ideology, engage in military activity, and contribute towards building the emerging 'State'.[289] This provides clear evidence of persecutive intent on an organisational level. The Da'esh fighters either volunteered or were coercively indoctrinated to share the same radical worldview and persecutive intent to commit the underlying persecutory acts and cause their result on a discriminatory basis.

In other words, the pattern of offences, coupled with the overall ideological policy and goal, provides commanding evidence of persecutory intent by all Da'esh fighters on an organisational scale.

6.1.3.3. Religious discriminatory intent

The taxonomy checklist asks: *Did the perpetrator's (or entity's) ideology and/or actions indicate a conscious, preconceived and deliberate exclusionary policy (explicit or inferred), against a targeted person or identifiable group or collectivity*

---

[288] OHCHR *Rule of Terror* (2014) par 17.
[289] Friedland Clarion project *Special Report: The Islamic State* (2015) 6.

based primarily (but not necessarily exclusively) on their actual or perceived religious identity, or lack thereof?

This question has three distinct elements *in casu*: (1) was *Da'esh's* ideology and/or actions conscious, preconceived and deliberate, (2) were their actions discriminately directed at specific civilian targets, and (3) were these targets specifically chosen because of their actual or perceived religious identity, or lack thereof? Although these three elements are interlinked, the following discussion will attempt to address each of these elements individually. It may be argued that for establishing and classifying persecution, this element is the most important, thus justifying a more detailed consideration.

The first and second elements are clearly established by the pattern of offences and religious ideological purpose of the armed group. The preceding evidence shows a manifest pattern of sectarian violence, deliberately directed against particular religious groups with the intent to curtail and control their presence within the caliphate.[290] This is based on the *Da'esh* ideology, for which the following summary may be suggested:

As a coordinated structure, the group's members are unified by a widely repudiated misinterpretation of the Islamic religion. Their radical, aggressive and terrorist *jihadi* ideology constitutes a fundamentalist and extremist disposition, which promotes sectarian violence, religious exclusion, and forcible resistance to moral or religious innovations (*bid'ah*) and foreign influence. Its members rigidly obey and brutally enforced this ideology in the areas formerly under its effective control, which affords them with religiously motivated justification and glorification for their human rights violations or abuses, mass crimes and atrocities.

What remains to be assessed in this regard, is the third element, which relates to the identity element underlying the discriminatory mindset of the armed group. To classify the persecutory conduct as religious persecution, the victims must have been deliberately targeted 'by reason of' the religious identity of the targeted group or collectivity, or lack thereof. This entails an assessment regarding specific and/or negative discriminatory intent at the hands of *Da'esh*, which will be discussed next.

---

[290] OHCHR *Rule of Terror* (2014) par 24.

a) 'By reason of' the targeted victims' lack of a certain religious identity

The 'Islamofascist'[291] nature of the Da'esh ideology provided religious justification, motivation and glorification for its egregious abuses against specific religious groups. This is evident from specific public statements, explicit policies and patterns of conduct. The foundation of Da'esh ideology is its posturing as an expansionist caliphate by implementing its restrictive and violent brand of Sharia, which provided divine authority and motivation to target religious communities it regards as infidels or heretics.[292] In terms of intra-denominational discrimination, the divine authority of Caliph Ibrahim to interpret the Islamic texts and condemn dissenting versions allowed Da'esh to employ the Islamic practice of takfir against all dissenting Muslim minorities, especially Shia Muslims. The treatment of non-Muslim religious minorities was based on an attempt to rid the caliphate of their presence through imposing discriminatory sanctions, systematically obstructing the exercise of basic human rights, undertaking coerced conversions, and deporting or killing those who refuse.[293] Consequently, Da'esh's religious views are self-righteous,[294] to the point that even the most inhumane acts against non-conforming religious identities are sanctified pursuant to or in furtherance of a policy of religious cleansing.[295]

Therefore, the first supposition is that, even if the evidence is unable to prove that Da'esh targeted particular religious groups, their public statements, explicit policies and patterns of conduct provide *indisputable evidence of a negative religious discriminatory intent*. In other words, Da'esh's religiously motivated attack was perpetrated with a 'blanket intent' to expel all non-conforming religious views from the caliphate. In Chapter Three, it was explained that such a blanket intent (negative intent) satisfies the discriminatory intent requirement in that the victims are targeted based

---

[291] Falk, A. *Islamic Terror: Conscious and Unconscious Motives*. ABC-CLIO (2008), pg 122.
[292] UN Human Rights Council, *Report of the Independent International Commission of Inquiry on the Syrian Arab Republic* (IICISAR). 13 August 2015, A/HRC/30/48, par 113.
[293] OHCHR *Rule of Terror* (2014) par 24.
[294] Terrorism Research and Analysis Consortium (TRAC) website – *'Islamic State (IS) / Islamic State of Iraq and ash Sham (ISIS) / Islamic State of Iraq (ISIS or ISIL, IS)'*: https://www.trackingterrorism.org/group/islamic-state-islamic-state-iraq-and-ash-sham-isis-islamic-state-iraq-isis-or-isil. Accessed 30/10/2018.
[295] Amnesty International *Ethnic cleansing on a historic scale* (2014) 4. Da'esh's military operations in the region were focused on expelling the 'near enemy', meaning Shia Muslims (whose beliefs it considers heretical) as well all secular, pro-Western presences in the Muslim world – TRAC *Islamic State*.

on the identity element. *In casu*, *Da'esh's* negative religious discriminatory intention implies that all divergent religious groups were targeted because they lacked the ideologically accepted religious identity of their persecutors and refused to convert to such an identity.

Although all religious and ethnic communities suffered as a result of the conflict, some "communities have been specifically targeted, with discriminatory intent, on the grounds of their actual or perceived religious and/or ethnic background".[296]

> Where ethnic or religious groups are believed to be supporters of an opposing warring faction, the entire community has been the subject of discrimination and, in some instances, violent attack.[297]

For the purposes of this study, not all of the affected religious groups will be considered. However, second only to the experience of the Yazidi community, Christians suffered an aggravated form of persecution as a result of their religious identity, as well as their perceived proxy for foreign or political influence on behalf of the 'Christian West'.[298] Consequently, it will be deliberated whether *Da'esh* acted with specific discriminatory intent towards Christians 'by reason of' their religious identity.

b) 'By reason of' the targeted victims' religious identity as Christians

Despite Christians being accepted by the moderate Muslim world as 'People of the Book', evidence of *Da'esh's* actions shows as a manifest pattern of offences and human rights abuses against Christians. The armed group labelled Christians as "slaves of the cross" whose women and sons should be enslaved.[299] The treatment of Christians was systematic and entirely consistent with these declarations:

> All the Christians, descendants of the indigenous Assyrian population that has inhabited Iraq for at least 3,000 years, were driven from Mosul. Their

---

[296] IICISAR A/HRC/30/48 (2015) par 110. It was mentioned previously that the treatment of the Yazidi community constituted particularly severe persecution to the extent that most authorities agree such conduct would constitute genocide. Therefore, the Yazidi community will not be considered in this discussion.
[297] IICISAR A/HRC/30/48 (2015) par 111.
[298] HRW *A face and a name* (2005) 35.
[299] Council of Europe, Parliamentary Assembly, *Resolution 2190 (2017) - Prosecuting and punishing the crimes against humanity or even possible genocide committed by Daesh*. Text adopted by the Assembly on 12 October 2017 (34th Sitting), par 4.

Appendix C

homes were marked with the Arabic letter nun, an abbreviation for Nazarene, referring to Christians.[300]

In Ar-Raqqah governate, Syria, IICISAR reports mention that *Da'esh* specifically targeted Christians because of their religious identities:

> While the ISIS attack on the Assyrian Christian villages formed part of the group's broader attacks... the group also targeted villagers on the basis of their religion. This discriminatory intent was demonstrated by the terrorist group's specific attacks on Christian symbols and the destruction of churches once ISIS was in control of the villages.[301]

In Iraq, Christians were targeted on the basis of their religion and suffered forced displacement, deprivation of property, the destruction of Christian churches and cathedrals, and Christian women were sold as slaves, based on publicised price lists.[302] A resolution of the Council of Europe noted that:

> [Da'esh] deployed members of Christian minorities as 'human shields', causing serious bodily or mental harm, and separated Christian children from their mothers, forcibly transferring them to another group.[303]

Along with the discriminatory nature of these practices against Christians, *Da'esh* made a number of clear statements of intolerant and violent intent.[304] Accordingly, the plain meaning of these discriminatory practices and statements, especially in context, clearly calls for the annihilation of Christians.[305] As Omtzigt bluntly states: "Daesh considers Christians as infidels, liable to be killed".[306] Consequently, Christians in *Da'esh*-occupied territories are faced with an appalling choice: pay the *jizya*, convert to Islam, leave, or be killed.[307]

These reported patterns of religiously discriminatory attacks against Christian communities in the region and beyond,[308] provide proof of a

---

[300] Friedland Clarion project *Special Report: The Islamic State* (2015) 27.
[301] IICISAR *A/HRC/30/48* (2015) par 120–122. See also OHCHR *Rule of Terror* (2014) par 25–26.
[302] Council of Europe *Omtzigt report on Da'esh crimes* (2016) 9.
[303] Council of Europe *Resolution 2190* (2017) par 3.
[304] See Knights of Columbus *Genocide against Christians in the Middle East* (2016) 8–10.
[305] Knights of Columbus *Genocide against Christians in the Middle East* (2016) 10.
[306] Council of Europe *Omtzigt report on Da'esh crimes* (2016) 10.
[307] Council of Europe *Omtzigt report on Da'esh crimes* (2016) 10.
[308] Various reports by the Clarion project indicate that Christians, in other countries where *Da'esh* had been active, were slaughtered in separate incidents, as depicted

religious discriminatory intent directed at individuals based on their religious identity. Although Christians were predominantly used as an example to illustrate *Da'esh's* religious discriminatory intent, it should not be overlooked that the group had undertaken a similar policy of imposing discriminatory sanctions on other religious minorities to either assimilate or flee; in the process destroying religious sites and systematically expelling minority communities.[309] For example, the group's discriminatory intent was made clear through the differentiation between Sunni's and Shia's after it had taken over control of Mosul in June 2014. Citing testimony from eyewitnesses and survivors, it was reported that the armed group massacred 679 Shia captives after having split them from Sunni prisoners who were later released. The UN High Commissioner for Human Rights noted that:

> Such cold-blooded, systematic and intentional killings of civilians, after singling them out for their religious affiliation may amount to war crimes and crimes against humanity.[310]

6.1.4. Summary and visual representation of checklist

In summary, *Da'esh's* religious discriminatory intent reflects a conscious, preconceived and deliberate attempt to target any dissenting or opposing religious identities. Its explicit discriminatory policy is evident at an institutional level and is based on a 'blanket intent' to expel all 'inconsistent' religious views from the caliphate. The group has systematically targeted persons and groups based primarily (but not necessarily exclusively) on their actual or perceived religious identity or lack thereof. *Da'esh's* attacks are based on the group's self-righteous religious ideology and are therefore committed in the name of a religious identity (religiously motivated persecution). The group's explicit ideological goal in the region meant that their actions were not only motivated by their self-righteous religious ideology, but were also deliberately directed at specific targets based on religious identity, thus constituting religious discriminatory intent. The religious discriminatory policy may be inferred from the group's explicit ideology and public statements, substantiated by employing religious motivation and justification for its violent actions. Such an intent may be at-

---

in videos released by these affiliated groups in Libya and Egypt – As referenced in Friedland Clarion project *Special Report: The Islamic State* (2015) 27.

[309] OHCHR *Rule of Terror* (2014) par 24.
[310] Harding *ISIS accused of ethnic cleansing* (2014).

tributed to each *Da'esh* fighter individually, considering that its membership is limited to those who share its worldview and recalling that they acted systematically under responsible command.

If this discussion is practically applied to the proposed taxonomy checklist, the flowchart may be illustrated as follows:

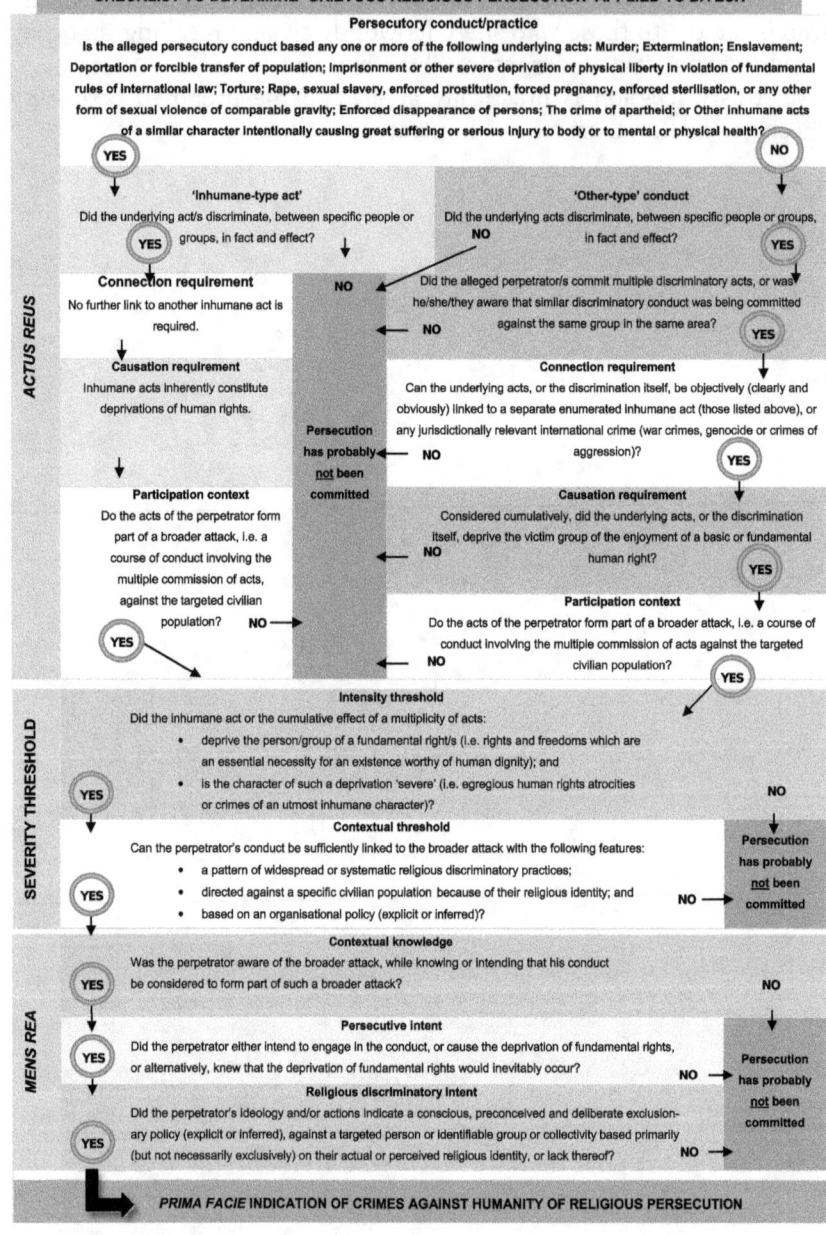

Appendix C

Based on the application of the taxonomy checklist for 'grievous religious persecution', the following substantiations were established:

- *Da'esh* embarked on a quest of religious purification of the area by leaving a trail of human destruction, terror and violence, in order to construct a 'pure State of Islam'.
- *Da'esh* used the divine authority of the caliph to enforce violent sectarian edicts against religious minorities.
- These 'attacks' were committed with absolute impunity, in a permissive environment created by ongoing armed conflict and inadequate governmental control.
- There is *prima facie* evidence to attribute religious persecutory intent to the conduct of *Da'esh* fighters as part of a manifest pattern of deliberate and calculated violent acts endorsed and directed by its leadership in accordance with an organisational policy, directed at religious minorities and dissenting religious groups in the region.
- The group clearly intended to separate the victim groups from the rest of the population and enacted discriminatory practices and violence in order to terrorise them into submission.
- *Da'esh* made derogatory public statements about various religious groups, which mirrored their religiously justified treatment of such groups as inferior infidels. This exclusivist policy, combined with the widespread and systematic approach with which, and the nature of the civilian population against whom, these atrocities have been committed, warrants the classification of such acts as crimes against humanity of religious persecution.
- Therefore, reasonable grounds exist to hold *Da'esh* members individually criminally accountable for such acts, particularly those who bear the greatest responsibility.

6.2. Multiplicity of the grounds of persecution

Having established that *Da'esh* acted with a religious discriminatory intent in committing 'grievous religious persecution', it should be noted that their religious motive for such actions not only intersected with non-conforming religious identities, but also other grounds of persecution. Thus, while religion constituted the primary ground of persecution, the armed group's religiously motivated persecution intersected with a number of other protected grounds, including persecution based political grounds, age, sexual orientation, profession, and ethnicity.[311] The intersection of religious motive with other grounds of persecution aggravated the experience of certain sub-categories of persecuted religious communities. In other words, 'religion' provided the primary basis for the differentiation of specific minority religious communities from the rest of the civilian population, whereafter the targeted group was further subdivided based on other aspects of individuals' identity. In the following discussion, some of these intersecting grounds of persecution, including gender-based discrimination, are briefly highlighted.

6.2.1. Gender-based discrimination

Apart from the corroborated witness statements indicating clear patterns of sexual and gender-based violence against women, the enforcement of strict *Sharia* law has meant that the religious persecution of women and girls has been aggravated on the basis of their gender. Even women and girls who are not part of religious or ethnic minorities were removed from public life and placed entirely under the control of male relatives, which impacted on various aspects of their lives.[312] Such religious edicts and their severe enforcement *"exacerbate the subordinate role of women in society, reinforcing patriarchal attitudes"*.[313] The women were further segregated based on their marital status and age.[314]

An appropriate example discussed earlier was the treatment of the Yazidi community. After having been segregated based on their religious identity, Yazidi community members were further subdivided. While men and older boys were summarily executed if they refused to convert, girls and women were generally subjected to sexual violence and slavery, *inter alia*. The differentiation on the basis of gender was also influenced by age, considering that boys over the age of 12 were forcibly recruited into the

---

[311] IICISAR *A/HRC/30/48* (2015) par 24.
[312] IICISAR *A/HRC/30/48* (2015) par 60-63.
[313] OHCHR *Rule of Terror* (2014) par 49.
[314] "Unmarried women – whom ISIS considers to be females over the age of puberty – pose a particular threat to the armed group's enforced social order. Parents of unmarried women and girls are terrified of their daughters being forced to marry ISIS fighters and as a result, early marriage is on the rise. Their fears are not unfounded. There are distressing accounts of fighters taking girls as young as 13 years old away from their families, resulting in violations of international humanitarian law and acts that amount to war crimes of cruel treatment, sexual violence and rape". – OHCHR *Rule of Terror* (2014) par 51.

Da'esh military,³¹⁵ while adolescent girls became eligible to be sold as slaves or forcibly married.³¹⁶

6.2.2. Discrimination on political grounds

In the context of the aftermath of the Iraqi invasion by the USA, many insurgent groups have argued that certain religious and ethnic communities are justified targets based on their actual or perceived political identity. The Human Rights Watch report states that:

> Attacks on Iraq's religious and ethnic communities—Shi'a Muslims, Kurds and Christians—are collective punishment for perceived cooperation with foreign forces and, in the case of Shi'a Muslims and Kurds, their assertions of national power.³¹⁷

Consequently, certain religious minorities who were targeted because their religious identity, were additionally perceived as a proxy for foreign or political influence. For example:

> Christians have repeatedly come under attack because they are viewed as supportive of the U.S. invasion, and many have taken jobs with the occupation authorities and various U.S. government entities. Insurgents may also have attacked Iraqi Christians as surrogates for the Christian West.³¹⁸

Based on reliable evidence, one report deems it reasonable to conclude that Da'esh had committed a pattern of attacks against those it perceives to be affiliated with the Iraqi Government or its allies, including police officers, members of the Iraqi armed forces, tribal and religious leaders, and those who had publicly criticised or were perceived to be opposed to Da'esh.³¹⁹ The report noted that:

---

[315] "ISIS has instrumentalised and abused children on a systematic scale. The deliberate nature of violations against children is apparent. By exploiting schools to indoctrinate children, the armed group fails in its obligations to ensure education and the protection of children from the dangers arising in war. In training and using children for combat roles, ISIS has violated international humanitarian law and perpetrated war crimes on a mass scale" – OHCHR *Rule of Terror* (2014) par 62.
[316] IICISAR *They came to destroy* (2016) par 82.
[317] HRW *A face and a name* (2005) 21.
[318] HRW *A face and a name* (2005) 35.
[319] UNHRC A/HRC/28/18 (2015) par 29.

Those violations were not based on perceived ethnic or religious identity but targeted Iraqis, usually Sunnis, deemed to be linked to the Government, or who refused to pledge allegiance to ISIL.[320]

It could be concluded that such targeted individuals were persecuted on the basis of their political affiliations.

6.2.3. Discrimination based on perceived 'immoral' behaviour

Da'esh imposes a strict worldview in line with a radical interpretation of Islam. Consequently, certain accepted human rights, such as the freedom of sexual orientation in the form of homosexuality, and perceived licentious recreational activities, are strictly forbidden. For example:

> ISIL-established Sharia courts in Mosul allegedly sentence people to such cruel, inhuman and degrading treatment as stoning and amputation. Two men accused of homosexuality were convicted by an ISIL 'court' and thrown from the top of a tall building... Thirteen teenage boys were sentenced to death for watching a football match.[321]

In conclusion, despite the obvious intersections of various identity factors, it was decisively argued that in most cases religious identity had been the primary basis for discrimination. While some individuals may have been targeted based on multiple aspects of their identity or intersecting grounds of persecution, it is indisputable that Da'esh's religious discriminatory ideology has specifically targeted identifiable religious minorities and communities. However, it is appalling to note that certain sub-categories within religious communities, especially women, have been subjected to multiple forms of discrimination and violence, further intensifying their suffering and physiological harm. These groups were not only persecuted based on their religion, but often based on intersecting persecutory grounds.

7. Conclusion

A clear and honest determination of the international core crimes is a vital step towards bringing the offenders to justice to the full extent of their crimes and preventing its recurrence.[322] This case study was aimed at applying the assessment platform set out in Chapter Six, to clearly and

---

[320] UNHRC A/HRC/28/18 (2015) par 29.
[321] UNHRC A/HRC/28/18 (2015) par 49.
[322] Council of Europe *Omtzigt report on Da'esh crimes* (2016) 5.

precisely determine the applicability of 'grievous religious persecution' in a given context. Within the broader taxonomy framework based on the definitional elements, this case study utilised the abbreviated checklist to test the viability of the taxonomy itself. The most important aim was to surmise the effectivity of the checklist by practically applying it to an appropriate case study.

Owing to a global trend of rising fear of Islamic extremism and religiously motivated persecution and violence, it was decided that the situation in Iraq and Syria would offer a relevant case study. It was inferred from various international reports that *Da'esh* constitutes a global threat to international peace and security, especially considering its role in the rise of sectarian violence and the ensuing escalation of 'Islamophobia' as a counter-effect thereof. To accurately assess the nature, scale and cause of the armed group's actions, it was necessary to examine the aftermath contextually. Initially, this required tracing the origins and evolution of the armed group.

The most important observations regarding *Da'esh's* background is that it had originated in a climate of deteriorating political unrest and foreign interference in the Arab peninsula, which, in the Islamic context, is impossible to separate from aspects of the Islamic faith. Consequently, these Islamic extremists consider themselves the 'protectors' of their religious heritage. The unstable situation in the region, combined with the armed group's clear organisational policy, common purpose, cohesive military structures, and rigid obedience to orders, resulted in rapid territorial gains. *Da'esh* thus proceeded to change the existing political order in the Middle East. In line with the group's intention of advancing their political, religious or ideological causes, it declared the areas under its control as a self-autonomous State or caliphate, and self-ordained their leader, Abu Bakr al-Baghdadi, as the supreme religious and political leader of Muslims worldwide. This provided Caliph Ibrahim with the 'divinely sanctioned authority' to interpret the Islamic texts, condemn dissenting versions, and employ the doctrine of *takfir* against perceived heretical Muslims. This religious authority, coupled with their *de facto* control over territory, provided *Da'esh* with the self-proclaimed religious and political legitimacy to initiate a military *jihad* against the perceived threat to, aggression against, or suppression of, the Muslim '*umma*'. In the name of this 'divinely sanctioned' extremist '*jihad*', militants sought to indiscriminately and brutally enforce their extremist ideology of *Sharia* law as the applicable legal, social and religious system in the caliphate. *Da'esh* fighters were 'divinely authorised' to commit widespread sectarian violence, acts of intimidation and terror, and systematic deprivations of basic human rights against opposing Muslim ideologies, unbelievers, apostates and dissenters renouncing the authority of Islam.[323] Ultimately, this premeditated and religiously motivated policy of ideological superiority aimed at oppressing or terminating any nonconformist views and creating a religiously homogenous religious State, resulted in either the extermination, assimilation or displacement of any dissenting religious identities from the region.

This global and unprecedented threat to international peace and security[324] triggered an international military intervention, but not before tens of thousands of civilians had been killed and hundreds of thousands had been displaced or kidnapped, resulting in a devastating humanitarian situation. It was established through reports based on credible evidence, that *Da'esh* had carried out acts of terrorism, egregious human rights abuses, violations of international humanitarian law and war crimes, genocide, and numerous crimes against humanity. The conscious, premeditated and deliberately discriminate nature of these inhumane acts, crimes and human rights atrocities established a pattern of religiously motivated offences on a colossal scale.

Da'esh's prima facie genocide of the Yazidi community was particularly heinous and clearly portrayed their religiously discriminatory ideology. Pursuant to the group's explicit self-righteous religious policy, the Yazidis were classified as an inferior *mushrik* group, and consequently faced destruction. Its ideologically enslaved fighters had a 'religious duty' to destroy the existence of Yazidism and proceeded to separate the Yazidi community from the rest of the population. Their divine religious ideology and superiority justified the commission of a manifest pattern of genocidal atrocities, intended to destroy the Yazidi community, in whole or in part. Consequently, the entire Yazidi community of Sinjar was either displaced, captured, or killed.

After having rounded up the Yazidi community, *Da'esh* turned their attention to other religious identities, such as Christians and non-Sunni Muslim communities. However, the same genocidal intent of extermination was not as clearly present in regards to these minority groups. However, its attempts at 'religious cleansing' in furtherance of its explicit ideological goal to create a pure State of Islam, and the brutal enforcement of *Sharia* law, had a similar far-reaching effect on these communities. Consequently, the armed group committed a manifest pattern of violent acts against these religious groups. The intention was clear: either expel them

---

[323] Mahmoudi *Islamic approach to international law* (2011) 391.
[324] UNSC *Resolution 2249* (2015).

from the region through forced displacement or forcibly integrate them through religious conversion. Either way, this religiously motivated policy would ultimately result in dismissing religious pluralism and creating a religiously homogenous region.

Importantly, *Da'esh's* strict doctrinally inspired religious methodology meant that it did not simply indiscriminately victimise the entire civilian population. In terms of religious edicts, fighters had to obey the group's interpretation of *Sharia*, wherefore the group acted as a coordinated force, replicating a methodical pattern of offences against specific religious communities throughout the region. The armed group's *jihad* was not a chaotic infliction of terror, but an orchestrated and planned execution of widespread and systematic terror against specific targets.

The proposed flowchart checklist posed a series of sequential polar questions with the intention of establishing whether each of the definitional requirements for crimes against humanity of religious persecution had been met, or not. Within this framework of understanding, the checklist for 'grievous religious persecution' was applied to the established pattern of offences committed by *Da'esh*, and provided the following summarised results:

- In terms of the *actus reus* it was found that during an organised 'attack' on religious minorities in the areas under its *de facto* control, *Da'esh* fighters had committed a pattern of 'inhumane-type acts', international core crimes, and 'other-type' acts, which constitute the underlying persecutory conduct. The 'inhumane-type' acts inherently constitute deprivations of fundamental rights, whereas the cumulative effect of the 'other-type' conduct systematically resulted in the denial of basic human rights and freedoms.
- The armed group was well organised, and those fighters who had pledged allegiance to it, obeyed its commands as manifested by the consistent and systematic nature of their crimes against specific civilian target groups. The individual acts and crimes by *Da'esh* fighters are clearly connected to an organisational policy and overall goal. As such, the pattern of persecutory conduct committed by *Da'esh* satisfy the *actus reus* requirements for crimes against humanity.
- In assessing whether the 'attack' satisfied the threshold of severity for crimes against humanity, it was established that the armed group committed the persecutory conduct on a massive scale and

in a methodical near-identical manner. Their large-scale victimisation of religious minorities through the systematic imposition of harsh restrictions on basic rights and freedoms is indicative of an underlying exclusivist policy. The nature and gravity of the 'inhumane-type' conduct inherently constitute a *severe* deprivation of *fundamental* human rights. Furthermore, the overall consequence of the enforcement of religious discriminatory practices, combined with restrictions on religious freedom and other human rights, constitute clear and substantial deprivations of fundamental human rights. As such, the pattern of persecutory conduct by *Da'esh* satisfies the intensity threshold.

- Regarding the final prong, *mens rea*, it was clearly evident that the armed group's actions show a consistent pattern of discriminatory intent. The group's organisational policy is rigidly enforced and consistently obeyed, resulting in a clear institutional ideology of religious superiority. It is reasonable to assume that each member of the group acted with the same common purpose, deliberately directing their underlying persecutory conduct at specific civilian targets. There seems to be no doubt that *Da'esh's* ideology, self-proclamations, and actions, indicate an explicit policy based on a conscious, preconceived and deliberate exclusionary targeting of persons or identifiable groups based primarily (but not necessarily exclusively) on their actual or perceived religious identity, or lack thereof.

- It is thus found that the nature and scope of the persecutory conduct, the severe consequences of this persecutory conduct on fundamental rights of those religious identities affected, and *Da'esh's* numerous declarations of doctrinally motivated religious discriminatory intent – which are all extremely well documented – is strongly suggestive, if not conclusive proof, of the deliberate commission of crimes against humanity of religious persecution.

- In regards to criminal accountability it was found that as an 'armed group', *Da'esh* exercised effective control over a certain territory and are therefore bound by the obligations imposed on *de facto* authorities under international human rights law, as well as the principles of international humanitarian law, both of which *Da'esh* clearly violated.

- Consequently, *Da'esh* leadership may be held responsible based on command or superior responsibility. Considering also that *Da'esh* fighters have consistently acted with the same common purpose derived from an accepted and explicit institutional ideology, such fighters shared the same religious discriminatory intent, for which they may be held individually criminally responsible on the basis of direct perpetration, or the basis of perpetration through a group (common purpose). It may be argued that this principle of common purpose may also be applied to other non-combatant members of Da'esh who played an important auxiliary role, such as spreading the group's propaganda through social media, providing direct or indirect funding, or otherwise aiding or abetting armed forces.

In light of these findings, it could be argued that the 'taxonomy checklist' proved to be an adequate framework with which to assess 'grievous religious persecution'. It should be noted that this taxonomy checklist is not the equivalent of a determination by an independent and competent court. It should also be reiterated that this checklist is based on a proposed taxonomy within the context of individual criminal responsibility before the ICC specifically. Furthermore, the checklist, including the assessment of Da'esh's 'grievous religious persecution', does not consider jurisdictional threshold questions regarding admissibility, permissibility and procedural matters before the ICC. Thus, the application of the checklist is premised on the presumption that the ICC has jurisdiction.

In the context of the relevant case study, neither Iraq nor Syria are parties to the *Rome Statute*, despite numerous calls for ratification,[325] and neither State is in a position to effectively prosecute these crimes under its domestic legal system. A referral of the situations to the ICC through the UNSC remains an important possibility; however, the lack of consensus amongst the permanent members necessitates the urgent consideration of establishing an international *ad hoc* tribunal.[326] Therefore, the primary responsibility for bringing Da'esh to justice rests with national courts of third States.

---

[325] See for example IICISAR *They came to destroy* (2016) 37; OHCHR *Rule of Terror* (2014) par 14; and UNHRC A/HRC/28/18 (2015) 17.
[326] UN Office of the High Commissioner for Human Rights (OHCHR), Report of the Independent International Commission of Inquiry on the Syrian Arab Republic (IICISAR). 5 February 2015, A/HRC/28/69, par 139.

Bibliography

South African law

Implementation of the Rome Statute of the International Criminal Court, Act 27 of 2002.

Prince v President, Cape Law Society & other 2001 (2) SA 388 (CC).

Books

Ambos, K. *Treatise on International Criminal Law: Volume II: The Crimes and Sentencing.* Oxford University Press, 1st edition (2014).

Ambos, K. *Treatise on International Criminal Law: Volume I: Foundations and General Part.* Oxford University Press, 1st edition (2013).

Andrews, J. *Identity Crisis: Religious Registration in the Middle East.* Gilead Books Publishing (2016).

Barrett, D. B. et al. *World Christian Encyclopaedia.* New York: Oxford University Press, 2nd edition, Vol 2 (2001).

Bassiouni, M. C. *Crimes Against Humanity in International Criminal Law.* Martinus Nijhoff: Dordrecht (1992).

Bassiouni, M. C. *Introduction to International Criminal Law.* Leiden: Brill | Nijhoff. (2012).

Bassiouni, M. C. & Wise, E. M. *Aut Dedere Aut Judicare. The Duty to Extradite or Prosecute in International Law.* Marthinus Nijhoff Publishers (1995).

Berman, P. *Terror and Liberalism.* W.W. Norton & Company (2003).

Bhuiyan, J. H. & Chowdhury, A. R. *An Introduction to International Human Rights Law.* Leiden: Brill / Nijhoff (2010).

Bielefeldt, H. *Freedom of Religion or Belief: Thematic Reports of the UN Special Rapporteur 2010 - 2016.* Religious Freedom Series of the International Institute for Religious Freedom, Vol 3, 2nd and extended edition, Bonn (2017).

Bielefeldt, H., Ghanea, N. & Wiener, M. *Freedom of Religion or Belief: An International Law Commentary.* Oxford University Press (2016).

Boot, M. *Genocide, Crimes Against Humanity, War Crimes: Nullum Crimen Sine Lege and the Subject Matter Jurisdiction of the International Criminal Court.* Volume 12 of School of Human Rights Research series. Intersentia nv (2002).

Boyd-MacMillan, R. *Faith That Endures: The Essential Guide to the Persecuted Church.* Sovereign World (2008).

Byron, C. *War Crimes and Crimes Against Humanity in the Rome Statute of the International Criminal Court.* Manchester University Press (2009).

Cassese, A. *Violence and Law in the Modern Age.* Princeton University Press. (1988).

Cassese, A. *International Criminal Law.* Oxford University Press, 1st edition (2003).

Cassese, A. (ed), *The Oxford Companion to International Criminal Justice*. Oxford University Press (2009).

Cassese, A. et al. *International Criminal Law: Cases and Commentary*. Oxford University Press (2011).

Cassese, A. et al. *Cassese's International Criminal Law*. Oxford University Press, 3rd edition (2013).

Cockburn, P. *The Rise of Islamic State: ISIS and the New Sunni Revolution*. Verso, London (2015).

Council of Europe, *Freedom of thought, conscience and religion: A guide to the implementation of Article 9 of the European Convention on Human Rights*, June 2007, Human rights handbooks, No. 9.

Cryer, R. et al. *An Introduction to International Criminal Law and Procedure*. Cambridge University Press (2007).

Davidson, L. *Cultural Genocide*. Rutgers University Press, New Brunswick, N.J. (2012).

Dawidowicz, L. S. *The War Against the Jews, 1933-1945*. Open Road Media (2010).

De Jong, C. D. *The freedom of thought, conscience and religion or belief in the United Nations (1946-1992)*. Volume 5 of School of Human Rights Research series. Intersentia. (2000).

Dörmann, K. et al. *Elements of War Crimes under the Rome Statute of the International Criminal Court: Sources and Commentary*. Cambridge University Press (2003).

Dugard J. et al. *International Law: A South African Perspective*. Juta, 4th edition (2005).

Durham, W. C. et al. *Facilitating Freedom of Religion or Belief: A Deskbook*. Springer (2013).

Evans, M. D. *Manual on the wearing of religious symbols in public areas*, Council of Europe manuals, Martinus Nijoff Publishers (2008).

Falk, A. *Islamic Terror: Conscious and Unconscious Motives*. ABC-CLIO (2008).

Ferguson, N. *The War of the World: History's Age of Hatred*. Penguin UK (2012).

Fest, J. C. *The Face of the Third Reich*. Published by Pelican (1979).

Fox, J. *Ethnoreligious Conflict in the Late Twentieth Century: A General Theory*. Lexington Books (2002).

Garner, B. A. *Blacks Law Dictionary*. Thomson / West Publishers, abridged 8th edition. (2005).

Grim, B. & Finke, R. *The price of freedom denied: Religious persecution and conflict in the twenty-first century*. Cambridge University Press. (2010).

Hauriou, M. & Gray, C. *Tradition in Social Science*. Amsterdam: Brill Academic Publishers. (2011).

Henckaerts, J. M. & Doswald-Beck, L. *International Committee of the Red Cross (ICRC), Customary International Humanitarian Law*. Cambridge University Press, Volume I: Rules. (2005).

Bibliography

Hoffer, E. *The True Believer: Thoughts on the Nature of Mass Movements*. HarperCollins (1951).

Hofstee, E. *Constructing a Good Dissertation: A practical guide to finishing a Masters, MBA or PhD on schedule*. EPE, Johannesburg (2006).

Holyoake, G. J. *English Secularism: A Confession of Belief*. The Open Court Publishing Company, Chicago (1896).

Horton, G. *Dying Alive – A Legal Assessment of Human Rights Violations in Burma*, a report co – funded by the Netherlands Ministry for Development Co-operation. Images Asia (2005).

Institute on Religion and Public Policy (ed.): *Know your rights: What is Religious Freedom?* Alexandria, Virginia, USA, September 2014.

Jary, D. & Jary, J. *Collins Dictionary of Sociology. Collins Dictionary of Series. Collins Internet-Linked Dictionary Of Series*. Collins, 3rd edition (2005).

Johnson, T. K. (editor). *Global Declarations on Freedom of Religion or Belief and Human Rights*. The WEA Global Issues Series, Vol 18. Verlag für Kultur und Wissenschaft Culture and Science Publ. Bonn (2017).

Kittichaisaree, K. *International Criminal Law*. Oxford University Press (2001).

Klamberg, M. (ed.). *Commentary on the Law of the International Criminal Court*, TOAEP, Brussels (2017).

Lemkin, R. Axis Rule in Occupied Europe: Laws of Occupation, Analysis of Government, Proposals for Redress. Carnegie Endowment for International Peace, Division of International Law (1944).

Lempert, R. & Sanders, J. *An Invitation to Law and Social Science: Law in Social Context Series*. University of Pennsylvania Press. (1989).

Lundgren, M. *Mediation in Syria: Initiatives, strategies, and obstacles, 2011-2016*. Contemporary Security Policy. Taylor & Francis (Routledge) (2016).

Mettraux, G. *International Crimes and the Ad Hoc Tribunals*. Oxford University Press (2006).

Morgan, K. W. (editor). *The Path of the Buddha: Buddhism Interpreted by Buddhists*. Motilal Banarsidass Publisher (1956).

Neusner, J. *World Religions in America*. Westminster John Knox Press, 4th edition (2009).

Nowak, M. *UN Covenant on Civil and Political Rights: CCPR Commentary*. Second revised edition. N. P. Engel (2005).

Office of the United Nations High Commissioner for Refugees, *Refugee Protection in International Law: UNHCR's Global Consultations on International Protection*. Edited by Feller, E. et al. Cambridge University Press (2003).

Orie, A. Accusatorial v Inquisitorial Approach in International Criminal Proceedings Prior to the Establishment of the ICC and in the Proceedings Before the ICC, in The Rome Statute of the International Criminal Court: A Commentary Volume 2 (Cassese, A. et al eds.). Oxford University Press (2002).

Pew Research Center. *Trends in Global Restrictions on Religion.* 23 June 2016. http://www.pewforum.org/2016/06/23/trends-in-global-restrictions-on-religion/#fnref-25807-1. Accessed 28/09/2016.

Pew Research Center. *Global Uptick in Government Restrictions.* 21 June 2018. http://www.pewforum.org/2018/06/21/global-uptick-in-government-restrictions-on-religion-in-2016/. Accessed 10/01/2019.

Philpott, D. & Shah, T. S. (editors). *Under Caesar's Sword: How Christians Respond to Persecution.* Cambridge Studies in Law and Christianity. Cambridge University Press. (2018).

Pikis, G. M. *The Rome Statute for the International Criminal Court: Analysis of the Statute, the Rules of Procedure and Evidence, the Regulations of the Court and Supplementary Instruments.* Marthinus Nijhoff Publishers (2010).

Plous, S. *The Psychology of Judgment and Decision Making.* Published by McGraw-Hill Education (1993).

Preti, A. & Cella, M. *Paranoia in the 'normal' Population.* Nova Science Publishers, Inc, New York (2010).

Rosenne, S. *Practice and Methods of International Law.* Oceana Publications, London and New York (1984).

Sandel, M. *Democracy's Discontent: America in Search of a Public Philosophy.* Harvard University Press (1998).

Schabas, W. A. *An Introduction to the International Criminal Court.* Cambridge University Press, 2nd edition (2004).

Schabas, W. A. *An Introduction to the International Criminal Court.* Cambridge University Press, 3rd edition (2007).

Sepúlveda, M. et al, *Human Rights Reference book.* University for Peace Publisher (2004).

Shaw, M.N. *International law.* Cambridge University Press, sixth edition. (2008).

Schirrmacher, T. *The Persecution of Christians Concerns us all: Towards a Theology of Martyrdom* [70 Biblical Theological Theses Written for the German Evangelical Alliance] Idea-Dokumentation, Idea e.V. Volume 2 of Studien zur Religionsfreiheit. Culture and Science Publishers, (2001).

Schirrmacher, C. *Islam: An Introduction.* Volume 6 of Global Issues Series, World Evangelical Alliance. Verlag für Kultur und Wissenschaft Culture and Science Publ. Bonn (2011).

Snyman, C. R. *Criminal law.* LexisNexis, fifth edition (2014).

Stefanus Alliance International: *Freedom of Religion or Belief for everyone.* Oslo (2012).

Swedish Mission Council: *What freedom of religion involves and when it can be limited. A quick guide to religious freedom.* Stockholm (2010).

Thames, K. H. et al. *International Religious Freedom Advocacy: A guide to Organizations, Law and NGO's.* Baylor University Press (2009).

Tieszen, C. L. *Re-Examining Religious Persecution: Constructing a Theological Framework for Understanding Persecution*. Religious Freedom Series, Vol 1 (2008).

Tieszen, C. L. *Towards Redefining Persecution*. Religious Freedom Series: Suffering, Persecution and Martyrdom. Vol 2. (2010).

Thouvenin, J. et al. *The Fundamental Rules of the International Legal Order : Jus Cogens and Obligations Erga Omnes*. Leiden: Brill, 2006. eBook Collection (EBSCOhost), EBSCOhost (accessed September 15, 2017).

Triffterer, O. & Ambos, K. *Commentary on the Rome Statute of the International Criminal Court: Observers' Notes, Article by Article*. Beck Publishers, second edition (2008).

Werle, G. *Principles of International Criminal Law*. The Hague: TMC Asser Press (2005).

Werle, G. & Jessberger, F. *Principles of International Criminal Law*. Oxford University Press (2014).

Zgonec-Rožej, M. (Principal author). *International Criminal Law Manual*. International Bar Association (IBA) (2013).

Book chapters

Brady, H. & Liss, R. *The Evolution of Persecution as a Crime Against Humanity*, in *Historical Origins of International Criminal Law: Volume 3*, Bergsmo, M. et al (eds). Torkel Opsahl Academic EPublisher, Brussels (2014).

Caceres, G. *Reasonable Accommodation as a Tool to Manage Religious Diversity in the Workplace: What About the "Transposability" of an American Concept in the French Secular Context?* From Alidadi, K. et al (eds), A Test of Faith?: Religious Diversity and Accommodation in the European Workplace. Ashgate Publishing, Ltd. (2012).

De Baets, A. *The impact of the Universal Declaration of Human Rights on the study of history*. History and Theory, Vol. 48, 20–43 (2009).

Deagon, A. *Towards a Constitutional Definition of Religion: Challenges and Prospects*. From Babie, P.T., Rochow, N.G. & Scharffs, B.G. (eds). *Freedom of Religion or Belief: Creating the Constitutional Space for Fundamental Freedoms*. Edward Elgar Publishing (2020).

Durham, W.C. et al. *Law and Religion: National, International, and Comparative Perspectives*. Aspen Elective Series, third edition (2010).

Durham, W.C. Jr. *Religious Freedom in a Worldwide Setting: Comparative Reflections*. Universal Rights in a World of Diversity: The Case of Religious Freedom. Glendon, M. A. & Zacher, H. F. (eds). The Pontifical Academy of Social Sciences (2012).

Kadayifci-Orellana, S. A. *Ethno-Religious Conflicts: Exploring the Role of Religion in Conflict Resolution*. The SAGE Handbook of Conflict Resolution. Bercovitch, J. et al (eds), SAGE, London (2008).

Lindholm, T. *Freedom of Religion or Belief from a Human Rights Perspective*. Freedom of Belief and Christian Mission. Aage Gravaas, H. et al (eds), Regnum Books International, Oxford (2015).

Reimer, R. *Persecution, advocacy and mission at the beginning of the 21ˢᵗ century.* Sauer, C. (ed). Religious Freedom Series: Suffering, Persecution and Martyrdom. Vol 2 (2010).

Journal articles

Acquaviva, G. & Pocar, F. *Crimes Against Humanity. Max Planck Encyclopedia on Public International law*, Wolfrum, R. (ed), Max Planck Institute for Comparative Public Law and International Law, Heidelberg. Published by Oxford University Press (2011).

Ambos, K. *General principles of criminal law in the Rome Statute.* Crim LF, 10 (1999).

Ambos, K. & Wirth, S. *The Current Law of Crimes Against Humanity: An Analysis of UNTAET Regulation 15/2000.* Crim LF, 13 (2002).

Anonymous author. *Nigeria: Persecution or Civil Unrest?* Full report annexed to World Watch Unit (WWU) of Open Doors International (ODI), *Is conflict in Nigeria really about persecution of Christians by radical Muslims?* June 24, 2013. Available at: https://www.worldwatchmonitor.org/old-site-imgs-pdfs/2576904.pdf. Accessed 03/12/2018.

Askin, K. D. *Crimes within the jurisdiction of the International Criminal Court.* 10 CLF 33 (1999).

Barrie, G. N. *Humanitarian Intervention in the Post-Cold War Era*, 118 SALJ 155 (2001).

Bielefeldt, H. *Misperceptions of Freedom of Religion or Belief.* Human Rights Quarterly, Volume 35, Number 1, pg 33–68. The Johns Hopkins University Press (2013).

Cassese, A. *Is the Bell Tolling For Universality? A Plea For A Sensible Notion of Universal Jurisdiction.* 1 J Int'l Crim Justice (2003).

Celso, A. *Jihadist Organizational Failure and Regeneration: The Transcendent Role of Takfiri Violence.* Political Studies Association Meeting. Manchester, England. April 14–16, 2014. Available at: https://www.psa.ac.uk/sites/default/files/conference/papers/2014/PSU%20presentation.pdf. Accessed 14/02/2016.

Chertoff, E. *Prosecuting Gender-Based Persecution: The Islamic State at the ICC.* The Yale Law Journal (2017).

Finnin, S. *Mental elements under article 30 of the Rome Statute of the International Criminal Court: a comparative analysis.* International and Comparative Law Quarterly, Vol. 61, No. 2, pp. 325–359. Cambridge University Press on behalf of the British Institute of International and Comparative Law (2012).

Fournet, C. & Pégorier, C. *'Only One Step Away From Genocide': The Crime of Persecution in International Criminal Law.* International Criminal Law Review, Vol. 10, Issue 5, pages 713 – 738. Marthinus Nijhoff Publishers (2010).

Fox, J. & Sandler, S. *Separation of Religion and State in the Twenty-First Century: Comparing the Middle East and Western Democracies.* Comparative Politics, Vol. 37, No. 3 (2005). http://doi.org/10.2307/20072892. Accessed 24/03/2016.

Bibliography

Frowein, J. A. *Ius cogens. Max Planck Encyclopedia on Public International law*, Wolfrum, R. (ed), Max Planck Institute for Comparative Public Law and International Law, Heidelberg. Published by Oxford University Press (2009).

Geiss, R. *Ethnic Cleansing. Max Planck Encyclopedia on Public International law*, Wolfrum, R. (ed), Max Planck Institute for Comparative Public Law and International Law, Heidelberg. Published by Oxford University Press (2011).

Grosby, S. The verdict of history: The inexpungeable tie of primordiality – A response to Eller and Coughlan. Ethnic and Racial Studies Review, Vol. 17 (1994).

Henckaerts, J. M. *Study on customary international humanitarian law: A contribution to the understanding and respect for the rule of law in armed conflict* – American Society of International Law Proceedings, 2005.

Kaul, H. *International Criminal Court (ICC). Max Planck Encyclopedia on Public International law*, Wolfrum, R. (ed), Max Planck Institute for Comparative Public Law and International Law, Heidelberg. Published by Oxford University Press (2011).

Kreß, C. *International Criminal Law. Max Planck Encyclopedia on Public International Law*, Wolfrum, R. (ed), Max Planck Institute for Comparative Public Law and International Law, Heidelberg. Published by Oxford University Press (2011).

Lippman, M. *The 1948 Convention on the Prevention and Punishment of the Crime of Genocide: Forty-Five Years Later*, TICLJ Vol. 8 No. 1 (1994).

Luban, D. *A Theory of Crimes Against Humanity*. Yale Journal of International Law, Vol. 29 (2004).

Luban, D. *Calling Genocide by Its Rightful Name: Lemkin's Word, Darfur, and the UN Report*. CJIL, Vol 7 (2006).

Mahmoudi, S. *Islamic approach to international law. Max Planck Encyclopedia on Public International law*, Wolfrum, R. (ed), Max Planck Institute for Comparative Public Law and International Law, Heidelberg. Published by Oxford University Press (2011).

Marshall, P. *Persecution of Christians in the Contemporary World*. International Bulletin of Missionary Research, Vol. 22 issue 1 (1998).

Nel, W. N. *Prosecuting Islamic extremism: Counteracting impunity for the armed jihad of the Islamic State group through international criminal justice*. International Journal for Religious Freedom, Vol 7, Issue 1/2, pages 55–76, (2014).

Onley, R. B. *Defending the freedom of expression – The danger and failure of the Organization for Islamic Cooperation's campaign for global anti-blasphemy laws*. International Journal for Religious Freedom, Vol 7, Issue 1/2, pages 31–53, (2014).

Politi, M. & Nesi, G. *The Rome Statute of the International Criminal Court: A Challenge to Impunity* (2001).

Polletta, F. & Jasper, J. M. *Collective Identity and Social Movements*. Annual Review of Sociology, Vol. 27 (2001).

Ramji-Nogales, J. et al. *Refugee Roulette: Disparities in Asylum Adjudication*, 60 STAN. L. REV. 295 (2007).

Rempell, S. *Defining Persecution*. Utah Law Review, Vol. 2013, No. 1 (2013).

Schabas, W. *Genocide. Max Planck Encyclopedia on Public International law*, Wolfrum, R. (ed), Max Planck Institute for Comparative Public Law and International Law, Heidelberg. Published by Oxford University Press (2011).

Schirrmacher, C. *Apostasy: What do contemporary Muslim theologians teach about religious freedom?* International Journal for Religious Freedom, Vol 6, Issue 1/2 (2013).

Shelton, D. *Human Rights, Remedies. Max Planck Encyclopedia on Public International law*, Wolfrum, R. (ed), Max Planck Institute for Comparative Public Law and International Law, Heidelberg. Published by Oxford University Press (2011).

The *Bad Urach Statement* published as part of the compendium on the *Bad Urach Consultation: Suffering, persecution and martyrdom - Theological reflections*. Edited by Sauer, C. & Howell, R. Religious Freedom Series: Suffering, Persecution and Martyrdom. Vol 2, Kempton Park: AcadSA Publishing / Bonn: VKW (2010).

Van Boven, T. *Racial and Religious Discrimination. Max Planck Encyclopedia on Public International law*, Wolfrum, R. (ed), Max Planck Institute for Comparative Public Law and International Law, Heidelberg. Published by Oxford University Press (2009).

Van Sliedregt, E. *Article 28 of the ICC Statute: Mode of Liability and/or Separate Offense?* New Criminal Law Review: An International and Interdisciplinary Journal, vol. 12, no. 3, (2009).

Vaughns, K. L. Taming the Asylum Adjudication Process: An Agenda for the Twenty-First Century. *30 San Diego L. REV. 1, (1993)*.

Wald, P. Genocide and Crimes Against Humanity. Washington University Global Studies Law Review 6, (2007).

Walter, C. *Religion or Belief, Freedom of, International Protection. Max Planck Encyclopedia on Public International law*, Wolfrum, R. (ed), Max Planck Institute for Comparative Public Law and International Law, Heidelberg. Published by Oxford University Press (2009).

Wiener, M. *The Mandate of the Special Rapporteur on Freedom of Religion or Belief—Institutional, Procedural and Substantive Legal Issues*. Religion and Human Rights - An International Journal, Issue 1-2, Volume 2, Marthinus Nijhoff Publishers, pg 3-17 (2007).

Online sources

Ambos, K. *Modes of Participation*. Oxford Bibliographies (2013). http://www.oxfordbibliographies.com/view/document/obo-9780199796953/obo-9780199796953-0068.xml. Acessed 08/09/2017.

Amnesty International, *Ethnic cleansing on a historic scale: Islamic State's systematic targeting of minorities in Northern Iraq*. 2 September 2014, Index number: MDE 14/011/2014. https://www.amnesty.org/en/documents/MDE14/011/2014/en/. Accessed 08/01/2015.

Bassiouni, M. C. *Crimes Against Humanity*. http://www.crimesofwar.org/a-z-guide/crimes-against-humanity/#sthash.xfVy1loq.dpuf. Accessed 27/02/2013.

Bibliography

Bell-Fialkoff, A. *A brief history of Ethnic Cleansing.* https://www.foreignaffairs.com/articles/1993-06-01/brief-history-ethnic-cleansing. Accessed 15/01/2019.

Burnard, M. *Understanding Persecution: Recalibrating a theology of suffering with the reality of Easter.* https://www.incontextinternational.org/wp-content/uploads/2016/09/1904-EasterPersecution.pdf. Accessed 26/07/2019.

Esposito, J. L. *Universal Islamic Declaration of Human Rights* (UIDHR). Oxford Dictionary of Islam. http://www.oxfordislamicstudies.com/article/opr/t125/e2435. Accessed 12/08/2018.

Friedland, E. *Special Report: The Islamic State.* Report prepared by Clarion Project, 10 May 2015. https://clarionproject.org/the-islamic-state-isis-isil/. Accessed 12/08/2016.

Ghamidi, J. A. *The Islamic Law of Jihad.* Studying Islam website: http://www.studying-islam.org/articletext.aspx?id=771. Accessed 20/08/2014.

Guptill, M. *Religious Persecution.* Model United Nations of the Far West, 50th Session – 2000. http://www.munfw.org/archive/50th/ga1.htm. Accessed 06/06/2012.

Hume. J. *Balance of Powers: Syria.* (2014). http://numun.org/blog/wp-content/uploads/2014/02/BOP-Syria-Committee-Dossier.pdf. Accessed 08/01/2015.

Imhoff, R. & Recker, J. *Differentiating Islamophobia: Introducing a new scale to measure Islamoprejudice and Secular Islam Critique.* https://www.academia.edu/545302/Differentiating_Islamophobia_Introducing_a_new_scale_to_measure_Islamoprejudice_and_Secular_Islam_Critique. Accessed 05/01/2014.

Johnson, T. M. & Zurlo, G. A. (eds.). *World Christian Database.* Leiden/Boston: Brill (2018). Extract available at: https://www.gordonconwell.edu/ockenga/research/documents/GlobalChristianity infographic.pdfPg1.pdf. Accessed 27/01/2019.

Lacabe, M. *The Criminal Procedures against Chilean and Argentinian Repressors in Spain.* Derechos Human Rights, 11 November 1998. http://www.derechos.net/marga/papers/spain.html. Accessed 20/04/2016.

Open Doors Analytical / World Watch Research Unit. *World Watch List 2016: Long version of all 50 country persecution dynamics.* January, 2016. http://opendoorsanalytical.org/wp-content/uploads/2014/10/WWL-2016-Compilation-2-Long-profiles-Edition-2016-02-01.pdf. Accessed 12/08/2016.

Open Doors Analytical / World Watch Research Unit. *World Watch List 2016: Compilation 3 – All WWL documents (not including country persecution dynamics),* January, 2016. http://opendoorsanalytical.org/wp-content/uploads/2014/10/WWL-2016-Compilation-3-All-WWL-documents-not-including-Country-persecution-dynamics-Edition-2016-01-28.pdf. Accessed 12/08/2016.

Open Doors Analytical / World Watch Research Unit. *World Watch List 2016: Compilation 2 – Long version of all 50 country persecution dynamics,* January, 2016. http://opendoorsanalytical.org/wp-content/uploads/2014/10/WWL-2016-Compilation-2-Long-profiles-Edition-2016-02-01.pdf. Accessed 12/08/2016.

Open Doors Analytical. *World Watch List Methodology.* November 2017. Available at: http://opendoorsanalytical.org/world-watch-list-methodology-latest-edition-november-2017/. Accessed 09/01/2018.

Open Doors Analytical / World Watch Research Unit. *World Watch List 2018: Compilation Volume 3 - Persecution Dynamics for Countries Ranking 1-25*. January, 2018. http://opendoorsanalytical.org/wp-content/uploads/2018/01/WWL-2018-Compilation-3-Persecution-Dynamics-of-countries-ranking-1-25-WWR.pdf. Accessed 28/01/2019.

Open Doors International / World Watch Research Unit. *World Watch List 2019*. January 2019. http://opendoorsanalytical.org/wp-content/uploads/2019/01/WWL-2019-Compilation-of-main-documents-excluding-country-dossiers-WWR-1.pdf. Accessed 25/01/2019.

Palmer, P. J. *The heart of a teacher: Identity and integrity in teaching*. (2008) Essay of edited excerpts from the Introduction, Chapter I, and Chapter V of Parker J. Palmer's, *The Courage to Teach: Exploring the Inner Landscape of a Teacher's Life* (San Francisco: Jossey-Bass Publishers, 1997). https://biochem.wisc.edu/sites/default/files/labs/attie/publications/Heart_of_a_Teacher.pdf. Accessed 04/07/2017.

Robbers, G. & Durham, W. C. (Editors). *Encyclopedia of Law and Religion Online*. In *Encyclopedia of Law and Religion Online*. Leiden, The Netherlands: Brill | Nijhoff. https://brill.com/view/db/elro. Accessed 25/01/2019.

UN Rapporteur's Digest on Freedom of Religion or Belief: Excerpts of the Reports from 1986 to 2011 by the Special Rapporteur on Freedom of Religion or Belief Arranged by Topics of the Framework for Communications. Geneva, March 2011. The Rapporteur's Digest is a compilation of relevant excerpts from thematic and country-specific reports produced by Angelo d'Almeida Ribeiro (serving from March 1986 to March 1993), Abdelfattah Amor (serving from April 1993 to July 2004), Asma Jahangir (serving from August 2004 to July 2010) and Heiner Bielefeldt (serving since August 2010). https://www.ohchr.org/Documents/Issues/Religion/RapporteursDigest FreedomReligionBelief.pdf. Accessed 09/08/2016.

University of Notre Dame – Under Caesar's Sword: Christian Response to Persecution. *In Response to Persecution: Findings of the Under Caesar's Sword Project on Global Christian Communities*. Report released on April 20, 2017 in Washington D.C. http://ucs.nd.edu/report/. Accessed 19/02/2018.

International Case Law

Appeal Judgement (*Kaing Guek Eav alias Duch*), Case File 001/18-07-2007/ECCC/SC, Extraordinary Chambers in the Courts of Cambodia, 3 February 2012.

Application of the Convention on the Prevention and Punishment of the Crime of Genocide (Bosnia and Herzegovina v. Serbia and Montenegro), Judgment, I.C.J. Reports (2007).

Arrowsmith v. The United Kingdom, 7050/75, Council of Europe: European Commission on Human Rights, 5 December 1978, 19 DR 5.

Campbell and Cosans v. United Kingdom, judgment of 25 February 1982, App. Nos. 7511/76, 7743/76, Eur. Ct. H.R.

Case concerning the Barcelona Traction, Light and Power Company, Limited (Belgium v. Spain); Second Phase, International Court of Justice (ICJ), 5 February 1970.

Decision Pursuant to Article 15 of the Rome Statute on the Authorisation of an Investigation into the Situation in the Republic of Kenya, Pre-Trial Chamber II, 31 March 2010.

Hasan and Chaush v Bulgaria (GC), App no 30985/96, ECHR 2000-XI, (26 October 2000).

Inter-American Court, *Compulsory Membership in an Association Prescribed by Law for the Practice of Journalism* (Arts. 13 and 29 American Convention on Human Rights). Advisory Opinion OC-5/85, 13 November 1985. Series A No. 5.

Jones v Ministry of Interior Al-Mamlaka Al Arabiya as Saudiya (The Kingdom of Saudi Arabia) & another (2004) EWCA Civil 1394.

Judgment (Kaing Guek Eav alias Duch), Case File/Dossier No. 001/18-07-2007/ECCC/TC, Extraordinary Chambers in the Courts of Cambodia, 26 July 2010.

Kjeldsen, Busk, Madsen and Pederson v. Denmark, App Nos. 5095/71, 5920/72, 5926/72, Council of Europe: European Commission on Human Rights, Judgement of 7 December 1976.

Kokkinakis v. Greece, App No. 3/1992/348/421, Council of Europe: European Court of Human Rights, 19 April 1993.

Larissis and Others v. Greece, European Court of Human Rights, Reports 1998-I, judgement of 24 February 1998.

Metropolitan Church of Bessarabia v. Moldova, App no. 45701/99, ECHR 2001-XII.

Nottebohm Case (Liechtenstein v. Guatemala); Second Phase, International Court of Justice (ICJ), 6 April 1955.

Prosecutor v Ahmad Harun and Al Kushayb, Decision on the Prosecution Application under Article 58(7) of the Statute, 27 April 2007 (ICC-02/05-01/07-1).

Prosecutor v Bagosora, Case No. ICTR-98-41-T, 18 December 2008.

Prosecutor v Blagoje Simić et al. (Trial Judgement), IT-95-9-T, ICTY, 17 October 2003.

Prosecutor v Blagojevic and Jokic (Appeal Judgment), Case No. IT-02-60-A, 9 May 2007.

Prosecutor v Clément Kayishema and Obed Ruzindana (Trial Judgement), Case No. ICTR-95-1-T, 21 May 1999.

Prosecutor v Dario Kordić, Mario Cerkez (Trial Judgement), Case No. IT-95-14/2-T, 26 February 2001.

Prosecutor v Dario Kordić, Mario Cerkez (Appeal Judgement), Case No. IT-95-14/2-A, 17 December 2004.

Prosecutor v Dragoljub Kunarac, Radomir Kovac and Zoran Vukovic (Trial Judgment), Case No. IT-96-23-T & IT-96-23/1-T, 22 February 2001.

Prosecutor v Dragoljub Kunarac, Radomir Kovac and Zoran Vukovic (Appeal Judgment), Case No. IT-96-23 & IT-96-23/1-A, 12 June 2002.

Prosecutor v Drazen Erdemovic (Sentencing Judgement), Case No. IT-96-22-T, 29 November 1996.

Prosecutor v Duško Tadić (Trial Judgement), Case No. IT-94-1-T, 7 May 1997.

Prosecutor v Duško Tadić aka "Dule" (Sentencing Judgement), Case No. IT-94-1-T, 14 July 1997.

Prosecutor v Duško Tadić (Appeal Judgement), Case No. IT-94-1-A, 15 July 1999.

Prosecutor v Georges Ruggiu (Trial Judgment), Case No. ICTR 97-32-I, 1 June 2000.

Prosecutor v Germain Katanga & Mathieu Ngudjolo Chui (ICC) Case No ICC-01/04-01/07, Decision on the Confirmation of Charges (30 September 2008).

Prosecutor v Jean Kambanda (Judgement and Sentence), Case No. ICTR 97-23-S, 4 September 1998.

Prosecutor v Jean-Paul Akayesu (Trial Judgement), Case No. ICTR-96-4-T, 2 September 1998.

Prosecutor v Kupreškić et al. (Trial Judgement), Case No. IT-95-16-T, 14 January 2000.

Prosecutor v Laurent Koudou Gbagbo (ICC) Case No ICC-02/11-01/11, Public redacted version of 'Decision on the Prosecutor's Application Pursuant to Article 58 for a warrant of arrest against Laurent Koudou Gbagbo' (30 November 2011) (*'Gbagbo Arrest Warrant'*).

Prosecutor v Milomir Stakić (Trial Judgement), Case No. IT-97-24-T, 31 July 2003.

Prosecutor v Milomir Stakić (Appeal Judgement), Case No. IT-97-24-A, ICTY, 22 March 2006.

Prosecutor v Milorad Krnojelac (Trial Judgement), Case No. IT-97-25-T, 15 March 2002.

Prosecutor v Milorad Krnojelac (Appeal Judgement), Case No. ICTY-97-25-A, 17 September 2003.

Prosecutor v Mladen Naletilic aka "Tuta", Vinko Martinovic aka "Stela" (Trial Judgement), IT-98-34-T, International Criminal Tribunal for the former Yugoslavia (ICTY), 31 March 2003.

Prosecutor v Miroslav Deronjić (Judgement on Sentencing Appeal), Case No. IT-02-61-A, ICTY, 20 July 2005.

Prosecutor v Miroslav Kvočka et al. (Trial Judgement), Case No. IT-98-30/1-T, 2 November 2001.

Prosecutor v Miroslav Kvočka et al. (Appeal Judgement), Case No. IT-98-30/1-A, 28 February 2005.

Prosecutor v Mitar Vasiljević (Appeal Judgement), IT-98-32-A, ICTY, 25 February 2004.

Prosecutor v Mitar Vasiljević (Trial Judgement), IT-98-32-T, International Criminal Tribunal for the former Yugoslavia (ICTY), 29 November 2002.

Prosecutor v Muthaura et al., ICC PT. Ch. II, ICC-01/09-02/11-382-Red, Decision on the Confirmation of Charges Pursuant to Article 61(7)(a) and (b) of the Rome Statute, 23 January 2012.

Prosecutor v Omar Hassan Ahmad Al Bashir (ICC) Case No ICC-02/05-01/09-1, Decision on the Prosecution's Application for a Warrant of Arrest against Omar Hassan Ahmad Al Bashir, Public Redacted Version (4 March 2009).

Prosecutor v Radoslav Brdjanin (Trial Judgement), Case No. IT-99-36-T, 1 September 2004.

Prosecutor v Radoslav Brdjanin (Appeal Judgement), Case No. IT-99-36-A ICTY, 3 April 2007.

Prosecutor v Radislav Krstic (Trial Judgement), Case No. IT-98-33-T, 2 August 2001.

Prosecutor v Radislav Krstic (Appeal Judgement), Case No. IT-98-33-A, 19 April 2004.

Prosecutor v Ruto et al., ICC PT. Ch. II, ICC-01/09-01/11-373, Decision on the Confirmation of Charges Pursuant to Article 61(7)(a) and (b) of the Rome Statute, 23 January 2012.

Prosecutor v Tihomir Blaškić (Trial Judgement), Case No. IT-95-14-T, 3 March 2000.

Prosecutor v Tihomir Blaškić (Appeal Judgement), Case No. IT-95-14-A, 29 July 2004.

Situation in the Democratic Republic of the Congo, in the case of the Prosecutor v. Thomas Lubanga Dyilo, ICC-01/04-01/06, International Criminal Court (ICC), 14 March 2012.

Situation in the Republic of Côte d'Ivoire, *Decision on the confirmation of charges against Laurent Gbagbo*, ICC-02/11-01/11-656-Red, 12 June 2014, Pre-Trial Chamber.

The Trial of German Major War Criminals, Proceedings of the International Military Tribunal Sitting at Nuremberg, Germany. International Military Tribunal, Judgment of 1 October 1946.

US Military Tribunal Sitting in Nuremberg, *US v. Altstötter et al.* (Justice Trial), Judgement of 3–4 December 1947.

Foreign law and case law

Fédération Nationale des Déportés et Internés Résistants et Patriotes and Others v. Barbie, Court of Cassation (Criminal Chamber), 20 December 1985, 78 I.L.R. 125.

Germany: Act to Introduce the Code of Crimes Against International Law [Germany], 26 June 2002.

Jacobellis v Ohio, 378 US 184, 197 (Stewart J).

United States of America: *International Religious Freedom Act of 1998*, Pub. L. 105-292, 27 October 1998. http://www.state.gov/documents/organization/2297.pdf. Accessed 19/10/2016.

United States of America: 2016 Amendment of the International Religious Freedom Act, cited as the *Frank R. Wolf International Religious Freedom Act* (H.R. 1150, Pub.L. 114-281).

United States of America: *Immigration and Nationality Act* (last amended March 2004), 27 June 1952 (INA), 8 U.S.C. § 1101(a)(42)(A). Available at https://www.law.cor nell.edu/ uscode/text/8/1101. Accessed 19/10/2016.

United States – *Genocide Convention Implementation Act of 1987* (the Proxmire Act). Public Law 100-606 (S. 1851).

International instruments

Assembly of States Parties to the Rome Statute of the International Criminal Court, *Rules of Procedure and Evidence*, ICC-ASP/1/3, at 10, and Corr. 1 (2002), U.N. Doc. PCNICC/2000/1/Add.1 (2000).

Control Council Law No. 10, Punishment of Persons Guilty of War Crimes, Crimes Against Peace and Against Humanity, 20 December 1945, Official Gazette of the Control Council for Germany, No. 3, 31 January 1946. Available at: http://avalon.law.yale.edu/imt/imt10.asp. Accessed 20/06/2016.

Council of Europe, *European Convention for the Protection of Human Rights and Fundamental Freedoms, as amended by Protocols Nos. 11 and 14*, 4 November 1950, ETS 5. (*European Convention on Human Rights*).

Council of Europe, *Protocol No. 11 to the Convention for the Protection of Human Rights and Fundamental Freedoms*, restructuring the control machinery established thereby ETS No. 155. Entry into force on 1 November 1998.

International Committee of the Red Cross (ICRC), *Geneva Convention for the Amelioration of the Condition of the Wounded and Sick in Armed Forces in the Field (First Geneva Convention)*, 12 August 1949, 75 UNTS 31.

International Committee of the Red Cross (ICRC), *Geneva Convention for the Amelioration of the Condition of Wounded, Sick and Shipwrecked Members of Armed Forces at Sea (Second Geneva Convention)*, 12 August 1949, 75 UNTS 85.

International Committee of the Red Cross (ICRC), *Geneva Convention Relative to the Treatment of Prisoners of War (Third Geneva Convention)*, 12 August 1949, 75 UNTS 135.

International Committee of the Red Cross (ICRC), *Geneva Convention Relative to the Protection of Civilian Persons in Time of War (Fourth Geneva Convention)*, 12 August 1949, 75 UNTS 287.

International Criminal Court (ICC), *Elements of Crimes*, 2011, Official Records of the Review Conference of the Rome Statute of the International Criminal Court, Kampala, 31 May–11 June 2010 (International Criminal Court publication, RC/11).

International Law Commission, *Draft Articles on Responsibility of States for Internationally Wrongful Acts*, November 2001, Supplement No. 10 (A/56/10), chp.IV.E.1. (UN Doc. A/CN.4/L.602/Rev.1).

International Law Commission, *Draft Code of Crimes against the Peace and the Security of Mankind 1991*, Yearbook of the International Law Commission, 1991, Vol II Part One, document A/CN.4/435 and Add.l.

International Law Commission, *Draft Code of Offences against the Peace and Security of Mankind with commentaries 1996*, Yearbook of the International Law Commission, 1996, vol. II, Part Two. http://www.legal-tools.org/doc/5e4532/. Accessed 13/02/2019.

League of Arab States, *Arab Charter on Human Rights*, 15 September 1994.

League of Arab States, *Arab Charter on Human Rights*, May 22, 2004, entered into force March 15, 2008.

Bibliography

League of Nations, *Covenant of the League of Nations*, 28 April 1919.

Negotiated Relationship Agreement Between the International Criminal Court and the United Nations. ICC-ASP/3/Res.1. Adoption: 04.10.2004. Entry into Force: 22.07.2004.

Office of the United Nations High Commissioner for Human Rights. (OHCHR). *Professional Training Series No. 7, Training Manual on Human Rights Monitoring*. United Nations Publication. (2001). https://www.ohchr.org/Documents/Publications/training7Introen.pdf. Accessed 16/01/2019.

Office of the United Nations High Commissioner for Human Rights. *Study of discrimination in the matter of religious rights and practices, by Arcot Krishnaswami, Special Rapporteur of the Sub-Commission on Prevention of Discrimination and Protection of Minorities*. E/CN.4/Sub.2/200/Rev.1. (1960).

Office of the UN High Commissioner for Human Rights: *Rabat Plan of Action on the prohibition of advocacy of national, racial or religious hatred that constitutes incitement to discrimination, hostility or violence*. Conclusions and recommendations emanating from the four regional expert workshops organised by OHCHR, in 2011, and adopted by experts in Rabat, Morocco on 5 October 2012. http://www.ohchr.org/Documents/Issues/Opinion/SeminarRabat/Rabat_draft_outcome.pdf. Accessed 27/09/2016.

Organization of American States (OAS), *American Convention on Human Rights, "Pact of San Jose"*, Costa Rica, 22 November 1969.

Organization of American States (OAS), *Convention to Prevent and Punish the Acts of Terrorism Taking the Form of Crimes against Persons and Related Extortion that are of International Significance*, 2 February 1971, OAS, Treaty Series, No. 37.

Organization of American States (OAS), *Inter-American Convention on the Forced Disappearance of Persons*, entered into force 28 March 1996, 14861 UN Treaty Collection 1015.

Organization of African Unity (OAU), *African Charter on Human and Peoples' Rights ("Banjul Charter")*, 27 June 1981, CAB/LEG/67/3 rev. 5, 21 I.L.M. 58 (1982).

Rome Statute of the International Criminal Court, Doc. A/CONF.183/9 of 17 July 1998 in force 1 July 2002 (2002).

United Nations, *Charter of the United Nations*, 24 October 1945, 1 UNTS XVI (*UN Charter*).

United Nations, *Charter of the International Military Tribunal – Annex to the Agreement for the prosecution and punishment of the major war criminals of the European Axis ("London Agreement")*, 8 August 1945.

United Nations, *Charter of the International Military Tribunal for the Far East*, 19 January 1946. https://www.loc.gov/law/help/us-treaties/bevans/m-ust000004-0020.pdf. Accessed 20/06/2016.

UN Committee on the Elimination of Racial Discrimination (CERD), *Report of the Committee on the Elimination of Racial Discrimination*, 26 September 1997, Supplement No. 18 (A/52/18).

United Nations, *Statute of the International Court of Justice*, 18 April 1946, established in terms of Chapter XIV of the *Charter of the United Nations* (*ICJ Statute*).

United Nations, *Final Act of the International Conference on Human Rights, Tehran*, 13 May 1968.

UN, *Vienna Convention on the Law of Treaties*, 23 May 1969, United Nations, Treaty Series, vol. 1155, p. 331.

UN Economic and Social Council (ECOSOC), *United Nations Convention Against Illicit Traffic in Narcotic Drugs and Psychotropic Substances*, 19 December 1988.

UN Committee on Economic, Social and Cultural Rights (CESCR), *General comment No. 20: Non-discrimination in economic, social and cultural rights (art. 2, para. 2, of the International Covenant on Economic, Social and Cultural Rights)*. E/C.12/GC/20, 2 July 2009.

UN Human Rights Committee (HRC), *CCPR General Comment No. 23: Article 27 (Rights of Minorities)*, 8 April 1994, CCPR/C/21/Rev.1/Add.5.

UN General Assembly, *Convention on the Non-Applicability of Statutory Limitations to War Crimes and Crimes Against Humanity*, 26 November 1968, A/RES/2391(XXIII).

UN General Assembly, *Declaration on the Elimination of All Forms of Intolerance and of Discrimination Based on Religion or Belief*, UNGA Res 36/55, 73rd plenary meeting, 25 November 1981.

UN General Assembly, *Declaration on the Rights of Persons Belonging to National or Ethnic, Religious and Linguistic Minorities*, 20 December 1993, A/RES/48/138.

UN General Assembly, *International Convention on the Suppression and Punishment of the Crime of Apartheid*, U.N Doc. A/Res/3068 (XXVIII), 30 November 1973 entered into force on 18 July 1976.

UN General Assembly, *Declaration on Territorial Asylum*, A/RES/2312(XXII), 14 December 1967.

UN General Assembly, *Convention for the Suppression of Unlawful Acts Against the Safety of Maritime Navigation*, 10 March 1988, No. 29004.

UN General Assembly, *International Convention on the Elimination of All Forms of Racial Discrimination*, 21 December 1965, United Nations, Treaty Series, vol. 660.

UN General Assembly, *Resolution 95(1) on the Affirmation of the Principles of International Law Recognized by the Charter of the Nuremberg Tribunal*. 11 December 1946, A/RES/95.

UN General Assembly, *Convention on Offences and Certain Other Acts Committed on Board Aircraft* (1963) 704 U.N.T.S. 219.

UN General Assembly, *Declaration on the Elimination of All Forms of Intolerance and of Discrimination Based on Religion or Belief*, UNGA Res 36/55, 73rd plenary meeting, 25 November 1981 (*Religious Discrimination Declaration*).

UN General Assembly, *Elimination of all forms of intolerance and of discrimination based on religion or belief: resolution / adopted by the General Assembly*, 16 March 2009, A/RES/63/181. (*UNGA Res. Discrimination based on Religion*).

UN General Assembly, *Declaration on the Protection of All Persons from Forced Disappearance*, 18 December 1992, UN Doc. A/Res/47/133 47 U.N GAOR Supp. (No. 49), at 207.

Bibliography

UN General Assembly, *Report of the International Law Commission on the work of its 48th session: resolution / adopted by the General Assembly.*, 30 January 1997, A/RES/51/160.

UN General Assembly, *Report of the International Law Commission on the work of its forty-third session*, 29 April – 19 July 1991, Official Records of the General Assembly, Forty-sixth session, Supplement No. 10. Extract from the Yearbook of the International Law Commission: 1991, vol. II(2).

UN General Assembly, *International Convention on the Suppression and Punishment of the Crime of Apartheid*, U.N Doc. A/Res/3068 (XXVIII), 30 November 1973 entered into force on 18 July 1976

UN General Assembly, *Convention on the Rights of the Child*, 20 November 1989, United Nations, Treaty Series, vol. 1577.

UN General Assembly, *Resolution 103(I) Persecution and Discrimination*, 19 November 1946.

UN General Assembly, *Universal Declaration of Human Rights*, 10 December 1948, Resolution 217 A (III) (*UDHR*).

UN General Assembly, *Setting international standards in the field of human rights*, Resolution 41/120 of 4 December 1986, 97th plenary meeting, A/RES/41/120.

UN General Assembly, *Convention on the Non-Applicability of Statutory Limitations to War Crimes and Crimes Against Humanity*, 26 November 1968, A/RES/2391(XXIII).

UN General Assembly, *Convention on the Prevention and Punishment of the Crime of Genocide*, 9 December 1948, United Nations, Treaty Series, vol. 78, pg 277 (*Genocide Convention*).

UN Commission on Human Rights, *Resolution 2005/40 on Elimination of All Forms of Intolerance and of Discrimination Based on Religion or Belief*, 19 April 2005, E/CN.4/RES/2005/40.

UN General Assembly, *Convention on the Prevention and Punishment of the Crime of Genocide*, 9 December 1948, United Nations, Treaty Series, vol. 78, pg 277.

UN General Assembly, *International Covenant on Economic, Social and Cultural Rights*, 16 December 1966, United Nations, Treaty Series, vol. 993, pg 3 (*ICESCR*).

UN General Assembly, *Convention on the Law of the Sea*, 10 December 1982.

UN General Assembly, *Convention against Torture and Other Cruel, Inhuman or Degrading Treatment or Punishment: resolution / adopted by the General Assembly*, 10 December 1984, A/RES/39/46.

UN General Assembly, *International Covenant on Civil and Political Rights*, 16 December 1966, United Nations, Treaty Series, vol. 999, p. 171 (ICCPR) and its two Optional Protocols (Optional Protocol to the International Covenant on Civil and Political Rights, 16 December 1966 entry into force 23 March 1976; and Second Optional Protocol to the International Covenant on Civil and Political Rights, aiming at the abolition of the death penalty, 15 December 1989.

UN General Assembly, The United Nations Global Counter-Terrorism Strategy: resolution / adopted by the General Assembly. 20 September 2006, A/RES/60/288.

UN General Assembly, *Elimination of all forms of religious intolerance*, Interim report of the Special Rapporteur on freedom of religion or belief, A/66/156, 18 July 2011.

UN General Assembly, *Elimination of all forms of religious intolerance*, Interim report of the Special Rapporteur of the Commission on Human Rights on the elimination of all forms of intolerance and of discrimination based on religion or belief, A/56/253, 31 July 2001.

UN General Assembly, *Elimination of all forms of intolerance and of discrimination based on religion or belief: resolution / adopted by the General Assembly*, 17 March 2010, A/RES/64/164.

UN General Assembly, *Report of the Special Rapporteur on Freedom of Religion or Belief, Heiner Bielefeldt*. A/HRC/28/66, 29 December 2014.

UN General Assembly, *Report of the Special Rapporteur on freedom of religion or belief, Asma Jahangir*. A/HRC/13/40, 21 December 2009.

UN General Assembly, *Implementation of General Assembly Resolution 60/251 of 15 March 2006 entitled "Human Rights Council"*. A/HRC/2/7, 2 October 2006.

UN General Assembly, *Elimination of all forms of religious intolerance*, Interim report by the Special Rapporteur of the Commission on Human Rights on the elimination of all forms of intolerance and of discrimination based on religion or belief. A/55/280, 8 September 2000.

UN General Assembly, *Resolution adopted by the Human Rights Council S-23/1: Atrocities committed by the terrorist group Boko Haram and its effects on human rights in the affected States*. A/HRC/RES/S-23/1, 21 May 2015.

UN General Assembly, *Report of the United Nations High Commissioner for Human Rights: Violations and abuses committed by Boko Haram and the impact on human rights in the countries affected*. A/HRC/30/67, 9 December 2015.

UN General Assembly, *Report of the independent expert on the situation of human rights in Somalia, Shamsul Bari*. A/HRC/18/48, 29 August 2011.

UN General Assembly, *Elimination of all forms of religious intolerance: Report of the Special Rapporteur of the Commission on Human Rights on freedom of religion or belief, Asma Jahangir*. A/60/399, 30 September 2005.

UN General Assembly, *Elimination of all forms of religious intolerance*, A/73/362, 5 September 2018.

UN General Assembly, *Declaration on the Right and Responsibility of Individuals, Groups and Organs of Society to Promote and Protect Universally Recognized Human Rights and Fundamental Freedoms: resolution / adopted by the General Assembly*. A/RES/53/144, 8 March 1999.

UN Human Rights Committee (HRC), *CCPR General Comment No. 5: Article 4 (Derogations)*, 31 July 1981. (*UNHRC: General Comment No. 5*).

Bibliography

UN Commission on Human Rights, *Commission on Human Rights resolution 2000/61 Human rights defenders*. E/CN.4/RES/2000/61, 27 April 2000.

UN Human Rights Committee discussion on 24 July 1992, Summary Records of the 1166th meeting of the forty-fifth session.

UN Human Rights Committee, *General Comment No. 22: The Right to Freedom of Thought, Conscience, and Religion in terms of Article 18 of the ICCPR*. CCPR/C/21/Rev.1/Add.4, Adopted by the Committee at its 1247th meeting (forty-eighth session), 20 July 1993. The UN International Human Rights Instruments, *Compilation of General Comments and General Recommendations Adopted by Human Rights Treaty Bodies*, 12 May 2004 HRI/GEN/1/Rev.7. (*UNHRC: General Comment No. 22*)

UN Human Rights Committee, *General Comment No. 24: Issues relating to reservations made upon ratification or accession to the Covenant or the Optional Protocols thereto, or in relation to declarations under article 41 of the Covenant*, par 10. From the UN International Human Rights Instruments, Compilation of General Comments and General Recommendations Adopted by Human Rights Treaty Bodies, 12 May 2004, HRI/GEN/1/Rev.7. (*UNHRC: General Comment No. 24*)

UN Human Rights Committee, *General comment No. 29: Article 4: Derogations during a state of emergency*. From the UN International Human Rights Instruments, *Compilation of General Comments and General Recommendations Adopted by Human Rights Treaty Bodies*, 12 May 2004, HRI/GEN/1/Rev.7. (*UNHRC: General Comment No. 29*).

UN Human Rights Council, *Combating intolerance, negative stereotyping and stigmatization of, and discrimination, incitement to violence and violence against, persons based on religion or belief : resolution / adopted by the Human Rights Council*, 15 April 2014, A/HRC/RES/25/34.

UN Human Rights Council, Forum on Minority Issues. *Protecting minority rights to prevent or mitigate the impact of humanitarian crisis*, speech before the 9 Ninth session of the Forum on Minority Issues on *Minorities in situations of humanitarian crises*, 24 November 2016.

UN Human Rights Council Resolution 7/8 *Mandate of the Special Rapporteur on the situation of human rights defenders*. A/HRC/RES/7/8, 27 March 2008.

UN Commission on Human Rights, *Implementation of the Declaration on the Elimination of All Forms of Intolerance and of Discrimination Based on Religion or Belief*, 10 March 1986, E/CN.4/RES/1986/20.

United Nations General Assembly Resolution 429(V) of 14 December 1950, UN High Commissioner for Refugees (UNHCR), *Convention and Protocol Relating to the Status of Refugees*. https://www.unhcr.org/3b66c2aa10. Accessed 13/02/2019. (*Refugee Convention of 1951*).

UN High Commissioner for Refugees (UNHCR), *The Refugee Convention, 1951: The Travaux préparatoires analysed with a Commentary by Dr. Paul Weis*, 1990.

UN High Commissioner for Refugees (UNHCR), *Guidelines on International Protection No. 6: Religion-Based Refugee Claims under Article 1A(2) of the 1951 Convention and/or the 1967 Protocol relating to the Status of Refugees*, 28 April 2004, HCR/GIP/04/06.

UN High Commissioner for Refugees (UNHCR), *Expert Meeting on Complementarities between International Refugee Law, International Criminal Law and International Human Rights Law: Summary Conclusions*, July 2011, Available at: http://www.refworld.org/docid/ 4e1729d52.html. Accessed 17 April 2016.

UN High Commissioner for Refugees (UNHCR), *Handbook and Guidelines on Procedures and Criteria for Determining Refugee Status under the 1951 Convention and the 1967 Protocol Relating to the Status of Refugees*, December 2011, HCR/1P/4/ENG/REV. 3.

UN High Commissioner for Refugees (UNHCR), *Procedural Standards for Refugee Status Determination Under UNHCR's Mandate*, 20 November 2003.

UN Security Council, *Report of the Secretary-General Pursuant to Paragraph 2 of Security Council Resolution 808 (1993) [Contains text of the Statute of the International Tribunal for the Prosecution of Persons Responsible for Serious Violations of International Humanitarian Law Committed in the Territory of the Former Yugoslavia since 1991]*, 3 May 1993, S/25704.

UN Security Council, *Statute of the International Criminal Tribunal for the Former Yugoslavia (as amended on 17 May 2002)*, 25 May 1993.

UN Security Council, *Statute of the International Criminal Tribunal for Rwanda* (as last amended on 13 October 2006), 8 November 1994.

UN Security Council, *Security Council resolution 955 (1994) [Establishment of the International Criminal Tribunal for Rwanda]*, 8 November 1994, S/RES/955 (1994).

UN Security Council, *Security Council resolution 1526 (2004) [on improving implementation of measures imposed by paragraph 4 (b) of resolution 1267 (1999), paragraph 8 (c) of resolution 1333 (2000) and paragraphs 1 and 2 of Resolution 1390 (2002) on measures against Al-Qaida and the Taliban]*, 30 January 2004, S/RES/1526 (2004).

UN Security Council, *Security Council resolution 1377 (2001) [threats to international peace and security caused by terrorist acts]*, 12 November 2001, S/RES/1377 (2001).

UN Security Council, *Security Council resolution 2178 (2014) [on threats to international peace and security caused by foreign terrorist fighters]*, 24 September 2014, S/RES/2178 (2014).

UN Security Council, *Security Council resolution 1500 (2003) [on the situation between Iraq and Kuwait]*, 14 August 2003, S/RES/1500 (2003).

UN Security Council, *Security Council resolution 1770 (2007) [on extension of the mandate of the UN Assistance Mission for Iraq (UNAMI)]*, 10 August 2007, S/RES/1770 (2007).

UN Security Council, *Security Council resolution 2368 (2017) [threats to international peace and security caused by terrorist acts]*, 20 July 2017, S/RES/2368 (2017).

UN Security Council, *Security Council resolution 1373 (2001) [on threats to international peace and security caused by terrorist acts]*, 28 September 2001, S/RES/1373 (2001).

UN Security Council, *Security Council resolution 2379 (2017) [on establishment of an Investigative Team to Support Domestic Efforts to Hold the Islamic State in Iraq and the Levant Accountable for Its Actions in Iraq]*, 21 September 2017, S/RES/2379 (2017).

Bibliography

UN Security Council, *Security Council resolution 2354 (2017) [on implementation of the Comprehensive International Framework to Counter Terrorist Narratives]*, 24 May 2017, S/RES/2354 (2017).

UN Security Council, *Resolution 2421 (2018) [The situation concerning Iraq]*, 14 June 2018, S/RES/2421 (2018).

UN Security Council, *Security Council resolution 1660 (2006) [International Tribunal for the Prosecution of Persons Responsible for Serious Violations of International Humanitarian Law Committed in the Territory of the Former Yugoslavia since 1991]*, 28 February 2006, S/RES/1660 (2006).

UN Security Council, *resolution 2161 (2014) [on threats to international peace and security caused by terrorist acts by Al-Qaida]*, 17 June 2014, S/RES/2161 (2014).

UN Security Council, *Report of the Commission of Experts Established Pursuant to United Nations Security Council Resolution 780 (1992)*, 27 May 1994 S/1994/674.

UN Security Council, *Security Council resolution 2253 (2015) [on renaming of Al-Qaida Sanctions Committee as "1267/1989/2253 ISIL (Da'esh) and Al-Qaida Sanctions Committee" and the Al-Qaida Sanctions List as "ISIL (Da'esh) and Al-Qaida Sanctions List" and on extension of the mandate the Office of the Ombudsperson for a period of 24 months from the date of expiration of its current mandate in Dec. 2017]*, 17 December 2015, S/RES/2253 (2015).

UN Security Council, *Security Council resolution 2195 (2014) [on preventing and combating terrorism, including terrorism benefitting from transnational organized crime]*, 19 December 2014, S/RES/2195 (2014). http://www.un.org/en/ga/search/view_doc.asp?symbol=S/RES/ 2195%20(2014). Accessed 06/02/2015.

UN Security Council, *Security Council resolution 2170 (2014) [on threats to international peace and security caused by terrorist acts by Al-Qaida]*, 15 August 2014, S/RES/2170 (2014).

UN Security Council, *Security Council resolution 2199 (2015) [on threats to international peace and security caused by terrorist acts by Al-Qaida]*, 12 February 2015, S/RES/2199 (2015).

UN Security Council, *Security Council resolution 2233 (2015) [on extension of the mandate of the UN Assistance Mission for Iraq (UNAMI) until 31 July 2016]*, 29 July 2015, S/RES/2233 (2015).

UN Security Council, *Security Council resolution 2249 (2015) [on terrorist attacks perpetrated by ISIL also known as Da'esh]*, 20 November 2015, S/RES/2249 (2015).

UN Security Council, *Resolution 808 (1993) Adopted by the Security Council at its 3175th meeting, on 22 February 1993*, S/RES/808 (1993).

UN Security Council, *Security Council resolution 2299 (2016) [on extension of the mandate of the UN Assistance Mission for Iraq (UNAMI) until 31 July 2017]*, 25 July 2016, S/RES/2299 (2016).

UN Security Council, *Security Council resolution 2332 (2016) [on the humanitarian situation in the Syrian Arab Republic and renewal of authorization of relief delivery and monitoring mechanism until 18 Jan. 2018]*, 21 December 2016, S/RES/2332 (2016).

UN Security Council, *Security Council resolution 2367 (2017) [on extension of the mandate of the UN Assistance Mission for Iraq (UNAMI) until 31 July 2018]*, 14 July 2017, S/RES/2367 (2017).

UN Security Council, *Security Council resolution 2195 (2014) [on preventing and combating terrorism, including terrorism benefitting from transnational organized crime]*, 19 December 2014, S/RES/2195 (2014).

UN Security Council, *Security Council resolution 2258 (2015) [on the humanitarian situation in the Syrian Arab Republic and renewal for a period of 12 months of two decisions of Security Council resolution 2165 (2014)]*, 22 December 2015, S/RES/2258 (2015).

UNWCC, *History of the United Nations War Crimes Commission and the Development of the Laws of War* (London: United Nations War Crimes Commission by His Majesty's Stationery Office, 1948). Available at http://www.unwcc.org/wp-content/uploads/2014/11/UNWCC-history-contents.pdf. Accessed 02/07/2016.

Organization of the Islamic Conference (OIC), *Convention of the Organisation of the Islamic Conference on Combating International Terrorism*, 1 July 1999, Annex to Resolution No: 59/26-P.

Vienna Declaration and Programme of Action, World Conference on Human Rights. 5, U.N. Doc. A/CONF.157/23 (25 June 1993).

International Criminal Court communications and reports

Office of the Prosecutor of the International Criminal Court, *Report on Preliminary Examination activities*, 13 December 2011.

Office of the Prosecutor of the International Criminal Court, *Policy Paper on Sexual and Gender-Based Crimes,* June 2014. https://www.icc-cpi.int/iccdocs/otp/otp-policy-paper-on-sexual-and-gender-based-crimes--june-2014.pdf.   Accessed 14/02/2017.

Situation in the Republic of Côte d'Ivoire (ICC-02/11-01/11-1) – *Warrant Of Arrest For Laurent Koudou Gbagbo*. https://www.icc-cpi.int/iccdocs/doc/doc1276751.pdf. Accessed 14/04/2016.

Summary of Statements made in Plenary in Connection with the Adoption of the Report of the Working Group on the Rules of Procedure and Evidence and the Report of the Working Group on Elements of Crime, Preparatory Commission document PCNICC/2000/INF/4, 13 July 2000.

Reports and communications

Abrams, E. *The Persecution of Christians as a Worldwide Phenomenon*. Testimony of Elliott Abrams, U.S. Commission on International Religious Freedom before the Subcommittee on Africa, Global Health, Global Human Rights, and International Organizations of the House Foreign Affairs Committee, 11 February 2014.

Amnesty International, *Amnesty International Report 2014/15: The State of the World's Human Rights.* 25 February 2015, Index number: POL 10/0001/2015.

Bibliography 489

Amnesty International, *Amnesty International Report 2017/18: The State of the World's Human Rights*. 22 February 2018, Index number: POL 10/6700/2018.

Amnesty International, *Northern Iraq: Civilians in the line of fire*. 14 July 2014, MDE 14/007/2014.

Amnesty International, Punished for Daesh's Crimes – Displaced Iraqis Abused by Militias and Government Forces. 18 October 2016, MDE 14/4962/2016.

Annex to the letter dated 14 August 2017 from the Chargé d'affaires a.i. of the Permanent Mission of Iraq to the United Nations addressed to the President of the Security Council, 16 August 2017, S/2017/710.

Annual Report of the U.S. Commission on International Religious Freedom. April 2013 (Covering January 31, 2012 – January 31, 2013) p 6. www.uscirf.gov.

Australian Security Intelligence Organisation. https://www.nationalsecurity.gov.au/Listedterroristorganisations/Pages/IslamicState.aspx. Accessed 19/10/2018.

Council of Europe, Committee on Legal Affairs and Human Rights report to the Parliamentary Assembly, presented by the Rapporteur, Omtzigt, P. *Prosecuting and punishing the crimes against humanity or even possible genocide committed by Da'esh*. Doc. 14167, Reference 4251 of 25 November 2016.

Council of Europe, Parliamentary Assembly, *Resolution 2190 (2017) - Prosecuting and punishing the crimes against humanity or even possible genocide committed by Daesh*. Text adopted by the Assembly on 12 October 2017 (34th Sitting).

Council of Europe, Parliamentary Assembly, *Resolution 2091 (2016) - Foreign fighters in Syria and Iraq*. Text adopted by the Assembly on 27 January 2016 (6th Sitting).

Comprehensive international framework to counter terrorist narratives. Annex to the Letter dated 26 April 2017 from the Chair of the Security Council Committee established pursuant to resolution 1373 (2001) concerning counter-terrorism addressed to the President of the Security Council, 28 April 2017, S/2017/375.

Final Report of the Commission Of Experts Established Pursuant to Security Council Resolution 780 (1992), 27 May 1994 (S/1994/674) as an annexure to Letter Dated 24 May 1994 From The Secretary-General To The President Of The Security Council. http://www.icty.org/x/file/About/OTP/un_commission_of_experts_report1994_en.pdf. Accessed 26/02/2013.

Human Rights Watch Briefing Paper. *The Rwandan Genocide: How It Was Prepared*. April 2006. http://www.hrw.org/legacy/backgrounder/africa/rwanda0406/rwanda0406.pdf. Accessed 14/02/2016.

Human Rights Watch. *Flawed Justice – Accountability for ISIS Crimes in Iraq*. 4 December 2017. https://www.hrw.org/sites/default/files/report_pdf/iraq1217web.pdf. Accessed 15/10/2018.

Human Rights Watch. *A Face and a Name: Civilian Victims of Insurgent Groups in Iraq*. 3 October 2005, E1709. https://www.hrw.org/report/2005/10/02/face-and-name/civilian-victims-insurgent-groups-iraq. Accessed 12/08/2016.

Human Rights Watch. *"They Are Not Our Brothers" Hate Speech by Saudi Officials*. September 2017. https://www.hrw.org/report/2017/09/26/they-are-not-our-brothers/hate-speech-saudi-officials. Accessed 15/10/2018.

Kikoler, N. *'Our Generation is Gone': The Islamic State's Targeting of Iraqi Minorities in Ninewa*. Bearing Witness Trip report to the Simon-Skjodt Center for the Prevention of Genocide, United States Holocaust Memorial Museum, (2015). https://www.ushmm.org/m/pdfs/Iraq-Bearing-Witness-Report-111215.pdf. Accessed 22/10/2018.

Report of the Commission of Experts Established Pursuant to United Nations Security Council Resolution 780 (1992). May 27, 1994 (S/1994/674).

Report of the Special Rapporteur on Freedom of Religion or Belief. Jahangir, A. http://daccess-dds-ny.un.org/doc/UNDOC/GEN/G09/102/10/PDF/G0910210.pdf?OpenElement. Accessed 16/08/2018.

Report submitted by the Special Rapporteur on freedom of religion or belief in re *Examination of the consequences of the events of 11 September 2001 as regards tolerance and non-discrimination*. Outcome of the 2001 International Consultative Conference, 14 March 2002, E/CN.4/2002/73.

Report of the Committee on the Elimination of Racial Discrimination. General Assembly Official Records: Forty-Fifth Session, Supplement No. 18 (A/45/18), chap. VII,

Report submitted to Secretary of State John Kerry by the Knights of Columbus and In Defense of Christians. *Genocide against Christians in the Middle East*. 9 March 2016, pg 6. http://www.stopthechristiangenocide.org/en/resources/Genocide-report.pdf. Accessed 31/01/2019.

Storms, R. A. *Korea, North*. Encyclopedia of Law and Religion. General Editor Robbers, G. First published online in 2015 at http://dx.doi.org/10.1163/2405-9749_elr_COM_00000055. Accessed 23/11/2018.

UN Committee on the Elimination of Discrimination Against Women (CEDAW), *General recommendation No. 30 on women in conflict prevention, conflict and post-conflict situations*, 1 November 2013, CEDAW/C/GC/30.

UN Docs. CCPR/C/45/CRP.2 (1992).

UN General Assembly, *Report of the International Law Commission, 66th session* (5 May–6 June and 7 July–8 August 2014), 2014, Supplement No. 10, A/69/10.

UN General Assembly, *First report on crimes against humanity by Sean D. Murphy, Special Rapporteur, at the 67th session* (4 May–5 June and 6 July–7 August 2015), 2015, A/CN.4/680 and Corr.1.

UN General Assembly, *Report of the International Law Commission, 69th session* (1 May–2 June and 3 July–4 August 2017), 2017, A/72/10.

UN Security Council, *Letter dated 13 November 2014 from the Chair of the Security Council Committee pursuant to resolutions 1267 (1999) and 1989 (2011) concerning Al-Qaida and associated individuals and entities addressed to the President of the Security Council*, 14 November 2014, S/2014/815 (2014). (Hereafter referred to as 'The Report on the threat posed by the ISIL').

Bibliography

UN Human Rights Council, Report of the Special Rapporteur on freedom of religion or belief, Addendum: Mission to Viet Nam (21 to 31 July 2014), 30 January 2015, A/HRC/28/66/Add.2.

UN Office of the High Commissioner for Human Rights (OHCHR), *Independent International Commission of Inquiry*, established pursuant to UN Human Rights Council Resolutions S-17/1, 19/22 and 21/26, 20 December 2012.

UN Office of the High Commissioner for Human Rights (OHCHR), *Report of the Independent International Commission of Inquiry on the Syrian Arab Republic (IICISAR). Rule of Terror: Living under ISIS in Syria*, 14 November 2014.

UN Office of the High Commissioner for Human Rights (OHCHR), *Report of the Independent International Commission of Inquiry on the Syrian Arab Republic (IICISAR)*. 5 February 2015, A/HRC/28/69.

UN Office of the High Commissioner for Human Rights (OHCHR), *Free & Equal Campaign Fact Sheet: Intersex*. 4 March 2016. https://www.unfe.org/wp-content/uploads/2017/05/UNFE-Intersex.pdf. Accessed 07/12/2018.

UN Human Rights Council, Report of the Independent International Commission of Inquiry on the Syrian Arab Republic (IICISAR). "They came to destroy": ISIS Crimes Against the Yazidis. 15 June 2016, A/HRC/32/CRP.2.

UN Human Rights Council, *Report of the Independent International Commission of Inquiry on the Syrian Arab Republic. (IICISAR)*. 13 August 2015, A/HRC/30/48.

UN Security Council, *Final Report of the United Nations Commission of Experts Established Pursuant to Security Council Resolution 780 (1992)*, 27 May 1994, (S/1994/674/Add.2 (Vol. I), annex II), (S/1994/674).

UN Report, *United Nations World Conference against Racism, Racial Discrimination, Xenophobia and Related Intolerance*, Declaration, 31 August to 8 September 2001, UN DocA/CONF.189/12.

UN Human Rights Council, *Report of the Office of the United Nations High Commissioner for Human Rights on the human rights situation in Iraq in the light of abuses committed by the so-called Islamic State in Iraq and the Levant and associated groups*, 13 March 2015, A/HRC/28/18.

UN Commission on Human Rights, *Report of the Special Rapporteur on the implementation of the Declaration on the elimination of all forms of intolerance and of discrimination based on religion belief*, 15 December 1995, E/CN.4/1996/95.

UN Commission on Human Rights, *Report submitted by the Special Rapporteur on freedom of religion or belief, in accordance with Commission on Human Rights resolution 2002/40*, 15 January 2003, E/CN.4/2003/66.

UN General Assembly, General committee: *Resolution on persecution and discrimination: Request for the inclusion of an additional item in the agenda / from the delegation for Egypt*. A/BUR/51, 11 November 1946.

UN General Assembly, Report of the Special Rapporteur on Freedom of Religion or Belief, 14 February 2011, A/HRC/16/53/Add.1.

United Nations Office at Geneva. *Intra-Syrian Peace Process.* https://www.unog.ch/unog/website/news_media.nsf/(httpPages)/4d6470dbeaf92917c1257e59004fac2d. Accessed 22/10/2018.

United States Commission on International Religious Freedom, *Annual Report of the U.S. Commission on International Religious Freedom.* April 2018. https://www.uscirf.gov/sites/default/files/2018USCIRFAR.pdf. Accessed 20/12/2018.

Websites

Amnesty International website. *Country profiles: Iraq.* https://www.amnesty.org/en/countries/middle-east-and-north-africa/iraq/. Accessed 26/10/2018

Amnesty International website. *Country profiles: Syria.* https://www.amnesty.org/en/countries/middle-east-and-north-africa/syria/. Accessed 26/10/2018.

Australia National Security website: https://www.nationalsecurity.gov.au/Pages/default.aspx.

BrainyQuote website, Don Miguel Ruiz. https://www.brainyquote.com/authors/don_miguel_ruiz. Accessed 17/10/2017.

Freedom of Mind Resource Center. *Steve Hassan.* https://freedomofmind.com/about-us/steven-hassan/. Accessed 20/12/2018.

Genocide Watch website: www.genocidewatch.org.

History Place website: www.historyplace.com.

Human Rights Watch – *World Report 2015.* http://www.hrw.org/world-report/2015.

Human Rights Watch website. *Daesh.* https://www.hrw.org/publications?keyword=Daesh&date%5Bvalue%5D%5Byear%5D=&country%5B%5D=9637&country%5B%5D=9648. Accessed 26/10/2018.

International Christian Concern Organization website: www.persecution.org.

International Criminal Court website: http://www.icc-cpi.int/Menus/ICC.

International Criminal Tribunal for Yugoslavia website: http://www.icty.org/sid/10415.

Jubilee Campaign website: www.jubileecampaign.org.

New York Times website: www.nytimes.com.

Open Doors World Watch List website: www.opendoors.org.

Spartacus Educational: https://spartacus-educational.com/PRholyoak.htm. Accessed 24/01/2019.

Terrorism Research and Analysis Consortium (TRAC) website – '*Islamic State (IS) / Islamic State of Iraq and ash Sham (ISIS) / Islamic State of Iraq (ISIS or ISIL, IS)*': https://www.trackingterrorism.org/group/islamic-state-islamic-state-iraq-and-ash-sham-isis-islamic-state-iraq-isis-or-isil. Accessed 30/10/2018.

The Global Coalition against Daesh website. http://theglobalcoalition.org/en/home/. Accessed 12/10/2018.

Bibliography

United Nations Human Rights Council website: http://www.ohchr.org/EN/Pages/WelcomePage.aspx.

UN Human Rights Council website. *Independent International Commission of Inquiry on the Syrian Arab Republic.* https://www.OHCHR.org/EN/HRBodies/HRC/IICISyria/Pages/AboutCoI.aspx. Accessed 26/10/2018.

United Nations website: http://www.un.org/en/.

UN Office of the High Commissioner for Human Rights (OHCHR): https://www.ohchr.org/en/hrbodies/sp/pages/welcomepage.aspx. Accessed 28/01/2019.

UN Office of the High Commissioner for Human Rights (OHCHR) website. *Human Rights Bodies - Complaints Procedures.* http://www.ohchr.org/EN/HRBodies/TBPetitions/Pages/HRTB Petitions.aspx. Accessed 16/02/2018.

UN Office of the High Commissioner for Human Rights (OHCHR) website. *Iraq.* https://www.OHCHR.org/EN/Countries/MENARegion/Pages/IQIndex.aspx. Accessed 26/10/2018

UN Office of the High Commissioner for Human Rights (OHCHR) website. *Syrian Arab Republic.* https://www.OHCHR.org/EN/Countries/MENARegion/Pages/SYIndex.aspx. Accessed 26/10/2018.

US Central Intelligence Agency, *World Fact Book.* Middle East / Iran. https://www.cia.gov/library/publications/the-world-factbook/geos/ir.html. Accessed 09/01/2019.

Vocabulary.com Dictionary, *Persecution.* https://www.vocabulary.com/dictionary/persecution. Accessed 17/10/2017.

World Watch Monitor website: www.worldwatchlist.us.

Media and other sources

Abi-Habib, M. *Iraq's Christian Minority Feels Militant Threat.* The Wall Street Journal. 20/08/2014. https://www.wsj.com/articles/iraqs-christian-minority-feels-militant-threat-1403826576. Accessed 08/01/2015.

Al-Jazeera news. *Iraq government loses control of Fallujah.* (4 January 2014). https://www.aljazeera.com/news/middleeast/2014/01/iraq-government-loses-control-fallujah-20141414625597514.html. Accessed 12/10/2018.

Al Jazeera News. *Syria's civil war explained from the beginning.* 14 April 2018. https://www.aljazeera.com/news/2016/05/syria-civil-war-explained-160505084119966.html. Accessed 22/10/2018.

Al-Salhy, S. & Arango, T. *Sunni Militants Drive Iraqi Army Out of Mosul.* The New York Times, 10 June 2014. https://www.nytimes.com/2014/06/11/world/middleeast/militants-in-mosul.html. Accessed 12/10/2018.

American National Counterterrorism Center – *Report on Terrorist Incidents 30 April 2006* – https://web.archive.org/web/20090326171214/http://wits.nctc.gov/reports/crot2006nctcannexfinal.pdf. Accessed 16/07/2017.

Afsaruddin, A. *Jihad: Islam*. Encycloaedia Britannica. Last updated on 15 January 2019. https://www.britannica.com/topic/jihad. Accessed 01/02/2019.

Author unknown, *Convert, pay tax, or die, Islamic State warns Christians*. The Guardian. Reuters. http://www.theguardian.com/world/2014/jul/18/isis-islamic-state-issue-ultimatum-to-iraq-christians. Accessed 20/08/2014.

Barnard, A. et al. *As Atrocities Mount in Syria, Justice Seems Out of Reach*. The New York Times, 15 April 2017. https://www.nytimes.com/2017/04/15/world/middleeast/syria-bashar-al-assad-evidence.html. Accessed 30/01/2019.

Bradley, M. M. *An analysis of the notions of 'organised armed groups' and 'intensity' in the law of non-international armed conflict*. LLD thesis at the University of Pretoria (2017).

Convention (II) with Respect to the Laws and Customs of War on Land and its annex: Regulations concerning the Laws and Customs of War on Land. The Hague, 29 July 1899.

Crabtree, V. *Religious Extremism* (2017) The Human Truth Foundation website: http://www.humanreligions.info/extremism.html. Accessed 21/06/2018.

Dettmer, J. *Al-Qaeda Denounces Syrian Jihadis*. The Daily Beast, 2 March 2014. https://www.thedailybeast.com/al-qaeda-denounces-syrian-jihadis. Accessed 12/10/2018.

Duthiers, V. et al. *Boko Haram: Why terror group kidnaps schoolgirls, and what happens next*. CNN International, 2 May 2 2014. https://edition.cnn.com/2014/04/24/world/africa/nigeria-kidnapping-answers/index.html. Accessed 29/01/2018.

Elbagir, N. et al. *Boko Haram purportedly pledges allegiance to ISIS*. CNN, 9 March 2015. https://edition.cnn.com/2015/03/07/africa/nigeria-boko-haram-isis/. Accessed 12/10/2018.

Harding, L. *ISIS accused of ethnic cleansing as story of Shia prison massacre emerges*. The Guardian website. http://www.theguardian.com/world/2014/aug/25/isis-ethnic-cleansing-shia-prisoners-iraq-mosul. Accessed 17/02/2015.

Hill, J. N. C. *Boko Haram, the Chibok Abductions and Nigeria's Counterterrorism Strategy*. Combating Terrorism Center – CTC Sentinel, July 2014, Vol 7, Issue 7, pg 15. https://ctc.usma.edu/app/uploads/2014/07/CTCSentinel-Vol7Iss75.pdf. Accessed 14/02/2017.

Hsueh-Hua Chen, V. *Cultural identity: Key Concepts in Intercultural Dialogue*, No. 22, 2014. https://centerforinterculturaldialogue.files.wordpress.com/2014/07/key-concept-cultural-identity.pdf. Accessed 04/11/2017.

Jubilee Campaign. *Jubilee Campaign Engages the International Criminal Court at The Hague*. http://jubileecampaign.org/iccmay21/. Accessed 06/06/2012.

Ochab, E. U. *Bringing Daesh To Justice – A Real Action At Last?* Forbes, 21 September 2017. https://www.forbes.com/sites/ewelinaochab/2017/09/21/bringing-daesh-to-justice-real-action-at-last/#1fc093c32622. Accessed 12/10/2018.

Ochab, E. U. *Netherlands joins UN Security Council to shine light on IS genocide*. January 11, 2018, World Watch Monitor. https://www.worldwatchmonitor.org/2018/

Bibliography 495

01/netherlands-joins-un-security-council-shine-light-genocide/. Accessed 22/10/2018.

Public dialogue on *"Forging a Convention on Crimes Against Humanity"*, organized by the Human Sciences Research Council in collaboration with the Konrad Adenauer Foundation, Johannesburg Holocaust and Genocide Centre, 21 February 2019.

Radio Free Asia. *China Jails Six Protestants in Yunnan Amid Massive Crackdown on 'Evil Cult'.* 18 January 2018. https://www.rfa.org/english/news/china/protestants-01182018110902.html. Accessed 31/01/2018.

Rathje, W. L. *Why the Taliban are destroying Buddhas.* 22 March 2001. USAtoday.com: https://usatoday30.usatoday.com/news/science/archaeology/2001-03-22-afghan-buddhas.htm. Accessed 29/01/2018.

Remarks on *Da'esh* and Genocide by Secretary of State John Kerry, Washington DC, 17 March 2016. https://2009-2017.state.gov/secretary/remarks/2016/03/254782.htm. Accessed 24/10/2018.

Spencer, R. *Islamic State justifies its jihad against Yazidis.* Jihad Watch website. August 21, 2014. http://www.jihadwatch.org/2014/08/islamic-state-justifies-its-jihad-against-yazidis. Accessed 23/08/2014.

Sookhdeo, P. *Editorial: The Two Faces of Islam.* (2014). https://barnabasfund.org/news/Editorial-The-Two-Faces-of-Islam. Accessed 09/02/2015.

Statement by former President Barack Obama, Martha's Vineyard, Massachusetts on 20 August 2014. http://www.whitehouse.gov/the-press-office/2014/08/20/statement-president. 22/08/2014.

Statement of the Special Rapporteur on minority issues on conclusion of her official visit to Iraq, 27 February to 7 March 2016. https://www.ohchr.org/EN/NewsEvents/Pages/DisplayNews.aspx? NewsID=17157&LangID=E. Accessed 22/10/2018).

Storey, H. *What constitutes persecution: Towards a working definition of persecution.* (2014), pg 1. Paper for European Chapter Conference, Goteborg, Sweden, 21–22 November on Recent Developments in European Asylum Law Conference, in cooperation between the Migration Courts in Sweden and the IARLJ. This paper is based on the article by Storey, H. *Persecution: Towards a Working Definition*, in V. Chetail & C. Bauloz (eds.), Research Handbook on Migration and International Law, Cheltenham: Edward Elgar Publishing (2013).

The Age. *Islamic State completely 'evicted' from Iraq, Iraqi PM says.* 10 December 2017. https://www.theage.com.au/world/islamic-state-completely-evicted-from-iraq-iraqi-pm-says-20171210-h01x2r.html. Accessed 12/10/2018.

The Middle East Media Research Institute website, Video clip: *ISIS Justifies Its War on Yazidis: We Called on Them to Convert to Islam First.* http://www.memri.org/clip/en/0/0/0/0/0/0/4438.htm. Clip #4438 Broadcast: August 20, 2014. Accessed 23/08/2014.

United States Holocaust Museum. *The Nuremberg Race Laws.* https://www.ushmm.org/outreach/en/article.php?ModuleId=10007695. Accessed 21/09/2017.

UN News Centre "Adopting resolution, Security Council approves sanctions against militants in Iraq, Syria" http://www.un.org/apps/news/story.asp?NewsID=48494#.U_br6WMdMuM. Accessed 22/08/2014.

UNESCO – *What is meant by "cultural heritage"?* https://web.archive.org/web/20160316203151/http://www.unesco.org/new/en/culture/themes/illicit-trafficking-of-cultural-property/unesco-database-of-national-cultural-heritage-laws/frequently-asked-questions/definition-of-the-cultural-heritage/. Accessed 29/01/2018.

World News – RT International. *All you need to know about ISIS and what is happening in Iraq.* (2 July 2015). https://www.rt.com/news/166836-isis-isil-al-qaeda-iraq/. Accessed 12/10/2018.

Worley, W. *At least 100 European Isis fighters 'to be prosecuted in Iraq, with most facing death penalty'.* Independent, 7 October 2017. https://www.independent.co.uk/news/world/middle-east/isis-foreign-fighters-iraq-prosecuted-death-penalty-families-mosul-a7987831.html. Accessed 18/10/2018.

www.ingramcontent.com/pod-product-compliance
Lightning Source LLC
Chambersburg PA
CBHW052046290426
44111CB00011B/1640